Adrian Smith is Senior Lecturer in History at the Univer
access to the Mountbatten papers within the Broadlands
the Royal Military Academy Sandhurst and the University of Kent. An established
author, broadcaster and journalist in the fields of modern British political, social
and cultural history, his books include *The City of Coventry: A Twentieth Century Icon*
(I.B.Tauris), *Mick Mannock, Fighter Pilot: Myth, Life and Politics* and *The New Statesman:
Portrait of a Political Weekly, 1913–1931*.

MOUNTBATTEN

Apprentice War Lord

ADRIAN SMITH

I.B. TAURIS
LONDON · NEW YORK

Published in 2010 by I.B.Tauris & Co Ltd
6 Salem Road, London W2 4BU
175 Fifth Avenue, New York NY 10010
www.ibtauris.com

Distributed in the United States and Canada Exclusively by Palgrave Macmillan
175 Fifth Avenue, New York NY 10010

ISBN: 978 1 84885 374 4

A full CIP record for this book is available from the British Library
A full CIP record is available from the Library of Congress

Library of Congress Catalog Card Number: available

Printed and bound in Great Britain by CPI Antony Rowe, Chippenham
from camera-ready copy edited and supplied by the author

FSC
www.fsc.org
MIX
Paper from
responsible sources
FSC® C013604

To Sean Greenwood, Colin Seymour-Ure, Graham Thomas, Derek Crabtree,
and Peter Hennessy – with thanks

CONTENTS

ILLUSTRATIONS

PREFACE

It is perhaps unusual for a book of this nature to have quite so many dedicatees, but Sean Greenwood, Colin Seymour-Ure, Graham Thomas, Derek Crabtree, and Peter Hennessy, have together exercised a profound influence over my endeavours to make sense of Britain in time of peace and war. Without their teaching, support, and advice across nearly four decades it is hard to imagine that I would have had the confidence to tackle such a challenging subject as Mountbatten of Burma. The fact that I did is largely thanks to Frank Cogliano ('It's a dirty job, but someone's gotta do it ...') and Miles Taylor ('We're going to put on a Mountbatten conference, and no doubt you'll want to give a paper ...'). As always, I'm especially grateful to Jane McDermid for her usual wry take on events and her good-humoured encouragement. In addition to Professors Greenwood, Seymour-Ure, and Hennessy, a number of modern British historians contributed to this project in a whole variety of different ways, including Ian Beckett, David Edgerton, Dil Porter, Andrew Lambert, Eric Grove, Richard Holt, David Kynaston, Miles Taylor, Alex Danchev, Huw Richards, Matthew Kelly, and Martin Polley. My thanks to all of them, and my apologies to any expert in the field whom I might have overlooked. This project has expanded and contracted since I first embarked upon writing about Mountbatten, and I'm grateful to Ian Talbot for helping me clarify in my own mind the final shape of the book.

Among my colleagues at Southampton, as well as Jane, Matt Kelly, and Ian, I'm especially grateful to Anne Curry, Tony Kushner, and John Oldfield for their advice, and to Sarah Pearce and Mark Cornwall for ensuring that my study leave in the first half of the academic year 2007–8 was followed by a light timetable in the second half – only thanks to their intervention was I able to complete the book by the following autumn. Mike Hammond and Ray Monk (and in Kent, Simon Fox) were the perfect running companions, providing competition, good humour, and an abundance of ideas – both around Southampton Common *and* through the five boroughs of New York. As an experienced and highly esteemed biographer, Ray's sound advice with regard to getting the book into print is especially valued. In this respect I am yet again indebted to Peter Hennessy.

Gill Coleridge demonstrated why she is the doyenne of non-fiction agents; and at I.B.Tauris both Liz Friend-Smith and Lester Crook for a second time ensured their author's sincere appreciation of all their efforts. The eagle-eyed, ultra-efficient Pat FitzGerald effortlessly converted my manuscript into a book – I stand in awe. My thanks must also go to Jayne Ansell for overseeing the final stages of publication.

Chris Woolgar, head of special collections in the Hartley Library at the University of Southampton, his deputy Karen Robson, and their impressively proficient assistants, were all heroic in their efforts to ensure easy and speedy access to the Mountbatten and Campbell-Johnson papers. Quite simply, without the help of Professor Woolgar and his team this book would not have been written, and I thank them profusely. Archivists and librarians at a variety of institutions, most notably the National Archives and the Imperial War Museum, have all been extremely helpful; but a special mention must be made of library staff in Southampton, and most especially, Lymington – Hampshire Libraries, along with its civic counterpart, provides an astonishingly speedy (and cheap) service in retrieving long-forgotten titles from across the county. Support your local library, and cut down on your inter-library loans!

I had the delight of discussing mid-century British cinema with the late Lord Brabourne, and equally memorable were my conversations with his widow, the Countess Mountbatten. The latter gave me every encouragement, and the present Lord Brabourne has displayed an interest in the progress of the book. Naturally I am grateful to the family for their original decision that so many of the voluminous papers and photographs originally archived at Broadlands should find a new home at the University of Southampton. I must of course thank the Trustees of the Broadlands Archives for permission to use those quotations and photographs which are taken from the archival material held in the Hartley Library. Similarly, Crown copyright material is reproduced with the permission of the Controller of HMSO and the Queen's Printer for Scotland.

I have had the pleasure of talking about Mountbatten in a variety of venues. My thanks to the conference/seminar organisers for providing me with the opportunity to test out ideas; and also the secretaries of local history societies, Historical Association branches, and various other non-academic organisations who have invited me to speak. These invitations have been invaluable as in the audience there are always one or two people who knew or met Mountbatten; encountering veterans of the *Kelly* has been a particular thrill, and a great privilege.

My students at Southampton have lived with Mountbatten for the past few years, and I hope to goodness they feel this project has improved and informed my teaching. I have endeavoured not to bore colleagues and undergraduates, but my greatest fear has been relentlessly imposing Dickie on friends and relatives. Hopefully, I've shown due restraint, and I thank all of them for their patience, indulgence, and expressions of interest. Above all, I must express my heart-felt gratitude to Mary and Adam. Both of them have, as so often in the past, been incredibly supportive, and always full of really good suggestions – there may well be more Mountbatten to come, Mary, but only after a decent pause. I promise.

Adrian Smith
Lymington, Hampshire
November 2008/September 2009

PART ONE

DICKIE MOUNTBATTEN, CONSUL, COURTIER, CHARMER, AND CHANCER

1

INTRODUCTION

The imperious Mountbatten: at home in the empire

This is a story that begins and ends with an empire tested by war. When His Serene Highness Prince Louis of Battenberg was born at Frogmore House on 25 June 1900 the army of his great-grandmother, the Queen Emperor, was far from home and struggling to maintain imperial authority. Nevertheless, however costly the final outcome, and inauspicious the long-term prospect, Boer power in South Africa was finally contained. Forty-three years later, when Acting Admiral Lord Louis Mountbatten arrived in the Far East as the Allies' Supreme Commander South East Asia, a restoration of the imperial status quo appeared a remote prospect: Japanese forces had usurped Britain's colonial authority in every corner of southern Asia, besieging India and threatening the very survival of the Raj. Remarkably, Mountbatten and his outstanding field commander, Bill Slim, transformed a punch-drunk empire's demoralized and defeatist army into a fighting force capable of facing up to and defeating a formidable enemy. The 14th Army that fought its way to Rangoon was in every respect Slim's creation, but tempering Mountbatten's exaggerated claims for its success need not entail a total dismissal of his role in restoring Britain's credibility as a military power east of Suez. Yet, for all the heroics of the 'Forgotten Army', after the Second World War the challenge was simply too great: the ferocity of nationalist sentiment in the Indian sub-continent and beyond signalled the eclipse of European hegemony.

In some cases, such as the Dutch East Indies, the end came soon. In others, for example, Malaya, several years would pass before the flag was finally brought down. Either way, the writing was on the wall.[1] No wonder the Americans mockingly christened SEAC 'Save England's Asian Colonies'. Mountbatten's direct contribution to the withdrawal from empire – from tension with France and Holland once the war in the Far East was over, through to Indian independence and partition two years later – lies beyond the focus of this book. The present volume concludes with Churchill increasingly fearful that imperial decline was the inevitable price of grand alliance.

Nevertheless, this is a tale told against the backdrop of a liberal-imperialism which, even with the departure from Delhi, still envisaged slimmed-down survival. This was after all an era when a bankrupt yet victorious Britain could briefly enjoy the moral high ground. That smeared window of opportunity – for a *British* Commonwealth that in reality could never be – lasted from Ernie Bevin's first musings on the global altruism of a social democratic 'Third Force' to Anthony Eden's last hurrah on the banks of the Suez Canal. These were the years when the Colonial Office's never very convincing optimism collapsed in the face of ground nut fiascos and ferociously-fought 'emergencies'.

The Second World War clearly accelerated this janus-like surrender of power – bloody and painful in the field, yet generating remarkably few tensions back home. Nevertheless, despite more prescient commentators' early mutterings of disquiet, the British Empire still appeared *the* major global force throughout the first half of Mountbatten's life. This was most obvious in the 1920s, at a time when 'imperial over stretch' was no more than a dark cloud on a very distant horizon. The Anglicised Lord Louis had spent his adolescent years on active service, protecting the imperial heartland from the Teutonic threat across the North Sea. In his early twenties he accompanied the Prince of Wales on flag-flying tours of cousin David's far-flung future domains. Resuming his naval career, Mountbatten's late twenties were focused upon technical proficiency in communications, and postings to that most visible symbol of extended power, the Mediterranean Fleet. Edwina Ashley, his glamorous and wealthy wife, had been acquired courtesy of a courtship that climaxed, most appropriately, with a proposal of marriage in the Viceregal Lodge. In the course of the following decade the tyro destroyer commander swapped deck for desk, lobbying for the restoration of the Fleet Air Arm and calculating the full impact of Axis air power on an overstretched surface fleet. His flotilla scattered or sunk, in May 1941 Mountbatten lost his own ship as a shredded imperial army surrendered Crete in a maelstrom of heroism and hysteria. Combined Operations would at last see the Empire strike back, but such an ambition could only be achieved at the cost of Canada's finest. A much-criticised chief of staff always defended Dieppe as a costly but necessary first step towards D-Day, that almighty but all too brief final display of British military might. By then operational planning of an equally impressive feat of arms – the recovery of Burma – was well advanced, with the supreme commander ultimately swapping the security of Ceylon for the more salubrious comforts of a liberated Singapore.

From the autumn of 1943 Mountbatten found himself a pro-consul, charged with hurling the barbarians back and reclaiming the distant territories of a great yet fading empire. A trusted general rebuilt the legions and recaptured the eagles, but final victory relied upon the military might of a new and increasingly assertive ally – an emergent imperial power still stubbornly refusing to accept itself as such. Despite his relative youth (a handsome face belied encroaching middle age), Mountbatten's three years as a war lord marked the culmination of a lengthy apprenticeship. Admittedly his ascension to supreme commander was astonishing given that as recently as the spring of 1941 he was still a relatively junior captain – command of a destroyer flotilla scarcely reflected his modest placing in the Navy List. And yet, he had been in uniform for almost the whole of his life. For all his faults, and there were many,

Figure 1.1: HRH going native in Japan with Lord Louis and 'Fruity' Metcalfe, April 1922

Mountbatten's glamorous lifestyle was rarely at the expense of his career. The obvious exception is globetrotting with the Prince of Wales, but he clearly drew a line in the sand at the conclusion of the second tour. His return home marked the re-awakening of a scarcely dormant ambition that in the ensuing years became ever more single-minded – Dickie Mountbatten was a driven man, and, while it may seem clichéd to suggest that matching his father's achievement and becoming First Sea Lord was the prime motivation, every facet of his career suggests that here was someone with one simple objective. This book examines every aspect of that career, taking particular note of the fact that Mountbatten fought not just one but two world wars. For the first time the legacy of his experience in the Great War is fully explored, returning to inform the final part, when the book climaxes with 'Operation Jubilee', the second most contentious event in a career dogged by controversy: two chapters consider in detail the raid on Dieppe mounted by Combined Operations on 19 August 1942. Given the scale of Canada's losses, perhaps no other event since Confederation has placed as great a strain on relations between Britain and her most vital imperial ally.

The last viceroy was, of course, far more than, in David Cannadine's memorable phrase, the 'imperial undertaker who never wore black' – someone who rose to fame on the back of empire, and yet with unusual prescience sensed which way the winds of change were blowing.[2] As flotilla captain, frontline commander, grand strategist, naval reformer, Whitehall moderniser, and Windsor *eminence grise*, for nigh on six decades he operated at the very heart of power. Almost as long as the tally of jobs he did take on is the list of posts Mountbatten claimed to have turned down: Minister of Defence in both Labour and Conservative governments, as well as several governor-generalships, including post-UDI Rhodesia. Here was someone adamant that he could do a better job running the country than Attlee.[3]

It's ironic that both Clem and Harold Wilson saw Lord Louis as a safe pair of hands, as adept at handling Ian Smith as Mahatma Gandhi.[4] As has been said, controversy dogged Mountbatten throughout his career; assassination at the hands of the IRA in August 1979 only momentarily silenced his critics. That Irish republicans should murder someone so synonymous with colonial concession is of course a cruel irony, especially when their victim saw reunification as 'the only eventual solution'.[5] Mountbatten's pragmatic (for imperial apologists, wholly cynical) view of empire reflected a calculated ability to soak up and even embrace the forces of modernity: to adjust and to adapt to change, while never, however briefly, renouncing the physical security, psychological reassurance, and material comfort of tradition and privilege.[6] Here was an aristocrat in an ostensibly meritocratic era, who, by dint of personality and professional training, found himself still wielding an extraordinary degree of influence. Yet in many respects Admiral of the Fleet the Earl Mountbatten of Burma was an Orléanist, protected from the harshest consequences of social revolution.[7] After the war he was quick to acknowledge a new spirit of egalitarianism, albeit heavily qualified. However, in reality he was too elevated and then too old to experience any significant shifts in the tectonic plates of British society, most obviously the demise of deference.[8]

The Ubiquitous Mountbatten: At Home in Hampshire

Tropical kit neatly pressed, peaked cap at trademark rakish angle, sleeves rolled ready for action, the Supreme Commander South East Asia stares meaningfully across Grosvenor Square. Given that Mountbatten made so little use of public transport throughout his 79 years it's ironic that his statue stands on the former site of the Southampton bus station. On many maps of the city the 'square' is not even marked, despite the tastefully disguised multi-storey car park and the gentrified corporate buildings. The setting contrasts markedly with Lord Louis' very public presence in Whitehall. Here Franta Belsky's severe statue stands on Horse Guards Parade, suitably adjacent to the Foreign Office – Dickie Mountbatten, anti-appeaser and last viceroy, master of both gun boat and diplomacy. In central London Mountbatten is only one on an avenue of heroes, a tourist-trail pantheon of leaders on air, sea and land who together led their country to victory in two world wars. The Southampton statue is in its own quiet way a shrine and a sanctuary, commissioned by a property developer in 1990 but taken over by the Burma Star Association eight years later: the original sculpture and a later memorial tablet were both unveiled by the veterans' vice patron, Patricia, the Countess Mountbatten. Within Burma's famous 'forgotten' 14th Army Mountbatten could never enjoy the loyalty and affection felt for 'Uncle Bill', the future Field Marshal Lord Slim. Yet – as at every stage of his career – goodwill in the ranks more than cancelled out the suspicion or even outright hostility felt by those who operated in close proximity to him; and yet remained resistant to the easy charm, the cultivated mix of relaxed manner and urgent command, and the seductive charisma of a man apparently at ease with the trappings of power and privilege. Mountbatten could of course generate fierce loyalty within the wardroom or the mess, and it would be simplistic to suggest that here was someone whom one either loved or loathed (for his biographer a day in the archives can produce a whole range of emotions, from indignation at the level of conceit through to astonishment at the scale of achievement). Whether weary ships' companies, fledgling commandos, or revengeful Chindits, Mountbatten demonstrated a remarkable ability to surmount an enormous divide of wealth and status when dealing directly with the forces under his command. Surmounting the cynicism – including perhaps that of his immediate subordinates – he had the capacity to deliver a convincingly clear-cut, and on the whole bullshit-free, operational briefing: a rallying exhortation which would leave a lasting presence in terms of raising collective and individual morale. For this reason alone the veterans of Kohima and the Arakan treat Grosvenor Square with the same respect as remaining members of the *Kelly*'s mess decks view their captain's final resting place in Romsey.

Distance breeds indifference if not disenchantment, and the passage of time has seen even as striking a monument as the Grosvenor Square statue merge in to a blurred, seemingly unchanging – and thus dimly perceived – urban landscape. Yet for those who care to register his presence Lord Mountbatten retains a permanent high profile, from Romsey to Ryde, and from Pompey to Poole. Nor should an earlier memorialisation of Edwina be forgotten, particularly in hospitals and schools. If the Broadlands estate lies at the heart of this sprawling, scarcely registered regional homage, then Southampton provides a model of civic commemoration: several offices, two university research centres, a major arterial road, a retail park, a Salvation Army refuge, and even a pub opened by the great man himself – as indeed was the building in which I write. By comparison, Admiral Jellicoe, the Grand Fleet's commander at Jutland and a First Sea Lord actually born in the city, is rewarded with nothing grander than a blue plaque. Only the Isle of Wight, where Mountbatten proved a popular governor, can match such ubiquity. It may be the republican norm across France, the United States, and even Australia, but the naming of roads, places and buildings after politicians and military commanders is scarcely commonplace in Britain: few French towns would dare to ignore Clemenceau and De Gaulle, and yet at home Lloyd George is invisible and Churchill more likely to give his name to a major institution than a minor thoroughfare. So why is Mountbatten the exception to the rule, certainly so far as the south of England is concerned? To say that he remains closely associated with the Solent and the Test Valley goes some way to explaining why his name survives in so many varied places. Yet almost certainly it was his intimate involvement with the Royal Family which bestowed on him a unique status, even while he was still alive. The brutal nature of Mountbatten's death further strengthened his posthumous credibility, reinforcing the case for numerous public buildings and roads to tap the last vestiges of deference and respect.

Hampshire may remain the epicentre of a fast-fading memorialisation, but recollection of Mountbatten continues to stir emotions wherever his legacy survives, most obviously in southern Asia – events marking the sixtieth anniversary of independence and partition offered a sharp reminder of critics' readiness to demonise, *and* of admirers' undiminished eagerness to applaud.[9] Yet for a man so obsessed with reputation the judgement of posterity stretched far beyond parochial debate over the relevance of the Mountbatten name to the twenty-first century. If he desperately needed to be the centre of attention in life then he yearned to remain so in death.

The meticulous Mountbatten: at home in the archives

Mountbatten planned his biography in the same way that he planned his funeral. In retirement at Broadlands he and his staff ceaselessly shifted and sorted official papers and private correspondence. Even before his departure from the Ministry of Defence in 1965 a few spare hours could always be found to scrutinise the files. Here was the archival lode which his official biographer would one day mine. Sudden, tragic death brought no abrupt end to the process of collection and cataloguing; a mass of posthumous material left the family facing a fresh challenge of filtering out the trivial and dealing with the downright hostile. Mountbatten's operating rule had been 'when in doubt, retain', and he was remorseless in hunting down even the most remotely relevant documents and artefacts. As for the controversial and contentious, he regularly rallied the Praetorian Guard of old comrades and trusted cronies to draft favourable briefing papers or to track down supportive evidence. Those closest to him, such as his former press attaché, Alan Campbell-Johnson, were lifelong keepers of the flame, ensuring Dickie's case for the defence survived beyond the grave.[10] Yet nearly two decades after his death even Campbell-Johnson could concede that, 'without Edwina there to cut him down to size, his surface vanity flourished. He did a lot of damage to his own reputation in those years'.[11] Sadly, Hugh Massingberd's account of his spring 1979 interview with an indiscrete, obsessive, vainglorious 'Polonius of the Court' is horribly convincing.[12]

Mountbatten's determination to ensure that any future researcher would recount the 'right' story was made that much more difficult by the introduction of the 'Thirty Year Rule' in 1967. Now he had to make certain any criticism of his actions that might eventually enter the public domain, for example, the Admiralty's rather jaundiced view of his first year in command of the 5th Destroyer Flotilla, would be discredited once his own version of events, then and later, was made available to a sympathetic and open-minded nation. Thus, when judged appropriate, he would speedily respond to any slur on his reputation; but otherwise he played the long-game, certain that eventually the 'truth' would come out, with every course of action, big or small, seen to be necessary and correct.

Clearly the choice of authorised biographer was crucial, and Mountbatten spurned premature efforts to bestow the imprimatur, however elevated the author. After all, during and after the war a generally supportive press, encouraged from

1942 by Lord Louis' formidable PR team, did more than enough to maintain the myth. An officially sanctioned volume might perhaps prove a hostage to fortune, revisiting such sensitive events as the crippling of HMS *Javelin* or the losses sustained at Dieppe. More crucially, any hint of hagiography would reinforce the view of senior staff inside the Service that Noel Coward's tribute to the *Kelly*, the highly successful 1942 feature film *In Which We Serve*, was an act of shameless self-publicity.[13] In any case, in the mid-1940s the Mountbatten saga was nowhere near conclusion, with the eventual elevation to First Sea Lord and the consequent revival of naval fortunes an anticipated climax to the story.

Not surprisingly, therefore, Mountbatten rebuffed Whitehall efforts to blunt the United States' instinctive suspicion of British imperial endeavour. One idea was to commission C.S. Forester to chronicle the rising star's life from single-minded cadet to supreme commander. Popular on both sides of the Atlantic, and a proven propagandist for both the Pentagon and the Admiralty, Forester was an obvious choice. Oddly, Mountbatten claimed him as a 'boyhood friend of mine' – yet, while the novelist was busy honing his cricketing skills at Dulwich College, the younger Battenberg would have been at the other end of the country preparing for life with the Grand Fleet.[14] When HMS *Kelly* was attacked by Stukas for the final time Mountbatten was absorbed in *Ship of the Line*, perhaps seeking inspiration from his favourite character in fiction, Horatio Hornblower. Forester sent Mountbatten a replacement copy, and first editions of subsequent volumes: *The Ship*, published in 1943 and based upon the writer's brief spell aboard HMS *Penelope*, was gratefully received. Predictably the gift generated three pages of corrections; although HMS *Artemis* is a light cruiser, and the action takes place a year after the *Kelly* sank off Crete in May 1941, there is a familiar Mediterranean setting. There is also a certain familiarity surrounding the *Artemis*'s captain. Miles Ernest Troughton-Harrington-Yorke – a handsome-looking aristocrat apprenticed in Beatty's navy, and identified as a high-flier at staff college – is a proven leader of men, both in and out of action. He has learnt to control a fierce temper and is 'profoundly interested in the art of living' – although, unlike Mountbatten, he has a taste for German symphonies and Dutch masterpieces. Given Forester's admiration of Mountbatten it's not fanciful to suggest that the central character in *The Ship* draws upon the heroic image at the heart of *In Which We Serve*.[15]

Working freelance for the Office of War Information and other quasi-military agencies in Washington, Ray Murphy was well-connected, wealthy, bright, and ambitious. A glamorous and handsome correspondent whose university experience included both Yale and Edinburgh, he had reported on MacArthur's Manila meeting with Mountbatten in July 1945. Impressed by this 'dynamic, if contradictory, personage', and yet suspicious of such a rapid rise to the top, Murphy talked to everyone at home who knew anything about Churchill's protégé. Puzzled that the response, even among British service personnel, was almost universally negative, he decided to find out for himself. To Murphy's amazement a major in the Joint Army Staff suggested he might like to write a biography, and straightaway secured him a flight to Singapore. The importance placed on Murphy's mission was reflected in the recruitment of Eisenhower's chief of staff, Walter Bedell Smith, to write a letter of recommendation. However, no-one thought to inform the man himself, and Mountbatten remained adamant that no official biography should be written. Yet clearly he was persuaded by Campbell-Johnson and Fleet Street veteran Mike Wardell, as well as by his closest friend and adviser Peter Murphy, that an *un*authorised biography would do him no harm; and could go a long way to killing off damaging prejudices and misinformation, especially in the United States where newspaper coverage was surprisingly hostile. Mountbatten's media men, like their master, found Ray Murphy 'very charming'.[16] Wined and dined in style, he left SEAC Headquarters armed with letters of introduction and firm promises that he could travel with the supreme commander's entourage, talk to Edwina, and be given access to a host of interested parties with a story to tell. Mountbatten was as good as his word, and in the preface to *The Last Viceroy* an impressive list of old friends, comrades, patrons, and political allies are thanked for their advice and assistance. He justified his support for Murphy by viewing the book as a *fait accompli*; and that therefore it should be 'written in as friendly a spirit as possible so as to help Anglo-American relations'.[17]

The assiduous American had a long briefing session with Mountbatten in August 1946, giving his subject a sextant as a mark of appreciation. Murphy interviewed him again two months later. At the same time he kept regular contact with another key member of Mountbatten's staff, his personal secretary at SEAC and again in India, Captain Ronald Brockman. The book's appearance in Britain was delayed to allow brief reference to India; but not even independence for the sub-continent could convince New York's Anglophobe publishers that their readers might be interested in the life of a silver-spooned imperial consul, however enlightened his views. Mountbatten became reconciled to East Coast hostility, lamenting *Time* and *Life*'s instinctive antipathy towards the Royal Family: in 1953 he blamed Henry Luce's magazines for distorting information culled from *Manifest Destiny*, a deeply deferential family biography written by Brian Connell, a writer whose respectful tone and bland prose is curiously reminiscent of *Hello!*.[18]

Six years earlier Ray Murphy tested Mountbatten's affection to the limit by relying on another, equally ruthless press baron to maintain his fashionable Manhattan lifestyle. From late June to early August, with public attention focused upon Mountbatten's minute to midnight negotiations in New Delhi, Lord Beaverbrook's *Sunday Express* published lengthy extracts from Murphy's manuscript. Initially Mountbatten was impressed, even if the first instalment 'made me squirm a bit'. Peter Murphy was similarly relaxed, but otherwise family and friends were appalled, with Brockman taking time off from affairs of state to insist on amendments in advance of the book's final publication. Attention focused upon the final instalment, where headlines and skilful sub-editing drew as much attention to the viceroy's weaknesses ('vanity and flamboyance') as his qualified strengths ('supreme self-confidence'). The ludicrous claim that in Burma he had applied fake tan before addressing the troops was forgivable in Mountbatten's eyes, if not Brockman's – the American had been an innocent abroad, set up by old enemies inside the Service. Nevertheless, the now ex-viceroy admitted privately to Peter Murphy that the allegation was hurtful and deeply damaging: 'it is the sort of malicious story which will be told against me to my grave, and do untold harm among the "he-men" of the Navy who despise Pansies'. No doubt there are those who read such a letter and see all their suspicions confirmed. A.N. Wilson, for example, has insisted that rumours within the Service of homo-sexual affairs were justified, with the future admiral of the fleet nicknamed 'Mountbottom'. Michael Bloch has even gone so far as to suggest a wartime penchant for sado-masochism.[19] If there was a perceivably homo-erotic element in his dealings with openly gay men such as Murphy, Tom Driberg, and Noel Coward this did not of itself indicate that Mountbatten was anything other than heterosexual; unlike, for example, his close friend the Duke of Kent, whose bisexual nature was an open secret by the mid-1930s.[20] In his 1947 letter to Murphy – a man who for the time was remarkably open about his sexuality – Mountbatten was simply using the robust language of the day to articulate an ever-present fear of thwarted ambition: the road to the top could easily be blocked by those elements within the Admiralty who still placed a premium on 'character', hierarchy, inflexible discipline, and above all tradition.

Mountbatten clearly liked Ray Murphy, witness the fact that his grovelling apology attracted such a gentle admonishment. Of more concern was the suggestion made in the *Sunday Express*, and more explicitly in American *Vogue*, that Mountbatten had taken the initiative in having his story told, with cooperation extending to Princess Elizabeth's fiancé being specially invited to Broadlands in order to talk about Uncle Dickie over dinner. By now installed as India's first governor-general, Mountbatten wrote to Murphy insisting that he reiterate no formal arrangement had ever existed: 'I do hope that you will not depart from our understanding again, as it would grieve me very much to find I had been mistaken in you.'[21] Veiled hints were absent from *The Last Viceroy*, and in the opening chapter its author goes to great pains to establish the basis on which he came to write the book. This is a biography long since confined to specialist bookshops and special collections, but it's actually rather good. Murphy is respectful but in no way over-awed by his subject, and he tells a good story. The writing is fresh, vibrant, and fast-paced, while not unduly journalistic; notwithstanding the attractiveness of the subject, a fresh and dynamic mid-Atlantic style would have appealed to austerity-era readers tired of solemn prose and authorial gravitas.

Serialisation of *The Last Viceroy* had left Mountbatten sensitive to public misgivings over his handling of Indian independence, especially when criticism emanated from within Express Newspapers. His quarrel was with the proprietor, not his staff: at Mike Wardell's invitation, *Evening Standard* editor Frank Owen had launched *SEAC*, the forces newspaper for the Far East; while columnist Tom Driberg had become a close confidant of the supreme commander when visiting Singapore and Saigon in the early autumn of 1945 – two years later, within and without Westminster he laboured hard at the viceroy's behest to stifle Labour criticism of a costly royal wedding and a continental groom.[22] At the same time Mountbatten sought legal opinion when the *Daily Express* mentioned his name alongside Nehru in an editorial insisting that, 'in all the world we have few more dangerous enemies'. Beaverbrook dismissed the allegation of libel, just as throughout the postwar years he rubbished the notion that his papers deliberately targeted Mountbatten: he was merely as vulnerable as any other figure in public life who, like the last viceroy, 'might transgress the high principles which the *Express* sets in all matters concerning the British Empire'. Unlike Churchill, Beaverbrook was wholly unforgiving of the man held directly responsible for 'the betrayal of Burma, refusal to let the Dutch back into Indonesia. And over everything the sack of India'. By the early 1950s Mountbatten had proved himself to be 'the biggest menace to the Empire', and a man who 'should never be given power and authority'. Yet evidence suggests the press baron had turned his back on Dickie and Edwina long before their departure for India. They had become friends with Beaverbrook in the mid-1920s, partly because Edwina's closest chum at the time, Jean Norton, was the Canadian's mistress. In May 1926 the two women helped run the *Express* switchboard during the General Strike, and both accompanied him to Russia in August 1929 – bizarrely, the Soviet authorities took an especially keen interest in the visit as the GPU believed Lady Louis to be a sister of the late Tsar. Another member of Beaverbrook's entourage for this first meeting with Stalin was the dashing Michael Wardell who, although briefly Edwina's lover, had joined Express Newspapers in 1926 at Dickie's instigation. Wardell quickly gained Beaverbrook's trust, and, apart from wartime service with SEAC, survived as managing director for over 30 years.[23] He proved more than capable of serving two masters, and acted as intermediary and peacemaker when relations between Max and the Mountbattens soured. Captain (D) was both grateful and embarrassed when the *Express* newspapers lavished 'extravagant praise' on his record as a flotilla commander; but in the winter of 1941–2 he felt increasingly irritated by offers of 'help in the Whitehall jungle', let alone the suggestion that his appointment to head Combined Operations was solely at Beaverbrook's suggestion. Perhaps it was this annoyance which, when viewing the rushes of *In Which We Serve*, stopped Mountbatten from vetoing a prominent shot of the *Daily Express* floating in the quayside slime with its notorious 1939 masthead declaration of 'No War This Year' clearly visible. A Fleet Street backlash, even before the film came out, saw Noel Coward pay a harsh price. In the Caribbean after the war he unashamedly courted Beaverbrook – the favourable reviews reappeared, but his friendship with Dickie and Edwina was never the same again.[24]

In the spring of 1958 Beaverbrook instructed the younger Max Aitken that no quarter be given to the departing First Sea Lord. Macmillan intended to appoint Mountbatten the first Chief of the Defence Staff, enjoying *primus inter pares* status within the Chiefs of Staff Committee. Beaverbrook had almost certainly been warned that this announcement was imminent, just as he was all too well aware that Mountbatten had barely disguised his opposition to the Suez expedition 18 months earlier. The newspaper proprietor instructed his son:

> Print these statements. Don't trust Mountbatten in Any Public Capacity. Together with a further quotation from Mountbatten's speech in Canada where he said he took full responsibility for Dieppe. Four thousand set forth and three thousand did not return.[25]

Beaverbrook's first love was always to his native country. The passage of time served only to strengthen his conviction that the Chief of Combined Operations had been directly responsible for the decimation of Canadian assault troops at Dieppe on 19 August 1942. Yet in the immediate aftermath of the disaster, both the *Daily Express* and the *Evening Standard* remained consistent to their owner's call for a 'Second Front Now', hailing the raid as clear evidence that relief for the Soviet Union could come sooner rather than later. As evidence mounted that all had been far from well, attitudes shifted. Beaverbrook became increasingly suspicious that such a poorly mounted operation was deliberately intended to undermine his case for an early Second Front. At a dinner party on 27 October hosted by Averell Harriman, Roosevelt's eyes and ears in London, the press baron tore in to Mountbatten. Shocked by Beaverbrook's intemperate language, the other guests largely accepted the CCO's defence that he bore full responsibility for drawing up the plans, but not for their execution. Looking back on the incident 30 years later, Mountbatten concluded that this was the night he and 'the Beaver' became firm enemies. That enmity lasted until 1963 when Macmillan – who ten years earlier had confided to his diary a similar distrust of Mountbatten – orchestrated a chilly reconciliation.[26]

Tom Driberg – as 'William Hickey', the *Daily Express*'s first gossip columnist – wrote a revealing biography of his old boss in the mid-1950s. By this time several but by no means all bridges had been burnt, so the reader still enjoyed the authentic voice of 'the Beaver': '"Mountbatten is vain, not clever. The woman is clever, not vain."' Although tempted to silence someone privy to so many secrets, Beaverbrook first of all reined in his libel lawyers – and bought the serial rights. This canny move gave him considerable influence over his renegade biographer, whose extravagant lifestyle had left him teetering on the edge of bankruptcy. Next, pressure was put on the similarly cash-strapped publishers, whose own lawyers were already demanding a radical revision of an increasingly sanitised manuscript. The book survived, but substantial cuts were made, particularly in the chapter dealing with Dieppe and Beaverbrook's subsequent vendetta. Needless to say, first to go was the charge reportedly made at Harriman's stormy dinner party: 'You murdered my Canadians in order to wreck my Second Front campaign!'. Driberg now acknowledged that there had been a *rapprochement* in 1944–5: Beaverbrook had generously given Mountbatten advice on how to, firstly, set up SEAC's formidable PR operation, and, secondly, forge good relations with the Kuomintang. Thus the author accepted Beaverbrook's denial of 'uninterrupted hostility', while still stressing the depth of 'personal resentment'. There was an 'emotional basis' to a vendetta so capricious as to rally Fleet Street rivals in a spirited defence of the First Sea Lord. Driberg quoted the *Observer* and the *News Chronicle*, and in his own column for *Reynolds News* he was to fight a running battle with former colleagues throughout the 1950s. Constrained by libel laws, and his fawning relationship with Mountbatten, Driberg could do no more than imply that Beaverbrook's friendship with young Dickie had ceased long before October 1942.[27]

A.J.P. Taylor, who of course knew his subject well, suggested that, 'Something about Mountbatten touched Beaverbrook on a raw nerve'. Disingenuously, he claimed there was more to this than met the eye, but that no close friends had any idea as to why. As keeper of his late patron's papers Taylor was almost certainly aware that when Jean Norton died in 1945 evidence had emerged that her relationship with Mountbatten might have entailed more than merely offering a shoulder to cry on whenever Edwina was away courting a stream of admirers.[28] Driberg, in his posthumously published autobiography, identified Jean Norton as the cause of the quarrel, but only because she cancelled an engagement with her lover to dine with the Mountbattens. Janet Morgan, Lady Mountbatten's official biographer, dismissed any notion of a brief fling as fanciful; but whether or not an affair took place is immaterial. Rather, the question is, did Beaverbrook believe that his mistress had been doubly deceitful – to her husband, and to her lover? Here therefore was possibly the real reason why Beaverbrook pursued Mountbatten with such ferocity – and yet also on occasion with such subtlety, witness the casuistical manner in which Ray Murphy's honest assessment of his subject was reworked so that, to the casual reader on a Sunday morning in the summer of 1947, the vices demonstrably outweighed the virtues.

Murphy's biography was a premature expedition in to virgin territory, but no comparable volume appeared for the remainder of Mountbatten's active career (admirals of the fleet technically never retire). Not that Mountbatten wholly dismissed the notion of an authorised biography appearing in his lifetime: in 1964 he systematically recorded a series of reminiscences with a view to Alan Campbell-Johnson embarking upon a major overview of his life. These recordings were typed up as an official record, and old colleagues were urged to give Campbell-Johnson their full cooperation if he sought an interview. The one-time press officer was given full access to the burgeoning Broadlands archives.[29] Given his fascination with the mechanics of film-making, and his growing involvement with television via his son-in-law John (Lord) Brabourne, it was scarcely surprising that from 1966 to 1968 Mountbatten devoted much of his time to a 12-part account of his *Life and Times*. The on-screen appearance of the subject, the pioneering use of colour, the juxtaposition of current and contemporary footage, the extensive filming on location, and the narrator's emphasis on narrative *and* explanation, can all be seen in other blockbuster series of the period, notably Kenneth Clark's *Civilisation* and Jacob Bronowski's *Ascent of Man*. Although broadcast on ITV and not commissioned by BBC2, the series' director, Peter Morley, appears to have been under very little pressure to cut and compress. Mountbatten is suitably indulged, and there are several scenes that cry out for ruthless editing, for example the long speech to the 1966 gathering of survivors from the *Kelly* which takes up the second half of episode four.[30]

The choice of scriptwriter was astute as John Terraine was both a scion of public service broadcasting and a highly respected – if, given his rehabilitation of Haig, somewhat controversial – military historian. By 1966 he had gathered various prestigious awards for the BBC's pioneering documentary series *The Great War*. Although his attention still focused upon the Western Front, Terraine was hugely knowledgeable about warfare in the twentieth century, as a succession of later books would readily confirm. He was by no means an easy person to work with, but he clearly had huge respect for Mountbatten; and the slim volume which accompanied the television series gave both voice and vital context to its subject. Terraine thereby provided the interested viewer with a succinct, semi-official – and thus sanitised – account of Lord Louis' life.[31] His text formed the core of a coffee-table book that appeared shortly before the tragedy at Mullaghmore. *Mountbatten Eighty Years in Pictures* drew upon an immense collection of photographs, today housed at the University of Southampton. Its subject rightly acknowledged the herculean efforts of his ever-present, ever-patient, ultra-discreet secretary, John Barratt, and of the Broadlands archivist, Mollie Travis. In the foreword Mountbatten made clear that at no time had he contemplated writing his memoirs, and he reiterated his refusal to authorise a biography.[32]

Admirers of the 'family album' eager to learn more were directed towards Terraine, and those books in which their hero had taken a particularly keen interest. Attention was drawn to *Freedom at Midnight* by Larry Collins and Dominique Lapierre, an exciting and very readable account of Indian independence which became a best-seller both sides of the Atlantic and inspired a TV documentary. Published in 1975 the book was quickly discredited by serious historians of partition, if only because the authors relied so heavily on lengthy interviews with a man well in to his seventies whose version of events was firmly rooted in solipsism, sweeping generalisation, and a suspect memory. Mountbatten's partial recall and contentious views were left unchallenged, not least his longstanding prejudice towards Jinnah and his more recent dismissal of Wavell's performance as viceroy from 1943 to 1947.[33] Given that so much of the book read like the ramblings of a vain old man, Patrick French is perhaps entitled to claim that, 'By attempting to create his own myth with such assiduous care, Mountbatten sowed the seeds of its posthumous collapse'.[34]

The posthumous Mountbatten: at home in the authorised biographies

Also included in Mountbatten's list of recommended reading was a biography of his parents, *Louis and Victoria*.[35] The author was Richard Hough, ex-fighter pilot, former publisher, father of future novelist Deborah Moggach, and neighbour and Garrick Club drinking companion of Kingsley Amis. Hough lived by his pen, with a rate of composition almost as impressive as his range of contacts. He first met Mountbatten in 1971, by which time he was already cultivating other members of the Royal Family. His letters to Mountbatten expose him as an outrageous name-dropper, who delighted in the fact that his daughter was in the same class at Gordonstoun as Prince Andrew.[36] The two men clearly got on very well, to the extent that by July 1975 they were on first-name terms. Hough was no doubt very good company, if only because he shamelessly massaged his new patron's ego – witness his readiness to traduce Anthony Pugsley, the captain of HMS *Javelin* who held Mountbatten directly responsible for the destroyer's near destruction in November 1940. Having enjoyed access to the Broadlands archives in order to write his book on Prince Louis and Princess Victoria, in the mid-1970s he worked closely with Mollie Travis on an ancillary project, a collection of Queen Victoria's letters to her granddaughter.[37]

Throughout the late 1970s Richard Hough spent many hours talking to Mountbatten, and in the process gathered a large body of material, by no means all of it factually correct. Some but by no means all of these conversations were recorded. Hough's career as a freelance writer necessitated the ability to write fast, and his putative subject's sudden death on 27 August 1979 released him from any promise not to produce a biography in Mountbatten's lifetime. His intention was that Weidenfeld and Nicolson publish the book on the first anniversary of the Mullaghmore tragedy. He met the deadline, with five extracts serialised in the *Sunday Telegraph* across the summer of 1980. This was despite the family's concerted effort to stop publication, orchestrated by Lord Brabourne. John Brabourne was married to Patricia, who as the eldest daughter had by special dispensation inherited the title of Countess Mountbatten. He had only recently recovered from the appalling injuries sustained when his father-in-law's boat, *Shadow V*, was blown up; and was still coming to terms with the murder of his mother and of his son Nicholas. Publication of *Mountbatten Hero of Our Time* must have seemed both insensitive and exploitative, and the family sought a court injunction when promotional material quoted Hough's claim that, 'The biography is the book he [Mountbatten] wanted me to write. It is the fruit of this material, of related sources, and of interviews and correspondence with his contemporaries'. Hough contested the case, and, while clearly sympathetic to the plaintiffs, the judge was not wholly convinced by either side.[38]

The outcome was a compromise foreword to the book which was the maximum the author would concede and the minimum the family would accept: 'Given that the official biography is still several years away, I feel that there is now room for an informal study of Lord Mountbatten's life.' Hough acknowledged that his subject had been extremely supportive of research into his parents' lives, but had always insisted no 'informal biography' chronicle his own.[39] However, *Mountbatten Hero of Our Time* is written as if the writer was Lord Louis' closest confidant, recording every word of the great man's recollections. It's a very workmanlike book, and the strong narrative drive leaves all but the most sceptical reader indifferent to the fact that Mountbatten's first-person account of events had often been reconstructed. Hough repeatedly crosses the line from reported speech to direct quotation – a line which, a much more distinguished biographer has argued, separates fact from fiction.[40]

The extent to which Richard Hough relied upon his subject's own words, real or reinvented, contrasted with the more orthodox approach of a complementary volume published in 1983. An unrepentant Hough, by now wholly indifferent to the views of the Mountbatten family, strenuously defended his life of Edwina: its authenticity rested upon 'the knowledge and support of many of those who knew her'. However, his acknowledgements were very much a B-list of the great and the good, and the credibility of his one trump card, Mary (Ashley), Lady Delamere, was later called into question by her sister's official biographer. The thoroughness of Hough's research was disputed when Edwina's cousin and close friend, Marjorie (Jenkins), the Countess of Brecknock, provided Lord Brabourne with a detailed (and scathing) list of factual errors. Needless to say, the family's fierce criticism did not enter the public domain.[41] Instead, *Edwina* appeared to confirm Hough's reputation as a competent man-of-letters whose thoroughness of research and genuine respect for his subject prevented modest revelation from degenerating in to dubious speculation. Thus, the critics had no obvious reason to be hostile. Indeed, the warm reception given to *Mountbatten Hero of Our Time* had encouraged Pan to publish a best-selling paperback edition in 1981. When Richard Hough died 16 years later, he was toasted by his Grub Street peers as a true professional. Within Broadlands he remained an *arriviste* who not once but twice had betrayed the trust of one-time friends and patrons. Wholly unrepentant, on the dustjacket of one of his later books – on Churchill – Hough still described himself as the Mountbattens' 'official historian'.[42]

Lord and Lady Brabourne's keen sense of betrayal clearly did not extend to another freelance writer familiar to senior members of the Royal Family, the broadcaster Brian Hoey. In the early 1990s Hoey, by now an experienced biographer, wrote a respectful but very readable thematic study of Mountbatten. Despite the publisher's inflated claims and a mildly provocative title, *Mountbatten The Private Story* revealed nothing new. Mountbatten's two daughters, Patricia and Pamela, their partners, and their children, had all rightly assumed that the author would invariably err on the side of caution – anyone whose list of publications included the official guide to Buckingham Palace was unlikely to behave in the same caddish manner as Richard Hough.[43]

Someone who did leave himself open to such a charge was the disgraced junior minister turned author, Lord Lambton. Hoey's book may possibly have been a family-inspired broadside, intended to sink a very odd volume written by Anthony Lambton a few years earlier. *The Mountbattens* claimed to uncover those 'long hidden truths' an absurdly ambitious royal mountebank had sought to suppress with regard to his German ancestors. A second volume was promised, its main purpose being to dissect the late Lord Louis' 'fantasies which, when intertwined with a complaisant memory, made nonsense of the truth'. Perhaps not surprisingly Lambton berated a secretive Brabourne for denying him access to the archives, and praised his fellow *persona non grata*, Richard Hough as a pioneer in shedding light on a man of modest talent's grim determination to reach the top. Writing a history of the Battenbergs was primarily a vehicle to attack Mountbatten at every opportunity, and Lambton was disarmingly honest as to his purpose. His main motive appears to have been the question that has rumbled on since 1952 regarding the correct surname for the Queen's descendants – Windsor, Mountbatten, or a combination of the two? Lengthy appendices confirmed an obsession with matters of genealogy, constitutional precedence, and royal nomenclature matched only by the great egotist himself.[44] All this blue-blooded eccentricity served only to generate a much simpler question: given the absence of any commercial argument for accepting such a rambling, unstructured, and occasionally unreadable book, what on earth convinced Constable of the case for publication?

Hoey's singularly unshocking examination of the man behind the medal ribbons was quickly followed by a no-nonsense explanation of how Mountbatten came to be the most decorated officer in the Senior Service – and, indeed, in any other service. Vice-Admiral Sir Ian McGeoch's *The Princely Sailor* was a worthy tome, offering the reader a convenient distillation of relevant information, and an admirably succinct account of Mountbatten's career. Only a former flag officer with a formidable CV could have gained access to such a distinguished array of interviewees. McGeoch had first encountered Mountbatten in 1944 when appointed to a staff post with the Pacific Fleet. By that time his exploits as a formidable submarine commander in the Mediterranean had earned him the DSO, the DSC, and a mention in dispatches, the latter acknowledging his breakout from a German POW camp. As well as a serial escaper lauded by MI9, McGeoch was a genuine submarine ace. He might easily have viewed Mountbatten's mixed fortunes at sea as confirmation that here really was, to use the Service's most pejorative label, 'the master of disaster'. In fact the very opposite was the case, and *The Princely Sailor*'s safe service perspective belied the tenacity with which Sir Ian could cross swords when defending his hero. No gold-braided warrior was too elevated to escape his wrath should circumstance dictate. For example, Andrew Cunningham, the Royal Navy's most successful fighting admiral since Nelson, and Dudley Pound's successor as First Sea Lord in 1943, was soundly taken to task by McGeoch: he berated Cunningham for criticising Mountbatten's operational command of his flotilla in the Mediterranean, and for creating the conditions which had left the *Kelly* so fatally exposed to air attack off Crete on 23 May 1941.[45]

The complex, interconnected working and personal relationship between 'ABC' and Mountbatten is clearly integral to the story told here. As shall be seen, even after he became First Sea Lord and no longer feared Cunningham's veto, in public Mountbatten encouraged an impression of conviviality, intimacy, and mutual respect – of a deep friendship evolving over time as the eager learner attained near equal status with the benevolent master. Beneath the wardroom politeness the reality was often very different, with the mastermind of Taranto and Matapan privately convinced that, for all the drive, energy and imagination, Dickie Mountbatten simply wasn't up to the job. Mountbatten knew this, in retirement recalling his mentor's fury that he should be distracted from an orthodox naval career not once, but twice: theirs was a 'love-hate relationship', with ABC scarcely disguising his antagonism between 1941 and that point in the mid-1950s when he was finally persuaded Mountbatten should become First Sea Lord – after which advice and goodwill again flowed freely.[46] Cunningham shared his scepticism with another grand strategist honed in combat, Alan Brooke. The Chief of the Imperial General Staff from December 1941 felt he owed nothing to Churchill, who in turn awarded his formidable foil a wary respect. Mountbatten on the other hand appeared to owe everything to Churchill. Like Cunningham, the CIGS remained firmly convinced that precocity, flair, and easy access to palace reception rooms, were no guarantee of senior command.[47] Brooke rightly saw Churchill as a *deus ex machina* figure in the lives of both Mountbattens, ever-present and ever ready. Winston's fascination with Dickie and Edwina – according to Janet Morgan evident even before they were born – was rooted in romance, genuine affection, a recognition of talent, and, in obeisance to Sir Ernest Cassell and Prince Louis of Battenberg, a curious legacy of gratitude, remorse, and respect.[48] The warm relationship between Churchill and Mountbatten – cracked but by no means wholly shattered by the events of March 1947–May 1948 – lies at the heart of this book.

The volume of literature specifically about Mountbatten is remarkable; and yet moored alongside this raft of biographies lies an argosy of specialist studies where one man is invariably the focal point. Subjects may range from nuclear strategy to functionalist management systems (on both of which naturally he claimed to be an expert), but India remains the principal reason – some would say the only reason – why scholars remain keenly interested in someone whose life and lifestyle seem so at odds with the contemporary world. For post-colonialists in Britain and on the sub-continent the sixtieth anniversary of independence and partition yet again placed the Mountbattens centre-stage – literally so in *The Last Durbar*, Shashi Joshi's distinctly post-modernist revisiting of partition ('It is only the dramatic genre of writing history that allows us to recover the complexity of such a process and frames the atmosphere of the concentrated moment').[49] Dramatising the events of 1947 is of course nothing new: the viceregal couple may have been late arrivals in Richard Attenborough's 1982 epic *Gandhi*, but on the small screen 25 years later they dominated Channel 4's drama-documentary *The Last Days of the Raj*, while back in the mid-1980s 'the immense, enduring affection felt for Lord Mountbatten and his wife Edwina' inspired a mid-Atlantic mini-series complete with tie-in novel.[50] As we shall see, British film-makers are sure there remains an audience for a big budget movie that convincingly recreates the public and private lives of Viceroy House's final and most glamorous denizens.

2007 certainly saw a renewal of interest in Mountbatten, however modest. Stanley Wolpert, the well-respected biographer of India's and Pakistan's founding fathers, launched a late-career attack upon the last viceroy. *Shameful Flight* is so relentless in its criticism of Mountbatten's handling of partition that the overall effect is counterproductive – one is left feeling no-one could be *that* bad, and survive with his career intact. Infuriated by the great panjandrum's casual dismissal of Jinnah when Wolpert met him for the first and last time in 1979, the veteran American academic deemed the time right to wreak revenge. In producing such an unbalanced and intemperate account of 'Mountbatten's frenzied rush to retreat', Wolpert did his reputation no favours.[51]

Not that anyone either noticed or cared. *Shameful Flight* was quickly forgotten. Unlike *Indian Summer The Secret History of the End of an Empire*, which rightly attracted rave reviews.[52] Shrewdly, the producers at Working Title had already bought the screen rights, in anticipation that Alex von Tunzelmann's lucid and lively book would be well received. *Indian Summer* is a remarkable debut, its young author sharing the same verve, panache, wit, and irreverency that Patrick French had displayed when first writing about India.[53] French is an obvious influence, but von Tunzelmann has her own voice – and very much her own opinions. She doesn't pull punches, mixing a healthy respect for Churchill and Gandhi with clear evidence that both men all too often exercised a malign influence over events. Mountbatten's increasingly painful dealings with Churchill are revisited, but von Tunzelmann also gives due attention to Clem Attlee's characteristically no-nonsense handling of someone whom he could never take entirely seriously ('rather a Ruritanian figure, don't you think?').[54] Her judgement is generally sure-footed, although attempts to link twenty-first century *jihad* with Winston's courting of Jinnah are presumably at the behest of the publisher; and the claim that Dickie advanced the date of Indian independence to impress Edwina fails to convince.[55]

The tortured nature of the Mountbatten marriage is explored intelligently and intuitively, but where the book really scores is in its authoritative and revealing portrayal of the 12-year relationship between Edwina and Jawaharlal Nehru. The former, for all her faults, is seen as a woman driven by a keen sense of injustice and a deeply-held humanitarian concern for the dispossessed of southern Asia, while 'Panditji' remains throughout a flawed visionary, a complex mix of atavistic passions and secular sanity. Nehru and Mountbatten may be 'two of the twentieth century's greatest men', but von Tunzelmann has no illusions about the latter.[56] While rejecting Andrew Roberts' insistence that the last viceroy was singularly lacking in both competence and integrity, she recognizes that here was a man unduly ill-disposed to the fledgling Pakistan, whose judgement was clearly clouded by his antipathy for Jinnah and admiration for Nehru. Agreeing to remain as governor-general had some merit, notably in moderating Indian militarism, but in the final analysis staying on was a mistake. In any case Mountbatten had personally contributed to ensuring cross-border tension over both Kashmir and the Punjab. A year after her book attracted a chorus of praise from young Turks like Miranda Seymour, old India hands like William Dalrymple and patrician biographers like Sir Martin Gilbert, Alex von Tunzelmann reflected on Dickie in Delhi: 'He's a funny one … a ridiculous figure in lots of ways – obsessed with trivial, infuriating things like protocol – but he had a progressive attitude towards postcolonial matters and he could get on with people. What you've got to look at is, could anyone else have done better at that particular job? I believe he was the right man and I don't think anyone else could have done better.'[57] Her musings were prompted by the announcement that filming would soon start on *Indian Summer*, and one aspect of Mountbatten's 'hinterland' which she rightly draws attention to is his obsession with the movies – and that, for all the significance of *In Which We Serve* in forging the Mountbatten myth, another Lean/Coward masterpiece, *Brief Encounter*, offers a subtle insight into Dickie and Edwina's fragile yet enduring alliance.[58]

Indian Summer provided a precedent for royal marriages embracing three not two. Although attention in the summer of 2007 naturally focused upon India and Pakistan, the tenth anniversary of Princess Diana's death revived the question of how much 'Uncle Dickie' had been a malign or a positive influence upon Prince Charles, and before that Prince Philip.[59] Eighteen months earlier, royal biographer Penny Junor was insistent that Charles Windsor would not have married Diana Spencer had his 'Honorary Grandfather' still been alive. This frequently aired nostrum was complemented by the implicitly contradictory claim that a dire warning from Mountbatten had left an impressionable Prince of Wales for ever haunted by the fear that he might find himself on the same slippery slope as 'Uncle David', his less than illustrious predecessor.[60] November 2007 marked the fiftieth anniversary of the Princess Elizabeth's marriage to Lieutenant Mountbatten, with Channel 4 twice airing a mildly sensationalist documentary: the general public's zenophobic suspicion of Prince Philip was greatly exaggerated, as was his uncle's role in masterminding the royal engagement.[61] It's clear that across the three decades since the great man's death a broad spectrum of commentary and polemic, from the respectful to the vitriolic, has flourished in the face of public indifference and growing ignorance – how many under the age of 50 have even heard of Mountbatten, or know anything about him other than that he had some connection with the Royal Family, witness an apparent indifference to the thirtieth anniversary of his assassination? Yet clearly Working Title believed there remains a strong interest. Evidence to support such an assumption is that August 2009 was not an occasion for total apathy: Timothy Knatchbull's memoir of childhood trauma, prompting a painful yet revealing exploration of the events surrounding the death of his twin brother, Nicholas, generated a wider media interest in the principal target of the IRA attack.[62]

What might loosely be termed 'a Mountbatten discourse' remains heavily indebted to not one but two monumental works of scholarship: Dickie and Edwina's authorized biographies. Philip Ziegler's magnum opus was matched – and arguably surpassed, in terms of in-depth investigation and insightful observation – by Janet Morgan's 1993 life of Edwina. This was a book written with the full cooperation of the family by an experienced author and former don. A one-time member of the Cabinet Office, Janet Morgan had cut her teeth in the corridors of power shepherding Richard Crossman's diaries through to publication. The meticulous editorship of four weighty volumes was clear evidence of their standard bearer's learned credentials. Her steadfast refusal to be intimidated by Whitehall mandarins had confirmed that here was a scholar of stamina, armed with grit and integrity. Someone so well qualified – and, as Lady Balfour of Burleigh, so well connected – offered the family reassurance that any revelations regarding Edwina's eventful private life would be handled in a sensitive and unsensationalist fashion. Janet Morgan adroitly squared the circle, revealing intimate details with regard to Edwina's interwar affairs while at the same time attracting plaudits from the Countess Mountbatten for the manner in which genuinely fresh information was uncovered.[63]

Morgan doubtless gained approval through the polite but brusque manner in which she dismissed Richard Hough's more speculative judgements regarding moral laxity in the Mountbatten household. Thus she nailed for dead the commonly held belief that, although Edwina won her 1932 libel case against the *People*, the newspaper had simply identified the wrong 'coloured man' as her paramour, implying Paul Robeson instead of the popular nightclub artist 'Hutch'; the fashionable black pianist had played at the Mountbatten's extravagantly refurbished Park Lane residence, Brook House, and been rewarded with a silver cigarette case. Hough had suggested that Edwina and Nehru embarked upon a full-blown affair in the late 1940s, but Morgan persuasively argued this not to be the case[64] Yet *Edwina Mountbatten* is anything but a whitewash. The middle chapters are particularly revealing, and yet never prurient. With a brutal elegance the author details the harsh reality of the strains placed upon the Mountbattens' marriage as Edwina sought emotional and physical solace in the company of smooth, brilliantined lovers like Laddie Sandford and Bunny Phillips. In terms of what had previously been a very rocky relationship the Second World War was clearly a watershed, and the second half of the book is as revealing as the first, but for very different reasons. Here the attention focuses far more upon the public than the private, its subject no longer of interest solely to gossip columnists but perceived at home and abroad as the partner of a power-broker, and as a formidable mover and shaker in her own right.

Morgan's portrait of Edwina is convincing, instructive, and on balance sympathetic. She is very good on context, not least in providing a persuasive picture of life in the fast set at the height of the Depression, with fashionable clubs and West End theatres facilitating a glitzy alternative to languorous weekends in the country and long summers on the Riviera – or in the more exotic parts of the globe increasingly favoured by Edwina as the 1930s progressed. Prolonged absence from Patricia and Pamela echoed their mother's own bleak experience as a child, and perhaps for this reason alone Janet Morgan never falls into the trap of being judgemental. Here is an impressively frank biography, and Mountbatten's failings and emotional inadequacies are explored in the same forensic yet intuitive fashion as those of his wife. Yet at the same time the book can be very funny, albeit on occasion unintentionally so: appeasing the indignant chef at the family's Valetta villa is pure Wodehouse.[65] Janet Morgan's unequivocal success in recreating the Mountbattens' private lives between the wars negates the need to do so here. Everyday life at Adsdean, Broadlands, and Brook House, let alone the catering arrangements at the Casa Medina, are recreated with such confidence and panache that the focus in this particular book has to be upon Lord Louis in uniform, albeit by no means exclusively so. Any exploration of Mountbatten's military career must of course embrace both the public and the private, but with the personal seen as secondary to the political.

As a couple the Mountbattens have been well served by their official biographers. It is easy to see why Lord Brabourne and his fellow trustees saw Philip Ziegler as ideally qualified to quarry the Broadlands archives: Eton, Oxford, the Diplomatic Service, and an editorial post at the Church of England's favoured publisher. Establishment credentials aside, Ziegler was a prodigious researcher who held his nerve in the face of a vast array of primary sources and an intimidating checklist of interviewees. He was promised full editorial control and unrestricted access to 'the treasure-house of Mountbatten's personal archives'. An impressive support team ranged from the Broadlands secretarial staff to such eminent military historians as Michael Howard and Stephen Roskill. Ziegler was promised access to anyone he wished to interview, from the royal house of Windsor to the rajmata of Jaipur; and in the course of the next five years he spoke to over 200 colleagues, acquaintances, friends, and rivals. The final outcome is an 800-page masterpiece, the author demonstrating impressive powers of self-discipline and concision in producing a single volume biography which, while eschewing any claim to be definitive, is remarkably comprehensive. Crucially for such a big book, while no page-turner, it is nevertheless very readable. In Ziegler's own words, 'The result is massive but not, I hope, intolerably so'. *Mountbatten The Official Biography* was very much a product of its era, skillfully blending a traditional, respectful 'life and times' model with the more inquiring, intrusive approach pioneered by Michael Holroyd in his life of Lytton Strachey. Ziegler pre-empted any charge of hagiography, defending his 'generally favourable portrait' as a fair and balanced assessment which would almost certainly have infuriated Mountbatten: 'To suppress his weaknesses would have been to discredit the account of his formidable strengths.'[66]

This was definitely not the authorized biography Mountbatten had in mind; but to meet his criteria for 'balance' and 'accuracy' would have been to produce an amplified version of Terraine's Whiggish account of triumph over adversity. The critics were right to point out that the judicious Ziegler had pulled off an exceptionally tricky task.[67] The worldly ex-diplomat would where appropriate give his man the benefit of the doubt, most controversially over the handling of partition. Nevertheless, Ziegler refused to temper his criticism where he felt it necessary, for example, regarding Mountbatten's operational command of the 5th Destroyer Flotilla. With remarkable deftness Ziegler navigated his way through Mountbatten's private life, hinting at marital tension, but avoiding any charge of undue prurience, and addressing head on suggestions of homo-sexuality or bisexuality. The latter charges he dismissed, but he wasn't afraid to explore the intense nature of Mountbatten's relations with close male friends such as Murphy and Coward, as well as his often obsessive fascination with bright beautiful women like Shirley MacLaine. Ziegler's only mention of Tom Driberg was in the context of Edwina enthusiastically endorsing his attacks on Ernest Bevin's arms-length approach to nationalist demands in south-east Asia. Yet only a few years later Francis Wheen felt confident enough to suggest that the postwar Labour Party's most openly gay MP and the Royal Navy's most high-profile serving officer, 'had much in common, including a sexual preference for men'.[68]

Not that rumours of Mountbatten being gay hadn't been aired openly while he was still alive: in 1975 his name was linked with a *Daily Mirror* exposé of deviant behaviour in the Life Guards' barracks, prompting a private protest that, 'I might have been accused of many things in my life but hardly of the act of homosexuality'. Noel Coward's letters to his 'dear dainty Darling' are gloriously camp, but with no clear hint of a private agenda.[69] Peter Murphy's are surprisingly businesslike – he was a long-term lodger, not a live-in lover. Indeed, entertaining Edwina was probably the main reason why both men were such frequent house guests between the wars. Noel was such a sweetie, and he may have had the gayest of times *chez Mountbatten*, but no correspondence held by the University of Southampton contains any obvious suggestion of a homo-erotic relationship. Mind you this is scarcely surprising as any intimate letters would remain firmly under lock and key at Broadlands.

In a lengthy essay for the *New York Review of Books* David Cannadine paid tribute to a 'fairminded' volume which left the reader with a clear idea of why Mountbatten could generate both deep admiration and fierce enmity; the latter reflected envy of a man for ever reluctant to rest on his laurels: 'On the whole the British prefer their royalty to be ornamental and impotent rather than ornamental and important.' Building on the neat aphorism, Cannadine identified Mountbatten's unique credentials within British royalty for closing down great institutions, both on the far frontier and closer to home. Thus, the flood of honours was not the usual consolation for a loss of personal esteem and influence, but a governing elite saying thanks for making Britain's demonstrable – and in the postwar era seemingly unavoidable – loss of power so palatable to a nation still easily impressed by someone so charming and well connected. Nearly 20 years later Cannadine remained adamant that wherever our man found himself – in the Viceregal Lodge or the Admiralty penthouse – Dickie Mountbatten remained ever faithful to his task as the 'pioneering and pre-eminent *de*-imperialist'. If there was a flaw in Ziegler's monumental, magisterial volume then it was an absence of reflexivity – there needed to be a keener awareness of perspective, 'namely a broader historical sense of just what it was that he was really doing'; and Cannadine's observation might be applied as much to the author as to his subject.[70]

This book makes no claim to match Philip Ziegler's official biography in terms of breadth, and in any case it covers only just over half of Mountbatten's crowded life. However, for forensic exploration of those first 43 years its author is happy to challenge the master: the intervening quarter of a century has seen a ceaseless stream of relevant secondary literature, and increased access to catalogued papers and diaries, many now available in hard copy or on-line. Crucially, the present volume addresses Cannadine's call for context, hence the initial claim that here is an imperial story. Opportunity is taken to step back periodically and, as well as reflecting upon familiar areas of controversy, to consider less obvious questions; exploring, for example, Mountbatten's fascination with applied science, or his readiness to embrace popular culture as a key myth-making tool.

Conscious that an authorized biographer needs to embody a demonstrable air of dignity and gravitas, Ziegler adopted a deliberately non-combative approach. He provided a generally low-key reaction to critics of Mountbatten whose work appeared prior to publication of his own book. Years later he noted his subject's unique 'capacity to inspire unbridled animosity in those who criticized him', citing Nigel Hamilton as an early example: Montgomery's biographer saw Mountbatten as a virtual psychopath and a 'master of intrigue, jealousy and ineptitude'.[71] This view was shared by the Ottawa historian Brian Loring Villa, whose excoriating account of how the Chief of Combined Operations bore total responsibility for the disaster at Dieppe Philip Ziegler found particularly distasteful.[72] Speaking in 1995 he highlighted what he saw as extenuating circumstances with regard to the raid, refuting Andrew Roberts' claim that operational errors were attributable to the 'overall commander'. Ziegler insisted that Mountbatten did not enjoy control over events in the field, reiterating the point in his foreword to the unamended 2001 paperback edition.[73] He refrained from any point by point response to Roberts' truly ferocious assault upon the 'mendacious, intellectually limited hustler' whose irresponsibility extended even to endangering his own family's lives through a vainglorious indifference to Garda advice.[74]

Perhaps Ziegler felt it would have required another book to see off Andrew Roberts' cold-steel character assassination. However, he was also aware that by the time *Eminent Churchillians* was published in 1994, he could no longer give Mountbatten the benefit of the doubt over an allegation that in August 1947 the viceroy secretly persuaded Cyril Radcliffe to make a last minute concession to India over the Ferozepur headwaters. Mountbatten insisted that Radcliffe, the supposedly inscrutable and incorruptible lawyer, whose reputation as a man of integrity was matched only by the scale of his ignorance regarding the geography of India, had been appointed on the clear understanding that he would remain at arm's length from the British authorities. Both barrister and viceroy reassured all parties at the time, and indeed for the rest of their respective lives, that the frontiers between India and Pakistan were the consequence of a scrupulously honest process of demarcation. Ziegler conceded that evidence accrued since the completion of his biography, particularly the testimony of the Boundary Commission's secretary, Christopher Beaumont, had forced him to accept that Mountbatten foolishly and unnecessarily jeopardized the position of scrupulous neutrality he had established since his arrival in India. Even worse, he had sought to disguise his démarche. The only defence Ziegler could offer to the myriad of Mountbatten critics, of whom Roberts was merely the most intelligent and articulate, was that, 'the Viceroy was physically exhausted and had been for months subject to the most gruelling psychological pressure' – to the extent that he erroneously 'convinced himself that the entire settlement was at risk'. Ziegler knew these mitigating circumstances were unlikely to sway the jury; and in the final analysis he fell back on a familiar plea that, despite Mountbatten's many errors of judgement and personal rectitude, 'if the scales of justice could be perfectly adjusted, he would be found to have done much more good than harm'. Despite one *very* foolish indiscretion, the summer of 1947 had seen Dickie Mountbatten at his best. Ziegler remained convinced that, for all his faults ('on the grandest scale'), the last viceroy had proved to be a genuinely great man.[75]

Philip Ziegler consciously avoided discussion of what actually constitutes 'greatness' – he had, after all, a very long book to finish, and the end was thankfully in sight. Yet, before exploring the first half of Mountbatten's career in depth, it is worth pausing to reflect upon his biographer's claim, carefully modulated and qualified, that here was someone wholly deserving of a place in the pantheon. Mountbatten spectacularly failed to match Ralph Waldo Emerson's basic criteria for greatness, namely a disdain for creature comforts, a readiness to embrace the simple life, and an indifference to public acclaim. His lifestyle was scarcely modest or his behaviour 'natural and poetic'; and yet he clearly matched Emerson's insistence on 'good humour and hilarity'. Both New England philosopher and old England patrician would have agreed that 'self trust is the essence of heroism'; as, the Transcendentalist adds, are persistency and consistency. Mountbatten would certainly have seen the latter as marked features of his viceroyalty and, no doubt, of his extended tenure as Chief of the Defence Staff. Emerson famously concluded that 'all heroes eventually become bores'. Those close to Mountbatten, especially in his later years, would no doubt concur. Stories abound of his endlessly repeating tedious tales of derring do, and the final volume of his published diaries unwittingly confirm this to be the case. One suspects that 'Lilibet' regularly displayed the patience of a saint, not least when hosting Uncle Dickie on *Britannia*.[76]

For Tolstoy great men, in the words of Sir Isaiah Berlin, deny their real cosmic insignificance only because they are 'ignorant and vain enough to accept responsibility for the life of society'. Thus great events unfold, and 'History' assigns to her heroes roles which are wholly disproportionate to their actual, in truth quite modest, contributions. To adhere wholeheartedly to the Tolstoyan diminution of the 'great man' (incidentally, note the absence of great women from this distinctly nineteenth century discourse), and yet devote so much attention to the life of Lord Louis, suggests a wholly paradoxical approach to historical determinism. Yet Tolstoy's deeply sceptical view of Napoleon's direct impact on the ebb and flow of battle offers a healthy rejoinder whenever the biographer is tempted to make too many claims regarding the significance of his or her subject, especially when the person in question is an omnipresent establishment figure like Dickie Mountbatten.[77] Tolstoy famously provided Isaiah Berlin with the intellectual dilemma of deciding whether the great novelist was a hedgehog or a fox: 'The fox knows many things, but the hedgehog knows one big thing.' Mountbatten was of course the quintessential fox: a 'centripetal rather than centrifugal' figure 'moving on many levels, seizing upon the essence of a vast variety of experiences and objects' and eschewing a 'unitary inner vision'.[78] He may have encouraged the left-leaning image, however superficial the reality, and yet no-one maintained a healthier respect for the prescribed role of both public official and gentleman officer within the British state. In public he scrupulously respected conventions of command and control. Behind the scenes it was of course a very different matter, and his semi-royal status proved an invaluable means of protection. Thus, from Munich to Suez Mountbatten unhesitatingly bent the rules whenever circumstances were deemed to justify bucking the system. Courting controversy and taking risks – is this the mark of the 'great man'? Except that the last viceroy's fiercest critics rarely perceive the risk-taking as genuine; if only, they argue, because a privileged safety-net would always cushion the machinating maestro's fall from grace.

Having concluded that here really was a great man, the official biographer courted criticism by suggesting that his ageing admiral died in appalling yet appropriate circumstances. In making his claim Ziegler chose his words carefully. Mountbatten had died at sea in truly memorable circumstances: he had left this world 'not with a whimper but with a bang that reverberated around the world', thereby avoiding the heaviest burdens of physical and mental decrepitude.[79] Mountbatten may have known nothing of his demise, but the cost to his family and that of local lad Paul Maxwell was unacceptably high: a total of four deaths, and serious injuries to Lord and Lady Brabourne and their other twin son.[80]

If the IRA's 'legitimate target' had been left to die with dignity, and with all his faculties still intact, then there would have been no more suitable time than the summer of 1982, once the union flag was again flying over Port Stanley. How Mountbatten would have relished the Falklands war as a reflection of all he considered crucial to effective amphibious operations: close land-sea-air liaison, attention to logistical detail, appropriate kit, meticulous training combined with necessary improvisation, flexible deployment of elite forces, a clear command structure (with the Royal Navy in the driving seat), and unequivocal political direction. Above all the Falklands campaign would have proved a purgative experience – a stark contrast to the angst of the Suez crisis when the First Sea Lord twice offered to resign, and privately pleaded with Eden to respect the UN and halt the invasion ('You can imagine how hard it is for me to break with all service custom and write to you in this way, but I feel so desperate about what is happening that my conscience would not allow me to do otherwise.').[81] A quarter of a century later, with Hampshire taking such a prominent role in the dispatch of the Task Force, one can picture a very different scenario: the nation's best known admiral of the fleet standing bolt upright in full dress uniform on the dockside at Southampton relishing his self-appointed ceremonial role of despatching the *QE2* and *Canberra* south, and of welcoming them home three months later. Truly, Lord Louis died before his time was up.

2

LORD LOUIS MOUNTBATTEN – A ROYAL PARVENU?

From Battenberg to Mountbatten

The funeral gave Grandpapa his final, glorious moment. If he had died a slow lingering death through illness, it wouldn't have been nearly so dramatic or touched the public's heart in the same way. But in a peculiar way, the method of his dying and the magnificent occasion of his funeral elevated him back into the limelight in a way he would have relished.[1]

Grandpapa's funeral on 5 September 1979 was a state occasion in everything but name. For all his protestations that the final farewell would be a private affair Mountbatten planned events in London and Romsey secure in the knowledge that Her Majesty was happy to grant his every wish. Each moment of a closely choreographed programme was dutifully anticipated and recorded. A bulky and much amended file was housed in the Lord Chamberlain's Office; a detailed blueprint to be referred to ceaselessly once news of its subject's demise had been telephoned through.[2] On the day itself everything went according to plan: the cortège progressed solemnly from the Chapel Royal to Westminster and then on to Waterloo Station; the service in the Abbey effortlessly stirred deep emotions of genuine grief and national pride; the coffin arrived at its final resting place promptly; and the obsequies of the private interment in Romsey took place quietly, discretely – and precisely on time. Everyone whom Mountbatten had intended to be there was there: from the extended family of Victoria and Albert to the old comrades of Burma and the *Kelly*. A crowd of 50,000 lined the streets in London, but even those paying their respects at home could sense from the televised proceedings that here was a potent and powerful mix of pomp, ceremony, dignity, collective mourning, and private grieving – gravitas, respect, shock, and regret, but also warmth and good humour. The latter was equally evident at the unveiling of Mountbatten's statue in Whitehall four years later, his eldest daughter echoing Barbara Cartland's post-funeral observation: 'Wouldn't Dickie have loved all this?'[3]

Dickie had seen his every demand satisfied because the denizens of Balmoral were in wholehearted agreement with the immediate family that this should be so. Clearly the funeral marked the British state making a loud and unequivocal statement – to the IRA, to Republican sympathisers on both sides of the Atlantic, and to a global audience – that gross acts of political violence could not sway government or popular resolve. Nevertheless, Mountbatten was always determined to be buried in the grand manner, whatever the circumstances in which he might pass away, and, given the resolve of the Royal Family, there is every reason to believe that at any other time this would still have been the case. If it is possible to set aside the manner of his death then one might argue that this was the last state or quasi-state funeral where there was no obvious sub-text: no elegiac end of an era as with Churchill in 1965; no family feuding and future of the monarchy agenda as with Diana in 1997; and no tacit acknowledgement of down-sized mourning as with the Queen Mother in 2002.

George VI's widow was of course in attendance. The absence of his elder brother's spouse was not the consequence of any deliberate snub, but simply because the Duchess of Windsor was incapable of leaving her bedroom let alone crossing the Channel to say goodbye to someone she probably had just cause never entirely to trust. Thus the long shadow of the Abdication fell short of the September ceremonials, no doubt to the relief of all concerned. Wallis Simpson's absence meant no reminder of a key figure in the young Mountbatten's formative years immediately after the First World War. 'David', Prince of Wales and future Edward VIII, rated scarcely a mention in the post-Mullaghmore encomiums, and yet until December 1936, and arguably even after, he was a major presence in the lives of both Dickie and Edwina. The newly-married Windsors' pro-Nazis sympathies – all too evident from their much-publicised visit to Germany in October 1937 – placed an obvious strain upon their relations with the anti-appeasement Mountbattens. The Duke's position was of course seriously compromised as a consequence of his 'Phoney War' peace initiatives, and he became a genuine security risk following the fall of France. While, privately and publicly, Mountbatten endeavoured to rescue his cousin's reputation after 1945, during the war he quite rightly distanced himself from someone he still believed was a 'spell-binder … [whose] charisma, his magic always worked'.[4]

Unlike Churchill the veil never wholly fell from Mountbatten's eyes, with normal relations resuming after the Windsors took up permanent residence in France. However strained those relations might on occasion prove to be, the couple did stay at Broadlands in June 1967 when the Queen invited them to an unveiling of a centennial plaque for her grandmother, Queen Mary. One source of tension was Mountbatten's growing concern over what would happen to the Duke's posthumous papers and most personal possessions. He repeatedly suggested that these be left to Prince Charles, encouraging the latter to make singularly awkward visits to his great-uncle.[5] 'David' died on 28 May 1972, and there was no argument over who would meet the Duchess at Heathrow when she flew in for her husband's deliberately low-key funeral at Windsor – Prince Charles was gently elbowed aside. By the time of her arrival Mountbatten had persuaded a deeply reluctant Buckingham Palace that refusing the BBC's request for a tribute to the Duke on grounds of precedent

Figure 2.1: The *Kelly* carries the Duke of Windsor home from France,
12–13 September 1939

might reflect badly upon the Royal Family. Rather like the controversy over whether
the standard at Buckingham Palace should fly at half-mast to mark Diana's death,
the Queen was eventually convinced of a change of heart by her private secretary,
granting Mountbatten permission to broadcast so long as he was muted in his praise.[6]

Reassured that the grave at Frogmore would one day accommodate her, the
Duchess hastened home to the Bois de Boulogne. Always deeply suspicious of Dickie,
she famously remarked of his wish that Edwina be interred in true naval fashion: 'What
can you say about a man who throws his wife into the sea?'.[7] Mountbatten's frequent
visits fuelled a mounting fear that he and/or the rest of the Royal Family were intent
on retrieving lost treasures once she was dead. The unwelcome house guest became
more and more focused upon his late cousin's estate, while an increasingly fragile
Duchess became obsessed. On 9 December 1974 her doctor instructed Mountbatten
to make no more cross-Channel visits. In the spring of 1979 her formidable, and
today notorious, attorney, Maître Blum, claimed Mountbatten had ordered a break-
in at the Windsor villa in order to steal confidential papers. These wild allegations,
fuelled by senile dementia and litigious greed, were ironic given that both conspiracy
theorists and respectable historians have long suspected Buckingham Palace of
employing questionable methods in the summer of 1945 to extract from Germany
any incriminating evidence that might link the Nazi leadership with the Duke of
Windsor – and with his younger brother and enthusiastic appeasement envoy in the
late 1930s, the late Duke of Kent.[8]

That the former Prince of Wales remained a great Germanophile despite his
experience of the Western Front was scarcely surprising. He continued to visit
Germany regularly after the Great War, speaking the language fluently. Furthermore,
he conducted a regular, if not always wise, correspondence with close confidants

among the imperial and aristocratic families being forced to come to terms with the harsh reality of the Weimar Republic. As a direct descendant of Queen Victoria, and the heir to the British throne, 'David' considered himself at the heart of a continent-wide social network that proved more than capable of surviving conflagration and revolution. As for the Saxe-Coburgs, so too for the Battenbergs. At Mountbatten's funeral the astonishing array of royal mourners, from Scandinavia to the Balkans, was testimony to the genealogical complexities of a bruised yet resilient European pan-monarchy, its teutonic epicentre transcending divisions of family and frontier. Crowded into Westminster Abbey were the crowned heads or immediate heirs of around a dozen countries, of whom at least half were still on the throne.[9] Most had some family connection, however distant, with Mountbatten. Almost all were, either directly or through marriage, related to the *Hochadel* or high nobility which, driven by Prussia, had in the first 70 years of the previous century forged a powerful nation state.

Twice in living memory that same nation state had sought hegemonic control of the European land mass. On both occasions the British Royal Family and its aristocratic subsidiaries had repositioned themselves as the very embodiment of patriotic fervour and purposeful national endeavour. For the first time in two centuries they established themselves as unequivocally British, hence the decision to drop all German surnames in 1917 – the year Battenberg was neatly anglicised to Mountbatten. Yet, unless German relations had demonstrably become 'the enemy', in both deed and thought, rarely were familial ties sacrificed; merely suspended for the duration. (Ironically the one continental family that did suffer fatal isolation was a wartime ally – the Romanovs.) Not even membership of the Nazi Party ruled out discreet wartime contacts, witness the Mountbattens' intermittent exchange of news with both branches of the Hesse family up until 1943 – defeat at Stalingrad, followed 18 months later by Claus Von Stauffenberg's failure to assassinate Hitler, prompted National Socialism to rediscover its radical roots and turn on a by now fatally compromised nobility.[10] Not that all German aristocrats were Nazi members or sympathisers, and Mountbatten drew strength from the fact that so many of his relatives deliberately remained aloof from day-to-day politics: if in wartime they took up arms then this constituted a laudable patriotism, no different from their fathers' readiness to defend the Reich in August 1914. However, second time around German armed forces were waging a very different sort of war, especially on the Eastern Front: any claim to be a simple soldier, adhering always to a martial code rooted firmly in chivalric values and the Geneva Convention, invariably rang hollow.

Of Victoria and Albert's nine children, two married into the Prussian imperial family and four into *Hochadel* royal houses, with the second son, Prince Alfred, doubling up as Duke of Edinburgh and of Saxe-Coburg and Gotha. His elder brother, the future Edward VII, may have eschewed the German connection, but his successor to the throne, George V, maintained the family tradition by marrying Princess Mary of Teck – no wonder the Prince of Wales enjoyed an impressive command of German, as indeed did his close friend and second cousin, the younger son of Prince Louis Alexander of Battenberg: although by instinct and intent unshakably loyal to the British crown, both of Mountbatten's parents were by birth German. Queen Victoria's second daughter, Princess Alice, married the Grand Duke of Hesse, their eldest child, Princess Victoria, finding the love of her life along yet another branch of the ever-more complex Hessen family tree, the Battenbergs. Prince Louis was a career sailor from a land-locked state who had left home to join the Royal Navy in 1868. He was an adopted – but by no means wholly assimilated – English aristocrat who, even as a chief of staff, still saw Hesse as *heimat*, home. Yet as an officer he overcame early hostility, successfully subsumed his German roots, and progressed towards the very pinnacle of command. Like so many of Their Lordships, including his second son, Prince Louis consolidated his reputation in the Mediterranean. Yet it was as Director of Naval Intelligence that he had first proved himself an unashamed moderniser within the Admiralty. The architect of the Dreadnought revolution, Jackie Fisher, became convinced that here was a man with the ideas, intellectual capacity, and above all the temperament, to maintain the momentum of reform. He rubbished any rumblings in the gutter press that his protégé's first loyalty might still be to Germany: 'In reality he is more English than the English ....'[11] Something of an exaggeration perhaps, but crucially Churchill was of the same opinion, in December 1912 orchestrating Battenberg's early elevation from Second to First Sea Lord. Over 60 years later Mountbatten insisted his father was, 'almost the last Admiral Churchill loved in World War I', thereby leaving open the question of who actually was the last, while glossing over the fact that by November 1914 Prince Louis was already *hors de combat*.[12] A skilful diplomat, in peacetime he deftly mediated between an interventionist First Lord and his uniformed colleagues on the Admiralty Board. As with the son, so with the father – Battenberg's success or failure as a chief of staff depended upon his partnership with Churchill. Like Dudley Pound, First Sea Lord in 1939–40, he became adept at curtailing or delaying Winston's wilder suggestions.[13] He was equally adept in easing tensions between the newly-established Naval War Staff and its army equivalent, and in facilitating discreet yet productive conversations with the French *Marin*. It's noticeable that top-down initiatives at this time encountered surprisingly little resistance given that the Royal Navy remained a generally conservative institution. It was known that Prince Louis neither took nor caused offence, and his easy temperament and obvious efficiency ensured a hard-won respect among his colleagues.[14]

That respect was complemented by affection for Princess Victoria, someone with an easy-going manner, a readiness to air her views, and an obvious appetite for knowledge. Domesticity not dynasty lay at the heart of the Battenbergs' marriage – a genuine partnership, with Prince Louis acknowledging his wife as a critical factor in his eventual success.[15] Mountbatten was born eight years after his elder brother, Prince George. He in turn was younger than Princess Louise, who married the future King Gustaf VI of Sweden, and Princess Alice who forged further ties with Germany by marrying the distinctly non-Hellenic Prince Andrew of Greece. The latter couple's four daughters all acquired aristocratic German husbands, their much younger brother, Prince Philip, visibly breaking tradition by marrying the future Queen Elizabeth II.

Figure 2.2: The six-year-old Prince Louis Battenberg on parade in Gibraltar, 1906

Thus, via his grandparents, and as a consequence of two nieces' marriages, Mountbatten was closely related to both branches of the Grand Duchy of Hesse and the Rhine: Darmstadt, and the more junior Kessel. He could boast family connections with several other houses prominent in the *Almanach de Gotha*, and – looking eastwards – throughout his life Mountbatten made great play of the fact that one of his mother's sisters had married Tsar Nicholas II (glossing over the fact that another had married the Kaiser's brother). However, within this complex web of endogamy the Hessen connections stand out, and, as Jonathan Petropoulos demonstrated in *Royals and the Reich*, this was especially problematic. The rise of the

Nazis presented genuine dilemmas, yet in the 1930s Dickie and Edwina maintained regular if sometimes uncomfortable contact with the extended family in Hesse, several of whom were intimately connected with the ruling regime. The Grand Duke George Donatus, whose funeral the couple attended in November 1937, was a late and perhaps pragmatic recruit to the party. In contrast, the present Duke of Edinburgh's brother-in-law, Prince Christoph of Hesse-Kassell, was a protégé of Göring and head of the secret signals intelligence agency, the *Forschungsamt*, until his ultimately fatal decision to join the *Luftwaffe* when war broke out. Three other princes were enthusiastic Nazis, while Philipp von Hessen, head of the family from 1940 and King Umberto's son-in-law, was a key figure in Axis diplomacy and for a long time a trusted confidant of Hitler. Reluctantly returning from Rome in 1933 to serve as *Oberpräsident* of Hesse-Nassau, his incarceration in a concentration camp following Italy's surrender highlighted the extent to which most aristocrats who served the Nazi Party had by late 1943 been denounced as potentially subversive and undermining the war effort. Prince Philipp was only distantly related to Mountbatten, but strong suspicions remain that, via his friend the Duke of Kent, he was an intermediary between Hitler and the Duke of Windsor.[16]

In maintaining regular correspondence and reciprocal visits with Dickie's German relatives, the Mountbattens displayed very real affection for the von Hessen-Darmstadt family. Along with their two daughters they holidayed at Schloss Wolfsgarten in August 1937, with Prince Christoph their principal host. Earlier in the year the posting of Prince Ludwig to the German Embassy prompted an intimate family party at Brook House, Dickie and Edwina's newly refurbished home in Park Lane. 'Prince Lu' was known to be unusually close to Joachim von Ribbentrop, yet diplomatic niceties meant that Stanley Baldwin and his Foreign Secretary, Anthony Eden, expressed no objection to the presence of King George VI and Queen Elizabeth.[17] Basic civilities had to be maintained, and if as a by-product Anglo-German relations improved then all well and good; but the Mountbattens were unusual among their 'set' in not deluding themselves about what was going on inside the Third Reich. From the outset they acknowledged the deeply oppressive nature of National Socialism, not least in its treatment of the Jews. Edwina, herself half Jewish, could scarcely fail to be affected by the brutal nature of Nazi persecution even prior to *Kristallnacht*, while her husband was able to see for himself the speed with which the German military machine was rebuilt once the last vestiges of the Treaty of Versailles had been cast aside. Mountbatten had no illusions regarding Germany's ambitions and its military potential, hence a consistent opposition to appeasement. In this respect he differed profoundly from all of George V's sons, including the Duke of York. Where the future George VI differed significantly from his elder brother was in not translating his faith in the National Government's conduct of foreign affairs in to a pro-active belief that the Nazi seizure and consolidation of power could be mutually beneficial to Germany and to the United Kingdom. As we shall see, Mountbatten set out to persuade the Prince of Wales before and after he acceded to the throne that Hitler constituted a very real threat to national and imperial security. He clearly failed, and the Germanophile mentality of the once and former king came to acquire an implicitly ideological dimension.[18]

Mountbatten's suspicion of German intentions after 1933 echoed the fears of his father from the spring of 1913 when calls for a naval holiday fell on deaf ears, both sides of the North Sea. In a relatively junior position within the Admiralty from 1936 to late 1938, and yet with connections at the very highest level of political control and military command, Mountbatten urged that the Royal Navy be put on a war footing. A very real criticism of Prince Louis and his senior colleagues in August 1914 was that, for all their reforms, the Admiralty remained institutionally ill-prepared to fight a world war. A particular criticism of the First Sea Lord was that, despite his initiative on 26 July in halting the Grand Fleet's dispersal once its test mobilisation and royal review were over, he allowed Churchill far too much influence over operational planning and implementation. Furthermore, he failed to improve the coordination of and communication with his senior commanders at sea.[19] The mixed fortunes of the Royal Navy in the first two months of the war, and the fierce pressure that the Unionist opposition and its Fleet Street supporters were already placing on Asquith's administration, made Battenberg an obvious target. Jingoist rags like Horatio Bottomley's *John Bull* saw treason not misfortune whenever the Service faltered. Prince Louis was now a political liability, and for the First Lord of the Admiralty it became expedient to sacrifice his most senior professional adviser. The two men had already clashed over Churchill's insistence on personally organising the defence of Antwerp. Having dealt directly with Battenberg while the First Lord was directing operations in Belgium, Asquith now shared Churchill's view that a change at the top was urgently required. In the end an 'emotionally crushed' First Sea Lord took the initiative, tendering his resignation on 28 October 1914. Any delay in announcing the decision was a consequence of George V's deep reluctance to see his cousin make way for Jackie Fisher. In departing the Admiralty Prince Louis appears genuinely to have believed that he could resume active service once the war was over. The reality was of course very different, and he finally resigned in January 1919. Being promoted to Admiral of the Fleet in September 1921 was scant consolation for being the first, but by no means the last, victim of a virulent Germanophobia, fuelled by an unforgiving and unscrupulous popular press.[20]

Writing from his flag ship at Rosyth, David Beatty summed up the view of the Grand Fleet: 'Prince Louis departed not for the reason given but to save the politicians.'[21] Andrew Roberts was by no means the first to wonder whether, up until Mountbatten's appointment as Viceroy, Churchill assuaged a keen sense of guilt by offering disproportionate support: 'He was to repay this debt of honour to the son often and heavily, until he came bitterly to regret it.' David Cannadine has suggested that Churchill could easily empathise with Mountbatten's 'inordinate ambition' because he too was driven by a 'burning desire to vindicate his father's unjustly slighted reputation'. David Reynolds identified a human cost to Churchill's efforts at making amends, pointing to the scale of losses at Dieppe: 'It was thanks to him [the PM] that this egregious social climber had been so absurdly over-promoted.'[22] In later life Mountbatten avoided any attack on Churchill for not doing more to protect Prince Louis in the autumn of 1914. His father had himself been remarkably generous towards the apparent orchestrator of his downfall, preferring to see Asquith as the real villain in the piece.[23] Mountbatten somewhat implausibly argued that a universal suspicion of ethnic Germans fighting for the Allied cause had ignored the Wilhelmine Reich's internal politics: the Hessen-Kassel branch had seen its lands confiscated by Bismarck following military defeat in 1866, and 'My father was 12 years old when this happened, so he had good reason to detest the Prussians from a very early age ... the very people he had come to England to avoid!'. Churchill in *The World Crisis* similarly encouraged this view that Battenberg felt antipathy not obligation towards an imperial state created three years after he had left for England.[24]

In his television memoirs Mountbatten made scant reference to the popular mythology surrounding his father's enforced resignation: the shaken young naval cadet alone by the flagstaff at Osborne wiping away the tears, and vowing to make amends for the great injustice done to his family by emulating Prince Louis' achievement in becoming First Sea Lord. Indeed, in an interview with the *Observer*'s Kenneth Harris a few years earlier he categorically denied the story. Back in April 1955 most newspapers had recounted the story when reporting Mountbatten's appointment as head of the Royal Navy.[25] Contrary to popular assumption, in the autumn of 1914 there was no taunting – the bullying accusations of pro-German loyalties endured by Mountbatten on his arrival at Osborne 18 months earlier were thankfully short-lived.[26] The Royal Naval College – located, ironically, in the grounds of the Prince Consort's summer retreat – was in every respect a tough school: the range of teaching was generally of a high standard, witness Mountbatten's designated tutor ending his teaching career as headmaster of Harrow; but a crowded, intense curriculum was underpinned by fierce discipline, with all movement undertaken at the double.[27] Fights were common, with Mountbatten on one occasion obliged to risk punishment by taking on a senior boy. Cadet Battenberg was seen as unjustifiably bumptious given his very average performances in the college's relentless succession of academic and practical tests, and his failure to stand out in 'games'. He was thus by no means universally popular, and yet his father's resignation did not serve to make him a victim.[28] Both staff and students recognised that a fundamentally decent man, popular within the Service, had been forced to fall on his sword. Nevertheless fellow cadets later confirmed Mountbatten's confident assertion that he could best vindicate his father by one day taking his place. Colleagues from various stages in Mountbatten's career confirmed that the memory of his father's humiliation drove him on, witness his insistence on returning to the Royal Navy's regular career path in 1946 and again in 1948. He himself readily admitted to Richard Hough that, 'I must obviously have had a great urge ...'. No doubt 'Fame was the spur because shame was the spur', but it would be foolish to attribute Mountbatten's immense ambition – naturally for the relentless Roberts, 'all-consuming' – solely to the nation's shameful treatment of Prince Louis. Here was a man who, by dint of character and personality, would have wanted to get to the top whatever his family circumstances; and yet it would not be an exaggeration to describe Cadet Battenberg as deeply and permanently affected by his father's enforced resignation as First Sea Lord.[29]

One consequence of Prince Louis' inequitable treatment was that Mountbatten made himself more British than the British. Yet, as several contemporaries observed, his mode of behaviour was distinctly un-English – he tried just that little bit too hard, and he made it too obvious that he wanted to win. Serving with the Mediterranean Fleet in the 1930s his insistence that HMS *Wishart* should be the top destroyer in every single competition was not viewed kindly – such naked ambition simply wasn't the done thing.[30] Similarly, Mountbatten consciously set out to work his way from the periphery to the heart of the Royal Family. Although clearly well-connected, the Battenbergs were undoubtedly drawn from the second division of the Hessen hierarchy. An isolated figure back home as a consequence of his decision to join the Royal Navy, Prince Louis nevertheless made a good marriage. Yet, notwithstanding the direct line back to Victoria, on the whole the Battenbergs stood respectfully at the edge of court life. Through prodigious energy, no little scheming, and sheer will power, their second son changed the status of the renamed Mountbatten family, creating a popular impression that he and his closest relatives were an integral part of the Windsor dynasty, and not merely a support act. As we shall see, Prince Albert had a minor role to play in bringing Dickie centre-stage. Yet the principal player was clearly the Prince of Wales.

Switching allegiances: Dickie and David … Dickie and Bertie

Mountbatten was always impressed by the fact that the Duke of York, five years his senior, had served at Jutland. Yet, despite the difference in age, at Cambridge in the winter of 1919-20 Dickie was clearly the dominant character – he was confident, articulate, good-looking, and above all, unconstrained by the strict rules George V had laid down for the varsity education of his younger sons. It's scarcely surprising therefore that the ambitious Mountbatten persuaded 'Bertie' to lobby the King on his behalf: at a time of enormous uncertainty within the Royal Navy nothing was to be lost career-wise by accompanying the Prince of Wales on his first major tour of the Empire; and indeed much could be gained by spending several months as aide-de-camp and close confidant of the next King-Emperor. At a dance in December 1919 Mountbatten was over-joyed to hear the Prince ask him to join the tour 'down under'.[31] If he did not consciously set out to bask in the reflected glory of the world's most eligible bachelor then Mountbatten did little to avoid this happening, even at the cost of antagonising several more senior members of the Prince's travelling entourage. There was no ruthless severing of ties with Prince Albert, witness an intermittent yet ongoing correspondence whenever Mountbatten was abroad. After the Duke of York married Elizabeth Bowes-Lyon and started a family he had little involvement with the Mountbattens and their racey, hard-living set. Perhaps there was the occasional muttering of disapproval, but the Yorks and the Mountbattens seemed to get on well – they just didn't see much of each other outside of formal engagements and social gatherings.[32] The glamorous Lord Louis may have displayed quiet admiration for the stammering, serious-minded, celebrity-eschewing Prince Albert, but it was the heir to the throne who demanded – and duly received – Mountbatten's complete loyalty and lasting affection.

The Prince of Wales, only recently returned from a triumphant tour of North America, had no wish to visit Australia and New Zealand, but he came under intense pressure to do so from his father and from Lloyd George. Economic recession had succeeded postwar boom, and, like Britain, both countries were experiencing serious labour unrest. In the view of a still immensely powerful Prime Minister a royal tour was the most effective way of countering claims that ANZAC sacrifices had been solely for the benefit of a now indifferent 'mother country'. Further dates on this global adventure included the Pacific colonies and the West Indies. Once home, preparations could begin for yet another tour; this time to India, Ceylon, Burma, and Japan.[33] The Prince loathed the notion of being separated for months from his worldly-wise mistress, Freda Dudley Ward. From the outset Mountbatten's principal task was to stop his besotted master descending into prolonged fits of depression, where 'he'd shut himself in his cabin for days, alone, face drawn, eyes brooding'.[34] Prior to the battle cruiser HMS *Renown*'s departure in March 1920 Mountbatten promised Mrs Dudley Ward that if a shoulder was needed to cry on then his was permanently available.[35] Within days the Prince was reassuring her that, despite the difference in age, his new friend was proving admirably supportive: 'As for the rest of the staff they are all as nice as ever but I haven't got the same bond with them and they don't know you ....' The two men became almost inseparable, with Mountbatten granted a degree of familiarity denied more senior members of the Prince's staff. Appalled by the brashness and breeziness of 'The Boy', they despatched a list of his 'misdeeds' to the admiral's cabin. Mountbatten's formal posting was as flag lieutenant to Rear Admiral Sir Lionel Halsey, Comptroller of the Prince's Household. Halsey's hale and hearty demeanour disguised a sharp brain. Sir John Jellicoe's fleet captain at Jutland, he combined his formal duties with the far less public role of inducting the King's sons into 'the Craft' – given his initially strained relations with Mountbatten he could scarcely promote the bumptious young pup as a fast-track entrant in to the closed world of freemasonry.[36]

Halsey and his staff captain, Dudley North, made clear in no uncertain terms what was and was not acceptable behaviour when socialising with the Prince. If Mountbatten had any sense then he would have realised that, however helpful royal patronage might prove in the future, antagonising senior officers within the Service was not a sound career move. Over time Mountbatten and Halsey were to develop a close working and personal relationship, as confirmed by the latter's despairing letter in the aftermath of the Abdication.[37] More immediately, the Prince continued to rage that his 'little brother' had been reined in, and was subject to such intense jealousy and dislike: 'I'm so fond of that boy and he means so much to me when I'm away from TOI [Freda Dudley Ward], far more than Bertie has or ever will ....'[38] Mountbatten's record of events hints at these tensions, but is never as explicit as his letters home to his mother. In terms of confidentiality and revelation his diary is a hybrid. At the start of the tour Mountbatten was asked by Halsey to keep an unofficial record, which could be printed on board and read for amusement. Intent on entertaining his shipmates he displayed a frankness certain to generate controversy if any entries were read beyond their intended audience; and yet for obvious reasons the diary was never as intimate and revealing as the more personal journal he maintained throughout his second sojourn with the Prince.[39]

Less than halfway through the tour 'David' was already insistent that his youthful soul-mate must accompany him to India and the Far East. Mountbatten himself was soon pulling strings at home, even before the *Renown* reached Australia. The case for keeping him was helped by the fact that he clearly did have a calming effect on the brooding and highly temperamental Prince, much to the relief of Halsey, North, and the other heavyweight members of his support team. Playing both Jeeves and Wooster, at moments of crisis Dickie wiped the fevered brow, leaving his more auspicious colleagues to liaise with local grandees and officials. Everyone was happy, despite the occasional frayed tempers and the odd nursery tantrum. To the relief of all the dominions proved as docile as the colonies proved convivial – all were only too glad to welcome the heir to the throne, particularly someone so skilled in working a crowd.[40]

What emerges from Mountbatten's private record of the second imperial tour, beginning in October 1921, is that he was far less his master's lackey and much more his own man. He was now Halsey's flag lieutenant in rank as well as in name, and, despite mutterings over HRH's insistence that Mountbatten always occupy the cabin/room next to his (resulting on occasion in severe discomfort, to the glee of colleagues), far less resentment was expressed over young Dickie's unique status among the staff.[41] Mountbatten's diary, while often eye-brow raising to the contemporary reader, indicates a lot of growing-up has taken place. Yes, there remains a brashness and bluster, reinforced by the predictable prejudices of a highly privileged young aristocrat let loose on the Raj – someone in a position where he can do almost anything, and meet almost anyone, on equal or near equal terms – but there are also signs of maturity and reflection, climaxing in an informed and reflective commentary upon Japan.

Two key developments in 1922 contributed to Mountbatten's more responsible, rather less jolly approach to life. As noted in the next chapter, his father, since 1917 the first Marquess of Milford Haven, died suddenly in July after visiting Mountbatten on his interim posting, HMS *Repulse*. The former Prince Louis of Battenberg was, in Ziegler's words, a 'repository of infinite wisdom and authority', his influence and example undiminished – and if anything enhanced – by the circumstances surrounding his departure from the Admiralty so early in the Great War.[42] The Earl of Medina, previously Prince George, inherited the title. Here too a powerful role model exited prematurely: a gifted engineer who set his younger brother off on a career in communications, 'Georgie' died in early 1938. Mountbatten had already contemplated marriage – to the debutante Audrey James – and then drawn back, but by mid-1922 he was convinced that he had found the woman he wanted to wed: Edwina Ashley, daughter of a reactionary Tory MP and grand-daughter of Edward VII's banker, Sir Ernest Cassell, was exciting, energising, enchanting, and enticing. She had brains and beauty, which was more than enough for a captivated Mountbatten, who had assiduously courted her since their first meeting in Cowes the previous August; but in addition she was an heiress. Cassell had been no distant patriarch, but something of a second father, providing comfort and security during the long periods that Edwina's distracted parents entrusted her to a succession of nurses and governesses. In drawing up his will Sir Ernest had bequeathed her a small fortune. When Cassell died in the summer of 1922 Edwina became extremely wealthy, with the prospect of becoming even wealthier: eventually she would inherit from an aunt the residue of her grand-father's estate, including the huge family mansion in Park Lane. She was also heir to Broadlands, once home to Lord Palmerston but lately the residence of her father, Colonel Wilfred Ashley, the future Lord Mount Temple.[43]

Proposing to Edwina Ashley would be anything but a private affair, particularly if one was the second cousin of the Prince of Wales and technically required the King's permission. Out of consideration for his grieving mother, Mountbatten promised to postpone the engagement until his arrival home from the Far East. He changed his mind when Edwina decided that she too would visit India, at the invitation of the Viceroy, the Marquess of Reading. Partly by fate but more by design, she found herself in Delhi at the same time as the royal party. On 13 February 1922 Mountbatten seized his chance. While still awaiting the final word from Buckingham Palace, within the viceregal residence their engagement was soon an open secret. Within days the gossip columnists at home were speculating on the date of a formal announcement: from the outset Mountbatten, with his matinee-idol looks and royal connections, and Edwina, with her wealth and beauty, were portrayed in the popular press as a golden couple. As Cannadine dryly noted, 'Sociologically, the match was perfect: she had wealth; he had status; they both had ambition'.[44]

Edwina was a happy distraction, and in consequence Mountbatten took his eye off the ball. Their happiness served only to remind the Prince of Wales that his paramour was several thousand miles away. With his friend quite literally engaged elsewhere, 'David' succumbed to prolonged depression and a succession of psychosomatic illnesses: 'Unfortunately only Mountbatten was close enough to understand his moods … The Prince luxuriated in his own sense of isolation.' Relief came only in the form of Edward 'Fruity' Metcalfe, a hard-drinking, hard-riding cavalryman destined to succeed Mountbatten as a sworn friend for life, and whom everyone inside Buckingham Palace, from the King downwards, viewed as a pernicious influence.[45]

Occurring only two years after the Amritsar massacre, and with Congress consolidating its status across the sub-continent as a broad coalition of nationalist sentiment, the royal tour was seen as vital in acknowledging the contribution of those Indians still loyal to the crown. Gandhi greeted news of Edward's arrival by ordering a peaceful boycott. However, this had only limited impact because the proportion of time spent in directly-ruled 'British India' was reduced in order to enjoy the extravagant entertainment of the princely states. While the Prince of Wales' natural instinct was to abandon protocol and make contact with the crowds, unreconstructed guardians of the imperial status quo like Metcalfe reinforced all his worst prejudices: given the Indians' manifest inability to rule themselves the secretary of state's reforms were a recipe for unrest, offering a green light to the subversive 'Non-Co-operationists' holding sway in the Congress Party. Not surprisingly, the reform-minded member of the Indian Civil Service posted to the Prince's party as his principal speech-writer was the subject of sustained criticism.[46] It would not have gone unnoticed that the India Secretary, Edwin Montagu, and his Viceroy, the ennobled Rufus Isaacs, were not only bruised survivors of the great Liberal schism, but were also both Jewish.[47]

HRH was invariably 'in the blackest rage' whenever his over-anxious hosts sought to keep him away from the 'Ghandiists': everyone from the Viceroy's secretary down would be lambasted for creating the impression that he had 'funked it'. The enthusiastic reception he received in Rangoon reinforced Edward's view that, unlike India, the authorities in Burma had the right idea – the smack of firm government, and scant meddling with reform. Ironically, in the light of Mountbatten's very different handling of Burmese nationalism in 1945–6, this was a view which the Prince's ADC wholeheartedly endorsed. Ceylon was seen as further confirmation that dealing exclusively with the local elite remained a fundamental principle of imperial rule: 'David now held a Durbar of the Chiefs' at Kandy – the King's Pavilion would have particular significance for Mountbatten in that two decades later it became his first staff HQ when appointed to command SEAC.[48] Again with hindsight, the royal visit to Japan had lashings of irony. Mountbatten was especially struck by the generosity of their Anglophile host, the young Regent and heir to the throne, Crown Prince Hirohito. The Prince of Wales was at his most charming and relaxed, for the first time on tour displaying obvious signs of pleasure and interest. These were the dying days of the Anglo-Japanese alliance, and there was still tangible evidence of close military cooperation: in conversation with Mountbatten veterans of the Royal Naval Air Service took particular pride in their role establishing naval aviation at the core of Japan's offensive potential.[49]

Back home the tour was seen as a great success. Fleet Street and newsreel coverage of the royal companion, plus news of his engagement to Edwina, ensured Mountbatten a high profile.[50] When the couple married later in the year the Prince of Wales was Dickie's best man – at the suggestion of the bridegroom's elder brother, who had been his first choice. Career commitments meant Mountbatten saw less of his friend, and yet they were still in regular communication, their paths crossing at parties, first nights, and royal engagements. Over the next decade the Mountbattens, either separately or sometimes together, pursued their own crowded lives, while 'David' maintained his own singularly incoherent lifestyle – a remorseless, Ruritanian schedule of reviews, receptions, and regimental reunions relieved only by Riviera escapism and revue-bar entertainment. Adulation and adultery was a damaging mix, yet by the mid-1930s the Prince of Wales for the first time in his life enjoyed a degree of stability. Fort Belvedere, in the Home Park of Windsor Castle, could lay claim to be a genuine home, and not just a convenient bolt-hole. Typically Mountbatten had taken a keen interest in decorating the Fort, and when in England would stay overnight about once a fortnight. He could scarcely fail to notice the other reason for the Prince appearing at one with the world: Wallis Simpson drew on his affections in a manner matched by no previous mistress, not even Freda Dudley Ward. The speed with which the latter was dropped had distressed Mountbatten, not least because he more than anyone had witnessed how much the Prince after the war had come

Figure 2.3: 'Bertie' welcomes 'David' home, HMS *Renown*, 21 June 1922

to depend upon her. Other women in the Prince's life, like Thelma Furness, were disqualified from becoming queen, and traditional candidates held scant appeal. Yet in the early 1930s Mountbatten was given a bizarre commission, being asked to draw up a list of eligible European princesses, the age range stretching from 33 to 15. One can imagine the sheer delight with which he undertook the commission, but also his realisation that it was a pointless task. Within the Prince's circle there was a growing belief that he would never marry – which made it that much more shocking when his real intentions regarding Mrs Simpson became clear. The Mountbattens were as surprised as everyone else.[51]

Over 30 years later Mountbatten privately noted that, from the moment his friend met the future Duchess of Windsor in January 1931, 'he lost all sense of reason'. There is more than a hint of disapproval in this recollection, compounded by the suggestion that its author already had reservations over the future monarch's fitness to rule. Yet at the time neither Dickie nor Edwina were over-critical; nor did they intimate to friends or close relatives any reservations regarding Edward's qualities as a king in waiting. With Mountbatten on station in the Mediterranean, most socialising with the Prince and his American lady friend took place in the south of France. Meetings in England were few and far between, although a rather uncomfortable dinner was held for the couple at Adsdean, the Mountbatten's pre-Broadlands country retreat. Janet Morgan is very good at comparing the insecure *arriviste* from the New World with Lady Louis, wholly comfortable with her admittedly unorthodox upper-class lifestyle: 'The newcomer's manner and appearance seemed contrived; Edwina was natural and assured.' As for Lord Louis, 'Socially ambitious herself, Mrs Simpson recognized careerism when she saw it'.[52]

In late May 1936 the Mountbattens were among the guests at the new King's first official dinner, organised primarily with the intention of introducing Mr and, more significantly, Mrs Simpson to the Prime Minister. This was the occasion on which Mountbatten claimed to have warned Baldwin of the growing threat from Germany.[53] The presence that night of the First Sea Lord, and of Samuel Hoare, First Lord of the Admiralty, at a similar dinner six weeks later, reflected one area where Edward VIII was impressive, namely his interest in the well-being of the Royal Navy. Here, as shown in Chapter Four, Mountbatten was shameless in encouraging the King to lobby Baldwin on the key issue of an autonomous Fleet Air Arm. He secured the appointment in July 1936 of Charles Lambe as an equerry, partly as a career boost for an old friend, but primarily so that the Senior Service was permanently represented inside Buckingham Palace. In the light of this preoccupation, it's perhaps ironic that Mountbatten and Admiral Chatfield sat across the dinner table from the aviator Charles Lindbergh – an isolationist scornful of British air power until silenced by the aftermath of Pearl Harbor. It's also ironic that Charles Lambe – a future First Sea Lord – soon changed his mind about the King. Initially very positive, from close observation he came to the conclusion that Edward VIII lacked bottom, and that any lasting liaison with Mrs Simpson would prove disastrous for both himself and his country. With no residual affection or sense of obligation, Lambe would have had no hesitation in pointing out to Mountbatten that a major crisis was looming.[54]

Beaverbrook may have secured silence in Fleet Street, but from New York Noel Coward told Mountbatten what he already knew – that throughout the summer of 1936 every newspaper and magazine in America had given the King's affair blanket coverage. On holiday in Europe Edward had acted as if totally indifferent to what anyone, including his government, thought about his behaviour, and this attitude continued at Balmoral in September. Traditional guests such as the Prime Minister and the Archbishop of Canterbury were excluded, but the lengthy list of aristocrats deemed *simpatico* included Dickie and Edwina.[55]

Their worst fears must have been fulfilled, not least when, at the end of their stay in Scotland, Mountbatten engaged in a long heart-to-heart with the King on the train journey south. However deep his doubts, Mountbatten's overriding sense of loyalty to his second cousin left him supportive until the final act. They had little or no contact in the late autumn of 1936, Mountbatten only attaching himself to crisis talks inside Fort Belvedere at the bitter end. Even then he was excluded from the key negotiations, not least because neither party – Edward and his closest adviser Walter Monckton, and Baldwin and his most senior cabinet colleagues – would have considered Mountbatten's presence a priority: what did he have to contribute, as opposed to the royal advisers and the King's three brothers, all of whose presence was deemed vital? Within the royal household 'Tommy' Lascelles had few illusions regarding Edward VIII. He would have found Mountbatten's exclusion unsurprising. The King's second secretary dismissed his royal master as a shallow man, whose shabby treatment of both staff and friends was to leave him, 'tragically and pitifully alone. It was an isolation of his own making: and the responsibility for it is entirely his own'. Thus Mountbatten's modest role as the great drama unfolded was to observe Mr Monk, the royal chiropodist, cut the King's corns: 'so as to get his feet as comfortable as possible when he was in exile.' He then vacated Fort Belvedere, more than mildly irritated: instead of chauffeuring the former monarch down to Portsmouth as originally arranged, he had been asked to ensure that none of the royal suitcases had gone astray.[56]

For over 50 years the idea has persisted that Mountbatten launched an abortive last-minute attempt to reverse the Instrument of Abdication. Even Philip Ziegler took seriously the suggestion that Mountbatten might have persuaded his second cousin to reconsider the idea of a morganatic marriage; and then plotted to discredit Baldwin's government in order to persuade the British public that their king could after all marry a commoner, even a divorcée. There is an irony here in that the Battenbergs, 'had genealogical flaws in their ascendance which rendered them imperfect princely, a fact which Mountbatten strove to conceal': in 1851 his grandfather, Prince Alexander von Hessen-Darmstadt, had defied his brother-in-law, Tsar Alexander II, and diluted the blood royal by marrying the lowly Julia Hauke.[57] Ziegler first suggested that the motive for action might be a morganatic marriage, and an authority on Wallis Simpson then ran with the idea that a change of heart was the consequence of the now ex-monarch belatedly appreciating the financial consequences of his actions.[58] As the authorised biographer Ziegler may of course have had access to confidential papers still held at Broadlands. Surprisingly perhaps, he seems to have taken seriously Claud Cockburn's claim as long ago as 1956 to have conspired with Mountbatten in order to influence public opinion.

Cockburn was a renegade upper-class journalist whose CV included a stint at *The Times* and a *Daily Worker* posting to Paris as Comintern propagandist for the beleaguered Spanish Republic. He ended his days in Ireland filing copy for *Private Eye*, his column an acknowledgement of how much Lord Gnome was inspired by Cockburn's legendary pre-war scandal sheet, *The Week*. Mimeographed on a creaking second-hand duplicator, *The Week* was sent out to a remarkably wide range of subscribers, all of whom were eager to digest news and information no mainstream journal would dare to publish – not least because so much Cockburn and his fellow-travelling hacks served up was scurrilous and potentially libelous. As befits the man who first coined the term 'the Cliveden set' to describe the Astors and their Thames-side Germanophile côterie, the editor of this gloriously muck-raking *samizdat* was fiercely opposed to appeasement. So too were the Mountbattens. They not only subscribed to *The Week* but they urged their friends to read it too. In his memoirs Cockburn insisted that one of these friends was Edward VIII.[59]

Cockburn claimed that a rich bookseller, 'of central European origins' and supposedly acquainted with Lord Louis Mountbatten, had approached John Strachey with a bizarre request. Strachey, author of the British left's most popular critique of a demonstrably creaking capitalism, *The Coming Struggle for Power*, and co-founder of the Left Book Club, was probably the country's most high-profile Marxist – and thus erroneously assumed to be a Communist. Never formally a party member, Strachey was the archetypal fellow traveller. Although after the war a minister in the Attlee government, a decade earlier he was harshly critical of the Labour Party's seemingly half-hearted response to the rise of the right across continental Europe. As 'Tom' Mosley's closest confidant in the Labour Party and then the short-lived New Party, Strachey enjoyed a unique insight into the messianic appeal of supposedly charismatic leaders. His strident Popular Front-style demands for a grand anti-fascist alliance with the Soviet Union brought him in to contact with a growing number of bipartisan groups, for example Focus, whose founders assumed Churchill to be a valuable if unholy ally in urging the case for serious rearmament – an assumption swiftly reconsidered following the great romantic's disastrous response to Baldwin's Commons statement on the Abdication.[60]

In March 1936 – the same month that Hitler ordered the remilitarisation of the Rhineland – Strachey supposedly passed on to Cockburn a message from Mountbatten asking him to draw up a potted autobiography. This would then be passed on to the new King as evidence that 'the editor of the obscure scandal-sheet was one of the Right People'. His Majesty would in consequence continue to read *The Week* whenever Mountbatten passed on his copy, and over a period of time would begin to see the Nazis for their true worth. Cockburn duly obliged, learning later that the last resort of Fleet Street's finest whenever a salacious story was spiked had become 'required reading at Fort Belvedere'. If Cockburn was telling the truth – and, by his own admission, between the wars he told some whoppers in the interest of the class struggle – then this was a ploy that proved spectacularly unsuccessful given the Duke of Windsor's scarcely disguised admiration for Nazi Germany. Mountbatten, by now First Sea Lord, chose not to rubbish the story when first revealed 20 years later, although in March 1936 he had yet to depart his posting in Malta. In the early 1970s Strachey's distinguished biographer, Hugh (now Lord) Thomas, assumed Cockburn was telling the truth. Furthermore, Thomas also took as gospel Cockburn's even more astonishing allegation – that Strachey and Mountbatten had conspired to keep the King on the throne.[61]

This time, according to Cockburn, Strachey passed on Mountbatten's promise of a scoop: if strictly confidential material 'of a particularly sensational character' entered the public domain courtesy of *The Week* then an embarrassed government might be faced with a dramatic shift in public opinion. With Strachey acting as a conduit, a plan was hatched that an anonymous dispatch rider would bring the sensational secret information straight from Fort Belvedere; and within hours a special issue would be hand-delivered to a 'selected list of influential subscribers' in and around the capital. In the event, after a long delay all that materialised was the unadorned message, 'The situation has developed too fast'. In her history of *The Week* Cockburn's wife tried to explain why such a diehard republican had been prepared to act in this way. The man himself claimed that it was essentially an act of mischief-making in the face of 'pompous discretion', and that anyway Mountbatten seemed a 'bonny fighter who ought to be encouraged'. Ziegler for some reason summarised this remarkable story without adding comment. Charles Higham, whose biography of Wallis Simpson was considerably 'sexed up' when republished in 2004, took Cockburn's claim to know nothing about the nature of his scoop as the basis for a very different interpretation of events. This was nothing to do with securing a volte-face by Baldwin, and his belated agreement to a morganatic marriage. In Higham's version the King had in fact been kept in the dark as Mountbatten and Strachey intended to disclose details of Mrs Simpson's highly discreet parallel affair with the ex-Guardsman and Ford car salesman, Guy Trundle. Bitter and betrayed, Edward would quickly have given up any idea of marrying the two-timing American, and a wave of sympathy would have secured a reversal of the Abdication: 'Popular with the working classes, he would, they [Strachey and Mountbatten] thought, serve the cause of Labour better than the Conservatives. But at the last minute the conspirators panicked and backed off from the plan'.[62]

Higham's interpretation of events, assuming of course that they happened in the first place, beggars belief. He depicts *The Week* as a conventional leftist magazine, reinforcing this impression with his description of Cockburn as a 'well-known Irish left-wing editor'. This was not some mass-circulation rival to the *New Statesman*; and neither was, 'The Labour Party … particularly anxious for the king to reverse the abdication' – Baldwin's strength lay in the fact that the opposition leaders wholeheartedly supported his adroit handling of the affair. Having followed Mosley into the political wilderness in 1931, Strachey was *persona non grata* in the Labour Party, and had no influence at all over Attlee and his colleagues. Neither was Mountbatten close to Clem at the time, not least because the Leader of HM Opposition had fought the 1935 general election on a platform of continued disarmament. Strachey was of course friends with both Desmond Bernal and Solly Zuckerman, but, given that Combined Operations' most distinguished scientists only met their patron and staunch defender in late 1941, neither of them could have acted as a channel of communication between Mountbatten and his alleged co-conspirator.[63]

In 1969 Mountbatten could scarcely ignore the Abdication in his television memoirs. He claimed to have become aware of Edward VIII's intentions regarding Mrs Simpson as late as November 1936, on the occasion of a visit with the King to the Home Fleet. Audiences at the time may have been convinced, but it's hard to believe that at that point Mountbatten still had no idea his friend considered marriage a serious proposition. The regretful courtier went on to distinguish between respect for the strength of His Majesty's feelings, and a firm belief that 'his duty to his country should have come first'. Implicit was the suggestion that, despite the

obvious pain, any monarch worth his salt would have sacrificed 'the woman I love'.
He expressed similar sentiments to his private secretary, John Barratt, indicating that
his own duty to the country required a swift switch of allegiance.[64] No wonder the
Duchess came to dread the arrival of 'Tricky Dickie', especially the occasion when he
booked a small studio in Neuilly and invited the Windsors to view 'their' particular
episode of *Life and Times*.[65]

Mountbatten described to viewers how he personally stiffened the Duke of
York's resolve when it became clear 'Bertie' must succeed his brother. Clearly the two
men spent a lot of time together at Fort Belvedere while the King was consulting
with his inner circle, or engaging in fruitless hard bargaining with Baldwin. In 1958
George VI's official biographer attributed Mountbatten with providing the same
encouragement that Prince Louis Battenberg had given to the future George V. A
decade later Mountbatten maintained that he had indeed given the now former Duke
of York a firm but gentle talking to: 'I was sure that a naval training was the best
possible preparation for being a king.'[66] It's certainly the case that the following day
he wrote to the apprentice monarch conveying the satisfaction of the Admiralty that
a 'Sailor King' was again on the throne: 'Heartbroken as I am at David's departure
and all the terrible trouble he has brought on us all I feel I must tell you how deeply
I feel for Elizabeth and you having to shoulder his responsibilities in such trying
circumstances. Luckily both you and your children have precisely those qualities
to pull this country through this ghastly crisis.'[67] Critics would see such a letter as
quintessentially Mountbatten, effortlessly switching allegiance in a platitudinous
expression of sympathy and admiration, underpinned by an inclusive implicit
criticism of the lost leader ('all the terrible trouble he has brought upon *us*'). In the
early weeks of the new reign he and Edwina do seem to have seen an awful lot more
of the King and Queen, and even had the two princesses come to tea.[68]

Perhaps one should try to suppress an understandable cynicism and note that,
with charming naivety (or simply pushing his luck?), Mountbatten went well beyond
the reciprocal gesture of offering to be the Duke of Windsor's best man. In actual
fact 'Fruity' Metcalfe was the preferred choice. Previous biographers have suggested
that Mountbatten took it upon himself to secure the presence at the wedding of
the Dukes of Kent and Gloucester, and indeed of the King himself. However, he
privately insisted in 1966 that his purpose in visiting his cousin's baroque bolt-hole,
Schloss Enzesfeld, in March 1937 was to break the news that no brothers could be
present: George VI had unhesitatingly given him permission to go; and indeed there
was no absolute veto on visiting as, although the Duke of Kent had been ordered not
to go, the Princess Royal had already paid her respects. The now ex-King wanted 'a full
royal wedding', with the groom splendidly dressed as Colonel of the Welsh Guards
– except that, as Mountbatten tried to explain, he was no longer entitled to wear the
uniform. The Duke could not believe 'Bertie' was a party to the Abdication, or was
directly responsible for the subsequent decision to deny the Duchess of Windsor
'the title, style or attribute of Royal Highness'. As Mountbatten later reported to
Harold Nicolson, 'the Duke is still completely unable to comprehend why it is that
everybody, including Queen Mary, did not welcome Mrs Simpson'. He could not

bring himself to tell 'David' that the break with his family and with his country was irreparable – Mountbatten's misery and mortification was marked by the seasoned traveller being violently sick on the flight home.[69] It's clear that the former monarch seriously underestimated his successor, believing his brother to be under the malign influence of the palace secretariat and the Prime Minister. Lord Wigram, the King's acting private secretary, insisted that if anyone from the Royal Family attended the wedding then this would mark the end of the monarchy. He chose to give Walter Monckton, the Windsors' legal adviser, the impression that the refusal to attend, and the denial of HRH to the Duchess, were decisions made in Downing Street. Yet, as Sarah Bradford has pointed out, given George VI's longstanding fascination with the nitty-gritty of English constitutional law, he may well have taken the initiative in denying his future sister-in-law a royal title. Mountbatten's private reminiscences three decades later appear to confirm this.[70]

Thus cabinet and palace were in agreement that the King's presence – and that of his brothers – at the wedding in Candé was out of the question. Mountbatten was scarcely an innocent in the corridors of power, and must surely have known this. Did the letter he sent to the Duke on 5 May regretting the veto placed on his plans for a family wedding constitute no more than the end of a grand and pointless gesture? If so, was this token expression of continued loyalty and affection for the 'king o'er the water' rendered even more fraudulent by Mountbatten's promise that he was doing all he could to be present in person? For all intents and purposes there was no way that an officer on active duty at the Admiralty, and with a formal responsibility as his service's aide-de-camp to the King, could have absented himself to attend a ceremony deliberately ignored by every leading figure among the nation's political and landed elites. If Mountbatten was indeed wholly disingenuous then perhaps the Duke should have called his bluff, and taken up the original offer to act as best man.[71] As it is, the jury remains out on just how much, in the first half of 1937, a calculating cousin sought to salve his conscience and still serve two masters.

At court Mountbatten worked his way back into favour, adroitly distancing himself from the old regime. As far back as their brief period together at Cambridge after the war, he had always got on very well with George VI. He flattered the still deeply insecure new King, treating him, albeit with suitable deference, as a fellow son of the sea and man of the world. This continued in to the war, with Mountbatten insistent that the arrival of the King in uniform was always a great morale-booster for the men under his command – he deeply regretted Churchill vetoing a royal inspection of the 14th Army when Rangoon fell in the spring of 1945. At the end of the war Mountbatten encouraged the King to think of himself as the 'old experienced campaigner' ready to keep Attlee's fledging government on the straight and narrow.[72] 'Bertie' was no fool, but presumably judged it more expedient to accommodate rather than alienate someone so clearly destined for the top – in future years Mountbatten might usefully keep his monarch in touch with events in the wider world, in a way no prime minister ever could or would. George VI had no illusions, and yet, while never an even-tempered man, he clearly bore no grudge towards Mountbatten over his rapid switch of loyalty. His wife viewed matters differently. Still deeply resentful of the impact her brother-in-law's passion had had upon the life of herself and her family, Queen Elizabeth was less reluctant to embrace one of Edward VIII's closest associates. Historians of the Royal Family are generally in agreement that she never felt especially warm towards either Dickie or Edwina, and that, beneath the polite patina of family sociability and civility, there was a similar coolness on the other side.[73]

The reluctant consort sat secure in her sense of being British; a titled, land-owning North Briton in an era when Unionism remained the dominant ideology astride the Forth and north of the Glen. One suspects that, for someone from such a well-established, semi-feudal, deeply conservative landscape, the Mountbattens were unflinchingly modern, and disconcertingly cosmopolitan (it's worth noting that as well as its literal meaning 'cosmopolitan' was a coded reference in upper class parlance to being Jewish). For Queen Elizabeth, and for many of like mind, Dickie and Edwina carried far too much baggage. Here was a couple for ever papering over the cracks in trying to reconcile an all-pervasive family-orientated social conservatism with the moral laxity of their own unorthodox lifestyles – a roving Edwina was unashamedly an absent parent throughout the interwar period. As with the rest of the nation, 1940 saw a marked change of circumstance, and a marked change of character: a war-weary Queen Elizabeth defended her indifference to the uniformed, re-energised Lady Louis on the grounds that, 'There's nothing more tiresome than a reformed rake!'. The Mountbattens were cosmopolitan *and*, to use a very 'thirties term, metropolitan – the latter of course a contributory factor in the former. While never 'bright young things' à la *Vile Bodies*, their world was an ultra-sophisticated reflection of the *zeitgeist* that Waugh, Huxley, and Firbank so neatly deconstructed up to the mid-1930s – at which point Noel Coward stepped in, offering a much sharper, subtler, more pointed brand of satire.[74]

Yet the Mountbattens' exhausting engagement with life took them far beyond Knightsbridge and the Embassy Club – clearly they lived life to the full in a privileged, wholly artificial London, with the East End a distant locale and the Depression a fuzzy backdrop; and yet at the same time their youth and position facilitated an enthusiastic embrace of the wider world, at variance with an older, more parochial generation of landed aristocrats, content to escape the capital courtesy of the family estate. Partly this global agenda was a consequence of Dickie's career, but it was also because Edwina was so restless; and she enjoyed the means to fund her roaming, and that of her travelling companions. What's striking about both of them is, firstly, just how many countries they visited between the wars, and secondly, how comfortable they seemed to be wherever they were in Europe. West or east of the Danube they felt equally at home, and it's this indifference to British isolation and detachment, other than in time of war, that defined the Mountbattens as continental in outlook and in mentality – and thus at sharp variance with the dominant insularity of interwar Britain, as exemplified, for example, in the Prime Minister's expressed relief that an 'English' nation whose value system remained rooted firmly in common sense could keep at arm's length those dark forces currently convulsing mainland Europe.[75] The Mountbattens found themselves, partly by birth and partly by design, at ease in the ruling elite of Mr Baldwin's archipelago-wide 'England'; and yet, indirectly in the case of Edwina, and directly in the case of Dickie, they were products of a very different national – even trans-national – culture. The German legacy was ever-present, even when repackaged as Hessen – or more narrowly represented as the ostensibly anti-Prussian Hessen-Kassel. National stereotypes are invariably fallacious and misleading, hence the folly in portraying Mountbatten as 'characteristically German'. Plenty of non-Germans have been, and continue to be: single-minded in their intentions, ferociously ambitious, demonstrably proud of their achievements, studious in the acquisition of technical expertise, and unashamedly frank regarding their intention to come out top in every task and contest they undertake. The elementary point is that all too often the reality is sharply at variance with individual and collective perspective: Mountbatten's peers – whether at Windsor or within Whitehall, or, equally crucially, in the wardrooms of the Home and Mediterranean Fleets – rooted their criticism of the man in an easy yet wholly erroneous assumption that those character traits which constituted both his very real strengths *and* his very obvious weaknesses were somehow symptomatically German. No they were not, and yet, just as one can scarcely ignore the imperial backdrop when examining Mountbatten at war, neither can one airbrush out of the story the fact that here was someone synonymous with the full panoply of the British state, who, to his credit, recognised the social, psychological, and cultural influences of an extended family firmly embedded in the heartland of continental Europe. Less readily acknowledged were the public and private tensions these family ties generated before, during, and after the two cataclysmic conflagrations that engulfed Europe in the first half of the twentieth century.

PART TWO

MOUNTBATTEN AT WAR, 1914–39

3

THE FIRST WORLD WAR
AND THE 1920s

With the Grand Fleet in the Great War, 1914–18

In July 1914 George V reviewed the Grand Fleet off Spithead. Prince George, serving on the battle cruiser *New Zealand*, invited his younger brother to view proceedings from the bridge. The test mobilisation extended even to the Royal Naval College, and technically Cadet Battenberg was on active duty. Twelve months later he was back on board the *New Zealand*, wrestling with chronic sea sickness in weather which, even by North Sea standards, was unusually rough. Mountbatten's first leave after entering Dartmouth in January 1915 provided an early acquaintance with the war at sea.[1] His very presence in the mine-strewn waters off Heligoland aptly illustrated how a quiet word in the right quarter ensured openings and opportunities denied to officers drawn from humbler origins. Given his background and upbringing it is scarcely surprising that throughout his life Mountbatten took privilege and patronage for granted. If the chance was there then it should be grabbed, and exploited to the full. What was important was not to waste that opportunity – take away the talent, and serendipity counted for nought. Luckily for Mountbatten his father could still pull strings inside the Admiralty, witness an initial posting to HMS *Lion*, flagship of Sir David Beatty's Battle Cruiser Fleet.[2] For all his unbounded energy and enthusiasm, there had been no sign at either Osborne or Dartmouth that here was an outstanding junior officer who could anticipate fast-track promotion. Later critics of Mountbatten's seamanship could point to a flawed record from the outset, but more surprising is the apparent absence of technical expertise: in the 1920s he earned respect within the Service by becoming the paramount authority on signalling, and yet as a cadet this was his weakest subject. Had the duration of Dartmouth's regular two year course not been halved then the evidence suggests that Mountbatten's star would have risen: while never a class captain his final ranking was a creditable fourteenth place – this was despite an ankle injury resulting in hospital and having to sit examinations with his leg in plaster. More significantly, an unexpected and much resented period of study at Keyham engineering college in Devonport provided Mountbatten with a fresh chance to test his intellectual mettle. Much to his annoyance, joining the Grand Fleet had been delayed for a term.[3]

While still stressing the centrality of technology to waging industrial war at sea, by broadening the curriculum at Keyham the Royal Navy dimly perceived a key weakness in the make up of both junior and senior officers: as Churchill acknowledged in *The World Crisis*, the paradigm shift in naval technology of the late nineteenth century had left less imaginative staff officers eager to break with the past but too ready to place their faith in equipment as yet untested in combat; hence their failure to draw on lessons learnt in the age of sail when formulating current strategy. One obvious example was the belated adoption of the convoy escort system, with the Admiralty for too long ignoring the great American naval strategist A.T. Mahan's use of history to argue against individual ships seeking out surface raiders and submarines.[4] Mountbatten clearly resented spending the spring of 1916 in the classroom. Had he been posted direct to the *Lion* then, like his elder brother, he would have fought at the Battle of Jutland. He would not, however, have enjoyed the considerable boost to his confidence of passing out first overall. Keyham set a pattern for the future, whereby Mountbatten would endeavour to finish every training or staff course top of the class. Excellence became the benchmark. Even if the in-service tuition was wholly unrelated to naval proficiency the same principle had to apply, witness his achieving first place in both French and German on a 1933 language course, and then going on to secure the highest mark in the Civil Service Commission's exam for advanced interpreters. Almost certainly no other officers on these courses could boast such a cosmopolitan family background, but Mountbatten's linguistic prowess confirmed an enviable ability to shut out all distractions and to focus upon the task in hand. Whatever he may have lacked in aptitude and natural ability he more than compensated for in application and endeavour; as Princess Victoria readily acknowledged when applauding her son's belated scholarly success.[5]

However formative his subsequent six months at Cambridge, Keyham College was the first step in granting Mountbatten – to use Denis Healey's oft-quoted phrase – a hinterland. If the Admiralty Board were endeavouring to foster well-rounded officers with imagination and the potential for initiative then, in Mountbatten's case, this coda to the hot-house environment of the Britannia Royal Naval College in time of war succeeded spectacularly. Mountbatten, like his close friend and near contemporary at Dartmouth, Charles Lambe, met a pressing need for energetic, ambitious and prescient young officers, alert to the potential of new technology but sensitive to the strategic and tactical limitations of undue reliance on a single orthodoxy – in 1916 still the big gun philosophy of Sir John Jellicoe and his fellow 'champions of the line'. In 1961 Stephen Roskill, a year below Mountbatten and Lambe at Dartmouth, recalled for a Cambridge audience how Jellicoe's bulky Grand Fleet Orders had in his view inhibited original thinking, encouraged the evasion of personal responsibility, discouraged initiative, and compounded those institutional weaknesses which had left the Senior Service so surprisingly vulnerable in August 1914, most notably the operational efficiency of an unduly bureaucratic Admiralty War Staff.[6]

Mountbatten's brief spell aboard his brother's ship offered a crash course in the harsh reality of enforcing economic blockade close to shore. The first year of the war had demonstrated the destructive potential of both U-boats and dense minefields, with the Royal Navy tactically and materially deficient in anti-submarine warfare and in mine-sweeping/laying. By April 1917 these deficiencies were to prove critical as evidence mounted that an imperial island nation was more vulnerable to remorseless *guerre de course* than a central European rival reliant on continental not colonial commerce.[7] The *New Zealand*'s presence in German waters was unusual as a chastened Jellicoe, shocked by the scale of early losses, had ordered North Sea patrols to avoid risky in-shore blockading. This distant control of sea lanes reinforced a strategic stalemate evident well before Jutland, as even an ostensibly 'Nelsonian' admiral like Beatty shared his commanding officer's view that preservation of the Grand Fleet was paramount and that cruisers or battleships could not risk being sunk by mine or submarine – any challenge to Germany's High Seas Fleet should take place in open waters, with the Royal Navy's presumed superior gunnery determining the outcome. By instinct the German Naval Staff was not as cautious, but from the Kaiser downwards there was a deep aversion to being sucked into a battle akin to that fought off the Falklands in December 1914: without submarine and aerial support – and despite rapid, accurate fire of powerful armour-piercing shells exposing the vulnerability of Beatty's fast but arguably thin-plated cruisers – sheer weight of numbers would ensure the Grand Fleet's ultimate victory.[8] In this respect Vice-Admiral Reinhard Scheer's reluctance in the final 18 months of the war to risk another decisive encounter can be seen as a vindication of an unglamorous, unflattering strategy: the Royal Navy controlled its home waters, and in partnership with allied navies protected merchant shipping from a now non-existent German threat. Whatever the merits of this seemingly inglorious refusal to engage with the enemy, officers and men shared a war-weary nation's keen sense of disappointment and anti-climax. Younger, more adventurous commanders such as Sir Roger Keyes feared that the Royal Navy's offensive tradition was being undermined, with profound consequences for its longer-term power and influence relative to not one but now two rival services.[9]

The Royal Navy's early triumphs were deceptive. Beatty's mixed fortunes off the Dogger Bank on 24 January 1915 demonstrated the value of code-cracking, but they also highlighted the high quality of German gunnery by comparison with that of the Battle Cruiser Fleet, the poor standard of British signalling, the inability to maintain effective reconnaissance in poor weather, the difficulty of controlling events from afar, and above all, the vulnerability of large warships to torpedo attack. At Jutland 15 months later these deficiencies were even more evident, and were compounded by: the Admiralty's mixed record in communicating vital new information; Jellicoe's reluctance to maintain the courage of his convictions and continue taking the fight to the enemy; the Grand Fleet's failure to train for fighting at night; and the speed-conscious Dreadnought designers' dual failure to maximise potential firepower and to prevent gun turret hits generating flash ignition of a ship's magazine. To be fair, there were key areas where British technology proved superior, witness warships

Figure 3.1: Elder brother 'Georgie' on the eve of war, HMS *New Zealand*, July 1914

capable of moving faster and for longer than their German equivalents, torpedoes
that were both reliable and difficult to detect, and systems of damage control which,
while primitive, preserved vessels in near-terminal condition. Also, Jellicoe's second-
day disengagement when under attack by German destroyers did make sense given
earlier losses (three battle cruisers and seven destroyers, with no less than 5672 men
dead). With an added threat from U-boats and mines, safeguarding his fleet remained
the key consideration; an early return to Scapa Flow and Rosyth meant damaged ships
could be speedily repaired and returned to action.[10]

The survival of the High Seas Fleet preserved German control of the Baltic, and thwarted plans for redeploying spare destroyers to escort duty in the Atlantic. Also, the loss of two further cruisers in August 1916 encouraged the Admiralty to accept Jellicoe's advice that henceforth his fleet engage with the enemy only if shielded by a demonstrably comprehensive destroyer screen.[11] Yet, despite such a remarkably passive policy – restated by Beatty in the final year of the war – a case can be made that Jutland was a decisive encounter, albeit not in a manner capable of satisfying either the politicians or the general public. Trafalgar was an obvious manifestation of maritime supremacy, but only with hindsight could naval strategists judge Jutland a comparable victory, in that never again did Germany offer a credible challenge to British control of the North Sea and the English Channel. In October 1805 Nelson and his captains drew on years of experience in fighting similar engagements, although rarely with so many 'wooden walls' at their command. In stark contrast, over a century later Jutland was the nearest thing to 'total war at sea'; and not even the Russian and Japanese admirals who contested Tsushima in May 1905 could empathise with Jellicoe and Scheer, both straining to retain control of two vast, dispersed manifestations of industrial might. No wonder the Grand Fleet's C-in-C informed the First Lord of the Admiralty that 'The whole situation was so difficult to grasp as I had no real idea of what was going on …'.[12]

A turret commander, by the time he fought at Jutland Prince George had already seen action at Heligoland Bight early in the war and off the Dogger Bank in January 1915. In briefing his younger brother on the great clash of 31 May–1 June 1916, he could rightly claim his ship had performed with considerable credit: first to sight the enemy, HMS *New Zealand*'s relentless and unusually accurate shelling had disabled two enemy cruisers and sunk another. Fast manoeuvring had left the battle cruiser relatively unscathed, unlike the *Lion*, which not for the first time had sustained serious damage. When Midshipman Battenberg arrived at Rosyth dockyard on 19 July Beatty's flagship was, 'in a pretty good mess. There was a gaping hole where the centre turret had been, and cordite fires had left their marks all over her'.[13] Built in 1909, the 26,000 ton *Lion* boasted considerable fire-power (13.5 inch guns) and an impressive turn of speed (25 knots), but the price was armour plate up to six inches thinner than on a battleship. The inspiration for these 'armoured cruisers', Sir John Fisher, had been keen that, once spotted, the enemy could be caught *and* outgunned. Thus the soon to be renamed battle cruisers functioned as both scouts and ships of the line. Given their base in the Firth of Forth, let alone the Royal Navy's dismal record of close communication, Beatty's cruiser squadron acted as if a separate force from the main body of the Grand Fleet, which remained at Scapa away from the action and yet still vulnerable to submarine attack.[14] Unlike Mountbatten's next ship, the oil-driven *Queen Elizabeth*, HMS *Lion* burnt coal. Here was, for its day, a sophisticated and complex weapons system, with a power source dependent upon intense manual labour more appropriate to the dawn of the Industrial Revolution: coaling could take up to half a day, with as much as 400 tons shifted in one hour. No-one in the ship's company was exempt, with blackened, dust-choked midshipmen bagging up coal in the bowels of the collier or redistributing it across the huge holds of Jackie Fisher's voracious leviathan.[15]

Life as a 'snottie' veered from the brutal (gun room bullying became so bad it required Beatty's intervention) to the glamorous (ward room functions seemed untouched by wartime deprivation). The midshipmen Beatty brought with him to the *Queen Elizabeth* were given a rough reception, reflecting the firm view of Jellicoe loyalists that the battle cruisers should bear the blame for their hero's failure to annihilate the High Seas Fleet at Jutland.[16] It is clear that the younger Battenberg was by no means universally liked among his peers. Whether over-compensating for nervousness, or displaying that grating self-confidence so unique to the adolescent English upper class, he could easily give the impression of being both ambitious and arrogant. However unfair, here was someone clearly keen to succeed, and who would benefit from early entry in to an elite network. Other junior officers, not unnaturally, envied that easy access to the corridors and drawing rooms of power. Later, that envy would be tempered by service acknowledgement that Mountbatten had genuine ability, let alone a talent for man management that somehow complemented (and at least partially compensated for) his firm belief in the value of exclusivity to public and private life.[17]

The pleasure of a plum posting was compounded by appointment as general factotum or 'doggie' to the *Lion*'s captain, Ernie – Alfred – Chatfield. 'Aloof, austere and magnificent', this imposing figure of authority nevertheless 'had a certain paternal atmosphere about him which made youngsters trust and like him'.[18] While Beatty's benevolence was clearly of value in the short term, making a positive impression on Chatfield would stand the teenage Mountbatten ('a very promising young officer') in good stead later in his career.[19] Knighted in 1919 and ennobled 18 years later, Chatfield not only served as an outstanding First Sea Lord for most of the 1930s, but in January 1939 he accepted the Prime Minister's invitation to succeed Thomas Inskip as Minister for the Co-ordination of Defence. An unhappy tenure in an unsatisfactory post ended with abolition of his hybrid ministry in April 1940 and Chatfield's well-timed departure from a war cabinet where there could only ever be room for one 'Former Naval Person'. Yet Churchill was by no means alone in admiring Chatfield as a sailor, if not as a cabinet colleague. Indeed he enjoyed widespread respect across Whitehall and Westminster, while his wartime record underpinned a well earned reputation for efficiency within the Service. Someone who was proving to have 'a good war', Chatfield was a worthy patron, and later correspondence confirms a keen interest in Mountbatten's career: he evidently considered his one-time messenger an exceptionally able officer, and, like so many ageing admirals, was charmed by Edwina. In 1922, it was Chatfield who protected his protégé when the 'Geddes Axe', wielded by cost-cutting First Lord of the Admiralty, Sir Eric Geddes, nominated no less than 350 lieutenants to be paid off. Officers with a private income were prioritised for retirement, and the Prince of Wales's cousin and touring companion was seen as a prime candidate. Mountbatten himself believed that to give up his career for the benefit of a less fortunate officer would be in neither his nor the Navy's best interest. Buckingham Palace discreetly made its views known, but Chatfield insisted that his selection committee took Mountbatten's name off the list because it was 'for the good of the Service for him to stay'. He may well have seen the father in the son, Chatfield sharing the view of most captains in 1914 that the 'brilliant' Prince Louis was 'perhaps the outstanding officer on the flag list'.[20]

As Chatfield's 'doggie' Mountbatten found himself on the fore-bridge whenever battle stations were called. Already 'one of his most ardent hero-worshippers', he was now able to judge for himself just how cool Beatty really was when under fire. Such moments came only rarely as for the most part patrolling the North Sea was a tedious and uneventful affair. However, just a month after joining his ship Mountbatten witnessed the last crucial engagement of the war when, having lost two cruisers, and seen his own flagship, the *Iron Duke*, narrowly avoid being torpedoed, Jellicoe signalled his vice-admiral to disengage: 'I thought Beatty was going to blow up; he blasphemed and cursed and said the most terrible things.' Ignorant of grand strategy the junior midshipman echoed a widely-shared view that Jellicoe lacked 'guts and leadership'. Only later did he change his opinion, and come to appreciate why Prince Louis had so greatly admired this 'insignificant little man in old-fashioned clothes'. From his prime vantage point Mountbatten could appreciate just how exposed the *Lion* was even before she lost her screen: one of three torpedoes fired at the cruiser had 'missed us by a matter of feet' only because a warning of mines had prompted Chatfield to order the helm hard over. Beatty had in fact been extremely lucky to escape obliteration. With Scheer already heading for home, further pursuit would have been foolhardy.[21] Unlike Churchill in *The World Crisis*, an older, more experienced Mountbatten came to appreciate why on 19 August 1916 the man 'who looked rather like a tapir' had been right to insist the cruiser squadron exercise caution and retreat to Rosyth. Yet admiration was still tinged with regret: a meeting with Jellicoe in Malta shortly before his death in 1935 confirmed for Mountbatten 'what an outstandingly competent, brave and brilliant man he was, though I still have wished he had steered for Horns Reef'.[22]

In December 1916 Jellicoe became First Sea Lord, leaving Beatty to take over the Grand Fleet. One small consequence of the broader changes in the chain of command was the arrival on the *Lion* of Lieutenant Battenberg. Newly married in to the Russian royal family, and a role model rather than a rival, he shared his brother's charm but not the fierce ambition and the ceaseless self-motivation. Yet Prince George's hands-on fascination with new technology had already made a deep impression – here was someone who could have complemented the sole surviving film of Jutland had he been allowed to leave A turret and collect his cine camera. His elder brother's elaborate film screenings aboard *New Zealand* and *Lion* inspired Mountbatten to explore the potential of cinema as an agent of education and enlightenment.[23] The climax of this campaign was the creation of the Royal Naval Film Corporation in April 1939, but as early as February 1920 a precocious, super-confident sub-lieutenant sought Admiralty approval to shoot an instructional film 'training officers and men in Flag Signalling and Fleet Tactics'. Impressed by the shooting script – if not the working title – their Lordships were happy that *The Mountbatten System of Manoeuvre Tuition* be filmed and then piloted in Portsmouth at

HMS *Excellent*.[24] Thus, at the age of 20, a familiar blend of imagination, industry, and shameless self-promotion began to emerge. In contrast, Prince George, although similarly inventive, was far less driven. His posting to the *Lion* necessitated a further move: a policy of brothers serving on separate ships meant Mountbatten's transfer to Scapa Flow, and service aboard Beatty's flagship, the *Queen Elizabeth*. He soon found himself again serving under Chatfield, who was summoned from HMS *Lion* to provide Beatty with a captain whose first loyalty was to him and not the former commander-in-chief.[25]

While Mountbatten later came to have mixed views about Beatty, his early career clearly benefited, if only indirectly, from being under the eye of a future Chief of Staff. Although actually very different in character and personality, with hindsight the two men had much in common: unlike Jellicoe, neither stood out at Dartmouth, and yet both gained from prestige postings as midshipmen, enjoyed unusually rapid promotion to captain, attained senior command courtesy of Churchill, drove their ships far too fast, dressed stylishly, played hard and to win, generated mixed feelings across the Service, and maintained unconventional marriages (not that the increasingly demented Ethel Tree had much in common with Edwina Ashley, other than good looks and a family fortune).[26] In the 1920s a shared passion for polo gave Mountbatten an excuse to maintain contact with the First Sea Lord, inviting him to become president of the Royal Naval Polo Association. Looking ahead to the next stage of Mountbatten's career, it is worth noting how polo was to prove a useful means of networking and of maintaining a high profile, not least because his teams rode hard, invariably won, and were captained by a master tactician. Another polo-mad admiral, Sir Roger Keyes, became the RNPA's vice-president. Stationed in Malta as C-in-C Mediterranean, in 1928–9 Keyes encouraged his star player to establish a service-wide regulatory body and secure Admiralty approval for his initiative. Beatty, recently retired and delighted with his honorary post, signalled a continued interest in Mountbatten's career.[27]

Yet over time it was Jellicoe who made a lasting impression. From the older, less flamboyant Grand Fleet commander Mountbatten learned the need for even very senior officers to understand how the Service's most complex and sophisticated equipment actually worked; that driving the procurement process was an urgent, ceaseless need to maintain the technological initiative, whether in ships, communications, or weaponry. Thus, unlike his vice-admiral, the C-in-C had begun the war fearful of superior German ordnance, recognising his ships' vulnerability to high trajectory shelling.[28] Mountbatten may have emulated Beatty's single-minded determination to reach the very top, but increasingly he came to embody Jellicoe's professionalism, his attention to detail, and, perhaps above all, his genuine interest in the well-being of the lower deck.

Although initially known more for his earnestness than his intellect, the son of Prince Louis Battenberg was bound to attract attention in both the wardroom and the admiral's quarters. Establishing a ship's magazine did his reputation no harm, particularly when the *Chronicles of Queen Elizabeth*'s Christmas edition boasted seasonal greetings from Sir David himself. Mountbatten edited four issues of this sea-going equivalent of a public school magazine, full of worthy yarns and rugby reports (our man played in the pack); and in the same spirit he joined the chorus of *Three Peeps*, a 'Musical Muddle in Three Acts' staged to entertain the chaps. Shows, magazines, and team games reflected the Navy's determination to keep crews busy *and* entertained during long periods of inaction. With large numbers living in cramped and austere conditions, often in remote ports, the maintenance of morale was crucial. In such circumstances harsh discipline had to be tempered by the paternalistic exercise of authority and control. Recreation and competitive sport were intended to foster fierce loyalty to the ship, and encourage a genuine camaraderie and *esprit de corps* between officers and men. Although most sailors were volunteers, and likely to remain in the Service for most of their working lives, they were by no means isolated from the profound social and political changes taking place in Edwardian Britain, and the very real boost the war had given to the power and influence of organised labour. The Home Front was marked by a demonstrable challenge to hierarchy and deference, and even a disciplined, stratified organisation like the Royal Navy could not ignore a very real prospect of dissent, if not, as in Germany, outright mutiny.[29]

Mountbatten quickly perceived the importance of keeping a ship's company if not blissfully happy then at least reasonably content. Yet editing a newsletter or staging a show was scarcely a chore – it was in fact frightfully jolly. It is therefore to his credit that a brief visit to the Western Front in July 1918 left him deeply uneasy over the way waging war at sea – moments of acute danger, but otherwise only modest discomfort – should contrast so starkly with the daily struggle in the trenches to survive: 'Now I was able to understand about war on land – what the casualty lists really meant, and the horrors of the conditions in which those enormous numbers of men were fighting and dying.' It is perhaps worth noting that the Royal Navy lost in total around 20,000 men during the First World War, which is only a few thousand more than died on the first day of the Somme, 1 July 1916. The fact that illness resulted in his spending a mere two days actually at the front (on the Ypres salient, with the BEF counter-offensive gaining momentum) simply added to Mountbatten's unease. It need hardly be added that an appointment at GHQ with Sir Douglas Haig was built in to the itinerary, the Field Marshal making 'a deep impression' in the course of what one can only assume was a very short meeting.[30]

Mountbatten was clearly sensitive to the absence of surface action in 1917–18, describing submariners as 'practically the Only People Who Fight'. His enthusiasm was the result of two months away from the *Queen Elizabeth* serving as a senior midshipman aboard the K6, one of the Royal Navy's more advanced submarines. To the surprise of the vessel's senior officers, on the eve of his departure their previously unremarkable snottie revealed a full working knowledge of the ship's operational capabilities and potential. Mountbatten sought his father's support for a transfer to the Silent Service, the Marquess of Milford Haven advising that a spell on a small surface vessel should be a prerequisite. Note that by this time Prince Louis Battenberg had acquired his new title and the family name had been anglicised. The change of name in June 1917 followed the example set by the Royal Family, and, while the elder son was renamed the Earl of Medina, the younger bore the courtesy title of 'Lord

Figure 3.2: Prince Louis Battenberg, retitled Marquis of Milford Haven, on board
P31 at the end of the Great War

Louis Mountbatten' until his ennoblement in 1946: 'It was all rather ludicrous. I'd
been born in England, and I'd always felt completely English. Having an English
name didn't make me any more English. But such was the mood of the times ....'
What proved a painful experience for his parents, each of them fiercely proud of
their German ancestry, yet at the same time deeply sensitive to the prevailing mood,
was bound to impact far less upon Mountbatten. While by no means indifferent to
family history and tradition, he was a young man on active service, and therefore had
more pressing matters on his mind – like whether or not to become a submariner.[31]

Although briefly schooled in Portsmouth on how to launch a torpedo attack, the freshly promoted Sub-Lieutenant Mountbatten ended the war trying to sink submarines, not drive them. On 13 October 1918 he finally left the *Queen Elizabeth* to serve on the Dover Patrol. In accordance with his father's wishes he joined one of the smallest vessels in the Royal Navy, HMS P31, serving as second-in-command of 50 officers and men. For the first time Mountbatten enjoyed freedom of responsibility, and the exercise of proper authority. He was in command for long periods of time, not least in the early weeks of 1919 when the ship was between captains. Highlights of his year with the humble P31 were conspiring with the captain to keep the ship in service, and – classic Mountbatten – persuading Princess Mary to bring her father aboard as part of London's Peace River Pageant on 4 August 1919. However, independence also meant accountability, as became clear only two days after his arrival on board. Already aware that escorting troop transports across the Channel entailed regular accidents, the novice officer of the watch was alarmed to find his passage out of Le Havre blocked by a French steam hopper, the *Yves*. Critics will no doubt see the consequent damage as early evidence of his poor seamanship, yet Mountbatten appears to have convinced the Treasury Solicitor that his commanding officer was on the bridge at the time of the incident, and that if anyone was at fault it was the litigious skipper of the *Yves*. Mountbatten's argument was that, while technically he was in command of the P31, in practice his lieutenant commander should be expected to account for what had taken place. Passing the buck might have been more excusable had the officer in question been the next captain of the P31. Here was someone who could applaud the efforts of a 'zealous and efficient executive officer' to maintain a happy ship, but who also abused his still very raw sub-lieutenant in front of the men. Mountbatten claimed that the lesson of this humiliating experience was never to behave in a similar fashion himself, and yet, as Philip Ziegler noted, later subordinates saw this precept 'to have been more honoured in the breach than the observance'.[32]

Securing a much-publicised visit by the King ensured the P31's survival when so many other small ships were being either mothballed or sent for scrap. She formed part of a flotilla ordered to the Baltic, thereby making her own modest contribution to counter-revolutionary intervention in the Russian Civil War. Given the fate of the Imperial Family, and Mountbatten's deep affection for both his cousins and their parents, this could have been a sensitive posting. Perhaps this was the reason why the Admiralty included his name in a list of 400 junior officers whose wartime service entitled them to recharge their intellectual batteries. He found himself completing his education at Christ's College, where, surprisingly, he chose not to study science.[33] Had he been at Oxford in the winter of 1919–20 such a move would have made sense given the poverty of physics prior to Lindemann's arrival. Cambridge, however, boasted the Cavendish Laboratory, with Thompson, Rutherford and Chadwick all viewing the undergraduate curriculum as crucial to their long-term research plans. No fewer than 50 uniformed young men were accepted into the Laboratory, their technical and scientific studies at Dartmouth and Keyham providing the necessary preparation to commence Part I Natural Sciences. Lieutenant Patrick Blackett, future Nobel Prize laureate, resigned his commission only three weeks after arriving in

Cambridge. Early recognition as a brilliant, if often controversial, physicist ensured Blackett's eventual appointment as an adviser to first the British and then the Indian governments. He first got to know Mountbatten at Combined Operations, later contact focusing upon issues such as nuclear proliferation and support for India's fledgling scientific establishment. Yet the two men only became close friends in their final years, drawn together by Blackett's belated desire to recall in detail his short but eventful career as a junior officer, and Mountbatten's wish to know why anyone who saw action at Jutland *and* Coronel could ever contemplate leaving the Royal Navy.[34] Neither knew each other at Cambridge, the younger man having no cause to set foot in the Cavendish. As an admiral agonising over the very real possibility of nuclear annihilation Mountbatten would one day find himself faced with the consequences of Cambridge science, but not in October 1919. Instead, he chose ethnology and, revealingly, English literature.[35]

The English Tripos had only recently been established, and in the course of the 1920s the faculty would be transformed. However, Mountbatten arrived in Cambridge too soon to encounter F.R. Leavis or William Empson. Precocious evangelists of 'Prat. Crit.' such as I.A. Richards must have seemed remote and intellectually intimidating. Not that Ivor Richards ignored the officers in his own college, Magdalen. He made Patrick Blackett his personal protégé, introducing him to Cambridge's most iconoclastic debating society, the Heretics.[36] More to Mountbatten's liking was the old guard of Georgian men-of-letters, ever ready to engage in gentlemanly discussion of worthy works with a well-connected war veteran. Although an unexpected advocate of the new curriculum, the veteran 'Q' – King Edward VII Professor of English Literature Sir Arthur Quiller-Couch – felt more at home in his Devon yacht club than in London's most fashionable literary salons. No wonder the Navy felt so relaxed about its 'war babies' reading Byron and Browning on the banks of the Cam. Mountbatten made the most of his two terms at university, progressing through minor debating societies to become an accomplished speaker at the Union.[37] In an Inter-Varsity debate his speech against an early Labour government ensured the motion's comprehensive defeat. His guest speaker that night was the man who, as First Lord of the Admiralty, had orchestrated proceedings at Spithead six years previously. In July 1914 Mountbatten, although already launched upon a life at sea, was still no more than a boy. Churchill's critics of course said the same about him. A flamboyant minister riding for a fall, he would have a marked impact on the future career of Prince Louis's younger son: indirectly in the short term, by providing a bitter incentive to strive for success, and directly a quarter of a century later when seeking out a fresh Beatty, similarly combative and equally charismatic. The tyro orator and the Westminster wordsmith, together vanquishing champagne socialists in the Cambridge Union, could scarcely envisage the symbiotic relationship that lay ahead. The impact of the Great War upon Churchill's political fortunes had been plain to see. The four year conflagration had, for Mountbatten, proved a tough if scarcely searing experience, and yet the lessons were no less profound.[38]

The most obvious lesson for a midshipman whose battle station had been on a flag-ship fore-bridge was the centrality of clear signalling to overall command and fleet manoeuvring. Even before Mountbatten joined the *Lion*, Beatty's ability to maintain operational control had been seriously undermined by unreliable signalling – most notoriously at the Dogger Bank in January 1915.[39] Good communications depended upon reliable intelligence, and, while the Great War placed Britain in the vanguard of code/cipher-breaking, there was an obvious deficit in visibly identifying and reporting the enemy. The Germans had demonstrated all too clearly the value of effective reconnaissance. Even while still at Cambridge Mountbatten identified signalling and wireless as fields which, once mastered, he could make a major contribution to. It was by building upon the advances made during the war, but only haltingly applied across the Service, that he very slowly gained the respect of his sceptical peers. If communications dominated the 1920s then the application of air power to the war at sea became Mountbatten's major preoccupation in the final years of the following decade. He had learnt to fly in 1918, but could see no way of pursuing his enthusiasm within the Royal Navy.[40]

The Service's readiness in April 1918 to surrender control of naval aviation to the newly-created RAF was soon seen as ill-advised, but in the short term deemed irreversible. In the winter of 1917–18 a strong case could have been made to General Smuts' investigative committee that, with the Royal Navy retaining full responsibility for carriers, a genuinely integrated command would require full authority over the aircraft operating off them. The Admiralty proved slow in pressing for an effective Fleet Air Arm, its tardiness all too evident in September 1939 when the Royal Navy went to war with only one purpose-built carrier (*Ark Royal*) and an assortment of obsolete biplanes (most famously, the Swordfish). Yet in November 1918 there were no fewer than 12 adapted and specially designed carriers; and the Royal Naval Air Service had attacked German targets as early as the second month of the war. Had Churchill still been at the Admiralty in the winter of 1917–18, and junior admirals such as Keyes and Tyrwhitt exercised greater influence, then the RNAS may have retained its separate identity. Like Churchill inside the Commons, after joining the Naval Air Division in July 1936 Mountbatten drew upon his wartime experience to lobby at the very highest levels for a wholly autonomous Fleet Air Arm: a major advantage enjoyed by the High Seas Fleet had been its air superiority in the skies above the North Sea, providing Scheer with an offensive option, and most crucially, a regularly updated picture of the British squadrons' locations and intent. Incredibly, in 1939–40 Mountbatten's continued high standing within the NAD facilitated personal use of a Swordfish for aerial reconnaissance and AA gunnery practice. The pilot and observer of 'Swordfish 5' accompanied their flotilla commander around the British coastline, flying out of whichever was the nearest RAF or FAA airfield.[41]

Like Churchill and Keyes – and, he claimed, his father, but that is debatable – Mountbatten did not see the 250,000 casualties sustained at Gallipoli as discrediting amphibious operations within a broader, flexible maritime strategy. A lack of political will and an absence of credible inter-service planning explained the poor kit and inadequate logistical support, the inconsistent performance of both naval and military forces, and the demonstrably poor leadership exercised by field commanders and general staff. With minimal training in how to secure hostile, well-defended terrain, it was scarcely surprising that when, as at Suvla, there was an element of surprise, the opportunity to break out from the beachhead was lost. Failure at the Dardanelles signalled the end of peripheral sea-based assaults, and strengthened the argument that a continental strategy demanded Britain's full focus upon the Western Front. The largely unsuccessful attacks on Zeebrugge and Ostend orchestrated by Keyes in April 1918 seemed to reinforce the case. Yet, if a lesson was to be learnt from belated attempts to contain U-boat operations in the Channel, it was that these were not latter-day cutting-out operations which the Navy could conduct unilaterally. Here was a lesson lost on Andrew Cunningham who as First Sea Lord continued to argue in 1943–4 for Combined Operations to be subsumed within the Admiralty. Suitable training, military expertise, and specialist equipment necessitated systematic inter-service planning – out of failure (within Mountbatten's Combined Ops HQ 'the ghosts of Gallipoli still haunted us') emerged a concept of properly combined operations. That concept, with piquant if cruel irony, was made real by Churchill in 1940 following the Army's demonstrable failure to emulate the first BEF and contain German aggression within the continent of Europe.[42]

In terms of grand strategy, one final and uncomfortable lesson of the war was the extent to which the Admiralty had become dependent upon allied navies in the Mediterranean and the Far East – or even closer to home with the presence of American warships in the North Sea for the final 18 months of the war. The USA constituted the greatest long-term challenge to British maritime strategy, but more immediately impressive was the range and potential of the Imperial Navy. Japan's surface fleet consolidated Allied control of the Pacific and the Indian Ocean, but in so doing exposed the emptiness of Royal Navy pretensions to remain a credible guardian of the entire imperial domain. If in November 1918 Mountbatten was only vaguely aware of Japan's significant contribution to the war effort, within four years he had become convinced that 'here was a power to be reckoned with'.[43] In April 1922 the Prince of Wales and his entourage arrived in Yokohama, where his ADC noted that, 'Next to our own service I have never seen such fine ships. Any one of them could have taken us on, on equal terms'. A visit to the training college at Etajima, and the dockyard/arsenal at Kure, reinforced his view that here was a navy which combined efficiency, flexibility, and innovation – the latter two qualities illustrated by the conversion of a battleship in to a state-of-the art aircraft carrier, and the development of Beatty's holy grail, reliable high impact shells. The conversion was a consequence of the disarmament agreement recently concluded at the Washington Conference, where Japan had been prepared to 'trade' Britain two cruisers in order to retain her latest battleship, the 34,000 ton *Mutsu*. In the absence of her captain, and with no visible sign of naval expertise, Mountbatten was allowed to inspect this 'wonderful ship. I take my hats off to the Japs for her!' He was especially impressed by the 16 inch gun turrets and the well protected magazine, the latter illustrating just how much Japan had learnt from the Royal Navy's vulnerability in the face of accurate German shelling. Ironically, those same lessons were not being acted upon at home, where Treasury retrenchment and rigid adherence to the terms of the Naval Limitation Treaty constrained Admiralty efforts to upgrade the surface fleet's larger warships, let alone commence the construction of their state-of-the-art successors. There was thus a very real threat of the Royal Navy lapsing into obsolescence. Eager to avoid a naval race with the United States, the British Empire now accepted parity with another power. The Treasury's refusal to sanction a two-ocean Royal Navy confirmed the demise of Britain's pre-war maritime supremacy. One obvious consequence was a very real threat to imperial security once Tokyo chose not to renew the 1902 alliance. As the royal party sailed away Mountbatten recorded in his diary that the visit had been a revelation regarding Japan's military might. There was evidence of growing social tension as a consequence of rapid industrialisation, but his prescient conclusion was that, 'A war might save them, as the people are still ultra-patriotic: this is the war I fear'.[44]

Interregnum: a captain's apprenticeship, 1920–36

From March 1920 to January 1923 Mountbatten's naval career was on hold. For much of that time he was touring the Empire as ADC to the Prince of Wales, after which he spent nearly six months on honeymoon in Europe and North America. His imperial globe-trotting was interrupted by an interim posting to HMS *Repulse*, the fastest, most heavily armed battle cruiser to enter service in the course of the First World War – although destined for destruction in the Second, along with the *Prince of Wales*. Again Mountbatten served under a future First Sea Lord, Dudley Pound, and yet again he forged a lasting – if by 1941 increasingly fraught – friendship. In the summer of 1921 Pound marked a shame-faced government's belated promotion of the Marquess of Milford Haven to Admiral of the Fleet by inviting him to sail up the east coast on the *Repulse* – a kindly gesture which Mountbatten never forgot. When C-in-C Mediterranean, Pound continued to correspond with his most flamboyant destroyer captain after Dickie and Edwina had returned home in the summer of 1936. By the end of the decade Britain's most senior admiral would be staying as the couple's house guest at Broadlands. Inviting chiefs of staff down to Romsey for a weekend shoot exemplified Mountbatten's indifference to rank and hierarchy – a self-confidence and self-belief enjoyed by accident of birth, and reinforced as a consequence of marriage. After 18 July 1922 he had position, privilege, *and* wealth. He also had potential: the charm and extravagant hospitality would have counted for little had Mountbatten been merely competent, let alone mediocre. Yes, the likes of Pound, Chatfield, and Somerville would have been rude not to reply to his letters, but they were under no obligation to write at such length, and with such demonstrable gestures of affection.[45]

Mountbatten's actual time aboard *Repulse* was quite short. Wage cuts and the premature return of the coal industry to private ownership brought the miners out on strike in the spring of 1921. The prospect of the railwaymen and transport workers joining them prompted Lloyd George's coalition government to declare a state of emergency. The Triple Alliance famously collapsed on 'Black Friday' – 21 April 1921 – but not before the Navy was deployed alongside the Army in providing, to use the correct technical term, Military Aid to the Civil Power. Mountbatten, encamped with his platoon of ratings outside Liverpool, was quietly relieved that the Merseyside police required no assistance: 'I just hoped that we would never have to be used against unfortunate people who were trying to obtain better pay and conditions.' Back on *Repulse* he had the pleasure of hosting his father; and yet within days he was quitting the ship to organise the Marquess's funeral. Although in poor health, the former Prince Louis had died unexpectedly of a heart attack. With his older brother serving abroad Mountbatten, still in deep shock, was obliged to oversee settlement of the estate. Imminent departure for India concentrated the mind wonderfully, leaving little time to mourn – the long journey east provided a welcome opportunity to grieve and reflect.[46]

In 1923 the newly-married Mountbatten hoped for a home posting, and ideally on a destroyer. Instead he found himself on yet another big ship, in the eastern Mediterranean, and under the command of a captain who resented having a conceited playboy foisted upon him. Like his fellow officers, Gilbert Stephenson, the captain of the *Revenge*, knew almost nothing about Mountbatten. Newspaper reports and service gossip suggested a very shallow person, never slow to flaunt the trappings of wealth or to exploit his privileged position within high society. Was he a lightweight, whose career to date had depended heavily upon friends in high places? Would his weaknesses soon be dissected by service professionals indifferent to the extravagant claims of society columnists? The familiar combination of charm and fierce concentration upon the task in hand won over all but the deepest sceptics, including Stephenson: 'tremendously intelligent … full of life and vivacity … he was, in fact, the most successful of all my officers when handling difficult men.'[47] To gain acceptance, and, more crucially, respect, Mountbatten simply worked harder than anyone else. As in all his jobs he first created a system, and then he rigorously applied it. Thus notes were kept on the 160 men in his charge, with faces memorised and key facts learnt. He worked the crew of his gun turret hard, countering the claim that he was unduly competitive by organising entertainment for the whole ship. Emulating his brother, the celluloid-starved film fan converted the quarter-deck in to a temporary cinema, having first secured from Douglas Fairbanks a print of the newly-released *Robin Hood*, and then persuaded the celebrated C.B. Cochran to provide *Revenge*'s band with a freshly arranged film score. Young Dickie was clearly well-intentioned, but it would have been understandable had his peers pointed out that such impressive and extravagant gestures were possible solely because of who he was. Lieutenant Mountbatten was no easy touch, but his demonstrable interest in the welfare of the lower deck had been recognised throughout the *Revenge* long before he left. Not surprisingly therefore, on his departure for London in August 1924 he was given a fond, even extravagant, farewell from the whole ship's company.[48]

Mountbatten came home to spend a year at the Royal Navy's Signal School in Portsmouth. By this time he was the proud father of a baby girl, Edwina having given birth on 14 February to the first of the couple's two daughters. Patricia was born at Brook House, the Mountbattens' opulent London base inherited from Sir Ernest Cassel and soon to be extravagantly refurbished. From Park Lane they sallied out to immerse themselves in a relentless and surely exhausting series of golf challenges, polo matches, tennis tournaments, fancy dress balls, discrete dinner parties, film and theatre premieres, palace functions, and nightclub extravaganzas, as well as Royal Ascot, Wimbledon fortnight, Cowes week, and every other obligatory event in the seriously rich's summer calendar. This was a regular diet of society functions maintained throughout the interwar period, and interrupted only by Edwina's presence on postings abroad or her frantic search for speed and ever more exotic bolt-holes. In the 1920s she appeared to be everywhere, motherhood scarcely curtailing her love of the fast life or her repeated need to get away – within a month of having Patricia she was in Antibes. Already, potentially fatal tensions had emerged within the marriage, as became obvious when the couple rowed repeatedly on an autumn trip to America with the Prince of Wales. A month of shows and cocktail parties on the East Coast did little to raise Dickie's spirits as he was dogged by tonsillitis and acutely depressed by Edwina's frenetic lifestyle, her repeated absences in the company of ostensibly exciting young men, and her eventual insistence on remaining in New York.[49]

Yet Mountbatten could not have been too down-hearted as at the end of his signals posting in Portsmouth he secured the highest marks in his class – no easy feat given the length and density of the course, with an examination every fortnight. His always hectic schedule had been made that much easier by the convenient location of Adsdean, the house in West Sussex which he and Edwina rented from late 1924. This was no modest retreat in the shadow of the South Downs. Some idea of the size of the grounds – and the couple's determination to make the estate a real home – is shown in their radical redecoration of the house, and their ignoring the owners' strenuous objections to the construction of a nine-hole golf course, a tennis court, and a polo ground. Adsdean brought Edwina in to closer contact with Dickie's fellow students, although she made strenuous efforts to avoid socialising with more senior officers, and most especially their wives.[50]

Mountbatten's Signal School triumph for the first time secured him a prestige posting on merit alone. However, first he had to master the Higher Wireless Course at Greenwich. Signals training, with its bizarre mix of algorithmic calculation and rote-learning, fostered fierce competition. Whether mind-numbing detail or brain-stretching theory, the dedicated student took it all in his stride. Faced with a relentless diet of applied physics, advanced mechanics, and pure mathematics, lightened only by the odd visit to a valve factory or a wireless station, Mountbatten was forced to draw on deep reserves of motivation. If he lacked an innate ability to tackle 'deep' science, he did have a remarkable capacity to be one minute focused totally on solving a highly complex technical problem, and then the next be off partying, practicing for polo, or playing with Patricia. Every day was meticulously planned, as if life was a permanent time and motion exercise. This obsession with utilising every moment of the day – from leaping into the shower when woken, to instant slumber once the lights dimmed in his on-shore replica cabin – was to remain with him for the rest of his days. Sleeping in a bunk at Brook House, with bedroom windows converted to portholes, model ships twinkling Morse signals, and a primitive sound system replicating the hum of a ship's engines, was bizarre; and yet in a strange way it helped Mountbatten compartmentalise his life – if he ever needed a sharp reminder of his priorities he could stare across the room at the glass case in the corner displaying Prince Louis' full dress uniform. Dickie's efficiency in detaching himself from Edwina's very public lifestyle whenever the Service demanded his full attention helped smooth the day to day course of their marriage; but when unavoidable absences seriously disrupted social and family arrangements then problems inevitably arose. A key factor of course was having a bevy of servants on hand to support this dual existence; naturally his chauffeur was on permanent call, with the Barker Cabriolet Rolls Royce – a wedding gift from Edwina, complete with signalman in place of silver wraith – specially adapted to ensure its owner snoozed in maximum comfort. As far as other motorists were concerned this was the ideal arrangement: Mountbatten's personal record for driving the Rolls from Park Lane to Portsmouth Barracks was one hour and 32 minutes. The speed and frequency of this nerveless single-lane south coast commuting was matched only by T.E. Lawrence on his Brough Superior a year or two later; in the case of 'Aircraftsman Shaw' the only mystery surrounding his death is why it didn't occur sooner. Is it too fanciful to imagine that, on the occasion Mountbatten gave a lift in his motor launch to designer R.J. Mitchell, he took time off from watching Supermarine's S 6 seaplane prepare for the Schneider Trophy in order to swap stories of motoring madness with Lawrence of Arabia? Perhaps the Arabist turned marine engineer gave his fellow speedster technical advice on how to get a few extra revs out of *Shadow II*, albeit complaining that Mountbatten had commissioned the craft from America rather than employ Hubert Scott Paine's yard in Hythe, where Lawrence tested air-sea rescue boats for the RAF.[51]

John Terraine, military historian turned documentary scriptwriter, neatly summed up his subject's inclusive, imaginative interpretation of communications; progressing beyond the basic requirements of signalling, wireless, and telegraphy, and embracing the revolution in film, radio, and telecommunications which occurred in the course of his lifetime: 'Mountbatten had found more than a trade: he had found a vocation.' Not only that, he now had focus, direction, and a clear career path. His success gave him a reputation for excellence in a rapidly expanding area of technical expertise; it offered a foundation upon which, sooner rather than later, he could stake his claim to command a destroyer. Here yet another well-known admiral acted as a role model: James Somerville, Mountbatten's flotilla commander a decade later, first attracted attention as a pioneering signals officer before consolidating his reputation on destroyers in the 1920s.[52]

Mountbatten left Greenwich in the spring of 1926, and marked time in the Reserve Fleet battleship *Centurion*. While awaiting his next major posting he shared Edwina's astonishing succession of minor ailments (given their wealth and relative youth at this time they experienced surprisingly poor health – perhaps a consequence of their late night lifestyle); masterminded weekend entertainments for the Prince of Wales and his retinue; invented even more electronic gadgetry; and worked on his golf swing. Above all he played polo, a sport first enthusiastically embraced when touring India with the Prince of Wales. As with everything new, there was the usual single-minded determination to overcome an absence of innate talent by focusing upon technique. Mountbatten scrutinised slow motion film of top players in order to analyse and then to improve upon individual and team tactics. Having access to fast, specially-bred ponies was clearly a big advantage, as was the invention and adoption of a more ergonomically efficient mallet. Yet the essence of winning consistently was for a team to maintain unprecedented levels of performance, and to do so meant adopting wholly new methods of preparation: an effective leader who on and off the field demonstrated both inspiration *and* tactical nous; a concept of teamwork that drew upon more than mere *esprit de corps*; and a programme of coaching that assumed each player's commitment to long hours of practice. Such an approach scorned the prevailing values of the amateur gentleman, and it is scarcely surprising that many of Mountbatten's contemporaries saw him as a subversive intruder. In an era when for the landed and professional classes the term 'professional' retained deeply pejorative connotations a captain who could go so far as to lobby that team members not be posted abroad seemed guilty of distinctly caddish behaviour. Poor show indeed; and yet, ironically, those blazered defenders of tradition who complained that the *arriviste* of Adsdean took the game (never 'sport' of course) far too seriously were the first to welcome his coaching manual *Introduction to Polo* when it first appeared under a *nom de plume* in 1931. Mountbatten viewed every chukka as equivalent to a naval engagement, with each successful shot akin to a direct hit. Perhaps not surprisingly therefore, his guide to playing polo bore a remarkable resemble to his instruction manuals, and in at least one instance 'Marco's' advice on how to operate efficiently as a team was directly replicated. The book proved a modest bestseller, with several editions and at least two translations. One reason for its long shelf life was that Mountbatten recruited Peter Murphy, the one seriously close friend he had acquired during his brief experience of university, to refine his own distinctly utilitarian prose style. In 1946 Murphy was to fulfil a similar, but far more controversial, role when he redrafted the supreme commander's final report on operations in South-East Asia Command.[53]

Peter Murphy was said to be the impressionable young Dickie's radical conscience at Cambridge, ostensibly maintaining this role for the rest of his days – he died in 1966. Infirmity meant the two men wrote regularly but saw little of each other in Murphy's later years, by which time Mountbatten's secretary, John Barratt, was maintaining a similar if more formalised function of aide and gate-keeper. Barratt was quite clearly a subordinate, in a way that his supremely confident predecessor never was: 'Few people actually knew what Murphy's role was in Dickie's life, but his real position was as a sounding board. He was brilliant at spotting mistakes in something that Dickie was planning, and he wasn't afraid to speak up … He wasn't always right, but he did manage to show Dickie that there were alternatives to the things he proposed.'[54] In the 1920s Murphy was a bright, amiable Irishman with plenty of time on his hands. Briefly a subaltern in the Guards, his private income was just sufficient to facilitate the role of cosmopolitan court jester within the Mountbatten set. A polymath and a brilliant linguist, Murphy voiced *outré* opinions in order to outrage gullible strangers, entertain his wide circle of well-heeled friends, and earn his – invariably luxurious – board. He relished his status as the definitive 'champagne socialist', not least because he was never asked to fork out for the Dom Perignon. Whether ensconced at Adsdean or crossing the Atlantic in a conveniently adjacent cabin, Murphy was a semi-permanent presence – in the boudoir a convenient shoulder to weep on when the going got tough; in the study a calculating mind to pay heed to whenever crisis loomed; and in the salon a ready wit capable of lightening even the darkest domestic tiff. In time he would move on from the role of marriage counsellor, go-between, and children's entertainer, and come to be seen as Mountbatten's *eminence gris*, even serving on his staff in the Far East. Enemies underestimated Murphy, dismissing him as a lightweight crony, and encouraging the rumour that he maintained a homosexual relationship with Mountbatten. Ironically, MI5 at the onset of the Cold War did not share the commonly held view that a 'queer' Irishman with dangerously radical views must by definition be a Communist spy. Murphy scarcely disguised the fact that he was gay (as was also the case for John Barratt), although he never gave any indication in public or even in private that his very close friendship with Mountbatten was anything but precisely that – a relationship based on trust and close proximity, but not physical intimacy. His sexuality (and conveniently his lack of good looks – even as a young man a fast receding hairline and rapidly expanding girth) was in many ways a bonus, as Dickie never found him a threat. Indeed between the wars he proved invaluable to Mountbatten as a comforter, travelling companion, and confidant of Edwina. In this respect Peter Murphy earned his keep, which, had it ever been calculated, would have constituted a considerable sum. To sum up, he was the sort of chap who wouldn't be seen dead on a polo pony but with consummate ease could provide his best chum with 50,000 words on how to ensure a triumphant afternoon in the saddle at either Beaufort or Cowdray.[55]

Captaining the finest polo team ever to grace the colours of the Senior Service was the mark of a coming man, but for any ambitious young officer the Mediterranean was the place to be. When the C-in-C, Sir Roger Keyes, first learnt that the next assistant to his fleet wireless officer would be Dickie Mountbatten he said no. Both brothers would be on station at the same time, and for Keyes that was one minor royal too many. When the young buck finally arrived he was told to his face that only guilt and a keen sense of debt to the late Marquess had forced a change of heart. Mountbatten started his new appointment with one disadvantage – quite simply, who he was – and two very obvious advantages: familiarity with Keyes's flagship, the *Queen Elizabeth*, and an immediate superior whose dual lack of motivation and ambition provided the apprentice signaller with an opportunity to make his mark.[56] He was convinced that all but his closest friends and colleagues believed him to be over-promoted and out of his depth: 'If I do come out to Malta and work like a beaver people won't believe it, and if I am seen on the polo-ground, they will say "I told you so".' In many respects his fears were justified as many in the Service did indeed see the high-profile Lord Louis as a polo-playing playboy who, even if quite bright, would simply not be around for the long haul.[57] The problem was that Mountbatten carried a great deal of baggage, metaphorically and literally. The villa in Valetta as big as the admiral's, the necessary complement of servants, the two 'runabout' cars, the famous Rolls with its silver signaller on the bonnet, the equally famous 66 ton yacht *Shrimp*, and of course the polo ponies shipped from England, were all bound to fuel resentment, especially among the many officers and their spouses who found themselves excluded from the glitzy dinner parties, the fashionable soirees, and the lavish balls that constituted nightly entertainment at the Casa Medina. That mixture of envy and irritation was compounded by Edwina who, when not back in London liaising dangerously with Mike Wardell and Laddie Sandford, was following the fleet around the Mediterranean: Mountbatten really did have a girl in every port, albeit the same one, and usually to be found waiting on *Shrimp* with cocktails and a warm welcome for the very smartest members of Sir Roger's entourage. Here was, to use the inevitable cliché, a golden couple who, from a distance, appeared arrogant and only too eager to flaunt their wealth. Under close scrutiny they probably still came across as insensitive to the feelings of those outside their social circle, and indifferent to any suggestion that their lifestyle might be seen, in terms of officer morale, as somehow divisive or even provocative. These charges may well have been unfair, and of course the Mountbattens' high profile and undeniable charm ensured a general absence of ill-will among the ratings. As in his previous posts Mountbatten generated – but rarely courted – popularity among the men, and the same was true for his apprentice signallers. Midshipmen and petty officers found him a born teacher, and many of his methods only became commonplace decades later. One obvious example was distributing précis of every presentation, thus encouraging students to focus upon content and not on taking notes. Typically, having edited and expanded these lecture summaries, he convinced the Admiralty that his work should become one of the Navy's standard textbooks.[58]

Soon Mountbatten was given the opportunity to display his skills as a communicator on a grander stage, but before leaving the Mediterranean he served for a short time as wireless officer for the 2nd Destroyer Flotilla. Although brief this was invaluable experience, filling an obvious gap in his service record. It was during this period that Edwina gave birth to the couple's second daughter, Pamela: prematurely on 19 April 1929 at the Ritz in Barcelona, where Dickie was leading his Bluejackets team in a polo tournament.[59] Transfer to the flotilla had been marked by promotion to lieutenant commander, a rank matching his subsequent appointment as the Signal School's chief wireless instructor. Mountbatten was based in Portsmouth, off and on, from the summer of 1929 until mid-1931: 'years of very intense activity for me.' Yet these were also the years when Edwina's absences and infidelities, and Dickie's occasional infatuations, brought their marriage to the brink of break-up. Indeed a report in the American press that the Mountbattens were separating prompted much soul-searching, but finally the decision to keep going. Ironically, one of those infatuations, the chic and petite Yola Letellier, was in effect hijacked by Edwina, and dragged around Europe from one fashionable health spa to another. In time she became a solid and loyal friend of both Mountbattens, recognised as Dickie's closest female companion – yet to describe her as his mistress is misleading, not least because of Yola's friendship with Edwina and the fact that her elderly husband, the French newspaper proprietor Henri Letellier, himself became part of the extended family. A devoted Mountbatten was extremely generous to Yola Letellier throughout his life, although once widowed she was very wealthy in her own right. However, there was never any thought – on his part, or hers – that they might marry following

Edwina's death in 1960. Nearly 30 years earlier she was, along with Peter Murphy, a key member of the Mountbatten support team, helping to keep the rackety show on the road as war loomed ever closer.[60]

With time on his hands Mountbatten took the first steps to qualifying as an interpreter four years later. In early 1930 he secured his pilot's licence. At Portsmouth he ran the Long Signal Course, but also lectured at Greenwich on the Royal Naval College's more advanced programme. Like all good teachers he enjoyed showing off, boasting the ability in both lectures and individual tutorials to put across complex ideas in a simple, straightforward, and invariably entertaining fashion. Nor did he rest on his laurels, reforming and updating the curriculum, as well as creating a single definitive instruction manual from a myriad of dense, poorly presented handbooks. His priority was 'a new and simplified way of laying out electrical diagrams, to make them more easily understandable', and a drawing school was established to replicate circuits in a uniform design and to the very highest technical specification. The result was a wholly new edition of the *Admiralty Handbook of Wireless Telegraphy*, largely authored by Mountbatten. He claimed similar proprietorial rights over an even more ambitious project, *The User's Guide to Wireless Equipment*, a full colour, loose-leaf volume published largely as a consequence of Mountbatten personally printing a pilot edition in order to convince Whitehall of the necessity for such a lavish format.[61] Other initiatives while at Portsmouth included the introduction of sub-focal flashing lamps to speed up morse transmission, and of typewriter keyboards to complete the mechanisation of semaphore signalling – simple, but highly effective, inventions. Not surprisingly, when he left the Signal School his superiors acknowledged someone with 'a great future in the service' – 'a natural leader, who exerts a strong influence and constantly inspires keenness'.[62]

4

FAST-TRACKING IN THE 1930s

Apprenticeship with the Mediterranean Fleet, 1931–6

August 1931 was perhaps not the most auspicious month in which to commence a fresh appointment, but arrival in Malta as Fleet Wireless Officer offered the chance to escape economic gloom at home – the deepening sterling crisis would quickly lead to the fall of Labour's second minority administration, a split within the party leadership, and Ramsay MacDonald accepting George V's invitation to form a National Government. In its abortive attempt to remain on the Gold Standard the Conservative-dominated coalition extended deep cuts in public expenditure to a 10 per cent reduction in service pay. On 15 September sailors of the Atlantic Fleet at Invergordon mutinied. Bizarrely, in later life Mountbatten attributed the mutiny to hire purchase, claiming that the cut roughly matched the amount many men paid out each week to buy furniture. In this unique analysis fear of the bailiffs was the principal cause of dissent. Unlike in Scotland, the Mediterranean Fleet had commenced its autumn cruise, making communication between ships' companies that much more difficult. Mountbatten and his team monitored fleet wavelengths continuously, confident that no illicit messages could be transmitted without their knowledge.[1]

There clearly were rumblings of discontent, and on 29 September he advised the C-in-C's Chief of Staff that Sir Ernle Chatfield should continue to keep his ships at some distance from each other. This much is clear because Mountbatten noted in his diary the meeting with Rear-Admiral Sidney Bailey, a C-of-S unusually close to his admiral and on the whole more receptive to uncomfortable news than the *Queen Elizabeth*'s flag captain, R.C. Davenport. Astonishingly, assuming that such a meeting actually took place, he did not record a crisis summit of senior officers at which, on the Commander-in-Chief's orders, he was present. In retirement interviews with Robin Bousfield and Richard Hough, Mountbatten claimed to be the man who alone prevented mutiny from breaking out in what Chatfield himself once described as, 'the heartland of the Royal Navy'. When asked by this 'very remote man' why no other officer was prepared to be so blunt about the threat of action on the lower deck, Mountbatten ostensibly replied that there was a systemic fear of endangering one's career by speaking out: as a man of private means, "'I don't need to buy my promotion by silence. What I do care about is the truth, and that you should know

it." It may be coincidence that I was promoted next shot'. Chatfield clearly did have
a role in securing his promotion to commander in October 1932, but principally
because he thought it vital for Mountbatten to be fast-tracked in to a less specialist
post, not because '… you've got the courage to tell me when nobody else has'.
Needless to say there was no mention of this frank exchange of views in Chatfield's
memoirs, published in the middle of the Second World War: his force gathered off
Crete in the late autumn of 1931 to learn of 'my appreciation of the steadiness of
the Fleet under the severe test of discipline caused by the sudden cuts in pay'. Fear
of mutiny was clearly not the non-event Chatfield described for his wartime readers,
but this whole episode suggests the ageing Mountbatten indulging in extravagant
myth-making. It is scarcely surprising that Hough replicated his subject's version of
events without comment, but it is noticeable that a sceptical Philip Ziegler quoted a
1970 letter from Michael Hodges, Mountbatten's assistant at the time and a lifelong
friend: 'I never felt that we were close to mutiny. I never heard, nor did you tell
me, of any attempted communication between what you call "mutineers".' It is also
worth noting that, when presented with Mountbatten's lengthy account of events
Chatfield's biographer toned down the more extravagant claims in drafting his own
narrative.[2]

Mountbatten's reputation went ahead of him, and he rarely disappointed.
Prejudices were speedily confirmed or high expectations swiftly met; mixed emotions
were the exception. Nowhere was this better illustrated than during his two year
tenure at the Castille, headquarters of the Mediterranean Fleet. The family's lifestyle
was similar to their previous stay on Malta, although, in keeping with the spirit of
the times, not quite so ostentatious and garish: the accountants, appalled by the
imbalance between extravagant outgoings and a shrinking investment income, had
advised a grand auction and a two year tax exile.[3] In any case the demands of work
left Mountbatten with far less time to indulge in a hectic social life. The spectacle
and excitement now derived from a whirlwind tour of the fleet, resulting in a bank
of data regarding key personnel and equipment, and a post-orientation assessment
as to how the prevailing system of wireless communication could be upgraded. The
focus was as much upon improving skills as modernising kit, with ships required
to compete against each other and a signals training centre established ashore.
Mountbatten was terribly possessive regarding his telegraphists, fostering an *esprit de
corps*, a fierce personal loyalty, and a shared determination to maintain high standards
of transmission and reception. He viewed them as the unsung heroes aboard ship,
endeavouring to raise their profile as part of a wider process of education: as his
experiences during the Great War had painfully confirmed, efficient communications
remained the key to any successful naval operation. In the brave new world of signals
intelligence wireless discipline was crucial to evading detection and to coordinating
a large strike force. As 'a bit of a showman', Mountbatten relied on 'dramatic
demonstrations' to get his message across: 'We simulated battle, by getting the ships
themselves to transmit action signals; we had aircraft up and submarines submerged,
and we fed in all their signals through loudspeakers as they came in. This is all old hat
now [1969]; but it was very new then, and I think our lords and masters were duly

impressed.' The C-in-C himself was party to these 'stunts' being invited to orchestrate fleet manoeuvres using only ships' call-signs, and to exchange pleasantries with his colleagues in London regarding the weather. Mountbatten's *coup de grace* was to ensure that all 70 ships were able to hear the King's first address to the nation on Christmas Day 1932, and he took enormous delight in meeting what at the time was a uniquely testing technical challenge.[4]

Chatfield had by this time returned home to become First Sea Lord, but in August 1932 his imminent departure had been marked by a visit from the Prince of Wales and the Duke of York. Needless to say, Mountbatten was deputed to be master of ceremonies. He orchestrated proceedings in his usual flamboyant yet generally efficient fashion, but could do little to reduce Chatfield's stress levels when the two princes flew off *Glorious* and were immediately lost in an unexpected bank of fog. Disaster was averted largely because of regular radio contact between the pilots and the aircraft carrier – a point not lost on the acting ADC to the heir to the throne, and no doubt expressed forcibly in the wardroom that night.[5]

The winter of 1933–4 was spent in Paris preparing to qualify as an official interpreter. By this time Brook House had been demolished, eventually to be replaced by a block of luxury flats, with the façade designed by Sir Edwin Lutyens no less. To respect the terms of Sir Ernest Cassell's will the Mountbattens would occupy a huge two-floor penthouse of the new Brook House. However the 30-room 'apartment', with its spectacular view of Hyde Park, was still two years from completion. For all but six months of this time Edwina was globe-trotting, usually in the company of the laid-back Bunny Phillips, her lover throughout the 1930s and into the war. Having emerged triumphant from a high-profile libel case Lady Mountbatten needed to exercise discretion, and travelling in remote regions ensured the absence of prying eyes. Dickie consoled himself with Yola Letellier, his daughters, polo, and above all, the feeling that his career remained firmly on track.[6] Confirmation of the latter came in his selection for the Naval Training School's Training Cruiser Course.

For at least the first ten years of its existence the School focused upon why the Grand Fleet had failed to annihilate the enemy in the course of the Great War ('Naval strategy and tactics were largely conditioned by a determination to make the next Jutland a Trafalgar – when a second Jutland was highly improbable'.) Mountbatten's cohort received a visit from not one but two former First Sea Lords. The 'wash-up' on the great battle took place over two days. On 13 February Jellicoe, supported by his one-time chief of staff, Sir Charles Madden, gave a briefing on the daylight action, drawing heavily upon information recently acquired from senior commanders in the former High Seas Fleet. Mountbatten found his worst fears about the 1916 clash of titans confirmed: intelligence had been abysmal and communications appalling. This was confirmed by discussion of the night-time action on 9 March, to which Mountbatten invited his cousin: 'The Prince and I went home shaken and depressed', both men lamenting the Service's stifling of individual initiative in the century following the defeat of France. On 1 June 1916 only the C-in-C's intelligence and intuition had saved the Grand Fleet from total disaster: 'I completely changed the immature emotional view I had absorbed about him when I was a midshipman.

I now realised what an outstandingly competent, brave and brilliant man he was, though I could still have wished he had steered for the Horns Reef.' Beatty's stock fell further, not least because he declined to travel south to Portsmouth. This was scarcely surprising given Beatty's fractious relationship with Jellicoe, and his firm belief that previous inquiries into the Grand Fleet's performance at Jutland had treated him unkindly.[7]

With the spring came Commander Mountbatten's first wholly independent command. By incredible good fortune he found himself 'a bit dazed but feeling very grand' on the bridge of HMS *Daring*. The 'D' class destroyers, 1350 tons and capable of cruising at over 35 knots, had only recently entered service. With four 4.7 inch guns, eight 21–inch torpedo tubes, and a crew of 140, *Daring* was, 'even more marvellous than I had imagined possible … a complete small cruiser'.[8] Given Mountbatten's lifestyle, playboy image, and seemingly modest credentials (at that time most officers still looked down their noses at the technical specialist), the wardroom viewed the arrival of their new captain with a mixture of scepticism and suspicion. He risked approbation at the outset by ignoring the advice of his flotilla commander and declaring that the ship should maintain the very highest level of hospitality and entertainment; he personally would ensure individual mess-bills remained at an acceptable level. Yet, rather than causing offence, Mountbatten's naïve gesture was greeted with good humour and, no doubt, relief. An initial readiness to give him the benefit of the doubt was reinforced the following Sunday when for the first time the new captain addressed the whole ship's company. Predictably, Mountbatten had done his homework, and his apparent familiarity with the personal circumstances of individual ratings ensured a lasting popularity on the lower deck. Those officers won over by his charm found him from the outset 'very human and approachable'. Once at sea even the sceptics conceded that here was a captain who – while over-fond of fast, somewhat flashy manoeuvres – was a surprisingly capable seaman, particularly given the size and speed of his command.[9] At this point it is perhaps worth noting that, for all the criticism Mountbatten attracted when in command of the *Kelly*, the quality of his seamanship in the Mediterranean in the mid-1930s was deemed exemplary by his superiors. From the outset he set himself a high standard of station-keeping, keenly aware that in peacetime a captain's prospects for promotion were influenced as much by his ship's smartness of appearance and manoeuvre as by his men's reputation and behaviour.[10]

With a happy ship, the growing respect of his peers, and the chance to test the full potential of a genuine state-of-the-art design, Mountbatten could scarcely believe his luck. The euphoria ended, emphatically, on 17 December 1934, when the crew of the *Daring* swapped their ship for an older, lighter, and demonstrably slower destroyer, HMS *Wishart*. The flotilla had been despatched to Singapore with a view to upgrading the quality of destroyers serving on the China Station. The ships now joining the Mediterranean Fleet were not especially ancient, but they had been built with undue speed in the course of the war and, far from home for an extended period, had been poorly maintained. Hiding his disappointment Mountbatten's first task was to rebuild the morale of his men, an obvious priority being the complete overhaul of their neglected and rather battered new home. There swiftly followed a succession of on-board competitions, shows, and that old favourite, the ship's newspaper. Acknowledged as a hard taskmaster and a disciplinarian, on the long, slow journey back to Malta the *Wishart*'s captain drew heavily on his infectious enthusiasm, and on a paternalistic patrician manner intended to charm even the most surly and suspicious.[11] Who knows whether this avuncular authoritarianism won over the most class-conscious members of the lower deck – unlike their fellow ratings on the *Kelly* at the end of the decade, the crew of the *Wishart* have never been rescued from Thompson's 'enormous condescension of posterity'. Even Brian Hoey, ever eager to explode the Mountbatten myth, simply echoed earlier biographers' insistence that arriving in Valletta was an unusually 'happy and efficient ship's company'.[12] There appears to be a blanket acceptance that anyone who ever served at sea under Mountbatten responded positively to his highly individual style of command, and anecdotal and documentary evidence supports the view that most sailors did. Yet it is naïve to assume universal approval, and, while expressions of dissent among his fellow officers can readily be found, evidence of any similar feelings among petty officers and ratings is far less likely to have survived.

Like Jack Aubrey, Mountbatten stressed the value of gunnery practice in relieving the tedium of long periods at sea.[13] Back in Malta the *Wishart* was given an early opportunity to demonstrate in competition her accuracy of fire. Eschewing the Grand Fleet tradition of speedy assault with all guns blazing, Mountbatten's gunners took their time, conserved their shells, and defied their many critics by emerging clear winners. The case against destroyers firing fast and indiscriminately appeared vindicated, and yet Captain (D) – an old shipmate of Prince Louis, H.T. Baillie-Grohman – complained long and loud about the *Wishart*'s reluctance to enter in to the spirit of the exercise. An uneasy relationship was further soured by Mountbatten's refusal to accept criticism: 'When I pointed out that we would probably have sunk any one of our fast-shooting rivals before they had even hit us, I think this was regarded as being in rather bad taste!'. With hindsight, it's scarcely surprising that, following his brief tenure at Combined Operations in 1942, Baillie-Grohman became a fierce and relentless critic of Mountbatten.[14]

Triumph in the gunnery trophy was an obvious morale-booster, but the *Wishart*'s captain warned against complacency. In the spring of 1935 he set the whole ship's company, including himself, the challenge of winning every prize at the flotilla's annual regatta on 4 September: in the full view of the Mediterranean Fleet, with all wives and families in attendance, the *Wishart* would sweep the board in the rowing and be declared 'Cock of the Fleet'. Just as the slide rule proved the case for firing less shells but securing greater accuracy, so the captain's calculations demonstrated the need to adopt a significantly faster stroke than was normal practice when crewing the Royal Navy's Chatham whalers. Later, when accused of encouraging an inelegant and unattractive method of rowing, Mountbatten claimed to have replied: 'I'm sorry. I hadn't realised that style was an important thing. I'd assumed that the thing that mattered was to be first past the winning post.'[15] It was ostensibly un-English remarks like this that encouraged dark mutterings about the chap displaying a decidedly Teutonic single-mindedness. Fair enough, Dickie played to win, but in displaying such fierce competitiveness did he respect the spirit of the game? Critics later pointed to the *Wishart* crews deceiving their rivals by only practising the new, shorter stroke at dawn and dusk. Furthermore, a rowing machine was secretly placed in the fo'c'sle, with officers and men alike – including the captain – furiously pulling to the rhythm of a manically ticking metronome.[16]

Blistered but unbowed, on the great day Mountbatten's men revealed the heterodox 38.5 strokes a minute, thereby securing total success. He and Edwina were exultant, relishing the colour and drama of a genuine spectacle. As the ship's band fanfared and the crew caroused (how many destroyers could boast Noel Coward as *de facto* musical director?), a hapless cock found itself lashed to the mast, and the captain read out a 'surprise' congratulatory telegram from His Majesty. Baillie-Grohman, again appalled by Mountbatten's indifference to tradition and accepted practice, offered grudging congratulations. In contrast, Andrew Cunningham, as Rear-Admiral, Destroyers, offered unqualified praise – for an ambitious captain intent on early advancement, the approval of 'ABC' constituted the ultimate accolade.[17] In an era when 'gentleman' and 'amateur' were synonomous, Cunningham appealed to Mountbatten as someone unembarrassed by being labelled totally professional. In this respect the latter believed they had much in common, notwithstanding the older man's understanding that very public displays of wealth and privilege were frankly incompatible with gravitas and authority. In the mid-1930s the Mountbattens had yet to appreciate that, for those forced to observe from afar, brilliance and bravura could easily be mistaken for mere braggadocio. Aboard the *Wishart* even the humblest able seaman could see that the captain had style, but the real reason for his popularity was obvious: Mountbatten could be judged by results – he was a winner, and he made sure that those who served under him could enter any bar or brothel in Valletta secure in the knowledge that they too were winners. It would be interesting to know how many fights on shore were generated by sailors from other ships irritated by the (singularly appropriate) cockiness of the *Wishart* lower deck. In this respect their captain failed as a role model, his very public pleasure in achieving success suggested conceit and immodesty, and disguised that sensitive side of his character which made him so successful in dealing with ordinary seamen on a one-to-one basis. He encouraged triumphalism not humility in his men. The will to win was a very real strength, but only if tempered by a genuine respect for the efforts of one's rivals. A man not prone to rigorous self-examination, Mountbatten rarely found time to reflect upon the negative impact of such behaviour, nor the fact that a lifestyle which he took for granted might strengthen his critics' deepest prejudices.[18]

Whatever their later feelings towards him, neither Cunningham nor his successor James Somerville subscribed to the view that Dickie was over-ambitious and flaunted his wealth. In his lengthy autobiography (700 pages), *A Sailor's Odyssey*, Cunningham scarcely mentioned Mountbatten, except briefly in the context of evacuating Crete in May 1941. If he could wholly ignore his colleague's service at Combined Operations and SEAC, it is scarcely suprising that Cunningham made no reference to his pre-war command of Mountbatten when in the Mediterranean. Needless to say, the latter painted a very different picture of their initial relationship, studiously ignoring ABC's jaundiced view of him after 1941. A 1967 memoir claimed that service under Cunningham was 'a real thrill', and that any congratulations from 'this absolute wizard' as to how Mountbatten had handled *Daring* or *Wishart* was praise indeed. During one particular exercise he had been invited to join the flag-officer whose 'fame in the destroyer world was legendary', and an admiring Mountbatten observed 'the greatest one-man performance I have seen on the bridge of a ship'.[19] His claim that Cunningham in the 1930s was by no means a distant hero does seem to be borne out by their private correspondence. They shared a fascination with signalling, even, if, unlike Sommerville, Cunningham was only interested in the operational and not the technical aspects of naval communications. All three men discussed the future tactical role of the destroyer, emphasising the destructive potential of the torpedo, and the centrality of effective signalling to offensive operations by day *and* night: near total victory off Cape Matapan in March 1941 would vindicate ABC's insistence on taking the battle to the enemy every hour of the day. During his brief tenure as Deputy Chief of Naval Staff in the winter of 1938–9, Cunningham was the most senior figure inside the Admiralty endorsing Mountbatten's establishment of the Royal Naval Film Corporation.[20] Cunningham was by no means an easy man to work with or under, and yet his outstanding powers of leadership, especially at sea, could generate fierce loyalty. In Mountbatten he would have recognised, if not a junior version of himself, another highly motivated officer displaying a familiar combination of abundant energy and supreme confidence in his own judgement. A man with no time for pleasantries, ABC was no doubt sincere when congratulating Mountbatten on his promotion to captain in the summer of 1937: 'No one in the Service has earned it more than you have and I am so pleased that that was recognised in the right quarters.'[21]

While eager to enhance his captains' ability to communicate with each other, and with him, Cunningham was generally wary of new technology. His own mental and physical attributes were so impressive, not least his phenomenal eyesight, that technical improvements not directly related to the waging of war were often dismissed as superfluous; witness his indifference to the 'Mountbatten Station-Keeping Equipment', a gearing system designed to assist destroyers keep correct station.[22] ABC was by no means alone in his suspicion of Mountbatten's invention, but a sympathetic procurement officer with a background in naval architecture secured Admiralty endorsement. The device was installed on three classes of destroyer, while another Mountbatten design, the enclosed bridge, became a standard fitting. Service on two very different destroyers provided an enormous body of direct experience to draw upon, and Mountbatten methodically identified design faults and potential remedies. In Malta, and later in London, he worked closely with a rising star in the Royal Corps of Naval Constructors, A.P. Cole. Ironically, the two men's working relationship was sparked by a blazing row. Yet anger swiftly made way for mutual respect, with Cole's technical training in Germany seen as confirmation that here was someone well worth working with. The young designer, drawing heavily upon Mountbatten's advice, was directly responsible for the new, much-improved, generation of destroyers that entered service at the start of the Second World War. He insisted, in the teeth of conservative opposition, that a single-funnel, two-boiler ship could enjoy greater space and a lower silhouette without any significant loss of speed. Typically, his collaborator claimed direct responsibility for this revolution in destroyer design: cocktails at Adsdean saw the Controller of the Navy converted to Cole's initiative.[23] Theory and practice neatly complemented each other, with Mountbatten fascinated by the engineering problems encountered in building or refurbishing a warship, from the initial design stage right through to the final fitting out. Three years later the *Kelly* would allow him direct involvement in the latter stages of the production process. Mountbatten was insistent that co-authoring with Cole a set of damage control instructions unique to the 'K' class destroyers ensured his ship's survival when badly holed by a German torpedo on 9 May 1940. Another key factor was his colleague's promotion of longitudinal hull framing as a guarantor of sturdiness and rigidity for destroyers on extended patrol in exceptional weather conditions.[24] As their correspondence confirms, this was a relationship rooted in mutual respect, and more than a hint of conspiracy: 'Dear Mountbatten ... It is difficult to talk to you from the office, as there are others in the room.'[25]

The fact that very senior officers were happy to socialise with Dickie and Edwina is scarcely surprising: sipping cocktails with minor – or even major – royals and well-known show business personalities at Adsdean or aboard the *Shrimp* revealed a glamorous world few admirals post-Beatty would normally enter. What is striking is the degree of intimacy revealed in correspondence with Mountbatten, even prior to his 1937 promotion. Thus Cunningham, writing from Alexandria on 16 September 1935, was remarkably indiscreet in revealing how he would play the long game in order to avoid conflict with Italy once the Duce's forces crossed into Abyssinia (the order was given a fortnight later). The future hero of Taranto and defender of Valletta, whose reputation as one of the great naval commanders would rest on an unblinking resistance to relentless Axis assault in 1940–2, confided to Mountbatten that 'I would abandon the Mediterranean and stop the holes at Suez and Gibraltar. Leave Malta with only the garrison'. This admittedly 'cold-blooded' treatment of the Maltese would reflect badly upon Britain, but might pre-empt any aerial attack and would be forgotten in the aftermath of an eventual roll-back of Italian influence and military might: 'This may sound a defeatist policy but it holds the chance of preventing a European conflagration which I think is all important and of course the Abyssinian adventure comes to a stop for want of refuelling.' To be fair to Cunningham, he added the rider that 'we can always alter it (our policy) at short notice'; and he did after all reflect the shared view of the Chiefs of Staff.[26]

Indeed Chatfield judged an air assault on Malta acceptable if it diverted enemy aircraft from attacking fleet operations intended to isolate Italy's expeditionary force. The Royal Navy's capacity to undermine Mussolini's hegemonic ambitions across the Mediterranean and in the Horn of Africa was taken as read. Where the Admiralty agonised was over the damage sustained in securing ultimate victory, particularly given the absence of a major force east of Suez. As early as April 1931 the First Sea Lord had warned ministers that the previous year's Treaty of London further compromised the Royal Navy's capacity to keep sea communications open, particularly if tension with Japan necessitated a major deployment in the Indian Ocean. Ironically, the first demonstrable signs of increased spending – traditionally symbolised by the abandonment of the Ten Year Rule in 1932 – compounded the problem, in that construction of the Singapore dockyard could now be completed. A combination of treaty obligations and the Depression ensured a loss of designers and skilled shipbuilders, so that, even if the National Government did agree to expand the surface fleet, the industry had no spare capacity. As it transpired, a major expansion programme only really kicked in as late as 1936–7. Anyway, by international standards British shipyards were slow, and in the mid-1930s still found difficulty replacing vessels, let alone building a new generation of battleships. Cunningham recognised that even a destroyer like the *Daring* lacked cutting-edge weaponry, notably in ASW, while the Mediterranean and Home Fleets' capital ships were arguably under-gunned by global standards. Ironically, prioritising ship maintenance in an era of retrenchment had meant downgrading the equipment and defence of naval bases, so that by 1930 no overseas port, including Grand Harbour, was deemed capable of providing adequate fleet support in time of war. Five years later not that much had changed, hence Their Lordships' warning to the Foreign Office that Malta would be hit hard by an Italian air strike. Indeed, all Mediterranean ports were deemed vulnerable given the acute shortage of anti-aircraft ammunition. Equally exposed was the fleet itself, with Admiralty planners predicating a scenario whereby the loss of warships in the Mediterranean would expose the hollowness of the British deterrent to Japanese expansionism in China and south-east Asia.[27]

It is hard to think what was more disturbing to Mountbatten: his commanding officer's readiness to retrench and regroup, or the *Wishart*'s illuminating and deeply depressing visit to the Tunisian port of Bizerta in December 1935. On 30 October and again on 22 November the Admiralty had been assured by the French Navy that Bizerta and Toulon would provide full dockyard facilities should the Mediterranean Fleet be forced to quit Grand Harbour. Yet Mountbatten's attempt to discuss contingency plans with the vice-admiral appointed as Bizerta's Prefect started badly, and proceeded to get worse. The French authorities were keen to avoid antagonising a large Italian community, hence their refusal to be seen in public with British service personnel: any civil disturbance would fuel indignation across the border in Libya. This fear that a further deterioration in relations with Mussolini might finally drive him into the German camp was soon echoed at a much higher level. Naval conversations in the New Year were to prove little more than a statement of good intentions. Back in Bizerta Mountbatten was at last allowed ashore, but had to dress in suitably Mediterranean civilian dress, and speak only French. It transpired that senior staff officers lacked detailed knowledge of the harbour's defences, largely because they 'had no concrete War Plan and did not seriously contemplate ever having to put these arrangements into operation'. The dockyard engineer proved far more cooperative, and back on the *Wishart* remarkably detailed charts were drawn up. Indeed, what is striking about the final report is its length and substance given the lack of cooperation: this was hard intelligence, and it is scarcely surprising that the technical data was widely circulated within the Admiralty and the Mediterranean Fleet, with relevant extracts forwarded to the Foreign Office. Mountbatten had found his supposed allies personally offensive and 'completely uncooperative. I realised then how fragile the Anglo-French Alliance might prove to be, and how doubly dangerous the situation was'.[28]

The Bizerta visit coincided with negotiation in Paris of the notorious Hoare-Laval climb-down over Italian aggression in Abyssinia. Although swiftly disowned by Prime Minister Stanley Baldwin in the face of public indignation, the 'compromise' agreed by Foreign Secretary Sir Samuel Hoare and his odious equivalent in the Quai d'Orsay further undermined Geneva's ostensibly tough line towards Mussolini. No wonder that, writing to Mountbatten in the spring of 1936, ABC concluded, 'The present emergency seems to be in a state of suspense and one thing only emerges and that is that whatever one does we don't propose to go beyond talking, strong action is entirely out of the question'.[29]

Yet six months earlier the rapid imposition of sanctions in response to Italy's flagrant flouting of the League Charter had suggested an Anglo-French readiness to enforce the post-Versailles interpretation of collective security. With all leave cancelled, and a very real fear of pre-emptive attack, the bulk of the Mediterranean Fleet was deployed to safer anchorage in Alexandria. *Wishart* and the other creaking ships that made up the 1st Destroyer Flotilla were deemed expendable and remained in Valletta to reassure the local population that Britain had not abandoned them. Had they been privy to ABC's private thoughts then presumably the Maltese people's faith in their imperial guardian, so crucial to the island's survival in 1941–2, would have disappeared overnight. With the Admiralty unwilling to challenge RAF advice that Italy might bomb the Grand Harbour, the families of service personnel were encouraged to leave for the duration of the crisis. Edwina refused, and did her bit to maintain morale by broadcasting news bulletins and stirring messages on the island's newly established wireless station.[30] The 'do or die boys' were detailed to harass and delay any attempted invasion or naval bombardment. Looking back on what might have been, Mountbatten had no illusions as to his flotilla's chances of inflicting serious damage, although he took heart from the performance of the Italian Navy after June 1940. Losses at Taranto and Cape Matapan left Mussolini's surface fleet invariably out-gunned and out-manoeuvred by the Royal Navy. Yet prior to the war the assumption in Whitehall was that such a fast and well-designed force constituted a major threat, in both the eastern and the western halves of the Mediterranean. If war did break out then the Royal Navy would undoubtedly emerge victorious, but at what cost? Notwithstanding the capacity of Italian submarines to inflict serious damage, the crisis over Abyssinia was, in Paul Kennedy's words, 'the first real acknowledgement by their Lordships that air power had arrived'. The absence of adequate anti-aircraft emplacements was as evident in Alexandria as in Valletta. However obsolete Italy's bombers may have appeared in 1940, five years earlier Naval Intelligence deemed them a genuinely potent threat to land bases and warships alike. The Admiralty advised a 'softly softly' approach, on the basis that even in defeat the Italians could reduce naval strength below the level necessary to retain full control of the Mediterranean *and* in an emergency deploy a credible force east of Suez. Only during Roger Backhouse's brief tenure as First Sea Lord did a less passive view of the Italian threat prevail, and Dudley Pound's appointment in May 1939 saw plans for a pre-emptive strike on Taranto temporarily dropped.[31]

After Mountbatten returned to London in April 1936, with the valedictory cheers of *Wishart*'s lower deck still ringing in his ears, both Somerville and his new commander-in-chief, Dudley Pound, wrote expressing their fear of Fascist support for Franco securing a permanent – and formidable – military presence in the Balearic Islands. Again, note the level of frankness in very senior officers' correspondence with Mountbatten. Like Cunningham, each admiral wrote to say thank you for his signed copy of an elaborate souvenir book recording *Wishart*'s achievements over the previous two years. Such a gesture could easily have been dismissed as typical of a conceited, over-ambitious young man with more money than sense. Yet, rather than scribble a token message of appreciation, Somerville and Pound each provided Mountbatten with chatty yet detailed accounts of naval operations off the coast of Spain. One is struck as much by the tone as by the content – the degree of intimacy was remarkable, reflecting Mountbatten's social standing as well as his fast-track status.[32] In fact both aspects of his career and character interacted, as for example when, upon his return from George V's funeral, he briefed Pound and the outgoing C-in-C, William Fisher, on current strategic thinking inside the Admiralty and across Whitehall. Not surprisingly, Somerville enthusiastically supported the rapid promotion to post-captain of an 'exceptionally capable and gifted officer and an excellent leader of officers and men', echoing these sentiments in his subsequent message of congratulation.[33] Keyes and Cunningham shared Somerville's delight that the Admiralty had chosen to ignore age and reward ability.[34] Indeed, what was striking about the dozens of letters and telegrams Mountbatten received following the formal announcement of his promotion in June 1937 was the very real affection displayed by his friends and fellow officers. Rarely formulaic, most messages of congratulation were long and full, with the natural envy of longer-serving colleagues skilfully disguised – as the Service's most precocious post-captain gleefully noted in his diary, seniority was usually attained in one's mid-forties, with 37 more often the age for promotion to commander.[35]

Interregnum: the Admiralty at the height of appeasement, 1936–9

By now, things were obviously hotting up. One didn't feel that one was in a 'peacetime' Navy any more, but rather an 'eve of war' Navy.[36]

Although Mountbatten left Malta aware that he was in line for rapid advancement, his early promotion was in part an acknowledgement of how much he achieved in his first year working at the Admiralty. In January 1936, when home for the late King's state funeral, Mountbatten was encouraged by a friend and fellow polo enthusiast, Connolly Abell-Smith, to come and join him in the Naval Air Division: a post was becoming vacant, Chatfield was committed to regaining full control of the Fleet Air Arm, and who was better qualified to argue the case than the son of the first admiral to recognise air power's future importance for the Navy? Abell-Smith was too junior to issue such an invitation without authority – others, more senior, would have noted Mountbatten's capacity to exploit his social connections, *and* the fact that he could fly.[37] However, he said no, under the mistaken impression that a job awaited him in the Plans Division, the elite advisory unit within the Naval Staff. Mountbatten was mistaken, but, suppressing disappointment, he pronounced himself better suited to the Air Division. He duly took up his new position in July 1936, four months after Hitler had remilitarised the Rhineland, and within days of the Nationalists' abortive coup dragging Spain in to three years of bloody civil war. Exactly a year earlier Churchill had signalled a renewed interest in the future size and composition of the Royal Navy, vigorously denouncing the recently signed Anglo-German Agreement. In the same Commons debate Hoare, commencing his brief tenure at the Foreign Office, rejected his old enemy's charge that the National Government had given Germany *carte blanche* to rebuild its navy. Remarkably, when Hoare returned to office in the summer of 1936, one of his first decisions as First Lord of the Admiralty was to agree that Churchill should be fully briefed regarding the Naval Staff's future plans. While relations with Chatfield became distinctly chilly post-1939, three years earlier the First Sea Lord recognised a ready ally, particularly when it came to convincing first Hoare, and then his cabinet colleagues, that the Royal Navy had to regain full control of ship-borne aircraft in order to facilitate a rapid programme of modernisation. RAF control of naval flying had resulted in obsolete, biplane aircraft, with the dynamic leadership of the US Naval Arm, and above all the Japanese Air Arm, demonstrating an urgent need for ministers to sanction an Admiralty-driven expansion of the FAA. One of the first papers to cross Mountbatten's desk asked:

> Can anyone doubt that if we went to war tomorrow, complete chaos would reign in the Navy's Air Services? Where are the machines? Where is the trained personnel? Where is the up-to-date material? They simply don't exist. There is not a squadron of aircraft about today with aircraft of a type which was not in service three years ago. There is not a squadron with a type whose design is less than ten years old.[38]

In tandem with Sir Roger Keyes – as a Tory backbencher no less loud and eccentric than when in uniform – Churchill promised Chatfield that he would do all he could to help. Thus a key part of Mountbatten's new job was to ensure Winston kept to the task in hand. One-time allies in the Cambridge Union, now Churchill and Mountbatten argued a far more serious case, ignoring constitutional niceties and even calling on the new King to intervene in support of their cause.[39]

    Debate over the future tactical use of ship-borne aircraft had focused upon the Mediterranean Fleet, and so Mountbatten – a torpedo enthusiast – was already aware of how limited their current role was. With priority given to the RAF's shore-based aircraft, there was little incentive for the Navy to develop the Fleet Air Arm as an innovative strike force, especially in ASW and convoy defence. Nor, prior to December 1937, was it entirely clear where Coastal Command's operational responsibilities ended, and the FAA's began. Yet a dependence on under-powered biplanes and the launching of only one purpose-built carrier – let alone the absence of a fast carrier force with an offensive capacity – was as much the fault of the Admiralty as the Treasury. However prescient Beatty himself may have been regarding air power, his colleagues seriously under-estimated the potential of air power. Thus in 1924 the Admiralty Board had given grudging agreement to the present arrangement. The 'battleship complex' had encouraged inertia, not least because traditionalists feared an independent tactical air component would drain resources away from the big guns. Naval procurement was the main casualty once air power as *the* key factor in destroying enemy resistance became the new strategic orthodoxy. (Amphibious operations similarly suffered, given the assumption that aerial bombardment rendered sea-borne assaults no longer feasible.)[40] Until the creation of a Flag Officer (Air) in 1931 the Naval Staff rarely challenged the CID's most vocal exponents of air power, or tested the full potential of naval aviation for waging war at sea.[41] A need to extend the Mediterranean Fleet's offensive capability beyond dependence on its 'big guns' was reinforced by the anticipated redeployment of capital ships should tension rise east of Suez: the 1937 Imperial Conference restated the centrality of Singapore to Commonwealth security (although two years later planners quietly but substantially reduced the size of the task force intended to deter Japanese aggression).[42]

Yet the latest strike *and* reconnaissance aircraft, the Fairey Swordfish, had a maximum speed of 115 knots, and reflected an inter-war preference for multi-purpose machines designed to fly off any carrier. Thus no aircraft in service on the eve of the Second World War could offer adequate fighter cover, or the capacity to protect merchant shipping from submarine attack. Responsibility for design and manufacture lay with the Air Ministry, which, given the low level of funding and support provided by the Admiralty, invariably subordinated Fleet Air Arm needs to those of the RAF. There was little sympathy within the Air Ministry for the Royal Navy's struggle to restore full autonomy, not least because the Admiralty sought control of shore-based aircraft operating over the sea, in other words, the newly-designated Coastal Command. Nor was Hoare, in his year chairing the Admiralty Board, prepared to add his weight to such a demand. On more than one occasion Chatfield hinted at resignation, but no member of the Government was prepared to support such a marked diminution in the RAF's operational mission. To placate the First Sea Lord an internal enquiry was set up in April 1936, chaired by Sir Thomas Inskip, the newly-appointed Minister for the Co-ordination of Defence. Baldwin received Inskip's initial recommendations in November, at which point Chatfield sought a second, more sympathetic report. This prompted a more detailed enquiry, with Lord Halifax and Oliver Stanley adding weight to Inskip's attempts at arbitration. It was at this point that Churchill chose to intervene.[43]

However prescient Prince Louis had proved regarding air power, the key figure in establishment of the Royal Naval Air Service was of course Winston Churchill. In March 1937 Mountbatten sent him an 11-page memorandum justifying the

Admiralty's maximalist position: the RAF should surrender all involvement in aerial operations over the sea, other than the training of personnel and the provision of anti-aircraft defence for the Navy's shore establishments. On a visit to Chartwell Inskip was given a copy of Mountbatten's paper. Churchill later furnished the minister with his own views on the future of naval aviation, articulating a less abrasive view of the Admiralty position. He saw sense in the RAF training all 'air chauffeurs and mechanics', with naval personnel then returning to an autonomous Fleet Air Arm for more specialist tuition. *All* bases should be protected by an inter-service 'Anti-Aircraft Command' under the ultimate authority of the Air Ministry. Churchill's functionalist compromise was ahead of its time, but at least signalled the potential for a common-sense solution acceptable to all. The former First Lord endeavoured to assist the Admiralty in a number of matters at this time, most notably the armament of the 'King George V' class battleships. Yet, as David Reynolds has demonstrated, events were to prove Churchill's pre-war thinking on naval strategy – as revealed in a March 1939 memo to Chamberlain – woefully wrong: the threat to capital ships from submarine or air attack had not been met, Singapore was not secure, war in the Mediterranean would not be shortlived, and so on.[44]

Relations between Inskip and the Air Ministry became strained, while in May 1937 Baldwin was succeeded as Prime Minister by Neville Chamberlain. For all the former Chancellor's prioritising of RAF demands, he supported Inskip's cabinet recommendation that the Royal Navy regain full control of ship-borne aircraft. This change of heart was accepted by the Secretary of State for Air, Lord Swinton, once Chamberlain reassured him that Coastal Command, although in future working closely with naval staff, need surrender no equipment or operational autonomy. Crucially, Hoare kept his promise to Mountbatten, and backed Inskip's report, even though no longer First Lord. Hoare's successor at the Admiralty, Duff Cooper, was one of Dickie's closest friends, and thus unusually well briefed when the Cabinet made its final, favourable decision in July 1937.[45] An announcement to the Commons was swiftly followed by the appointment of a Fifth Sea Lord/Chief of Naval Air Service. His new department initiated major training and procurement programmes. The Fleet Air Arm formed a new branch of the RNVR, with an intended establishment of 10,000 regular and reserve personnel by the autumn of 1939. Crucially, six purpose-built carriers were commissioned, all entering service in the early years of the war.[46]

Mountbatten was too junior to support the view of those admirers who see him as a founding father of the modern Fleet Air Arm. Real power lay in the hands of Ernle Chatfield, not least because all governments move heaven and earth to avoid the embarrassment of a chief of staff resigning. He clearly indicated to Baldwin in June 1937 that this was no idle threat. Ziegler's measured assessment was surely right: if not crucial, then Mountbatten's was nevertheless a very useful contribution, and 'far more than could have been expected from an officer of his seniority'.[47] After Inskip submitted his first, unhelpful report, the First Sea Lord drew on every weapon in his armoury. Mountbatten's immediate superiors encouraged him to lobby the King, with a view to 'David' questioning Baldwin as to the future of the Fleet Air Arm. The Abdication crisis quickly intervened, but by that time the Prime Minister had been suitably swayed by royal intervention, with Inskip duly instructed to launch a second enquiry.[48] The final decision was based solely upon political and military considerations, but at a critical juncture royal intervention had given the debate fresh impetus, and for this the Admiralty Board had reason to be grateful. By the time Mountbatten's promotion was announced, the Air Division had every reason to believe that restoring full autonomy to the FAA was a foregone conclusion. He had due cause for double celebration.

If, as has been suggested, an unashamed ethos of anti-intellectualism was all too prevalent inside the interwar Admiralty, then Mountbatten was more than capable of advancing new ideas without giving the impression that he secretly scorned his superiors' individual and collective intelligence. In this respect his social skills and political nous distinguished him from the Naval Staff's more arrogant and less astute advocates of fresh thinking.[49] Needless to say, he had his finger in a number of pies, each of which absorbed a great deal of time and energy. It was almost as if, once the Fleet Air Arm had its freedom, then Captain Mountbatten had a roving commission. For all the talk of imminent war, frenetic activity was invariably followed by intensive rest and recuperation, witness an extended period of leave in the winter of 1937–8, during which the pleasure of captaining his team in a Caribbean polo tournament was tempered by news of his brother's cancer – in April 1938 George died. His son David, having already followed the family tradition by entering the Navy, became the third Marquess of Milford Haven. The loss of such 'a brilliant man ... a real hero to me', left Mountbatten shattered, with work providing a welcome distraction. A project especially close to his heart at this time was the formation of the Royal Naval Film Corporation, a scheme whereby Wardour Street provided free of charge a regular stream of new releases. As early as 1915 Prince George had experimented with on-board cinema projection to relieve the tedium of life at sea, and the RNFC marked the culmination of a 20-year project to utilise film for education and entertainment: the inaugural screening took place in April 1939 aboard HMS *Ark Royal*.[50]

Throughout their lives both brothers were demonstrably gadget men, and the final years of peace exposed Mountbatten to a variety of fresh ideas and new technology. In later life he claimed an early interest in rocketry, the consequence of a short-lived acquaintance with inventor Robert Esnault Pelterie. Attempts to interest the Admiralty in the military application of missiles – especially French missiles – proved predictably fruitless.[51] Mountbatten was still fascinated by the potential for faster and more secure signalling, and he became a great admirer of the RAF's enciphering machine, the Typhex. He made a persuasive case for piloting these machines, but failed to secure approval from the Admiralty Signals Department for their introduction across the Service. The system was not universally adopted until as late as 1942, when American concern over repeated security lapses forced a belated reappraisal of signalling needs. Typhex's unpopularity was not down to any technical deficiency, but because it was so closely associated with the RAF. Such a blinkered example of inter-service rivalry deepened Mountbatten's conviction that hidebound tradition and blind prejudice had no place in the modern military environment. The seeds of his unequivocally functionalist approach to defence management a quarter of a century later could be found in pre-war squabbling over resource allocation and procurement.[52]

The Naval Staff's belated realisation of the threat to surface vessels from air attack encouraged rapid development of a long-range anti-aircraft gun. But only in 1937, after senior officers had visited the first pocket battleship, the *Deutschland*, did the value of concentrated close-range weaponry first become apparent. Nevertheless, great faith was still placed in the ability of long-range fire to break up formations of enemy bombers. Furthermore, it was assumed that the smallness of each target, let alone its speed and manoeuvrability, would provide a reassuring level of protection.[53] Mountbatten was clearly unimpressed by such complacency, witness his championing of the rapid-firing, armour-piercing Swiss gun, the Oerlikon. In May 1937 the gun's co-inventor, Antoine Gazda, brought his company's promotional film to London. At the suggestion of a colleague, George Ross, who had met Gazda in Tokyo two years previously, Mountbatten attended a screening. Like Ross, another 'young Turk' inside the Admiralty and someone who had already seen the new gun in action, he was singularly impressed. However, the Royal Navy placed great faith in the half-inch Vickers, a slower and less destructive weapon. To demonstrate the superiority of the Oerlikon, Mountbatten arranged with Vospers for the Swiss gun to be installed on a motor torpedo boat. New weapon and new vessel together proved an impressive combination; and yet, when testing in the Solent ended, the Navy insisted that a Vickers gun replace what had proved a demonstrably superior substitute. As always in such circumstances Mountbatten took his complaint to the very top, finding a sympathetic ear in Sir Roger Backhouse. The new First Sea Lord was a gunnery specialist, and the same admiral whose tour of the *Deutschland* had set alarm bells ringing inside the Admiralty. On 12 July 1938 Mountbatten organised a meeting between Backhouse and Antoine Gazda, facilitating several visits to the Admiralty over ensuing months. Even after his posting ended in October 1938, he remained a vocal supporter of the Oerlikon gun, and was recognised as such throughout Whitehall. In some quarters eyebrows were raised that a serving officer should form so close an association with someone who, for all his intelligence and good manners, was a foreign arms dealer. However, he was by no means alone in this, witness the remarkable array of senior officers Oerlikon invited to Zurich, where test firings were combined with guided tours of the Alpine slopes. In general Mountbatten's promotion of the Oerlikon was viewed in a favourable light, and an order for 500 guns in May 1939 was seen to vindicate a relentless two-year advocacy. When the *Kelly* was recommissioned in December 1940, having been virtually rebuilt as a consequence of her torpedoing six months earlier, she carried twin Oerlikons.[54]

Throughout the Czech crisis Mountbatten was on extended leave, the death of his brother in April 1938 forcing him to focus upon family affairs. The winter of 1938–9 saw him embark upon a succession of fast-track staff courses at the Royal Naval War College in Greenwich. For four months he studied intensively on the inter-service War Course, after which he spent a spare fortnight in Paris working up the first draft of a French/English naval dictionary. The need to minimise the risk of mutual incomprehension was becoming ever more apparent, and it's typical of the man that he deemed himself uniquely qualified to facilitate clarity of signalling between Allied ships. An assessment of his performance at the Air Division had identified someone who, blessed with the talent to reach the very top, could scarcely contemplate failure – either that of himself, or of anyone else. Here was 'a naïve simplicity combined with a compelling manner and dynamic energy'. Such a perceptive judgement was spot on, recalling Mountbatten's insistence that the *Wishart* win everything, and his consequent indifference to complaints of unsporting behaviour. This excess of enthusiasm, with an almost child-like need to be seen to excel, was evident even when Mountbatten was 'competing' against the best and the brightest of all three services. The calibre and seniority of officers attending the April 1939 Higher Commanders Course gives an insight into the level at which he was now operating. While the Royal Navy sent five captains to Aldershot, the War Office provided no less than seven major-generals, including ABC's brother, A.G. Cunningham, and, from the Indian Army, Claude Auchinleck.[55] By now Mountbatten was on familiar terms with most flag officers, but this was his first opportunity to network with senior staff drawn from the rest of the armed forces. When first introduced to 'The Auk' could he have imagined that only eight years later they would both be battling to maintain order across a whole sub-continent?

With news of his next appointment imminent – he was confirmed Captain (D), in command of the 5th Destroyer Flotilla, on 27 June 1939 – Mountbatten viewed his staff training as vital preparation for a war now seen as inevitable. The German Army's entry into Prague in March 1939, and the resulting Anglo-French guarantee of Polish sovereignty, were seen as confirmation that Munich had provided no more than a breathing space. In his TV life Mountbatten made great play of his credentials as an anti-appeaser: from as early as 1935 he and his wife had been vocal 'crusaders, and, like all prophets of doom, rather unpopular ones'.[56] That someone whose mother was Jewish loathed the Nazis was scarcely surprising. As for her politics, Edwina's late-blooming left-leaning instincts had led her from deluded strike-breaker in May 1926 to duped fellow-traveller ten years later. She visited Russia in 1929 as part of Beaverbrook's entourage, admiring chastened kulaks and smiling Stakhanovites from the warmth of a luxury-class couchette. A return visit in the winter of 1935–6 saw Popular Front sentiment prevail over healthy scepticism and commonsense: 'the people on the whole are contented and the young ones happy and enthusiastic.' While not especially gullible, and by no means an innocent abroad, Edwina nevertheless surrendered to the controlled itinerary and the Intourist factsheet.[57] Scarcely touched by ideology, her political opinions were well-meaning but full of contradictions – at breakfast she scanned the court page of *The Times*, not the court reports of the *Daily Worker*. Mountbatten shared his wife's instinctive sympathy for the poor and dispossessed, and was clearly moved by the poverty, social deprivation, and relentless misery so evident in those parts of the country hardest hit by the Depression. Pragmatic and meritocratic, his faith in an interventionist response to social deprivation was the gut instinct of a man for whom organisation was literally the order of the day. If short on intellectual rigour, Mountbatten's basic thinking nevertheless paralleled the ideas of that broad spectrum of centre-left politicians and opinion-makers who, with their Keynesian belief in planning for full employment and social justice, came in from the cold after May 1940. Groups such as The Next Five Years, PEP, and above all, Focus, combined a forensic critique of the National Government's domestic agenda with a deepening unease over cabinet reluctance to confront fascist aggression.[58]

Mountbatten had no illusions about Hitler or Mussolini, and feared the consequences of a third hostile force on France's borders. After only four months of civil war he confided to Robert Bruce Lockhart his preference for 'a Left victory in Spain – even Communist'. While Edwina 'became rather a tub-thumper', Mountbatten preferred a more circumspect approach, talking 'mostly to people who shared our views and might be able to get something done'. As a serving officer discretion was the order of the day, quietly cultivating sympathetic sections of the press. Thus he made a deep impression on Beaverbrook's henchman and Edwina's one-time paramour, Mike Wardell. The *Evening Standard* was something of a maverick within Express Newspapers and generally hostile to appeasement, not least because it boasted David Low as its cartoonist. Wardell, the *Standard*'s general manager, assumed that Mountbatten worked in Naval Intelligence. In September 1936 Wardell passed on to a sceptical Bruce Lockhart news that the Admiralty had knowledge of a secret treaty between Franco and the two fascist dictators. Rex Fletcher, an old colleague of Bruce Lockhart inside MI6, soon rubbished the story, and doubtless rubbished Dickie's credentials as an intelligence source. It was about this time that, at a Buckingham Palace banquet, Mountbatten secured himself a place next to the Prime Minister. Baldwin politely pooh-poohed any suggestion from the King's second cousin that so many new airfields in north-west Germany signalled a future attack across the North Sea. Nor did he share Mountbatten's belief that the Nazi leader's survival depended on military aggression: '"Hitler is like a man on a bicycle," I remember saying. "He's got to go on pedalling or he'll fall over; he can't maintain himself stationary".' [59] Mountbatten was convinced that, 'if Hitler pushes us beyond a certain point, no British government could survive that did not accept his challenge and fight'. Yet appeasement sent the very opposite message to Berlin, encouraging German expansionism in central and eastern Europe. Immediate surrender of the Sudetenland at the Munich conference in September 1938 simply reinforced Hitler's belief that Chamberlain would invariably choose acquiescence over resistance.

Mountbatten consoled himself with the thought that, 'Thank God I'm not a German'.[60] Given that he expressed this sentiment to a cousin who was a privileged member of the Nazi Party it was difficult to convince oneself that aristocratic disdain for the new regime was all-pervasive at Wolfsgarten, the ancestral seat of the Hesse dukedom. Indeed, at this point the very opposite was the case. The Mountbatten family visited the castle in August 1937 for a short holiday. An early return was necessary the following November. This final pre-war visit to Germany was in order to attend the funeral of Georg Donatus von Hessen and his family, all of whom had been killed in a plane crash. The Hereditary Grand Duke was Mountbatten's cousin on his mother's side, and, like too many in the Hessen extended family before the war, he was an enthusiastic and ambitious member of the Nazi Party. In consequence his funeral was a grand affair, a presumably uneasy Mountbatten marching through the crowded streets of Darmstadt in a funeral cortege of SS or SA uniformed aristocrats and party dignitaries. The event was considered of sufficient importance that Prince Louis' patron, von Ribbentrop, flew back from the London embassy to attend. The procession was carefully orchestrated – with only mixed results – to imply the new order's triumph over an outmoded feudal authority.[61]

Yet, ironically, Edwina suffered family embarrassment even closer to home. Her father – like many other deeply conservative members of the landed classes – was courted by Ribbentrop during his stay as ambassador in London. Wilfred Ashley met the Nazi leadership, including Hitler, on the eve of the 1936 Nuremberg Rally. His frequent letters to *The Times* and his presidency of the Anglo-German Fellowship had echoes of Lord Darlington in *The Remains of the Day*; and indeed, while ambassador in London, Ribbentrop was invited to spend the weekend at Broadlands. Lord Mount Temple's scarcely qualified enthusiasm for the Reich ended only with the terror of *Kristallnacht*: while remaining a member of the Fellowship, he resigned as president in November 1938. Given that his first wife was Jewish it is astonishing that Mount Temple remained so close to Hitler's regime for so long. His reluctance to make the break is especially puzzling given that he was objecting to Nazi anti-semitism as early as April 1933, when he accepted the newly-formed Jewish Emergency Committee's invitation to chair its first public meeting – and received hate mail from Berlin as a result.[62] Mount Temple clashed with his son-in-law over Munich, seeing the surrender of the Sudetenland as a necessary stage in the consolidation of the Reich as a 'truly national entity': Hitler was to be congratulated on fulfilling Bismarck's dream of uniting all ethnic Germans under a single flag.[63] Mountbatten saw his continental ancestry as giving him a unique insight in to the German *mentalité*, warning his fellow-countrymen against complacency. In this respect Mountbatten had much in common with Churchill's fellow cassandra, Frederick Lindemann, and the Foreign Office's fiercest advocate of war in August 1914, Eyre Crowe – the warning voice that says, 'I know and fear these people, precisely because I'm one of them'.[64]

In the spring of 1939 the *March of Time*'s London office, invariably hostile to the Chamberlain Government, sought Mountbatten's advice on newsreel coverage of the Royal Navy. This was at precisely the time when within the Foreign Office Rex Leeper was placing heavy pressure upon Fleet Street and the British newsreel companies to maintain at least neutral coverage of the embryonic Axis. With Franco victorious, the Admiralty viewed a now permanent Italian presence in the Balearics as further evidence of the need to keep diplomatic channels open.[65] In London, pending the final fitting out of the *Kelly*, Mountbatten stayed up all night and drafted a detailed shooting script, complete with bibliography: Hitler was compared with Napoleon; a large and powerful surface fleet seen once more as the only credible means of defending our island race. In fact the film, *The Battle Fleets of Britain*, was not released until the following November, by which time the onset of war demanded a script very different from Mountbatten's original.[66] Yet *March of Time*'s request for help had offered the über-screenwriter a triple opportunity: to highlight Hitler's real intentions and to argue the case for increasing the size of the Navy, and of course to become involved in professional film-making, however modest the role.

The television life of Mountbatten made no mention of its hero's experiment in scriptwriting 30 years earlier. It did, however, portray him as one of a select few anticipating disaster unless the National Government accelerated rearmament and the adoption of new weapons systems.[67] In this respect the relevant episode, broadcast early in 1969, echoed the dominant discourse on the eve of the Thirty Years Rule transforming appeasement historiography: the ultimate survival of the nation dependent upon Churchill and a handful of fellow anti-appeasers, ready when the call came in September 1939, and more especially in May 1940. It is worth recalling that, although the *Kelly* never went to Dunkirk, *In Which We Serve* portrays HMS *Torrin* rescuing exhausted Tommies from the beaches in a scene of high drama reminiscent of the opening chapter in *Guilty Men*; and when at the onset of war Chamberlain asks his wireless audience to, 'imagine what a bitter blow it is for me', John Mills as ABS 'Shorty' Blake fires back a lower deck riposte: 'Well it ain't exactly a bank holiday for us.'[68]

On paper Mountbatten was still a very junior captain, and yet he visibly wielded a degree of influence wholly disproportionate to his rank. He socialised with the most powerful figures within the nation's ruling elite; off-duty he was treated by his commanding officers as an equal; and at court in the late 1930s he retained the trust of the new King, if not necessarily his spouse. His lifestyle had little in common with the day to day lives of ordinary people, including most of his fellow officers. He was privileged in that the Admiralty tolerated his criticism of government policy in a manner unthinkable had any other junior officer engaged in such scarcely-disguised expressions of dissent. But then no other junior officer would have been able to lobby ministers and mandarins in the manner of a Dickie Mountbatten. He enjoyed mixing with men of power and influence, and more and more he considered himself a figure of similar weight and gravitas. That sense of being not just a party to history, but of actually making it, was reinforced by his closeness to the two cabinet ministers nearest his own age: Anthony Eden and Duff Cooper.[69] After the latter became First Lord of the Admiralty in 1937 he signalled to his old friend that, so long as Mountbatten exercised a degree of discretion, he could raise with him any matter of concern. Not for the last time Mountbatten petitioned his minister to fix a knighthood, in this case for an old shipmate of his father. The Chief of Naval Staff was furious, but powerless to protest. Even after Duff Cooper resigned over the Munich agreement – the only cabinet minister to do so – he maintained a backbench interest in the Navy, acting on Mountbatten's request to press for speedier expansion of the Fleet Air Arm.[70] The day after Duff Cooper informed Chamberlain that he could no longer remain in office ('I think he was as glad to be rid of me as I was determined to go'), Mountbatten was one of several serving officers to express intense disappointment at his departure, and immense admiration for his courage in refusing to be swayed by the huge tide of public emotion and relief: 'Your going at this time is a cruel blow to the Navy; none knows better than I, who enjoyed to a certain measure your confidence.'[71] Duff Cooper quoted this letter at length in his memoirs, making clear elsewhere how close he was to Mountbatten at this time. Given their friendship there are surprisingly few letters from this period that survive, not least because, despite the displeasure of his constituency association, the former First Lord now allied with Eden's motley group of back bench dissidents, the so-called 'glamour boys'. This was despite Duff Cooper's dislike of Eden: he envied his rival's early success, and was convinced that he could have done a better job as Foreign Secretary. While the Eden Group pursued a still cautious line of dissent inside Parliament, its most distinguished new recruit adopted a more aggressive stance, calling for an immediate alliance with the Soviet Union in a series of articles for the *Evening Standard*.[72]

Figure 4.1: 'Dickie with backhander 1939'

Equally surprising is the dearth of pre-war correspondence between Mountbatten and Eden. When Mountbatten's life finally appeared on television in 1969 Eden begrudgingly agreed to pay testimony to their friendship: 'We were of the same generation, and we were among the few who took exactly the same political view at the time in the Czech crisis.' Yet in *Facing the Dictators*, Eden's lengthy defence of his record in and out of office, he had made no reference to Mountbatten, and indeed he scarcely mentioned his erstwhile friend in the succeeding volume. Clearly, in 1962 the wounds of Suez had yet to heal, with an embittered Lord Avon reluctant to acknowledge how close he had once been to someone he now saw as having stabbed him in the back.[73] In 1938–9 Eden sought solace and advice at Brook House and Adsdean, his ego and wounded pride gently massaged by Dickie if not by his wife: no great admirer, Edwina was in any case invariably abroad with Bunny Phillips. Back in 1922 Eden had seen Edwina Ashley's engagement to the young Lord Louis as 'a waste'. This was particularly ironic given the deterioration in their relations over the next three decades. A weekend at Broadlands in February 1955 proved especially chilly, with Eden finding his hostess 'so very left and so full of prejudice', and Edwina dismissing the heir apparent thus: 'So nice and charming but so weak.'[74] Eighteen months later, at the height of the Suez crisis, the First Sea Lord was asking himself if Eden was mentally as well as physically ill. In retirement both men enjoyed a polite but uneasy relationship, Mountbatten privately noting that it was 'staggering what one mad PM can do'.[75]

One of Mountbatten's first acts upon returning from the Caribbean in the spring of 1938 had been to congratulate the former Foreign Secretary and his junior minister, Lord Cranborne, the future Marquis of Salisbury, for no longer tolerating Chamberlain's continued courting of Mussolini. He later claimed responsibility for persuading both men to resign, but in fact he was out of the country at the time.[76] That summer Eden retreated to a remote Antrim castle, far from the frenetic diplomatic activity engulfing Paris, Prague, and London. A long chat with his successor, Halifax, had left him gloomy as to the outcome of the Czech crisis. His mood was scarcely improved by reading *The Week*, which Mountbatten prescribed as necessary holiday reading. For Eden being away from the Foreign Office for the first time in eight years was agonising, but this inability to influence events 'will be a different matter in the autumn, if we reach that situation'.[77] Was he suggesting to Mountbatten hopes of an early return to office – which of course Eden's critics suggest tempered his treatment of Chamberlain before and after Munich? Or, was the reluctant rebel signalling that his 'glamour boy' admirers on the Conservative back benches would consolidate their opposition to government policy in the next parliamentary session?[78] Mountbatten no doubt interpreted his friend's comments as the latter. Despite collaborating with Churchill over the future of the Fleet Air Arm, he knew just how isolated Chamberlain's most trenchant critic was within a party still overwhelmingly loyal to its leader (only after Sir John Simon poured scorn on Eden's March 1939 call for a broader National Government and a Soviet alliance did his group embrace Churchill's tiny clan).[79]

With Bevin and Dalton unable to commit the Parliamentary Labour Party to a coherent, united anti-appeasement *and* pro-rearmament policy, Eden appeared the best, and, from the perspective of Brook House, the only credible voice of opposition. Duff Cooper was constrained by virtue of his office until October 1938, and, while a powerful resignation speech enhanced his authority and credibility, he attracted little personal loyalty, hence his deferring to Eden's leadership inside the Commons. For Dickie and Edwina, it had to be the former Foreign Secretary, witness a sinews-stiffening assignation at Broadlands as the Czech crisis reached its climax: Eden joined 'Bobbety' Cranborne in promising to speak out once back in London. A post-Munich weekend at Adsdean saw Eden reviewing recent events in a 'free and frank way'; and yet his still muted voice in the spring and early summer of 1939 must have come as a disappointment – unlike the Mountbattens, he believed there were still circumstances in which war could be avoided.[80] The first clear indication of a change of mind was Eden's decision to rejoin the Territorials, and yet as late as 2 September he chose not to challenge the Prime Minister's astonishing assurance to MPs that peace was still possible – despite Duff Cooper urging him to stand up and join Arthur Greenwood in 'speaking for England'.[81] One can only speculate, but perhaps the summer of 1939 saw the Mountbattens' never easy relationship with Eden enter one of its periodic troughs: Dickie was preoccupied with work, while, following her father's death on 3 July, Edwina was orchestrating the family's move from Adsdean to Broadlands.[82] Anyway, prince charming was increasingly distracted by an end to his exile. War having finally come, a despairing Prime Minister at last bowed to public opinion and brought Eden back into government – a return to office barely noticed by a Royal Navy too busy digesting the news that 'Winston is Back'.[83]

PART THREE

MOUNTBATTEN AT WAR,
FLOTILLA CAPTAIN 1939–41

5

HMS *KELLY*, 1939–40

The *Kelly* goes to war

So the war has started with all its horrors and destruction. In August 1914 I was thrilled, excited and pleased – now I have a home and family to think of and I'm worried.[1]

Excluded from the heart of government, Eden fretted. Churchill on the other hand exerted a disproportionate influence over the conduct of the war, not least because in the winter of 1939–40 only the Royal Navy appeared ready and eager to engage with the enemy. Aghast at the First Lord's idea of a Baltic offensive, senior officers schemed and stalled, focusing Churchill's attention on the U-boat menace and the more immediate threat of German surface raiders.[2] By the time the Mountbattens dined at Admiralty House on 5 December, attention was already focused upon an anticipated clash with the *Graf Spee* somewhere in the South Atlantic. Churchill, entranced as always by Edwina, could hardly fail to be impressed by Dickie's insistence that the Service needed to raise its game in terms of self-promotion, and that the war at sea was there for the winning. Here was the kind of commander who, hopefully, down in the South Atlantic was preparing to destroy Germany's premier pocket battleship: Mountbatten offered an apparent model of controlled aggression, positive thinking, scrupulous planning and preparation, and inspirational leadership.[3] Churchill was surrounded by caution and constraint, and Mountbatten doubtless shared many of his superiors' fears and apprehensions. A closer acquaintance with Dudley Pound enabled him to see how adroitly the First Sea Lord played the long game in seeing off Churchill's wilder proposals.[4] Yet across the dinner table the old romantic saw only what he wanted to see: a seafarer, a swashbuckler, a man of style and substance, and a stalwart companion of not one but two sovereign cousins. Why, Churchill speculated, were there not more winners at the highest levels of command – men who, like Beatty then and Mountbatten now, embodied the offensive spirit of Nelson's fighting navy? Harold Nicolson concurred. Lunching with his old friend two days later, he found Mountbatten 'so keen that it is like a breath of fresh air'.[5]

With Duff Cooper flying the flag in America, and Hore-Belisha elbowed out of the War Office, Eden remained 'the only man of our generation in the Cabinet' – could he reassure Mountbatten about the state of French morale, and could he convince his fellow ministers that here was a very different conflict from the '1914 Edition'? In January 1940 a mildly irritated Secretary for the Dominions warned against undue alarmism. Eden insisted that whenever the test came France, its army and its people, would hold firm. Dickie could take comfort from the fact that this was a view shared across Whitehall and throughout the BEF. The fall of France only six months later vindicated Mountbatten's concern that too much faith was being placed in the Maginot Line. However, by the mid-1970s he was portraying himself as a one-time voice in the wilderness: having been right over Appeasement he had spent the period of the phoney war urging an early offensive against a Reich still consolidating its victory in Poland.[6] This suggests a level of influence which he simply did not have in the twilight months of the Chamberlain Government. Eden was isolated, and Churchill receptive but preoccupied.[7] Besides, Captain (D) had his own war to fight, leading the 5th Destroyer Flotilla in to a series of escapades, from the Arctic Circle to the Western Approaches.

The captain's command consisted of eight 'J' and 'K' class destroyers, their actual complement determined by how many were sea-worthy at any one time. Of the 12 ships built only a quarter survived the war, with four sunk by the time Mountbatten handed over responsibility for the 'the fighting fifth' in late May 1941. HMS *Kelly*, named after a redoubtable Great War admiral, was the first of its class to enter service. She was the brainchild of the formidable Albert Percy Cole, arguably the finest naval architect of his generation. As shown in the previous chapter, A.P. Cole was in no way awed by Mountbatten, and each man's healthy respect for the other bred an effective design partnership. For all his independence of mind Cole had to work within the specifications laid down by the Naval Staff, for whom the balance of firepower had shifted from guns to torpedoes. Thus, the *Kelly* and her sister ships boasted two quintuple torpedo tubes, but only six twin-mounted 4.7 inch guns. Critically – and ironically given Mountbatten's oft-voiced fear of aerial assault – these supposed state of the art destroyers relied on only modest anti-aircraft armament, with the main guns' elevation limited to 40 degrees.[8] The *Kelly*'s twin Oerlikon cannons were finally installed in December 1940, but limited finance and availability meant they could not become a standard fitting across the flotilla. Thus, despite an unusually low silhouette, a maximum speed of 32 knots, and a unique 'longitudinal system' of hull construction intended to provide greater strength, these ships were highly vulnerable to air attack. A further irony was that, while the procedure for firing the guns seemed relatively sophisticated, the system for launching torpedoes remained remarkably haphazard and wasteful: with such a high margin of error, success depended upon a scattergun principle of simultaneously firing as many torpedoes as possible.[9] Although Cole's unorthodox approach to structural design prioritised resilience and damage control, beyond the bridge there was precious little provision for extreme weather conditions, witness the absence of heating on the mess decks. Sodden sailors froze in Arctic conditions, the deckhead dripping with condensation and the lockers soaked by sea-water pouring down the ammunition hoists. Conversely, in the Mediterranean or the tropics the heat below deck could be unbearable.[10]

Nevertheless, the *Kelly* was built to the very highest standards, partly because Mountbatten (and Cole) would tolerate nothing less and partly because it was the measure by which the rest of the flotilla, under construction in other yards, could be judged. Thus the installation of No. 615's twin engines and boilers, developing no less than 40,000 shaft horse-power, was overseen by one of the Service's most senior surface fleet engineers. Mountbatten himself spent much of 1939 inspecting those yards where ships of his new command were being built.[11] Since the previous October he had been a frequent visitor to the north-east. In the week leading up to the *Kelly*'s launch on 25 October 1938 her first and only captain quickly forged a warm working relationship with the managers and workforce at Hawthorn Leslie. This was the small shipbuilding firm whose yard was to become synonymous with one of the wartime Navy's most enduring legends. These were the proud men (and women) of Hebburn, County Durham, who built HMS *Kelly*, provided both the ship and its crew with a genuine home, and then found themselves in the almost unique situation of having to rebuild their pride and joy only two years after it first slid effortlessly down the slipway and came to rest on the banks of the Tyne.

It was only on 27 June 1939 that the Admiralty formally appointed Mountbatten as the *Kelly*'s captain, but for nearly eight months he had been absorbed in the minutiae of fitting out his new-found pride and joy. With Edwina away, and the children occupied and cared for, he could devote a disproportionate amount of time to ensuring Hawthorn Leslie fulfilled his every need. No client was ever so demanding, but then, as far as the board was concerned, no client was ever so deserving. Mountbatten in characteristic fashion flattered and seduced the managing director, Robin Rowell. What was at first a marriage of convenience turned into an enduring friendship. Similarly, upon their arrival in Hebburn each of his officers and petty officers 'chummed up' with their civilian counterparts: 'We became great friends all the way down the line ....' Mountbatten's respect and admiration for Hawthorn Leslie was genuine and well-documented. He judged the workforce to be scrupulously honest, applauding their frankness and integrity. Managers and men were seen as demonstrating a quality of teamwork normally akin to the armed forces – for Mountbatten surely the ultimate accolade.[12]

Rarely had a future ship's company set such an exacting standard of finish. At least once a month Mountbatten arrived to review progress, exchanging detailed notes with the shipyard manager and with 'Egg' Burnett, the fledgling destroyer's first lieutenant. Loyal and trustworthy, Lieutenant-Commander Philip Burnett had first encountered Mountbatten in 1930 when studying at the Signal School in Portsmouth. He was impressed, noting the extent to which the students' favourite instructor belied his playboy image. As an anti-submarine officer Burnett had the necessary qualification to serve as a flotilla leader's first lieutenant. At Adsdean in June 1938 the tyro captain had sounded him out about a new job. Meeting in Weymouth three months later Mountbatten decided that Burnett was definitely the man to oversee the *Kelly*'s preparedness for sea. This was a key appointment given that Captain (D) would be focused upon the flotilla, often at the expense of his own ship, and that design features incorporated in to the *Kelly* would be shared with the other destroyers under construction, starting with the *Jervis*, in which both men took a particularly keen interest. Mountbatten's letters to Burnett reveal an assumption that, with war imminent, both men would serve together for an unusually long time. He clearly rated him highly, urging 'Dear No. 1' never to hold back when expressing his opinions, even when critical of superior officers – including his captain. Nevertheless, Burnett never felt wholly relaxed in his dealings with Mountbatten, always remaining somewhat in awe of him despite a distinguished war record and elevation to rear-admiral. Every week throughout the winter and early spring of 1938–9 Burnett exchanged long and detailed letters with his commanding officer. The captain's correspondence invariably contained diagrams, measurements, hastily scribbled pencil notes, and sketches, their subject matter ranging from key facets of the *Kelly*'s fighting efficiency (Asdic location, embryonic radar lashed to the mast, and above all, Mountbatten station-keeping equipment) through provision of creature comforts in the captain's cabin (electric razor socket, fitted book shelves) to the cooking and storage space for potatoes (a larger galley stove, and moving the oilskins out of the decontamination store). Needless to say fitting the cinema screen and installing the projector were high priorities. Particular attention was given to a tailored bridge seat (on a long watch comfort facilitates efficiency, explained its future occupant), and to the décor of the guest cabins. The provision of a bathroom and the stowage of a ceremonial awning 'forced' Mountbatten to request Hawthorn Leslie's painters take unusual care over decorating the wardroom and cabins: the King and Queen intended to visit Belgium on a state visit the following September, and he had offered to wing them across the North Sea in the *Kelly*. This would, he hoped, not be the last occasion on which the Windsors could enjoy the services of a speedy and salubrious alternative to the royal yacht.[13]

A fellow recipient in Hebburn of Mountbatten's missives was the *Kelly*'s chief engineering officer, Lieutenant-Commander Mike Evans. It was Evans who regularly found himself explaining to the shipyard manager why Mountbatten and Cole were so insistent on radical last-minute design changes.[14] By late spring the captain himself could apologise for placing so much pressure on the Hebburn workforce. He focused his attention on the *Kelly* while still keeping an eye on the progress of her sister ships. At the same time he needed to foster a keen sense of identity among those who were to lead 'the fighting fifth' into battle. Adsdean and later Broadlands proved invaluable in providing the right kind of atmosphere in which captains and specialist officers from across the flotilla could get to know one another, and hopefully then bond in the true Nelsonian tradition. Meanwhile, when necessary, members of this embryonic 'band of brothers' were duly and dutifully despatched to such bleak but uplifting training establishments as the Admiralty Fuel Experimental Station – in this particular instance it was deemed essential that all engineers be metaphorically and literally up to speed with twin boiler technology.[15]

In early May 1939 Mountbatten had completed his choice of officers for the *Kelly*. Among the successful candidates were Lieutenants Maurice Butler-Bowdon and Edward Dunsterville, respectively navigator and signals officer. Both men were to retain close contact with Mountbatten throughout the course of his career, and well beyond. Because their responsibilities embraced the flotilla as a whole they were ever present, even when the *Kelly* was out of commission. On any matters related to the 5th Flotilla Butler-Bowdon was seen by his old captain as a sounding-board, a sniffer dog, and a reliable source of knowledge and advice. As we shall see, this was especially the case whenever Mountbatten felt obliged to defend his handling of the action on 29 November 1940 which saw HMS *Javelin* severely damaged. 'Dusty' Dunsterville, like his new boss a former signals instructor, was at Mountbatten's right hand from June 1939 until the moment the *Kelly* finally sank below the waves on 23 May 1941. As 'Flags' he was in theory – if not always in practice – party to all the captain's plans and intentions, and in that capacity he served Mountbatten well. So well, that Mountbatten took Dunsterville with him to SEAC and to the Mediterranean in 1952, and as First Sea Lord made him Director of Signals.[16] Another *Kelly* veteran, the gunnery lieutenant, Alastair Robin, benefited from Mountbatten's belief that the effort entailed in finding out who could best meet his particular needs must not be wasted. Robin was also posted to SEAC, providing with Dunsterville a pair of old comrades to whom the C-in-C could let off steam secure in the knowledge that his indiscretions would go no further.[17]

Like many other career officers, Alastair Robin found himself benefiting from Lord Louis's interest and, when necessary, his readiness to pull strings. Mountbatten's own rapid promotion, and the range of contacts he acquired across an ever more integrated armed forces, rendered him a highly persuasive and powerful patron. Nor was his eagerness to place favoured colleagues in plum posts restricted to the Service – if he could secure a comfortable civilian appointment for a deserving case then he would move heaven and earth to do so. Mountbatten's papers are full of requests for help, followed by the despatch of suitably supportive letters to prospective employers. In all this there was the familiar fusion of laudable altruism, *noblesse oblige*, and infuriating ego. Certainly, if the old man had done his 'homework' on you, concluded that you had what it takes, and by your subsequent performance felt vindicated in his decision, then potentially you stood to gain in terms of promotion. Potentially, in that Mountbatten generated such intense dislike among so many senior officers, civil servants, and politicians, that to be identified as one of Dickie's chaps was by no means a guarantee of advancement. As early as 1939 Mountbatten's bank of knowledge regarding naval personnel was formidable. Furthermore, he was on the whole a good judge of character, witness the quality of those who served aboard the *Kelly*, both officers and men. He valued initial impressions, and of course he himself endeavoured to convey a favourable first impression – whether that be indulging the great and the good, or inspiring the wounded and wary. Thus in June 1939 he found himself charming the cabinet secretary in to making a 300 mile journey north simply to sample life at sea, and less than two months later he was convincing Chatham's finest that the *Kelly* draft was their dream come true.[18]

Figure 5.1: The 5th Flotilla's captain with his navigator, Lt. Maurice Butler-Bowdon, HMS *Kelly*, August 1939

Sir Edward Bridges was a bizarre guest to entertain while conducting five days of intensive sea trials. Cole's presence on the bridge at this time made a lot more sense. The acceptance trials in mid-August concluded with a formal hand-over and the *Kelly*'s departure south. As with the skeleton crew assembled in Hebburn, everyone who joined the ship in Chatham was interviewed by a well-briefed captain: while the emphasis had to be on team-work each man would be dealt with on an individual basis, and in consequence judged on his own merits. Every member of the ship's company had a role to play, and Mountbatten saw it as his business to ensure that even the humblest rookie felt the captain valued his contribution to the wellbeing of the ship.[19] Few commanders in modern times have generated so much unashamed hagiography, and yet all those who served under Mountbatten on the *Kelly* clearly regarded it as a unique and unforgettable experience: 'His whole life was wrapped around his ship and his men, officers as well as we on the lower deck. Nothing seemed to be done at all on that ship unless the lower deck knew about it.' In the words of another ordinary seaman, 'He made me feel like an Admiral'.[20] Mountbatten was accessible and approachable, seemed genuinely interested, asked informed questions, placed a premium on the welfare and wellbeing of dependents, and ensured adequate rest and recreation. As with previous postings he ensured his ship enjoyed first-class projection facilities, and he quickly initiated a regular news bulletin.[21] Furthermore, Lord Louis shamelessly used his social connections to reinforce a widely shared belief that serving on this particular ship was something extra special – after all, how many other destroyers on active service entertained royals and film stars? At the same time he was of course totally demanding. Loyalty had to work both ways – the captain would do all within his powers to satisfy the needs of the men under his command, but in return he expected *everyone*, without exception, to meet his high expectations. He was rarely unreasonable, and so individuals were entitled to make mistakes – after all, he himself was by no means infallible. Those who erred might well be given a second chance. They were rarely granted a third.

Mountbatten's commissioning address on 25 August 1939 was immortalised by Noel Coward only three years later. While *In Which We Serve* owes much to David Lean's quiet command of cameras and cast, the thinly-disguised story of the *Kelly* is very much Coward's film – his performance as Captain (D) silenced the critics, and his screenplay convinced most if by no means all of Mountbatten's deeply sceptical colleagues. As suggested in Chapter Six, the film is at its most empathetic and evocative in those scenes set on or around the *Torrin*. At Dickie's insistence, Captain Kinross was a fictional creation and no mere impersonation. Yet, free from the family and back on the bridge Coward's character draws heavily upon its original inspiration. The script is rooted firmly in Mountbatten's own words, albeit transcribed by Coward after his friend returned from the Mediterranean in the summer of 1941 eager to recount his adventures. Kinross's initial, inspirational briefing to his men has, in successive biographies, become the authorised version.[22] However, we shall never know precisely what the 230 who gathered aft on the new destroyer's lower deck heard their captain say. Some had served with him before, and knew what to expect. They dutifully told Mountbatten 'what sort of a ship they thought I wanted … And that is exactly what we got: a happy and efficient ship'.[23] News of the Nazi-Soviet pact had already broken, and with the situation in Poland deteriorating rapidly, war was imminent. Mountbatten wanted his ship commissioned before the Fleet was mobilised. He calmly announced that, instead of the normal three weeks commissioning time, the job would be done in three days: loading and painting would be carried out round the clock, and other than the cooks all personnel would be directly involved. With the job done, the ship would sail round into the Channel for working-up. What most impressed those previously unacquainted with Mountbatten was that, while never risking over-familiarity, and a consequent undermining of authority, he cheerfully pulled his weight when it came to even the dirtiest and most demanding jobs: all the officers, including the captain, could be found painting the ship a bizarre shade of 'invisible' pink, mercifully replaced by battleship grey once war was declared. The sight of Lord Louis leading by example was clearly conducive to fostering an early sense of collective identity, but morale was dependent upon effective teamwork under pressure and in action: gunnery trials off Portland Bill gave every indication that here was an experienced and reliable body of regular seamen, but the real test would come under fire.[24]

There are competing accounts of the way in which Mountbatten learnt Britain was at war. The more prosaic version, courtesy of the man himself, has him over the side repainting the ship. A more appealing, and thus oft-repeated, anecdote has him interrupting yet another lecture on the eponymous station-keeping equipment in order to read a signal. Mountbatten continues, informing the audience that his final sentence would normally be along the lines of, '... I have given you the basic principles of operating my gear. If war should at this moment break out, you know enough about it to work it'. Officers and POs hang on the captain's every word, and at last he continues: 'Well, war has at this moment broken out.'[25] One can hear Coward's clipped tones. No wonder Mountbatten, when reading this version of events a quarter of a century later, gave his implicit approval. Yet its author, Kenneth Poolman, had based his history of the *Kelly* upon stories first heard aboard the *Kimberley* long after her sister ship had gone down. While 'the only captain she ever had ... [who] knew and loved her from the time of her birth when her keel was laid until the keel was the last thing visible as she sank beneath the waves' clearly had no problem with instant mythologising – it would have been strange and wholly out of character if he had – the now First Sea Lord adopted a consciously inclusive approach in his preface to Poolman's stirring tale of derring do. Sensitive to the personal criticism prompted by *In Which We Serve*, and eager not to cause offence throughout the surface fleet, he insisted that to remember the *Kelly* was in fact to pay 'tribute to all the destroyers that fought so gallantly and well in the days when we still had our backs to the wall'.[26]

Unlike many of the men under his command Mountbatten knew what it was like to be on the receiving end of a torpedo attack, even if that experience derived from a very different kind of war to the one anticipated in September 1939. An elementary lesson learnt standing on the bridge beside Ernle Chatfield nearly a quarter of a century earlier had been the need for eternal vigilance. Mountbatten hammered home the importance of relentlessly scanning the waves for any sign of enemy activity: the almost immediate loss of the liner *Athenia* highlighted the gravity of the U-boat threat, so better the embarrassment of a false alarm than an unanticipated explosion below the water line. Typically, with the war only 24 hours old *Kelly*'s captain signalled the Admiralty that a submarine attack had been successfully rebuffed, with the enemy presumably sunk by depth charges. Burnett argued strongly against submitting such a tenuous claim, but Mountbatten was insistent. Confident that no U-boats had been anywhere near the ship an amused Naval Intelligence Division anticipated a flurry of imaginary 'kills' once the 5th Flotilla was fully operational.[27] It was this 'up and at 'em', ever optimistic attitude which colleagues found either comical or conceited. Churchill on the other hand considered it Mountbatten's most endearing and inspirational character trait – hence the readiness to promote, even when his protégé demonstrably lacked necessary experience and seniority. Nor could the royal connection ever be wholly forgotten, witness the choice of the *Kelly* to bring the

Duke and Duchess of Windsor back to England in the second week of the war. Churchill and Mountbatten were the obvious partnership to orchestrate the former monarch's low-key return, Buckingham Palace preferring to keep its distance from a necessary but potentially difficult operation.

The events of 11–12 September 1939 might have been scripted by Evelyn Waugh. Consider the cast: representing his father, a whisky-fuelled Randolph Churchill, his questionable status as a subaltern in the 4th Hussars symbolised by the pair of spurs strapped on back to front; bemusing the bridge, a Pooterish ex-King, never slow to pose the most banal of questions; indifferent to the rigours of war, a luggage-laden Riviera refugee adamant that not one item of her wardrobe remain in Cherbourg; and finally, three cairn terriers whose indifference to the natural order and appearance of a Royal Navy destroyer was more than evident by the time they scampered down the gangway in Portsmouth. Apparently Mountbatten was concerned that officers and men would be seduced by the charm and glamour of 'cousin David' and Wallis Simpson. Nothing could have been further from reality, 24 hours with the Windsors proving a test of everyone's patience, not least that of the captain.[28]

Having completed his mission in tact and diplomacy, Mountbatten returned to the task in hand, namely forming the 5th Flotilla. Home in the early autumn of 1939 was Devonport. The frequent, often seemingly purposeless, excursions of the *Kelly*, *Kingston*, and *Kandahar* into the Western Approaches reflected the extent to which the First Lord had reverted to type. Both Churchill and a compliant Dudley Pound ignored the lessons learnt countering the U-boat menace last time around, and the tactical debate encouraged by the Admiralty throughout the late 1930s. The centrality of Asdic, air cover, close convoy protection, and above all, playing the long game, to effective anti-submarine warfare was ignored by an impatient Churchill intent on subverting the Service's 'defensive obsession'. Ever-optimistic, he was convinced that sizeable hunting groups, where necessary including aircraft carriers, could successfully scour the eastern Atlantic for submarines.[29] Early evidence of the folly of this high-risk approach was the narrow escape on 14 September 1939 of the Royal Navy's only modern carrier, *Ark Royal*, and the sinking of HMS *Courageous* only three days later. Fleet carriers were subsequently withdrawn from such operations, but hunting groups continued to seek out the enemy instead of forcing him 'to reveal his presence within range of immediate counter-attack'.[30] The *Kelly* was about 40 miles from the *Courageous* when she went down, 350 miles west of Land's End. Despite appalling weather the destroyer reached the rescue area in just over an hour. Among the 47 seamen transferred from the two neutral liners first on the scene was the stricken carrier's Commander (Flying) and most senior surviving officer, Connolly Abell-Smith.[31] For Mountbatten, being reunited with his old friend in such circumstances must have been especially poignant. It was Abell-Smith who nearly four years earlier had urged him to join the Naval Air Division. Both men had shared an enthusiasm for new ideas, not least the pursuit of genuinely integrated air-maritime operations – the antithesis of the costly tactics currently holding sway.

The following five weeks were divided between convoy duty in the Channel and chasing largely imaginary U-boats west of the Scillies. However, on at least one occasion depth charges did drive a submarine to the surface; but what should have been an easy 'kill' slipped back beneath the waves before the *Kelly*'s startled gunners were ready to fire. All aboard were still on a steep learning curve, and Mountbatten focused upon building up the fighting efficiency of his own ship and of the flotilla as a whole. Nevertheless, in his unusually affectionate letters to Edwina he found time to combine requests for vital supplies with anxious queries regarding the move to Broadlands. Family business and a rekindling of old love was conducted as much in person as by post, given that the captain's wife travelled down to Devon from Romsey no less than four times in six weeks.[32] Although they had no idea at the time, the winter of 1939–40 was to see the Mountbattens spending, by their standards, unusually long periods of time in each other's company. Not that this seemed likely when, on 20 October, Captain (D) was ordered north, to Loch Ewe on the west coast of Ross and Cromarty.

Figure 5.2: A family portrait prior to Patricia and Pamela leaving for America in July 1940

The 5th Flotilla had not actually arrived in the Pentland Straits when the Admiralty sent several ships in to Norwegian waters for the purpose of recovering the SS *City of Flint*, a captured American freighter en route to Germany. Success would mean the release of those crews taken on board the pocket battleship *Deutschland* after their ships had been sunk in the Atlantic. The mission demanded discretion as much as valour given that the German prize crew was intent on remaining within the three-mile limit, and Norway was still at this time a neutral country. Mountbatten felt himself admirably equipped to deal with such a delicate situation, and anyway he desperately desired the plaudits – and the DSO – which would rain down on whoever freed several hundred merchant seamen. Racing across the North Sea he hoped to intercept the freighter at a point along the Norwegian coast where shallow waters would force it out into the open sea. The *Kelly* was indeed first to the scene, only to be ordered out of the coastal zone by a Norwegian gunboat. There then followed one of those moments which admirers see as confirmation of their hero's style and *savoir-faire*, and enemies dismiss as further evidence of an egotist simply incapable of resisting any opportunity to show off: speaking in German via a loudhailer Mountbatten informed his opposite number that the *Kelly* would comply, but could he, 'Please give my compliments to my cousin, Crown Prince Olaf'?[33] There then followed the first of several acknowledged or alleged errors of judgement which when taken together render Mountbatten's record as captain of the *Kelly* a contentious mixture of the brilliant, the banal, and the utterly bemusing.

Two days of fast patrol necessitated refuelling in Sullom Voe. Returning to Norway, Mountbatten relied on intuition rather than calculation. He pointedly ignored the advice of his signals and navigating officers, identifying a position of interception behind rather than ahead of the *City of Flint*. In consequence, unlike the much-publicised rescue of the *Altmark*'s prisoners the following February, 600 civilian seamen found themselves facing five years in a German internment camp. In private Mountbatten apologised to Dunsterville and Butler-Bowdon for not heeding their advice. Later in life an unforgiving 'Flags' continued to insist, 'It is absolutely basic that in any intercepting situation like this you go to the position furthest on your target could have reached and then work back. But Mountbatten would have none of this. He wanted to catch the ship first and at once, to make a splash'.[34] To make matters worse, an impatient and no doubt irritated captain then compounded his error by setting course for Scotland at a cruising speed of 28 knots. Gale-force winds and heavy seas demanded a rate of knots perhaps half that at which the *Kelly* was travelling when she turned homeward and hit a huge wave. The sharpness of the turn left the ship rolling as much as 50 degrees starboard. Incredibly, one lucky sailor on deck at the time was swept into the sea and then washed back onboard; another, not so fortunate, was never seen again. Guardrails, davits, and boats all disappeared, leaving the length of the *Kelly*'s starboard side a mangled mess.[35] There had been loss of life and significant material damage, and yet Mountbatten emerged relatively unscathed from the episode. Attention focused upon the exceptional weather conditions and not the excessive speed of the ship. It was almost as if this had been a necessary test, vital in order to vindicate the robustness of Cole's revolutionary design. Thus Cole himself wrote in confidence to Mountbatten that colleagues within the Naval Construction Department believed 'the combination of sea and speed could quite conceivably have caused your roll (which I believe is a record), and that very few ships would have survived it'.[36]

That the *Kelly* had come through appeared to militate against a robust and extended inquiry into why the accident took place, let alone the circumstances surrounding the failure to trace and recover a slow, lumbering, and unarmed freighter. Mountbatten could consider himself lucky that the Admiralty let him off so lightly, Their Lordships' reluctance to pursue the case perhaps influenced by a refusal to provide William Joyce with any further opportunity to taunt the Royal Navy: judging by the former Blackshirt's remarkably well informed broadcasts, if Mountbatten's colleagues had yet to mark his card then 'Lord Haw-Haw' certainly had.[37] To be fair to Mountbatten, at this early stage in the war even the most cautious destroyer captains found the removal of speed and fuel restrictions 'exhilarating'.[38] Also, 'Egg' Burnett, with the authority of a retired rear-admiral, defended his captain's decision not to dawdle on the way home: 'By the morning we were within range of enemy aircraft and we wanted to get out of the range, so we turned and went as fast as we could.' As an experienced commander, not afraid to criticise Mountbatten's handling of his ship when appropriate, Burnett articulated the case for the defence, namely that it was better to sustain a tolerable degree of damage than risk losing the whole ship: 'We were perfectly seaworthy. All we'd done was lose our boats.'[39]

HMS *Kelly* returned to Hebburn for repairs, and, with Churchill still looking to mount operations in a now ice-bound Baltic, the opportunity was taken to reinforce plating on her hull. A brief return to sea – involving, perhaps now not so surprisingly, a minor collision – preceded three weeks back at Hawthorn Leslie while the boilers were cleaned out. A fortnight's leave at Broadlands was interrupted by Admiralty briefings, 'bore war' socialising, and enthusiastic support for Edwina as she laboured to silence the sceptics and secure a worthy and worthwhile appointment.[40]

In mid-December Mountbatten motored back up to Tyneside blissfully ignorant that within days he would be back in Romsey, and that he would remain in Hampshire for the next six weeks. While readying the *Kelly* to sail some time over the next 48 hours, he received a signal from the C-in-C, Rosyth Area, ordering him to sea immediately. Under his overall command all available destroyers were to hunt down the enemy submarine which had torpedoed not one but two oil-tankers, now on fire off the entrance to the Tyne. While the *Kelly* and HMS *Mohawk* put workmen ashore and raised steam, Mountbatten consulted the charts – given the depth of water at the mouth of the river, it was more likely that the two ships had struck recently laid magnetic mines. In any case, by the time he reached the stricken tankers the U-boat would have long gone. The local flag officer concurred, but, upon telephoning Scotland to query the purpose of the order, he was told in no uncertain terms that Mountbatten should stop bellyaching and get to sea. Yet again the *Kelly* proceeded at undue speed down river, by Jarrow Staithes narrowly avoiding a spectacular collision with an incoming merchantman. Much more cautiously, and with the *Mohawk* safely half a mile astern, Mountbatten edged towards the nearer of the two blazing tankers, the *Athol Templar*, signalling his intention to take off survivors.[41] By this time he was convinced that they were in the middle of a minefield, and confirmation came when, 'we heard a mine grating along the bottom, just under the bridge; that was very unpleasant. It grated along midships, then under the wardroom, and finally went off

Figure 5.3: The torpedoed Kelly's starboard waist looking aft, North Sea,
13 May 1940

between the propellors. The whole ship was shaken, we were knocked off our feet
…'.[42] There was a violent shock and brief confusion, after which damage control
procedures quickly brought the situation under control. The propellors had been
smashed, the tiller flat flooded, and the whole stern section wrenched out of line due
to the force of the explosion. The *Kelly* was powerless and rudderless, and yet she
could count herself lucky – a faulty proximity fuse had meant the ship was not fatally
holed. Her captain soon realised just how close he had come to losing his pride and
joy, while ruefully noting that his own quarters had sustained the worst damage. As
the *Mohawk* gingerly moved in to recover the tanker crews, two tugs arrived to tow
Mountbatten's crippled destroyer back up to Hebburn.[43]

As the *Kelly* limped home Mountbatten addressed the ship's company. He delivered the second of the two speeches through which, courtesy of *In Which We Serve*, his persona as the nation's best-known destroyer captain – dashing *and* fair – established itself in the collective psyche of wartime Britain. By this time everyone on board knew that a young frightened stoker, hearing the mine bump against the hull, had fled the engine room. Aged 17 at the time, in Coward's film this sorry figure was played by a suitably haunted Richard Attenborough. As Mountbatten pointed out to his comrades gathered on the lower deck, 'Out of 260 men, 259 behaved as I expected they would'. The single reprobate acted in the full knowledge that the penalty for deserting one's post was death.[44] In reality, as well as in re-creation, Mountbatten's address was a measured performance, teetering on full melodrama but always just pulling back from the edge. The extended pause, the careful deliberation, and the slow, purposeful crowd-scanning gaze reinforced both the gravitas of the speaker and the grave nature of the offence. Those present would later look back on a moment when all Mountbatten's many faults were stripped away; when he displayed a sensitivity, an acknowledgement of human frailty, and a comprehension of the thin carapace of courage.[45]

Philip Ziegler suggested his subject lacked the imagination to be seriously frightened, his extrovert, optimistic temperament enabling him to wipe out any long-term reflection upon what might have been: 'A tranquil mind may not be the most important quality of a great warrior, but it is a pre-requisite.' Such an argument is less than convincing, not least because more than once Mountbatten readily acknowledged his capacity to feel real fear. Thus, when reminding *Kelly* veterans that the same panic-stricken stoker later won the DSO, he expressed genuine sympathy for someone who after the war turned down repeated invitations to attend reunion dinners: 'no wonder he was frightened. I was too.'[46] On that dismal, grey evening in December 1940 conscience and humanity informed Captain (D)'s preferred course of action:

> ... you may be surprised that I propose letting him off with a caution – or rather two cautions: one to him, and one to me, for having failed to impress myself sufficiently in three months on all of you, for you to know that I would never tolerate such behaviour. Nobody will ever again leave their post. I will never give the order, 'Abandon Ship'. The only way in which we will ever leave the ship will be if she sinks under our feet.[47]

The words are Mountbatten's, recalled in retirement. A fuller, more familiar version appeared originally in Kenneth Poolman's 1957 tribute to the *Kelly*. That speech, drawing heavily upon Noel Coward's 1942 rendition, while technically more accurate, in that the figures for the crew and the length of training are correct, was nevertheless a reconstruction.[48] Yet Mountbatten was more than happy with Poolman's version of events as he read the whole manuscript and in the book's preface praised its author. Yet the veracity of the text scarcely matters – what really counts are the consequences. This was a moment of high drama, at the time witnessed by relatively few, and yet within a surprisingly short period of time both the magnanimous gesture, and the announcement of it, were to become foundation stones in the building of the Mountbatten legend. With the release of *In Which We Serve*, life became art, and then, in a stream of biography across the second half of the century, art contrived to become life: precisely where did Kinross/Coward end and Captain Lord Louis Mountbatten begin?

Captain (D) arranged for his flotilla staff to transfer to HMS *Kelvin*, still in Portland. *Kashmir* and *Kingston* remained on patrol off the Orkneys, sharing in the sinking of at least one enemy submarine.[49] The *Kelly* was in dry dock for 11 weeks, and for much of that time Mountbatten was at Broadlands, his leave extended as a consequence of contracting jaundice. A sympathetic crew wished him a speedy recovery, their goodwill towards the captain and his wife reinforced by Lady Louis' generous gesture upon hearing that their ship was again out of action. Scarcely expecting a further lengthy period ashore, most of the men had little spare cash and had used up their travel warrants. All had anticipated being at sea over Christmas, now less than a fortnight away. Edwina solved their dilemma by offering to pay the return fare of any seaman who wished to be at home with his family throughout the holiday period.[50]

While Dickie convalesced Edwina at last found a job to match her talents as a celebrity go-getter: the new president of the London Nursing Division of the St John Ambulance quickly revealed a remarkably capacity to raise money and to revamp what, for all the exigencies of war, remained a worthy but creaking organisation. Appropriately, in April 1940 she also took on the presidency of the Hampshire Nursing Division. Thus began a commitment to the Order of St John which in many respects shaped the final two decades of a crowded hectic life – just how crowded and hectic is shown in the way Edwina still found time to oversee extensive building work at Broadlands and to fit in a flying trip to Paris on the eve of Germany's offensive in the west.[51]

In mid-February Mountbatten was well enough to return to sea. So too was the *Kelly*, and in early March Captain (D) found himself providing a destroyer screen for the Home Fleet. On convoy duty off the Shetlands a week later, in the middle of an early morning snowstorm, disaster struck again. The *Kelly* ran into the stern of another destroyer, HMS *Gurkha*, sustaining a 35-foot gash in the aft upper deck. At Scapa a metal plate was riveted over the damage inflicted by *Gurkha*'s propeller. With Hawthorn Leslie too busy, the wounded destroyer was despatched south, spending six weeks under repair in the London graving dock at Blackwall. Mountbatten chose not to make an example of the officer of the watch, even though he was partly, if not entirely, to blame.[52] What really annoyed him was the fact that the accident-prone *Kelly* was fast becoming a joke throughout the Service. To make matters worse he had ordered his radio operators to react to any exceptional sound by sending the signal, 'Have been hit by mine or torpedo'; to which in this instance was added, 'Am uncertain which'. A rapid transmission made sense, in that the Admiralty would have some indication as to why the ship had sunk. In this instance, unfortunately for Mountbatten, someone on the *Gurkha* had the wit to reply, 'That was not mine but me'. Since the commencement of hostilities the Home Fleet had suffered a succession of calamities, but none involved such a prominent and unashamedly ambitious officer – for too many of his colleagues here was a high-flier who deserved his come-uppance. In no time at all every wardroom in the Home Fleet was talking about the *Kelly*, but for all the wrong reasons.[53]

Party to service gossip and anecdote, biographer and fellow admiral Sir Ian McGeoch noted those occasions when efforts were made to catch his hero out or to fault his seamanship. Yet, as in the Mediterranean five years earlier, Mountbatten's delicate and responsive handling of his ship when in confined spaces confounded the critics. As for the Thames in the middle of March 1940: 'Old ex-dockers still admire the way Mountbatten handled his ship into the narrow dock without assistance.'[54] Most of the crew were granted leave, a handful remaining for one of the more bizarre episodes in the *Kelly*'s short and chequered history. The ship had arrived in London bearing not the wounds of war, but the scars of incompetence. Yet no less a personages than the King and Queen, accompanied by the Duke and Duchess of Kent, were invited aboard to inspect the damage. The royal party enjoyed the best of the Navy's wartime hospitality and then Mountbatten delivered his *coup de theatre*, the private premiere of Charlie Chaplin's *The Great Dictator*, despatched across the Atlantic by United Artists as a favour to an old friend. It was moments like this that convinced both officers and men the *Kelly* was no ordinary ship. Yet at the same time such an extravagant gesture was seen by some senior officers as confirming their belief that the 5th Flotilla – and its captain in particular – still had much to prove.

The *Kelly* was out of action for six weeks, and as the 'phoney war' drew to a close Mountbatten observed the opening stages of the Norwegian campaign from the sidelines. While having no desire to sacrifice himself needlessly, how he must have envied Guy Warburton-Lee, leading 2nd Destroyer Flotilla into Narvik harbour at dawn on 10 April. The chances are the outcome would have been no different: two enemy destroyers swiftly sunk, but then two of the flotilla lost and one badly damaged in a surprise counter-attack. Like Warburton-Lee, who was awarded a posthumous VC, Mountbatten's eagerness to engage would surely have seen him ignore the five German destroyers hidden in adjacent fiords.[55] In 1977 Stephen Roskill suggested that a signal direct from the First Sea Lord to 2nd Flotilla had sealed its fate, in that the force commander aboard *Renown* then chose not to intervene. In a long-running battle with the doyen of naval historians, Arthur Marder, Roskill restated the argument made in his official history, namely that an ailing Sir Dudley Pound should never have been appointed to head the Royal Navy, and that this was evident as early as the spring of 1940. Roskill's view that Pound was exhausted, and thus unduly compliant in his dealings with Churchill, was illustrated by the failure of senior staff to secure cancellation of 'Operation Wilfred', the on-off-on enterprise to lay mines in Norwegian waters and to force vessels carrying Swedish iron ore out to sea, where they could be captured. This was action Mountbatten had been urging since the New Year, justifying a violation of international law on the grounds that Germany did not hesitate to sink neutral shipping.[56] Returning to the Admiralty late on the evening of 7 April, Pound was obviously incapable of thinking clearly, let alone confronting a 'well dined' Churchill. Why was Sir Dudley 'dead beat', and thus indifferent to his planners' advice that, with alarming evidence of intense German naval and air activity, imminent mine-laying off Vestfiord be cancelled? Because he had spent the day fly fishing on the Test at Broadlands.[57] Mountbatten had tired him out, and no doubt exulted that in cabinet Winston had at last got what he wanted – at precisely the moment that the First Lord's flawed strategy was being overtaken by events.

Although a frequent visitor to the Admiralty throughout April 1940 Mountbatten was a peripheral figure in terms of decision-making. Close personal relations with the ministry's two most senior figures rarely if ever secured him access to the Operational Intelligence Centre – the War Room. At this stage in his career he may have had the ear of the First Sea Lord (an asset not to be dismissed given Pound's reputation as a centraliser who was poor at delegating), but his influence upon the Service's senior hierarchy was far less than staff officers of equivalent rank who were at the heart of operational planning. It is this distance from real power which makes Mountbatten's rapid advancement from late 1941 so astonishing – only 24 months later, while still holding the substantive rank of post captain, he would be a serious candidate to succeed Pound as First Sea Lord.[58] That he should find himself in such an elevated position was of course thanks to the patronage of the Prime Minister. Churchill's enemies saw a cruel irony in the Norwegian campaign bringing about a change of government. Neville Chamberlain's many admirers at Westminster and in Whitehall complained that the new coalition was headed by a maverick politician who bore much of the responsibility for what had gone wrong.[59] The First Lord's handling of almost every aspect of the operation was open to criticism, not that this would be immediately apparent to anyone reading the relevant chapters in his history of the Second World War.[60]

Norway vindicated Mountbatten's prewar insistence that, without adequate fighter cover, the Royal Navy could no longer guarantee an expeditionary force its absolute command of coastal waters. In the absence of demonstrable air superiority, any troops being disembarked, and crucially any warships transporting and/or supporting them, had to have credible anti-aircraft protection – in a largely pre-Oerlikon era this was manifestly not the case. Nowhere was this more evident than in the deployment on 14–17 April of Allied troops north and south of Trondheim, a key objective if control of central and southern Norway was to be snatched away from an enemy by now present along the entire coastline. On 27 April, while Mountbatten and his crew made the *Kelly* ready for sea, up river in Downing Street the War Cabinet acknowledged the inevitable and ordered an immediate withdrawal of 11,000 beleaguered French and British troops. Admiral Sir Charles Forbes, C-in-C Home Fleet, despatched a large task force under Vice-Admiral John Cunningham to Namsos, a tiny port north of Trondheim where half of 'Maurice Force' was concentrated. The commander on the ground was the eccentric one-eyed hero of the Great War, Adrian Carton de Wiart VC DSO. Carton de Wiart was to be immortalised as Colonel Ritchie-Hook in one of the funniest books in the English language, Evelyn Waugh's *Men at Arms*. While the major-general would always have his suspicions about the French, the *Chasseur Alpin* was the only brigade trained and equipped to fight in the surrounding mountains. Under relentless aerial bombardment this elite unit was forced to fall

back on a port by now in flames. If Carton de Wiat felt his chaps could no longer
biff the Hun then it really was time to call it a day. He advised evacuation, treating
the Admiralty's promise to get all his men out with deep scepticism: 'I thought it was
impossible, but I learned a few hours later that the Navy do not know the word.'
Astonishingly, Churchill later regretted that 'Operation Hammer' was not given more
time to succeed. Had ministers procrastinated then the expeditionary force would
almost certainly have been wiped out.[61]

Having steamed north to Scapa Flow at breakneck speed, Mountbatten was
ordered by Cunningham to lead a vanguard of five destroyers into Namsos harbour,
clearing the way for three French transports to disembark the troops over two nights,
1 and 2 May. With the task force still some distance from Norway the *Luftwaffe*
launched a high-altitude bombing assault. None of Cunningham's ships were hit, but
the inadequate elevation of the 4.7 inch guns highlighted the vulnerability of those
destroyers chosen to operate close to shore.[62] Early on the morning of 1 May the
task force heaved to near the entrance to the Nansen fiord, at a point still some 70
miles from Namsos. Mountbatten requested permission that his division press on at
speed, taking advantage of the dense fog that had closed in overnight. Cunningham
presumably had no idea the *Kelly* would proceed in poor visibility at around 26 knots,
narrowly avoid destruction on half-submerged rocks, and leave the four captains
following in her wake astonished that Mountbatten was not only willing to risk the
lives of his own crew but theirs as well. Particularly perplexing was the fact that even
when enveloped in a fog bank the ships were still being bombed. In fact the Stuka
pilots were spotting the destroyers' mastheads, which stuck out of the fog and were
clearly visible in the morning sunlight. Once the fog cleared the fiery shell of Namsos
could be seen at the end of the fiord; but HMS *Maori* had been hit and the intensity
of the bombing forced Mountbatten to withdraw. In the sanctuary of thick fog the
division slowly worked its way back out to sea, this time relying a lot more on Asdic
bearings and a lot less on native intuition.[63]

By nightfall all fog had cleared, and Philip Vian on the destroyer *Afridi* was
entrusted with leading a flotilla of rescue ships into Namsos. Vian had made his
name seizing the *Altmark* two months earlier – an achievement Mountbatten had
previously failed to match when he allowed the *City of Flint* to get away. Free to
operate independently of the main force, here was a second opportunity in 24 hours
to make a name for the *Kelly*. With 'dark blue sky overhead and black, towering cliffs
on each side' the destroyer raced up 'the deep magnificent fiord', entered Namsos
harbour, 'blazing like a Hollywood film set', and lifted off the quay 229 *Chasseurs
Alpins*.[64] In reality it was presumably whoever had been ordered to embark first,
but the rescue of tough combat-hardened Frenchmen adds a suitably cool and
cosmopolitan touch to a good story. So too does the fact that Mountbatten found
time to exchange warm greetings with a grateful eye-patched general before the latter
disappeared back in to the night.[65] Coward should have incorporated this episode
into *In Which We Serve* instead of veering away from reality and sending the *Torrin* to
Dunkirk. How ironic that while Dickie was impressing the *Chasseurs*' commanding
officer with the fluency of his French, Edwina was demonstrating to Parisian shop-

girls her own formidable linguistic prowess.[66] Far crueller is the irony that at first light the Stukas returned and sank Vian's ship. The *Afridi* had been the last to leave Namsos, having delayed her departure to rescue survivors from the stricken French destroyer *Bison*. Trapped in the fiord and burning badly, she simply rolled over and disappeared beneath the waves, taking 100 men with her. Meanwhile the *Kelly* reached open water, and the opportunity for evasive manoeuvring so long as Cunningham's convoy remained in range of the dive bombers.[67]

The evacuation from Namsos, notwithstanding the loss of the *Bison* and the *Afridi*, was rightly judged to have been a success. It was perhaps the campaign's only success given that Norway was a triumph of incompetence from start to finish. Rather like Jutland, with hindsight the Royal Navy might claim that Germany's surface fleet had suffered severely; but unlike 1916 the enemy now enjoyed a marked strategic advantage in that his base for attacking the Atlantic convoy routes had moved a thousand miles westward. A further parallel was that the Service could claim to have destroyed or badly damaged key elements of the enemy's attacking force, and yet had itself incurred heavy losses – by the time action in the North Sea ceased on 9 June 1940 a fleet carrier, two cruisers, and nine destroyers (with, crucially, a further 12 in urgent need of repair).[68]

With hindsight, there were obvious conclusions for Mountbatten as a future Chief of Combined Operations. The clearest lesson was that so much learnt during the Great War, and in particular at Gallipoli in 1915, had been forgotten. There was still no integrated command structure to facilitate the effective formation and deployment of an invasion force. There were no regular units properly trained and equipped to participate in amphibious operations, and thus no vessels suited to landing troops speedily and securely in a hostile environment. Unlike the Dardanelles an absolute priority was the ability to provide effective air support from the outset. Collaboration between the RAF and the Royal Navy in Norway had been heroic but chaotic. The Fleet Air Arm's destruction of the cruiser *Konigsberg* was scant consolation given the *Luftwaffe*'s repeated success in disrupting operations to land or evacuate Allied ground forces: the bomber pilots of *Fliegerkorps* X were specially trained to attack shipping, and were quickly in action once Norway's airfields came under German control. Without air superiority, and ideally – as in Normandy four years later – air supremacy, forces on land and support vessels operating in coastal waters would remain highly vulnerable, and thus incapable of consolidating any immediate tactical advantage. At the same time capital ships could not be risked within range of enemy bombers, thereby withdrawing any protection they might offer hard-pressed destroyers and cruisers. In the spring of 1940 this cautious approach, while understandable, left the Navy heavily dependent upon its submarines to disrupt the enemy's North Sea supply lines – with little or no aircraft cover, there was no alternative. A year later Mountbatten was to witness the same scenario all over again, with the defence of Malta, and critically, the fall of Crete.[69]

Less than a week after the action at Namsos there occurred a sequence of events which, taken together, consolidated Mountbatten's reputation in the eyes of the general public as a sea-going warrior aristocrat. That same sequence of events, with a slightly different outcome, might just as easily have left a calamitous captain desk-bound and side-lined, his dreams of a glittering career dashed courtesy of a damning inquiry or even a court martial. After Norway the *Kelly* was ordered to the Clyde for refuelling. On 8 May she returned to action, leading the *Kimberley* and the *Kandahar* back in to the North Sea. HMS *Kandahar*'s captain was Geoffrey Robson who, while previously senior in rank, now found himself under Mountbatten's command. Typically, on his appointment the latter had seen no cause for tension, paying tribute to 'Commander W.G.A. Robson, who is one of my greatest friends' – but not, one suspects, one of his greatest admirers. Mountbatten genuinely held Robson in high esteem. Otherwise he would surely have intervened to prevent his late brother's son, the third Marquess of Milford Haven, joining the *Kandahar*'s wardroom in February 1940.[70]

With growing evidence of an imminent offensive in the west, Admiralty intelligence monitored a parallel increase in naval traffic. Mountbatten was directed to rendezvous with Vice-Admiral Charles Layton's cruiser, *Birmingham*, and join four other destroyers assigned to disrupt mine-laying operations off the Jutland peninsula. The long yet predictably speedy journey from Clydebank saw the core of 'the fighting fifth' reinforced by an ageing but equally fast destroyer, HMS *Bulldog*. All four ships were expected to liaise with Layton somewhere off the island of Sylt. Just after seven o'clock on 9 May, while in London Churchill prepared to assume the reins of power, an RAF patrol reported spotting a U-boat and forcing it to dive. *Kelly* and *Kandahar* were released from the *Birmingham*'s anti-submarine screen in order to substantiate the report. An optimistic reading of Asdic led to depth charges being released, but no obvious sign of a U-boat. Under orders, Robson had no option but to remain with the hunt, even though the more time passed the more he suspected Mountbatten was glory-hunting – a definite 'kill' would deliver that elusive DSO. The *Kandahar* signalled her captain's wish to leave, but Mountbatten insisted upon a further 20 minutes.[71] Yet with night approaching there was a very real chance of not retaining close contact with the *Birmingham*, leaving the cruiser open to attack from fast, heavily armed E-boats, operating in home waters under cover of darkness. To make matters worse, steaming at 31 knots around the north of Scotland and across the North Sea had left the three 'K' class destroyers with scarcely enough oil to reach England and refuel. In consequence *Kimberley* had already been sent back to port. The situation was critical, but Captain (D) showed no urgency about rejoining the *Birmingham* until well after 8.00pm when a second aircraft reported enemy shipping in close proximity. While no doubt open to criticism he could provide a reasonable explanation for his actions up to this point, even if his signals officer did later insist that, 'Leaving the cruiser alone was about the worst gaffe Mountbatten ever committed'. The report of a U-boat in the area was reliable, and there was no guarantee that it had gone. In such circumstances an extended hunt was necessary in order to guarantee the cruiser maximum protection. Also, with no previous experience of tracking E-boats, none of the destroyers' Asdic operators knew that a hydrophonic effect could be caused by a motor torpedo boat travelling at high speed. Finally, with the *Birmingham* cruising at 28 knots the three destroyers' resumption of station was bound to take some time, and therefore Mountbatten was not especially tardy in resuming station. However, his subsequent behaviour was far more contentious.[72]

On a spring evening, in reasonably good weather, and patrolling close to the enemy coastline, an absolute black-out would appear crucial. Nevertheless the *Kelly* greeted the *Birmingham* with an Aldis signal: 'How are the muskets? Let battle commence.' The case for the defence was that mixed lighting conditions at dusk, the difficulty of liaising re where to resume station, and crucially, the apparent passing of an immediate threat, justified Mountbatten's use of V/S (visual signalling).[73] Not that this view was widely shared at the time, and Robson was incredulous at such seemingly cavalier behaviour. The flashing morse lamp could be seen for miles, but distance was immaterial as the shadowy E-boat had already spotted the offending vessel. Nemesis was swift and brutal. At 10.44pm the first torpedo was seen to pass beneath the *Kelly* on the port beam, followed almost immediately by a huge explosion as its partner ripped into the starboard side beneath the bridge and blew up the for'ard boiler room – a plume of smoke and steam poured skyward as water poured through a gaping 50-foot hole and flames engulfed the superstructure. Astonishingly, only 27 men had been killed, although many more were seriously injured. Far more would have died had the ship foundered, but this was that pivotal moment when all the hours of damage control training were vindicated. Not only had A.P. Cole mapped out procedures, but he had impressed on Mountbatten how, rather than endeavour to correct the list, he should 'try and stabilise the ship at the list she then had'. The key was to act fast and lighten the load. Despite a heavy list to starboard, no power, and no communications, Mountbatten and his crew contrived to keep the ship afloat and, courtesy of heroic endeavours in the tiller flat, even to steer it. Everything that could be discarded was, including ordnance and boats – the secret was to minimise the weight on deck and above the waterline, relying on ballast to keep the ship from rolling. Astonishingly, given the extent of the *Kelly*'s self-inflicted wound, the removal of all unnecessary top weight ensured her immediate survival.[74]

On the bridge of the *Kandahar* David Milford Haven could only look on with horror, his first instinct being to search for survivors.[75] Geoffrey Robson's first instinct in the immediate aftermath of the explosion was to preserve his ship. The late Guy Warburton-Lee had argued strongly that in the event of a torpedo attack the priority was to minimise losses, hence all other ships had to distance themselves from the scene of the attack as speedily as possible. In accordance with the new orthodoxy the *Kandahar*'s grim-faced captain left Mountbatten's men to fend for themselves. Robson did absolutely the right thing, even if the captain of the *Kelly* was convinced that, had the positions been reversed, he would have stayed to assist. Indeed off the Friesian Islands on 31 August he was to risk both *Jupiter* and *Javelin* when a couple of minelayers were themselves sunk by mines.[76] As luck would have it, the *Bulldog* steamed into the area and was able to take the crippled ship under tow.[77] Layton and Scapa Flow were informed that the intention was to bring the *Kelly* in, and two tugs were requested. Mountbatten later wrote that in his opinion, 'the handling of the *Bulldog* was a supreme display of seamanship', witness her crew renewing a severed cable twice during the hours of darkness. That first night gave a clear indication of what was to come, with the mercurial E-boat making a bizarre high speed return to the scene of its former triumph. Apparently out of control, and with her 20 mm gun firing wildly, the enemy vessel bounced off the *Bulldog* and roared along the *Kelly*'s semi-sunken starboard side, shearing off the davits and guard rails before disappearing back into the night.[78]

By the time Robson returned to discover the *Kelly* was still afloat she was ready for him to receive the wounded. As the most senior officer present his first thought was to inquire, 'Is Captain (D) alive?'. How Mountbatten must have relished Robson reading the return signal, with its now familiar formula of surface jolliness scarcely hiding the all too pointed message: 'Yes, you are not in command of the Flotilla yet!'. He claimed to have adopted a similarly jaunty but direct tone in dismissing Admiral Layton's advice that he open the seacocks and scuttle the ship. In reality it must have been obvious that this was not the best time to throw caution to the wind and make fresh enemies. Arriving on the scene at first light Layton's first thought had been that the risks were far too great to justify the *Kelly*'s salvage value. It was only as he left the three destroyers to transfer casualties, bury the dead, and fend off the *Luftwaffe*, that the reason for Mountbatten's stubbornness became clear – rather than bring the *Kelly* back to be scrapped, he had every intention that she would go home to Hebburn and be restored to her former glory.[79] The notion of rebuilding a stripped-down, burnt-out, waterlogged destroyer at precisely the moment that the BEF was coming face to face with the full might of the German war machine could be seen as mad or irresponsible, or both. As a morale-booster and propaganda tool it was to prove an act of genius. There was no way Mountbatten could have guessed this at the time, but standing alone on a half-wrecked bridge drinking his beloved cocoa he must surely have mused on the myth-making dimension of such an enterprise. Yet neither calculation nor reason dictated the desire to bring the *Kelly* home. In the words of Edwina's biographer, 'It was all instinct, the reaction of a captain who loved his ship and was determined not to lose her to the enemy'.[80]

The second night, with the *Kelly* listing at five degrees in a heavy swell and help still several hours away, the end appeared nigh. The price of greater stability was to lose more top weight, and yet everything other than the machine gun ammunition had already gone. At this point the captain 'had a brainwave'. Transferring 230 officers and men to the other destroyers, albeit while under heavy attack from Dornier light bombers, left the ship lighter by around ten tons and therefore much higher out of the water. Cole, who journeyed north to greet the *Kelly* on her return, calculated that, had the ship not been abandoned, she 'would undoubtedly have gone over before we got her back'.[81] When the tugs arrived the following morning six officers and 12 volunteers went back on the *Kelly* to handle the ship, renew the tow-wire, and man the machine guns. The captain took his turn firing off ·5-inch rounds at the enemy aircraft that plagued the long painful journey back to Hebburn: 'And so we came home, after ninety-one hours in tow: home to Hawthorne Leslie's, and I'll never forget the heart-warming cheer from all the shipyard workers as we came into the Tyne.' The whole ship's company was stunned by their reception – to anyone manning the riverbank these were bona fide heroes, at a moment when the news from France and Belgium already appeared bleak. Humbled by the warmth of the welcome, and assured that suitable arrangements were in place for interment of the dead and treatment of the wounded, an exhausted Mountbatten at last surrendered his command. He joined Geoffrey Robson for dinner, which one can only surmise was a somewhat tense affair. From the *Kandahar* he wearily made his way, 'no luggage, unshaven and filthy', to the Station Hotel and the 'heaven' of a real bed. It quickly became clear that his ship would have to be stripped down to her bare structure and rebuilt almost from scratch. The *Kelly* would be out of action for at least six months. Such a prolonged period out of the water meant that she had to be decommissioned. Thus, most of the officers and all of the men awaited fresh postings across the Home Fleet. With the dead resting in Hebburn cemetery and the wounded safe in hospital Mountbatten addressed the remainder of the crew for the last time. All present 'volunteered to remain on or come to any other ship with me', and indeed over the next few months 22 lower deck correspondents sent respectful, even affectionate letters to their old captain asking him if he could fix a return to the *Kelly*.[82]

Although by now fully immersed in her nursing activities, Edwina found time to travel north and see for herself just how much damage had been inflicted on the 'poor old *Kelly*' ('Amazing feat to have got her back, 300 miles'). Dickie returned home with her, but with Brook House shut and Broadlands poised to be taken over by the Army he almost immediately motored up to Immingham, near the mouth of the Humber. Here, in the County Hotel, he met up with the *Kelly*'s flotilla appointments, and for the next four months maintained his staff headquarters. Easy access to first-class links rendered the small port a surprisingly comfortable base from which to thwart an imminent invasion. As usual he worked hard, putting in a 12-hour day; but he also played hard, finding time to convey Edwina by RAF flying boat to a fortieth birthday dinner party – celebrated, it must be said, in the distinctly unromantic setting of the Station Hotel, Hull. Having abandoned elaborate plans for mother and daughters to flee the Germans courtesy of a chartered yacht, conversation focused upon Pamela and Patricia's impending departure for America. They were due to depart on an evacuee ship, the *Washington*, on 4 July, their parents fearful that a successful invasion would see the Gestapo target the family because of its royal connections, and also because Edwina was half-Jewish. Long separations from the children were by now the norm, and any doubts were stilled by the readiness of wealthy East Coast families to provide a temporary home (in succeeding months it became clear that much of this alarmingly extravagant hospitality would at some point require recompense).[83]

Ensconced in Immingham, and deprived of his ship's on-board screen and projector, the cineaste suffered withdrawal symptoms. He ordered the fitting out of a personal picture palace. On the *Kelly* attendance at screenings, although closely monitored, was optional.[84] Ashore, joining Captain (D) for his daily celluloid fix was non-negotiable, fellow officers enduring the most primitive conditions while marvelling at Mountbatten's total absorption in every film, good or bad. The three-line whip extended to the dank, dingy cinemas of Devonport when 5th Flotilla moved south in late September. Most officers opted for sleep as soon as the lights dimmed, but along with the rest of the crew Mountbatten sat enthralled. One of the few things captain and men had in common was a seemingly indiscriminate love of the silver screen, hence back on board their bridge-building discussions of whatever was on general release – after which the crew rolled in to their hammocks and 'the old sybarite' returned to his cushy billet in Admiralty House.[85]

Away from the movies Anthony Pugsley, captain of the *Javelin*, admired Mountbatten's ability as a highly efficient administrator, capable of undertaking 'multifarious other activities, social and political, by working at a tremendous pressure, expecting his staff to do likewise'. Writing in 1957 Pugsley offered a pen portrait of the man whom, as we shall see, he held responsible for the *Javelin* losing her bow and stern. Noting that rapid advancement to the viceregal palace and the Admiralty penthouse had required extraordinary talents, Pugsley deftly and meaningfully observed, 'Whether these were discernible in the destroyer captain, it is hard to say'. While no fewer than 32 destroyers were either sunk or damaged during the evacuation of the BEF from Dunkirk, further north the remains of 'the fighting fifth' were, at least for the present, intact. The 5th joined other destroyer flotillas in round the clock sweeps of coastal waters south and north of the Thames estuary, thereby denying the Germans even the briefest of opportunities to launch a cross-Channel assault. Prior to each patrol Mountbatten's captains waited nervously to hear whether he would be sharing their bridge and claiming their cabin. Pugsley acknowledged Captain (D)'s tact in a difficult situation, and also his approachability. Yes he had genuine charm, rooted in 'good looks and easy manner', but he had the ability to talk to anyone, and crucially, he was never patronising. On the lower deck he was considered straight and willing to listen, and in the wardroom, 'My officers would crowd round him to enjoy his conversation with far less diffidence than they would show with other senior officers'.[86]

Mountbatten's critics saw little to question regarding his man management skills. They focused instead upon the series of misfortunes that had bedevilled the *Kelly*, not least the torpedo attack which so nearly sealed her fate. A growing belief that Mountbatten was something of a Jonah was quickly dismissed, as was the reassuring and oft-quoted observation of a conveniently anonymous admiral that, 'I know of nobody I'd sooner be with in a tight corner than Dickie Mountbatten, and I know of nobody who could get me into one quicker'.[87] Why, queried the sceptics, had Mountbatten exposed his ship – and indeed all the other ships in the vicinity – to such obvious danger? Far too much time had been taken up in a fruitless undertaking, during the course of which he had lost visual contact with the flag ship; and then in order to rectify the situation he had alerted the enemy by reckless use of the signal lamp. As already suggested, there is a case for the defence, and this was argued forcefully by Mountbatten and his allies at the time. The success of their advocacy is shown in the generous and frankly unconvincing conclusion of a report on the affair submitted to Admiral Sir Charles Forbes, C-in-C Home Fleet. The view of the inquiry was that the *Kelly*, along with her companions, had been victims of a well-executed trap.[88] Such a judgement may have been hard to believe – and for some no doubt hard to stomach – but a generous interpretation is that it reflected the Navy's tactical naivety regarding the offensive role of E-boats. Weighing heavily in

Mountbatten's favour were the courage displayed in bringing his charge home, the physical endurance required to remain awake and in control no matter how testing the conditions, and the 'consummate seamanship' necessary to keep his wounded warship afloat and on course.[89]

Beyond Tyneside few were aware of Mountbatten's apparent triumph. The Admiralty withheld the story of the *Kelly* until the first week in December, by which time the Royal Navy needed a good-news story – public attention was focused upon the Blitz, and memories of the Battle of Britain remained fresh in people's minds. The *Daily Mirror* offered a centre-page spread to mark the *Kelly*'s return to active service, revealing 'an epic story that will live for ever in British naval history'. With multiple references to Nelson, much was made of the fact that here was a 'hero of the last war … cousin of the King' capable of displaying the common touch: 'a captain who found time in the thick of battle to leave his bridge to murmur words of comfort to a dying seaman ….'[90] The *Mirror*'s twin geniuses of photo-journalism, Guy Bartholomew and Hugh Cudlipp, had created a template for any subsequent coverage of the photogenic 'MAN WITH THE NELSON TOUCH'. For example, in July 1941 a dull *Picture Post*-style magazine called *Everybody's Weekly* published an unintentionally hilarious profile of a polo-playing man of the people who eschewed luxury and indulgence, and whose favourite meal was 'the old seaman's diet of salt pork and bread' washed down with lime juice! Insistent that here was a member of the Royal Family who had genuinely earned his honours, one Lawson Carr gushingly concluded:

> If he hadn't so much blue blood in his veins, Lord Louis Mountbatten would probably have higher rank than he has now. But rapid promotion might invite jokes about favouritism and influence, and in these days that is something the Navy must avoid. So the man who might be Admiral remains a Captain. He himself prefers it that way, for it gives him the life he loves – in the little ship on the dangerous seas.[91]

By the time this article appeared Mountbatten's adventures aboard the 'little ships' were at an end. Anyone inside No. 10 familiar with the course of his career in the six months between the rescue of the *Kelly* and her return to service would have read Mr Carr's conclusion, and smiled wryly. On the top floor of the Admiralty the response would have ranged from indignation to incredulity.

Delaying a press release may have revealed the Navy's previously hidden talent for effective news management, but it surely reflected a deep division within Whitehall as to whether Mountbatten's actions warranted heavy reprimand or generous reward – or indeed both. Philip Vian, a more clear-cut hero, had no doubt as to the scale of his colleague's achievement, writing on 4 June to express his, 'unbounded and unstinted admiration for your perversity and obstinacy in hanging on when you must have had every possible kind of inducement to let her go'. Five days earlier Charles Forbes had sent Mountbatten a lengthy, hand-written, and apparently genuine letter of congratulations: 'You had a tough time getting the Kelly in and we all admired the way you stuck to it. It was worth it more from the morale point of view even than the material.'[92] Forbes was of course proved correct in that first of all the Service, and then later the British people, would take enormous pride in Mountbatten's refusal literally to roll over and die – here, in the minds of many, was a symbol of the whole nation, single-minded and resolute in the face of overwhelming odds.

Yet Forbes was equally insistent that Mountbatten's actions did not justify the award of that much-desired DSO. The C-in-C Home Fleet may have been right to point out that, 'owing to a series of misfortunes – mine, collision, torpedo – *Kelly* had only been to sea 57 days during the war', but he was surely on shakier ground in claiming that other destroyer captains were more deserving and that all would have displayed the same grim determination to bring their ship home. Forbes must have been under enormous pressure, given that the First Sea Lord's preferred option was to keep Churchill happy – why, asked the Prime Minister, had this brave and brilliant young officer be denied the most appropriate award for his undoubted gallantry? The simplest answer was that, for all his bravery and brilliance, Lord Louis should not have placed his ship in a situation where there was a strong possibility of being torpedoed – and nor was this the first occasion on which his actions lay open to a charge of poor judgement.[93] Perhaps not that surprisingly, behind-the-scenes lobbying by the Duke of Kent, scarcely a figure of weight and gravitas, fell on deaf ears. Beaverbrook, by now Minister of Aircraft Production, and thus in daily contact with Downing Street, fuelled Mountbatten's belief that, '... the powers working against me must be very strong indeed ... There is never smoke without fire'. As the only Captain (D) without a DSO he encouraged Edwina to press his case within the right circles, but always to exercise maximum discretion ('learn up the arguments by heart and make out you got them from any of my officers direct'). He was sure that, effusive congratulations notwithstanding, Forbes felt this bumptious individual needed bringing down a peg or two.[94]

Mountbatten was clearly a bitter man, even if he wore his sense of injustice lightly. The medal would no doubt come – as indeed it did, sooner rather than later – and the immediate controversy served only to convince the old romantic in No. 10 that here was a cousin of the King uniquely endowed by dint of birth and character to wage war in true Nelsonian fashion. Churchill, sympathetic to a growing belief within Whitehall that the C-in-C no longer enjoyed the full confidence of the fleet, agreed with his chiefs of staff that to deter invasion warships should be concentrated in coastal waters. Forbes, reluctant to strip Atlantic convoys of their escorts, was vocal in his opposition. His refusal to give Mountbatten a medal, however minor the episode, simply strengthened the Prime Minister's resolve. Forbes had to go, and on 2 December 1940 Admiral J.C. Tovey returned from the Mediterranean to assume command. By either coincidence or intent, later that week the story of the *Kelly*'s exploits was released to the press, and a fortnight later her captain had his DSO: unusually, the citation made no reference to a specific action or service, but rather 'the wholehearted devotion to duty' of an officer noted for his 'outstanding zeal, patience and cheerfulness'. Mountbatten attributed his belated success to Edwina's

Figure 5.4: Despite a 65 ft long hole, HMS *Kelly* limped home to Hebburn, and Hawthorn Leslie's dry dock

courting of Albert Alexander, First Lord of the Admiralty in both the coalition and postwar Labour governments.[95]

A.V. Alexander had an unusually close relationship with the Prime Minister, displaying a degree of loyalty matched only by his affection and respect for Clem Attlee. Whatever their private reservations, it is unlikely that either the First Lord or the First Sea Lord would have strenuously objected when Churchill proposed fast-tracking Mountbatten in to a senior appointment.[96] Of the two men most likely to object, Andrew Cunningham was in Malta and Charles Forbes was in retirement. Dudley Pound even repeated the offer after Mountbatten, invited up to Chequers on 8 December, was 'staggered' by Churchill's 'flattering' proposal, firmly but politely stating his preference to remain at sea.[97] Philip Ziegler surmised that the post must have been Vice Chief of Naval Staff, a position so vitally important that Mountbatten's acceptance at such a critical moment would have sent shock waves across the Service. Ziegler was no doubt right to suggest that, despite some disappointment over Pound preferring not to press the matter, Mountbatten must have experienced a sense of enormous relief.[98] Churchill had entertained his bold captain at Chequers knowing there was no longer any risk of Forbes quietly taking his revenge. The premier's intentions were twofold: to reward Mountbatten's gallantry, and to see the Admiralty employ his talents to the full. Yet again young Dickie had caught Churchill's imagination, Fleet Street following up its picture splash coverage of the *Kelly* with reports of a second ship saved from the cemetery of the sea. Yet again the story was not all it seemed, and this time there was no equivocation: no less a person than the Vice Chief of Naval Staff – the very person Churchill chose his protégé to replace – deemed Mountbatten directly responsible for the near sinking of Arthur Pugsley's much-loved destroyer, HMS *Javelin*.

Far from the *Kelly* but not from controversy: commanding 5th Flotilla, autumn 1940

The late autumn of 1940 saw ships of the 5th Flotilla at sea day and night. Captain (D) often found himself obliged to remain ashore, and a later criticism was that he failed to recognise the extent to which combat performance could be undermined by fatigue.[99] However, Mountbatten did command the flotilla's first major deployment in the Western Approaches and across the Channel; no less than seven destroyers supported and screened the battleship *Revenge* in an intense bombardment of Cherbourg. Forty-eight hours later, on 17 October, the 'fighting fifth' fought its first, inconclusive engagement with a force of German destroyers. Two aspects of the encounter were notable: firstly, the audacity of the enemy in sending four ships to the mouth of the Bristol Channel, and secondly, the ease with which their superior speed facilitated escape. The flotilla looked to a more decisive action, in open water off the Brittany coast and in conditions which would negate the German destroyers' three knots advantage. However a more immediate threat came from the RAF: patrolling off Brest the 5th found itself under attack. The claim of a contrite Blenheim pilot that he had been badly briefed simply confirmed Mountbatten's jaundiced view of Coastal Command.[100]

The *Kriegmarine* continued its aggressive tactics across the Western Channel into the winter. On 24 November three of the four destroyers encountered the previous month sank a couple of merchant ships off Plymouth. Four nights later a second sweep of the Cornish coast saw a coaster and two tugs sunk. At 5.30 on the morning of Friday, 29 November the *Karl Glaster*, *Beitzen*, and *Hans Lody* turned for home. Signals intelligence confirmed that the *Karl Glaster*'s flotilla commander, Hans Bartel, had set course to reach Brest by daylight. However, Mountbatten and his force of five ships had already spotted faint gun flashes on the eastern horizon. Led by the *Javelin*, the flotilla headed south-westward in chase of its quarry. Turning north to intercept, Mountbatten located Bartel's ship and the *Beitzen* at 5.40am. The Germans' first visual sighting was at roughly the same time, but thanks to EMII, their powerful short-range radar, they had already spotted the enemy. Only the *Javelin* and the *Jackal* had comparable kit, but their RDF ('radio direction finding') equipment was cruder and less reliable, failing to operate in tandem throughout the course of the next – ferociously intense – ten minutes. Both sides over-estimated the distance between them, judged by the *Javelin* to be 7,000 yards and closing. In such circumstances, where speed of response was absolutely critical, reliability and accuracy of radar gave the enemy an obvious superiority. Furthermore, the Germans' sophisticated fire control system facilitated the accurate despatch of multiple torpedoes via a fan-shaped salvo. The irony is that at the time they were unaware just what advantages they enjoyed. If anything Bartel was too cautious, erroneously assuming that a cruiser and a destroyer screen were en route to reinforce the attacking flotilla. In reality, with almost no moon, only intermittent access to RDF, *and* a faulty wireless transmitter on the *Javelin*, the solitary British ships were finding difficulty in maintaining contact with each other, let alone three hostile destroyers (having stayed to confirm the coaster's destruction, the *Hans Lody* was by now steaming rapidly towards the scene of engagement).[101]

According to Mountbatten, as 'two darkened vessels were sighted fine on the starboard bow, crossing ahead of our line from starboard to port', the RDF briefly kicked in and he became aware that the distance was now only 3,500 yards. However, the *Javelin*'s Principal Control Officer still assumed the radar was faulty and thus the range much greater. This breakdown in communications was central to Captain (D)'s explanation of why the *Javelin*'s first salvo failed to secure a direct hit. Had all equipment worked then his unorthodox approach to endeavouring to 'get as close to the enemy as possible, to ensure inflicting damage quickly, whilst remaining between him and his Base', would have been vindicated. Anthony Pugsley, standing beside Mountbatten on *Javelin*'s bridge, had assumed standard naval procedure for a night action: with respective forces closing at nearly 2,000 yards a minute he awaited the order to fire ahead at the most immediate target. To Commander Pugsley's astonishment Mountbatten ordered the flotilla to turn 90 degrees to port: placing his ships on a parallel course to a faster enemy would ensure an optimum engagement at the earliest opportunity, with minimal risk of friendly fire and the possibility of a follow-up torpedo attack. Inflicting maximum damage upon Bartel's destroyers before they escaped out of range made sense in daylight, but in the dark the risks were enormous; not least because a sharp change of direction at high speed necessitated retargeting the enemy. For Mountbatten the delay proved fatal, compounded by the Germans' ability to launch a pre-emptive torpedo strike: the first salvo sailed over the *Karl Glaster*, at the very moment her fan of torpedoes slammed into the *Javelin*'s bow, stern and midships.[102]

The ship was hurled over on her side, but astonishingly, given that a fierce explosion in the magazine had set the fuel tanks ablaze, she righted herself. The stern was 'a mass of tangled, blazing wreckage' and the forecastle and forward gun turret had been blown away, but the engine and boiler rooms remained largely intact. Yet again Cole's insistence on building destroyers that could survive massive structural damage had been vindicated – here was a ship that from each end had lost no less than 44 per cent of its original length, and it was still afloat. Sadly the good news did not extend to the casualty list, with three officers and 43 ratings lost. In addition a significant number were badly wounded, some as a consequence of being blown overboard but then picked up by the *Jackal*. The latter was the dim and distant target of a speculative torpedo strike by the *Hans Lody*. Meanwhile Bartel ordered his guns to fire a valedictory salvo; the Germans were already making smoke and gathering speed. Virtually unscathed and mightily relieved, they soon turned south and set course for Brest. For Captain (E) and his comrades 'Operation Seydlitz' could be considered an unqualified success, although ironically their superiors in the German Naval Staff interpreted events very differently. As in 1916–18 caution prevailed, and operations in the Channel were significantly reduced – with so small a surface fleet on active duty the risk to the *Kriegmarine* of losing one or more destroyers was deemed to be too great.

For the British all was chaos. The lack of flashless cordite, and the dazzling light generated by the explosion in the *Javelin*'s magazine, both blinded and bemused the *Jackal* and the *Jupiter*. The former broke away but failed to intercept the *Hans Lody* which had already crossed her line. In a similar knee-jerk reaction the *Jupiter* fired her torpedoes, but with all three Germans gaining speed to port may well have been targeting the *Jackal*. Understandably, the captain of the *Jupiter* had assumed the end of the *Javelin*. Meanwhile, his more senior counterpart on the *Jackal* remained unaware of the urgency of the situation, and that the flotilla now looked to him for orders. Ironically, his location so far west of the other ships was read on the German radar as evidence of a second group. The *Jersey* was similarly isolated, while the *Kashmir* endeavoured to remain on station. Her captain, Henry King, labouring under the misapprehension that it was the *Jupiter* which had been hit, fretfully awaited orders from a frustratingly silent and invisible Mountbatten. At around 6.00am, with the first glimmer of daylight, crucial minutes were wasted in establishing who was where, and which captain was now in command. *Jackal*, in close support of the crippled *Javelin*, and fearful of an E-boat attack, nevertheless despatched her sister ships in a fruitless chase down to Ushant. By late morning all five destroyers were reunited, with Fighter Command seeing off any inquisitive enemy aircraft. For Mountbatten it was déja vu. First one and then a second tug arrived from Falmouth, the *Javelin* taking over 14 hours to crawl back to Devonport. She wallowed patiently in Plymouth Sound, held afloat and upright by her two tugs until suitable space was found for her within the dockyard. Only then, in the middle of yet another air raid, did a quietly indignant Commander Pugsley step ashore.

Two decades later, at a reception in Singapore, the Chief of the Defence Staff's first remark on being introduced to Anthony Pugsley's son was, 'Your father never forgave me for that night action in the *Javelin*'. By that time Mountbatten would have read *Destroyer Man*. Its author, a retired rear-admiral with a CB and two bars to add to his DSO, scarcely pulled his punches. While never directly criticising his one-time flotilla commander Pugsley depicted the decision to run parallel with the enemy as a disastrous and wholly unavoidable course of action. Nor was he alone in insisting that Mountbatten's gamble was rash and unwarranted. If anything, Henry King was even blunter in his view that given the conditions a sharp turn to port was indefensible.[103]

Within days of the action Pugsley submitted a largely neutral appendix to Captain (D)'s report on their unfortunate encounter with the enemy. Attack is supposedly the best form of defence, and Mountbatten was unrepentant – indeed, it could be said that he had no choice. He depicted an intensity of fire far greater than was later proved to be the case, and insisted that any failure to inflict serious damage upon the enemy was a consequence of systemic communications breakdown, over which he had no control. Yet he insisted that two German destroyers had been hit. Pugsley refrained from endorsing this claim, simply pointing out that, 'The Captain personally observed two distinct hits', one of which must have been an unknown fourth destroyer given that no British warship was so far east. In his summary Mountbatten ran roughshod over his junior's healthy scepticism. Thus the superiority of British gunnery had forced the Germans to make 'full use of the traditional advantage which a fleeing enemy has over his pursuer in firing torpedoes'. Nevertheless, he recommended initiating any future attack with a coordinated torpedo launch. Not for the first time Mountbatten bemoaned the Service's inadequate experience of fighting in the dark, noting pointedly that the *Javelin* had been absent from the flotilla's most recent night exercise. Apparently, morale within the flotilla remained high, not least because of a common belief, 'that our ships are as nearly unsinkable as human ingenuity can make them'. The problem therefore lay, not with the ships, but with the kit: flashless charges, effective R/T, and reliable RDF aboard every destroyer were absolute priorities if such a regrettable incident was not to occur again. Similarly a more disciplined adherence to flotilla formation was recommended, with Captain (D) and his most senior commander henceforth advancing in line astern and avoiding any early exposure to attack. Here Mountbatten pulled no punches – he clearly identified the *Jupiter* as responsible for the fiasco that followed his enforced absence from command, although to be fair this indictment did note the inexperience of her captain. The advantage of being able to focus upon the flotilla while Pugsley sailed the ship was duly noted, but with none of the compliments courtesy demanded. Mountbatten's version of events was a remarkable document, somehow rendering newspaper reports of a victory for the Royal Navy in the Channel less fantastical. Was the episode no more than a necessary lesson on a steep and unavoidably expensive learning curve? Photographs of a decapitated, amputated *Javelin* provided a much-needed reality check. Yet even here the machinery of mythologising rolled effortlessly on, once again depicting Lord Louis as the sailor who, however hard the task, would always bring his ship – and his men – safely home to port.[104]

Admiral Dunbar-Naismith, C-in-C Western Approaches, may have been the perfect host, but he was appalled by his house guest's report. A confidential covering letter found Mountbatten guilty of failing to organise his attacking force correctly, and of a tactical misjudgement in ordering a 'line of bearing' rather than penetrating the enemy 'line ahead'. Furthermore, Dunbar-Naismith disputed Mountbatten's explanation as to why searchlights were not employed as well as star shells. Yet the admiral found himself in a difficult position as he had failed to secure the support of Philip Vian, the senior captain in attendance when Mountbatten was debriefed. Although pressed hard by Dunbar-Naismith, Vian undermined the case for the prosecution by refusing to comment. Nevertheless, as report and commentary ascended through the Admiralty hierarchy, accompanying criticism became terser and more forthright: an unnecessary and ultimately costly manoeuvre had wasted precious time, and, in the words of no less an authority than the Vice Chief of the Naval Staff, it was 'elementary that one should open fire first at night'.[105] Reading these remarks one can only wonder why no further action was taken, and yet the answer is obvious. Mountbatten was a high profile naval hero at a time when Britain needed every hero she could muster – even the mildest reprimand might undermine national morale should news leak out, while just the slightest hint of an inquiry could guarantee a torrent of indignation from both 'the old man' and from his sovereign. Indeed, as we have seen, for Churchill his protégé's latest adventure merited medals and a senior staff appointment.

Mountbatten, despite escaping censure, was always deeply sensitive to any suggestion that he bore personal responsibility for the near-destruction of the *Javelin*. In 1962 he used his authority as CDS to secure the flotilla's navigation officer access to relevant Admiralty files, including Bartel's postwar briefing by Naval Intelligence. (When Viceroy he had found time to read the latter in 1947, and gained grim satisfaction in learning how much the Germans had relied on their radar.) Butler-Bowdon compiled a report that contested Pugsley's account of events in *Destroyer Man* and encouraged Mountbatten to dispute the Admiralty's critical view of his conduct. Later, when Robin Bousfield drafted a private history of the *Kelly*, Mountbatten contributed a feisty defence of his tactics, albeit conceding that he should have turned two or three minutes earlier: 'but I was obsessed with the idea of getting to point blank range to force a decisive action ....' He continued to insist that the 'true disaster' was the flotilla's failure to regroup; and felt vindicated when told in confidence that Charles Firth, commander of the *Jackal*, had seen the *Javelin* hit but then hesitated to take command.[106] In 1971, a letter from an officer on the *Hans Lody* briefly convinced Mountbatten that the *Javelin* had in fact been hit by the third and not the first German destroyer, which 'would account for the hitherto inexplicable circumstance of being torpedoed unobserved'. Butler-Bowdon listened sympathetically to his master's latest excuse, and then gently rubbished the notion that any ship other than the *Karl Glaster* had launched the original salvo. Even after his most trusted envoy wrote his own, ostensibly definitive account, Mountbatten would not rest, resuming his quest for total vindication as late as the summer of 1976.[107]

The *Javelin* episode was in many ways a model for later controversies, usually of a much grander nature. Mountbatten rarely if ever needed to convince himself that he was correct in whatever course of action he chose to pursue. Far more important was that his judgement be seen to be right – and if, publicly or even privately, he was subject to criticism then every path had to be pursued in order to secure approbation. No matter how distant the event his critics must be silenced, with the record left unblemished. A similar mentality extended to the keepers of the flame, Richard Hough being the most obvious example, although on this occasion even he could appreciate the case for the prosecution. Philip Ziegler, scarcely his subject's harshest critic, adopted a judicious tone in assessing whether Pugsley and the Admiralty had been right to complain, duly noting that, 'The weight of naval opinion is that Mountbatten blundered'. Even this was too much for Admiral Sir Ian McGeoch, insistent that his man had taken an acceptable risk, and that the consequent reluctance of German destroyers to roam the Channel bore out the need for aggressive tactics. Had Pugsley still been alive he might have considered legal action against his unequivocally hostile fellow admiral. For Mountbatten's acolytes and admirers even a hint of criticism was sacrilegious and deserving of the deepest scorn: to confirm the justice of his case McGeoch noted that the damning Vice Chief of the Naval Staff was in fact Tom Phillips, a veteran 'big guns' disciple whose sceptical view of air power sealed the fate of the *Prince of Wales* and the *Repulse* only 12 months later.[108]

6

HMS *KELLY*, 1941

From the Western Approaches to the Med: the final six months of the *Kelly*, December 1940–May 1941

If the higher echelons of the Admiralty still questioned Lord Louis's credentials as a flotilla captain, no such doubts remained regarding his wife's capacity to energise and organise London's hard-pressed nurses and volunteers. Rapid elevation to number three in the St John hierarchy reflected the extent to which Edwina had become a pivotal figure in the capital's ARP and first-aid provision, her daily diary crammed with shelter inspections, ministerial lobbying, recruitment initiatives, ceaseless admin, and the regulation requirements of a stylish aristocrat determined that even in time of war standards must never slip. Fear, fatigue, and family friction all took their toll, with rest and recreation at Broadlands marked by a previously dormant passion for market gardening and an unashamed relief that henceforth the house would serve as a hospital and not a barracks.[1]

Throughout the winter of 1940 and into the spring Mountbatten spent little time away from his ship. He was preoccupied with the *Kelly*, having returned to Hebburn in late November to admire the repairwork, and to initiate an intensive, month-long training programme. Chatham's finest had all but disappeared, with 170 of the 260-man ship's company 'HO' rookies – almost all of these 'Hostilities Only' recruits had no experience of going to sea, with predictable results. Some old hands found themselves back below deck, but not as many as their old captain would have wished. Several of the *Kelly*'s original crew had written requesting a transfer, only to be informed by Lord Louis that, sadly, such matters were beyond his control. However, evidence emerged that in some cases a blinkered Lord Louis had discretely approached men he especially wanted back on board. Such soliciting proved wholly counter-productive, providing his enemies with yet more evidence that here was a lightweight charmer as unscrupulous as he was incorrigible.[2] For someone clearly capable of displaying shrewd judgement and careful calculation, Mountbatten did have a remarkably capacity for letting his enthusiasm and single-mindedness get the better of him. Did it not even for one moment cross his mind that encouraging *Kelly* veterans to request a transfer would become common knowledge across the Service, further damaging his reputation?

The men of *Kelly redux* had much to absorb and little time in which to do so, as Captain (D) made clear in his commissioning address. Beneath the usual exhortatory rhetoric was a steely message that all aboard had to learn fast if their ship was to lead by example and serve as an effective flotilla leader. New recruits' perception of their skipper changed markedly when they read in the *Daily Mirror* of the *Kelly*'s earlier adventures.[3] Throughout the period of reconstruction Mountbatten's flotilla officers had remained with him. Continuity on the bridge was a major factor in bringing the ship's company up to speed so quickly. However, one significant change of personnel was Philip Burnett's replacement as first lieutenant by Lord Hugh Beresford, scion of a wealthy Anglo-Irish family who for two centuries had sent its sons to sea. The new Number One was related to Admiral of the Fleet Lord Charles Beresford, a singularly unattractive Germanophobe who in August 1914 had incurred Churchill's wrath by publicly demanding Prince Louis's dismissal.[4] For Mountbatten the sins of the great uncle in no way prejudiced his opinion of Burnett's successor, whom he held in the highest esteem. While gently mocking 'the other lord' for his religious beliefs and natural reserve, from the outset he appreciated that here was someone who generated universal respect, whether among the workers at Hebburn or the apprehensive HOs fresh from basic training. A simple, unqualified blend of honesty and integrity shone through, generating a quiet authority that ideally complemented the captain's more extrovert yet also more abrasive style of leadership. Hugh Beresford's avoidable death in the aftermath of the *Kelly*'s sinking affected Mountbatten deeply, as indeed it impacted upon the whole crew – here was a destroyer unusual in having successive executive officers as popular on the lower deck as within the wardroom.[5]

The speed with which the first lieutenant earned Mountbatten's respect is reflected in the pivotal role he played throughout the five weeks of intensive training prior to Captain (D) rejoining his flotilla. Beresford was left in command over Christmas, striking just the right note in his seasonal address to a muster of HOs fearful, freezing, and still in shock following a storm-tossed trip from Scapa Flow to the Faeroes. Not that the maiden journey north from Hebburn had been uneventful, with a predictable collision even before the *Kelly* left the river – ramming a merchant ship, SS *Scorpion*, had required rapid reshaping of the previously painstakingly restored bows. When finally the ship did depart the Tyne Mountbatten had found himself forced to direct his 170 wretched and retching rookies to action stations – fearing a German destroyer directly ahead, to his relief Rosyth signalled a belated warning of night-time gunnery practice. Muted yuletide festivities in Torshavn were enlivened by news that, with trials complete, the *Kelly* had been ordered south to Plymouth.[6]

It was at this point that Mountbatten finally secured his beloved Oerlikons. He also acquired someone to fire them – Petty Officer Ted West. After the war, in the course of which he gained the DSM, West wrote a short but revealing account of his time on the *Kelly*. While still in Hebburn he and his fellow non-commissioned officers had been told in no uncertain terms that, while formalities must always be respected, the captain would consider them no different from the denizens of the wardroom – and would therefore have the same high expectations. With such a raw crew the role of the CPOs and their colleagues was deemed crucial to the ship's survival,

Figure 6.1: HMS *Kelly*, 23 August 1939–23 May 1941

hence West's nervousness when ordered to oversee the mess decks. Another lifelong admirer of Lord Louis was 'Rocky' Wilkins. Able Seaman Wilkins was an experienced gunner, but he had no idea just how much energy and emotion had been invested in providing the ship with added protection from air attack. The captain's keen interest made a deep impression, as did his support for Mrs Wilkins when the Blitz claimed the family home. The two men established a lifelong rapport; a friendship made that much easier by Wilkins' easy deference and Mountbatten's patriarchal – some would say patronising – sense of humour. While both went their very different ways after May 1941, nine years later a fresh and genuinely warm relationship developed after Wilkins invited his old captain to become patron of the Kelly Reunion Association. We must return to Mountbatten's involvement with the Association, but his first encounter with Rocky Wilkins deserves mention, not least because for 30 years the two men were in regular correspondence, and literally toured the world together.[7]

On 18 January 1941 the 5th Flotilla – *Kelly*, *Kashmir*, *Kipling*, and *Jersey* – rejoined the Western Approaches Striking Force. While weather conditions in the Channel and out into the Atlantic were at least marginally better than in the far north, the physical demands made upon such an inexperienced crew were arguably worse. The flotilla was on two hours for steam, with intermittent shore leave invariably curtailed by urgent orders to report back on board. More effective submarine-tracking – a consequence of improved RDF, closer liaison with Coastal Command, and a breakthrough at Bletchley in cipher-breaking – generated frequent sightings, and the subsequent deployment of all available destroyers. While attention focused upon the now ever more debilitating U-boat threat, in the early spring of 1941 a fresh fear was the potential for surface raiders operating out of France's Atlantic bases to inflict serious losses upon Allied merchantmen. 'Operation Berlin' in early 1941 saw the battle-cruisers *Scharnhorst* and *Gneisenau* scouring the North Atlantic for easy targets, but frustrated in their attempts to break up larger, well-protected convoys; in fact, in two months they only sank or captured 22 ships. Evading Somerville's Force H, despatched from Gibraltar to scour the eastern Atlantic, the German squadron headed for home. The Admiralty assumed Admiral Lutjens would choose one or other of the northern passages, and deployed the Home Fleet accordingly. On 20 March the enemy was spotted 600 miles west-north-west of Finisterre, and a second sighting 24 hours later confirmed speculation that Brest was the intended port: within a day the raiders were safe within the inner harbour having repeatedly evaded interception.[8]

According to Mountbatten, Western Approaches Command saw St Nazaire as a suitably large and convenient bolt-hole. Captain (D) ostensibly informed the 'fighting fifth' in a gloriously gung-ho announcement that he intended to intercept and destroy no less than six capital ships plus however many destroyers were screening them. As always the *Kelly*'s chroniclers have preserved for posterity her captain's exact words ('I know I can depend on each and every one of you'); but, whatever he did or did not say, and whatever his reason for inflating the size of the task force, it's clear that Mountbatten was portraying a wholly unreal scenario. The reality was that his destroyers faced decimation in the face of overwhelming firepower, with odds far longer than those granted the *Graf Spee*'s adversaries 13 months earlier – assuming of course that this version of events has any veracity. Mountbatten claimed that Admiralty orders failed to specify St Nazaire, and he therefore felt free to follow his gut instinct. The 5th headed for Brest, as of course did the Germans. But was St Nazaire not specifically mentioned because by 20 March *Scharnhorst* and *Gneisenau* had been spotted on a more northerly course? In any case, until that point the Home Fleet had anticipated Lutjens would head home via the *Kriegmarine*'s preferred route, between the Faeroes and Iceland. As already seen, two days later the raiders arrived in Brest. However, heavy cloud cover meant a long delay before the RAF could confirm their arrival. According to Mountbatten no less a person than the First Sea Lord was apoplectic that the 5th had not set course for the mouth of the Loire; while Dunbar-Naismith was said to have signalled his cavalier captain that, should aerial reconnaissance reveal a task force safe and snug in St Nazaire, he could consider himself relieved of his command. Ostensibly vindicated, exultant, and more to the point, still alive, Mountbatten made a second calculated guess. According to Hough, with no intelligence to support his theory he confidently assumed that the *Admiral Hipper* had continued north in an attempt to reach Norway under the cover of bad weather. In actual fact the *Hipper* had never at any stage been part of the taskforce, and had slipped out of Brest a week ahead of the two battle-cruisers' arrival. The only incentive Mountbatten might have had was that the Admiralty lost track of this solitary cruiser until her arrival in Kiel on 28 March. Richard Hough in recounting this episode clearly drew on Robin Bousfield's unpublished account, which was based almost entirely on Mountbatten's version of events. It's a good story, but it doesn't bear close scrutiny – and, like so many events in which the *Kelly* is supposed to feature prominently, goes unrecorded in the official history of the war at sea, published while Mountbatten was still a serving officer.[9]

Whether or not engaged on a wild-goose chase, the flotilla suffered atrocious conditions in the Irish Sea, with the *Kelly* again rolling 70 degrees, this time losing two boats and incurring now familiar damage along the starboard deck. Predictably, the other ships remained intact, resuming regular ASW patrols while the *Kelly* was being patched up in Plymouth. One week later the full flotilla found itself back off Brest escorting the fast minelayer *Abdiel* in a concerted effort to tighten the blockade. Night-time confusion saw the *Kelly* drift within range of the outer harbour's shore batteries, and the resulting exchange of fire alerted the *Luftwaffe*. Dawn saw the Oerlikons' first real test as a *geschwader* of Stukas caught up with the four destroyers. For a majority of Mountbatten's men this was their first taste of dive-bombing. It was a chastening experience, and one which over the next two months was to become all too familiar.[10]

A royal visit to Plymouth at the height of the Blitz embraced a visit to the *Kelly*, an exhausted crew returning from an all-night operation to learn that the King would be aboard within three hours. Unlike his brother, George VI actually knew his way around a ship, and, unlike his envious cousin, he had taken part in the Battle of Jutland. Keenly aware of the form on such occasions, the second of the sea-going Windsors asked if the ship's company could be granted shore leave – he could scarcely have chosen a worse night, and at dawn, with the city still in flames, shocked and hung-over sailors regained the relative safety of their ship.[11]

Another great port brought to its knees but by no means out for the count was Valletta. By early January 1941 it was clear that Germany had every intention of intervening decisively in the Mediterranean: plans for the invasion of the Soviet Union were increasingly disrupted by an all too obvious need to stiffen Italian resolve in both Greece and Africa. Without early intervention the British would complete their seizure of Libya and consolidate control of a huge swath of North Africa and the Horn. To ensure the safe passage of German reinforcements Malta had to be neutralised. Grand Harbour could not expect to carry on providing a secure base from which to attack Axis convoys, especially once the decision had been made to deploy the *Afrika Korps*. The arrival on Sicily in early 1941 of *Fliegerkorps X*'s 150 Stukas and Junkers 88s signalled the first serious reversal in Andrew Cunningham's struggle to secure effective control of the Mediterranean. The *Luftwaffe* put steel in the Italian bombing campaign, encouraging low-level attack, particularly at sea, and thus a much higher strike rate. Over the next three months numbers grew, until Kesselring's *Luftlotte* deployed around 800 aircraft from the Adriatic to the Aegean. Although his next great triumph after Taranto – the Battle of Cape Matapan – did not take place until the end of March, ABC was already well aware that the pendulum had swung firmly in favour of the enemy. German air superiority in the spring of 1941 confirmed the vulnerability of the surface fleet, the fragility of the Allied convoy system, and the relative ease with which naval operations out of Malta could be put at risk. Relations with both Downing Street and the Admiralty were never easy, witness the very obvious reluctance with which Somerville's Force H fired on the French capital ships at Mers el-Kebir in July 1940. Similarly, Cunningham questioned the wisdom of despatching 58,000 troops to Greece in early March 1941, notwithstanding the Royal Navy's ability to disembark such a large number of men at short notice – and to evacuate most of them six weeks later. However, an added strain was placed on the Commander-in-Chief's relations with the Prime Minister and his First Sea Lord when Churchill insisted on a more aggressive approach to disrupting the enemy's north-south lines of communication. With a shortage of submarines, surface ships would be even more exposed to air attack, notwithstanding Dudley Pound's readiness to reinforce Cunningham's over-stretched fleet. One consequence was that Mountbatten and his six destroyers – *Kelly, Kipling, Kelvin, Kashmir, Jackal,* and *Jersey* – were despatched to Gibraltar, from where they made the hazardous journey in to the heart of the Mediterranean. Meanwhile, the German 12th Army spread out across Greece and southern Yugoslavia. On 28 April, with battle still raging in the southern Peloponnese and Rommel rapidly regaining vast areas of lost territory in Libya, the newly designated Force K at last arrived in Valetta. For both officers and men the raids on Plymouth were a picnic when compared with what greeted them once they stepped on to dry land.[12]

Mountbatten was piped ashore in the middle of an air-raid, with up to 70 bombers pounding the fortifications and installations around Grand Harbour. This was par for the course as he explained later to an old friend from his polo-playing days, Robert Neville – with an average of six raids every 24 hours, 'I won't pretend it's fun. It's altogether different when the ship is at sea and "alive", to being a sitting target. But the morale of my chaps is really magnificent and has never showed up better'.[13] Nevertheless, after an initial act of defiance – or bravado, take your choice – when he dismissed the suggestion that all but the gunners seek cover, Mountbatten ordered each destroyer to ensure that everyone spent one night out of two sheltering ashore. He himself remained aboard: 'I didn't like to think what people would say if the *Kelly* was sunk in harbour, and when they asked where Dickie Mountbatten was, were told that he had been in an air-raid shelter.' In retirement he readily confessed to a TV audience that 'I've never been so frightened in my life'. Fear ('all of us have had many narrow shaves'), lack of sleep, and a general feeling of helplessness fuelled irritation and frustration.[14] He railed at the seeming impugnity with which the *Luftwaffe* laid magnetic mines at the mouth of the harbour, his frustration compounded by a total absence of enemy convoys whenever the destroyers finally managed to make open water. Five days of fruitless searching culminated in the *Jersey* striking a magnetic mine at the entrance to Grand Harbour. With no minesweeper to call on Force K languished in port until an enterprising torpedo officer suggested that depth charges could detonate the mines and create a safe-channel. This simple solution released the flotilla, and helped raise Mountbatten's spirits pending the eventual arrival of a magnetic-minesweeper, HMS *Gloxinia*.[15]

The *Kelly* had moored at Parlatorio Wharf, until recently occupied by Mountbatten's next, albeit short-lived, command, HMS *Illustrious*. The arrival in

Malta of the crippled carrier on 10 January roughly corresponded with the Axis air forces initiating a more intensive, more methodical bombardment of the island. As Cunningham acknowledged, the demise of the *Illustrious* confirmed an obvious absence of Allied air power, with reinforcement of a paltry fighter presence on Malta dependent upon the slow trickle of Hurricanes arriving courtesy of a crate or off a flight deck. In Egypt a fatalistic ABC echoed the view of Malta's governor, William Dobbie, that the Royal Air Force was doing the best it could in the circumstances. While Mountbatten at this point saw no cause to question his admiral's judgement, he begged to differ. Not that he was alone – inter-service tension was at its height on the island, with every wardroom and mess deck convinced that, yet again, the RAF was failing to do its job. Few chose to protest at the highest level, but, predictably, Captain (D) took action within days of the 5th's arrival. Not only would he cable his complaints to Alexandria and the Admiralty, but he renewed old friendships with those of the island's movers and shakers eager to get rid of General Dobbie. One of Mountbatten's first appointments was lunch at the Governor's Palace, in the course of which he was singularly unimpressed by his host's overly frank assessment of the situation – even though he himself shared the general's view that without more aircraft Malta could do little by way of taking the battle to the enemy. Mountbatten came away with a much higher opinion of the newly arrived lieutenant governor, Sir Edward Jackson. He agreed with Mabel Strickland, long-time pillar of Maltese society and owner/editor of the staunchly pro-British *Times of Malta*, that Dobbie was unduly defeatist and had to go. The master of pulling strings, old pal Dickie helped Strickland petition Churchill to dismiss a man whose integrity was indisputable and who every day displayed great personal courage. Thus began a rather shoddy year-long campaign, orchestrated by Mabel Strickland in consultation with Mountbatten, which ended only when a high-powered delegation were advised by Jackson and Vice-Admiral Malta that Dobbie had to go: Walter Monckton, minister of state in the Middle East and an acquaintance of Mountbatten since advising Edward VIII at the time of the Abdication, recommended a major shake-up of the island's emergency executive, starting at the very top.[16]

Blissfully unaware that Tom Phillips had been appalled by his handling of the 5th's attack on the German destroyers six months earlier, Mountbatten vent his spleen to the Vice-Chief of the Naval Staff. Ironically, Phillips was likely to provide a sympathetic ear. He scarcely disguised his view that the expedition to Greece was a major distraction from the Navy's main focus of operations in the Mediterranean basin. Deeming Dudley Pound too acquiescent to the wishes of the Prime Minister, the VCNS would have sympathised when Cunningham insisted that destroyers alone could not disrupt Axis convoys to Libya, particularly given the acute shortage of fuel in Valletta.[17]

A fortnight later Cunningham warned Mountbatten there could be 'no rest for destroyers in the Mediterranean', while conceding that three weeks in Malta was about as much as any crew on a small ship could tolerate. Cunningham seemed sympathetic, to the point of promising Force K brief respite in Alexandria. However, Captain (D)'s conspiring and complaining coincided with the moment at which his commander-in-chief began openly to express reservations regarding his powers of leadership. Less than two months before, Cunningham had confided to Pound how much 'I like and admire Mountbatten', but by mid-May the seeds of doubt had been sown. There had always been a healthy respect but never unreserved admiration – such as Mountbatten demonstrated for Cunningham, in public at least – and henceforth the equivocation became ever more obvious. After all, by writing to Phillips, having already received reassurance from his superior, Mountbatten had for all intents and purposes gone over Cunningham's head. ABC doesn't appear to have been someone who bore grudges, but he was clearly a man with a long memory. Only two days after Mountbatten complained directly to the Admiralty, Cunningham voiced his disappointment that the 5th Flotilla had failed to exploit a night-time attack on Benghazi by lingering long enough to pick up four incoming vessels. Instead, 'They were dive bombed by moonlight and legged it to the northward'. The implication was clear: by ignoring orders to sweep south of the port, Mountbatten had cut and run at the first sight of a Stuka. This was probably unfair, and Cunningham's judgement that the loss of a destroyer constituted an acceptable price for wiping out a convoy suggests a surprisingly gung-ho appraisal of the situation. Nevertheless, the operation had undoubtedly been flawed by poor navigation, for which Mountbatten bore ultimate responsibility.[18]

The 'fighting fifth' only once made the 760 mile round trip to Benghazi. Germany's airborne invasion of Crete on the morning of 20 May 1941 was containable, provided the Navy could prevent rapid reinforcement by sea. The success of the Mediterranean Fleet, and of British and Anzac troops defending the island, was dependent upon adequate air support. Thus, the assault could have been rebuffed, had not the *Luftwaffe* enjoyed virtual air supremacy. In the 11-day battle for control of Crete air power was the critical factor, wearing down an initially heroic defence and severely denting the offensive potential of Cunningham's surface fleet. Thus, while a convoy transporting 2,300 German troops was decimated on the night of 21–22 May with minimal damage to the attacking force, attempts the following day to follow up this initial success saw the loss of a destroyer and two cruisers with heavy damage to three other capital ships. All were the victims of bomber squadrons based in southern Greece.[19]

Ordered to rendezvous off Crete with the two squadrons endeavouring to thwart a full-scale invasion, Mountbatten briefed his captains, gave them lunch, and then sent them back to their ships. Aboard the *Kelly* the lower deck was cleared, and the captain gave the ship's company a frank assessment of what lay ahead. Finally, on the afternoon of 21 May the 5th Flotilla left Malta for the last time. Before leaving a pessimistic Mountbatten had his wardrobe emptied, and a bulging suitcase deposited dockside. If – or, more likely, when – the *Kelly* sank then he could at least find some consolation in having two expensively tailored and beautifully cut uniforms, monogrammed underwear and pyjamas, *and* a toothbrush preserved and accessible; a prescient move, partially stymied by the RAF promptly despatching the case to London.[20]

The following morning Mountbatten's five destroyers arrived in the now lethal waters west of Crete, just in time to see a bomb smash through the starboard batteries of the veteran flagship, the *Warspite*. The Junkers 88s soon turned their attention to the new arrivals. Much-practiced evasion tactics saw the flotilla survive intact. The *Kandahar* and the *Kingston*, operating as part of a separate force, were already searching for survivors from the destroyer *Greyhound*; the cruisers *Gloucester* and *Fiji* were deployed to provide covering anti-aircraft fire, but by early evening they themselves were abandoned and ablaze. That night the *Kelvin* and *Jackal* looked for men from the *Gloucester* while the rest of Mountbatten's command sought survivors of the *Fiji*. These orders were soon countermanded and, reunited, Mountbatten's now much diminished flotilla steamed north through the Antikithera Channel to patrol the coastline west of Suda Bay. It was at this point that the *Kipling* developed a steering defect, and withdrew to the south-west. Arriving in Canea Bay, the *Kelly* and the *Kashmir* poured fire on to requisitioned caiques carrying German troops. The soldiers, heavily weighed down by their kit, abandoned ship in orderly fashion, and were promptly drowned. With the battle nevertheless turning firmly in the enemy's favour, Mountbatten pressed on with his task of raking hostile positions around the Meleme aerodrome. Stationed just over a mile off-shore the two destroyers hit their targets with commendable accuracy, none of the Anzac trenches coming under 'friendly fire'. In fact the bombardment was so successful that it enabled the Australian and New Zealand forces to press forward, if only to retreat to a fresh line of defence once airborne reinforcements launched a counter-attack. Whilst pulling out of Canea Bay, the two ships spotted and shelled another loaded caique; carrying fuel and munitions, it exploded in a huge ball of flame. It would prove a pyrrhic victory: with the airfield again secure the Germans were pouring reinforcements into the Meleme redoubt.[21]

By dawn on 23 May the *Kelly* and the *Kashmir* were sailing southwards roughly a mile apart; and with their sister ship repaired, at full steam, and only six miles astern. Their crews exhausted, all three destroyers were by now off Crete's south-west coast, having withdrawn at a rapid rate of knots from what appeared to be the area of maximum danger. A key factor in Cunningham's decision to cease operations to the west and north of the island, and if necessary to withdraw all forces to Alexandria, was the 'Most Immediate' message he had received late the previous evening. The hand-written signal indicated an acute crisis of AA ammunition on the surviving battleships, leaving the destroyers stripped of protection from sustained aerial attack. Typed confirmation the next day indicated exactly the reverse. It transpired that there was still 'plenty' of short-range ordnance. But by then it was too late – the order to pull out had been given, and the Navy was firmly on the back foot. Crucially, Mountbatten and his tiny command were isolated, exposed, and bereft of concentrated protective fire.[22] Cunningham's order, for which he accepted full responsibility, was well-intentioned, whatever its calamitous consequences for the remnants of 'the fighting fifth'. The eventual outcome confirmed a deeply felt misery regarding the absence of effective air cover, witness the commander-in-chief's later revelation to Mountbatten that he, 'felt like going out in a destroyer into the thickest of the bombing and getting killed'. Not being at the heart of the action was bad enough, but frustration and anger was compounded by the unprecedented level of interference from London, with the First Sea Lord too slow to defend Cunningham in the face of an impatient and unreasonable Churchill. In such circumstances it is scarcely surprising that, once the evacuation of Crete was complete, ABC indicated to Pound his willingness to surrender command of the Mediterranean. Service rivalry was cast aside when an 'outraged' Cunningham found that his popular Air Force counterpart was deemed a more suitable scapegoat.[23]

Friday 23 May 1941 marked Prince Louis Battenberg's eighty-seventh birthday, had he still been alive. How he would have relished the day – the Home Fleet had at last set out from Scapa Flow in hot pursuit of the *Bismarck*, now only 24 hours away from its cataclysmic rendezvous with the *Hood*. In the Mediterranean, only ten minutes beyond first light, a spotter plane appeared high above the *Kelly* and her two companions. The Ju88s swiftly followed, their high altitude at the moment of attack offering a better chance of dodging the bombs: 'But at about eight o'clock that morning ... our doom appeared on the horizon, in the form of twenty-four Junkers 87 dive-bombers.'[24] From 8000 feet, in waves of three – targeting first the *Kashmir*, and then the *Kelly* – each Stuka dutifully took its turn, a revengeful orc arcing in to a steep, siren-screaming, single-minded dive. The two ships accelerated to 34 knots in a desperate attempt to avoid the fatal impact, frustrated gun crews cursing behind flash shields until those precious few seconds when at last the enemy came within their restricted elevation. Any slim chance of escape depended upon their shipmates releasing a relentless stream of machine gun fire, the *Kelly* alone having the benefit of its twin Oerlikons. Tracer from the latter ripped through the fuselage of at least one aircraft, but by then it was too late. The lead bomber in each wave released its load with clinical efficiency, and both ships were hit almost simultaneously – struck amidships a broken-backed *Kashmir* sank almost at once. On Mountbatten's command, the *Kelly* turned hard to starboard, her speed causing a heavy list to port. Momentarily safe on the bridge Mountbatten and Dunsterville watched with horror as in an instant the second bomb sealed their fate. It crashed through the X gun-deck, obliterating the crew of the 4·7 inch gun in a split second, and exploding adjacent to the engine room. Orders screamed down the voice-pipes met with zero response, while the one meaningful command – to keep firing – was wholly unnecessary: led by a manic Beresford, everyone who could man a gun was peppering the sky with shells and tracer. Already, blackened and burnt survivors were emerging from below decks; but many trapped beneath either drowned as the rising water wiped out an air-lock formed in the engine room, or escaped via an upper deck hatch once the ship turned turtle and they could swim to the surface. Because the destroyer was travelling so fast the water poured in like a tidal wave. In every account of the *Kelly*'s final seconds Mountbatten always insisted that his sole preoccupation was that he be the last to leave, hence his dawdling on the bridge even as the ship rolled to an alarming 90 degrees. Appropriately he climbed up on the station-keeping gear ('which I had invented and which was fitted in the Flotilla'), then clung hopelessly to the gyro-compass pedestal:[25]

And then the sea came in a roaring maelstrom. I saw officers and men struggling to get out of the bridge, then I took an enormously deep breath as the water closed over my head … Somehow I managed to flounder and work my way across the upside-down bridge until I got to the bullet-proof bridge screens. Here I had to pull myself under, and up to this moment it was horribly dark. A faint glimmer of daylight appeared on the other side of the bridge-screens but the water was churning around and I could distinguish nothing.[26]

With his lungs near to bursting Mountbatten wrapped his hands across his mouth and nose, kicked hard against the superstructure, and in the last seconds of life shot to the surface. Gasping for breath he looked round and was horrified to discover that he and Butler-Bowdon were in imminent danger of being cut to ribbons by the propellers as the stern descended upon them. He screamed to his navigator to swim away, and, once safe, ordered everyone in the water to head for the one Carley raft released before the *Kelly* turned over. Edward Dunsterville also found himself uncomfortably close to the descending propellors, with Rocky Wilkins exercising a vice-like grip on his lifebelt: 'There were a lot of us bobbing about and we found bits of wood to hold on to. The water was very warm, but the oil was awful. It got into your stomach and mouth and gummed up your eyes.' Dunsterville was more than happy to indulge his captain whenever Mountbatten told the oft-repeated story of how an oil-soaked Stoker Garner, 'took one look at me and said, "Funny how the scum always comes to the top, isn't it, sir?"' Where he drew the line was when Mountbatten, lamenting an over-speedy decision to jettison his tin hat, recalled the Stukas turning back to machine-gun the survivors – a version of events mythologised courtesy of *In Which We Serve* when 'Shorty' Blake is martyred at the hands of the *Luftwaffe*, and Mountbatten's insistence to his first biographer that this was the moment when, 'I learned … that you don't fight on your own terms, or on any preconceived old-fashioned ideas of chivalry, but you fight on the enemy's terms'. Dunsterville was by no means alone in insisting, firstly, that Mountbatten was mistaken in contrasting his own behaviour when the caiques were sunk with that of the Stuka pilots, and secondly, that none of the nine officers and 121 men lost when the *Kelly* went down died as a consequence of machine-gun fire. On the other hand, the *Kipling*'s captain, Aubrey St Clair-Ford – if not his fellow officers – maintained that several men did indeed die as a consequence of random Stuka fire; and John Knight described dragging machine-gunned ship-mates on to his raft. The cynical signalman also recalled how nobody moved when 'Louis' ordered some survivors to switch rafts: 'They were all thinking "If you want someone to swim to that other raft, mate, you lead the way".'[27]

Having secured the wounded within the raft, and overseen the gruesome business of removing the dead, Mountbatten endeavoured to raise spirits with a rendering of 'Roll Out The Barrel', only to silence his ragged chorus with a cry of 'Three cheers for the old ship' as she finally – and silently – slipped beneath the waves. Unfortunately, just as the *Kelly* was about to expire the freshly-arrived *Kipling* had crashed into her while desperately avoiding one last Stuka attack. Thus rescue of

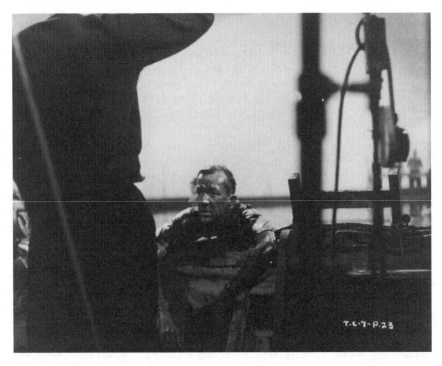

Figure 6.2: *In Which We Serve* saw Noel Coward restage the Kelly's sinking off Crete in May 1941

Mountbatten and his men was carried out by a ship listing severely to starboard and with a gaping hole in urgent need of repair six feet beneath her bow. The damage was so extensive that her maximum speed was drastically reduced – a critical factor when later the bombers returned. The *Kipling* lowered scrambling nets and the oil-soaked, half-blind, choking survivors found themselves dragged on board. Mountbatten had in tow a badly wounded seaman, but by the time he reached the ship the man was dead and so he had no choice but to let him go. Psychologically as well as physically shattered he collapsed on deck, pulled himself together, knocked back a stiff whisky, and made his way to the bridge. Greeting the *Kipling*'s captain – 'a brave, brilliant and very competent man' – he formally resumed command of the flotilla, and then left St Clair-Ford to recover those men still in the water.[28] The biggest problem was lifting the wounded and dying out of the Carley raft. All this took time, and meanwhile a mile away men and officers of the *Kashmir* awaited rescue in and around their five rafts. Arguably it was their experience, rather than that of the *Kelly*'s crew, which bore the closest resemblance to the central conceit of *In Which We Serve*: the film is built around Captain Kinross and his comrades' prolonged exposure to the elements and to the enemy, their individual memories generating the flash-backs that together constitute the history of the *Torrin*.

In Mountbatten's words, 'Now everything resolved into a battle of wits between St Clair-Ford and the bombers', with something like 100 high-level attacks carried out across the long hours of rapid evasion and painfully slow recovery. Eventually both men decided to try and speed up the process by utilising the *Kipling*'s fast motor-boat, rather than continuing to manoeuvre the destroyer alongside the rafts. Lowering and releasing such a big boat was a complex business, but once in the water its rope falls had to be unshackled by hand. With a bomber approaching and the 'Full Ahead' order given, Mountbatten called for the ropes to be cut, and too late made clear he had meant the after falls. Fatally, the foremost falls were slashed first, so that, as the destroyer raced forward, the bows of the motor-boat turned out and it began to capsize. Hugh Beresford, and his fellow first lieutenant on the *Kipling*, John Bush, had rushed to the after falls but the weight of the sinking vessel meant 'the after davit was pulled right over and seemed to crush them as the falls tore away and the boat sank …'. The loss of Beresford was an especially heavy blow, not just for Mountbatten who had followed his career since 1927, but for everyone who had served under him on the *Kelly* – as his captain made clear in *The Times* two months later.[29]

The *Kipling* resumed the long and dangerous business of evading bombardment and evacuating the rafts, both captains insistent that everyone in the water must be brought on-board whatever the risk to the ship. Captain (D) could now find time to visit the sick-bay and the mess decks, each section of the ship packed with casualties; in counselling and comforting the *Kelly*'s most seriously wounded, his reassuring familiarity with every man's personal circumstances proved invaluable as a morale-booster. In the whole of his career this was arguably Mountbatten's finest hour, at least partially redeeming the outrageous conceit and arrogance, and explaining why those who served under him in 1941 remained to the very end so fiercely loyal. It was another four hours before a crowded, crippled *Kipling* could at last slowly and painfully make her way to Alexandria. Still plagued by rogue bombers, but with now the pick of the flotilla's gunners to draw upon, the ship waited for dusk and a brief escape from the attention of the *Luftwaffe*. Diesel was critical if come the dawn the *Kipling* was not to find itself a sitting duck, but early on the morning of 24 May – Empire Day – the net-laying ship *Protector* provided sufficient fuel to allow a sad but triumphant arrival in Egypt just a few hours later. Every deck of every ship within the Mediterranean Fleet, recently returned and licking its wounds, was packed with men cheering and waving caps as St Clair-Ford guided his charge through the boom gates and on to pier 46. Along with the trucks and ambulances, the drivers, dockers and orderlies, on the quay waited no less a person than the C-in-C himself. Also present was Prince Philip, then a young midshipman and plucked off the battleship *Valiant* in order to welcome home his uncle – the magnificently tactless nephew roared with laughter on spotting the civilian-suited Mountbatten's oil-blackened face, hastily offering explanation and apology in the face of an incipient tongue lashing. Cunningham drove his two captains, plus Dunsterville, back to the Residency.[30] Over the next few days ABC proved sensitive, supportive and sympathetic. To a man whose ship now lay at the bottom of the Mediterranean, along with over half her crew, his host was 'kindness itself … Cunningham made me feel that their loss had been worthwhile, and that the Navy had never put up a finer show'.[31]

The admiral fixed him up with a suitably well-tailored tropical uniform and – most important – the appropriate medal ribbons, so that Mountbatten cut an impressive figure when the survivors of the wardroom gave their captain a farewell dinner. For his sister 'the evening was a tremendous success'; but he confessed to his daughter that 'with more gaps than places it was a sad affair'. Still immaculately dressed – and skilfully disguising the worst effects of ingesting so much oil – he was driven the following day to Dhekeila, the stripped down yet reassuringly secure Fleet Air Arm station from which his men would be dispersed to their next postings. Mountbatten moved among the ratings, as always on such occasions saying all the right things – no defeat, magnificent fighting spirit, fresh opportunities, reassurance not apprehension, and so on. He had arranged for the ship's company to be guests of the Gezira Sporting Club, and the prospect of pool-side recuperation was generally well received. At last the *Kelly*'s first and last captain clambered on to a wooden crate and delivered an honest and moving elegy to 'the ship we loved' and the lost comrades who lay beside her: 'what a grand way to go … There may be less than half the *Kelly* left, but I feel that each of us has twice as good a reason to fight … her spirit will go on inspiring us until victory is won.' Insistent that he would be 'proud and honoured' to serve again alongside any seaman present, Mountbatten wished them all good luck, thanked them 'from the bottom of my heart', and in a voice shaking with emotion said goodbye. Writing to his sister he noted the finality of the occasion, and yet somehow the spirit of the *Kelly* would survive, simply because, 'we had all loved the ship so much and were such a happy band of brothers. I have never known a ship with such a tremendously high ship's spirit and I don't suppose I ever will again'.[32] Here truly was the Nelsonian touch. In fact this was to prove *au revoir* not *adieu*, and after 1950 he would see most if not all of these men at least once a year for the rest of his life. Nevertheless, for all present there seemed every reason to believe that this was a very real farewell – the size of the Royal Navy and the nature of the British class system being such that the possibility of them reconvening at some point in the future looked unlikely, if not inconceivable.

The next morning Mountbatten was en route to Cairo, yet again risking life and limb by flying without a parachute in a Blackburn Skua, the failings of which he would have been all too familiar with from his prewar stint at the Admiralty. At the Headquarters of Middle East Command he infuriated RAF staff with the ferocity of his complaints, choosing to ignore the very obvious absence of long-range fighters in the Nile delta. He continued to vent his spleen at the Embassy, no longer lambasting the Air Force on the ground, but the Chiefs of Staff for 'keeping the Middle East so bare of air'. A sympathetic ambassador supplied Mountbatten with a briefing paper to accompany the long memorandum of complaint Cunningham had asked him to deliver personally to Churchill – a course of action fully endorsed by James Somerville, Force H's commander: 'I'm glad you've sent Dickie Mount B home to report matters. He's forceful and has the gift for putting a case.'[33] On 1 June 1941 the absurdly disguised 'Mr Lewis Mountain' left Cairo for London via Lagos. Required to travel by flying boat it took Mountbatten over a fortnight to get home. The journey might have been shorter had he been on a boat, but this was deemed out of the question for security reasons.[34] Mountbatten finally reached Downing Street on 21 June, just in time for lunch. Apart from the Prime Minister the only other person present was Beaverbrook, still on balance an admirer of Mountbatten, if not for very much longer. Arriving 20 minutes late their host confided to his waiting guests that Germany would invade the Soviet Union the very next day. Although eager to depart for Chequers, Churchill nevertheless listened sympathetically to Mountbatten, even if later events confirmed his continued failure to appreciate how much air cover had become a vital element in the war at sea. He promised Dickie that his ship's sacrifice off Crete would not go ignored, and soon proved true to his word. Mountbatten returned to Broadlands, where he spent the night fire-fighting: several incendiaries landed on the roof, and as many as 25 landed on the estate causing extensive damage.[35] The bombing was particularly untimely given Edwina's recent offer to convert part of the house into an annexe of Southampton General Hospital, providing around 75 beds, staff accommodation, an operating theatre, and x-ray facilities. The scale of this provision significantly enhanced the ability of overstretched Hampshire hospitals to provide adequate surgical and medical support for civilian as well as service patients.[36]

Over the next few days much of Mountbatten's time was spent at the Admiralty, including high-level briefings of both Dudley Pound and his minister, A.V. Alexander. Later in life Mountbatten recalled how enthusiastically he had defended Cunningham's conduct of naval operations off Crete, and there seems no reason to question his insistence that, 'I was fanatically devoted to him and all that he stood for and had achieved'. Not that the admiration was reciprocated in print – across 700 pages of autobiography Cunningham's only mention of Mountbatten is a passing reference when regretting the loss of the *Kelly* and *Kashmir*. In June 1941 the young pretender had no inkling of how much he had irritated ABC during his stay at the Residency; his over-eagerness to accentuate the positive in the aftermath of tragedy confirming the admiral's belief that Dickie Mount B was still nowhere near the finished product. Cunningham was the professional par excellence, but he was uncharacteristically indiscreet at dinner the day after Mountbatten's departure, informing Dunsterville that, 'The trouble with your flotilla, boy, is that it was thoroughly badly led'.[37]

In noting Cunningham's remark Philip Ziegler expressed sympathy for the overall sentiment. The great sin of the official biographer is hagiography, and to his considerable credit Ziegler readily acknowledged Captain (D)'s failings as a flotilla commander. The charge that he drove his destroyers far too fast was a familiar one; but here was a leader who, while undoubtedly courageous under fire and quite brilliant in his handling of the men directly under his charge, was deemed to lack focus, judgement, patience, and above all, 'that mysterious quality of "sea sense", the ability to ensure that one's ship is in the right place at the right time'. These observations were clearly based upon conversations with officers serving on destroyers at the time, as Ziegler acknowledged in his ultimate judgement: this was 'as good a captain as most and better than many of his contemporaries', but his peers were unanimous in believing the commander of the 5th Flotilla to be 'no better than second-rate'. Surprisingly, Richard Hough, in his history of the *Kelly*, endorsed Ziegler's view of Mountbatten's record on the bridge, rather than revisiting the no flaws portrayal to be found in his own life of the great man. Vice-Admiral McGeoch's blustering argument that by mid-1941 Lord Louis had proved himself a 'first-rate naval officer' rested largely on the fact that the author had spent 40 years in a Service notoriously suspicious of bright, ambitious young men, and Philip Ziegler hadn't. Revisionism is probably too strong a term, but in this version of events Cunningham was clearly the villain, not merely resenting Mountbatten's ebullience but revealing yet again his deep-rooted suspicion of technological innovation – rather than ABC the greatest fighting admiral since Nelson, here was a man whose championing of 'seamanship' at the expense of modernity had damaged the fighting efficiency of Destroyer Command in the 1930s and of the whole Mediterranean Fleet in the early years of the war. McGeoch's loyalty was laudable, but his endeavours to deny Cunningham the triumphs of 1940–41, most notably Cape Matapan, and to find Mountbatten blameless for every one of the 5th Flotilla's several mishaps, served only to undermine his case.[38]

It's this very refusal to countenance that at least in some respects mistakes may have been made which fuels scepticism when examining Mountbatten's own interpretation of events – most obviously in the case of the *Javelin*. To be fair, he was very unlucky, and yet all too often we make our own luck: for the *Kelly* a reputation for bad luck invariably disguised the consequences of her captain's impetuosity. Yet that same impetuosity was generated by an infectious enthusiasm, which was manifestly a powerful motivating force at every level within his own ship, if not necessarily beyond. For most on the mess decks the patrician captain could do no wrong; yet within the wardroom was displayed a range of emotions, from healthy respect for a born leader, through amused tolerance of the old man's ego and eccentricities, to the unspoken fear that here was someone whose style of command was inspirational but potentially fatal. Admiration was never unconditional, not even for the likes of Burnett and Dunsterville, so that the closer one found oneself to Lord Louis the deeper the reservations.[39] In the early summer of 1941 such doubts were not to be aired openly, not least because of the courage and leadership Mountbatten so visibly displayed on the final voyage of the *Kelly* – the panache scarcely hid the pain, and even his harshest critic would concede that his conduct throughout those final days and hours was a manifestation of substance as well as style, bravery as well as bravado.

Mountbatten's flotilla had been scattered or sunk, and yet his early elevation to command a big ship – the aircraft carrier *Illustrious*, late of Malta and now under repair across the Atlantic – was a clear sign that his career remained on track. Nevertheless, no ship before or after could replace the *Kelly* as the focus of his affection: with only ever one captain, she was an object of love and devotion which he never had to share, other than with his shipmates – and perhaps his wife. Almost his first act on arriving in Alexandria had been to cable Edwina: 'Once again all right but this time heart broken'. One of *In Which We Serve*'s most moving scenes is when Celia Johnson as Alix Kinross toasts her husband's other great love – Mountbatten's bleak if reassuring telegram was wholly in that spirit, and for Noel Coward in July 1941 an obvious inspiration.[40]

The myth of the *Kelly* (1) – the filming of *In Which We Serve*

Dickie told whole story of the sinking of the *Kelly*. Absolutely heart-breaking and so magnificent. He told the whole saga without frills and with a sincerity that was very moving. He is a pretty wonderful man, I think.[41]

How Captain (D)'s command of the *Kelly* inspired his friend Noel Coward to film 'a patriotic tribute and a panegyric to his favourite service' is a familiar story.[42] Not always appreciated is the degree to which, at such a critical point in the war and with Combined Operations still to bed down, Mountbatten became directly involved in the pre-production, the filming, and the promotion of *In Which We Serve*. A novice in the studio Coward could not have made the film without the technical expertise of David Lean, rightly credited as co-director. Nor, at critical moments in the course of shooting the movie, would Lean and his cameraman Ronald Neame have been able to carry on filming had Mountbatten not intervened in order to remove a host of bureaucratic obstacles.

In April 1938 Mountbatten had secured Coward a jaunt around the Mediterranean Fleet, ostensibly to discover what sort of films would go down best on the lower deck (home-grown not Hollywood comedies it transpired). Little of any consequence emerged from the trip other than to publicise the case within both Whitehall and Wardour Street for a final agreement on free film distribution across the Service. As has been seen, intensive lobbying at last saw the launch of the RFNC in the spring of 1939. Two years later Mountbatten enabled Coward to acquaint himself with decklife in wartime by fixing a tour of the Home Fleet.[43] The result was a long, lumbering, unfocused, and wholly unfilmable script. In October 1941 the final draft of 'White Ensign' had been radically reworked by David Lean, and preparations for a spring shooting schedule were well advanced.[44] Unfortunately, this was the very moment at which Coward was found guilty on two separate charges of flouting wartime currency regulations. Mountbatten ignored advice to distance himself from Coward, who felt the press had unfairly called his patriotism into question.[45] Rather, he rode to the rescue whenever his friend encountered Whitehall opposition, particularly after the court case when both Brendan Bracken, the Minister of Information, and the head of the MoI's Film Division, Jack Beddington, were adamantly opposed to Coward's continued involvement, especially if he insisted on playing the lead role.[46] The minister was persuaded once he had seen the final script, almost certainly because his patron in No. 10 was insistent he should give the go-ahead. An exultant Mountbatten later reassured Coward that Bracken felt *In Which We Serve* to be 'a first-class film and was only too delighted to find that his judgement had been better than his film advisers!'[47] When necessary Mountbatten made shameless use of the direct line to Buckingham Palace, securing the King's support for the film and facilitating newsreel coverage of the Royal Family's afternoon on the set at Denham. George VI's enthusiasm, and a bruising encounter with his cousin, forced even the redoubtable Beddington to give way and back the project.[48]

Having helped cast the crew of the fictional HMS *Torrin*, Mountbatten brought from Portsmouth real sailors to lick them in to shape. Once shooting started he wasn't averse to taking time off from Combined Ops in order to resolve supply problems: a logistical, technical, and financial nightmare, production soon fell behind schedule. When on set the original Captain (D) added his voice to those of a destroyer commander and a *Kelly* veteran released at his request by the Admiralty – he arbitrated over the telephone if ever advice from the bridge clashed with that of the fo'c'sle. From February to June he viewed the rushes every weekend, providing Coward and Lean with detailed feedback on dialogue and action. By not objecting at the time Mountbatten offered tacit endorsement of the shot which would so enrage Beaverbrook – producer Tony Havelock-Alan's suggestion of the *Daily Express* floating in dirty dock water with the visible headline 'NO WAR THIS YEAR'. Perhaps disingenuously, after the film's premiere Mountbatten told an irate, threatening, and unappeased press baron that he had sought but failed to secure the shot's removal from the finished print.[49]

In Which We Serve attracted universal critical acclaim when premiered in September 1942, and was perhaps the most popular British feature film of the whole war. Despite soaring studio costs, it cleared £60,000 in the UK and grossed $180,000 in the USA, where Coward was awarded several honours, including a 1943 Academy Award. *Kelly* veterans deemed the drama to be 'astonishingly accurate', and in November 1943 a Mass Observation survey found the film the most popular of the previous 12 months.[50] In the early weeks of release Mountbatten attended a succession of screenings in order to promote the film – and, his critics quietly suggested, to promote himself. Brian Loring Villa, in blaming Mountbatten directly for the Dieppe disaster, insisted that an unhealthy preoccupation with the making of *In Which We Serve* adversely affected planning for the raid.[51] Such a claim is both inaccurate and unfair, and yet one has to ask why someone carrying so much rank and responsibility should – and could – invest so much time and effort in such a peripheral project. Shameless self-promotion maybe, but Mountbatten clearly saw Coward's original idea as a valuable means of raising service morale, particularly on the lower deck, which in the film attracts as much attention as the wardroom and the bridge. Furthermore, the plot's juxtaposition of ship and shore, the explicit endorsement of a cross-class 'People's War' agenda (as exemplified on stage by *This Happy Breed* and in song by 'London Pride'), and the prevailing understatement so characteristic of 1940s English drama, together ensured that here was a film far more than the sum of its parts. *In Which We Serve* went well beyond a simple (in reality, extremely ambitious) tribute to the Royal Navy: as Coward and Mountbatten anticipated, it boosted the morale of the whole nation, at a time when Britain had little to celebrate and much to mourn. Taranto and Matapan notwithstanding, throughout 1941 and well in to 1942 this was especially true of the war at sea – the tide was still to turn in the Battle of the Atlantic, and pride in the sinking of the *Bismarck* was clearly outweighed by the shock of losing the *Hood, Prince of Wales, Repulse*, and so on.[52] In insisting that cinema-goers on the Home Front and in the rest of the armed forces would once again appreciate just how much was owed to the Senior Service, Mountbatten and Coward were spectacularly vindicated. 'The most gratifying thing of all is that even the commonest journalistic mind has observed that it really is a dignified tribute to the Navy ... a definite contribution to the war effort by showing the public what the Navy really is like', the co-director noted in his diary. *In Which We Serve* encouraged other intimate yet exciting portrayals of the nation in uniform, notably *The Way Ahead*, Carol Reed's tribute to Churchill's citizen army.[53]

In Which We Serve reclaims the Royal Navy's special place in the hearts of an 'island race', and, although the audience's response to the triumphs and travails of the *Torrin* must indeed be a keen sense of 'eternal and indomitable pride', Leslie Howard's commentary restates that message as the story draws to an end. At the same time, for all his protestations, the film's widespread popularity provided a timely boost to the fast-growing Mountbatten legend. The tale of the *Torrin* is the story of the *Kelly* with all the embarrassing bits removed: there is no gung ho exposure to enemy fire, or unfortunate collisions, and Captain Edwin Kinross is clearly a far more cautious – and indeed a far better – sailor than Lord Louis Mountbatten. In this respect Coward adhered to his friend's early insistence that the familiar persona of limousine-chauffeured, land-owning, aristocratic 'Captain (D)' be transformed in to 'a simpler character altogether, far less gifted than he, far less complicated, but in no way, I hope, less gallant'.[54] A surface gloss of wealth and privilege was stripped away, but Dickie's character and personality remained essentially intact. Kinross is supposedly a solid and reliable pillar of the professional middle class, but even before the *Torrin*'s maiden voyage we find replicated Mountbatten's familiar, relaxed rapport with the other ranks, and hear the now all too familiar commissioning address. The sensitive handling of the young stoker who panics under fire is the archetypal example of Mountbatten man management, although of course audiences at the time were not to know such an incident had actually occurred.[55]

Coward confided to arguably Britain's greatest wartime director, Michael Powell, that 'I'm a snob, I know it. I couldn't bear to have anyone else play Dickie!'; and, to be fair, his performance was by no means as bad as his homophobic critics in Fleet Street gleefully anticipated.[56] In uniform, and with his mentor's battered cap set at just the right angle, the hours of careful scrutiny and the scrupulous attention to detail ensured, in the words of his biographer, a credible 'approximation of a naval captain, a Cowardian impression'.[57] While on the bridge or quarterdeck Coward just about pulls it off, in the wardroom and the lounge his brittle characterisation invariably degenerates into caricature. He may have been born in Teddington but his notion of bourgeois domesticity is hilarious, partly because he has no understanding of the everyday banalities of parenthood, and partly because he can not avoid lapsing in to 'gay' revue-type dialogue. What is striking about the Kinross's pre-dinner cocktail chat is the similarity with the Gilpins' smart, snappy, super sophisticated exchanges in Coward's 1935 satirical depiction of Dickie and Edwina, *Hands Across the Sea* (loathed but then embraced by the Mountbattens once they were reminded that all publicity

Figure 6.3: Mountbatten provided Noel Coward with real sailors to ensure the authenticity of *In Which We Serve*

is good publicity).[58] In his memoir, *Future Indefinite*, published in 1954 when relations with the Mountbattens, especially Edwina, were somewhat strained, Coward was both revealing and cautious about the nature of their friendship. He acknowledged his debt to Dickie in seeing the project through to completion ('From the beginning he saw the idea as a tribute to the Service he loved, and he supported me through every difficulty and crisis until the picture was completed.'), but implied that the character of Kinross was entirely his own creation.[59] By this time 'darling Noel' saw Dickie and Edwina very intermittently. Appropriately, regular contact with his one-time hero was re-established in 1966 after Coward was invited to a *Kelly* reunion and inaugurated as an honorary member of the ship's company – an idea which could only have originated at Broadlands.[60]

Coward's insistence that Kinross was a product of his own imagination had been in response to a request from Mountbatten who, following promotion to full admiral in 1953, now saw the ultimate prize in his sights. Sensitive to a groundswell of hostile opinion within the Service, not least the widely-shared view that *In Which We Serve* constituted a misleading and sanitised account of real events, Mountbatten confided in Coward that, 'You may not realise it, but I have been greatly criticised, chiefly among my brother officers, for being a party to the making of a film which apparently was designed to boost me personally'.[61] Was the man being disingenuous, or was he genuinely surprised? The latter would imply a degree of naivety wholly at odds with his general character and demeanour. Of course Mountbatten in 1942 perceived *In Which We Serve* as potentially a massive boost to his reputation and standing, at a time when cinema audiences – let alone the British public at large – were desperate for heroes. Henceforth popular perception of this ostensibly unique leader of men blurred the edges between fiction and reality, and the same applied to his late ship: the tale of the *Torrin* is an idealised history of the *Kelly*, but over time it assumed the mantle of the 'truth' – in postmodernist jargon the preferred text within a heroic meta-narrative of the war at sea. The views of those who actually served on the *Kelly* may have ranged from quiet pride to outright scorn, but in practice Coward and Lean's film complemented and even underpinned their own noble version of events.

The myth of the *Kelly* (2) – the *Kelly* Reunion Association, and Hebburn's refusal to forget

Within a year of the *Kelly*'s sinking a memorial tablet had been laid in Hebburn Cemetery as a symbol of the close ties between the community and all those who had served on the ship, in either her first or second incarnations. Mountbatten ensured that the immediate relatives of all those lost off Crete would receive photographs of the tablet, the entire company on the eve of leaving Malta for the last time, and the 27 graves of those killed in 1940. Included was a covering letter, sent to mark the first anniversary of the ship's demise. At Broadlands a year earlier Mountbatten had penned letters of condolence, plus an account of 'The Kelly's last fight', promising nearest and dearest that their loved ones would never be forgotten. Immediately afterwards he had instigated plans for a simple memorial to be established in the north-east, and his second letter marked a vindication of that promise. Other than the establishment of a permanent commemoration there was of course nothing unusual in a commanding officer communicating directly with the families of service personnel lost in action. What was unusual perhaps was the volume of correspondence. The letters and cards Mountbatten received throughout the summer of 1941, and again the following year, were – no surprise really – highly deferential in tone. All were of course exceptionally moving, 'His Lordship' firmly and yet with great sensitivity disappointing all those desperately hopeful that a much-missed son or husband might still be alive. Especially striking, however, is the body of testimony to Mountbatten's standing on the lower deck. So much has been written about the *Kelly* and the special rapport the captain enjoyed with his crew that it is easy to become cynical, particularly when the man himself went to such great lengths to foster the legend. Yet these letters of appreciation all confirm how popular and highly regarded he really was, with a constant theme being the pride felt by the writer's dear departed in serving under a commander who knew everyone by sight, name, and reputation.[62]

The quiet, dignified pride of the relatives that their loved one served on the *Kelly* was shared on Tyneside by those who built or serviced the ship. For over 40 years after the war a very real effort was made to keep the memory of the *Kelly* alive, with a special welcome to veterans every Remembrance Sunday. Often that weekend's memorial services were marked by distinguished guests from Broadlands, and in the final year of his life Mountbatten himself was present to inspect the Sea Cadets and pay his respects to the fallen. One reason for his presence in 1978 may have been a concerted effort to distance the three ceremonies of remembrance (church, town war memorial, ship memorial) from a local Orange Lodge which, responding to the deteriorating situation in Northern Ireland, had endeavoured to hijack proceedings. Mountbatten was appalled by this development, which simply adds to the cruel irony of his death at the hands of blinkered Republicans the following August; a cruel irony reinforced by the fact that his 'fighting fifth' sweatshirt – a final gift of the *Kelly* Reunion Association – helped police to identify the body.[63]

The sweatshirt presented to Mountbatten in 1978 (and which he insisted on wearing for the rest of the reunion dinner) marked an important year in passing on the story of the *Kelly* to the next generation. On Sunday 12 February BBC2 broadcast a primetime account of the ship's adventures. The programme, in 'The Lively Arts' series, juxtaposed reminiscences of veteran sailors and shipbuilders with a backstage account of how writer Tom Kelly and musician Alan Price returned to their Geordie roots for a Jubilee-inspired celebration of the local community. *Kelly – A Musical Documentary* was staged on 15 July 1977 in South Shields. However, Hebburn was well-represented in a large cast of largely amateur actors and musicians, with Price starring as narrator at a time when the ex-organist of local heroes The Animals was at the height of his fame. Mountbatten was literally an off-stage presence, heard but not seen welcoming 'Jack' to the ship and amazing the Cockney newcomer with how much he already knew about him (Jimmy: 'He does that with every man, he knows everyone's name. He's not just any old skipper and this isn't just any old ship you know ... Mind Louis expects the best from you and he'll get it'). Tom Kelly had clearly spent a lot of time talking to Rocky Wilkins, who needless to say headed a deputation of veterans present on the night. Also attending were ex-officers James Turnbull and Ralph Scorer, who dutifully despatched to Broadlands favourable reviews of the show, and of Sir Bernard Miles' equally creditable performance at a Jubilee wreath-laying ceremony in Hebburn – the *Torrin*'s fictional chief petty officer substituting for the *Kelly*'s actual captain marked yet another step in the blurring of fact and fiction so crucial to an enduring popular perception of the 'People's War'. Surprised and delighted by the scale and sentiments of the show, Mountbatten promptly secured a script and programme for the Broadlands archive. He was happy to be photographed with Alan Price at a BAFTA press screening in the week prior to the documentary's transmission, and, perhaps predictably, irritated the BBC by highlighting the needs of his family as well as his archive – where ever-indulgent film producers were once ready to oblige, now cost-conscious programme-makers remained indifferent to Lord Louis' insistence on the need for not one but two complimentary recordings.[64]

The distancing of events has seen memorials merge in to the immediate landscape, ever-present yet rarely registered. The generation that eulogises the *Kelly* as the most special ship ever built at Hawthorn Leslie will soon have gone, their collective memory having already been incorporated into a broader, more public history, or for the cynics scanning Hebburn's civic website another Home Front opportunity for England's burgeoning heritage industry (embracing the breweries, witness at least six Mountbatten or *Kelly* theme pubs and hotels). The same would be true of the *Kelly* corner – for the George Cross island's largely post-independence population now a quaint section of Fort St Elmo's Malta War Museum. Physical manifestation is increasingly complemented, or simply replaced, by virtual memorialisation and commemoration, which in its own way can become a more dynamic means of recalling and celebrating the past – and, indeed, has to be once all protagonists have at last passed on.[65]

This is particularly true of the *Kelly* Reunion Association. Although established in 1950 with the captain's encouragement and approval, this was very much a lower-deck initiative. Thus officers were present at annual dinners by invitation and not by right, and while Mountbatten's support was crucial in maximising membership, Rocky Wilkins was very much the driving force. The honorary secretary and the association president worked closely together, albeit not always in harmony, witness a misunderstanding as late as 1978 over sympathetic handling of the stoker who – courtesy of Richard Attenborough's fictional depiction – famously left his post when the *Kelly* struck a mine, and yet later in the war was awarded the DSM. Association business notwithstanding, the Mountbatten papers hold voluminous correspondence between the captain and his former shipmates, much of it concerning advice and assistance from the one man who in 1940–41 always seemed to have an answer. Clearly old habits died hard. Mountbatten's obsession with his funeral arrangements naturally extended to the presence of the Reunion Association. In September 1979 Wilkins, already shattered by the circumstances surrounding his hero's death, was mortified that so few members were invited to march, and that they were placed so far back in the order of procession. Resilient to the end, and supported by high-ranking survivors of the *Kelly* wardroom, he ensured a prominent presence at the subsequent memorial services, in Romsey and Westminster Abbeys respectively. The last great public display of pride, perhaps even defiance in the face of old age and public indifference, was the Association's presence at the 1983 unveiling of the nation's permanent and most visible commemoration of Mountbatten, his statue in Whitehall.[66]

Perhaps the last word should be left to Mountbatten himself. The Association's 1980 reunion was a sombre affair addressed by the Prince of Wales ('Now your Captain is dead. And we have all lost a very special friend.'). The intention had been to mark Lord Louis' eightieth birthday by presenting him with a painting of the *Kelly* at Namsos by the distinguished marine artist Mark Myers – predictably, before his death Mountbatten bombarded the painter with advice and even sketches drawn on holiday in Norway.[67] Despite the assassination (in defiance of?) all known surviving veterans of the *Kelly* still received a framed print of the ship under fire off the Norwegian coast, and with it her captain's final tribute:

> To me she was quite unlike any other ship I served in ... I knew and loved her from the time of her birth when her keel was laid until the keel was the last thing visible as she sank beneath the waves.[68]

PART FOUR

MOUNTBATTEN AT WAR, CHIEF OF COMBINED OPERATIONS 1941–43

7

FROM ADVISER TO CHIEF OF COMBINED OPERATIONS, 1941–2

Autumn 1941 visit to the United States

Early in the war Edwina had moved in to her mother-in-law's grace-and-favour flat in Kensington Palace. Broadlands was proving an ever more uncomfortable bolthole, and eventually she found her own rented accommodation in central London. Then Dickie arrived back in England. With Brook House in ruins, the couple looked for a new home: 15 Chester Street was a Mayfair town house conveniently placed for Edwina to make her way to Brigade HQ in Belgravia, or to head east and deal with the consequences of the latest raid. By now she was for all intents and purposes number three in the St John Ambulance, with special responsibility for London. Within 18 months she would be Superintendent-in-Chief, an astonishing rise and one based primarily upon ability not rank. Lady Mountbatten did not suffer fools gladly. Cold *and* compassionate, she had a remarkable capacity to berate hopeless council officials on behalf of the bereaved, bemuse hapless cabinet ministers on behalf of the bombed-out, and beguile helpless admirers on behalf of just about any cause that she felt needed their support and needed it now – and to carry out all three functions comfortably between a lunchtime manicure and an early evening snifter. Each morning Edwina left the house promptly at eight, often working a ten-hour day. However, by mid-1941 she no longer saw the need to spend every night touring the East End. In consequence, throughout the summer months she saw more of Dickie than at any other time during the war. He still irritated and infuriated her, not least because he remained excessively uxorious and singularly incapable of exercising discretion; but for the first time in their married life Edwina could comprehend why her husband applied himself so single-mindedly to the task in hand. Long since dismissed as a lover and boon companion, respect and affection for Mountbatten now rested on his value as an executive role model.[1]

For the Ambulance Brigade's most formidable recruit, the Blitz fostered both courage and conviction. Alex von Tunzelmann is surely right in insisting that, 'Edwina did more than just waft around impressing Cockneys with her personal grooming'.[2] Even the most cynical proletarian was left noting the impeccable cut of her bespoke black uniform, *and* the fact that she articulated the dispossessed's fears and needs with the ardour of the freshly converted. Edwina's beliefs were rooted in instinct and experience, with scant regard for policy and ideology. Her ideas were aspirational and well-intentioned, but at heart empty and contradictory.[3] Yet she surfed the tidal wave of Home Front radicalisation and party disenchantment that marked British politics in the testing 18-month interregnum between the waning of the Blitz and the Empire's valedictory triumph at El Alamein. This of course was that strange period in the war when Sir Stafford Cripps, returning in triumph from his tenure at the Moscow embassy, could flaunt his continued expulsion from the Labour Party and yet still be seen as a credible challenger to Churchill should an already dire situation worsen.[4] It's not surprising, therefore, that Edwina would become friendly with Isobel Cripps, their respective spouses finding a common cause in tempering and accommodating Congress's more extreme demands.

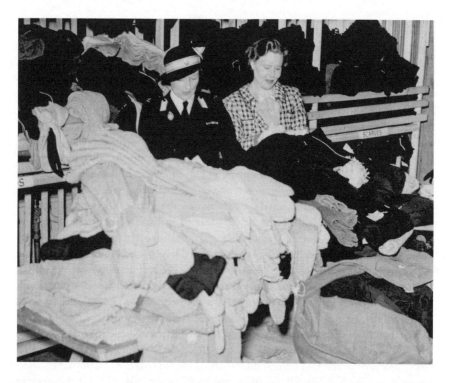

Figure 7.1: Edwina Mountbatten leading by example early in her St John's Ambulance career

Lady Mountbatten's chums judged her champagne egalitarianism and anti-colonial effrontery as at best amusing and at worse hypocritical. One evening in February 1942 millionaire backbencher and unrepentant Chamberlainite 'Chips'

Channon found himself downing dry martinis in the Dorchester with the Greek sovereign, his distant cousin, and 'Edwina M … now a complete Socialist, which for anybody in the position of a millionairess, a semi-royalty, and a famous fashionable figure, is too ridiculous'. She may have spent the day haranguing bureaucrats and checking latrines, but she looked 'a dream of beauty' and, perhaps more surprisingly, 'seemed fond of Dickie'. Propping up the bar with the King of the Hellenes and this 'cool, chic and completely charming' couple, a gloomy Channon insisted that the Government was doomed and the nation faced disaster.[5] Ironically, only hours earlier Mountbatten had secured the Chiefs of Staff's approval for what he later saw as one of his greatest wartime triumphs, the commando raid on St Nazaire.[6]

But demolishing the lock gates of the Normandie Dock was just another item on an Admiralty wish list in June 1941. Admiral Syfret, the First Sea Lord's Naval Secretary, had precious little time to worry about the *Tirpitz* when he had Captain Mountbatten energetically petitioning him for command of a capital ship.[7] A brand-new cruiser was his for the asking, but Churchill's most favoured sailor lobbied for an even greater challenge. His eventual reward was the Royal Navy's most recently launched aircraft carrier, HMS *Illustrious*. For the British, if not the Americans, this was a seriously big ship, weighing nearly 29,000 tons, carrying up to 40 aircraft, and bearing a complement of around 1,300 officers and men. The contrast with *Kelly* could scarcely be greater. This was most definitely not the normal posting for a destroyer captain with a by no means unblemished record. Although the carrier only joined Cunningham's fleet in August 1940, she soon lived up to her name: it was *Illustrious*'s Swordfishes that had flown to Taranto. In January 1941 she was repeatedly attacked by the *Luftwaffe* off Malta, the assault continuing when she sought shelter inside Grand Harbour. Altogether, *Illustrious* sustained nine direct hits, and several damaging near misses. A three-inch armoured flight deck had ensured the carrier's survival, allowing her to limp back to Egypt, and then escape via the Suez Canal. In the summer of 1941 *Illustrious* was undergoing an extensive refit at the US Navy Yard in Norfolk, Virginia. By November she would be ready to cross the Atlantic, and rejoin the Mediterranean Fleet.[8]

For Mountbatten this was a dream posting. His valet duly and dutifully packed the two tin trunks, the hand-stitched leather suitcase, and the made-to-measure action stations helmet container. The *Illustrious*'s freshly-appointed captain found out all he could about his new command, and immersed himself in Fleet Air Arm tactics and procedures. Assuming a seat was available he would be flying out on 15 August. Their Lordships were more than happy to see him go. The Prime Minister was of course delighted to see him go. Churchill had great plans for Dickie in America. As a former Secretary of the Navy, Roosevelt would surely provide a warm welcome in the White House. Shore-based admirals in the capital and around the country could scarcely skip an opportunity to meet someone whose experience of battle conditions at sea was so recent. Crucially, the American public might heed the call for intensifying material aid to battered, brave, and beleaguered Britain if the speaker was a charming, blue-blooded, and immaculately groomed war hero.[9]

As it transpired, Mountbatten experienced scant opportunity to fulfil this overtly propagandist role. The person who did was in fact Edwina. Dickie persuaded her that here was a rare chance to make a significant contribution to the war effort without feeling in any way guilty about temporarily vacating Brigade Headquarters. He overcame her fears about addressing large audiences by providing a master class in the art of memorising key points and then appearing to speak spontaneously; all the other tricks of the trade, of which Mountbatten was a master when it came to seducing an audience, she would acquire through experience. The couple had quarrelled over Edwina's eagerness to bring Pamela and Patricia home. Mountbatten believed that, by providing her with an opportunity to see the girls, she could be convinced that they should remain Stateside. Accompanying him to America allowed Edwina to enjoy quality time with her daughters, to liaise closely with the American Red Cross, and to thank personally the myriad of organisations in both the United States and Canada whose material and financial aid had flowed across the Atlantic in the first two years of the war. Boot-like, Dickie stepped aboard the clipper still fretting over his luggage. With Manhattan fashion houses beckoning, Edwina chose to travel lightly. Assured every item of jewellery was aboard and secure, she sat back, switched off, and relished the four day flight from austerity – by the evening of 19 August 1941 she was back on Fifth Avenue, rediscovering high balls in the cocktail bar of the Plaza.[10]

From New York and a joyful reunion with the children, Mountbatten flew down to Norfolk and his first encounter with the crew of *Illustrious*. Not everyone in the wardroom was unfamiliar, not least because true to form the new captain had pulled strings to secure a few familiar faces from the *Kelly*. Officers unacquainted with Mountbatten would almost certainly have known how he had championed the Fleet Air Arm before the war. The circumstances in which he had lost his ship off Crete made those sceptics who still saw him as an over-promoted glamour boy more circumspect when passing judgement on the new arrival. Nevertheless, their suspicions would have been fuelled by the fact that over 40 press photographers snapped the new captain being piped aboard for the first time – Lord Louis was news, and the MoI's propagandists saw his presence on the eastern seaboard as a PR windfall. While energising the ship's company with his enthusiasm and eagerness to get on with the job, Mountbatten needed to exercise tact, and even a degree of humility. He had an awful lot to learn about carrier warfare, and with the US Navy yet to enter the war, he was heavily reliant upon his own staff. Up to this point he had appraised the potential of air power from the perspective of the victim, but now he needed the tactical acumen of the aggressor. He would be heavily dependent upon the expertise of his senior airmen, forcing him to make far fewer unilateral decisions than he was used to as a destroyer captain, or even a flotilla commander. First impressions were favourable, not least because Mountbatten was so demonstrably enthusiastic about his new command. The ship's company must have been delighted that a priority was improving entertainment at sea, with arrangements put in place for a state-of-the-art projector to be shipped out from England.[11]

While Edwina criss-crossed America on an astonishingly packed itinerary, Mountbatten based himself in Washington. A joint visit to Rhode Island had marked Edwina's baptism of fire, with a well-received, confidence-boosting address to the Newport chapter of the Red Cross. Dickie meanwhile was busy giving a guest lecture at the Naval War College, focusing upon his direct experience of 'Destroyer Warfare'. Back on the Chesapeake Bay he delivered a rip-roaring address to over 1,000 midshipmen at Annapolis, the US Navy's equivalent of Dartmouth. Although he ensured there was sufficient spare time to spend with his children, Mountbatten found himself tied in to a hectic schedule of inspections and formal visits. With repairs to *Illustrious* still far from complete, Mountbatten was free to fly the flag at a wide variety of military bases and munitions plants.[12] On one occasion he bumped into his old crony, Antoine Gazda, who by now was selling Oerlikons in large numbers on both sides of the Atlantic. The embassy was especially delighted with his 50-minute briefing to the Overseas Press Club on the war in Europe, and the courting of key opinion-formers extended to a lengthy session with the doyen of the Washington press corps, Walter Winchell. Mountbatten listened patiently for over two hours while America's most influential syndicated columnist put the world to right, and then, 'did more in half an hour to make Winchell appreciate the attitude of a typical officer in the Royal Navy towards the war than ten million words of print could ever achieve'.[13] As Churchill had anticipated, Mountbatten charmed FDR. Inside the Oval Office he met the aides and generals with whom he would work closely over the next four years, and beyond. This was almost certainly the first time he encountered Harry Hopkins, Roosevelt's closest confidant and most trusted emissary. Mountbatten had arrived for dinner at the White House bearing a shellac 78 as the presidential gift – Noel's morale-boosting hit, 'London Pride'. Roosevelt was a great fan of Coward, and his lengthy post-port rumination on how to wean a wary nation off isolationism was lightened intermittently by the scratched sounds of 'The Master' emanating from the West Wing gramophone.[14]

With the situation in the Far East already critical, the US Navy was ostensibly only one step from a war footing. Senior staff in Norfolk, Newport, and Washington were eager to learn from someone so well-connected, and with so much recent combat experience. Mountbatten was a frequent visitor to the Naval Department, urging fleet commanders like Ernie King to extend convoy protection in the North Atlantic and to liaise more closely with their Canadian and British counterparts. In a letter to the First Sea Lord, Harold Stark, Chief of Naval Operations, pointed to Mountbattan's 'genuinely beneficial' visit as confirmation of the need for closer collaboration between the two navies. Here was someone who had been 'outstandingly helpful in every way ... His knowledge of his profession, his keen observation of our methods, his frank statements of his thoughts of them, his telling us of the British Navy methods and comparison with our own, his sincerity, frankness and honesty have not only won our liking, but also our deep respect'.[15] Praise indeed. The 'frankness and honesty' was especially evident when Mountbatten spent the last week in September with the US Pacific Fleet at Pearl Harbor.

As an exhausted Edwina arrived back in Washington, Dickie flew out on the 1940s forerunner of the redeye express, TWA's 'transcontinental' Boeing 307 Stratocruiser. He had been invited to Honolulu by Admiral Husband E. Kimmel, fleet commander *and* Navy Chief of Staff. Given the rank and status of his host it's scarcely surprising that Mountbatten was lavishly entertained wherever he went. He was taken on a comprehensive tour of Hawaii's huge naval and air base, and he met senior personnel from the Army and the Marines, as well as assorted flag officers and their staffs. In the light of subsequent events, it's ironic that whenever possible he pumped carrier veterans for advice – at this stage in the war he would have learnt a lot more on the far side of the Pacific. Mountbatten was expected to sing for his supper, and when bad weather delayed fleet manoeuvres he delivered three lectures to huge audiences – one largely to soldiers on the battle for Crete, and two on destroyer tactics and wider aspects of the war at sea. Finally the bad weather lifted, and Kimmel's special guest spent four days on exercise with one of the fleet's three task forces (each one of which, to Mountbatten's surprise, only went on exercise every three months). The eager student based himself on William 'Bull' Halsey's flagship, the aircraft carrier *Enterprise*; although the skipper of the destroyer *Balch* had the mixed blessing of Captain Mountbatten alongside him on the bridge throughout his squadron's battle fleet attack.[16]

It seems somehow fitting that the man who received the Japanese surrender of Singapore on 11 September 1945 should have flown with the USAAF/USN air group that launched a dawn attack on Pearl Harbor just under four years earlier. Gathered in a vast hangar below the *Enterprise*'s flight deck, the ship's company whooped and cheered whenever Mountbatten speculated on the US Navy soon fighting alongside their British comrades. Such prescience was less well received by their commanding officers, many of whom objected to Mountbatten's blunt assessment of their combat readiness. He was appalled at how complacent and unprepared the Americans were, and how vulnerable Pearl Harbor was to a surprise airborne assault. Pointing to the large number of aircraft neatly lined up beside every runway, he confidently predicted that all would be lost in the event of an attack. At a post-exercise wash-up some officers complained that he was being unduly alarmist, but a grateful Kimmel endorsed Mountbatten's suggestion that coordination of the islands' defence be secured via dedicated telephone lines and the centralisation of operational staff in a bomb-proof headquarters. This was clearly the lesson of Malta; but before changes could be initiated the Japanese arrived, quite literally out of the blue.[17]

Dickie flew to Los Angeles for a curtailed R and R with Edwina. Although their stay in Beverley Hills was brief, various attractions and entertainments were organised by old friends, and, in the case of Douglas Fairbanks Jnr, a future colleague. With stars in his eyes the white-jacketed, bemedalled movie buff dined in the company of Norma Shearer and danced the night away in the arms of Rita Hayworth. The fantasy soon ended, even if the sashaying sailor never lost his fascination with Hollywood actresses. Advised by the British consul in LA that the Admiralty wanted him back in Washington as soon as possible, Mountbatten headed east. He and Edwina would soon be reunited, as honoured guests of the President. Their stay at the White House was short, Churchill personally apologising to Harry Hopkins for having denied FDR such congenial company.[18]

On 7 October Mountbatten had been called to the embassy, and to his intense disappointment learnt that *Illustrious* was no longer his. Instead, the Prime Minister wished to brief him as soon as possible on, 'something which you will find of the highest interest'. There was talk within the chancery of a post in Combined Operations. In other circumstances this would have been an enticing prospect, but Mountbatten resented losing his command, and feared that such an unorthodox career move might sabotage his dream of one day becoming First Sea Lord. To Churchill's intense irritation he refused to return home immediately, pleading a formal dinner at the White House and the need to make one final visit to Norfolk: as well as bidding farewell to the entire ship's company, he felt it necessary to appease those comrades from the *Kelly* he had seduced away from their precious destroyers for service aboard an aircraft carrier.[19] Meanwhile the President smoothed Churchill's ruffled feathers, insisting that, 'Mountbatten has been really useful to our Navy people'. Already both men regarded 'Dicky' as a reliable emissary, Roosevelt trusting him to convey details of some nefarious scheme for undermining the Vichy regime, with which at this point the United States retained diplomatic ties.[20]

Mountbatten left New York on 21 October. With Edwina still to embark upon the Canadian leg of her marathon tour, the couple would not meet again until early December. When she did return Pamela accompanied her, with Patricia planning to follow in six months time once she had completed high school. A two-day island hop, via Bermuda and the Azores, brought Dickie to Lisbon, where he made a deep impression on the Ministry of Economic Warfare's adviser to the ambassador, the future Tory education minister David Eccles. The feeling was clearly mutual as Eccles would soon find himself joining the staff of Combined Operations.[21] On the final leg of the flight home – his feelings an uneasy mix of regret, irritation, apprehension, and excitement – Mountbatten steeled himself for an uncomfortable appointment with the Prime Minister.

Combined Operations – creating a new headquarters

A despondent and deposed carrier captain reached London on 25 October 1941. Pausing only to assure his mother he was fit and well, Mountbatten made his way to Chequers and a painful encounter with Churchill. The latter was both angry and astonished when the newly designated 'Adviser on Combined Operations' appeared singularly ungrateful that the premier saw him as the best man for the job. Although the post meant promotion to commodore, Mountbatten indicated how he would far rather be at sea in *Illustrious* given that he knew so little about waging war on land. An incandescent Churchill questioned his sanity, with a sharp reminder that past experience suggested terra firma might offer a safer and more suitable path to glory: 'Here I give you a chance to take a part in the higher leadership of the war, and all you want to do is to go back to sea! What can you hope to achieve, except to be sunk in a bigger and more expensive ship?'[22]

Mountbatten acknowledged that this was indeed a remarkable opportunity to do great things; but he was left under no illusion as to the enormity of his task. Warming to his subject, and with no chiefs of staff present to temper his remarks, the Prime Minister outlined a twin-track programme of launching increasingly ambitious raids on mainland Europe, while at the same time initiating detailed preparation for a return to France. The former flotilla commander was expected to mastermind a dramatic rise in cross-Channel attacks, in itself a formidable challenge. Yet, he was also charged with nothing less than planning a full-scale invasion.[23] Mountbatten was easily persuaded, and disappointment over the loss of *Illustrious* drained away.

His enthusiasm for the job was scarcely dented when it became obvious that the Chiefs of Staff Committee (COSC) did not share Churchill's vision of the Adviser's role and responsibilities. Indeed, inspection of the three service chiefs' directive, as agreed on 16 October 1941, may have settled the nerves, and offered assurance that he was anything but alone in shifting the military imperative from national survival to full-scale offensive. Mountbatten no doubt anticipated a stealthy expansion of his empire, but in the short term he was content to remain the Chiefs of Staff's 'technical adviser', attending COSC only when required. That same advisory function, re 'the technical training of their forces', extended to force commanders, who were nevertheless obliged to seek Combined Operations' advice when planning major operations. Contrary to Churchill's understanding of his role, Mountbatten only held full responsibility, including the appointment of force commanders, for 'raids on a very small scale'. However, the Special Service troops responsible for those raids did operate under his authority, even if some or all of these forces could conceivably be transferred to a separate command structure for particular operations. The Adviser enjoyed complete discretion over instruction in combined operations for the three services, with full control of all recognised schools and training centres. He was instructed to 'direct and press forward' all relevant R and D, and crucially, to 'Study tactical and technical developments in all forms of combined operations varying from small raids to a full-scale invasion of the Continent'. This final responsibility, liberally interpreted by the Prime Minister, lay at the heart of Mountbatten's remit – certainly, as far as Churchill was concerned, if not necessarily, his chiefs of staff.[24]

In addition to Dudley Pound, the other two chiefs were the RAF's cerebral advocate of strategic bombing, Charles Portal, and the Army's quietly respected architect of a fit for purpose command structure, Sir John Dill. The Chief of the Imperial General Staff (CIGS) reacted badly to the Prime Minister's truculent treatment of his generals, while Churchill found 'Dilly Dally' near impossible to work with. By October 1941 Dill's days were numbered, and over Christmas he would make way for the brilliant but acerbic head of Home Forces, Alan Brooke.[25] Despite a readiness to forget their differences when socialising, in committee Brooke and Mountbatten rarely saw eye to eye. The former applauded the latter's enthusiasm, while at the same time finding his penchant for the grand gesture deeply irritating. As we shall see, Brooke suspected Mountbatten's ability to perform at the very highest level – was Dickie in any way capable of matching his own high standards of organisation and sagacity? But the head of the Army also questioned Mountbatten's interpretation of his status and authority vis-à-vis the three service chiefs, and in this Brooke drew heavily upon the directive approved by his predecessor. Dill may have found Churchill unnecessarily confrontational, but he wasn't intimidated by him. Neither were Portal and Pound, and Mountbatten's arrival at Combined Operations Headquarters (COHQ) was largely because the Chiefs of Staff had found the previous regime intolerable.

The directive of 16 October 1941 had stipulated that the head of Combined Operations would work 'under the directions of the Chiefs of Staff'. This was acknowledged in a change of title, and constituted a significant shift from the previous arrangement, whereby the Director of Combined Operations had also reported to Churchill, in his capacity as Minister of Defence. The Director's refusal to accept this new inferior status, and to see his semi-autonomous organisation down-graded to an essentially service role in relation to the three armed services, created the vacancy for Mountbatten. The man he replaced was a sexagenarian Admiral of the Fleet, member of parliament, knight of the realm, and Great War hero – the redoubtable, heavily decorated, and deeply opinionated Sir Roger Keyes. Scourge of Chamberlain in the Norway debate, Keyes was a disciple of the unorthodox who applied harsh lessons learnt at the Dardanelles to planning – and leading – the Royal Navy's assault on the U-boat base at Zeebrugge in April 1918. Keyes' eagerness to attack, even at the darkest hour (whether that be at the height of the Hindenburg Offensive, or in the wake of Dunkirk), endeared him to Churchill. His friendship and loyalty in 'the wilderness years' was deemed to warrant due reward.[26] Chartwell's unashamed romantic saw glamour, panache, and the pursuit of glory in brave young warriors like T.E. Lawrence, or Dickie Mountbatten, or even Orde Wingate; but he also relished the prospect of proven heroes dusting down their uniforms, revisiting past glories, and then setting out to surpass them. From Jackie Fisher's unhappy return to the Admiralty in the First World War through to a succession of superannuated sailors early in the Second, Winston failed to recognise the folly of the second coming – he was the exception to the rule, and in many respects he had never gone away. In Downing Street in June 1940 the barnstorming Roger Keyes seemed an obvious choice to initiate, 'a vigorous, enterprising and ceaseless offensive against the whole German-occupied coastline'.[27] Here, in Churchill's mind, was someone with sufficient clout and courage to challenge the natural caution of the service chiefs: 'How wonderful it would be if the Germans could be made to wonder where they were going to be struck next, instead of forcing us to wall in the Island and roof it over! An effort must be made to shake off the mental and moral prostitution to the will and initiative of the enemy from which we suffer.'[28]

However, if 'Enterprises must be prepared with specially-trained troops of the hunter class, who can develop a reign of terror down these coasts', then the Chiefs of Staff felt they already had the right man in place. On 14 June 1940 Alan Bourne, previously Adjutant-General of the Royal Marines, had been given an office in the Admiralty and put in charge of Combined Operations. Bourne was to oversee organisation, recruitment, training, and equipment development. His first job was to initiate raids by special forces as soon as possible. Crucially, his function was to *advise* the three services, and they in turn would offer whatever assistance Bourne needed to

launch his 'reign of terror'.[29] *Combined Operations, 1940–42*, a wartime booklet from
the Ministry of Information, placed two years of raiding in the context of a long
and honourable tradition, dating back to the days of Drake and Grenville. Yet even
the MoI had to acknowledge how amphibious operations had been forced to take a
backseat between the wars, witness a total complement of only nine landing craft in
September 1939. That same month had seen the closure of the Inter-Services Training
and Development Centre at Fort Cumberland, near Portsmouth. The ISTDC had
only been in existence since May 1938. Its instructors were frightfully keen chaps
who positively relished the fact that Combined Operations was a cinderella service
and a career graveyard. Their various activities in the final year of peace proved a
bizarre mixture of the farcical and the highly professional. Captain L.E.H. Maund,
the one man in the Royal Navy with recent experience of opposed landings, ran
the establishment and fought successfully for it to be re-opened. Astonishingly, the
ISTDC was shut down again in April 1940, when the Admiralty assumed Maund
might be put to better use in Norway. It was resurrected for a second time once
Bourne recognised that remarkably few people in the British armed forces knew
anything about amphibious operations, other than that Gallipoli had shown them to
be a jolly bad thing. Ironically, at this point in time most instructors were energetically
hauling troops off French beaches, not busy working out ways to land them.[30]

Bourne would soon be Keyes' number two.[31] As number one he had precious
little time to make his mark, although remarkably his embryonic organisation did
contrive to scorn the French armistice by sending 115 men across the Channel to
shoot a handful of Germans and come back unscathed. Churchill was singularly
unimpressed by 'pinprick raids' on Boulogne, and on Guernsey – an alarmingly
haphazard trip to the Channel Islands on the night of 14 July 1940 achieved nothing
other than to leave three volunteers as prisoners of war. The hapless three were
members of Lieutenant-General Bourne's lasting achievement, the Commandos.
The idea of tough, specially-selected, lightly-armed men in highly trained amphibious
units capable of inflicting disproportionate losses on the enemy was not in fact
Bourne's. Neither was the idea Churchill's, although he quickly claimed credit for
it. Ironically, the person responsible for selling the notion of special forces to the
Prime Minister was the much maligned Sir John Dill. There was in fact a precedent,
in the 'Independent Companies' sent to fight alongside the Royal Marines during
the Norway campaign. They continued operating in various formats until eventually
subsumed in to Brigadier Charles Haydon's umbrella commando body, the Special
Service Brigade. By mid-October 1940 the commandos, along with their landing
crews, had a recognised home – the Combined Training Centre at Inverary.[32]

HMS *Quebec* was Combined Operations' first training establishment outside the
south coast, and in time the highlands and islands of Scotland would become the
main focus of commando activity. From the outset Keyes was always in search of
improved accommodation and training facilities. In late August he established COHQ
on the ground floor of Richmond Terrace, an office block originally intended for the
Metropolitan Police. He had assumed the post of Director on 17 July 1940, and
almost immediately Downing Street demanded details of autumn raids. Churchill

was thinking in terms of a tenfold expansion in the size of the forces currently available. Yet in the aftermath of Dunkirk the War Office was reluctant to see manpower leaching away from the defence of southern England. Furthermore, the Army insisted on creating battalions out of the ten Commandos; this undermining of autonomy persisted until a more appropriate structure was restored in February 1941.[33]

Even if Keyes could secure a rapid increase in manpower, he still required specialist ships and landing craft. While he and his staff could initiate orders for the latter, Combined Operations needed assistance from the Admiralty to secure large landing ships. Here was a fledgling body heavily dependent upon the goodwill of the Navy, and headed by an old warrior the First Sea Lord judged singularly unsuited to the post. Pound was by no means the only admiral to lament the combative Keyes' return to active service.[34] Before the year was out he had clashed with Andrew Cunningham twice: over the disastrous Dakar expedition in September 1940, and three months later, the abortive seizure of Pantalerria, a rocky islet south of Sicily. Keyes had always been a maverick figure within the Service, and now he seemed a positive menace – why had he felt the need to vacate the Admiralty, and did he not appreciate where his first loyalties lay? Similar sentiments would of course be expressed regarding his successor. At the same time the CIGS and his most senior general on home soil, Alan Brooke, were wary of someone who seemed so intent on stealing their best men and equipment. Yet the suspicion and scarcely disguised hostility of at least two of the three service chiefs contrasted markedly with the loyalty and affection Keyes generated inside Combined Operations. Partly this derived from a system of patronage which saw a disproportionate number of old cronies manning a desk in Richmond Terrace or some godforsaken establishment north of the Great Glen.[35] In *Men At Arms* Evelyn Waugh wickedly recreates special forces' early misadventures, with eccentric bemedalled geriatrics grateful for another bash at the Hun.

Yet even the professionals respected Keyes' leadership and organisational ability. In his memoirs Lord Lovat, a commando legend and a hard taskmaster, was unstinting in his praise of Combined Operations' founding father.[36] It was after all hard not to like such a decent, warm-hearted, and larger than life character, and this made his eventual loss that much harder to swallow. Keyes' unique standing within the Special Service Brigade was reinforced by the fact that his eldest son was a popular commando, who was killed only a few weeks after his father resigned his position. The Commandos' commanding officers, Charles Haydon and Robert Laycock, were career soldiers in the Guards, yet staunchly loyal to Keyes. Both men dismissed the Army Council's rear-guard defence of regimental tradition, resolutely defending their fledgling force. What distinguished them from Keyes was that they quietly contested any challenge to the autonomy of Combined Operations, while their *capo* displayed a fatal indifference to tact, diplomacy, and deference. As an admiral of the fleet, accountable only to Churchill, Keyes believed himself immortal. In February 1941 'Pug' Ismay, of whom more anon, was instructed by an impatient Churchill to stop Keyes bombarding him with letters by redefining the Director's relationship with the service staffs. The outcome was a crucial amendment in March 1941 to the Chiefs of Staff directive, specifying that henceforth Keyes was under their direction as well as that of the Minister of Defence. For all intents and purposes this critical change was ignored. Clearly no student of civil-military relations, by the summer of 1941 the Director of Combined Operations was riding for a fall.[37]

Pound shared with Cunningham the firm belief that Keyes displayed the conceit and confused thinking of an old man. Unimpressed by the performance of 'Layforce', Bob Laycock's commandos in the Middle East, the C-in-C of the Mediterranean Fleet readily concurred. Clearly Cunningham felt prejudiced towards Combined Operations long before he succeeded Pound as First Sea Lord in October 1943.[38] Relations between COHQ and the Admiralty were plagued by constant turf struggles, while the Director's dealings with force commanders remained fractious and confused. Brooke and Keyes were engaged in a running battle over Home Forces' demand that the Commandos be reintegrated into the regular chain of command.[39] A succession of ever more elaborate operations came near to fruition and were then cancelled, fuelling further rows across Whitehall. However, one substantial raid did take place, in that on 3–4 March 1941 3 and 4 Commandos landed on the Lofoten Islands in the far north of Norway, destroying factories, ships, and oil reserves. The commandos and their Norwegian guides returned home with 225 prisoners, 314 local volunteers, and one English internee; and could rightly celebrate an operation that had gone off with scarcely a hitch. Yet a subsequent inquest revealed inadequate training, and the suspicion that, had there been organised resistance, the outcome might have been very different.[40]

Keyes was convinced he needed greater autonomy and authority, placing the resource demands of Combined Operations on a par with those of the three services. He clashed repeatedly with the commanders of 'Pilgrim Force', the formidable expedition put together in spring 1941 to seize the Canaries. As the prospect of Spain formally joining the Axis receded so too did the case for seizing her offshore islands. In early August at Scapa Flow the remnants of Pilgrim Force participated in the ambitious 'Exercise Leapfrog'. The force commanders had insisted on the time and place, and George VI was present to watch the whole complex exercise unravel. The King, despite the appalling Scottish weather obscuring most of the action, was well aware that he was witnessing a fiasco. A furious Keyes formally complained to the Minister of Defence that his authority was being undermined by the Chiefs of Staff, not least in their insistence that COHQ should exercise no control over force commanders.[41] In making a stand, he forced Churchill to take one side or the other, and there could only be one outcome.

The Chiefs were briefed by Pilgrim Force's commanders on their unhappy experience under the umbrella of Combined Operations. Consequently, in September 1941 the COS Secretariat drafted a fresh directive, severely curtailing Keyes' tasks and responsibilities. That the latter now signalled a subordinate role was reinforced by the emphasis upon the central role of C-in-C Home Forces, and his naval and air equivalents, in planning and training for any future invasion. In redesignating the Director as 'Adviser', the Chiefs of Staff quite clearly created a resignation issue.

That they should do so is scarcely surprising given Keyes' apparent propensity to inform them they were all cowards! The testy warrior reacted furiously to the COSC's initiative, sending several memos to Churchill, and insisting that his old friend meet him. The Prime Minister replied with an emollient but nevertheless firm letter. In a flurry of correspondence the premier consistently backed his service chiefs, and in the end Keyes was forced to concede defeat: typically, he begged Churchill not to feel guilty, promising to do all he could to assist his successor. Even so, he still kept complaining to No 10 that a traitorous Pound had contrived his departure – the news that on 19 October he must give way to a newly promoted Dickie Mountbatten simply confirmed him in his belief that he had fallen victim to an Admiralty coup.[42]

A fledgling Combined Operations needed someone of Keyes' calibre and near legendary status to establish itself independently of the three service ministries. The outgoing Director could never be dismissed as a gentleman amateur, witness the speed and efficiency displayed in consolidating the Commando structure, and in establishing a comprehensive training programme for amphibious operations.[43] Nevertheless, Keyes was too old, impatient, and idiosyncratic to accommodate the complex and bureaucratic decision-making apparatus required to withstand the hammer blows of 1942, form the basis for a viable joint command structure with the Americans, and facilitate the basis upon which Britain would turn unilateral defeat into collective victory. The Prime Minister either recognised this fact for himself, or was made to recognise it. All three chiefs were in agreement, and so was the man Churchill already had in mind as his next CIGS, Brooke. Running Combined Ops was a young(ish) man's job, and, so long as Mountbatten remained respectfully at arms' length from the COSC, not even Brooke queried whether his 'exploits and abilities seemed ... to fit him in a high degree for the vacant post'.[44] Dill's opinion was by now almost irrelevant, but it would seem he welcomed Mountbatten's appointment: like Brooke he assumed the elevation of such a junior officer would ensure compliance to the chiefs' wishes. The same seems to have been the view of Charles Portal – Mountbatten found the Chief of the Air Staff especially welcoming and supportive.[45]

Eyebrows were raised within the Admiralty, but, given several weeks' delay in announcing the handover, there was only muted discussion as to whether Dickie could fill Roger Keyes' sizeable shoes.[46] It was the First Sea Lord himself who queried the presence of a destroyer captain, however well connected, within the corridors of power. Pound was a traditionalist, guaranteed to object strongly should the new Adviser seek to flex his muscles at the expense of the Royal Navy. Mountbatten's style and bumptious self-confidence, as in inviting admirals to weekend at Broadlands, was previously unthreatening, and even mildly amusing. In new, very different circumstances, the *arriviste* at the top table was viewed with ever greater suspicion by someone already in the early stages of an increasingly debilitating, and ultimately fatal, illness. Sensitive to Service suggestions that he was unduly subservient to Churchill, Pound belatedly took the Prime Minister to task over Mountbatten's meteoric rise in rank. Dudley Pound may not have liked the cut of Dickie's jib. Almost certainly he saw him as a threat – and with some justification given the power of prime ministerial patronage. Yet at least on the surface the First Sea Lord was available, accessible, and generous in his advice. As Richard Hough pointed out, 'Mountbatten was the only officer below flag rank who could raise the telephone (as he often did) and speak to him personally at any time'. Direct access to the man at the top, from the Chiefs of Staff to the President of the United States, was a priceless asset. As in every other job he undertook, Mountbatten shamelessly exploited this privilege. His staff recognised this fact, which gave them added confidence in his ability to get them what they wanted.[47]

Within Combined Operations there was obvious enthusiasm for the new appointment. At least one junior officer, as yet unaware of Mountbatten's arrival, named him in a shortlist of RN captains ideally qualified to instil some sense of order and purpose into an organisation seemingly incapable of generating inter-service collaboration.[48] When finally the Adviser's appointment entered the public domain, Fleet Street on the whole responded warmly. Only the *Daily Express* was openly hostile, but by this time the Beaverbrook vendetta was building up speed. Not that Mountbatten had any idea of what was to come.[49]

Keyes was stoic and friendly when briefing the new Adviser, warning a sceptical Mountbatten that, 'the British have lost the will to fight'.[50] He held his one-time 'two-striper' in high regard, recalling his virtues as 'a most able staff officer'; but he questioned whether the younger man had, 'the guts to make big decisions'. Bitter and inconsolable, Keyes got it into his head that Churchill had granted the Young Pretender the breadth of authority he himself had been denied.[51] He was wrong about the timing, but entirely right to anticipate a swing in the pendulum – within six months his successor had exceeded any powers previously enjoyed by Keyes, and had himself become a chief of staff.

Not that such a dramatic development would have been obvious over the winter of 1941–2. Mountbatten drew on a natural ebullience in dealing with his new colleagues at Richmond Terrace, deftly blending an impression of supreme self-confidence and a readiness to learn. A degree of humility, real or cultivated, was clearly necessary when dealing with COHQ colleagues still technically senior to him. A readiness to display previously untapped reserves of tact and discretion was evident in occasional briefings of the Defence Committee, and more crucially, in Mountbatten's dealings with the Chiefs of Staff. On average once a week from the end of October 1941 through to the following spring he would attend meetings of the COSC, and speak to any relevant items on the agenda. Throughout this period Pound was in the chair, only making way for Brooke as Chairman of the COS on 5 March 1942. As far as the latter was concerned, this was the honeymoon period, with Mountbatten seen to be both competent and accommodating. The Adviser made various requests, usually related to resources, and when these were rejected he accepted each setback with good grace. The goodwill created in these early months, contrasting so starkly with the putrid atmosphere in the dying days of Keyes' reign, presumably made it that much harder for the service chiefs to protest when Churchill bestowed near equal status on Mountbatten. That decision coincided with Brooke being invited to succeed Pound, the Prime Minister implicitly making the point that concern over the conduct of COSC meetings had focused upon the performance of the somnolent chair, not its most junior attendee.[52]

On 19 November 1941 the Minister for Economic Warfare, Hugh Dalton, noted in his diary how the new man at Combined Ops was, 'having to start right at the beginning, as we had to more than a year ago, and fire practically all the existing top lot'. This was something of an exaggeration, but, before considering what changes Mountbatten did instigate at Richmond Terrace, it's worth noting the close relations he developed with Dalton. The latter was instinctively hostile to a fast-rising second cousin of the King, but Mountbatten won him over. Dalton was the minister responsible for sabotage experts the Special Operations Executive, a body envious of Combined Operations' representation on the COSC. Mountbatten invited SOE to locate a liaison officer inside his own headquarters, and when necessary would speak on the Executive's behalf at meetings of the Chiefs of Staff. He persuaded his counterpart, Robert Bruce Lockhart, to keep in touch via the ever reliable Peter Murphy ('the sixth best brain in England'!). The two 'outlaw' organisations, COHQ and SOE, had their roots in Churchill's defiant response to the fall of France, and both were viewed suspiciously by MI6. They had many common interests, and after Keyes' departure collaborated closely. For example, Special Operations supplied unorthodox munitions, most notably the tailor-made drip fuse that delayed the explosion of HMS *Campbeltown* at St Nazaire.[53] The key date in facilitating close collaboration was 9 January 1942 when Mountbatten spent an hour in the minister's office exchanging information and sharing prejudices, most notably towards the Diplomatic Service and Charles de Gaulle. Any differences over demarcation disappeared, SOE at one stage having claimed that raids of less than 30 men should be its prerogative. Dalton was too experienced not to spot a charm offensive, especially when Mountbatten endeavoured to paint himself as by instinct a champion of the workers. Yet Labour's most guileful representative in cabinet was at least partially won over. After all, here was someone 'amusing' and seemingly well-intentioned, who potentially could prove a very useful ally. Nevertheless, in his diary that night a prescient Dalton shrewdly noted that Mountbatten, 'may become, or be presented by others as, an uncomfortable acquisitive force ...'.[54]

Plotting a socialist revolution in Vichy France with the King's least favourite politician exemplified the chameleon tendency in Mountbatten's make-up. More importantly, creating an unholy alliance with Dr Dalton was a classic instance of Lord Louis the elite networker. He worked Whitehall and St James's assiduously, while at the same time extending his encyclopaedic knowledge of naval personnel to embrace both the Army and the Royal Air Force. Mountbatten had loyalty to King(s), country and family. He probably saw himself as equally devoted to close friends like Peter Murphy and Yola Letellier. Indeed, the latter, although hijacked by his wife in the 1930s, might reasonably be described as a Platonic mistress. Yet after the war he saw Yola less and less, and the same proved true of Noel Coward. More cruelly, Peter Murphy was in effect dropped once Dickie and Edwina embraced establishment respectability. Thus the parameters of Mountbatten's loyalty were actually quite narrow, and in consequence his respect for naval tradition became increasingly qualified. Clearly he loved the Royal Navy, and becoming First Sea Lord surpassed every other goal and accomplishment. But he abhorred a tunnel vision belief in the superiority of the Senior Service, and a slavish adherence to outmoded mores, rituals, and prejudices. His distaste for inter-service rivalry, which was especially prevalent within the Royal Navy, was never greater than in the latter years of his career, when, as Chief of the Defence Staff, he endeavoured to push through a wholly 'functional' system of defence management. The organisational structure of the Ministry of Defence adopted in 1964 fell far short of the integrationist model championed by the CDS, with compromise a wise course of action given the Canadians' disastrous single service experience.[55]

Mountbatten had the *savoir-faire* to feel as comfortable in the mess as in the wardroom, and Combined Operations offered an ideal opportunity to break down prejudicial service loyalties in such a way that every officer and NCO felt similarly relaxed wherever he or she might be posted. Within COHQ naval staff remained the worst offenders, with every effort made to curb cliquish tendencies and absurd conventions.[56] Across the whole of Combined Operations separate messes were discouraged, the intention being to counterbalance the disproportionate influence of a majority naval personnel. While some arch-defenders of naval tradition were either *in situ* or slipped through the net, Mountbatten scoured the armed forces for like-minded individuals sympathetic to his vision of unequivocal cooperation and a collective identity. Combined Operations was no place for single-minded careerists, not least the fainthearted officer unwilling to take on the Admiralty, War Office, or Air Ministry should the needs of COHQ become paramount.

This commitment to inter-service collaboration was especially evident on the operational side of Mountbatten's dual remit, set out in a memorandum submitted to the Chiefs of Staff five weeks after his arrival at Richmond Terrace. For most of that time he only left the building for meetings and inspections. Rarely taking time off, let alone retreating to Romsey, he remained at his desk all day and into the night, often sleeping on the office couch.[57] Yet, however crucial to Combined Operations' repositioning within the military apparatus, the policy document approved by the Chiefs on 9 December 1941 marked only a modest advance on a steep learning curve. Concise yet detailed, it laid out a complete organisational structure, building on the best of Keyes' initiatives yet at the same time establishing a fresh model for liaison with the service ministries. Of the latter, the Admiralty was clearly the principal partner, and the administrative arm of COHQ would comprise primarily of naval staff, appropriately tasked with overseeing personnel, material, and most critically, shipping. Thus, a key amendment to the final directive delineated Mountbatten's dual responsibilities as: 'Adviser on Combined Operations', responsible for liaising directly with force commanders and the staffs of the three service chiefs; and 'Commodore Combined Operations', with executive responsibility for those joint forces designated to undertake raids and longer-term, large-scale operations.[58]

The Chiefs of Staff gave their backing to changes which were already underway. Upon taking up his appointment Mountbatten was astonished to discover that the total complement of COHQ, including typists and messengers, was a mere 23. Keyes had been running a modest, hand-to-mouth operation, with the emphasis very much upon improvisation. Captain John Hughes-Hallett was appointed as Naval Adviser in December 1941, and within a year he would find himself leading the taskforce into Dieppe. Hughes-Hallett was as accomplished in the cockpit or on a bicycle saddle as he was aboard a boat. Yet ironically, it was driving a desk that brought out his finest leadership qualities. He felt strongly that the poverty of the former regime's planning provision reflected a lack of ambition – all the Director had wanted to do was launch a 'bigger and better Zeebrugge-type raid'.[59] Such criticism was clearly unfair, and Mountbatten's enemies no doubt contended that Keyes' stripped down, flat management structure contrasted favourably with the bloated, over-bureaucratic apparatus that came to occupy every available room within the Richmond Terrace complex.

Keyes had recruited a motley collection of Royal Navy staff, both active and retired. The latter were mostly dead wood, but alongside them were one or two younger officers who were both able and enthusiastic. Rear Admiral H.E. Horan, a former flag captain of Cunningham's, was an exceptionally able administrator who took the much junior Mountbatten's appointment in his stride. He soon found himself one half of the partnership masterminding a rapid expansion of Combined Operations' fleet of assault ships and craft. Commodore Guy Warren had already proved a miracle-worker in forming an embryonic invasion force, but along with Horan he was expected to establish a vital new element in Britain's offensive armoury. Commissioning an armada of state-of-the-art vessels from British and American yards was possibly the greatest achievement of Mountbatten's tenure at COHQ. In December 1941 Admiralty projections were for '500–700 tank landing craft and 2,000 smaller craft manned by 2,000 officers and 20,000 men within the next 16 months'. By April 1943 naval personnel was well over double the predicted numbers, with nearly 90 assault ships and around 3,600 assorted landing craft and barges.[60] A team of planners, both at home and in North America, facilitated this massive expansion in numbers.[61] However, Mountbatten can personally claim much of the credit for securing so many extra officers and men. He kept the Chiefs of Staff on side, outflanked Admiralty objections by persuading Ernie Bevin, the Minister of Labour, to amend the Manpower Services Budget, and toured training establishments convincing 'Hostilities Only' cadets that Combined Operations was no longer the Service's poor relation: in a good-humoured but hard-hitting address Mountbatten would insist that if he wasn't able to serve in destroyers then amphibious operations was the next best place to be – so, if Combined Ops was good enough for him, then it was good enough for the rawest recruit to the RNVR.[62]

Guy Warren may have been the right man for the job, but in many instances the job had not been created in the first place. Thus Keyes had never got round to appointing a chief of staff. Mountbatten filled the gap by recruiting a Royal Marines brigadier who had fought the Great War in the Royal Naval Air Service, G.E. Wildman-Lushington. Given his CV he could be guaranteed to squash any hint of inter-service rivalry. In the absence of the young master he could be relied upon to crack the whip. Also, his presence alongside Warren on the Dakar expedition had left him keenly aware of how not to mount a large-scale operation. Godfrey Wildman-Lushington was clearly the sort of chap who ran a tight ship. He was possibly the only soldier, other than Bob Laycock, who could lambast Evelyn Waugh, and not immediately become an enemy for life. One of the brigadier's earliest initiatives was securing an efficiency expert to create order out of the organisational chaos caused by over-hasty expansion.[63]

Order was duly imposed upon the administrative side. The same was true for the operational side, henceforth organised within a four-part structure: planning, training, communications, and intelligence. The always loyal Hughes-Hallett recalled an energetic Adviser 'infusing a new spirit … the operational planning side knew for the first time that their work was real and earnest: that the raids they were working on would in all probability be carried out'.[64] Not long after its establishment the Planning Section was split between teams working on imminent raids, and staff engaged in long-term preparation for a full-scale invasion of France. True to the new orthodoxy Planning was headed by officers drawn from all three services, of whom the most interesting was Robert Henriques. Born into a highly-regarded Jewish family of businessmen and intellectuals, Henriques had resigned his commission to establish himself as a writer and farmer. He returned to uniform when the first Commandos were formed, and became Charles Haydon's brigade major in the Special Service Brigade. Haydon himself, while deputising as brigade commander for the absent Bob Laycock, also acted as COHQ's Military Adviser. Even before the war ended Henriques began a series of semi-biographical novels, which are very much in the spirit of Siegfried Sassoon and Henry Williamson. The central character, 'Meego', is a thinly disguised version of the author, so naturally Mountbatten's HQ is the setting of a later volume.[65] Henriques was seconded to the Americans for the North African landings, 'Operation Torch'. He remained attached to the US Army, and ended the war a full colonel. Of the three novelists associated with Combined Operations – the others being Evelyn Waugh and Neville Shute, who at the time was an Admiralty researcher – Robert Henriques was the most prolific; and yet today he is the least known. Like Williamson his work warrants rediscovery and reappraisal.

The Training Section was headed by a vice-admiral and a major-general deemed too old for active service. Here Mountbatten might have experienced problems, but in fact the infrastructure was already in place, and so Training expanded on the back of earlier success.[66] Like Bob Laycock, Charles Haydon was a highly capable commander of the Special Service Brigade. His Commandos had pioneered the training and instruction of elite forces. Thus the priority for Combined Operations was to secure a similar level of competence and thorough preparation among naval personnel manning the assault ships and landing craft. This was to prove a herculean task, made that much more difficult by having to work in tandem with some of the more sceptical elements inside the Admiralty. The day-to-day headquarters for the Training Staff was not in London but, more sensibly, in Scotland. The Hollywood Hotel, otherwise known as HMS *Warren*, was conveniently located on the Firth of Clyde at Largs, and features prominently in Waugh's writings.

Training offered continuity, but the Signals Section was a wholly new invention. Not surprisingly, given his expertise, Mountbatten invested considerable time and effort in ensuring that all three services were following identical procedures and adopting complementary kit. Sensibly, the Chiefs had relocated an inter-service communications committee within Combined Operations. Again three representatives operated jointly, sharing an office with the Chief Signals Officer, Commander Michael Hodges. This was a team of problem-solvers, liaising with researchers at Malvern and the various other R and D establishments scattered the length and breadth of the country. The Signals Staff's principal task was to establish a coherent, pro-active programme of research and development; and an early example of how seemingly disparate improvements in communication could come together was the creation of a Headquarters Ship for force commanders masterminding a major amphibious operation. The first 'communications flagship' was an Australian ferry turned armed merchantmen, HMS *Bulolo*. Conversion work began early in 1942, but was not completed by the time of the Dieppe raid on 19 August. However, *Bulolo* and a companion ship, HMS *Largs*, did take part in the 'Torch' landings later that year. Their crews received instruction in a mock-up HQ ship at the Combined Signals School in Troon, part of a nationwide network of training establishments shared with the Royal Navy.[67]

The role of the Intelligence Staff was not in normal circumstances to gather material. Rather, its task was to collate, assimilate, synthesise, and interpret all information channelled into Combined Operations from the various intelligence-gathering agencies. Where necessary needs would be identified, and material requested, for example, via photo-reconnaissance. Comprehensive, up-to-date human and signals intelligence was absolutely vital to every raid planned by Combined Operations, which makes the appointment of Bobby de Casa Maury as Senior Intelligence Officer that much harder to comprehend. As we shall see, the Marquis de Casa Maury fell on his sword after the Dieppe raid, and intelligence officers inside the Admiralty and War Office felt vindicated, in that they strenuously opposed the presence of an intermediary between themselves and operational planners inside COHQ. Hughes-Hallett, never generous in his praise, defended Casa Maury as someone who was not only speedy and efficient in collating intelligence, but also imaginative and innovative in uncovering important information: who else would have discovered that gates for the St Nazaire lock and the Southampton dry dock were designed by the same engineer – an employee of the Southern Railway Company who kept all his old plans?[68] Even so, was Mountbatten wise to appoint a one-time playboy and admirer of Edwina, whose credentials rested largely on his success in revitalising Bentley Motors, and establishing the Curzon and the Paris as London's leading art-house cinemas? Admittedly Bobby had flown with the Royal Flying Corps and joined the RAFVR well before war broke out, but relevant experience was restricted to working as an air intelligence officer in the West Country.[69] It was in that capacity that he first angled for a job in Dickie's new outfit, so he must have been astonished when asked to head the Intelligence Section.[70] Overnight Flight Lieutenant Casa Maury found himself a wing commander, albeit acting and unpaid. When Bobby joined COHQ he brought the family. By marrying Freda Dudley Ward, the Marquis had become step-father to Bob Laycock's wife, Angela. The latter was always a favourite of Mountbatten, and she and her mother were invited to open the Combined Operations Restaurant. This proved to be a rip-roaring success, establishing Richmond Terrace as a convivial refuge for anyone with a big appetite and the correct security clearance.[71]

Whether a Cuban-born cinema owner with a fancy name was any good or not, was almost immaterial. Chaps with the right sort of background like Ian Fleming, or SOE's official historian, Michael Foot, could sign up for the duration and, if they were demonstrably up to the job, be inducted into the intelligence community.[72] A flamboyant character like Bobby de Casa Maury would have had to be exceptional in order to be accepted by the professionals. Perceived failures of intelligence in planning the Dieppe operation sealed his fate. Following previous raids no-one in the service ministries ever conceded that he might doing a reasonable job. Indeed he was *persona non grata* across much of Whitehall, the general feeling being that he was SIO only because he was one of Dickie's crowd. Nor was the Marquis the only pal to find a billet inside Richmond Terrace. To the horror of MI5, Peter Murphy flitted in and out of COHQ, fulfilling a shadowy liaison role on behalf of both SOE and the Political Intelligence Department.[73] Of the 400 personnel recruited by the summer of 1942, an exceptionally large number had been personally selected by Mountbatten. It's scarcely surprising that, as well as competence, a key criterion was whether he found a candidate congenial and collegial – and, crucially, did he or she appear to like him? Youth, good looks, and an attractive personality were all sound attributes; nor did an ability to boost the Adviser's ego go amiss. Not that Mountbatten's efforts were restricted to Richmond Terrace: he found convenient postings for pals on both sides of the Atlantic.[74] It was a perk of the powerful that he clearly relished. His personal correspondence over the next quarter of a century reveals the *deus ex machina* of Broadlands regularly finding friends a job or having a quiet word with someone who can.

To be fair, talent was always a key criterion, and a high proportion of Mountbatten's senior appointments at COHQ vindicated his selection. Micky Hodges was such a success as Chief Signals Officer largely because he and Dickie had worked so well together as fleet wireless officers in the Mediterranean a decade earlier: they shared the same ideas, and they spoke the same language.[75] Ronnie Brockman, eventually prized from the First Sea Lord's office to serve as Mountbatten's secretary, performed that function for the next 22 years with quiet efficiency: a vital buffer in the outer office, the ever-patient captain offered wise words at moments of crisis, and provided a calming influence whenever tempers frayed.[76] Yet Dalton wasn't the only person to hear rumours that the Adviser was surrounding himself with close associates who were not necessarily up to the job. Robert Henriques, whom Mountbatten treated appallingly, found 'this most genuine of War Lords' a strange paradox: how could someone so extraordinarily talented retain, 'a total inability to judge men correctly, whether they were his cronies or his subordinates, and yet with the power to command an uncritical loyalty from almost everyone ...'?[77] As someone who later served on George Patton's staff, Henriques could speak with authority on the military ego. Late in life a remorseful Mountbatten conceded that all too often he had treated staff abominably, 'flying off the handle too quickly, largely through overwork and inexperience'.[78] When Lieutenant-Colonel Lord Lovat descended on Richmond Terrace from his commando eyrie in order to be briefed on Dieppe, all his worst fears were confirmed. Venturing in to a veritable den of sin and iniquity, he espied, 'a fair proportion of drones among the inmates'.[79] Another soldier, the Communist journalist Goronwy Rees, gained a more favourable impression. Acting as Monty's eyes and ears, he was immediately struck by the number of people and by the scarcely disguised eccentricities. Yet at the same time he was singularly impressed by the fact that everyone was so well-informed about the finer points of amphibious warfare. Thus all shared a formidable body of technical knowledge, *and* a collective identity. Given that Rees was so scathing about most other aspects of the Dieppe raid, his sympathetic portrayal of the febrile atmosphere inside COHQ is worth taking on board.[80]

Not so sympathetic was Evelyn Waugh. The novelist delayed for a decade revisiting his painful experience as a commando: Guy Crouchback, previously encountered in *Men At Arms*, may suffer similar misfortunes, but he is of course a far nicer man than his creator. In *Officers and Gentlemen*, 'Marchmain House', the headquarters of 'Hazardous Offensive Operations', is, 'that bizarre product of total war which later was to proliferate through five acres of valuable London property, engrossing the simple high staff officers of all the Services with experts, charlatans, plain lunatics and every unemployed member of the British Communist Party'.[81] In this respect HOO HQ is out of the same mould as Waugh's Ministry of Information in the 'phoney war' novel, *Put Out More Flags* – in Mountbatten's own words, 'The only lunatic asylum in the world run by its own inmates'. The proliferation of bizarre acronyms within HOO reflects the crazy proliferation of initials throughout Combined Operations, with only the Adviser and the telephone receptionist able to discriminate between the SCOCO, the SEOCO, the SOCO, and the various SNOCOs. Waugh loathed 'Shimi' Lovat, and the feeling was mutual. It was the noble laird who orchestrated Waugh's exit from the Special Service Brigade in July 1943. Lovat left 'the world's biggest snob' haunting the corridors of Richmond Terrace, insistent that he be reunited with Bob Laycock in Italy. Mountbatten refused Waugh's plea to intervene, and Charles Haydon promptly sacked him for insubordination. Yet, for all the bad blood, Waugh would have warmly applauded his old adversary's dismissal of COHQ as, 'H.M.S. *Wimbledon* – all rackets and balls'.[82]

For the rest of his career allegations of empire-building, over-staffing, and extravagance would plague Mountbatten. The loudest complaints concerned the size of his staff in south-east Asia, and even during his brief tenure as Viceroy he was accused of finding jobs for the boys. While the charge carried less credence in 1947, Combined Operations did set a precedent for SEAC in terms of unnecessary posts, underemployed flunkies, and an over-elaborate headquarters. In his official biography, Philip Ziegler set out the case for the defence, arguing that, 'Elegance need not denote idleness or incompetence … Mountbatten being what he was, efficiency and extravagance went hand in hand'. To be fair, much of this criticism emanated from unreconstructed defenders of service autonomy. Hunkered down inside the War Office or the Admiralty these traditionalists articulated a blinkered and wholly outdated view of amphibious warfare, insisting that anyone seconded to an irregular, long-haired outfit like Combined Operations should never forget where their first loyalty lay. This after all was an organisation with the temerity to set up a 'rival navy', and was headed by a maverick always a law unto himself.[83] Woe betide anyone who went native, and found a residency at Richmond Terrace eventful and even on occasion fun. Unrepentant, an evangelistic Adviser's counter-strategy was to spread the word that working at COHQ was an exciting, if sometimes quirky, experience. Nowhere was the quirkiness more evident than in Combined Operations' scientific establishments, and, as we shall see in Chapter Ten, Mountbatten tacitly approved his boffins' indifference to military decorum.

Rumours of the old-boy network running rife within COHQ clearly reached the highest levels of government. In retirement Mountbatten loved to recall his retort when Churchill queried the appointment of Sir Harold Wernher as 'Co-ordinator of Ministry and Service Facilities' or, as the COSC first labelled the post, 'transport director'. Wernher was a former soldier and successful businessman who had married the sister of the Marquis of Milford Haven's wife, prompting an already sceptical PM to ask, "Isn't this fellow some relation of yours?" The swift reply was, "Not so close as Duncan Sandys is to you!" Here was a cocksure and super-confident Mountbatten drawing attention to the speed with which Churchill's son-in-law had achieved ministerial office after being invalided out of the Army. Wernher's early Whitehall battles brought only a modest return, with the notable exception of the jerrican, initially ordered via the Admiralty because the War Office was so obdurate: the savings in fuel, let alone the sheer convenience, were enormous, and successive generations of squaddies would be forever grateful to Dickie's brother-in-law twice removed. Far greater achievements would come in the build-up to D-Day, not least his liaison role in the construction of the Mulberry artificial harbours. Wernher ended the war a major-general, his rank reflecting the Army Council's belated admission that here was someone who from the outset had perceived the centrality of logistics to the waging of industrial war.[84] He wouldn't have found himself in the position he did without Mountbatten's strenuous lobbying of the Chiefs of Staff. On this occasion, at least, nepotism worked.

Raiding, and promotion to Chief of Combined Operations

As will become clear when considering the controversy surrounding the Dieppe raid, the Chiefs of Staff were never entirely successful in clarifying Combined Operations' remit re operational planning. In May 1942 a directive established the nature of Mountbatten's executive authority, not least the extent of his accountability to the COSC. Yet the order was open to interpretation, and the reality of mounting an operation invariably differed from what in theory constituted the correct procedure.[85] So long as raids remained relatively modest there was no obvious tension between force commanders and COHQ, and little evidence of divided loyalties. Problems arose once projected raids became far more ambitious in intent. Large-scale operations overseas in which Combined Operations played a substantial role, say in the Mediterranean or the Indian Ocean, saw differences hammered out on the spot with few serious reverberations back home. The framework for mounting raids would prove overly complicated and involve far too many intermediate commanders, but in January 1942 Jock Hughes-Hallett was deputed to coordinate all future operations. He and his staff liaised with the appointed force commanders through every stage of preparation and rehearsal, although those officers heading a designated operation were not obliged to accept COHQ's advice and material support. At the point of execution it was the force commanders who held direct responsibility for the success or otherwise of the raid.[86]

A last vestige of the old regime was a Boxing Day return to the Lofoten Islands, anticipated by the enemy and thus speedily curtailed; and, a day later, the hard-fought occupation of two islands located 300 miles down the coastline, Vaagso and Maaloy. Charles Haydon again lead a joint Anglo-Norwegian commando force, in a well-executed operation that demolished an assortment of factories and utilities, inflicted heavy losses on the Germans in terms of personnel and merchant shipping, and secured over 70 recruits for Norway's exile army. The scale of the dual operation, and crucially, the level of inter-service collaboration, were unprecedented. A transitional event, the Vaagso raid offered confirmation of all that Keyes had achieved, while signalling Combined Operations' future potential for success.[87]

For all Mountbatten's grand ambitions and fine intentions only ten raids were carried out in the first six months of 1942. As summer approached he and his staff were acutely aware that this remained a modest tally. Any sensitivity re accusations of underachievement arose out of the fact that the two most spectacular raids – at Bruneval and St Nazaire – were planned and executed much earlier in the year. However worthy, all other raids appeared something of an anti-climax, especially when matched against the ambitious schedule Hughes-Hallett had submitted to Mountbatten for approval on 23 January. An assault on Dieppe was already seen as the climax to this first phase of raiding, with the assumption that by June sufficient vessels would be available to land a division. Interestingly, in light of the fact that the actual raid on Dieppe was cancelled and then resurrected as the disastrous 'Operation Jubilee', Hughes-Hallett's original schedule envisaged a repeat raid. Like Mountbatten after the cancellation of 'Operation Rutter', he and his team argued that the enemy would be taken completely by surprise. In this version of events engineers reinforcing the port's defences after the initial raid would be wiped out. Clearly, no-one at this early stage could see that German sappers would be hard pressed to make Dieppe's fortifications better than they already were. Sadly, no-one ever did arrive at this conclusion. Yet the absurdity of attacking a convenient ferry terminal twice paled into insignificance by comparison with the major operation Hughes-Hallett planned for mid-summer: 'we visualised a landing on the south bank of the Somme to seize a beach head through which a large force of armoured cars could pass and make a quick dash towards Paris.' Six weeks later the captain answered Churchill's query as to what initiative might be taken should Russia buckle under the weight of the Germans' springtime offensive. This time Hughes-Hallett suggested seizing the Cherbourg peninsula and recapturing the Channel Islands. The Army saw this idea as confirmation that Combined Operations was wholly out of touch with harsh military reality. Brooke again articulated the absurdity of these ideas when torpedoing a subsequent plan for the Brigade of Guards to invade Alderney.[88]

Given that in July 1942 it would be Mountbatten who convinced FDR to curb his generals' enthusiasm for premature madcap incursions, it's ironic that less than six months earlier he was displaying a similar mentality, *and* rewarding his chief planner with an advancement as rapid as his own. Hughes-Hallett may have seriously underestimated the German Army's capacity for dogged resistance, but not that of his enemies inside Whitehall. Wisely, he declined his commanding officer's offer to arrange an early promotion to commodore.[89] This was Dickie Mountbatten, master of the universe. In the spring of 1942 he clearly felt that he could fix anything. Of course this was largely due to his appointment as a chief of staff. But it was also because a resurgent Combined Operations had got off to a flying start. The winter expedition to Norway could clearly be counted a success, and the raid on Bruneval, a tracking station north of Le Havre, was a brilliant *coup de main*. On the night of 27 February 1942 around 100 paratroopers, sappers, and technicians landed behind a large cliff-top villa and adjacent radar dish. It took less than three hours for the raiders to occupy the house and outpost, seize a vital piece of equipment, capture three operators, fight their way down to the beach, and be whisked away by waiting landing craft – all for the loss of one man killed, seven wounded, and seven missing. Both execution and planning were exemplary, and the atmosphere inside COHQ must have been exultant.[90]

Given that the raid on St Nazaire had strong echoes of Keyes' attack upon the U-boat pens at Zeebrugge, it's ironic that the destruction of the lock gate is regarded as Mountbatten's most audacious achievement at Combined Operations. After the war this was the operation he always highlighted, and it's no coincidence that as First Sea Lord he gave Peter Lucas Phillips all the help he could in researching *The Greatest Raid Of All*. The author's acknowledgements are a who's who of everyone who planned and participated in the raid, and the book is very much the insiders' account of what took place. Over six decades later the attack on the dry dock at St Nazaire retains its reputation as the ultimate Brits at their best adventure, and Dickie Mountbatten is still seen as the driving force behind the operation – the man who insisted that the ship ramming the lock gate could not simply be left there but would have to be blown up.[91] He always maintained that the idea of denying the *Tirpitz* access to the only Atlantic port available to such a huge battleship arose out of a lunchtime conversation with his close friend and confidant, Charles Lambe. As Director of Plans at the Admiralty, Lambe was acutely aware of the danger to Allied shipping if the captain of the *Tirpitz* felt confident that any damage sustained while raiding in the Atlantic could be repaired within the comparative safety of the Normandie Dock. Hughes-Hallett maintained that St Nazaire was already seen as a possible target: an expedition could arrive at the mouth of the Loire undetected, and retain an element of surprise by riding the estuary shoals on the spring high tide.

Explicitly in Hughes-Hallett's version, and implicitly in both Bernard Fergusson's and Lucas Phillips' semi-authorised accounts, the admiral seen as least supportive of the operation is Sir Charles Forbes. As C-in-C Plymouth, Forbes was technically responsible for the raid. A scarcely disguised scepticism reflected his generally poor opinion of the upstart Mountbatten. The latter encouraged the view that critical changes to the original plan, notably the transfer of commandos from the *Campbeltown* to the more vulnerable motor launches, were imposed by the Admiralty, largely at Forbes' instigation.[92]

Only four out of the 18 coastal craft that sailed from Falmouth on 26 March 1942 returned, and over half of the soldiers and sailors who stormed ashore the following night were taken prisoner. One in four who took part in the raid was killed, with a substantial number of survivors seriously wounded. A roughly comparable number of Germans died, the majority when the *Campbeltown* exploded at noon on the day after the attack; other casualties were sustained during the initial fighting, and when delayed charges destroyed key installations around the basin. With over 200 POWs and nearly 170 dead, British losses were exceptionally high, albeit modest when compared with the carnage of Dieppe.[93] An astonishing five VCs was scarce compensation for so much tragedy, especially as two of the awards were posthumous. Yet 'Operation Chariot' was a truly heroic enterprise, and for a hard-pressed nation a rare morale-booster at a time when all frontline news was consistently bad. Crucially, the raid left the Normandie Dock wrecked for the rest of the war, with the *Tirpitz* forced to remain in Norwegian waters.[94]

The third best-known raid, other than Dieppe, did not occur until the end of 1942, and yet its origins lie in developments earlier in the year. While Churchill had expressed his distaste for 'pinprick raids', Mountbatten had set a target of one minor assault every fortnight or so; if only to disrupt routine among the defenders, and remind them that an attack could occur at any time in any place. One tiny but brutally effective unit regularly crossing the Channel was the Small-Scale Raiding Force. This group was virtually a law unto itself, but normal procedure was for COHQ's Search Committee to submit targets to an Examination Committee. Chaired by Wildman-Lushington, and including future Tory minister Antony Head, this was a scrutiny body which recommended expeditions to Combined Operations' Council. Later renamed the Executive, the most senior committee inside COHQ would initiate an operational plan, and forward the more ambitious schemes to the COSC for final approval. Once an operation was up and running then Mountbatten monitored its progress assiduously, suffering the agonies of the helpless father while the raid was actually under way. He himself came up with some of the most outlandish ideas, all of which were quietly dumped by his indulgent junior colleagues.[95]

By the spring of 1942 COHQ's various committees were fast-tracking small-scale operations, while at the same time exploring the potential of new weaponry and equipment. Much of this kit was being developed in Southsea by Captain Tom Hussey's team at the Combined Operations Development Centre. Hussey was a near lifelong friend of Mountbatten's, the two men first meeting in 1917. The CODC was later incorporated into COXE, appropriately located at Appledore: north Devon was chosen for the Experimental Establishment as its coastline had several features similar to that of northern France. Hussey became the grandly named Director of Experiments for Operational Requirements, liaising with the Royal Navy in a distinctly hit and miss programme of weapons development: complementing COXE was the Admiralty's Directorate of Miscellaneous Weapon Development, known affectionately by all those who worked there as the 'Wheezers and Dodgers'. One of the latter's less eccentric department heads was N.S. Norway, an RNVR lieutenant commander better known as Nevil Shute. For the first 20 years or so after the war Shute was an enormously popular novelist in Britain and Australia, drawing heavily upon his expertise as an applied scientist in the 'warfare state'.[96]

A priority for Tom Hussey's original establishment was penetrating enemy-held harbours to attack shipping, and specially designed canoes were seen as the best means of securing entry.[97] H.G. Hasler, a Marine major attached to CODC, gained approval for an operation to disrupt blockade-running out of Bordeaux. In June 1942 Dalton's successor at the Ministry of Economic Warfare, Lord Selborne, urged action against vessels operating out of the Gironde estuary; and on 7 December Hasler led six folding two-man canoes (the 'cockles') up river and into the port. The idea was to attach limpet mines to any available merchant vessels. Although only Hasler and his canoe-mate survived, having crossed the Pyrenees and made their way through Spain to Gibraltar, it was discovered after the war that four ships had been damaged. Reports at the time suggested a positive impact inside Vichy France in terms of boosting support for the Resistance. Churchill of course found the whole enterprise absolutely splendid.[98]

It was no surprise that 'Blondie' Hasler made it back as he was the quintessential cat that walked alone, but 'Operation Frankton' was demonstrably a suicide mission. The final rehearsal had been a shambles, and, had it not been for Mountbatten's strong personal backing, the mission would almost certainly have been cancelled.[99] Not surprisingly, a raid which saw ten out of 12 die merited no mention in the Ministry of Information's 1943 history of Combined Operations – a surprisingly revealing booklet, which contrived to be both understated and triumphalist (sometimes in the same sentence), and which made remarkably few references to Lord Louis Mountbatten. By the mid-1950s, costly and questionable endeavour had become heroic self-sacrifice, arguably the dominant trope in British war films of the time. The filming of *The Cockleshell Heroes* depended heavily upon the cooperation of the Royal Navy, and, despite the use of fictional characters, José Ferrer's production offered a convincing portrayal of how the attack was planned and carried out. Yet, notwithstanding a particularly impressive performance by Trevor Howard, *The Cockleshell Heroes* enjoyed mixed fortunes on both sides of the Atlantic. Its British premiere was graced by the two survivors of the real raid and their families, all of whom dutifully lined up at the start of the evening in order to meet the Duke of Edinburgh and his uncle. Needless to say the First Sea Lord was the driving force behind the book of the film, featuring prominently in the early chapters of Hasler's collaborative effort with Peter Lucas Phillips, and contributing a brief foreword.[100]

The Prime Minister found 'Dickie's show at St Nazaire, though small in scale ... very bracing'.[101] Yet wrecking the Normandie Dock was seen as a vindication, not a reward: Churchill had already decided that Mountbatten should be redesignated Chief of Combined Operations (CCO). The former Adviser's promotion to Acting Vice-Admiral, with comparable honorary ranks in the Army and RAF, came as a complete surprise to the three service chiefs. The First Sea Lord, still absorbing the news that Alan Brooke was to succeed him as Chairman of the Chiefs of Staff Committee, objected strongly. The head of the Navy anticipated resentment and discontent, thereby undermining 'confidence in my leadership' – Pound would be seen as a party to Dickie's rapid advancement, or else appear powerless in the face of royal and/or prime ministerial patronage.[102] The head of the Army was less forthright, but he saw scant need for Mountbatten to attend the COSC, 'where he frequently wasted both his time and ours'. Brooke rejected the very principle of a 'Chief of Combined Operations' on the grounds that every operation was combined and that in essence Mountbatten fulfilled a support role for his three new colleagues: 'It was certainly not intended that he should direct combined strategy'.[103] The quality of the new chief's input to his first full COSC meetings merely fuelled Brooke's prejudice. Mountbatten already knew that in the CIGS he had more than met his match. Invariably he would defer to Brooke, viewing him in the same way as he viewed Andrew Cunningham.[104] Fading yet still astute, Dudley Pound must surely have seen that Mountbatten related to him in a more relaxed, and instinctively less deferential, fashion. Quiet resentment was fuelled by Churchill responding to the First Sea Lord's objections with a no-nonsense reply to all three chiefs, making clear that his mind was made up: the Chief of Combined Operations would attend COS meetings 'as a full member whenever major issues are in question', as well as for matters directly related to his own particular remit.[105]

An eagle-eyed Philip Ziegler noted that the Chiefs of Staff quietly made their point via the minutes of COSC meetings, with the Secretariat denying Mountbatten equal status until well into the summer. The solitary exception to this procedural revenge was on 20 March 1942 – the one occasion that the Prime Minister took the chair.[106] Mountbatten in later life was always eager to portray his dealings with the Chiefs of Staff as harmonious and productive. He told Richard Hough that Charles Portal was an especially close friend, and this was no doubt true. Less convincingly, he also claimed to enjoy a close working relationship with Dudley Pound. Interviewed by John Terraine, Mountbatten maintained a similar line. Endeavouring to be more honest with himself, he nevertheless portrayed his dealings with Alan Brooke in a very positive light. Again, the parallel with Andrew Cunningham emerges, in that posterity must record how highly the tyro war lord was viewed by these genuinely great men – mighty warriors unhesitatingly welcoming one of their own into the pantheon.[107]

The Chief of Combined Operations appears genuinely to have had no idea why his dealings with Pound were so painful. Thus he failed to appreciate just how much the First Sea Lord viewed him as a threat. When Andrew Cunningham came home from the Mediterranean in April 1942 he made a courtesy call at the Admiralty. He found Pound 'in great distress', and fearful that Churchill might force him out in favour of Mountbatten. An astonished Cunningham – perhaps the most obvious successor should the post become vacant – insisted that his old friend, 'glue himself to his chair'. Yet Pound was not a well man, and sickness fuelled insecurity. There is of course no clear evidence that the Prime Minister felt Dickie was ready for the top job. At the same time, the most powerful man in wartime Britain was more than capable of acting on a whim. Thus David Reynolds is not alone in speculating that appointment to the COSC could conceivably have been Churchill's first move in placing his own man at the head of the Navy. In 1964 John Godfrey, the wartime Director of Naval Intelligence, passed on Cunningham's claim to have stiffened Pound's resolve. Entering his final year as Chief of the Defence Staff, Mountbatten insisted that, in the unlikely circumstance of Churchill inviting him to become First Sea Lord, he would have refused: on the grounds that the whole Navy regarded Cunningham as uniquely qualified to assume the post.[108]

Churchill's eagerness to enhance Mountbatten's power and influence might possibly have been encouraged by his fellow Harrovian and anti-appeaser Leo Amery. The Secretary of State for India had after all been urging a revolution inside Whitehall from the moment Chamberlain resigned: the new administration had been a deep disappointment given the survival of so many ministers from the old regime. Amery's readiness to build on the 1935 Government of India Act – opposition to which had so nearly wrecked Churchill's political ambitions – simply fuelled prime ministerial impatience with his old crony's penchant for grand reform, whether that be in southern Asia or closer to home.[109] If the PM had great plans for Dickie then he had no need to draw upon the superior intellect of Leo Amery. The latter met Mountbatten for the first time on 8 February 1942, and came away convinced that, 'he is the kind of man who ought really to be made more use of in this war'. Two months later he was telling a doubtless sceptical Anthony Eden that Mountbatten was quite clearly the coming man. Amery went so far as to advise the Prime Minister that the time was right for a 'super Chief of Staff' to break what he saw as 'the logjam of the common denominator'. The diminutive imperialist sent Mountbatten a copy of his memo, inviting comments. The recipient wisely chose not to put his thoughts on paper. Amery was about 20 years ahead of his time, and it's just as well that he never had a chance to argue his case with Alan Brooke. The same is true for Jock Hughes-Hallett, who around the same time sent the CCO a lengthy paper on how to extend his personal authority, and at the same time orchestrate a radical restructuring of the Whitehall war machine. This ambitious, wholly unrealistic document was no bolt out of the blue as it clearly bore the Mountbatten stamp. Like Hughes-Hallett, it was obvious whom Amery had in mind for the task of super strategist; and across the dining table over the next few months Mountbatten portrayed himself as a twentieth-century Alexander, forever struggling to slice through the Gordian knot of wartime bureaucracy.[110]

Hughes-Hallett's initial optimism regarding Mountbatten's promotion clearly waned across the spring of 1942. Yet inside COHQ the Naval Adviser had been by no means alone in celebrating his boss's arrival at the top table: 'At one stride our organisation had penetrated the very centre and citadel of Power. We were now to work for a man with access to all secrets, and for one who could, and would, be an advocate at top level for any plan.'[111] Note the veiled reference to Enigma, and, as we shall see in the next chapter, Mountbatten for the first time gained access to the hidden secrets of Bletchley Park. No doubt discovering the full extent of Britain's cipher-breaking operations made a deep impression, but the greatest cause for celebration was becoming a vice-admiral at 41, an age three years below Beatty, and two years younger than Nelson. Although he raised his flag in an acting capacity, he knew that even at his substantive rank he was racing up the Navy List – with a firm promise from Churchill that an eventual resumption of normal duties would bring another *Illustrious*-type command. Equally pleasing was appointment as an honorary lieutenant-general and honorary air marshal. Mountbatten later denied that he was tempted to acquire the appropriate uniforms, but he would have done so given half the chance. How could someone so obsessed with costume and dressing up pass the chance to strut around in the full rig of not just one but two other services – especially when this privilege was normally reserved for the most senior members of the Royal Family? Somewhat disingenuously he informed his oldest daughter how the Army and the RAF were both keen for him to secure their uniforms, but that a lack of both confidence and coupons was holding him back![112] Edwina knew Dickie was straining at the leash to kit himself out with the full regalia, and that only service sensitivity held him back. She offered Patricia a sardonic slant on daddy's 'Triphibious Command': 'General Goering will be put into the shade by his manifold ranks, uniforms and decorations and dramatic and theatrical position.'[113]

Within weeks Patricia could judge for herself. Mountbatten fixed her a flight home so that she might join the Wrens. Now that the whole family was back in Britain, Edwina felt free to intensify her war work. Despite an already packed diary, in July 1942 she assumed full responsibility for the 70,000 volunteers and cadets who had swelled the wartime ranks of the St John Ambulance Brigade. As Superintendent-in-Chief of the Nursing Division, she had attained the most senior post available to a woman. Even allowing for the exigencies of war, Edwina's rapid rise to the top was remarkable. Her appointment was announced not long after news was finally released of Dickie's promotion.[114] The Mountbattens' friends and admirers applauded the duality of their dedication to the war effort, while privately expressing astonishment that a couple too often dismissed between the wars as lightweight and loose-living should now enjoy positions of exceptional power and influence.

Any enjoyment was tempered by the wartime loss of close friends and relations, not least one of Dickie's and Noel's closest chums, the Duke of Kent. George VI's younger brother died on 25 August when the Sunderland he was flying in smashed into a Scottish hillside hidden by mist, and then burst into flames. Four days later Coward and the King were in tears as the coffin was carried into Windsor Chapel. So too was the lachrymose Dickie, standing to attention beside a grim-faced but dry-eyed Edwina. For an hour or so he mused upon the death of a shallow, scandal-haunted royal sibling who, for all his moral peccadilloes, was guaranteed to liven up a wet weekend at Adsdean or Broadlands.[115] Yet surely Mountbatten's mind must have wandered in the course of the funeral service. Here he was mourning the loss of a single man, albeit a close friend, but only ten days before over 1,000 soldiers and sailors had died in the course of a single morning. Operation Jubilee, the resurrected attack on Dieppe, had been COHQ's most ambitious raid. It was also the organisation's costliest raid, for which – rightly or wrongly – the Chief of Combined Operations was held directly responsible. As he said his last goodbye to Prince George, offered Edwina a lift back into town, and steeled himself for a further round of inquiries into what went wrong, could it possibly have crossed Mountbatten's troubled mind that Dieppe was a controversy which would continue to rage long after his own sudden escape from earth's mortal coil?

8

THE DIEPPE RAID, 19 AUGUST 1942

> Mountbatten gave us [4 Commando] a lecture – said he wished he was going with us. Once we realised where we were going, I think 200 blokes thought, 'I wish he were going instead of us'. But yes, very nice talk. We cheered him – off he went.[1]

The bigger picture (1)

'It was the best of times, it was the worst of times … it was the spring of hope, it was the winter of despair ….' Dickens might well have been writing about Britain in 1942. Having escaped invasion and weathered the Blitz, both government and people could at last contemplate more than mere survival. With the United States and the Soviet Union now fighting alongside the British Empire, a bruised, weary, and petulant nation could hear Churchill talk of victory, and with some trepidation start planning for peace. Yet anticipating rapid defeat was manifestly absurd given the shattering extent of Japan's military success in the Far East; the ambition and sheer audacity of Germany's march on Moscow; the relentless, remorseless nature of Axis recovery in the Mediterranean; and the inexorable destruction of Allied shipping in both the Arctic and the Atlantic. While events conspired to fuel deep pessimism, most obviously the fall of Singapore, ministers and military could take heart from the United States' adherence to a strategy of 'Germany First', in other words placing a high priority on the war in Europe and endeavouring to contain Japan. Acknowledging that the Allies' first task was to destroy the strongest partner in the Axis had been a key outcome of the 'Arcadia conference', hastily arranged in Washington after America's entry into the war. Prioritising the war in Europe marked a major blow to the ambitions and intentions of the US Navy – its Chief of Naval Operations, Admiral Ernie King, was notoriously hostile towards the British and their empire. The same summit saw the establishment of a Combined Chiefs of Staff Committee. The CCS was intended to facilitate joint decision-making between the three service chiefs in London and their American counterparts, the Joint Chiefs of Staff.[2]

Despite a morale-shattering evacuation of the Pacific Rim, American strategists were surprised how speedily containment could convert to counter-attack. Admiral

Nimitz and General Douglas MacArthur's grinding assault on Japan's over-stretched fleet and remote conquests contrasted with the slow pace of 'Operation Bolero', the establishment in Britain of an Allied invasion force. Failure to initiate a large military build-up, so long as German U-boats continued to inflict major losses on mercantile shipping, was acknowledged by the Admiralty in April 1942, when George C. Marshall, the US Army's Chief of Staff, visited London for the first time. Marshall was surprised by his hosts' wariness regarding an early liberation of mainland Europe, and by the force with which Brooke and his colleagues urged caution. In July 1942 the Americans accepted postponement of their invasion plan, 'Operation Roundup', and conceded the case against 'Sledgehammer', their revised proposal for an emergency seizure of Cherbourg and its hinterland.[3] Both Churchill and Roosevelt were acutely aware that the British veto of a rapid return to France encouraged those voices in Washington insistent on Japan as the principal enemy. The two leaders recognised the need for GIs to see action across the Atlantic before the end of 1942. The result would be 'Operation Torch', intended to squeeze Rommel out of North Africa: in late autumn Anglo-American forces landed in Morocco and Algeria, and despite demoralising losses at the hands of the *Afrika Korps* engineered a successful link up with the Eighth Army. For generals like Mark Clark and George Patton, adamant that the British showed the Germans far too much respect, Tunisia offered a harsh lesson: the ferocity of fighting at Kasserine in February 1943 made Eisenhower appreciate why Brooke and his colleagues had dismissed Sledgehammer as sheer madness.[4]

The first year of formal alliance saw politeness, formality, and grand gestures of fraternity and bonhomie disguise irritation, impatience, misunderstanding, and incomprehension. This was a relationship that was 'special' for all the wrong reasons, hence the importance of the unique understanding forged by Churchill and Roosevelt. Both men endeavoured to reduce tension, minimise the differences, and keep everyone focussed upon the common cause. They looked to uniformed acolytes with the political nous to over-ride mutual suspicion, both in the boardroom and on the battlefield. Hence the importance to FDR of Eisenhower – and the value the Prime Minister placed on Mountbatten as an envoy welcome in Washington, not least in the White House. Not that Mountbatten at any point in the war enjoyed the power, influence, and respect enjoyed by Ike – although no doubt he was convinced that he did! Eisenhower enjoyed Marshall's trust and respect, but neither Brooke nor Cunningham could ever accept Mountbatten as an equal.

Dwight D. Eisenhower was one of a handful of planners inside the War Department who recognised that Britain's historic approach to securing victory in mainland Europe had been to wear down the enemy by exploiting the Empire's assets and naval mastery in order to impose a blockade, to attack on the flanks, and to support continental allies; scarce manpower would be conserved until such time as a clear military advantage ensured the necessary *coup de grâce*. The bloody experience of the British Expeditionary Force twice in two decades had highlighted the huge cost of a continental commitment.[5] With precious little prospect of defeating Nazi Germany on land, after Dunkirk both prime minister and service chiefs had reverted to type. Churchill did after all have a preference for prizing open Europe's 'soft underbelly', only this time his target was Rome not Constantinople. Britain had to play the long game by, firstly, engaging the enemy on the periphery, notably the Mediterranean and North Africa; secondly, encouraging resistance movements across a wide political spectrum; and thirdly, complementing blockade with a debilitating bomber offensive. Ideally, the German war economy would implode, maintaining military authority across such a huge land mass would become unsustainable, the Axis would collapse in the wake of Italian defeat, and the Third Reich would face political meltdown – at which point the Allied ground forces could intervene. A readiness to preserve life, and a recognition that neither Britain nor the Dominions had the manpower to wage 'industrial war' for more than a very short space of time, rendered such thinking remarkably resilient. This grim, gradualist belief in 'closing the ring' somehow survived the catastrophic failure of Bomber Command's initial offensive, the demonstrable success of the Germans in squashing resistance and ruthlessly exploiting the resources of occupied Europe, the ignominious collapse of colonial power in south-east Asia, and the arrival in London of American military planners eager to engage with an enemy only 22 miles across the Channel.[6]

Yet, it would be wrong to view such pusillanimous thinking as all-pervasive. The highest levels of command never questioned the case for invasion. It was simply that they did not accept an early return to France as the absolute priority, viewing a premature expedition as potentially catastrophic. Field commanders in 1940, such as Brooke and Montgomery, were adamant that so ambitious an undertaking should only go ahead when Allied troops were trained and equipped to fight – and to beat – the finest soldiers in Europe. Similarly, the number of craft and weapons systems required to land and then to support these 'citizen soldiers' would need to be of sufficient quantity as to compensate for most units' lack of combat experience. The deployment of untested troops necessitated exceptionally fine leadership, and both Brooke and Churchill saw a dearth of cool-headed, confident field commanders as further cause for delay. Indeed, without American resolution, an over-cautious prime minister would have postponed D-Day until the following year.[7]

The views and temperament of the CIGS contrasted sharply with his counterpart, who at the outset was deeply suspicious of British intentions. The US Army's Chief of Staff drew heavily upon the strategic thinking of his principal adviser in the War Department, Al Wedemeyer – a well-groomed young colonel whose style, respect for European ways (remarkably, two years had been spent at Germany's staff college, the *Kriegsakademie*), and clarity of thought appealed strongly to Mountbatten. By January 1942 a far more powerful influence was the newly-appointed head of the War Plans Division, Eisenhower.[8] Marshall interpreted 'Germany First' as meaning a massive build-up of men and material in Britain (Operation Bolero), and a coordinated strike on France as soon as the Allies could combine favourable conditions with an overwhelming display of military might: 'Behind such thinking lay the military traditions of the Civil War, and America's abundance of manpower and resources … the United States' classical strategy of applying overwhelming power to annihilate the enemy's forces ….' That 'classical strategy' was, of course, still intact in 1991 and again in 2003. Viewed from the War Department, a fading empire's enthusiasm for energy-draining operations in the Mediterranean and the Middle East was quite simply a distraction from the main task. Furthermore, British strategists' focus on the periphery constituted a critical dissipation of resources; and even the American arsenal, however huge, was incapable of meeting every demand in every theatre of war. Mounting Operation Torch appeased public opinion at home, no doubt to the pleasure of the President. Yet, to devote a significant proportion of America's fighting potential to the Mediterranean, especially when an easy conquest of Italy was such a huge leap of faith, was to acknowledge how quickly Marshall's belief in the one big punch had given way to waging war on a multitude of fronts.[9] Acknowledging this erosion of strategic first principles, in the summer of 1943 the Americans grimly conceded the case for postponing Roundup's successor, 'Operation Overlord', until the following spring.

The bigger picture (2)

That the British two years before D-Day should have blanched at American enthusiasm for a full-scale assault upon the Atlantic Wall is scarcely surprising. Here was a military apparatus finally facing the brutal consequences of imperial overstretch. The hammer blows inflicted since Pearl Harbor had seen the fulfilment of pre-war military advisers' worst-case scenarios. Retreat across the Western Desert would see an ashen-faced Churchill learn of Tobruk's surrender in the middle of an Oval Office meeting with the President.[10] The catastrophic losses of Burma and of the Malayan peninsula, as well as Hong Kong, had been prefaced by the sinking of the *Prince of Wales* and the *Repulse*. Mountbatten, incidentally, believed both ships could have been saved had their admiral, his old adversary Tom Phillips, finally acknowledged the critical impact of air power upon the war at sea.[11] British shipping losses for the first six months of 1942 exceeded those for the whole of 1941, partly because of American reluctance to use the same convoy system as the Royal Navy. As in the Mediterranean, early 1942 saw heavy pressure upon the Home Fleet, witness the success of the *Gneisenau*, *Scharnhorst*, and *Prinz Eugen* in running the gauntlet of Channel air and sea defences.

In such circumstances it seems remarkable that any discussion of invading mainland Europe could have taken place, and yet even before Marshall's first visit to England contingency planning was well under way. Combined Operations argued strongly, and persuasively, that in the medium-term there were simply not enough specialised landing craft to launch even a stripped-down invasion: to mount Sledgehammer would be extremely difficult, and at great cost, thereby delaying the invasion proper.[12] However, Mountbatten found himself in a minority over the issue of where a landing would take place, refusing in March 1942 to endorse the recommendation of the Pas de Calais made by his fellow Combined Commanders, Fighter Command's Sholto Douglas and the Home Forces' Bernard Paget. COHQ accepted the RAF's case that close proximity ensured adequate air cover, but insisted that much further west, on the Normandy coastline, conditions were far more favourable to landing and supplying an invasion force, establishing a firm bridgehead, and facilitating a disciplined withdrawal if required.[13] Brooke, reluctant in any circumstance to send men across the Channel, was sympathetic to Douglas's suggestion that a sustained air battle might force the Germans to redeploy *Luftwaffe* squadrons intended for the Eastern Front. Such a scenario would fulfil the function of a diversionary enterprise in the west without sacrificing an excessive number of British and Canadian troops: 'But to do this a landing must take place within our air umbrella, namely in vicinity of Calais or Boulogne. But Mountbatten was still hankering after a landing near Cherbourg where proper air support is not possible.' The Chiefs of Staff's meeting on 28 March had been 'difficult', and in his diary the CIGS feared that over dinner at Chequers that night Mountbatten might break ranks. Brooke later recalled that, 'Dickie's visits were always dangerous moments and there was no knowing what discussions he might be led into and what he might let us in for!' Yet at the same time Brooke conceded that in presenting a united front to Churchill he found Mountbatten 'most loyal', invariably seeking advice before departure for Chequers, and briefing the Chiefs at their Monday meeting on the Prime Minister's mood over the weekend.[14]

Needless to say, Mountbatten always insisted that his resolute opposition to the shortest route was a key factor in the final choice of the Normandy beaches. Thus, a decisive moment of high drama was when he asserted his authority as a chief of staff, in order to dismiss the Combined Commanders' case for the Pas de Calais. Like Cleopatra's nose there may be a tenuous chain of causality, but this is to ignore the enormous weight of events that separates the speculative planning of early spring 1942 from the detailed analysis that facilitated Overlord 26 months later. In his diary Brooke made no reference to Mountbatten ostentatiously distancing himself from his colleagues; and when Stephen Roskill pointed out the absence of any official record, the response from Broadlands was that 'the minutes rather blurred over the clash'! Clearly something happened as Jock Hughes-Hallett, in his capacity as Naval Adviser at COHQ, attended a Combined Commanders meeting at which Paget berated Mountbatten for 'disloyal and insubordinate' behaviour towards himself and Sholto Douglas. Hughes-Hallett recalled Mountbatten as keeping his cool, but the incident highlights the considerable antipathy and animosity felt towards him in so many quarters of Whitehall.[15] Making an enemy of Paget meant simply adding yet another name to an ever-lengthening list. Here after all was a general who believed that any half-decent soldier could without too much difficulty make his way ashore and engage with the enemy. However, antagonising the C-in-C Fighter Command probably wasn't a good idea given that on 8 April the Chiefs of Staff gave Douglas and Mountbatten responsibility for Roundup as well as Sledgehammer: once heads had been banged together, Brooke raced off to Hendon to welcome Marshall and his entourage.[16]

Here was an American delegation with an agenda largely determined by events unfolding at the opposite end of the European landmass. Given the British Empire's dire circumstances in the spring of 1942 it seems remarkable that the Soviet Union could make ever greater demands for military hardware; and that such a wide spectrum of informed opinion could have sympathised with the campaign for a

'Second Front NOW', orchestrated by that most unlikely of journalistic alliances, the *Daily Express* and the *Daily Worker*. Energised by his encounter with Stalin, and no longer a minister, Lord Beaverbrook delighted left-leaning mavericks on the *Evening Standard* like Michael Foot by endorsing the Communist Party's call for Britain to launch an offensive in the west so as to ease pressure on Soviet forces in the east. This of course was a view shared by Washington, with the President's closest advisers voicing the Joint Chiefs of Staffs' fears of an imminent Russian defeat.[17]

Those fears were increased once Stalin had signalled a readiness to discuss armistice terms with Germany if his allies in the west failed to accelerate aid and take positive action. Whether or not the General Secretary was bluffing, such provocative remarks could not be ignored.[18] Nor were they when Marshall and Harry Hopkins reached London in April 1942. Hopkins, an Anglophile 'New Dealer' and a key intermediary between Roosevelt and Churchill, conveyed FDR's concern over Britain's apparent indifference to the fragile state of the Red Army.[19] Hopkins summarised popular opinion back home as impatient for action across the Channel, and sympathetic to those arguing that the full weight of American firepower be directed against Japan.[20] Marshall submitted Eisenhower's proposal for Roundup, a full-scale invasion a year hence; and for a contingency operation, Sledgehammer. The latter was a diversionary assault on the French coastline, landing five British and American divisions before the onset of winter should the Soviet Union seem on the point of surrender. Brooke and his colleagues, although privately alarmed, calmly disguised their true feelings and played for time – the softly, softly approach was a convenient tactic for dealing with Churchill, and might similarly work with the Joint Chiefs of Staff. Force commanders were appointed, with an operational base inside COHQ: 'It only took them a fortnight to confirm that a large-scale Anglo-American landing in 1942 was out of the question.'[21]

Even if the British could contain and eventually curtail American enthusiasm for launching an invasion, whether large or small, it was more and more obvious that a gesture would need to be made. Irrespective of the strategic case for a major incursion across the Channel, a means of appeasing the Americans must be found. Sledgehammer eventually envisaged six divisions, but any operation conducted under the auspices of Combined Operations would by definition be a much more modest affair, albeit on a scale far greater than any raids to date. Furthermore, in late spring Churchill did feel obliged to commit British ground forces to 'a landing on the Continent in August or September 1942', subject to the availability of suitable landing craft.[22] This unexpected commitment was not in response to pressure from the United States, but in order to appease the Soviet Union,

Up to this point the Soviet ambassador in London, Ivan Maisky, had made little headway in advancing the case for a Second Front. Maisky, like his former boss, Litvinov, always maintained great affection for the British. The same could scarcely be said of Vyacheslav Molotov. The Soviet foreign minister flew to Britain in May 1942 to confront Churchill. The cold reception Molotov received in London contrasted with the warmer welcome he was given in Washington. The Roosevelt administration refused to make a clear commitment, but did accede to Molotov's request for a joint communiqué noting the urgent need for a Second Front.[23] The British saw Sledgehammer as dead and buried, but across the Atlantic it remained very much alive, abandoned only in late July after the Joint Chiefs signed up to Operation Torch.[24] Nevertheless, when Molotov came back to Britain both Downing Street and the Foreign Office remained adamant that no invasion was imminent. Yet clearly so stark a message could not be conveyed to the Kremlin, hence Churchill's confidential aide-mémoire. Drafted by the Chiefs of Staff and intended as a holding operation, the document was seen by Stalin as a hard and fast commitment:

> Clearly, it would not further either the Russian cause or that of the Allies as a whole if, for the sake of action at any price, we embarked on some operation which ended in disaster or gave the enemy the opportunity for glorification at our discomfiture. It is impossible to say in advance whether the situation will be such as to make this operation feasible when the time comes. We can therefore make no promises in the matter but provided that it appears sound and sensible we shall put our plans into effect.[25]

Never mind the rider, both Moscow and Washington could insist – and did – that the British were pledged to cross the Channel before the summer was out. The means by which they would do so was signalled in what one may assume was Mountbatten's contribution to the draft statement: not only would raids 'against selected points on the Continent ... increase in size and scope as the summer goes on', but the random nature of these raids would prevent the enemy from reinforcing his armies in the east.[26]

As we shall see, by this stage plans for 'Operation Rutter', COHQ's ambitious expedition to Dieppe, were at an advanced stage. Mountbatten was eager that there should be no misunderstanding among the Americans as to the limited nature of his forthcoming enterprise. Whereas in late spring 1942 the three service chiefs and the Prime Minister could see an advantage in not drawing attention to obvious differences over Sledgehammer and Roundup, the CCO argued that Washington should be in no doubt as to the real nature of any cross-Channel incursion. The Chiefs of Staff were still reassuring the Americans that Bolero was proceeding apace, but by late May mixed messages began reaching the White House. The Prime Minister fuelled alarm within the administration when he informed FDR of Mountbatten's imminent arrival in the United States: 'Dickie will explain to you the difficulties of 1942 when he arrives.'[27] Despatching Dickie to Washington was a brilliant move by Churchill, even though later in life Mountbatten suggested it was a case of his fellow chiefs of staff coming to appreciate that he was 'the only person' capable of fulfilling such a delicate mission: 'My job in Washington was probably the most important job I had to do in the war. I had to persuade Roosevelt and his advisers that American strategy and expectations needed re-thinking.' His task was made no easier by the two allies' contrasting fortunes in North Africa and the Pacific – on the day of Mountbatten's arrival, the Japanese Navy sustained a cataclysmic reversal of fortunes at the Battle of Midway. Understandably, both military and civilians were exultant, and in no mood to take lessons in grand strategy from an Englishman better qualified to speak as victim not victor in any discussion of air power at sea. Yet ironically, victory at Midway called into question Ernie King's argument that Japan remained in the ascendancy, and therefore America's capacity to wage war in the Pacific was still adversely affected by giving Europe priority.[28]

Even Admiral King recognised that Lord Louis Mountbatten was no ordinary visitor, and in the heart of the Republic the envoy's closeness to the Royal Family remained his strongest card. Roosevelt was no closet royalist, but he retained fond memories of the King and Queen's 1939 state visit.[29] In any case, Mountbatten had made a favourable impression on the President 12 months earlier. Indeed there were few movers and shakers in Washington who failed to take note of someone so close to both George VI and the Prime Minister. For this reason alone Mountbatten was a man worth cultivating, but both business and socialising were made that much easier by his open, easy-going personality. Ever the charmer, Mountbatten knew how to put on a show. Not only did he look good and could work a room, but a very real strength was the elimination of those character traits which for nigh on 200 years had rendered the English upper classes so deeply unattractive to all but the most Anglophile of Boston brahmins. Here was a man who, in the eyes of his hosts, appeared amiable, amenable, affable, and approachable. Part natural and part cultivated, this was someone who oozed self-assurance, but tempered his arrogance by making the most of his youthful image – he showed deference where necessary, and disguised his indifference or antipathy when an opponent failed to be convinced. Mountbatten's charm could be seductive, but, according to Marshall's shrewd aide and confidant, Al Wedemeyer, not that seductive: American commanders were well aware that his confidence in the Oval Office was at odds with his more humble standing in the military hierarchy back home.[30]

Wedemeyer and Mountbatten had been in regular contact since the previous April. The cerebral colonel saw Mountbatten as energetic, enthusiastic, and receptive to new ideas. That didn't necessarily mean he trusted him.[31] Indifferent to decorum, Wedemeyer and George Marshall had visited COHQ before being briefed by the three service ministries. Surprisingly, Marshall and his host had got on like a house on fire, even though they were never as close as Mountbatten claimed. Marshall rightly saw Mountbatten as very much the junior member of the Chiefs of Staff Committee. No doubt the CCO purposely distanced himself from his older, less affable colleagues – he was after all, to quote one recent writer on Dieppe, 'a very wily cove indeed'.[32] The tour of Richmond Terrace proved a great success, with the Chair of the Joint Chiefs singularly impressed by the degree of service integration. Mountbatten recalled cracking a weak joke about his staff all getting along fine because everyone spoke English:

> And then, suddenly, the penny dropped, and on the spur of the moment I said:
>   'Come to think of it, General, you Americans talk English too, after a fashion. Why don't you send some American soldiers, sailors and airmen to join us in this headquarters?'

The idea appealed to Marshall immediately, and that is how the first integrated Allied Headquarters came into existence.[33]

Within a month nine staff officers had crossed the Atlantic, headed by a brigadier-general: the secondment of someone as high-ranking as Lucian Trescott showed how seriously Washington viewed joint planning.[34] Mountbatten threw himself wholeheartedly into inter-allied collaboration, but for a long time he found himself battling with the military establishment's patronising, condescending view of 'the colonials'. Not being drawn from the English upper classes, and being himself an outsider, this almost sanctimonious air of superiority was always alien to him. Unlike so many of his peers he knew the United States very well, and many of his friends lived on the Eastern seaboard and the West Coast. He liked Americans – and crucially, they liked him.

Marshall and Hopkins had left London in April 1942 promising to meet Mountbatten's demand for twice as many landing craft, and up to 1,000 power units for Port of London barges.[35] Only a month later Eisenhower had arrived, eager to meet Britain's most assiduous student of amphibious operations: reportedly 'vigorous, intelligent and courageous', Vice-Admiral Mountbatten seemed ideally qualified to command an invasion force. Unfortunately Eisenhower announced Mountbatten's suitability as a supreme commander at his first meeting with the Chiefs of Staff. Brooke broke the embarrassed silence by politely pointing out that Mountbatten was in fact sitting across the table; and, without saying a word, made it perfectly clear what he, Pound, and Portal thought of their visitor's naive suggestion.[36] It need hardly be said that for Mountbatten it was love at first sight. He and the like-minded Ike forged a formidable partnership, formalised in June 1942 when the two men were given joint responsibility for the training of all forces intending to cross the Channel. Eisenhower continued to champion Mountbatten as a chief of staff enjoying near absolute authority for orchestrating the invasion. While Marshall was sympathetic to the suggestion, the three service chiefs in London were adamantly opposed to such an appointment.[37]

Mountbatten was clearly viewed as the coming man in Washington. Yet, after a private meeting with FDR on 9 June 1942, his stock fell sharply. The two men talked for over five hours, leaving Mountbatten delighted with the outcome.[38] George Marshall and the Secretary for War, Henry Stimson, had been denied the opportunity to contest the claim of this 'extremely articulate Britisher' that an invasion in 1942 was near inconceivable: the Allies could at a stretch deploy three American and 13 British divisions, and yet no less than 27 enemy divisions were currently based in France. Nor could the RAF, along with a token presence from the USAAF, match the *Luftwaffe*'s 1,500 front-line aircraft. However, the biggest constraint – and here Mountbatten could speak with authority – was the acute shortage of landing craft. A crude estimate was that only 4,000 men, around a third of a division, could be put ashore at any one time: the Americans envisaged a mighty task force, but in 1942 all Combined Operations could offer was a cross-Channel shuttle service.[39] It could be no consolation to those killed or wounded at Dieppe, but the raid was a brutal –

some will no doubt say callous – vindication of Mountbatten's presidential briefing. His private meeting with Roosevelt fuelled mistrust in Washington, with senior advisers and commanders revising their view of the Allies' rising star.[40] Mountbatten had to work his passage back into favour, but his task was made easier by the fact that he never alienated Eisenhower. Nor, crucially, would the President tolerate criticism of someone so close to Churchill; and someone so at ease with himself, even when assiduously brokering an agreement between two of the most powerful men in the world.

Wedemeyer memorably described Mountbatten as, 'John the Baptist laying the groundwork for the great strategic evangelist Winston Churchill'.[41] The Allied messiah had reason to be satisfied with his ambassador's lightning visit to Washington. After a gruelling over-night flight from Quebec, Mountbatten went straight to Chequers, where the Prime Minister interrogated him until first light. Philip Ziegler noted that five hours later the CCO was reporting to the Chiefs of Staff, after which he worked at Richmond Terrace until 9.30pm, by which time he must have been absolutely exhausted.[42] Mountbatten had reassured Churchill that Roosevelt would be receptive to landings in North Africa *if* they demonstrably provided GIs in England with sustained combat experience. Thus, when Churchill met FDR on 21 June he was confident of agreement on what would become Operation Torch.[43] What he did not anticipate was an assumption on the part of the President that a major raid on Dieppe might help him lever the Joint Chiefs into sacrificing Sledgehammer: had Mountbatten exceeded his brief in exaggerating the scale and significance of Operation Rutter? Churchill sniffed and snorted, but suppressed any suspicion that his emissary had proved himself a false prophet. In any case the PM had more urgent matters to consider – this was the day he learnt that Rommel had recaptured Tobruk.[44]

With the Prime Minister safely back in Britain, events now conspired to demand action sooner rather than later. By mid-summer the situation looked a little brighter, with the Eighth Army no longer in retreat, more convoys arriving from America unscathed, and Bomber Command beginning to inflict serious damage on German industry. However, the Russians were incandescent when aid was suspended while the Admiralty absorbed the lessons of Dudley Pound's disastrous decision to scatter the ill-fated Arctic convoy, PQ17. Churchill despatched a lengthy explanation to Stalin, reassuring him that action was imminent.[45] Visiting London in July 1942 Marshall, enthusiastically supported by King and Eisenhower, for the first time gave Sledgehammer a precise objective. He argued the case for a largely British operation to attack Cherbourg before the end of the year, and then to retain control of the Cotentin peninsula until the following spring. Ideally, a solid bridgehead would be created, providing a well-defended base for the launch of Roundup. This was a wholly unrealistic proposal, first floated by Beaverbrook before leaving for Moscow in September 1941. Churchill had ridiculed the original idea, and nearly a year later he saw no reason to change his mind. His chiefs of staff were equally appalled by the idea, and for three days in late July remorselessly challenged the American mission to come up with a convincing defence of a fundamentally flawed plan. Marshall in the end admitted defeat, and consequently accepted the case for despatching a sizeable force to North Africa – signing up to what became Operation Torch was a tacit acknowledgement that Roundup could not now take place in 1943, although the Americans delayed for as long as possible accepting that this was the case.[46] When Churchill met Stalin for the first time on 12 August, he insisted that the Torch landings would divert German reserves away from the Eastern Front. A charge of bad faith regarding promises made in the aide-mémoire was robustly dismissed; but on the eve of his departure Churchill cabled London to establish precisely when British forces would be setting foot on French soil.[47]

From Rutter to Jubilee – planning the raid

British forces were of course frequently setting foot on French soil, but had only really made their presence felt in the raid on St Nazaire. Of all the targets identified by COHQ in January 1942, the cross-Channel terminals had the strongest appeal. After all, every harbour from Calais to Le Havre was reassuringly familiar, and would no doubt provide planners with an abundance of intelligence. Crucially, unlike the Loire estuary, the ferry ports' proximity to the south coast negated the need for any hazardous night-day journey. Hughes-Hallett later acknowledged that Dieppe had no special significance, and that seizure of a port was not deemed a necessary learning experience ahead of the actual invasion.[48] The 'vital lessons' of Dieppe examined in the next chapter were only highlighted once the raid had taken place, and an obvious disaster necessitated a hasty rationale. To the end of his life Mountbatten was ultra-defensive about Operation Jubilee. He knew only too well that in any test of his credentials as a 'great man', Dieppe would rank second only to Indian independence. As we shall see, with the passing of the years he became increasingly assertive, dismissing the critics and insisting that from the outset he and his staff had clearly understood the purpose of the raid. No doubt, by the end of his life he had convinced himself that this was the case. Here after all was someone quite happy to state that, 'It is a curious thing, but a fact, that I have been right in everything I have done and said in my life'.[49] It's safe to say the jury is out on that particular claim, no doubt noting that there is no evidence of any rigorous appreciation being undertaken as to the principal aims of Operation Rutter. In other words, nobody at the outset put down on paper the arguments for and against mounting the operation. Nor, after Rutter's cancellation, did Combined Operations belatedly acknowledge the case for a proper appreciation of Dieppe's suitability as a place to attack.[50]

Throughout the early spring of 1942 COHQ worked on an outline plan for Rutter, justifying the choice of Dieppe on the grounds that it was not heavily defended and the beaches in and around the town were suitable for landing both infantry and armour. Seizure of both the town and its hinterland would facilitate the destruction of vital facilities and defences, including a radar station and an airfield. The assault force, including tanks and paratroopers, would have the capacity to hold its bridgehead across two tides, and then re-embark in a suitably orderly fashion.[51] St Nazaire notwithstanding, this was a major escalation in operational planning.

Nevertheless, Combined Operations' belief that the Chiefs of Staff would run with the idea was boosted by Mountbatten's elevation to near equal status on the COSC. The novelty of the plan prompted an exuberant Churchill to spend three hours ruminating over 'invasion possibilities'. Throughout an interminable lunch the indulgent Mountbatten left a fretful Alan Brooke with the task of bringing their well-oiled host back down to earth. Ten days earlier, on 13 May, the Chiefs had delegated evaluation of COHQ's plan to Bernard Paget. The general promptly passed it on to South Eastern Command, which in the event of the raid going ahead would provide the bulk of the assault force. Thus Operation Rutter formally passed into the hands of Lieutenant-General Sir Bernard Montgomery. To what extent Monty had already involved himself in planning for the raid depends, as we shall see, upon which account one chooses to believe.[52]

In retirement the nation's most famous general was remarkably adroit at disassociating himself from the Dieppe raid. First of all, he made it clear that Jubilee would never have gone ahead had he still been in England. Later, Monty bemoaned the absence of a designated task force commander, even suggesting that a hands-on Mountbatten might have pulled it off. His biographer interpreted the latter remark as an over-generous gesture to the real villain of the piece.[53] Nigel Hamilton was happy to absolve Montgomery of direct responsibility for the debacle, albeit conceding that his man should have taken a keener interest in the detailed planning taking place at Richmond Terrace. Montgomery's priority was the battlefield training of untested soldiers tasked with defending the south of England against a formidable enemy. He was too busy building an army to become immersed in fine detail. Thus, from the outset he seems to have distanced himself from Rutter, relying on his personal liaison officer to keep him apprised of what Combined Operations were up to. In the 1950s Goronwy Rees would become a scandal-haunted university principal in his native mid-Wales; three decades later exposure as a Comintern agent left his reputation in ruins. However, in 1942 Major Rees was a fellow-travelling newspaperman and novelist who at the onset of war had enthusiastically embraced military life. MI5 was later appalled to discover that such a close friend of Guy Burgess had served as an intelligence officer with Home Forces, and been seconded to act as Monty's eyes and ears inside COHQ. Rees observed at close quarters only one of the three force commanders charged with carrying out the raid.[54]

Trafford Leigh-Mallory, the air vice-marshal at the head of Fighter Command's front-line 11 Group, was an intermittent presence at COHQ and thus unlikely to bump into Monty's man. The same was true of the first naval force commander, who only arrived home in June: Rear-Admiral H.T. Baillie-Grohman returned to London from running the Combined Training Centre at Kabrit. In different circumstances he could have been flying back from the Middle East to succeed Keyes. Baillie-Grohman had an impressive CV, and crucially, both Andrew Cunningham and the First Sea Lord held him in high regard. Instead, in June 1942 he found himself appointed by Dudley Pound as Rear-Admiral Combined Operations. He was clearly the Admiralty's man inside Mountbatten's growing empire, keeping a wary eye on someone who until recently had been very much his junior. Indeed, Baillie-Grohman had previously been the CCO's commanding officer, so Mountbatten's unenthusiastic response to his appointment was scarcely surprising.[55] Goronwy Rees had more time to observe the ground force commander, Major-General Hamilton 'Ham' Roberts of the 2nd Canadian Division. While endorsing his master's high opinion of Roberts' chief of staff, Rees shared Monty's poor opinion of the divisional commander. Untested as a leader in battle, here was someone manifestly lacking the required initiative, mental toughness, and combat experience. The Canadian lacked the personality, ability, and seniority of rank necessary to establish his authority over the whole planning and operational process. Rees reported back that Roberts wasn't up to the job. Roberts would be hung out to dry over Dieppe – proving a convenient scapegoat for Mountbatten and his acolytes after the war – but Rees had every reason to believe that here was a man out of his depth. Furthermore, that belief was vindicated by the chaos he witnessed first hand on the day of the raid.[56] Having to deal with a triumvirate of force commanders (each boasting their own planning teams), plus Mountbatten and his staff, confirmed Montgomery in his view that there had been a fatal confusion of command – nobody, not even the CCO, bore clear responsibility for the whole show.[57]

Much has been made of Montgomery's brusque dismissal of Combined Operations' plan for flank landings in brigade strength (5,000 men) up to nine miles east and west of the town. At least one member of the planning staff for Rutter later dismissed Mountbatten's claim that COHQ's proposal was vetoed by the Army. Walter Skrine maintained that in early April his team had already recognised the folly of landing infantry and armour in two locations 18 miles apart, with the whole force expected to fight its way to the port inside 15 hours. Skrine was insistent that, despite serious misgivings over the quality of intelligence gathered by Bobby de Casa Maury and his team, COHQ began talking to Home Forces about the feasibility of a frontal assault several weeks before Montgomery dismissed the notion of flank landings as amateurish. Hughes-Hallett in his unpublished memoirs made clear that Mountbatten's Deputy at Combined Operations – the Guards general and commando chief Charles Haydon – always saw a direct attack as the only feasible option. Haydon chaired two meetings with the Army in mid-April 1942 at which the centrality of armour to the operation was seen to necessitate a frontal assault – there was too great a risk of tanks being marooned outside the town. Where Hughes-Hallett seriously differed from Skrine was in insisting that Montgomery was party to key decisions made at these meetings. In *The Full Monty*, a radically rewritten second edition, Nigel Hamilton drew heavily upon Walter Skrine's account of Rutter's birth pangs to refute Mountbatten's claim that Montgomery was the principal author of the frontal assault.[58]

According to the ever loyal Hughes-Hallett, Mountbatten missed Monty's call for a fresh operational plan, but made sure he was present to chair a second meeting, on 25 April. He defended the idea of a pincer movement on the grounds that it didn't matter if the port was not occupied so long as the landings and re-embarkation vindicated Combined Operations' fresh approach to amphibious warfare. Montgomery argued that, 'if we did not capture the town the operation would be represented for ever afterwards as a failure, and that from the intelligence at our disposal there should not be any great difficulty in a frontal assault'. If this version is to be believed then Mountbatten must have recognised that Montgomery, backed by Paget and enjoying Brooke's absolute trust, clearly had the upper hand.[59] He backed off, and a multitude of different planning teams pressed on with the central task of mounting an ambitious operation which already contained a fatal flaw: because of the density of naval traffic rendezvousing before dawn off Dieppe, flanking attacks to knock out enemy batteries east and west of the port would have to take place 30 minutes prior to the main force landing on the shingle beach adjacent to the town esplanade. Putting aside the key question of whether half an hour was enough time to destroy entrenched positions, these preliminary attacks would remove any element of tactical surprise. Troops and tanks rushing up the beach and on to the boulevard would not have the same shocking effect if the town's defenders had been given advance warning. To compensate for the absence of tactical surprise at the centre, there needed to be heavy air bombardment in advance of the main attack, and directed heavy shelling from a capital ship lying offshore.[60]

Bernard Fergusson's *The Watery Maze*, which, as we shall see, was very much Mountbatten's project, made no mention of Montgomery prior to a key meeting in early June. Goronwy Rees, writing at around the same time, recalled his bemusement over Monty's reluctance to become directly involved. Fergusson made clear that Mountbatten had accepted the Home Forces' case for a frontal assault only because he had been assured that a heavy bombing attack would significantly reduce the level of resistance. This was why the Chiefs of Staff agreed to the outline plan on 13 May without the need for any extended discussion – because Dickie assumed the Prime Minister would relax his rule forbidding night-time bombing of towns and cities in occupied Europe.[61] On 1 June, with a heavy heart (all those happy holidays with Clemmie in Dieppe!), Churchill sanctioned a preliminary air attack. However, at a joint planning meeting on the same day, an argument was made against bombing. Further discussion was postponed, and Mountbatten left for Washington. This meant the CCO was absent from a further meeting of the force commanders, held at Richmond Terrace on 5 June. Until this time preliminary bombardment had been implicit in the case for going directly to Dieppe. Now the use of heavy bombers was firmly ruled out. Leigh-Mallory argued that they were unlikely to hit precise targets, would remove the element of surprise, and might be better employed in diversionary attacks. Challenging someone as forthright in their views as Trafford Leigh-Mallory was no easy task: inside Fighter Command better men than 'Ham' Roberts had tried and failed.[62] Yet, astonishingly, on 5 June Roberts agreed. He feared that bomb damage would impede the main assault, with debris in the narrow streets preventing his tanks from advancing into the heart of the town. Mountbatten was not present to protest. In his memoirs Montgomery insisted that, had he been present, then he would never have accepted the change of plan. Not only was he at the meeting, but he chaired it – and, according to the minutes, he uttered not a word of protest.[63]

Although Mountbatten 'expressed his disagreement in the strongest terms' when back from America, it was already too late. In his absence planning had gone on apace, and Brooke made clear to him that he had no choice but to bite the bullet. According to Goronwy Rees, at the next big planning conference for Rutter the CCO, 'handsome and breezy, like Brighton at its best, announced that Mr Churchill had decided that, for political reasons, it would be inexpedient to undertake the bombing of Dieppe'. The last thing Mountbatten wanted was for it to be common knowledge that, not once but twice, he had been outmanoeuvred over key elements of the outline plan. In any case, neither he nor anyone else at COHQ involved in planning the raid saw the absence of aerial bombardment as a reason for cancellation. Using heavy bombers was problematic, and their absence simply highlighted the importance of directed shelling from the sea. The Chief turned on his formidable charm to reassure a veritable army of planners that the absence of Bomber Command was an opportunity not a setback.[64]

Fergusson, in his sanitised history of Combined Operations, glossed over the second major blow to Mountbatten's plans for vital fire-support. Forty years later, Nigel Hamilton saw the absence of a capital ship offshore as confirmation that no man was ever less qualified for the task in hand.[65] From Scapa Flow in 1939 to the Indian Ocean in 1941, every time the Royal Navy lost a big ship, parliament and press were awash with anguish and recrimination. To a First Sea Lord terminally ill and ever expectant of the next major disaster, COHQ appeared sublimely indifferent to the formidable striking power of the *Luftwaffe*: 'Battleships by daylight off the French coast? You must be mad, Dickie!'.[66] Once Baillie-Grohman came to appreciate why Pound viewed the loss of a battleship as a morale-sapping public relations disaster, he decided to take the initiative himself. The landing forces were by now training on the Isle of Wight for the actual assault. The island had been sealed off since late May. From Rutter's headquarters in Cowes, the naval force commander petitioned the C-in-C at Portsmouth to provide him with a couple of cruisers. When his request was rebuffed, he tried again. Baillie-Grohman's persistence made him unpopular with the Admiralty, and his reluctance simply to make the best of a bad job won him few friends inside COHQ. Hughes-Hallett was deeply suspicious of someone who scarcely disguised his scepticism regarding the operation, and who had arrived at Combined Operations with his own very clear ideas as to the recruitment and training of naval personnel. Quite clearly, Baillie-Grohman was not 'one of us'.[67]

This might easily have been the point at which wisdom prevailed, with Mountbatten displaying an impressive degree of moral fortitude in order to call the whole thing off. Both sympathisers and critics have lamented his failure to do so, albeit suggesting that Rutter now had a momentum all of its own.[68] If he could have foreseen just how ghastly the whole affair would turn out to be, he would surely have said enough is enough, and prepared himself for the inevitable flak. With Churchill's support he could have survived with his reputation reasonably intact, if only because the service chiefs viewed Dieppe as a minor show. Yes, he would have been unpopular inside the Foreign Office, where Eden and his permanent secretary, Sir Alexander Cadogan, would have struggled to appease Maisky and his masters. But a few chilly looks across the dinner table at Brook's or White's scarcely constitutes a career-shattering crisis.

The other person who might have displayed a laudable combination of foresight and principle was Major-General Roberts. He could have made clear that, without adequate air and naval support, there was a strong possibility that his men would be mown down before they even got off the beach. In other words, that this was a disaster waiting to happen, and that he was not prepared to risk the lives of the several thousand soldiers under his command. This would have taken a very brave man, not least because of the enormous pressure placed upon him by Andrew McNaughton and Harry Crerar, commanders respectively of all Canadian Forces in the UK and the 1st Canadian Army Corps. Both men had high expectations, with McNaughton articulating the view of an impatient federal government that the dominion making the greatest contribution to the war effort had seen the morale and fighting calibre of its troops ebb away in the face of inactivity. Canadian troops had been in Britain for over two years, and Ottawa's desire for action reflected the views of the general public, both English and French-speaking. For primarily political reasons – to meet the increasingly vocal complaints of Mackenzie-King and his cabinet – Combined Operations was forced to abandon its original idea of deploying the Commandos and the Royal Marine Division.[69] Yet again Mountbatten went along with the idea, despite the obvious risk in making such heavy demands upon keen yet wholly inexperienced soldiers. In later life he insisted that he had complained strenuously, suggesting that Monty bore the blame for selection of Roberts' division. Montgomery always denied responsibility – a view challenged by both Crerar and McNaughton.[70] Given a clear political as well as military agenda, and his bored, demoralised regiments' natural eagerness to see some action, Roberts' reluctance to stand up and be counted is understandable. Indeed, according to Hughes-Hallett, he displayed a curious and worrying naivety, in that the more obvious the difficulties the greater the enthusiasm.[71]

That enthusiasm was considerably dampened by Yukon I, the dress-rehearsal mounted along the Dorset coast. The operation was scheduled for 21 June, and Montgomery insisted on a dry run at Studland Bay eight days earlier. This was just as well given the Royal Navy's comprehensive failure to land troops in the right place, at the right time. The tanks arrived a whole hour after the infantry, for most of whom the experience of being dumped ashore in near total darkness by a coxswain with no clear idea where he should be had proved a rude awakening. Gung-ho Canadians, already hard hit by relentless and demoralising sea sickness, were already coming to terms with the harsh reality of battlefield action. Their generals remained upbeat, in stark contrast to Montgomery and Paget.[72] Mountbatten was away in America, but had he been present then there is no way he could have refused the Army's insistence on a second exercise. In any case, Churchill, always keen to be where the action was, had travelled down to Bridport, and had seen the chaos for himself. Combined Operations and the Royal Navy were given ten days to facilitate a dramatic improvement in the standard of inshore navigation. In practice, the only way effective control of 250 ships and landing craft could come about was by switching the main assault from nautical twilight to civil twilight. Crews could now see where they were and what they were doing, but the delay in going ashore further eroded the element of surprise. On 23 June the CCO, from the vantage point of his official yacht, watched

Yukon II slowly unfold. The general feeling aboard *The Sister Anne* was that this time around things had gone pretty well – a view shared down on the beach by Paget and Montgomery. All agreed that the raid would go ahead on the next appropriate tide, in early July. Monty saw cause for optimism once reassured that the Admiralty could adapt the RAF's GEE air navigational aid to guide the taskforce through a huge minefield the Germans had laid mid-Channel. In private he was increasingly anxious, learning from Ultra of the 10th Panzer Division's arrival at Amiens. That anxiety was shared by Churchill. Although, as we shall see, Brooke of all people quelled prime ministerial fears when they met with Mountbatten and Hughes-Hallett in Downing Street on 30 June.[73]

Summer tides gave Operation Rutter a brief window of opportunity during the first week of July. The whole force was at anchor in Yarmouth Roads, waiting to slip the Solent once the weather improved. With a fierce westerly, and driving summer rain, troops found the misery of killing time in cramped quarters a dispiriting experience. Conditions out in the Channel ensured cancellation on 7 July, and in any case that morning the invasion fleet had been spotted by a German reconnaissance flight: four Focke-Wolf 190 fighter-bombers had hit two of the largest transports, claiming the first casualties of the raid. The number of dead and wounded would have been much higher had the bombs not passed right through the assault ships before exploding. By the end of the day the operation was off, and weary, dispirited troops were returning to barracks.[74]

The actual order for cancellation was made, at Baillie-Grohman's request, by Sir William James, the Port Admiral. Despite the *Luftwaffe* raid, Mountbatten had ordered an evacuation of the two bombed ships, and their troops redistributed within the fleet. Did the CCO seriously envisage that the raid could still be mounted in the remaining 24 hours? Whether he did or not, Mountbatten was already giving serious consideration as to how Rutter might be resurrected. Four days earlier he had sent a message to Churchill warning that the weather forecast was not good, and that Combined Operations might therefore seek a second bite at the cherry. Despite a security-conscious PM discouraging any such notion, on 6 July Mountbatten secured agreement from the three service chiefs, 'that consideration should be given to the possibility of remounting'. Mountbatten's sternest critic has argued why neither he nor Hughes-Hallett used the COSC's cautious approval in order to justify Jubilee. Quite simply, the two men cultivated an assumption that they were responding to a post-Rutter request from the Prime Minister. In other words, they did not want to give the impression that they planned to remount the raid even while the ships were still hunkered down in the Solent; and, for obvious reasons, they had no wish to highlight Churchill's deep reservations.[75]

Baillie-Grohman moved fast to kill off any possibility of remounting an operation he had always viewed as a disaster waiting to happen. The two exercises had simply confirmed him in his belief that there had been no rigorous appreciation of an operation which served no obvious purpose. On 7 July, secure in the knowledge that Rutter was dead, he put his name to a lengthy and uncompromising memorandum prepared previously by his staff. Baillie-Grohman insisted that Mountbatten reject any notion of reviving the mission, and crucially, he persuaded 'Ham' Roberts to add his signature. Relations with the CCO and Hughes-Hallett, already bad, now slumped to an all-time low.[76]

Montgomery's relief at the collapse of Rutter had been palpable. From almost the outset there was a very strong risk that security had been compromised. Junior officers made alarmingly accurate calculations; and in any case it was common knowledge on the Isle of Wight that the Canadians were headed for Dieppe. Once the troops were dispersed then the planned target was for all intents and purposes in the public domain. Montgomery wrote to his immediate superior, the C-in-C Home Forces, recommending that no similar operation be contemplated in the future. When, not long after, he heard that serious consideration was being given to remounting the raid, Montgomery went and told Paget to his face that the whole idea was crazy. Almost immediately fate intervened – Brooke at last got the man he thought best qualified to reinvigorate the Eighth Army, and Monty flew to Cairo. Montgomery was impervious to Mountbatten's charisma and connections, and remained so all his life. He wasn't convinced by Dickie's credentials as a seafarer, let alone as a quasi-general. Even though the Canadians now enjoyed direct responsibility for remounting Rutter, Montgomery had the authority to subvert any deployment of forces ultimately under his command. To ask whether Operation Jubilee would have gone ahead had he still been in England is frankly a waste of time. Forget the counterfactual scenario. The truth is that from 10 August 1942 Monty was no longer in the frame.[77]

The week following the cancellation of Rutter saw morale inside COHQ at an all time low. For months the focus had been upon Dieppe, with little contingency planning. No blueprint existed for an alternative operation, of similar ambition, which could be mounted at relatively short notice. In other words, no headline-grabbing sortie comparable to St Nazaire could be staged before the end of 1942. Mountbatten had marched his men to the top of the hill, and then marched them down again. This clearly impacted upon inter-Allied relations as well as on morale at home; but a more immediate consideration was the damage done to the fragile reputation of the Chief of Combined Operations. After all rumours were flying round COHQ that Marshall was about to become Allied supreme commander in the UK, with Mountbatten as his chief of staff. A 'wash up' was held at Richmond Terrace on 8 July. Mountbatten made the 'unusual and, I suggest, rather bold proposal that we should remount the operation against Dieppe'. He dismissed all objections based on security by arguing that, even if the Germans had been anticipating an attack, they would never suspect that the British might restage exactly the same operation.[78]

Three days later, with the force commanders present, he restated the case for trying again. Neither his number two, Charles Haydon, nor his Royal Marines chief of staff, the now Major-General Godfrey Wildman-Lushington, thought much of Mountbatten's idea. They were politely scathing of the proposal, and initially enjoyed the support of all three force commanders. However, Mountbatten was too fierce an opponent to concede that he was outnumbered. He lobbied ferociously, and let Hughes-Hallett off the leash. Over the next fortnight the doubting Thomases within COHQ were isolated, a sceptical Leigh-Mallory came on board, Roberts was lent on by McNaughton, and Baillie-Grohman was levered out. By mutual consent the dissenting admiral joined the staff of Sir Bertram Ramsay, mastermind of the Dunkirk evacuation and designated naval commander for any cross-Channel invasion.[79]

It was Admiral Ramsay, no doubt encouraged by Baillie-Grohman, who wrote to Mountbatten on 25 July insisting that Combined Operations abandon any idea of remounting the raid. The CCO coolly dismissed Ramsay's threat to take the matter up with his fellow chiefs of staff. Hughes-Hallett shared Mountbatten's indifference to service etiquette and the sensibility of senior officers. His behaviour towards Roberts and Leigh-Mallory in the immediate aftermath of Rutter was incredible: claiming the support of Sir Stafford Cripps – in mid-1942 at the height of his wartime popularity – Hughes-Hallett threatened his superiors with an official inquiry into their conduct. Meanwhile, he continued to cultivate Admiral James, the C-in-C down at Portsmouth. Recognising that there was only one naval officer able to assume command and hit the ground running, James backed Mountbatten's decision to appoint Hughes-Hallett as Baillie-Grohman's successor. Now there were two destroyer captains masterminding Rutter *redux*, soon to be renamed Operation Jubilee. With security considerations paramount, there could be no further rehearsals. When Hughes-Hallett led his task force out into the Channel on or around 16 August, then it would be for real. The Canadians accepted the reality of the situation, but it didn't mean that they liked it. With Goronwy Rees gone, and Montgomery quietly relieved to be kept in the dark, Roberts and his increasingly apprehensive staff were left to figure out for themselves how a handful of untested battalions could fight their way into a now all too familiar target and then fight their way out again.[80]

There are many cruel ironies surrounding Jubilee. Surely the most bizarre is the fact that, although the actual planning of the operation generated an excess of paperwork, there is no single document signing off the operation. Mountbatten would always insist that, in the interest of security, all authorisation had been verbal. Hughes-Hallett was equally insistent, pointing to 'Pug' Ismay, Churchill's representative on the COSC, as the man who ensured that all parties were properly briefed.[81] As the next chapter will confirm, the lack of a killer document has generated an astonishing body of scholarship and speculation. The absence of a paper trail emanating from the Chiefs of Staff Committee, particularly a key meeting it held on 20 July, allowed Mountbatten to claim that his three colleagues, as well as the Prime Minister, had given him the green light. This claim was tested and contested from as early as 1950, but he was unswerving in his insistence that Jubilee enjoyed the full support of the two most powerful figures in the British war machine, Churchill and Brooke. The COSC minutes for 20 July 1942 referred to 'the next large-scale raiding operation', even if Jubilee was not mentioned by name; and a War Office note dated the same day actually labels the operation. In an environment where every minister on the Defence Committee was kept in the dark, and even the Vice Chief of the General Staff had no idea what was going on, the list of senior commanders Mountbatten gleefully left out of the loop far exceeded the names of those cognizant that a remounting of the raid was imminent.[82]

What the minutes of the COSC from the summer of 1942 do make clear is that Mountbatten was stopped in his tracks when insisting on a significant increase in his authority. Between 17 and 27 July the CCO made strenuous efforts to ensure that, 'he be vested with executive responsibility for mounting and launching the next large-scale raiding operations'.[83] If successful, Mountbatten would have enjoyed the final say in all aspects of operational planning, and could have initiated a mission without securing prior approval from above, namely the Chiefs of Staff. Some, of course, would argue that in practice this is precisely what he did at Dieppe. The other chiefs recognised that this would leave Mountbatten largely unaccountable for inter-service missions conducted under the auspices of Combined Operations, and insisted on retaining a system of checks and balances. Thus Admiral Sir William James retained a veto, as did each service's designated force commander. Dickie's longer-term ambitions had for the moment been thwarted, and yet the compromise agreed on 27 July required only for him to submit an outline plan in order to secure the Chiefs' approval.[84] Thus Jubilee remained a very real prospect, not least because no-one enjoying the power of veto wished to exercise it. The Port Admiral had expressed no fundamental objection to restaging the mission, and Leigh-Mallory's enthusiasm for taking on the *Luftwaffe* had returned. However deep his inner fears, Roberts recognised that out of duty to his division he must make the best of a bad job. Hughes-Hallett was of course supremely confident. His determination to hit Dieppe would be only too apparent when, after two postponements because of bad weather, on the afternoon of 18 August 1942 he confidently dismissed Admiralty forecasts and insisted it was time to go.[85]

Dieppe – what was supposed to happen

A key difference between Rutter and Jubilee was the replacement of airborne troops by commandos.[86] This decision not to use paratroopers because of adverse wind conditions was fortuitous – had they been deployed then the risk element would have been that much greater, and even more men and equipment would have been lost. After all, the performance of the commandos was one of the few pluses to emerge from the Dieppe raid. Royal Marine 'A' Commando, involved in the operation from the outset, was given a fresh task of penetrating the harbour, capturing the 40 invasion barges moored there, and sailing them home. The raid on St Nazaire had already exposed the cost of a classic 'cutting out' operation in an era of concrete pill boxes and automatic weapons. To elaborate an already complex plan in this fashion makes one wonder if Mountbatten had been re-reading his precious Hornblower. Clearly he needed Mr Bush to point out that this particular mission was dangerously over-egging the cake. With splendid irony the bulk of the Marines would maintain a great Nelsonian tradition courtesy of the French – seven heavily-loaded Chasseurs would slip their Isle of Wight moorings and proudly bear the cross of Lorraine back across the Channel.[87] The remainder of the Commando would sail on board the gunboat HMS *Locust*, commanded by Robert 'Red' Ryder, VC-winning hero of the St Nazaire raid.

Responsibility for eliminating the coastal batteries furthest from the port was now given to the two Army Commandos. These would be brought down from Scotland to take advantage of two new LSIs (the large 'Landing Ship Infantry' converted from Channel ferries to house the landing craft which conveyed troops to the beaches): with nine of these 'mother ships' now available every unit could be conveyed by sea. Not everyone could travel in comfort, and 3 Commando, along with two Canadian battalions, would cross in small, speedy but highly vulnerable LCPs (the wooden 'Landing Craft Personnel' originally known as the Eureka and intended primarily for in-shore operation).

Over 6,000 troops and 252 vessels were now committed to the operation. Varying ships' speeds, plus a complicated timetable for landing, meant that the fleet had to leave at different times, and then regroup off the French coastline before dawn. This was a major leap of faith, as was the assumption that re-embarkation of the entire force from Dieppe was now a credible option. Yet the significance of this final, crucial stage of the operation was rendered that much greater by a key decision now made at COHQ: the delay until mid-August meant the raid would have to take place over one tide and not two.[88] The length of this ever-more ambitious operation was thus reduced to a mere six hours – as it transpired, this change of plan was probably fortuitous. The seizure rather than the swift destruction of so many useless barges aptly illustrated the stubborn belief that, within a single cycle, a multitude of tasks might still be undertaken: no doubt such a dramatic gesture looked great on paper, but it exemplified the planners' dual failure to appreciate the harsh realities of time and tide, and to learn from recent experience.

The commando landings were scheduled for 4.50am, five minutes after the RAF's initial attack on the extensive artillery and anti-aircraft gun emplacements above and beyond the town. The frequency and intensity of the Hurricanes' bombing and strafing would grow over the next half-hour as the two colonels led each of their Commandos towards respective targets on the outer flanks. Under John Durnford-Slater, a veteran of Vaagso, 3 Commando would land on the two Yellow Beaches east of Dieppe, near the village of Berneval, and knock out the Goebbels battery. Meanwhile, the dashing disciplinarian Lord Lovat, would lead two detachments of 4 Commando up from Orange Beaches 1 and 2, located west of the port, and destroy the six 75mm guns behind the cliffs at Varengeville. Both these targets were around six miles from the harbour, and yet an assumption of total success dictated that both Commandos would make their way without too much trouble in to the town, and duly depart for home along with the rest of the expedition. What distinguished the Commandos from all other elements of the taskforce was their commanding officers' insistence on being given complete responsibility for the planning and execution of their contribution to the raid. Crucially, this included departing, if circumstances dictated, via the same beaches on which they had landed. The intensity of training and preparation reflected deep scepticism regarding the overall plan, and an acknowledgement that conditions would be harsh and resistance fierce. The contrast – and the contrasting fortunes – with almost all other military units would soon become painfully clear.[89]

Under cover of darkness, at the same time as the Commandos, the first two Canadian battalions would come ashore and attack the inner flanks. The Royal Regiment of Canada would climb up off Blue Beach, secure the village of Puys a mile east of Dieppe, and then swiftly eliminate all defences on the eastern headland. The twin objectives were four heavy guns and an anti-aircraft battery. As in every other element of the raid the planning was over-optimistic: the artillery would be turned against the Germans down in Dieppe, and the sights of the AA guns removed for closer inspection back home. Based on his Great War experience Douglas Catto, the battalion commander, was convinced the cliff top at Puys would be blocked by barbed wire, backed up by heavy machine guns. His request for advance bombardment was refused by Roberts on the grounds that aerial reconnaissance had not revealed any wiring of the gully behind the beach. The reality was that both the gully path and the sea wall had been sealed off, and that the four pill boxes defending Puys did indeed boast a formidable armament. The planners' only concession to caution was in providing a company of the Canadian Black Watch to protect the Royal Regiment's flank once the main assault began. This was the worst of both worlds: the company was no more than a token force, brought in only because Catto's battalion was seriously under strength, and yet it added to the numbers attempting to negotiate a thin stretch of beach at full tide in the dark. The problem with Puys was that it was an obvious landing place if the eastern headland was to be secured, which was precisely why it was so well guarded. Yet a combination of compact beach and steep, narrow gully gave every advantage to a relatively small number of heavily armed defenders. Barring heavy bombardment, or commandos capturing the pill boxes overnight, all the odds were stacked against the Canadians. Catto rightly feared that they would never get off the beach, and he was proved right.[90]

A parallel seizure of the western headland would see the South Saskatchewan Regiment land on Green Beach at Pourville, two miles to the west of the port. At 4.50am Canada's Cameron Highlanders would move through the secure beach-head, push up the valley of the River Scie, and attack the enemy airfield at St Aubin. The overall intention was to secure swift control of Dieppe's immediate hinterland, and its most threatening artillery and heavy machine-gun positions. Tactical surprise and speed of assault would thus neutralise the town's surrounding defences and isolate its local defenders from early reinforcement.

At 5.10am the four 4-inch guns of Hughes-Hallett's seven Hunt-class destroyers, boosted by the firepower of the exile Polish navy's *Slazak*, would shell the waterfront.[91] By now it would be daylight, and, after five minutes of very modest bombardment, the main assault could begin. Forces attacking on the flanks could all anticipate high chalk cliffs, broken by narrow clefts or deep river-mouths. Dieppe is itself an estuary, but with a relatively shallow harbour at the eastern end of the resort's mile-long beach. Here, a battalion of the Essex Scottish would land on Red Beach, while the Royal Hamilton Light Infantry would arrive further west along the shingle, at White Beach. Also landing would be 30 Churchill tanks, as yet untested in battle. They belonged to the 14th Canadian Tank Battalion, better known as the 'Calgary Tanks'. Their passage across the Channel would be courtesy of purpose-built LCTs (in command of the large, lumbering 'Landing Craft Tanks' was a young and enthusiastic Lieutenant-Commander Lord Beatty – an irony not lost on Mountbatten).[92] With armoured support, infantry would climb the sea-wall, cross 150 yards of lawns and flower beds, and secure the line of hotels and other buildings along the Boulevard de Verdun – never was a road more grimly and appropriately titled. With the western headland presumably secure, the large and imposing casino at the foot of the cliff could be swiftly seized, after which troops and tanks would move in to the main body of the town. Meanwhile, a team of sappers would be demolishing an ambitious list of waterfront targets. The francophone Fusiliers Mont-Royal, despite having crossed from Shoreham in the cramped and almost wholly unprotected LCPs, were designated to remain off-shore as Force Reserve. Did a farsighted staff officer with an unusual degree of political nous anticipate the destabilising effect of heavy casualties on Québecois public opinion? If so, such caution was to be cruelly over-taken by events.

Having achieved total success the entire taskforce would depart from Dieppe well before noon; and well in advance of Panzer or Waffen SS units arriving to eliminate any threat of a Second Front redoubt. The most immediate reinforcements would come from the *Luftwaffe*, its Focke-Wolf 190 and Me109 fighter pilots endeavouring to regain air superiority at the earliest opportunity. The RAF, supported by its Canadian counterpart, would seize the initiative in unprecedented numbers – 63 squadrons to be exact. The two squadrons of bomb-carrying Hurricanes would be boosted by five squadrons of Boston and Blenheim light bombers. In committing no less than 56 front-line squadrons to the operation, Fighter Command was deploying a force even greater than that with which it had fought the Battle of Britain. As in 1940, an astonishing array of nationalities would take to the skies, matched only by the diverse composition of the ground forces.[93] By seizing an early advantage Leigh-Mallory – an unrepentant advocate of the 'Big Wing' – intended to inflict maximum losses upon the enemy. The importance of the air battle was reflected in the seniority of his representative on HMS *Calpe*, and the presence on board of Tangmere's most experienced flight controllers. The RAF's force commander would remain at 11 Group's Uxbridge HQ, joined for the day by the Chief of Combined Operations.[94]

The two men were guaranteed a secure, continuous link to the *Calpe*, the destroyer hastily converted to a command and communications centre once it became clear the prototype Headquarters Ship, HMS *Bulolo*, would not be completed in time. Hughes-Hallett, Roberts, and their respective staffs would be based on the *Calpe*, but a back-up operation was established on another destroyer, HMS *Fernie*. The complexity of the operation demanded an ambitious communications system, with a very real risk of overload and partial or total breakdown. The *Calpe* had to liaise with the mainland while at the same time retain close contact with all other shipping, as well as the troops and tanks engaged in battle ashore.[95] A constant stream of reports would be coming in, with corresponding orders relayed to forces at sea, on the land, and in the air. Apart from the technological challenge, the three force commanders and their staffs would need to demonstrate an unprecedented degree of co-ordination. Any assumption that the course of the battle could be coolly monitored from the calm of the bridge ignored the brutal fact that with alarming speed the *Calpe* would find itself part of that same battle – in action *and* endeavouring to exercise effective command and control.

HMS *Fernie*, similarly festooned with ad hoc aerials, was an obvious home for Mountbatten's all-important press corps, as well as various Allied observers, including the brigadier-general seconded by Marshall to COHQ, Lucian Truscott. The Americans also provided a squadron of B17s to bomb the airfield, and a pioneering complement of newly-named US Rangers, fresh from commando training with their British counterparts. Also assigned to the *Fernie* was Commander Ian Fleming, from the NID's Operational Intelligence Centre. With a higher security clearance than even 007, Fleming was the one person on the raid 'indoctrinated' with regard to Ultra – a distinction he shared with Mountbatten who, as a chief of staff, received direct from 'C', the head of SIS, his daily digest of Enigma intelligence. Fleming had strict orders not to go ashore, and Bond devotees can only speculate on what he was expected to do if in danger of capture and interrogation. Flight Sergeant Jack Nissenthal knew exactly how he would avoid being taken prisoner: either crack open his cyanide capsule or wait to be shot by his 'comrades' – with echoes of Bruneval, the signals specialist and his escort would remove equipment from a radar station on the western headland and bring their state-of-the-art booty back for analysis. As it transpired, the platoon did no more than get within sight of its objective, and Nissenthal, despite nearly drowning, made it home without risk of suicide.[96] Appropriately, it was Ian Fleming who ensured that any future attempts to steal from the enemy would be conducted in a systematic and organised fashion, courtesy of his 'Red Indians', the Special Intelligence Unit (soon renamed 30 Commando, and later redesignated 30 Assault Unit). This semi-covert body of hi-tech plunderers quickly became a key element within Combined Operations but always remained an Admiralty organisation. Seven years after 30AU disbanded Commander James Bond made his debut in *Casino Royale*, a path-breaking story of cards, cads, Cold War espionage, and torture. Was it merely coincidental that Fleming set the novel in 'Royale-les-Eaux', an attractive Channel resort boasting a large gaming house?[97]

What is most striking about Jubilee's elaborate blueprint is the absence of flexibility and contingency planning – where was the provision for when the strict timetable slipped, as it surely would, and things began to go wrong? Did no-one speculate upon the fact that if the inner flanks were not secured at lightning speed then the Germans would be ready and waiting to rake White and Red Beaches with withering fire for nearly 30 minutes prior to the main assault force coming ashore? As Robin Neillands observed, fatal flaws in the tactical thinking multiplied, 'like some uncontrolled virus … there was a choice of difficulties, but either a heavy bombardment of the headlands or a landing in the dark at the same time as the flank attacks was a better option than the planners chose'. At his first briefing Lovat was appalled to learn of the late start, remaining adamant that the Commandos would not participate in a daylight attack. Yet the main assault force had no choice as COHQ and the Admiralty foresaw multiple collisions if inexperienced commanders and coxswains were asked to land such a large force before daylight: Yukon I, the shambolic inaugural exercise for Rutter, had confirmed amphibious operations' chilling capacity for organised chaos. Yukon II had marked a deceptive improvement in the control and in-shore handling of dense traffic, and yet the option of a full-scale landing before dawn remained out of the question.[98] On the day itself almost all naval personnel performed with great courage and professionalism – it offers scant consolation, but as far as the landing ships and craft were concerned, the cost in lives and equipment could have been far worse.

Dieppe – what did happen

Tuesday, 18 August 1942 was a day of queuing, confusion, and congestion in Channel ports from the Solent to Newhaven. The weather remained singularly unseasonal and squallish. This was no D-Day armada, but the fleet that gathered in the eastern Channel early on the Wednesday morning was nevertheless impressive. Minesweepers had cut two passageways through the huge mid-Channel minefield laid down by the Germans, and the main assault force steamed through unscathed. All parties regrouped at the 'lowering position' ten miles off-shore, and the LSIs prepared to release their landing craft. Thus the most successful aspect of the raid occurred at the outset – no similar operation had ever been undertaken at night. For all the feverish preparation and quayside second-guessing, there remained a strong chance of enjoying tactical surprise.[99]

This may have remained the case had HMS *Calpe* picked up Dover's two warnings that a small convoy was working its way south from Boulogne about seven miles off-shore. *Fernie* did pick up a signal but assumed the same was true for her sister ship. Here was the first serious systems failure in that no-one had perceived a need to check whether priority signals had been received. The two destroyers patrolling the eastern flank were thus unaware of an enemy convoy in their vicinity. It's worth noting here that Bletchley Park intercepted Convoy 2437's report of its encounter with British shipping, but by the time the decrypt arrived at the Admiralty it was too late to be of operational significance. The same was true of all cipher traffic that day: Jubilee occurred over a relatively short time-span, and it took three hours from interception to the relevant intelligence being received at sea. Similarly, the RAF gained little from close monitoring of Enigma because the air battle was so short. In addition, even though the Operational Intelligence Centre was being fed Ultra intercepts it was reluctant to pass unnecessary information on to Hughes-Hallett for fear of German code-breakers deducing that their own cipher had been broken.[100]

At 3.47am German armed trawlers fired off a star shell and attacked 3 Commando's motley assortment of boats. A brief but bloody engagement saw the group scattered. Damage to the escorting steam gun-boat meant a loss of radio contact with the force commanders. Her skipper and John Dunford-Slater set out in a Eureka to find the *Calpe* and to report that there appeared scant prospect of the Goebbels battery being put out of action. 3 Commando's most senior officer was to remain, to his subsequent deep disgust, *hors de combat*. Only when he at last got back to Newhaven did he discover that six of the LCPs actually got ashore. Five landing craft did reach Yellow Beach 1, but nearly half an hour late. An intense fire-fight to the north of Berneval, and within the village itself, saw the commandos keep fighting in the face of mounting casualties and dwindling ammunition. At 10.20am the survivors, including the first Americans to fight on mainland Europe, accepted the inevitable and surrendered.

Yet astonishingly, for at least two hours that morning the Berneval battery was effectively out of action, being forced to defend itself rather than focus upon the main assault. Only one group landed on Yellow Beach 2, but Major Peter Young fooled the enemy into thinking the guns were under attack by a much larger force. A timely retreat saw all 20 officers and men return safely to England. Their contribution to the raid as a whole was hugely disproportionate to their number, Hughes-Hallett rightly perceiving the attack as 'perhaps the most outstanding incident of the operation'. His despatch noted 'the exceedingly serious consequences' had the assault on the eastern battery failed. Yet, notwithstanding the minor miracle of Yellow Beach 2, and the commandos' remarkable fortitude in the face of overwhelming odds, it was a failure: the guns remained intact. Around a third of 3 Commando were listed as killed, wounded, or missing; and 82 highly trained soldiers spent the next three years in a prisoner-of-war camp. No wonder the absent Durnford-Slater was appalled by the loss of his best men – his worst fears about the raid had been confirmed.[101]

The naturalist Peter Scott, writing his impressions of the raid only a few days after his return home, remained sure that, had the German convoy not stumbled across 3 Commando, then the element of tactical surprise would have remained intact. As it was, the firing of the flare failed to trigger a full emergency. Nevertheless, defending forces were alert, if only because their generals judged mid-summer conditions conducive to Allied incursion. Furthermore, 18–19 August was the night of the Dieppe garrison's weekly 'stand to' exercise. All the evidence indicates that it was foresight not fore-warning that ensured a swift response. But not that swift, otherwise the Pointe d'Ailly lighthouse would have soon ceased flashing. Even though he could see ships ablaze on the horizon, Scott was in fact some distance from the initial debacle: his steam gun-boat was out on the western flank escorting 4 Commando.[102]

Lovat's men, like their comrades in 3 Commando, benefited from COHQ's very detailed appreciation of what they could expect. One recent chronicler of Dieppe has questioned why the Canadians never received comparable briefings; and why Mountbatten's number two, the vastly experienced Guardsman turned raider, Charles Haydon, didn't invite Lovat and Durnford-Slater to cast a critical eye over the Jubilee plan. They had after all already worked out where they were going, simply by reversing the picture postcards available at their initial briefing.[103] Lovat's Commando, including a handful of Rangers, had the luxury of travelling courtesy of HMS *Prinz Albert*, a converted Belgian ferry carrying eight LCAs (newly commissioned assault landing craft). The LSI was familiar from eight practice landings 4 Commando had carried out at Lulworth Cove. The rehearsals in Dorset had allowed Lovat to fine-tune his original plan, fixing a timetable but at the same time factoring in reversals and contingency arrangements – in stark contrast to the planners at Richmond Terrace and the field commanders at 2nd Division. Through his brigadier, Bob Laycock, he ensured that COHQ's cleverest intelligence officer, Antony Head, would provide an eve of mission briefing. He also insisted on the Navy's best available navigator, thereby ensuring that both groups hit the beaches at exactly the right place at exactly the right time. Nothing was left to chance, and the elimination of risk contrasts starkly with other units' experience. Lovat was seen by his second-in-command as having 'planned the attack on the battery brilliantly ... he was strong-minded enough to get his own way'. Furthermore, once the operation was underway, the chief of Clan Fraser 'led and controlled it perfectly'.[104]

In many respects Operation Cauldron was a dry run for the *coups de main* of D-Day, not least in the devastating combination of ground and air attack at a pivotal moment. 4 Commando displayed an invention, determination, and ruthlessness that literally blew the Varengeville garrison away. From a force of 252, 12 commandos died, with 34 wounded or missing. Most of the casualties came home, with one of them awarded the VC for his part in the final attack. By 8.30am Lovat's battered force was back in its boats. An exuberant colonel sent Mountbatten a rare glimmer of hope on a dismal morning: 'Hess battery destroyed, all enemy gun crews finished with the battery – is this OK with you?' Only when he rendezvoused with the *Calpe* were Lovat's original fears revived. The destroyer was already crammed with wounded men, and in danger of being sunk by the *Luftwaffe*. Like Lovat, Lieutenant Scott was awaiting further orders, but none came. Eventually, both gunboat and commandos were told to head home. Scott attributed an all too obvious paralysis of authority to the ferocity of the air attack, compounded by a near breakdown in communications: 'There was a terrible feeling of helplessness at this time, and also a strange aloofness from the awful happenings so close to us but hidden by the thick white curtain [of smoke].' Late in the afternoon a triumphant 4 Commando docked at Newhaven. Their brigade commander, Bob Laycock, offered a surprisingly downbeat welcome, insisting on discretion in the light of the Canadians' heavy losses. An exhausted Lovat was immediately driven to London, and a late-night meeting with the CCO.[105]

Due to brief the Cabinet the following day, Mountbatten must have been desperate for good news. Yet Lovat was far too tired to offer any serious insight into the course of the battle. However, in later years he was far more forthcoming. In his memoirs Lovat suggested that after St Nazaire Mountbatten had become 'over-bold and prepared to take unjustified risks' when planning his next great adventure. In a Canadian documentary shot around the same time the commando chief was unequivocal: 'You've got to start one day fighting the enemy, but you don't start by landing frontally in daylight at a defended port like Dieppe.' Yet if anyone was personally responsible for such a fundamental and catastrophic error Lovat appeared to blame the disingenuous Montgomery rather than the delusional Mountbatten.[106]

In the immediate aftermath of the raid Durnford-Slater was disappointed but phlegmatic. As for Lovat, he and his senior officers had little faith in COHQ's ability to identify viable missions, either before or after Dieppe. Through their own initiative they had benefited from a depth of intelligence superior to that enjoyed by the main assault force, and crucially, they had worked on the premise that a vigilant enemy would be of a higher fighting calibre than the Canadians were led to expect. A hazardous raid on Boulogne in the spring of 1942 had convinced Lovat that confident and experienced landing-craft crews were vital in ensuring punctuality and accurate navigation. Looking back on Operation Jubilee years later he blamed Hughes-Hallett for not ensuring that all naval personnel were of a uniformly high standard, and Mountbatten and his fellow chiefs of staff for not giving the Royal Navy enough training time. The Chiefs were equally to blame for bowing to political pressure and agreeing to deploy 'inexperienced beginners; all innocent of heart and unaware of withering fire power and the ferocity of war'. To compound the folly the Canadians had been expected to establish a beach-head in a battle zone almost untouched by preliminary bombardment. The experience of 4 and more especially 3 Commando on 19 August had been bloody, but these were elite forces, highly trained and in most cases battle-hardened. For Lovat the contrast with Roberts' 2nd Division could not have been greater – and it is to these 'inexperienced beginners' that we must now turn.[107]

Tactical surprise was crucial to every aspect of the Jubilee masterplan, but never more so than on Blue Beach. Less than 100 Germans held the cliff-top at Puys, but they boasted Spandau heavy machine guns and 81mm mortars. Already awake and on duty, officers and NCOs commanding the four pill boxes were alerted by the German convoy's noisy encounter with 3 Commando. Now an astonishing chapter of errors saw the pendulum swing even further in favour of the defenders. The converted cross-Channel ferries carrying the Royal Regiment arrived off France ahead of schedule, but then some of the landing craft followed an accompanying motor gunboat (MGB) towards the wrong beach. Once the error was recognised precious minutes were lost regrouping. Trying to make up lost time another escort set off too fast, leaving the slower craft way behind. Instead of guiding his convoy straight for Blue Beach, the second MGB's skipper, Lieutenant-Commander Harry Goulding, headed for Dieppe before turning north up the coast. This was disastrous, both in terms of German flares illuminating the invasion force, and the fact that the small boats' painful procession up the coastline was accompanied by a stream of relentless shellfire. It aptly illustrated Lovat's complaint that naval personnel were singularly deficient when it came to night-time, in-shore navigation.[108]

Even before first light the enemy had no problem sighting Douglas Catto's hapless raiders. Yet by the time the first wave finally got ashore, not long after 5am, dawn was breaking, and the German machine-gunners could enjoy a crystal-clear view of the entire beach. Their big, belt-fed Spandaus seriously out-gunned the invaders' magazine-fed Brens. Crucially, German mortar crews were not hampered by problems of elevation, unlike their Canadian counterparts who feared firing bombs at nearly 90° in case they came straight back down. The defenders' mortar bombs crashed in to the beach and on to the incoming craft, while machine-gun fire enfiladed the 50 yard stretch between the LCAs and the sea wall. Of over 250 men in the first wave, a pitifully small number made it across the shingle. Twenty minutes later, in full daylight, the second wave approached a beach littered with dead and wounded, many of them slumped across the bows of nine badly damaged death-traps. This was another occasion on which the assault should have been called off, the first being when it became clear that there could be no element of surprise and no cover of darkness. However, honour prevailed over common-sense, and Catto refused to sacrifice one half of his battalion in order to save the other. The result was carnage as bad as – or perhaps even worse than – the bloodiest moments on the Western Front: the first day of the Somme may be an obvious parallel, but more appropriate is Passchendaele, in that those not shot or shelled died of drowning. Of course a more apt comparison is the landing at Anzac Cove on the Dardanelles, the bloodiest day of a costly adventure which Mountbatten had sworn would never be repeated.

Just a handful from the second wave reached the fragile safety of the sea wall. A few, some would say wisely, only jumped ashore when forced to at pistol point. Their reluctance was to generate heated discussion in the immediate aftermath, and become a sensitive issue in the ensuing years. To Hughes-Hallett's subsequent regret, publication in the *London Gazette* of his post-raid despatch made a passing reference to some soldiers' reluctance to go ashore. This was in August 1947, since when controversy has surrounded, 'something which had best been allowed to slumber …'.[109] To what extent troops were coerced was one of the key issues discussed at an informal enquiry held only two days after the raid: convinced that events at Blue Beach had triggered a larger failure, Hughes-Hallett ordered every naval officer who had taken part in the landing to account for his actions. The enquiry noted with alarm the reluctance of the beachmaster to vacate one of the two heavy-duty LCMs (the slower, larger Landing Craft Mechaniseds). Unlike for the other beaches, the Royal Navy had not appointed a deputy – a failure tacitly acknowledged by the captain chairing the enquiry. For all its fulsome praise of the courage displayed in getting the Canadians ashore, his final report revealed a shocking picture of panic, confusion, and incompetence. Given the volume of hastily gathered evidence, and obvious grimness of proceedings, this document has an immediacy and frankness absent from later inquests into what went wrong.[110]

There was no obvious chain of command, and yet somehow a crazy, chaotic evacuation of the beach began. While LCAs were either abandoned or heroically relaunched under remorseless fire, the two bigger boats turned west towards Dieppe and liaison with any destroyers able to take off the wounded. The events at Blue Beach were so horrific that it is hard to imagine anything worse taking place. Yet it did – when the five LCAs carrying 'Edwards Force', the support company of the Black Watch, landed under the cliffs at the western end of the beach. Ironically, their location was their saviour as attempts to break cover generated a ferocious response. It had been a pointless intervention, the consequence of two junior officers losing radio contact and acting as they thought appropriate: the naval commander in consequence lost his life, while the army commander waited with his largely unscathed company to be taken prisoner.

When landing craft returned to the beach in the hope of evacuating more men, the scramble to get on board was so intense that at least one LCA failed to seal its bows and sank. Men were reduced to swimming out to sea in the feeble hope of being picked up. Most either drowned or were shot as they fought with a falling tide. Ironically, some were rescued by Eurekas of 3 Commando arriving on the wrong beach. It was now around 7.30am, and action along the shore had all but ceased. Yet, astonishingly, up at the head of the gully Douglas Catto had cut through the wire and led a small force of survivors to the edge of the village. Fierce house-to-house fighting followed until the Canadians cut loose and found cover. Late that afternoon, they came out of hiding and joined up with their comrades as the shattered remains of the 2nd Battalion Royal Regiment of Canada marched off into captivity. Of the 262 who surrendered, no less than 103 were wounded, of whom 16 subsequently died. A total of 65 officers and men got back to England, with half of them casualties. The battalion lost a shattering 88 per cent of the front-line infantry men who made up its four rifle companies. German losses amounted to two dead and nine wounded.[111]

What is really remarkable about this whole episode is how the force commanders on board HMS *Calpe* had almost no idea what was going on. There was a near total breakdown of communications from the moment the battalion signallers were shot as they stepped ashore. The destroyer *Garth*, having provided a pitiful bombardment prior to the first wave's arrival, intermittently sent Roberts largely speculative signals, but in reality had little idea what lay beyond the smoke-screen. Goulding, in the MGB, sent the *Calpe* such a wildly optimistic assessment that he was ordered to report directly to Hughes-Hallett. When Goulding repeated his crazy claim that three companies had landed with light casualties he was believed, and a positive signal despatched to Uxbridge at 7.40am. Where was the healthy scepticism, not to say downright cynicism? An injection of realism came much later when signals from the *Garth*, badly damaged but using the smoke-screen to good effect in providing covering fire, finally convinced Hughes-Hallett that the landing on Blue Beach had gone disastrously wrong. Around 9.00am he ordered Goulding to lead four LCAs in-shore and pick up anyone still alive and uncaptured. It was a pointless mission, as quickly became apparent – a landing was out of the question, and in any case there was no-one left to collect.[112] For one inner flanking attack to collapse had serious implications for the main assault, but should both fail then the consequences were catastrophic.

The *Calpe*'s first signal from Green Beach indicated that the South Saskatchewans had successfully landed while it was still dark. Sadly, this was also the last signal, and for the next four hours Roberts had little idea of what was happening in and around the village of Pourville.[113] The element of surprise lasted long enough for the four rifle companies, each facing a truly herculean task, to discover that half of them were on the wrong side of a river surrounded by marshland and crossed only via a narrow and heavily fortified bridge. As at Puys, Green Beach was an obvious place to land, hence the presence of a small but skilfully deployed defence force. By 6.00am the South Saskatchewans may have cleared Pourville and the western slopes above the village, but they paid a high price for failing to land troops east of the River Scie. Furthermore, intermittent contact with the escort vessels off-shore meant that naval support was directionless and irregular: direct hits on enemy positions were few and far between. Astonishing acts of heroism, not least by Cecil

Merritt, the battalion commander, saw the bridge finally secured – but not before the Cameron Highlanders belatedly came ashore at 5.50am. A half-hour postponement had been deliberate, the Camerons' CO not wishing to impede the advance guard's consolidation of the beach-head. Given that German gunners now had the precise range to rain fire down on the incoming craft this was a fatal error, and indeed the colonel paid the ultimate price the moment he stepped ashore. Most of this follow-up force landed west of the river, and yet it was the delayed assault upon the eastern slopes which was encountering the stiffest resistance.

Both battalions had started the battle significantly under strength, and increasingly they found themselves scattered across a wide area: they needed to regroup and, for the Camerons, restore a clear chain of command. In time the Canadians were able to concentrate their forces and renew their advance inland. Yet they had no idea how well the attack on Dieppe was progressing, and whether a planned rendezvous with the Calgary Tanks was still on the cards. Communications remained near non-existent, whether between units or via the beach to Roberts. The strength in depth of the enemy implied no Allied breakout, and thus no prospect of tanks appearing behind a rapidly strengthening German counter-attack. Resistance was now so great that not long after 9.00am the invaders began to fall back upon Pourville, anticipating a disciplined fighting retreat back down on to Green Beach. This the Canadian troops achieved, with great distinction, but as they vacated their positions the enemy returned. By the time the remnants of the two battalions reached the shoreline the Germans had reoccupied their defensive positions, and re-established their sight lines across the beach below.

When finally the *Calpe* heard news from Green Beach, it was a signal requesting the evacuation of casualties. This was at 8.46am, a time when almost every report reaching Roberts bore bad news. Assuming the worst at Pourville, he ordered everyone to get out at 10.30am. This would quickly become part of a decision to pull all the troops out, with the codeword 'Vanquish' signalled at 9.50am. Not long after, withdrawal was put back by 30 minutes, partly to ensure all troops had heard the order, and partly to give the RAF enough time to thicken the smokescreen. The postponement until 11.00am sowed confusion among the main assault force, not least because the revised time was now a whole hour later than that originally sought by senior officers in Pourville. The original idea had been that the Camerons and South Saskatchewans would withdraw through Dieppe, but now the landing craft would be needed back on Green Beach. All attempts to radio the boat pool failed, and frantic flag signalling attracted only a handful of craft. Two LCAs came and went, driven off by shelling and machine-gun fire. Just after 11.00am four landing craft drove on to the beach, instead of waiting in water deep enough to prevent grounding once the rescued rushed aboard. By this time the tide was all but out, and the Canadians faced a 200 yards dash under murderous fire. Those that made it to the sea found one LCA so badly holed that it had to be abandoned. In consequence a second boat became so overloaded that it capsized. The remaining two craft, crammed with men, remained seaworthy just long enough to unload survivors on to the nearest available destroyers. Further efforts to collect troops off the beach saw top-heavy landing craft so overloaded that they turned over – some swam, some drowned, and most died in a hail of machine-gun bullets. On the beach itself order and discipline had all but broken down, and with so many LCAs swamped by troops there came a point around noon where it was clear that the last seaworthy boat had limped away, and the covering rear guard had no option but to surrender.[114]

One hundred and twenty brave men remained on Green Beach to the bitter end. Among them were the four company commanders of the South Saskatchewan Regiment and their CO, the redoubtable Cecil Merritt. Of the battalion's 25 officers only six reached England unscathed. Out of 523 who left for Pourville, 353 made it back, but 167 of them were wounded. 84 men were killed, and another 89 made prisoner. Five hundred and three of Canada's Cameron Highlanders landed, and 268 came away, of whom 103 were wounded. 60 men died, and 167 became POWs. Only eight out of 32 officers returned home without one or more wounds. The joint losses for both battalions on Green Beach totalled no less than 39 per cent. As Robin Neillands has pointed out, such an appalling figure reflects the fact that there were simply not enough troops deployed to undertake a multitude of tasks: radar station, anti-aircraft battery, and airfield all remained intact. Given how far inland Colonel Merritt and his men penetrated, what they did achieve was remarkable: while a prisoner in Germany the battalion commander was awarded the VC for his courageous leadership. Similarly, the Camerons' acting commander, Major Tony Law, deserved praise for taking his men further than any other Allied unit that day – halting only when faced by well-organised and overwhelming firepower. Yet again, the planners had placed their faith in the element of surprise, and in an over-riding assumption that the enemy was incapable of a speedy response.[115] As at Blue Beach, the assurance and aggression of the defenders, especially when well dug-in, confounded a confident belief that German soldiers manning the Atlantic Wall were demonstrably inferior to their comrades on the Eastern Front.[116]

Success in the four flanking assaults ranged from modest achievement to total failure, and yet a frontal attack on Dieppe demanded complete control of the two headlands, and of the coastal batteries beyond. Even had this ambitious objective been achieved then ideally capital ships and heavy bombers would have obliterated the concrete defences overlooking the esplanade and the sea wall. The reality was that Hughes-Hallett's destroyers scarcely dented the town's principal defences, and the cannon-firing Hurricanes left several lethal pill-boxes intact and operational.[117] The German armament was formidable, both on and around the esplanade, *and* in the narrow caves which had been carved out of the chalk cliffs on either side, thereby remaining invisible to aerial reconnaissance. This was defence in depth, with even a potential weak-spot like the half-demolished casino demonstrating the enemy's ability to reinforce at short notice. As elsewhere, the planners had grossly under-estimated the level of resistance, as became evident even before the first troops landed at around 5.20am.[118]

Two hours earlier the Canadians had transferred from three assault landing ships to an armada of LCAs, their long journey to the shore cramped and uncomfortable. Alerted by events elsewhere, the German defenders opened fire once the landing craft emerged out of the smokescreen laid down by the RAF. At the eastern end of the esplanade, on Red Beach, the Essex Scottish took heavy casualties and were quickly pinned down behind the low sea wall. Down at White Beach the Royal Hamilton Light Infantry suffered equally heavy losses. Robert Labatt, the battalion commander, saw that the attack had stalled, and in a costly effort to regain momentum sent his men in to seize the casino: after an hour of fighting their way room by room through the half-lit, half-wrecked gambling house, the Hamiltons somehow or other got a message to the *Calpe* that the building had been cleared. Up to this point – 7.15am – all signals off the beach had been garbled and gloomy, but here at last was some good news. Learning that the casino had fallen, and clearly clutching at straws, Roberts convinced himself that at last enemy defences in Dieppe were starting to crumble. There was no fine line between exploiting success and compounding failure – the force commander's disastrous decision to deploy his reserve was based on the bare minimum of information, and was taken at a moment when mounting evidence indicated the operation to be failing on every front.[119]

Roberts was dependent upon a solitary scout car stranded halfway up the beach. The occasional signal from a beleaguered NCO was all that remained of a communications network shattered at the point of arrival. Yet even a signals corporal scared witless was aware that any sustained attack would derive little direct support from the 15 tanks that had belatedly staggered off the beach, over the wall, and on to the promenade. Anti-tank obstacles installed to seal off entry to the town remained largely intact. The sappers designated to destroy them lay dead or wounded on the beach – the Royal Canadian Engineers suffered a staggering loss rate of nearly 90 per cent. Leaderless and with nowhere to go, the stranded tank crews kept firing at enemy positions until they ran out of ammunition, after which they simply waited to surrender. They had neither the firepower nor the elevation to shell targets on the headlands, and more significantly, could provide no penetration for the infantry. Of the Calgary Tanks' remaining Churchills, in a chapter of accidents all but one got ashore, at the cost of five out ten LCTs (two other vessels were badly damaged, and it's worth noting that around half of David Beatty's crews were either killed or wounded). These landings were absolutely chaotic, with all senior officers left dead, wounded, or isolated. Considering that the Germans had no anti-tank guns they were remarkably successful at immobilising the Churchills, targeting their tracks and directing tracer fire at vulnerable fuel tanks. It was at this stage of the operation that the largest number of infantrymen refused to go ashore, notably a platoon on LCT6, last of the second wave and the only landing craft that saw all three tanks gain the promenade unscathed. The latter was a minor triumph in itself given the panorama of horror that greeted anyone scanning the seafront from the dubious safety of a villa on the Boulevard de Verdun.[120]

The lonely signaller on Red Beach reported that 30 or so soldiers of the Essex Scottish had finally got across the promenade. Their brief house-to-house foray in the direction of the harbour was as far as anyone got in Dieppe that day, but, along with good news from the casino, this was sufficient to convince Roberts that now was the right time to send in reinforcements. That such a decision should result from the solitary success of a battalion reporting 75 per cent casualties is tragic irony of Jacobean proportions. Roberts had no justification in assuming that the Calgary Tanks, along with the Essex Scottish, were at last advancing into the town. Every report, however garbled, indicated the contrary; and in any case the casualties mounting up on the *Calpe* and its companion destroyers were evident proof of disaster. Shattered landing craft struggled to keep afloat while waiting to off-load the wounded and report on the disastrous course of events ashore.

All the evidence suggested carnage, and yet Roberts nevertheless despatched the Fusiliers Mont-Royal to reinforce the Essex Scottish on Red Beach. The resulting slaughter was a consequence of the 26 LCAs providing such an easy target as the craft were swept westwards by the current to the furthest extreme of White Beach. Landing at around 7.00am the Fusiliers were further shredded by the stream of fire and hand grenades coming off the far headland. All but four of their 31 officers were killed, wounded or captured, and only a tiny number got back to England. With over 100 killed off-shore or on the beach, and dozens more wounded, just 120 out of the battalion's complement of 584 men contrived to avoid capture.[121]

Unlike the Québecois, the Royal Marine Commando did set out with the intention of landing on White Beach. Relieved of the crazy task of capturing invasion barges, its CO, 'Tiger' Picton-Phillips, had been ordered to transfer all his men on to LCAs and LCMs, land at the far end of the beach, skirt round the town, and attack the batteries on the eastern cliff. If it wasn't for the fact that the colonel lost his life frantically signalling to turn back, and that well over a third of 'A' Commando's officers and men were killed, wounded, and captured, such a command would be an absurdity worthy of General Melchett: 'This meant a mere walk of two and a half miles along the Rue de Sygogne, where no one had yet advanced 20 yards.'[122] Nothing highlights better how 'Ham' Roberts deep in the bowels of the *Calpe* was totally out of touch with events on the ground. In his unpublished memoirs Hughes-Hallett distanced himself from this decision, insisting that, 'my own picture of the general situation – confused though it was – was a good deal clearer than that of General Roberts who had nothing but a mass of garbled corrupt radio messages to go upon'. That may well have been true, but Hughes-Hallett's credentials as a master tactician were scarcely strengthened by a firm belief that 'A' Commando would have been better employed reinforcing Green Beach.[123]

If the Royal Marines paid a heavy price for being despatched on a suicide mission, their losses scarcely compared with the two Canadian battalions that bore the brunt of the fighting in the main assault. On White Beach the Royal Hamilton Light Infantry lost 372 men killed or captured, and many of the latter were casualties. Just half of the 217 men who got back to England escaped without injury, and only one officer. For the Essex Scottish, of the 555 men who landed on Red Beach a mere 52 made it back home: 121 died and 382 were taken prisoner, many of them wounded. These were truly devastating figures, but, as has been seen, on 19 August 1942 they were by no means unique.[124]

Lovat's farewell to Orange Beach may have been a textbook operation, but it was the exception to the rule – the withdrawal from Dieppe was both tragedy and farce.

In his memoirs Hughes-Hallett gave the impression that Roberts had become so detached from harsh reality that, before reluctantly accepting the case for evacuation, he had to be stopped from going ashore in a last desperate effort to rally his men.[125] Once the force commanders were in agreement that it was time to go, and their initial departure date had been hastily amended to 11.00am, the destroyers turned their attention to the twin headlands. Here was a forlorn attempt to cover the withdrawal by shelling the Germans' most visible positions. This was a desperate act, but at least it made sense. The same could scarcely be said for the lieutenant who interpreted 'Vanquish' as authorisation to head home. Not only did he command LCF1 ('landing craft flak'), but he also controlled a number of LCAs. Nor was he alone in his folly: not for the first time that day there was a failure to seek clarification of a crucial message from the *Calpe*. In consequence the officer commanding the boat pool led various LCPs and smaller vessels straight back to Newhaven. Given the scale of earlier losses, let alone the imminent destruction of several LCAs at Pourville, the premature departure of so many landing craft severely impaired efforts to maintain a lifeline between the town beach and the ships in action off-shore.[126]

The parallel withdrawals from Red and White Beaches were blighted by delay, and irregular communication between senior officers ashore and the *Calpe*. The shortage of boats meant that coxswains who had gone in under fire, lifted off a full load, and successfully made their way out to the waiting destroyers, found their relief turn to horror when ordered to go straight back. However dense the smokescreen it provided only partial cover, and as the cloud drifted inland the principal beneficiaries were the German gunners on the twin headlands. The loss of LCAs, not least as a consequence of too many troops rushing to clamber aboard, replicated the horrors of Green Beach: fixed lines of fire were wreaking havoc; the number of landing craft was rapidly diminishing; for all the courage and camaraderie order was breaking down; and the whole process was taking far too long. Many soldiers tried swimming to safety, with some drowning, a few succeeding, and most coming to terms with reality. Lethargy, exhaustion, and the need to preserve life dictated imminent surrender; by 1.00pm, when the *Calpe* briefly broke out of the smokescreen to make a bold but dispiriting survey of the seafront, it was clear that the battle was all but over. By early afternoon the long shingle beach was already empty of the living. It would be another week before the dead were finally gone, with each tide washing up yet more bodies.[127]

The remnants of Hughes-Hallett's armada limped back across the Channel, repeatedly harassed by the *Luftwaffe*. For the *Calpe*, carrying over 300 survivors, many of whom were seriously injured, the price of hanging on until the bitter end was extensive bomb damage. Nevertheless, she remained afloat and able to provide escort protection. In fact all but one of the Hunt-class destroyers sent to Dieppe survived. The exception was HMS *Berkeley*, which was so badly hit during the withdrawal that she had to be abandoned and then sunk by torpedo. When finally the fleet reached Portsmouth and Newhaven the authorities struggled to cope with the volume of casualties. It was not until the early hours of the following day that all the wounded were at last off the boats and en route to hospital. For those fit to remain with their regiments roll-call on 20 August was a revelation, and for many the first clear indication of how lucky they were to be alive and at liberty. It was true that around two-thirds of the original force had made it home, but this figure was distorted by the not inconsiderable number that never actually landed – most through no fault of their own, and some as a consequence of refusing to obey orders. In total, out of 6,000 combatants 3,367 were either killed, captured, or wounded, including 270 commandos and 550 members of the Royal Navy. Canada's 2nd Brigade suffered the loss of 56 officers and 851 men, a number of whom died in captivity. It's worth noting that German casualties totalled little more than 600. An equally revealing statistic is that more Canadians were captured in one morning at Dieppe than in the whole of the period they spent fighting their way up through Italy. The most obvious comparison is with the Great War, notably the Somme offensive; but one key difference is that Canada's fighting men on the Western Front enjoyed an enviable record of securing their objectives, most famously at Vimy Ridge.[128]

The initial report on the raid, submitted to the War Cabinet in mid-October 1942, insisted that the, 'most striking achievement was the success of the Royal Air Force in providing cover and inflicting casualties on the enemy'. Allied losses were largely accurate, with 106 aircraft lost and 153 personnel killed (including 71 pilots, of whom 44 were RAF); while the Royal Navy saved a handful of pilots, the RAF's own Air Sea Rescue picked up no less than 14, albeit at a cost of 29 crewmen dead or missing. Fighter Command sought to counter-balance a fairly bleak picture with a scarcely convincing estimate of enemy aircraft severely damaged or destroyed. The RAF came up with a statistic around two-thirds higher than what it stated was the Germans' own calculation of 170.[129]

Where the latter figure came from is not at all clear, but in the real world the *Luftwaffe* had lost a total of only 48 aircraft. Over half of the German losses were bombers. They flew at distance from their home bases and displayed a recklessness not seen since the Norway campaign. In actual fact most of the Heinkels and Dorniers destroyed had been at nearby Abbeville, still waiting to take off when the Americans' 91st Bomber Group attacked the airfield. The USAAF lost no B17s in its modest baptism of fire. The RAF in contrast had eight bombers shot down, with only minimal damage inflicted upon the enemy's concrete gun emplacements. Much greater success was achieved in laying down successive smokescreens, but even here Leigh-Mallory felt far more could have been achieved had the aircraft been available. Although Fighter Command clearly enjoyed numerical superiority, the ability of *Luftwaffe* fighter pilots to patrol for far longer periods forced a trebling of RAF squadrons in the skies above Dieppe. A key role was to ward off bomber attacks, but the Spitfire squadrons' principal task was to engage as speedily as possible with the 300 or so Me109s and FW190s flying in rota out of French airfields. The RAF was to lose no less than 88 fighters on 19 August 1942. The air battle over Dieppe cruelly exposed the inadequacies of the first generation Mustangs; but the same proved true for the previously much admired Spitfire Mk V in its first serious encounter with Focke-Wolf's latest creation: the outstanding performance of the FW190 sent Supermarine's designers straight back to the drawing board, working out how to maximise the performance of their new fast-climbing Mk IX. An added hazard for Allied fighters at Dieppe, especially the unfamiliar Mustang, was being hit by indiscriminate friendly fire. Two important lessons of the raid were improved aircraft recognition, and an acknowledgement that anti-aircraft gunnery needed to be more focused and less wasteful. Yet the most important consequence for the RAF was that no case could now be made for a concerted effort to bleed the *Luftwaffe* in the west, in order to ease pressure on Soviet fliers in the east. The cost was simply too great.[130]

9

DIEPPE – THE AFTERMATH, THE INQUEST, AND THE DEBATE

Dieppe – news management in the immediate aftermath of the raid
Before exploring news management in the immediate aftermath of the Dieppe raid, we need to note the symbiotic relationship between Combined Operations and the mass media. To employ contemporary parlance, Mountbatten was the master of spin. He was always happy to oblige the press – and yet he was never entirely blind to the fact that those who live by the sword can just as quickly die by the sword. He had of course relished the role of a dashing royal in a dashing destroyer, as portrayed via the Admiralty's impressive public relations operation. Fleet Street coverage of the *Kelly*'s fortitudes, whether at home or off Crete, had been in turns sonorous and sombre, but was never censorious. A mixture of rigorous self-censorship, urgent patriotism, and customary deference had ensured the absence of any awkward questions; after all this was a nation experiencing the greatest ever threat to its survival, and all acts of courage, however tainted by rashness, were to be loudly applauded. Someone so fascinated by the communications revolution was bound to prioritise public relations once the Prime Minister gave him carte blanch to revamp Roger Keyes' still fragile creation.

This was ironic as the admiral turned parliamentarian was himself never one to shun the limelight. Yet Keyes did appreciate that an embryonic organisation like Combined Operations needed to establish itself before enthusiastically embracing the special correspondent and the newsreel cameraman. Nor did Keyes wish to upset the Admiralty's formidable team of publicists, as soon became the case once he had moved on.[1] This is not to suggest that in COHQ's early days there had been no publicity, but it's clearly the case that Mountbatten and key members of his staff cultivated Fleet Street on a previously unprecedented scale. Nor were they satisfied with keeping the British press happy. Combined Operations made effective use of a sustained propaganda initiative in the United States, as well as the Dominions' ceaseless search for good news stories from the old country. In this respect special forces provided glamour, bravado, and an aura of cool-headed derring do which mirrored the public persona of their nominal leader – feature articles on both sides of the Atlantic portrayed the commandos as Churchill's creation and Mountbatten's not so secret weapon. Such stories were naturally short on detail and long on speculation, with reporters drip-fed information until such times as a Bruneval or St Nazaire provided solid evidence that the chaps selected to fight a shadowy war on the edge of occupied Europe really could give the Germans a bloody nose.

The commandos themselves hated the limelight, with two officers court-martialled for their treatment of the team sent to film and report the raid on Vaagso. Ever the professional, Lovat loathed the prevailing notion of his men as 'reckless, devil-may-care fellows who acted in a slap-happy and generally irresponsible manner'. He insisted his men have nothing to do with the press and anyone who disobeyed his orders was gone within 24 hours. For the Dieppe raid Lovat made an exception as a friend in Fleet Street was a first-class shot. Noting Mountbatten's love of the limelight, the clan chief turned commando was of the firm belief that, 'A good soldier – Montgomery was a notable exception – should avoid publicity and keep his mouth shut'.[2]

Lovat was no doubt irritated by the extent to which Mountbatten became so closely associated with the commandos once news broke in the spring of 1942 that he was Chief of Combined Operations. Churchill's carefully orchestrated announcement triggered what today would be labelled a media offensive.[3] Newspaper and magazine articles on both sides of the Atlantic – and even in Vichy France – felt free to make absurd and inaccurate claims regarding 'Commando Chief Lord Louis Mountbatten'. One splendidly Buchanesque cover story, later recycled in *Life*, had 'Cousin Dickie' disappearing from Brook's, only to reappear in the club several weeks later a fully qualified commando and a veteran of the Vaagso raid: 'Daring courage, a first-class brain and cool judgement rarely go together, but they make a wonderful fighting combination. Lord Louis Mountbatten has all three.'[4] In the United States *Time* and *Reader's Digest* matched *Life* in feeding Anglophile Americans' fascination with the warrior royal.[5] Needless to say, feature writers not war correspondents were responsible for fostering a cult of the personality that Mountbatten's men found either highly amusing or deeply irritating. In March 1943 Combined Operations' in-house magazine published a gentle reminder that anyone accredited to accompany special forces on active service had already earned their spurs, and were fully entitled to enjoy the commandos' trust and cooperation. Restricted circulation enabled the naming of widely-respected journalists, with the BBC's Frank Gillard singled out as a battle-hardened veteran of Dieppe now plying his trade in the desert.[6]

Mountbatten set up a machinery for news briefing which, in a more sophisticated form, would later become a key element within SEAC Headquarters. Relying heavily upon Alan Campbell-Johnson, the same system was resurrected in 1947 with the intention of representing clearly, unambiguously, and sympathetically, the Viceroy's day-to-day handling of the transfer of power. India was a distinctly British show, but back in 1942 Mountbatten's PR team looked to Hollywood for inspiration – although Douglas Fairbanks Jr. found his way from the West Coast to Richmond Terrace, as indeed did Darryl F. Zanuck, a far more useful recruit was Jock Lawrence, Sam Goldwyn's publicist. Lieutenant Fairbanks may have advised on how to get your message across – he had after all been a very public advocate of America entering the war – but his involvement in planning for the Dieppe raid was actually quite modest; even if it proved good experience for later work with the US Navy when mounting amphibious operations in the Mediterranean. In the summer of 1942 what Mountbatten really needed was a tough back-room operator like Lawrence, not an adulatory one-time matinee idol like Fairbanks.[7]

Just as he admired almost anyone connected with the movies, Mountbatten shared a similar affection for denizens of the 'Street of Shame'. He liked journalists, and he liked their bosses, witness his early friendship with Beaverbrook. Most newspapermen who worked for him were on the payroll of the 'Beaver', but by no means all. Thus one important recruit to COHQ in the summer of 1942 was David Astor, a young Royal Marine officer already fixed on an ambitious long-term goal of remoulding the *Observer*. Captain Astor was the press officer who never saw action: on four separate occasions he set his sights on France only to see the raid called off. To his credit, Mountbatten covered Astor's back when MI5 warned that here was someone frequently seen with German émigrés. Astor found Richmond Terrace a convenient base from which to mastermind the relaunch of his newspaper. Away from COHQ for a few hours he found time to network and recruit fresh talent; for example, weekly meetings in a Soho restaurant of the 'Shanghai Club' ensured regular acquaintance with left-leaning journalists and political commentators. Here was a handy supply of exceptional talent, and Astor energetically recruited several of the *Observer*'s best known columnists and feature writers.[8] Among the Tuesday night diners was George Orwell, already a close friend and occasional contributor.[9]

It was Fleet Street's coming man whom Mountbatten chose to brief the naval force commander as soon as the *Calpe* reached England. Astor made sure that Hughes-Hallett would exercise appropriate discretion when reporting to Admiral Sir William James, C-in-C Portsmouth. Already the CCO was ensuring that all sang from the same hymn sheet. Although one of the few owner-editors to retire with his reputation intact, David Astor does appear open to a charge of double standards. On the one hand he was working assiduously for Combined Operations, endeavouring to portray an obvious disaster in the best possible light, but on the other he was feeding information to the *Observer* newsroom. Indeed, if Orwell is to be believed, Astor succeeded in painting an even blacker picture than the actual chain of events – he even had the nerve to complain about press deception![10]

Surprisingly, Fleet Street had only one pool contributor at Dieppe. No doubt to the intense irritation of both Express Newspapers and the *Daily Mirror*, the worthy but uninspiring *Daily Herald* was selected. The solitary presence of the much-respected A.B. Austin on behalf of the whole British press hides the fact that a formidable body of reporters, photographers, and cameramen crossed the Channel. The Canadian Army's PR unit ensured that all the key newspapers in Ontario and English-speaking Quebec were either directly represented or had access to what today would be labelled an 'embedded correspondent'. With COHQ's enthusiastic approval, the Canadians also invited five Americans, including Associated Press's Drew Middleton and *Colliers*' Quentin Reynolds. Tellingly, no less than a quarter of the total number of journalists who went to Dieppe were drawn from the country with the smallest military representation.[11] After Ed Murrow, Reynolds was the USA's best known reporter in London, held in especially high esteem by the Ministry of Information for his contribution to the GPO Film Unit's portrayal of the early Blitz, *London Can Take It!*. In the autumn of 1940 Reynolds had not only provided a rousing commentary for the re-edited, renamed *Britain Can Take It!*, but back home in New York had enthusiastically endorsed the documentary's defiant message.[12]

Reynolds was a valuable asset, and he was well-acquainted with Mountbatten. Not surprisingly he was invited to join Hughes-Hallett aboard the *Calpe*. On his return from the raid he filed an overwhelmingly positive story – to his own paper, then one of America's leading weeklies, and later to *Reader's Digest*. The material was then repackaged to provide an early defence of Dieppe as a vital dress rehearsal for the imminent invasion of mainland Europe. Reynolds was insistent that preparation for the operation, if not the implementation, was flawless: Mountbatten's energy and enterprise had forged an organisation unparalleled in its efficiency, and it was hardly Combined Operations' fault if exemplary planning clashed with forces far beyond its control. Hilariously, Reynolds accepted without question Jock Lawrence's insistence that Lord Louis hated the glare of publicity.[13]

Austin was to write an even more gushing tribute to Mountbatten, going far beyond any wartime necessity to depict the operation as a qualified success.[14] Two other correspondents wrote similarly propagandist accounts of the raid, intended to reassure North American, especially Canadian, readers that the heavy casualties were a tragic necessity. Ross Munro, already a prominent journalist in Montreal, was shipped back home to address crowded receptions from coast to coast. Although troubled by the less than honest message he was forced to convey, he still managed to produce by the end of the war a distinctly upbeat version of events. Well before that there appeared Wallace Reyburn's best-selling tribute to the fallen. Although by birth a Kiwi, Reyburn was accredited to the Canadian press corps, writing for the weekly *Montreal Star*. He went ashore at Pourville with the South Saskatchewans, and, in a truly traumatic escape from Green Beach, had been lucky to sustain no more than a few minor wounds.[15] Entitling his story *Rehearsal for Invasion*, Reyburn echoed Reynolds in unquestioningly accepting Mountbatten's argument that lessons learnt would be invaluable when returning to France. In later life, as we shall see, Reyburn wholly rejected a defence of the raid formulated even before the operation was fully concluded. A quarter of a century later he witheringly recalled the speed with which this remarkably resilient line of argument was first constructed.[16]

The day after the debacle Mountbatten chaired a lengthy meeting at COHQ. All senior staff were expected to attend, and after lunch they were joined by several junior officers who had actually taken part in the operation. The presence of the latter ensured what diplomats tactfully label 'full and frank discussion'. It was probably the most uninhibited and brutally honest exchange of views generated by the raid. However, it was the earlier conversation which determined how Dieppe would be projected to a waiting world. Notable by their presence that morning was Whitehall's finest PR men and, crucially, the MoI's new minister, Brendan Bracken.[17]

For Combined Operations, Bracken's presence was crucial: not only was he the first politician to provide focus and direction to the Ministry of Information, but he retained a powerful presence within Fleet Street, and crucially, he enjoyed the full confidence of the Prime Minister.

In Cairo the PM was already aware that 'casualties have been heavy and that generally speaking objectives were not attained'. Yet, according to the CCO, morale was excellent, and all troops were 'in great form'.[18] Churchill was too sharp to be deceived by such platitudinous nonsense. He gave Mountbatten – and Bracken – every encouragement to snatch a spurious victory out of defeat: 'Consider it wise to describe "Jubilee" as quote reconnaissance in force unquote.' Two days later Churchill signalled to the War Cabinet his 'general impression' that 'the results fully justified the heavy cost. The large-scale air battle alone justified the raid'. This interpretation of events had already been conveyed to the King, and would be reinforced by Churchill's statement to the Commons on 8 September. Yet in the immediate aftermath of the raid both the Prime Minister and the CIGS were too preoccupied with matters in the Middle East to appreciate the sense of crisis at home. The Secretary for India was anything but sanguine when Mountbatten rushed from COHQ's initial inquest to reassure the Cabinet that the raid, 'while essentially unsuccessful in itself', had nevertheless destroyed a third of the *Luftwaffe*'s forces in France. When a sceptical Leo Amery asked why a less strongly defended location had not been selected, 'Mountbatten said that he had had a scheme of that sort but it had been vetoed'. Already the CCO was covering his back.[19]

The three communiqués released on the day of the raid had been little more than an acknowledgement of events. Following the meeting at COHQ a final, more detailed communiqué could be drafted. At the same time all reporters who went to Dieppe were given a belated, but definitive, briefing, and their stories finally cleared for publication. On the morning of 21 August readers and listeners at last received hard news regarding Operation Jubilee. But by this time German news agencies had released a stream of negative stories and a black propaganda station was putting its own unique spin on the more mainstream broadcasts out of Berlin. The Germans were presented with a unique opportunity to exploit inter-Allied tension when the initial guidance given to British editors by the Controller of Press and Censorship significantly under-estimated the Canadian contribution. Too often, both in Britain and the United States, initial coverage of the raid concentrated upon the heroics of the commandos and Fighter Command. Ill-informed, sensationalist reporting encouraged the short-lived popular assumption that Dieppe had somehow been a triumph. The astonishingly inaccurate stories that appeared in both the popular and quality press were replicated in American newspapers. This set an agenda, but at the expense of the principal participants – and of the other allies whose forces had taken part in the operation, most notably the Free French. At least the Canadians themselves could applaud their fighting men's first major contribution to the war effort, even if it quickly became obvious that information was being withheld regarding the number of lives lost. Official casualty figures were finally released on 15 September 1942, by which time no journalist or broadcaster in Canada could depict Dieppe as anything other than an appalling tragedy – already newspapers were asking how such losses could ever be justified.[20]

The truth was that Combined Operations' publicity machine had found itself fire-fighting from the moment news filtered back that the flanking attacks had stalled. For their German counterparts, however, the Dieppe raid had proved a huge propaganda coup. The photographs alone appeared a damning indictment of British hubris, with Churchill and Mountbatten depicted as cynical imperialists happy to sacrifice Canadian lives in order to preserve an obsolescent plutocratic and aristocratic power structure.[21] Exposing the emptiness of Lord Haw-Haw's charges was easy. The seriously challenging task for Mountbatten was convincing the service chiefs and the War Cabinet, as well as the wider world, that Combined Operations had conducted itself to the very best of its ability, that valuable lessons had clearly been learnt, and that direct responsibility for the failure of Operation Jubilee most certainly did not rest upon his own slender and impressively epauletted shoulders. Defending Dieppe to a success-starved public was not an insurmountable problem, especially when the likes of Ross Munro could be dragooned into convincing sceptical Canadians that the loss of their boys was a heavy but necessary price to pay. Notwithstanding the power of German propaganda, in the battle to maintain morale Quentin Reynolds and his fellow hacks could be relied upon to conjure triumph out of tragedy.

No, the real problem rested within Whitehall, where Mountbatten faced mounting criticism. Meeting in the specially designated 'Dieppe Room', COHQ's hastily convened 'Study Group' was tasked with providing a speedy analysis of what went wrong. Meanwhile, as a holding operation Hughes-Hallett's obligatory despatch to Sir William James skilfully pre-empted a number of awkward questions. With Roberts and Leigh-Mallory, he then drafted a joint memorandum for Mountbatten; this formed the basis for COHQ's November 1942 paper on lessons to be learnt from mounting such an ambitious assault. However, before that, on 15 October, the CCO signed off Combined Operations' official report. Here was a powerful – if not necessarily persuasive – point by point defence of the organisation's contribution to planning the raid. Veiled and not so veiled criticism of the Army, both British and Canadian, was apparent throughout the document. Not surprisingly, there was scant criticism of the Royal Navy; and the RAF's inflated claims were assumed to be authentic.[22] Accepting Leigh-Mallory's version of events was crucial for Mountbatten. The 'pre-invasion dress rehearsal' defence might be sold to a forgiving public, and would clearly gain credence post-D-Day, but a specialist audience simply wanted to know what went wrong, and whether any redeeming features could be identified – hence COHQ's quiet conspiracy with Fighter Command. By late autumn 1942 a formidable volume of literature on the raid had been generated. At this point the former Clerk to the House of Lords, Hilary St George Saunders, was invited to review all relevant documentation, and to scrutinise the integrity of COHQ's final submission.[23] Given that at least two key reports were the ultimate responsibility of the Chief of Combined Operations, this was an extraordinary turn of events – as Mountbatten clearly recognised when pointing out to the Prime Minister's closest aide that he and his staff had been given a clean bill of health.[24]

Dieppe – defending the indefensible?

Churchill was too shrewd a politician not to appreciate why every effort had been made, 'to make this business look as good as possible', but that didn't stop him wanting to know why Jubilee was such an unmitigated disaster.[25] This revival of interest in the raid was encouraged by Alan Brooke. The CIGS had access to the Ministry of Information's weekly reports on the level of morale across the Home Front: throughout the autumn they revealed a growing belief that the Germans had advance notice of Dieppe, and that the Government was disguising the full extent of the tragedy.[26] Over dinner at Chequers soon after his return from Cairo, Brooke had made clear to both his host and his fellow guest, the Chief of Combined Operations, how poorly he viewed preparation for the raid. Mountbatten responded angrily, insisting that the military, and Montgomery in particular, bore final responsibility for what had gone wrong. If the Army still felt disempowered then the only remaining remedy was to disband COHQ. Claiming that Brooke's complaint was a resignation issue, Mountbatten threatened to request from Churchill a 'full and impartial enquiry' – clearly no-one, including himself, would emerge from such an investigation with their reputation intact, but he knew only too well that this was the last thing Brooke wanted at such a critical moment.[27]

Throughout the autumn the Chief of the Imperial General Staff had other priorities, in that he and Churchill were preoccupied with Monty's counter-offensive in the Middle East. However, once the full extent of the Eighth Army's success at El Alamein became clear, the two men could again focus upon the bigger picture. Renewed discussion within the Chiefs of Staff on grand strategy reminded the CIGS why so many of Mountbatten's ideas were 'half-baked'. Brooke enjoyed Dickie and Edwina's company, but like Cunningham he found congeniality no criterion for promotion. Dudley Pound remained similarly sceptical, and three days before Christmas he backed Brooke in a 'heated discussion' over Mountbatten's suitability to command all naval forces involved in the eventual invasion of France. Nearly ten months after Mountbatten's promotion both men were still insistent that, 'his job is one of an advisor and not of a commander'. A very different view was held by Charles Portal. The Chief of the Air Staff was no doubt appreciative of the CCO's recognition that Bomber Command needed a greater resource allocation in order to pulverise Germany. The PM's Chief of Staff, 'Pug' Ismay, was similarly supportive of Mountbatten's credentials as a task force commander.[28]

The next day – 23 December 1942 – the CIGS saw a 'very bad' invasion plan for Sardinia as confirmation of Combined Operations' obvious failure to understand the unique requirements of amphibious warfare when waged on the grand scale. As with Dieppe, the men at the top were largely drawn from the Navy: Mountbatten or Hughes-Hallett were thus singularly unqualified to plan the land battle once troops had disembarked. This of course ignored the contribution of experienced army officers within COHQ such as Charles Haydon, and the fact that it was Eisenhower who had signed off the Sardinia operation.[29] Ismay had already warned Mountbatten that Brooke was encouraging Churchill to delve further into the reasons why the Dieppe raid had failed so spectacularly. He forwarded eight questions for which the Prime Minister required urgent answers. Ismay clearly envisaged Mountbatten dealing with the matter personally and discreetly, even offering to pop into Richmond Terrace with some handy advice prior to Dickie putting pen to paper.[30] In actual fact this by no means easy task was passed on to Haydon. Significantly beefing up his deputy's draft reply, an indignant Mountbatten pointed out that the CIGS was well aware how he had always seen preliminary bombing of Dieppe as a prerequisite of any direct attack upon the port: because all force commanders accepted the final military plan, and a frontal assault seemed increasingly necessary whenever the actual invasion took place, he had chosen not to veto the operation.[31]

Mountbatten's fury with Alan Brooke was understandable. As we have seen, a compelling criticism of the CCO is that, if he was so certain preliminary bombardment was crucial to a frontal assault, then he ought never to have sanctioned Operation Rutter, let alone Jubilee. In other words, Mountbatten should have matched conviction with courage, and steeled himself for the inevitable charge that Combined Operations was all talk and no action.[32] Yet the same charge can be made of Brooke, who also had it in his power to halt the raid. At a meeting in Downing Street on 30 June an unusually cautious Churchill had asked Hughes-Hallett if he could guarantee success. Brooke had intervened to state that such a request was unreasonable, in that if one knew the outcome then there would be little point in mounting the raid in the first place. For the CIGS, if not, ironically, for the planners at Combined Operations, the over-riding objective of the raid was to see if a major cross-Channel incursion could be mounted. The PM, keenly aware of conditions in Egypt and Burma, observed that this was, 'not a moment at which he wanted to be taught by adversity'. In that case, Brooke replied, he should forget about France, as without the results of such an operation 'no responsible general' could authorise a full-scale invasion. Churchill fell silent, and Rutter rolled on. Surprisingly, Brooke made no record of this exchange in his diary, and yet Hughes-Hallett's account remains both credible and convincing.[33]

Churchill's Christmas Day reading contained a robust defence of his protégé's conduct. As in COHQ's original report, Mountbatten focused upon the force commanders' direct responsibility from mid-May for detailed planning, and their refusal to reverse a decision made in his absence to abandon high altitude advance bombing: at Tangmere two days before the raid Roberts had again insisted to Mountbatten that bomb damage would disrupt the invaders' advance into the town. Asked by the PM for his opinion of Major-General Roberts, Haydon provided Mountbatten with a masterly put-down: Combined Operations had viewed him as, 'a brave man who was always prepared to give a definite opinion and as one who was tenacious in holding such opinions once he had expressed them'. He was assumed to be efficient, as why else would the 'Canadian Authorities' have appointed him? Churchill queried why the frontal assault had gone ahead without first securing the cliffs at either side. Mountbatten replied that, had the timetable been adhered to, then the headlands would have been under fierce attack at the moment the main landings were launched. Furthermore, 'the limitations of aerial photography' had left a big hole in COHQ's intelligence briefings: no available images had detailed the fire positions dug into the cliffs, nor the anti-tank guns hidden behind the road blocks on the esplanade. In answer to the Prime Minister's final query, Mountbatten made a persuasive case as to why tanks had not been employed in a pincer movement – and yet at the same time he was insisting to Ismay that this had always been his preferred option. The memo to No. 10 concluded with a rueful defence of the frontal assault on the grounds that securing well-defended ports on the French coast was now unavoidable: Dieppe had proved 'a most valuable guide', demonstrating, 'not only the care with which the enemy has disposed his garrisons, but the need for extremely close support if they are to be overcome and the troops put ashore in good order for the battle inland'.[34]

Yet nothing in the outline plan for Rutter, or in the final plan for Jubilee, indicated that the main aim of the operation was to test with what difficulty a port could be seized at the commencement of an invasion. Had the intention always been justified in this way then choosing such a heavily defended location might have made sense. In reality, there was a myriad of objectives – almost all of them unattainable – but no clearly-defined purpose. Presumably, if there had been minimal loss of life then Dieppe would have been depicted as no more than its original intention – a morale-boosting escalation in Britain's capacity to launch debilitating raids upon occupied Europe. Certainly Churchill's mantra description of the operation as a 'reconnaissance in force' would have sounded more convincing. In other words, by choosing such an ambitious target Combined Operations could have countered a widely-held view that British forces remained woefully ignorant of how to mount a successful inter-service amphibious operation. Instead, Dieppe confirmed the pessimists' worst fears. Therefore, the enormous cost of the operation, not least in lives lost, demanded a speedy redefinition of Rutter/Jubilee's *raison d'être*.[35]

Later, as we shall see, Dieppe was justified for exactly the opposite reason. Namely, that it confirmed Combined Operations' growing conviction that a continental invasion had to take place away from heavily defended harbours, and that technological ingenuity could resolve the logistical dilemma of how to maintain cross-Channel supply lines without first securing a port. Whatever the explanation, in the immediate aftermath, and in succeeding years, there had to be a discernible reason for mounting the operation. No senior officer, not least the Chief of Combined Operations, would concede that Dieppe was in fact something of a paradox. Given COHQ's planned withdrawal within the space of a single tide this was technically a raid – and yet a de facto invasion force was despatched across the Channel, tasked with nothing less than the seizure of not just the town but its immediate hinterland. Deployment of such a large force provided the problem, not the solution, forcing inexperienced planners to address major issues of manpower, supply, logistics, and above all, security. Not only did they have to get men and vehicles safely off the beaches, but they then had to orchestrate an efficient and disciplined withdrawal. Dollard Menton, despite multiple wounds the only battalion commander to make it back to England, was in no doubt that, 'the plan was too minute, right down to the last detail. And when so many things cannot be foreseen, you then can't adjust. You've got no alternatives … a plan like that, planned too long ahead of time, is bound to fail'.[36] No wonder all parties involved in this complex and demanding operation kept reassuring themselves that tactical surprise would seriously disrupt an already weak *Wehrmacht* garrison. Astonishingly, as late as mid-1942 some British planners had still not taken on board the most fundamental lesson of two world wars – never, ever under-estimate the Germans' ability to fight, and to keep on fighting.[37]

The under-estimation of German resistance did claim one victim: Bobby de Casa Maury fell on his sword in February 1943, and quit as head of COHQ's Intelligence Section a month later. The reasons for his departure were complex and murky: they ranged from the Air Ministry refusing him a third promotion in 12 months to an erosion of trust between the ex-playboy and his step son-in-law, Bob Laycock. Mountbatten was loyal as ever, devoting a disproportionate amount of time to shoring up his old chum's credibility within the intelligence community, but with precious little success. He found himself smoothing ruffled feathers within Freda de Casa Maury's extended family, and calling in old favours in order to secure Bobby a decent posting. The latter task continued well in to 1943 as, having been invalided out of the Air Transport Auxiliary, the now wingless wing commander hoped Dickie could fix him a job at Bush House, liaising with Peter Murphy from inside the Foreign Office's Political Intelligence Department.[38]

Within Whitehall de Casa Maury had enjoyed neither trust nor respect. Inside the service ministries he was *persona non grata*, and an obvious target once survivors of Dieppe revealed the all too obvious gaps in Combined Operations' intelligence briefings. In its final report on Dieppe, COHQ made a spirited defence of its *modus operandi*, rejecting claims that the Confidential Book circulated on 8 June 1942 had failed to provide planners with a comprehensive and up to date overview of terrain and defences.[39] This was certainly a complaint voiced after the war, but even at the time scientists inside Combined Operations such as 'Sage' Bernal took on board the need for far more detailed beach reconnaissance – no geologist had calculated the depth of shingle on Red and White Beaches, hence the painful progress of the Churchill tanks up on to the promenade. After the war Ernest Magnus, a Canadian staff officer, and Goronwy Rees, Monty's liaison officer at COHQ, were by no means alone in bemoaning the quality of information and interpretation provided by the marquis and his merry men: why had no-one realised how easy it was to dig into chalk cliffs and position heavy machine guns? Heavily dependent on aerial photography, analysts at Combined Operations had made little use of human intelligence: no suggestion was made to MI6 and SOE that agents or local resisters scour the bays and headlands for evidence of camouflaged defences. The consequence was a gross under-estimation of the enemy's potential to mount an effective resistance. Similarly, scant attention had been given to German radar provision, and it was pure luck that relocation of naval RDF equipment meant the landings took place within a temporary blindspot.[40]

Baillie-Grohman, the first choice naval force commander, had been singularly unimpressed by the polo-playing 'foreign grandee', whom he found 'utterly useless'. He shared Roberts' concern that COHQ Intelligence failed to filter and assimilate information: rather than act as a fast and efficient conduit, in actual fact it slowed

down transmission from source to user.[41] Ultimately, de Casa Maury paid the price
for Mountbatten's decision not to inform the intelligence services or the Inter-
Service Security Board that he was remounting the raid.[42] This was an astonishing
decision, and an incandescent Joint Intelligence Committee was insistent that
in future Combined Operations adhere to the normal procedures for ensuring
maximum security and pooling of information. In December 1942 the Chiefs of
Staff Committee over-rode Mountbatten's protestations and issued a directive that in
no circumstances should a major operation be mounted without first notifying the
ISSB.[43] Whitehall insiders had always dismissed de Casa Maury as inconsequential,
and by Christmas it was clear that he would have to leave. He was a liability, and his
quarrel with the head of special forces was the last straw. Mountbatten knew that he
needed a big hitter, acceptable to all three services and with an established rank of full
colonel, or the equivalent. Bobby was a lightweight, and a busted flush. Where once
he was the CCO's flamboyant problem-fixer inside Richmond Terrace, he himself
was now the problem. Laycock, the warrior 'that every man in arms should wish to
be', was too great an asset to antagonise.[44] For Mountbatten it was a painful task, but
the marquis had to go. To his credit he jumped before he was pushed. It's hard to
think of the ageing *flaneur* as a sacrificial lamb, but Philip Ziegler was surely right in
pointing out that, 'Casa Maury was Mountbatten's man, and the shortcomings of his
department were ultimately Mountbatten's responsibility'.[45]

'Ham' Roberts' fate was no doubt sealed well before Mountbatten despatched
to Downing Street his seasonal message of defiance. By the following spring the
Canadian had been relieved of his command and sent to run a recruiting depot. In
Mountbatten's correspondence with Ismay, and throughout Combined Operations'
official report, Roberts was clearly the main target in any implicit criticism of the
force commanders – for example, COHQ's claim to have warned that anti-tank guns
might be hidden from reconnaissance aircraft. Needless to say, no mention was made
of Leigh-Mallory's role in deciding not to request permission from the PM to bomb
a friendly civilian target.[46] Like Roberts, Leigh-Mallory was initially so keen to take
the battle to the enemy that he dismissed the need for preliminary bombing – indeed,
as we have seen, it was his advice that convinced the Canadian a heavy air assault
would prove counter-productive.[47] With no solid evidence to support his claim,
Leigh-Mallory always insisted that Fighter Command could inflict serious damage
upon the *Luftwaffe*. Yet at the same time he accepted the Admiralty argument that
the RAF's failure to secure air superiority over the Channel meant no capital ships
could be risked in an operation off the French coast. Again, as we have seen, had
this not been the case then sustained supporting fire from the Royal Navy's heaviest
guns might have compensated for the absence of aerial bombardment. The air force
commander emerged from the Dieppe inquest with his reputation intact, as did the
naval force commander – after all, both had powerful friends to protect them. In
his unpublished memoirs Hughes-Hallett made clear how poorly he rated the third
member of this hapless triumvirate. When the admiral turned MP suffered a serious
stroke in 1970, Mountbatten urged his secretary to send all papers covering Dieppe
to Broadlands. Revealingly, Mountbatten was sympathetic to the idea that a copy of

'Before I Forget' be housed at the Imperial War Museum, secure in the knowledge that Hughes-Hallett's reminiscences enhanced his own reputation at the expense of an obvious scapegoat like Roberts.[48]

A loyal yet independent-minded bureaucrat, Hughes-Hallett codified the lessons of Dieppe in his original despatch and in the various reports produced by COHQ in the autumn of 1942. Like his master, the diligent captain emerged from the whole experience relatively unscathed. His responsibilities within Combined Operations grew rapidly, and he was well placed for further advancement – his ultimate reward was appointment as Naval Chief of Staff for the real invasion. Hughes-Hallett articulated a number of key points: yes, defeating the Germans required much stronger military forces, including a large, swiftly deployable reserve, and yes, heavy naval and/or aerial bombardment was a crucial requirement before and after troops went ashore; but assault forces could only anticipate success if sharing standardised kit, landing procedures, and battlefield tactics, and if heavy shellfire and bombing was directed towards freshly identified 'targets of opportunity' (concealed heavy machine guns, for example). It was Hughes-Hallett who had convinced Mountbatten that, both publicly and privately, a solid case could be made for Jubilee – and that it really was a vindication of Combined Operations' approach to amphibious warfare. Had COHQ resisted pressure to launch a frontal assault then the losses would have been far less, and the positive outcomes that much more obvious. Next time, whether in the Mediterranean or back across the Channel, they would get it right. In his memoirs Hughes-Hallett voiced a familiar trope of post-war Dieppe apologists: over 4,000 survived the battle, albeit often as POWs, and although, 'This was a grim price to pay, yet it was cheap in comparison to the lessons learned, through which the Normandy casualties were enormously reduced'.[49]

Hughes-Hallett was articulating a position hammered out in the 1950s when he and Haydon had provided Mountbatten with a version of events more sympathetic to COHQ than that drafted by the Admiralty's in-house historians. The latter had listened carefully to Walter Skrine, a major in Combined Operations who had been at the heart of military planning for Dieppe and was then appointed a liaison officer with 2nd Division. Skrine, inconveniently, insisted that the switch to a frontal assault had not been initiated by the Army, and imposed by Montgomery, but was in fact a joint decision: early recognition that a flanking attack would be fraught with danger had meant that a more direct approach was always a serious option for Mountbatten's planning staff. In 1958 the First Sea Lord was well-positioned to undermine Skrine's alternative version, and in so doing ensure that the final draft of the Navy's staff history was no source of personal embarrassment.[50]

Mountbatten and Hughes-Hallett resolutely maintained the 'grim price to pay' line throughout the 1960s and 1970s. In public the previous decade had witnessed a discreet silence over Dieppe, with early anniversaries commemorated in a quiet and dignified fashion. In a more deferential era, and at a time when Diefenbaker's Canada was still mindful of her ostensibly unique and responsible position within the Commonwealth, hostile voices rarely gained a public airing. The twenty-fifth anniversary of the raid saw the first expressions of serious dissent, but four years earlier Mountbatten drafted a text which formed the basis for every public statement he made on Dieppe until the time of his death 16 years later. The Chief of the Defence Staff's message to a Ranger reunion was almost certainly written by Alan Campbell-Johnson, perhaps after consultation with Jock Hughes-Hallett, who in 1963 was still a year from losing his seat as an MP.[51] Similar sentiments were expressed in an uncontentious CBC film made the same year, and in a further four television documentaries broadcast between 1967 and 1977.[52] All five programmes met with Mountbatten's approval as he laid down strict ground rules regarding his contribution. Invariably the principal condition of his taking part was a respectful, formulaic interview at Broadlands. On each occasion the production company acquiesced as Mountbatten's presence was clearly crucial. Indeed, when the BBC cautiously commemorated the raid's thirtieth anniversary the grand old man was delighted to discover such a sympathetic and amiable director. Needless to say, *The Life and Times* saw its hero offer a short but spirited defence of Dieppe as a tragic but vital prelude to Overlord.[53]

Back in 1963 Mountbatten clearly decided that attack was the best form of defence. He was uncompromising in his defence of Operation Jubilee, and as the years passed he made ever more exaggerated claims[54]:

I believe it is impossible to over-estimate the value of the Dieppe Raid. It was the turning-point in the technique of invasion. Many vital lessons were learnt. Not only did we learn the right lessons, but what was equally important, the Germans drew the wrong conclusions. The Germans misread the lessons of Dieppe and fortunately for us went on strengthening their port defences and garrisons and left only a thin line holding the beaches. This enabled the Normandy assault to take place across the beaches, where all the Navy gunfire support and heavy air bombardment available could be turned on to flatten out the beach defences and defenders, without impeding our follow-up. It is generally acknowledged that the casualties among the vast assault force that landed in Normandy in 1944 were far lighter than anyone could have hoped for in 1942, and this can be directly attributed to the heavy casualties we suffered in the infinitely smaller force that landed at Dieppe. Those gallant men who gave their lives at Dieppe, by their supreme sacrifice gave to the Allies the priceless secret of victory in the subsequent assaults...I have no doubt that the Battle of Normandy was won on the beaches of Dieppe. For every one man who died at Dieppe in 1942, at least ten men or more must have been spared in Normandy in 1944.[55]

The notion that Jubilee unintentionally – let alone deliberately – deceived or mislead the enemy is highly contentious. Surely, the operation had to be a success, and the town seized, to convince the Germans that an Allied task force might head first for Cherbourg or Le Havre? In any case these towns were being turned into fortresses irrespective of the raid, so that, even had it proved a triumph, no credible invasion plan could anticipate swiftly securing a major port.[56]

Regrettably, these awkward questions were not addressed in *The Watery Maze*. Bernard Fergusson's commissioned history of Combined Operations from the fall of France to the Suez crisis was published in 1961. The Treasury had vetoed an official history, insisting that the story be incorporated into Stephen Roskill's account of the war at sea.[57] An internal history of COHQ had appeared around this time, while back in 1951 the then Fourth Sea Lord had encouraged Alan Campbell-Johnson to follow up *Mission To India* with the story of Combined Ops.[58] This idea was resurrected in 1957, backed by Antony Head and, remarkably, the Cabinet Secretary, Sir Norman Brook. As a serving officer, Brigadier Fergusson was not their first choice. However, his fame as a Chindit commander, and his status as a best-selling military historian, ensured the cooperation of all key personnel who had served in COHQ. As a former intelligence officer at NATO and director of psychological warfare during the Suez venture, Fergusson enjoyed the highest security clearance. Mountbatten devoted a great deal of time and effort to helping the future Lord Ballantrae, facilitating full access to confidential files, including his study group's inquest on Dieppe.[59] Drawing heavily upon Combined Operations' final report, and reading back from D-Day, Fergusson detailed the lessons learnt. These ranged from fresh means of ensuring that the enemy was reduced to a state of inert shock by the time troops stepped ashore (including a major increase in the firepower of LCTs); through a radical rethink of when to land armoured support, and how to breach shoreline obstacles; to an upgrade in beach piloting, and the establishment of 'Force J', a naval assault force on permanent stand-by and headed by Hughes-Hallett. The communications meltdown that had rendered the *Calpe* so completely helpless had highlighted the urgent need for building not just two but several Headquarters Ships.[60] Well tutored by Mountbatten, Fergusson saw life-saving principles emerge 'out of the fire and smoke and carnage on the beaches of Dieppe': crucially, the raid had 'lifted discussions about the invasion of Europe out of the academic sphere into the practical'.[61] For the CDS and his acolytes *The Watery Maze* had passed its keenest test, with flying colours.

Offering an insider's perspective, Mountbatten's most recent biographer has drawn upon service expertise to portray Dieppe as a vital testing-ground for new technology, especially in the twin areas of radar and electronic warfare.[62] Nevertheless, a powerful argument can be made that the technology and the tactics which contributed to the overall success of the Normandy landings (notwithstanding the heavy losses sustained on Omaha Beach) emerged irrespective of Jubilee; and that fresh ideas owed far more to experience gained in the Mediterranean landings.[63] There was simply too long a gap between Dieppe and D-Day, the former lying 'on the far side of the great divide in the course of the war formed by the winter of 1942–3'. All the evidence suggests that planning for Operation Overlord made surprisingly little reference to Dieppe, despite the heavy involvement of two of the force commanders and Mountbatten himself.[64] Nevertheless, 'it is perhaps legitimate to claim for Jubilee a pervasive but largely unspoken effect on the awareness of planners in the form of a salutary reminder of the irremediable consequences of a badly planned assault'.[65]

By 1963 Mountbatten already knew that his grandiloquent claims were open to challenge. That year Terence Robertson's *Dieppe: the Shame and the Glory* was published in Britain, its author already a controversial figure in his native Canada.[66] By now the carefully crafted orthodoxy was being challenged. Nevertheless, Mountbatten's remarks to the Rangers provided a template for his speech marking the twenty-fifth anniversary of the raid, and more crucially, a lengthy address delivered in Toronto on 28 September 1973. On the latter occasion the man synonymous with Operation Jubilee was faced with an especially testing and sensitive task – convincing the Dieppe Veterans and Prisoners of War Association that Canada's great sacrifice had not been in vain. Although publication of the speech generated a testy correspondence with Charles Stacey, the Canadian Army's official historian, on the day itself all went well, with the distinguished guest treated respectfully, if not always warmly.[67] To the end of his life Mountbatten was desperate to get his message across to Canadians 'why they should be proud of Dieppe', and yet at the same time he was perfectly capable of claiming privately that, 'They want to revel in their misery'. As Brian Loring Villa has rightly pointed out, the latter was a pretty outrageous remark, even allowing for the fact that Mountbatten was in his seventy-eighth year when he said it.[68]

In Britain the thin veil of discretion was seriously torn apart in the summer of 1967 when Wallace Reyburn wrote to the *Sunday Telegraph* bitterly denouncing Mountbatten's claim that Dieppe was a vital prerequisite of D-Day. No longer the dutiful propagandist, Reyburn recalled his own horrific experience on Green Beach in a remarkable letter, which lambasted everyone concerned with organising the raid. With an iconoclastic candour and lack of deference, he tore into Mountbatten – here was a man unapologetic over sacrificing more than 1,000 lives in order to learn lessons which his staff could quite easily have worked out for themselves.[69] Mountbatten, although no longer CDS still very much in the public eye, was clearly astonished by the vehemence of Reyburn's attack. Rather than allowing himself to be tarnished by association with this squalid quarrel, he asked Hughes-Hallett to reply. Drawing upon his supposedly unique position as Jubilee's naval force commander, the former MP's point-by-point refutation appeared a fortnight after the original letter. The delay was because Hughes-Hallett's recall of events was in fact drafted by John Terraine, and approved by Mountbatten. Reyburn hit back in a now characteristically belligerent and sarcastic fashion, reiterating his belief that Combined Operations was wholly to blame for what had been nothing less than a total disaster.[70]

This time Mountbatten sat down with Terraine to draft a second reply, which he then invited Campbell-Johnson and David Astor to comment upon. A further fortnight's delay, prior to publication on 1 October 1967, was partly because of the time it took to agree on a final text, and partly because the *Sunday Telegraph* considered the correspondence closed. Hughes-Hallett's letter only appeared when, advised by Campbell-Johnson and egged on by Mountbatten, he threatened the paper's editor-in-chief, Michael Berry, with a complaint to the Press Council and the prospect of litigation. Not only was Hughes-Hallett then given the satisfaction of the last word, but the following week the *Sunday Telegraph* reverted wholly to type, publishing a Navy backwoodsman's gushing tribute to Lord Louis, great man of history.[71]

What this incident illustrates is that, whenever the approved version of Dieppe was called into question, Mountbatten called upon all the resources at his disposal, and counterattacked with all guns blazing. The same would be the case whenever any facet of his career, or any aspect of his behaviour, was publicly criticised. As already evident in Mountbatten's sensitivity over his mixed fortunes as a flotilla captain, the official record had to be protected, underpinned, and even enhanced – and this was of course to prove a lifetime commitment.

Both Brian Loring Villa and Nigel Hamilton have seen Mountbatten's 'aristocratic insouciance' as the main reason why so many Canadians view Dieppe in the same way that Australians perceive Gallipoli: in each case the flower of their army was, 'squandered for Allied political purposes – but with the British failing to pick up the historical tab ...'.[72] This of course presumes Canada to be a homogenous entity, which is clearly not the case; and it suggests the raid remains firmly lodged within a powerful and widely-shared nation-building mythology, which is, to say the least, highly debatable.[73] Yet, when directly addressing a North American audience, Mountbatten himself encouraged the view that 2nd Division were tragic victims of a trans-Atlantic imperial game-plan. Thus, in a two-hour programme broadcast on Quebec television in November 1976 he insisted that Canadian forces were chosen solely 'for political reasons'. Courage was no substitute for experience, and, as confirmed by the commandos' virtuosity on 19 August, this was an operation that called for battle-hardened veterans.[74] Nor were Canada's most senior officers qualified to plan such an ambitious operation, and yet Brooke had been insistent that Mountbatten leave them free to make the final decisions.[75] There were few aspects of Rutter/Jubilee on which Montgomery agreed with Mountbatten, but in 1966 he was similarly candid in acknowledging that he should have protested more strongly over the choice of troops.[76] Such frankness was absent from Montgomery's memoirs, published eight years earlier, although a private note in 1962 detailed his serious misgivings over the quality and leadership of the 2nd Division.[77]

As previously noted, Monty's memoirs gave every indication that had he still been in England then Jubilee would never have gone ahead. He had after all advised Home Forces' C-in-C, Bernard Paget, in the aftermath of Rutter that a raid on Dieppe was now out of the question. Yet, in distancing himself from an operation which, while not taking place on his watch as he had left for Egypt, he nevertheless took an active part in planning, Montgomery must have known how Mountbatten would react. To add insult to injury, Monty insisted that he would never have agreed to dispense with preliminary bombing.[78] Yet, as has been seen, in his capacity as C-in-C South-Eastern Command, Montgomery had chaired the key meeting at COHQ on 5 June 1942 where Roberts and Leigh-Mallory had argued against an advance air strike. Stung by yet another hostile piece in the *Daily Express*, Mountbatten took Montgomery to task. Needless to say he got nowhere, but the joshing tone of the correspondence ensures an entertaining clash between two magnificent egos.[79]

A quiet revenge came in 1961 when, in *The Watery Maze*, a well-briefed Bernard Fergusson highlighted Montgomery's account of Dieppe: here indisputably was a passage 'where his memory has played him false'. Even Nigel Hamilton, when contrasting the meticulous and methodical Montgomery with a manipulative and malevolent Mountbatten, acknowledged that here was a mischievous rewriting of history. Yet for Hamilton the question of aerial bombardment was an irrelevancy. Monty's biographer pointed to the absence of capital ships as being of far greater significance. Thus, Mountbatten had quite deliberately conspired to convince the generals that his destroyers could provide adequate covering fire. Hamilton's chapter on Dieppe, first time around, directed a remarkable torrent of invective at 'a man whose mind was an abundance of brilliant and insane ideas often without coherence or consistent "doctrine"'. Yet, rather feebly, Montgomery was let off the hook solely on the grounds that, 'there was, in his own nature, a love of boldness that caused him to neglect the inherent impossibility of the plan'.[80]

Hamilton must have realised the thinness of his case in that he had a second stab at skewering Mountbatten, in a much fuller and more forensic treatment of Dieppe. Far less inhibited, and drawing upon a raft of fresh material, Hamilton completely rewrote the first half of his life of Montgomery 20 years after the original volume had first appeared. Revisiting Mountbatten's dark dealings over Dieppe, Hamilton undoubtedly delivered his reader a more scholarly indictment of the 'elegant, energetic, socially adept dilettante'. Yet the denunciation was relentless, and in places Hamilton still relied on speculation at the expense of evidence, not least in his insistence that the main motive for resurrecting Rutter was Mountbatten's secret ambition to be appointed invasion supremo ('harboured in his once-princely, machiavellian heart'). This assertion appears to be based upon a long footnote in Brian Loring Villa's demolition job on Dickie. Villa's footnote is itself based upon the flimsiest of evidence: Leo Amery's eagerness to extol Mountbatten's virtues when the two men first got to know each other in the spring of 1942.[81] Hamilton's dark lord is callously indifferent to the losses at Dieppe, and, when faced with the disastrous consequences of his single-minded drive to the top, schemes ceaselessly to implicate a largely innocent Montgomery.[82] Reflective of a less reverential era, Hamilton second time around was unsparing in his criticism of Churchill, Eisenhower, and even Alanbrooke – all had to some degree or another colluded with a man who for the rest of his life would 'cajole, charm and entice his former staff into a collective subversion of the record …'. This was certainly true, up to a point. What Hamilton underestimated was the extent to which Mountbatten's colleagues – yes, the temptation is to say cronies – freely collaborated with their old boss to maintain intact a powerful post-war myth surrounding Combined Operations; and to counter what they genuinely felt to be unfair criticism, invariably regarding Dieppe.[83]

Dieppe – Mountbatten's two fiercest critics

Considering the controversy that surrounds so many of his enterprises – and the degree to which his enemies loathed him – outside southern Asia the number of sustained and wholly uncompromising attacks upon Mountbatten has remained surprisingly few.[84] No-one has written a deeply hostile biography in the spirit of say Express Newspapers' reporting and editorialising in the 1950s: reiteration of a basic message that here is a man who not only can not be trusted, but is no good at his job.[85] Surprisingly perhaps, Dieppe illustrates how the circumstances in which Mountbatten died brought about a reluctance, in Britain at least, to demolish the myth and to destroy his credibility as an operational commander. Critics of the planning and execution of the raid have of course castigated Mountbatten, but not as often as one might expect. Yes, the decision-making process has been personalised, with the CCO seen as ultimately responsible for the debacle – and yet on only a handful of occasions has the original indictment translated into a full-scale assault upon the great man's basic integrity and overall behaviour. Clearly, Nigel Hamilton was more than capable of character assassination, but chronicling Monty's golden years offered precious little opportunity. From the summer of 1942 Montgomery and Mountbatten were rarely on the same continent, let alone in the same country; and, as has been seen, another decade would pass before jousting could resume on a serious basis. Hamilton's insistence on the psychopathically ambitious Mountbatten as 'a master of intrigue, jealousy and ineptitude', coldly playing with men's lives 'like a spoilt child', was of course an irresistible quote once Andrew Roberts' tidal wave of vitriol and indignation swept through Operation Jubilee.[86]

For Roberts, Combined Operations revealed Mountbatten at his most duplicitous; and yet one senses that Dieppe is but a prelude to the serious business of denouncing the last viceroy for his iniquitous boundary-fixing and callous disregard for human life. Coverage of the raid has the hallmarks of a neat yet over-hasty exercise in seeking confirmation of all one's worst prejudices – the assiduous researcher deploying his formidable skills and expertise to mount a prosecution as dependent upon innuendo as on solid evidence of malpractice. Thus Peter Murphy is rightly criticised for his insensitive recollection of how keen the Canadians were to participate in the raid ('… since it was they who (for exhibitionist and other reasons) had insisted on being murdered!!'), but the reader is left unaware that otherwise Mountbatten was offered shrewd and sensible advice on how to handle Tom Driberg.[87]

As noted in Chapter One, by the mid-1950s Beaverbrook's prewar protégé had scant respect for his old master, not least because the Canadian's vendetta against Mountbatten remained as intense as ever. A Labour backbencher, when not at Westminster Tom Driberg was busy at work on his unflattering and yet by no means ungenerous biography of the 'Beaver'. Edwina's wartime chum had ingratiated himself with her husband when he spent some time in Singapore and Saigon reporting on SEAC's role in the transition to peace. Mountbatten quickly came to appreciate that this new confidant offered a convenient conduit for his views, in both Fleet Street and Parliament. In consequence his response to nationalist demands across the Far East secured sympathetic coverage at home, courtesy of a grateful Driberg. Ten years later, having begun his book on Beaverbrook, Driberg sought Mountbatten's approval for his explanation of why Express Newspapers had maintained such an unrelenting campaign of abuse since August 1942. Mountbatten gave his old pal enthusiastic support at every stage of the book's production, yet it was Peter Murphy who perceived the potential damage to the First Sea Lord's reputation if his collaboration with a rather *risqué* figure like Driberg became public knowledge. The warning was vindicated in that 40 years later Andrew Roberts was not averse to dropping singularly unsubtle hints regarding all three men.[88]

The irony is that, had Roberts read one of his primary sources more thoroughly, he would have noted Peter Murphy's concern in the summer of 1942 that cross-Channel raids had a diminishing value in terms of Home Front morale; and that piecemeal action encouraged German propaganda in its insistence that any distraction from the great struggle in the east was an unnecessary sacrifice of Allied soldiers. Murphy had risen to quite a senior position within the Political Warfare Executive, and his percipient memo was borne out by Goebbels linking Jubilee with Churchill's parallel visit to Moscow ('a prisoner of the Kremlin'). Mountbatten would have been shocked by his close friend's astute yet implicitly critical reading of the runes. Presumably he never found out that Murphy, always supportive and enthusiastic, had in fact questioned Combined Operations' propagandist value to London and Washington's Manichean struggle with Berlin to secure global goodwill.[89]

Roberts was insistent that full responsibility for Dieppe lay with the Chief of Combined Operations, and him alone. He rightly pointed out that if the raid had been a success then Mountbatten 'would have claimed all the credit', and that if he 'thought it would fail, it was his duty to abort it'. This is, as already noted, and as Robin Neillands has argued so persuasively, the key charge against Mountbatten – that, when told there must be a frontal assault but no heavy bombardment from air or sea, he chose not to cancel the operation.[90] However, identifying Mountbatten's key failure provides no reason for denying the service chiefs and/or the force commanders any responsibility whatsoever – particularly when Roberts then went on to criticise the CCO for not being present at every stage of the planning process. Similarly, Bobby de Casa Maury, although an obvious target, could not be held personally responsible for every single failure of intelligence.[91]

Roberts not surprisingly drew upon a deeply sceptical Lord Lovat to support his case, but went on to suggest that later in the war the commando leader strongly resisted further service under Mountbatten. In fact personality was not the main consideration – Lovat felt certain his special forces were best qualified to fight across the Channel, and not in the unforgiving jungle of south-east Asia. Mountbatten suffered some selective quoting at Roberts' hands, but his exaggerated claims regarding Dieppe's importance when planning D-Day were rightly rubbished. Hughes-Hallett's reminiscences were clearly seen as the smoking gun; but one is left uneasy at the selection of material to support Roberts' argument. Like Brian Loring Villa he demonised the naval force commander, portraying him as callously indifferent to Canada's virgin soldiers. Yet had Roberts read more of the memoirs then he would have learnt how, prior to the first exercise, an anonymous Hughes-Hallett spent an enlightening and humbling week under canvas with the 2nd Division. It's difficult to feel sympathy for someone who was such a cold fish – Thomas Cromwell to Mountbatten's King Henry – and yet the harsh impression formed from Roberts' dexterous use of quotation was hardly fair.[92]

In the early 1990s Andrew Roberts was an ambitious young man, eager to capitalise on the favourable reception given to his first book, a spirited reaffirmation of Lord Halifax's centrality to British politics before *and* after Churchill's accession to the premiership in May 1940.[93] Unlike his heroine and guiding light, he recognised that Thatcherite faith in the free market was incompatible with publicly praising 'Winston'. Anyone prepared to go on television and argue that Britain suffered a crippling crisis of confidence by not seizing the whole of the Suez Canal in November 1956, and that the withdrawal from India eight years earlier had been premature, would undoubtedly consider the late Lord Louis an anathema.[94] Here was an obvious candidate for Roberts' iconoclastic, aggressively promoted collection of essays, *Eminent Churchillians* – Lytton Strachey, never slow to mock an admiral or accept a generous advance, would surely have approved. Roberts worked fast and inevitably took shortcuts, as soon becomes obvious to anyone consulting the relevant papers. Conversely, Mountbatten's other high profile critic, the Canadian academic Brian Loring Villa, took real pride in the lengthy gestation of his monograph on Dieppe – a scholarly underpinning of 38 pages of footnotes, plus two lengthy appendices on methodology and applied theory of organisational behaviour, provided solid evidence of eight years hard labour in the archives. In a crowded field Villa's epic is by no means the best book on why and how disaster struck, but it's arguably the weightiest. The only challenger is fellow Canadian John P. Campbell's dense argument as to the centrality of intelligence in understanding why the raid went so disastrously wrong.[95]

Villa's central thesis in *Unauthorised Action Mountbatten and the Dieppe Raid 1942* is that minutes of the Chiefs of Staffs' meeting on 12 August noted approval of 'the future raiding operation', but that this reference did not constitute a green light for Jubilee. If this had been the case, why did the Vice Chief of the Imperial General Staff, Sir Archibald Nye, who had attended the meeting in Brooke's absence, only learn of the operation as it was taking place? *Ipso facto* the raid was an unauthorised action on Mountbatten's part, and, to quote Campbell's neat description, 'Villa's book daringly rests on this one point like an inverted pyramid'.[96] So precarious a balancing act demands focus and clear concentration. Yet a fundamental weakness of Villa's magnum opus is that, for all the insistence on a rigorous methodology (the historian as a born again political scientist), seriously impressive documentary research is repeatedly undermined by an inconsistency of argument, and an undue readiness, in the final analysis, to speculate on the grand scale. Furthermore, he has an irritating habit of advancing a particularly remote and implausible suggestion at great length, before finally dismissing its validity – only to leave just a hint of suspicion in the mind of the reader, as in, '*Did* Mountbatten by the summer of 1942 really believe that he could become Churchill's supremo, reigning over all the other chiefs of staff?' No, of course he didn't, but nevertheless a dense, heavily-referenced footnote discusses the possibility at great length, before finally rejecting it.[97]

There are too many veiled suggestions scattered throughout Villa's book, even if, like his compatriot John Campbell, he convincingly dismisses a hoary canard of Andrew Roberts – that Bletchley Park had provided a convincing case for aborting the mission. At the same time he rejects any notion of a Sigint double-bluff, as advanced by Anthony Cave Brown and anyone else daft enough to believe Churchill calmly sacrificed the Canadians at Dieppe, along with the citizens of Coventry nearly two years earlier, in order to protect high-quality intelligence from Ultra and from MI6's dangerously exposed agents on the ground. Both Villa and Campbell endorse and amplify Stephen Roskill's dismissal of David Irving's characteristically controversial claim that the Germans were forewarned, *and* that the British knew this. Irving first made this claim as long ago as October 1963, in a series of articles for the *Evening Standard*.[98]

In the final analysis Villa's Mountbatten is unconvincing. When convenient to the argument, the all too recent destroyer captain displays the headstrong temperament and political naivety of the over-promoted tyro, desperate to establish his credentials within the very highest echelons of Churchill's uniquely tailored machinery for waging war. Yet for much of the book we find the vainglorious, drivingly ambitious *spinmeister* of Washington and Whitehall orchestrating proceedings and masterminding future events with a Clausewitzian calculation and a Machiavellian cunning. In consequence some sections read like a bedazzling fusion of *Othello* and *The Glass Bead Game*.[99] There are forgotten heroes (Keyes, Baillie-Grohman), obvious villains (McNaughton, Hughes-Hallett), questionable characters (Leigh-Mallory), and natural fall guys (Roberts). No member of the Government, not least the Prime Minister, emerges with his reputation intact. Beaverbrook is an especially malign and powerful influence, along with the Americans largely responsible for Mountbatten's elevation: the Canadian's hold over Churchill is a consequence of the latter flagging in the face of remorseless Axis advance, and the prospect of Cripps colluding with Eden and Attlee to seize power (a truly unholy alliance which illustrates the stream of speculation, selective quoting, and unsubstantiated claims to be found in Chapter Three).[100]

For Villa the service chiefs are worthy warriors, united in their determination to thwart Winston's wilder proposals for keeping Washington happy, but consequently failing to forestall tragedy for a far closer ally. Thus all three chiefs of staff are fatally flawed by their respective reasons for not vetoing the original proposal, and their not reining in Mountbatten once Pound and Portal had ruled out naval or aerial bombardment. The CCO is rightly criticised for not using his unique relationship with Churchill to put pressure on the First Sea Lord to provide stronger naval support, and yet on the same page Villa raises the possibility that Mountbatten, 'really did not care whether the Dieppe raid was a success or a failure'. On the previous page he reasserts a wholly unconvincing charge that completion of *In Which We Serve* was a fatal distraction. Again and again Villa undermines the credibility of what could be a persuasive argument regarding confusion of authorisation at the highest level, by adopting a scattergun approach: every shred of evidence, however questionable, must be advanced to support a largely indiscriminate list of charges against Mountbatten (and by implication, or on occasion explicitly, Churchill). Thus, close reading of documents such as the aide-memoire given to Molotov in June 1942, with its scarcely-noted promise that 'raids will increase in size and scope as the summer goes on', can be quickly followed by an unsupported explanation as to why Mountbatten chose not to seek Churchill's help: it would generate too many awkward questions, leading to ultimate cancellation. Mountbatten may have made such a calculation but we can not say with certainty because we simply don't know, and in any case the suggestion does not square with a parallel insistence on Churchill's eagerness to convince Stalin how serious the British were about significant cross-Channel action.[101]

Villa's insistence that Jubilee was mounted without proper authorisation by the Chiefs of Staff Committee implied a cover up. He claimed to find no convincing explanation in any of the published or unpublished official histories why the operation was revived. His answer, of course, was that no authorised historian could find documentary evidence of the committee's agreement to remount the raid. This gap in the official record explained why Churchill failed to call the raid 'Jubilee' when cabling from Moscow, and why Archibald Nye was incandescent when told the attack was under way.[102] In a persuasive explanation of events, and a fairly gentle riposte to Villa, fellow Canadian Peter Henshaw saw no special significance in Churchill's failure to use the correct codename given that even the most engaged staff officers sometimes employed obsolete terminology. In Nye's case confusion remained as to whether he was genuinely ignorant of Rutter's restaging, or simply that no-one had furnished him with a precise date.[103]

Nor did Henshaw feel that Stephen Roskill was disingenuous in maintaining Churchill's approval of the raid, even if the claim that 'nothing was committed to paper' was – as we shall soon see – clearly a Mountbatten-inspired canard. Combined Operations' in-house history suggested that on 27 July 1942 the COSC specified Dieppe when conceding to Mountbatten a revised procedure for all future raids. No the Committee did not, but Henshaw insisted that nothing 'strictly false' was stated. He showed a similar generosity to Sir James Butler, whose ostensibly definitive account of grand strategy was, if less open to a charge of being economical with the truth, nevertheless cryptic in its version of events. Sir Harry Hinsley, intelligence's keeper of the flame, was similarly vague, but in Henshaw's view not deliberately evasive. Thus, contrary to Villa's belief that Whitehall conspired to disguise Mountbatten's adventurism, Henshaw concluded that few statements in the official histories regarding the role of the COSC, '[are] demonstrably false; some are certainly misleading; but most seem reasonable enough, as far as they go, when the full scope of the Committee's deliberations in July 1942 are understood'.[104]

Henshaw questioned Villa's *modus operandi* of combing the archives for the Chiefs' specific decision to remount Rutter as Jubilee – and then citing failure to find any written record as conclusive evidence of Mountbatten's unauthorised action. His argument was that the revised procedure for the CCO to mount or remount a raid, as agreed by the Chiefs on 27 July, did not specify the need for final authorisation – this was an assumption, not a stated requirement. The COSC was still expected to approve an outline plan and the choice of field commanders, but this had already been carried out for Rutter; and prior to the first operation's final cancellation the Chiefs had agreed to try again at a later date. Mountbatten then generated 'legitimate confusion' by not only proposing to remount the raid, but on 17 July requesting a substantial extension of his executive powers to launch such an operation. When the service chiefs resisted the breadth of authority anticipated by their impatient colleague, Mountbatten scaled down his demands. Nevertheless he secured a wholly new procedure for organising large-scale operations. The COSC still had to see a final plan, but previous raids had already revealed this to be a grey area. Committee members no doubt assumed that they would be given the final say over Jubilee, but now, 'there was no procedural reason why Mountbatten should allow them further scrutiny of the plan'.[105]

The three service chiefs may have been treated cavalierly in that, by not keeping them better informed, Mountbatten followed the letter, if not the spirit, of the agreed procedure, 'as far as that procedure was defined'. However, argued Henshaw, the COSC was clearly cognizant of Jubilee's existence, as why else would members have approved Hughes-Hallett's appointment as a force commander. Further evidence perhaps lies in a reference to the outline plan for 'a future raiding operation' in the minutes of a meeting on 12 August. This may not of course have referred to Dieppe, or could it be that the Chief of Combined Operations was sufficiently vague as to mislead his colleagues re the imminent raid? Yet an obvious absence of detail may explain Nye's subsequent anger, because he sat in for Brooke at that particular meeting. The extent to which the VCIGS was kept in the dark, in a roundabout way reinforces Henshaw's conclusion that Mountbatten exploited to the full his freshly acquired discretionary powers in an irregular, even irresponsible fashion – and yet, 'there is little evidence to suggest that the authority of the Chiefs of Staff was ever *directly* [my italics] circumvented'.[106]

Villa had examined, not always convincingly, why each of the service chiefs, including even Alan Brooke, might support a substantial cross-Channel incursion in the summer of 1942. Henshaw on the other hand looked to the relevant commanders-in-chief. Their individual reasons for not torpedoing Mountbatten's plan might explain why there was no obvious last-minute deception of the COSC: Sholto Douglas's Fighter Command was eager to challenge the *Luftwaffe*; Andrew McNaughton's Canadian First Army was desperate to justify its existence; and Bernard Paget's Home Forces Command was sensitive to charges of timidity, and possible exclusion from future planning of the real invasion. Thus Mountbatten, anxious to realise his extravagant promises, found that, 'the men who might have expected to resist plans for the reckless employment of forces under their command actually urged their subordinates – the force commanders – to cast aside their doubts about *Rutter* and *Jubilee*'. With Baillie-Grohman replaced by Hughes-Hallett, and Leigh-Mallory as eager as ever to fill the skies with Spitfires, those doubts focused upon the Army; but it was 'Ham' Roberts who insisted that bomb damage in Dieppe would impede his tanks, and, as we have seen, whatever his later complaints, the outgoing Montgomery was uncharacteristically quiet. Henshaw's argument was that, because none of the commanders-in-chief made the prerequisite of aerial or naval bombardment a matter of principle – knowing that to do so would force the Chiefs to confront the issue and veto the operation – Jubilee went through on the nod. A 'procedural flaw' did not allow for every commander-in-chief opting to support an operation which was demonstrably problematic: the assumption was that there would be one or more objections, and on this basis the COSC would cancel the operation. This had already occurred when Bomber Command refused to support a large-scale landing on Alderney, and would again prove to be the case when plans for a raid on Lorient were dropped in 1943.[107]

In this way Henshaw rejected Villa's argument that the military bureaucracy by 1942 was too efficient to leave such a vital decision unrecorded, and therefore Mountbatten must have acted without authorisation, skilfully covering his tracks in the face of near total failure. Yet at the same time Henshaw refused to join those insistent that the Chiefs must have sanctioned the raid. His is a deeper, more complex explanation of events. He draws back from portraying Mountbatten as a shameless and malevolent schemer, but makes a persuasive case that here was someone who instinctively knew how to operate within a still embryonic apparatus of defence management; someone who relied upon the necessary tools of evasion and omission, yet only crossed the line with reluctance – a charmer, not a confidence trickster, if such a fine distinction can be made.

Considering that Philip Ziegler was writing Mountbatten's official biography, it's surprising that he devoted only 12 pages to the Dieppe raid. Ziegler has never given any indication that he read Henshaw's article, but his hostile review of Villa's book certainly added spice to the correspondence pages of the *Spectator* in the spring of 1990. Over a decade later, in the foreword to a fresh edition of *Mountbatten*, Ziegler happily jousted with Andrew Roberts over Dieppe and India. On Villa, there was not a word. He simply refused to take the Canadian seriously, arguing that to suggest Mountbatten was solely responsible for Operation Jubilee, without any explicit or implicit approval, was 'a spectacular red herring'. Ziegler insisted at a seminar in 1995 that the absence of a formal record, and the enforcement as high as the VCIGS of a need-to-know restriction on information, was in no way unusual – and by no means the final piece in the jigsaw that proved Mountbatten had acted unilaterally in launching the raid: even Villa conceded that it was physically impossible to conceal such a large operation from the three service chiefs (although it still seems astonishing that Nye had no idea of what was taking place). Ziegler was too quick to dismiss his bête noire's thesis, refusing even to concede a greyness regarding Dickie's ability to work the system. Yet Villa staunchly maintained his fundamentalist position, despite, ironically, seeming throughout his book to qualify its central thesis. Thus, early on in *Unauthorised Action* the author asks whether it was 'really possible that Mountbatten had broken all the rules', and offers only circumstantial evidence to support such a claim; later, he concedes that Jubilee generated a 'vast paper trail', leading all the way back to the War Office and the Admiralty. Nevertheless, the final conclusion is unequivocal, hence OUP's choice of title – and hence Ziegler's regrettable refusal to offer a much fuller critique of Villa's wilder claims.[108]

This reluctance to engage directly with the book, and with its author, survived in to the present century.[109] Back in 1995 Ziegler refused to accept Villa's account of how Churchill had signed off the brief, blame-free narrative of the Dieppe raid that appears in *The Hinge of Fate*, the fourth volume of his war memoirs. It seemed unbelievable that, through 'Pug' Ismay (as General Sir Hastings Ismay, the PM's representative on the Chiefs of Staff Committee, and then as Lord Ismay the last viceroy's chief of staff) and Sir Henry Pownall (previously SEAC Chief of Staff), Mountbatten could have convinced 'the old man' to endorse a version of events which was at best highly contentious, and at worst, manifestly false.[110] For Ziegler, if Churchill said that 'no records were kept' but that he personally had gone through operational plans approved at all levels, then that was evidence enough. Villa disputed such a claim, and argued that 'Mountbatten's account ... has served as a bedrock for virtually every subsequent history of the Dieppe raid'. As we have seen, over the next three decades Mountbatten and his sympathisers constructed an interpretation of events consistent with *The Hinge of Fate*'s insistence that D-Day confirmed the many lessons learnt from what was, 'a costly but not unfruitful reconnaissance in force ... Honour to the brave who fell. Their sacrifice was not in vain'.[111] Only one person could have added that final flourish to what quickly became the orthodox version. There is of course a parallel here to the way in which popular perception of Churchill's pre-war adversaries on the Tory front bench, was – and for many still is – moulded by their portrayal in volume one of *The Second World War*: appeasement historiography for well over a decade was moulded by, first, *Guilty Men*, the notorious post-Dunkirk polemic speedily put together by three stars in the Beaverbrook firmament, and eight years later, *The Gathering Storm*.[112]

Early in the new millennium, when writing his magisterial study of how Churchill came to write *The Second World War*, David Reynolds revisited the same archives as Villa, most notably the Ismay papers. Drawing upon his own research, not least privileged access to Churchill's personal archives, Reynolds compiled a convincing account of how, in the autumn of 1950, a genuinely alarmed Mountbatten 'substantially rewrote' Churchill's explanation of why the raid went wrong. Reynolds was able to compare respective drafts, noting how Mountbatten: played down the size of the losses; claimed to have discussed the operation personally with Churchill; and insisted that the chiefs had given verbal approval, no record being made for reasons of security.[113] Recognising that this was a wholly contentious version of events, Ismay anticipated a radical rewrite, only to find a distracted Leader of HM Opposition indifferent to further revision. Commenting upon the success of the 'egregious social climber' in slipping past Churchill a sanitized description of what may or may not have constituted an 'unauthorised action', Reynolds concluded, 'that the Chiefs of Staff did not approve the final plan ... On the other hand, if Mountbatten had been given authority to act alone, that makes him largely responsible for the shambles – hence his desperate efforts in 1950 to spread the blame'.[114]

Reynolds clearly vindicated Villa. Ziegler had rejected the latter's account on the grounds that Churchill was incapable of accepting a narrative which did not constitute a wholly accurate reflection of events. This was to underestimate the huge pressures on an old man sniffing an early return to power, but hounded by impatient publishers on both sides of the Atlantic – Mountbatten's rewrite had gone through on the nod, with neither Ismay nor the Cabinet Secretary willing to pursue the matter further. Knowing Mountbatten as he did, Ziegler could never depict his man as incapable of adopting pretty unscrupulous tactics in order to defend COHQ and his own reputation. As it transpired negotiating with Churchill and his aides provided a template for future confrontations. Relying upon such staunch allies as the ever-faithful Hughes-Hallett, Mountbatten would re-fight Dieppe again and again, always countering criticism with overwhelming force: to mix metaphors, he used every weapon in his armament, and he never took prisoners. Usually he relied upon intermediaries to make his case, especially when still in uniform, but later in life he would if necessary respond personally. Whenever possible he would take pre-emptive action. The mantra was always the same: 'No concession, no compromise … no Dieppe, no D-Day.'

10

'THE STEEL HAND FROM THE SEA' – COMBINED OPERATIONS AT ITS ZENITH

Reshaping Combined Ops

A sprawling organisation, within which certain elements worked well and others were notoriously inefficient, Combined Operations was a shape-shifter. It had a formal structure and yet, like any dynamic, multifaceted mechanism for waging war, it was in constant flux. Personalities and circumstances could more easily mould and remould an inter-service body uninhibited by tradition and convention. Periodically that formal structure would change, either quite profoundly or as a consequence of organisational fine-tuning. Changes might be in response to particular events, or because the CCO redesignated roles to acknowledge fresh priorities. The changes announced in May 1943 reflected a need for senior personnel within COHQ to enjoy clearer lines of command over what now constituted a substantial fighting force. With a total complement of around 5,800 officers, at least 100 were working at Richmond Terrace. The expansion of the Special Service Brigade, and the seemingly inexorable growth in specialist shipping, had created a fighting force of over 50,000 soldiers and sailors. Thus a key development early in 1943 had been the belated integration of the Royal Marine Division, and the consequent creation of 41 and 42 Commandos. A year earlier the RM Division had been withdrawn from the expedition to seize Madagascar, highlighting the fact that it no longer seemed to have a clear purpose. Despite the loss of so many Royal Marines at Dieppe, Mountbatten argued that these were men uniquely qualified to fight as commandos. The traditionalists finally backed down, and today's Royal Marine Commandos were born. Brooke's intense dislike of the Army Commandos ensured their demise at the end of the war, since when the iconic green beret has been synonymous with the Royal Marines.[1]

Given the size of his command the CCO recognised the need to delegate responsibility for executive action. Each branch of the armed forces inside COHQ required a greater degree of autonomy. He proposed therefore that the Vice, Deputy, and Assistant Chiefs of Combined Operations should enjoy parity of status, and their posts be retitled, respectively, Military, Air, and Naval Chief of Staff. Churchill agreed to the changes, but offered Mountbatten a stern if friendly warning not to undermine 'the integrity of the inter-Service organisation' which he himself had worked so hard to forge.[2] Charles Haydon remained a pivotal figure at COHQ, his power and influence enhanced by the much greater degree of discretion he enjoyed over military affairs. Although the balance of power had shifted slightly in his favour, Haydon's prickly relationship with his boss still veered alarmingly from outrage to adoration, and back again. Judging Haydon irreplaceable, Mountbatten responded to any threat of resignation with an irresistible barrage of charm and emotional blackmail.[3] Both men became a lot closer to each other once they were working apart. Mountbatten came to appreciate just how much he had depended upon Haydon in the aftermath of Dieppe, and he continued to rely upon his wise counsel across the next 30 years.

Haydon's naval equivalent was Rear-Admiral Charles Daniel, whose background in signals and destroyers strongly resembled that of Mountbatten; except that, like Charles Lambe, the newly designated Naval Chief of Staff had the added advantage of having served in the Admiralty as Director of Plans. Daniel's empire had grown so large that it was scarcely surprising Dudley Pound took advantage of Operation Torch in November 1942 to ask whether the Admiralty should assume most of COHQ's naval responsibilities. The landings in North Africa placed enormous strain upon Combined Operations, and a myriad of problems were compounded by preparation for 'Operation Husky', the forthcoming invasion of Sicily. Mountbatten was a realist, accepting that operational planning and implementation on the scale now demanded by the Allies was beyond the capability of his naval staff. All duties other than tactical innovation, and identifying new shipping and equipment requirements, were transferred back to the Admiralty. By mid-1943 the Royal Navy had secured most of the responsibilities ceded to Mountbatten 18 months earlier. Planning this transfer of tasks was largely the responsibility of the CCO himself: a new, harmonious working relationship between Combined Operations and the Admiralty was crucial if the first direct assault upon Axis territory was to succeed. This was a pragmatic response given the fact that COHQ was clearly no longer up to the job, every admiral west of Suez was railing against Dickie's 'private navy', and critically, Charles Daniel had declared himself in full agreement with the First Sea Lord. In August 1943 responsibility for Combined Operations' burgeoning invasion fleet, and its home bases, was formally transferred to the Royal Navy. Ready to welcome vessels and crews was a familiar face, Jock Hughes-Hallett having left COHQ the previous May to become the Senior Service's principal staff officer in the inter-Allied team planning 'Roundup', the prelude to Operation Overlord.[4]

Mountbatten's increasingly relaxed view of the Navy's demands must have been because he had one eye on his career post-Combined Operations. Churchill's protection and patronage could only take him so far, and would only last so long. An aspiring First Sea Lord had no desire to see his senior colleagues permanently label him as a loose cannon whose first loyalty lay outside the Service. After all, he had already experienced several run-ins with the mastermind of the Dunkirk evacuation, Sir Bertram Ramsay, who by now had been promoted to admiral and put in charge of the Royal Navy's contribution to a full-scale invasion of France. Ramsay must have known that Mountbatten was already lobbying to be naval commander whenever the great day came – and was no doubt equally alert to the fact that Pound and Brooke considered such an appointment preposterous. When Ramsay temporarily switched to planning Operation Torch, he reiterated his concern over the training and discipline of Combined Ops' naval personnel.[5] Given events at Dieppe, Mountbatten could scarcely protest.

Ramsay complained about training and discipline; and the dispersed nature of Combined Operations made it difficult to impose uniform standards. Endeavouring to be more than just a figurehead necessitated frequent visits to establishments scattered the length and breadth of the land. When the CCO wasn't on the road or in the air, then he was back at his desk wrestling with paperwork. All too often he found himself at Chequers, fighting to keep awake as Churchill greeted the dawn with an empty decanter and a succession of ever more outlandish demands. He could only maintain such a ferociously demanding lifestyle for so long, and Mountbatten's readiness to meet the Admiralty's demands coincided with a first intimation of mortality. A chronic workload left him exhausted and vulnerable to infection, so it was scarcely surprising that in April 1943 he was laid low for three weeks with pneumonia. Churchill had been similarly ill the previous month, and soon after Brooke would suffer an unusually severe bout of influenza – so wholehearted a commitment to direction of the war effort was bound in the end to take its toll. Philip Ziegler suggested that coming to terms with such a physically draining illness constituted a wake-up call, after which Mountbatten never again took his health for granted: the first hint of infection, and the doctor would be summoned. There was an added bonus: if Brooke's diary entries are anything to go by, then Dickie's absence from the COSC for almost a month had an obvious calming effect upon its chairman.[6]

Someone guaranteed to infuriate the CIGS even more than the Chief of Combined Operations was Charles de Gaulle. Brooke never changed his opinion that fundamentally the man was a menace. Mountbatten, however, was finally persuaded by Eden that de Gaulle constituted the Foreign Office's best hope of a free France avoiding a political vacuum, quickly filled by the Communists. The most critical issue COHQ had to address was security, with periodic reviews identifying Allied forces operating under the Combined Operations umbrella as the biggest source of leaks. Exhorting the Americans to be more discreet worked once the CCO himself took charge, but persuading the Free French to operate on a need to know basis was well-nigh impossible. De Gaulle's headquarters in Carlton Gardens was notorious for its lax security, and yet he demanded prior notice of all raids across the Channel, as well as full consultation on any proposed deployment of French special forces. These demands had an internal logic given de Gaulle's perception of himself as the walking embodiment of a free, sovereign France, but any concession to his demands constituted a severe compromising of operational security. Robert Henriques recalled a meeting at which *le général*, even more enigmatic and lofty (in every respect) than usual, remained impervious to his host's courtesy and affability: pressed for assurance that any information passed directly to him would go no further, de Gaulle said only,

'Je connais la guerre'; and, having affirmed four times his understanding of war, he walked out. On this occasion Mountbatten had more than met his match.[7]

Operation Torch had profound implications for de Gaulle as success meant the liberation of sovereign French territory, notably Algeria. This was the first great test of Anglo-American military collaboration, and Mountbatten's strong personal and working relationship with Eisenhower reinforced a belief inside Combined Operations that the organisation must make itself indispensable to the C-in-C and his joint planning staff. Even before Torch was finalised, Ike and Dickie were working in unison: until the Americans switched the main deployment of forces from Morocco to Algeria, Churchill proposed both men crossing the Atlantic to complain loudly that the original proposal was flawed.[8] With Dieppe still fresh in their minds, five planning syndicates inside COHQ studied the various options for coordinated strikes on the Vichy-controlled Mahgreb. Eisenhower requested access to a chastened Bobby de Casa Maury and his Intelligence Section, as well as the far less humble Tom Hussey and his assorted acronym-challenged research centres. Mountbatten's enthusiasm for working with the Yanks extended to sending George Patton, the American commander on the ground, a joint team of planners, headed by Lucien Truscott and Robert Henriques – the latter went native, going ashore in Morocco attired as a US Army colonel. Reluctant to become reacquainted with Richmond Terrace, Henriques opted to spend the rest of the war working for Patton.[9]

The capture of Casablanca, and the far less straightforward seizure of the Algerian seaboard, exposed deficiencies in landing craft crews and beach parties far worse than Ramsay had identified. With fiercer opposition and more intense fighting at the beachheads then, as Fergusson noted, with classic mid-century English understatement, 'our pattern of success would have been much more jagged'. In other words, it could have been a bloody shambles. While Dieppe had highlighted the need for overwhelming fire support, North Africa had exposed hopeless organisation once troops and equipment were ashore. Thus COHQ's priority over the winter of 1942–3 was establishing an effective organisational unit, the battalion-size Beach Group; while Hussey's COXE tested a pontoon raft, a range of beach recovery kit, and an American amphibious truck, the DUKW. All these innovations, along with rocket-launching and artillery-firing landing craft, were available for the invasion of Sicily the following summer. Also mobilised was a specially selected body of RN captains, trained to liaise closely with the army and to control every aspect of an individual landing, from initial training through to the final arrival of vehicles, stores and ammunition. These SNOLs (Senior Naval Officer Landing) kept their inter-service staffs stationed permanently on their ships, ensuring that everyone learnt from experience.[10]

Not that Sicily was Mountbatten's first choice for the Anglo-American assault on Fascist Italy. The Joint Planners saw Sardinia as a softer target, arguing that an invasion could be mounted at least three months sooner than for Sicily. By choosing Sardinia the Allies could maintain their momentum, and at the same time surprise the Axis by not attacking the most obvious target. Eisenhower initially supported Mountbatten, but Brooke found neither man convincing. The CIGS felt Sardinia could bring no tangible benefit, despite the claim that its airfields were better placed for bombing the mainland. He was convinced the Germans would experience greater problems placing reinforcements on Sicily, and that this would be a critical factor given the centrality of a speedy victory to triggering the collapse of Mussolini's regime. Also, leaving the island in enemy hands would disrupt Allied sea communications across the Mediterranean. Crucially, Brooke enjoyed Churchill's backing, and within the COSC he knew that he could always count upon Pound.[11] Mountbatten on the other hand was confident that Charles Portal agreed with him. Also, he felt confident that he could secure the support of senior planners among the Americans, such as Al Wedemeyer. Thus the question of Sicily or Sardinia became a key issue when the Atlantic partners met at Casablanca in January 1943.

The Casablanca Conference and beyond, January–July 1943

The Casablanca conference commenced on 14 January, with Churchill and the Chiefs holding a preliminary meeting the previous afternoon. Brooke, the key figure in presenting the British position on strategic priorities, was weary from a long flight on a converted Liberator. For most of the journey he had fought fiercely for space on the floor of the cabin with his sleeping companion: Mountbatten, as if at sea, slept soundly throughout, wholly oblivious to the discomfort caused whenever he turned over. The Chief of Combined Operations awoke refreshed, and eager to exploit the goodwill generated among the Americans by his organisation's contribution to Torch. A visible reminder of COHQ's importance in securing success was HMS *Bulolo*, serving as the conference's communications centre. The headquarters ship was moored in Casablanca harbour, and Mountbatten insisted that time be found for a tour of his pride and joy. With minimal US involvement at Dieppe, the events of 19 August were unlikely to cast a shadow over those negotiations in which the CCO was involved. Not that he was especially prominent in the ten-day wrangling over the conflicting resource demands of the Pacific and European theatres of operation. Harry Hopkins was not alone in suspecting that some chiefs of staff were more equal than others. At meetings of the Combined Chiefs Brooke would always take the lead, confident that his overall objectives accorded with the case Churchill was making to Roosevelt and his acolytes. The CIGS's insistence that the United States acknowledge the necessity of a sustained Allied offensive in the Mediterranean naturally required complete unanimity within the British delegation.[12]

After five days of hard bargaining a basis for agreement finally emerged, with Brooke delighted by the Americans making a specific commitment to 'Operation Husky', the invasion of Sicily as a prelude to an assault upon the Italian mainland. Yet after dinner on the evening of 21 January, the COSC found itself once again arguing over whether Sardinia might be a better option. Mountbatten, who in Brooke's mind 'never had any decided opinions of his own', was again articulating the preference of the Joint Planning Staff for an ostensibly more vulnerable island. The argument ranged for three hours, until near midnight an exasperated chairman decided the time had come to bang heads together. Brooke was adamant in his refusal to tell the Joint Chiefs that 'we did not know our own minds' and therefore now preferred Sardinia. A decade later he recalled pointing out to his colleagues that, 'such a step would irrevocably shake their confidence in our judgement. What is more, I told them frankly that I disagreed with them entirely and adhered to our original decision to invade Sicily and would not go back on it'.[13] Only 12 months in to the job and the CIGS was indispensable. A proven tactician in the field, and now a master strategist, 'Brookie' enjoyed Churchill's absolute confidence. Even a favoured son like Mountbatten was a mere mortal by comparison. Having stirred the embers of mutiny, the Chief of Combined Operations sensibly backed down.

At the Combined Chiefs' meeting the next morning Brooke gave no indication of division in his own camp, and by noon Operation Husky was up and running. Yet, astonishingly, Mountbatten would not let it go. Over lunch at the President's villa he complained to Hopkins that the service chiefs had stubbornly ignored the advice of himself and 'all the younger officers in the British lay-out'. No wonder he advised everyone at his table, 'not to say anything about his urging the attack on Sardinia instead of Sicily'.[14] Not for the first or the last time in his life, an inability to exercise common-sense and remain silent in the face of perceived injustice got the better of him. There is a fine line between indiscretion and disloyalty, and in this case the excitable admiral stepped over. Sound judgement fell victim to the adrenaline rush of finding himself, admittedly playing a peripheral part, at the very heart of great-power politics. This was no whispered mumbling in a shadowy corner of Rick's Café but a conversation in a crowded dining room. It would be surprising if Brooke did not learn about the exchange, and this might explain why his remarks about the CCO over the next few weeks were especially vehement.[15]

It's ironic that Mountbatten argued so strongly against a full-scale assault upon Sicily as when it took place, in July 1943, the sea-borne landings gave every suggestion that COHQ had finally got its act together. The airborne invasion was a far more costly affair, but this was beyond Combined Operations' remit. Seven and a half divisions were carried from a rendezvous south of Malta to the beaches west of Syracuse by an armada of 2,760 vessels. Both Antony Head and Robert Henriques were tasked with establishing what lessons could be learnt, and they were in agreement that on the whole disembarkation had gone to plan. The weather had been unseasonably stormy, but with no serious consequences other than chronic seasickness among those troops going ashore in the smaller landing craft. The gales' worst effects were on the parachute drops and the glider landings, the latter already severely reduced by premature release and friendly fire.[16]

The one obvious conclusion was that, for such a huge operation, all senior commanders needed to share the same headquarters. Instead of them being concentrated in Malta they were scattered around the southern Mediterranean. Had there been fierce resistance on the beaches then serious liaison problems would undoubtedly have occurred. This was an avoidable lapse, especially given that Charles Haydon had observed an absence of firm leadership during the Torch landings. Eisenhower had responded enthusiastically to Haydon's complaint; and his appointment as commander-in-chief for Husky, with Cunningham masterminding naval operations, was intended to ensure a clear chain of command. Yet communications at the very highest level broke down, witness Eisenhower's remark when he heard the BBC report that the C-in-C had just announced his forces' arrival in Sicily: 'Well, thank God: *he* ought to know!' Until he heard the wireless report Eisenhower had received no news of what was going on.[17]

Waiting for news with Ike in Valetta was Mountbatten. The COSC had agreed a month earlier that he could fly out to the Mediterranean and see for himself how well the forces under his command conducted themselves. This was a good time for Dickie to be out of the country as Bunny Phillips was on four months leave in England and occupying all Edwina's spare time.[18] However willing to indulge his wife, he could scarcely have relished the prospect of a Broadlands *ménage`a trois* every weekend through to October. As well as consulting with the commander-in-chief, he spent time with Ramsay in his convoy escort HMS *Antwerp*, before transferring to Cunningham's flagship for a tour of the British landing areas. On 11 July Mountbatten went ashore with Tony Head, experiencing his first taste of war on dry land for a quarter of a century.[19] Conditions were very different from the Western Front, but just as dangerous – driving behind the front line in Montgomery's staff car, Mountbatten was alarmed to find an enemy aircraft strafing every vehicle in sight: 'All of us at the back immediately flung ourselves down, but not so Monty who sat bolt upright and didn't even turn his head to look at the Messerschmitt … Monty never turned a hair and didn't seem to be afraid.'[20] The contrast with Rommel's experience the following year is striking, and counterfactualists can only speculate on the consequences had the *Luftwaffe* pilot secured the Humber in his sights. Equally alarming was Mountbatten's brief return to commanding a destroyer. *Plus ça change* – in a breakneck journey at 30 knots to liaise with the US Navy admiral, Kent Hewitt, he ploughed straight through a minefield the Americans assumed to be impenetrable. Hewitt's final report to Washington was warm in its praise for Combined Operations' contribution to the success of his mission. This was a view shared by other American senior staff, while their British counterparts were far less suspicious or openly hostile than a year earlier. As Bernard Fergusson, albeit over-egging the cake, neatly observed, 'Husky was an enormous triumph; and Mountbatten was much too human to suppress his delight at the part C.O.H.Q. had played in it'. Fergusson knew his man, yet no doubt the CDS read his conclusion in draft form, and blithely nodded agreement.[21]

COSSAC and D-Day planning

The irony was that the summer of 1943 in many ways marked the zenith of Combined Operations' eventful history. Even before Mountbatten departed for the Mediterranean he was well aware that the dynamics of defence decision-making were already shifting. More and more the focus was upon Roundup, and its eventual successor Overlord. Several admirals senior to Mountbatten considered their claims to take a naval task force across the Channel far stronger than someone whose command experience at sea was limited to leading a destroyer flotilla. In any case it was clear from the COSC that his appointment to such a senior post would be vetoed by the First Sea Lord. Thus, despite his title, any direct involvement in the invasion of France was as the head of a large, multi-purpose organisation which would service and supply the requirements of a powerful, overall planning body. Those services would include an advisory input, provided at every level from the CCO and his staff at the top to the coxswain and his crew at the bottom. While no supreme commander could yet be appointed (the main candidates were either in the Mediterranean or chairing the Chiefs of Staff Committee), the Casablanca conference recognised that a combined staff was now required to coordinate the extensive planning operation already well under way. Thus was created COSSAC (Chief of Staff to the Supreme Allied Commander), a post filled by Lieutenant-General F.E. Morgan.[22] Amiable, affable, and courteous, Freddie Morgan's diplomatic skills rendered him the ideal candidate for the job. He rarely set out to massage egos, but he was a masterly manipulator of the vain and single-minded. Crucially, he got on well with Mountbatten, who at the time held Morgan in high regard. In retirement, and eager to claim credit for just about everything, Mountbatten still acknowledged his great affection for Morgan, but dismissed him as a 'great disappointment', if only because he was 'virtually ineffective' within the Whitehall war machine. A key figure in maintaining good relations between Combined Operations, COSSAC, and the Navy would be the ubiquitous Commodore Hughes-Hallett. Having assumed a variety of roles since leaving COHQ, presumably Hughes-Hallett now felt the time was right to accept promotion.[23]

By coincidence, not design, COSSAC's staff started work while Mountbatten was seriously ill, in April 1943. Ultimately Morgan's planners would become the supreme commander's executive staff, but their original function was more wide-ranging. It was established at the outset that any large-scale operation, not just the eventual invasion, was now Morgan's responsibility. Had there been another Dieppe then in theory COSSAC would have been in the driving seat, with Combined Operations fulfilling a support role. Alan Brooke, who concluded his description of Morgan's new post with the scarcely encouraging 'Well there it is. It won't work, but you must bloody well make it', tellingly referred to him as the Chief Staff Officer for Cross Channel Operations.[24] Given their publication so soon after the war, Morgan's memoirs might easily be dismissed as a Whiggish account of D-Day's birth pangs – everyone behaved splendidly, and we were on track from the start. It's easy to be cynical, but the consistent sentiment of *Overture to Overlord*, and the tone of its author's correspondence with Mountbatten, together indicate an absence of resentment and a readiness to collaborate. The CCO was a proud man in every sense of the word, but in this instance he rarely appeared protective and proprietorial. Thus, as Morgan noted appreciatively, help was 'gladly and enthusiastically given. Virtually he put at our disposal the planning and intelligence sections of his own headquarters, than which nothing better could be imagined'. COSSAC staff could have trawled the services for fresh personnel, but Mountbatten's goodwill ensured an absence of overlap, plus provision of units which simply did not exist elsewhere. Thus Morgan's team came to rely heavily upon the beach reconnaissance of a unit placed on a regular footing after Torch, the Combined Operations Pilotage Parties. Reconnoitring potential landing sites and identifying hidden obstacles in a short space of time became a highly sophisticated exercise. Providing detailed geological analyses of beach samples tested even COHQ's keenest scientific minds, of whom more anon. Yet for all the dependence upon Combined Operations, by the summer of 1943 the COSSAC staff had become an impressive inter-service, inter-Allied organisation in its own right.[25]

COSSAC was given a detailed invasion brief as a consequence of the Trident conference, held in Washington throughout the middle weeks of May. Morgan was not invited to attend, and a more notable absentee was Mountbatten. It's a sign of how much the bout of pneumonia had taken out of him that he chose to stay at home. Instead, COHQ was represented by the magnificently monikered Major-General Minden Whyte-Melville MacLeod, a founding father of combined operations who in his time had served as a gunner on both the Western Front and the North-West Frontier. MacLeod had set up Combined Operations' Middle East training centre at Kabrit on the Great Bitter Lake, and had only been back in England since January. He was himself a convalescent, having cracked his spine in a crash landing when the aircraft carrying him home from Egypt was shot down over the Welsh coast. Heaven only knows what the Americans made of this Buchanesque Highland aristocrat, especially if he chose to wear a kilt and leant heavily on his stalking stick. No doubt the latter was not the case, with efficiency trumping eccentricity: the CCO was too sensitive to the American psyche not to choose the right man for the job. In Mountbatten's absence the Chiefs of Staff's meetings prior to negotiations with their US counterparts appear to have been brief and non-contentious. Given the very obvious tension within the Combined Chiefs, especially when attention focused upon the future direction of operations against Japan, the British delegation couldn't afford to give even a hint of internal division. Interestingly, in the light of later developments, for the first time the question arose of a supreme commander in southern Asia. Churchill clearly assumed that this would be a British appointment as he discussed the issue in the context of whether Wavell 'still had enough drive and energy' to carry on as Commander-in-Chief of the Indian Army.[26]

Churchill and Brook returned to London via Algiers. By the time they were finally home COSSAC had been briefed on Trident's discussions with regard to the invasion of Europe. Initial projections had been made as to the size of enemy resistance, and the number of American and British divisions required for the initial assault and for the break-out from the beachhead. At least 29 divisions were predicted, and this figure was later seen to be a significant under-estimate. The earliest an invasion force of this size could be assembled in the south of England was the spring of 1944. The pressure was on COHQ to ensure that in 12 months time as many as 4,500 fully crewed assault ships and landing craft would be ready to cross the Channel. Like Mountbatten, MacLeod was a 'can do' sort of chap. While still in Washington he ordered his team to have a first stab at anticipating each division's particular requirements. Nevertheless, the decisions arrived at by the Combined Chiefs and their staffs remained highly provisional. They did, however, offer COSSAC a framework within which to operate. Crucially, Morgan was still required to advise on the key question of which locations along the French coast were most suitable for landing a taskforce of such magnitude.[27]

Chapter Eight suggested that two parts hard evidence and one-part unashamed bullying had seen Mountbatten secure a general endorsement of Combined Operations' invasion choice, the Baie de la Seine. However, across all three services there remained vocal supporters of the shortest crossing. To resolve the dilemma, Morgan split one of his staff's three branches, Operations. He ordered his American planners to produce an outline plan for a Normandy invasion. Meanwhile their British colleagues would undertake the same task for the Pas de Calais. The latter was the most direct route to the Rhine, but it was also the most heavily defended. In any case most arguments for targeting the nearest stretch of coastline had by now been overtaken by events, not least the extension of fighter cover courtesy of long-range fuel tanks. The British team were happy to concede defeat when the Americans argued persuasively in favour of a landing on the beaches north of Caen. Yet within Home Forces Headquarters there were diehards still insistent on the Pas de Calais. Morgan's generous view was that these were generals moulded, 'by a lifetime of niggling, cheeseparing, parsimony, and making do'. Thus, they lacked the imagination to comprehend the sheer scale of American power and resources that would be deployed 12 months hence. Until the Calais lobby was finally silenced, no further progress could be made: 'From this appalling quandary we were rescued by the Chief of Combined Operations, always a leader of progressive thought and somewhat of an *enfant terrible* to his more elderly *confrères*.' Assuming Mountbatten actually read Morgan's book – and, given his modest penchant for reading anything other than technical manuals and tales of blue-jacketed derring do, that is a big assumption – how he must have relished his portrayal as a youthful, gold-braided man of action![28]

Mountbatten orchestrated the reworking of a regular Combined Operations course at HMS *Warren* into a four-day brain-storming session on every aspect of a cross-Channel invasion. Needless to say, he insisted on chairing proceedings, unphased by the age and seniority of his invited guests. This was, as he pointed out to Bernard Montgomery, 'my humble personal attempt to get a move on with OVERLORD'. Twenty years later Mountbatten shed the false modesty, insisting that no one else had the clout and connections to ensure commanders as senior as Paget, McNaughton, and the US Army's Jacob Devers could all be in the same place at the same time.[29] The 'Rattle' conference commenced on 28 June, with Largs in the middle of a heatwave. The presence of so many Americans and Canadians ensured that at some point formality, precedent, and procedure would break down; and a more relaxed, more productive atmosphere would henceforth prevail. This was exactly what happened, but it took a good 36 hours before the British contingent's stifling stuffiness and innate suspicion finally cracked. After that jackets were removed, even if ties remained firmly knotted, and Dickie was in his element. With his usual attention to detail every effort had been made to ensure the guests were comfortable and the atmosphere conducive to calm and consensual discussion. Whenever the atmosphere became tense or even fractious then the chair adjourned the meeting for tea or coffee on the lawn. Periodically the pipe band of the Argyllshire Home Guard would appear in order to smooth the ruffled brow and calm the nerves – in theory at least. As an admiring Morgan gratefully recalled, 'The showmanship could not have been excelled'. Mountbatten might wish to have been a studio boss had the Royal Navy not had first call, but he was also ideally qualified to run a five-star hotel. No wonder he was so relaxed when the idea was first aired of opening Broadlands to the public.[30]

Given the eminence of the assorted air marshals and air commodores, admirals, generals, and brigadiers, it's not surprising that one wag renamed Rattle 'The Field of the Cloth of Gold'. When Henry VIII met Francis I precious little was resolved other than that the latter was a better wrestler. Nearly four centuries later, the 75 temporary residents of the Hollywood Hotel demonstrated an enviable capacity for sticking to their agenda, and generating a remarkable sequence of action points: the minutes ran to 143 foolscap pages, and hard on their heels came COSSAC's final report to the Joint Planners, and with the latter's commentary, to the British Chiefs of Staff. Morgan's recommendations constituted a long and remarkably detailed document, which was unequivocal in its insistence that, 'we concentrate our efforts on an assault across the Norman beaches about Bayeux'. Among its many achievements, some of which we shall return to, the Rattle conference at last silenced those critics inside Paget's HQ insistent that seizure of Calais and Boulogne was a prerequisite of the invasion's ultimate success. Last ditch defenders of the Pas de Calais remained blind to the new consensus inside Richmond Terrace, and further afield: if no harbours were immediately available then the Allies now had the technology to take their own 'artificial anchorages'. The latter was another key recommendation when Morgan personally delivered his report to the COSC.[31]

At the time Morgan and Mountbatten spoke as one. The more flamboyant half of the partnership controlled events throughout the Rattle conference, but he regularly conferred with his genial general. The latter used conviviality to disguise the single-minded pursuit of a clear set of objectives. These chimed with COHQ's thinking over the previous 18 months, ensuring that Combined Operations' invasion initiatives complemented COSSAC's understanding of the bigger picture. Yes creative tension existed, but the relationship between Morgan's extended family and the cousins at Richmond Terrace was one rooted in continuity and a common identity. Harold Wernher insisted that forging the latter was very much in Mountbatten's mind when he first suggested placing key players from both sides of the Atlantic in a hothouse environment, both metaphorical and literal. Flying back to London from Largs, Wernher congratulated his brother-in-law several times removed on a conference which marked the climax of everything Mountbatten and COHQ had striven for since his arrival in the autumn of 1941: providing COSSAC with a clear path forward, and seeding the embryo of a 'coherent Invasion Planning Force', was a personal triumph, on the back of which Dickie should seek a fresh challenge. Henceforth, hands-on control of operational planning would be surrendered to commanders in the field, ensuring a diminution in Combined Operations' size and importance; as already signalled by the surrender of its 'private navy' to the Admiralty.[32] Mountbatten knew

Wernher was right, hence his lobbying for command of a big ship given that Pound had deemed his appointment as a taskforce commander to be out of the question. However, in the absence of any formal suggestion that it was time to move on, he continued the 16-hour day and the prioritisation of pet projects, almost all of which involved dealing on a daily basis with Combined Operations' formidable array of research scientists.

Boundary-breaking boffins on the Combined Ops front line (1): Dickie's scientific advisers

Patrick Blackett was last seen in Chapter Three, resigning his commission at the end of the Great War in order to stay on at Cambridge as a student of maths and physics. The future Baron Blackett may, in the opinion of another ennobled scientist, Solly Zuckerman, have been the 'father of operational research', but Dickie Mountbatten was the first senior commander to acknowledge the direct application of OR to land operations.[33] Operational research might loosely be defined as the systematic, scientific analysis of all aspects of waging war, from grand strategy right through to the most basic tactics in the field. Locating scientific method at the heart of industrial war was of course nothing new. Yet from the mid-1930s a growing number of British scientists, drawn from across the political spectrum, had identified a novel role for David Edgerton's 'warfare state': authorising and facilitating a rigorous and comprehensive investigation into the most resource-efficient means of eroding the enemy's offensive and defensive potential. Such an audit could be conducted by a variety of means, and with reference to a diversity of scenarios, large or small; but by definition it constituted operational research.[34]

Early in the war OR's most immediate application was to the strategic air offensive over Germany. Quantitative research into the consequences of bombing non-military targets dated back to the mid-1930s, and Henry Tizard's ill-fated inquiry into Britain's paltry air defences. The original Tizard Committee dissolved because of irreconcilable differences between its chairman and his former friend and fellow physicist, Frederick Lindemann.[35] A key member of the Air Ministry committee was Patrick Blackett, by now busy applying quantum mechanics to earlier research with Rutherford into tracking charged particles. With laboratory life a fading memory how Lindemann must have envied the younger man's international standing as an experimental subatomic physicist. He could see that Blackett had the finer mind in the field of particle physics, but wrongly perceived an inferior understanding of the real world when it came to practical politics. Not surprisingly, the conservative Lord Cherwell (the peerage came in June 1941) and the left-leaning Nobel laureate (the prize came in 1948) would clash repeatedly over the next 20 years.[36]

Mountbatten on the other hand found Blackett's politics surprisingly persuasive in that as an old man he came to share the same deep scepticism re the efficacy of nuclear weapons.[37] In earlier years the future First Sea Lord may have blanched at some of Blackett's more naive statements regarding Soviet science; but as India's Governor-General he had warmly applauded the readiness of an academic already so active in public life to support the new nation's embryonic scientific establishment.[38] Residual goodwill was rooted in the firm belief that Patrick Blackett was at heart always a Navy man, his remarkable achievement in having fought as a 'snottie' in the Falklands and at Jutland matched by his critical advisory role inside the Admiralty throughout the Battle of the Atlantic. For five years Mountbatten and Blackett were colleagues in the House of Lords, but they shared far more than a voice in Parliament: a common education (Osborne/Dartmouth/Cambridge); a raft of honorary degrees but no actual doctorate; the sovereign's esteem as both a Companion of Honour and a recipient of the Order of Merit; *and* fellowship of the Royal Society.[39]

Blackett just happened to be president of British science's most august body in 1966, the year Solly Zuckerman successfully proposed Mountbatten for election as a fellow. It's clear from a speech given to the Royal Society four years earlier that the then Chief of the Defence Staff was angling for an invitation to join – not least because Prince Philip was already an FRS. As Chief Scientific Adviser to the MOD, Zuckerman may well have felt that professional etiquette required his boss's retirement prior to his nominating Mountbatten under Statute 12, 'which provides for the election of persons who either have rendered conspicuous service to the cause of science or are such that their election would be of signal benefit to Society'. The newly elected fellow replied to the President's letter of congratulations by observing that, 'It must surely be unique in the annals of the Society for one sailor to propose another for membership, which adds greatly to the value of your invitation'.[40] Technically, Zuckerman had been the proposer, but the letter highlights how Mountbatten still viewed Blackett as a Navy man nearly half a century after he had so abruptly left the Service. Handsome in looks, and handsome in manner, both men were remarkably adroit in posing as outsiders, while seeming effortlessly to progress to the very top in their respective chosen professions – the President of the Royal Society warmly welcoming the Admiral of the Fleet as a fellow man of science somehow symbolises this mutual ascendancy. A key difference, however, was that 'Mr Blackett' cloaked a natural ability that bordered on genius inside a common man persona – much to Cherwell's chagrin, no doubt – whereas Dickie Mountbatten always had to work bloody hard and, for all his fine intentions, scarcely disguised an inherent sense of *noblesse oblige*.

Between the wars Blackett was a close associate of the crystallographer and founding father of British molecular biology, J.D. Bernal. Both men served on the reconstituted Committee for the Scientific Survey of Air Defence, and therefore remained close to Tizard, the National Government's most influential scientific adviser until May 1940.[41] Churchill's arrival in Downing Street brought due reward for Lindemann, whose friendship and loyalty throughout the wilderness years earned him a uniquely powerful role within the Prime Minister's inner circle. 'The Prof' had if anything been a more ardent anti-appeaser than Churchill, and his deep-rooted suspicion of Hitler's intentions paralleled those of Mountbatten: while Lord Louis was a scion of *mitteleuropean* aristocracy, Lindemann's ex-pat roots lay firmly in the Bavarian bourgeoisie. By coincidence, Lindemann was educated at the Lycaeum in Darmstadt, progressing to the Grand-Ducal Technical High School in 1905.

Connections with court through his father, and a precocious ability to play tennis at championship level, brought young Frederick into frequent contact with the Grand-Duke of Hesse himself. As a regular on-court opponent of Ernst-Ludwig, it's not entirely fanciful to suggest that Lindemann was present at Wolfgsgarten when the young Prince Louis made his first trip to meet mama and papa's grandest German relatives. Based at Berlin University from October 1908, after 14 years abroad the young researcher rapidly returned 'home' in August 1914, appalled by the Kaiser's hegemonic ambitions. Wartime research in Farnborough at the Royal Aircraft Factory was followed by the herculean task of restoring the Clarendon Laboratory's reputation for cutting-edge research; but Lindemann's readiness to resist German expansionism re-emerged with the collapse of the Weimar Republic.[42] Whether ensconced in Oxford or from September 1939 firmly established within Whitehall, the future Lord Cherwell took a keen interest in quantifying bomb damage. Urged into action by Desmond Bernal, his 1941 critique of Bomber Command's effectiveness as a strike force was pivotal in the RAF's strategic reappraisal of how best to bomb Germany.[43]

Yet Lindemann was by no means alone in gathering empirical evidence as to how the Blitz was impacting upon the Home Front. Bernal, a priapic polymath who somehow reconciled pathfinding biomolecular research with an enthusiasm for all things Soviet, was busily engaged in fieldwork. So too was the South African physiologist and anthropologist Solly Zuckerman. The two men had collaborated on several research projects since forging a deep friendship in the summer of 1931. When Zuckerman established his dining club and policy discussion group for left-leaning scientists and economists, 'The Tots and Quots', Bernal immediately joined. Blackett was a more half-hearted member, although he was active in a later, more broadly-based group called 'For Intellectual Liberty' – inspired by the Popular Front and claiming to be both pacifist and anti-fascist, the three points of the FIL triangle were Bloomsbury, Kingsley Martin's *New Statesman*, and politically engaged scientists such as 'Sage' Bernal, J.B.S. Haldane, and Julian Huxley. Franco's revolt gave the FIL a cause, but, like Mussolini's invasion of Abyssinia the year before, events in Spain forced Marxisant intellectuals to adopt either a position of absolute pacifism or to accept rearmament as the only credible means of resisting fascist aggression. The Condor Legion's assault upon Republican Spain acted as a spur to the 'Cambridge Scientists Anti-War Group', most of whose members were by 1937 anything but anti-war. Bernal, the CSAWG's president, was eager to investigate the physical and psychological impact of sustained bombardment upon civilian populations. For the final two years of peace he researched the subject with suitable academic rigour, while at the same time campaigning furiously with Haldane and the Left Book Club's John Strachey to secure adequate air raid precautions.[44]

Bernal and Zuckerman had known Strachey since his pre-Marxist days as Tom Mosley's bag carrier in the New Party. While the Prosector of London Zoo and Fellow of Christ Church College retained a deep suspicion of political dogma, he liked Strachey as a person. Bernal on the other hand saw the author of *The Coming Struggle for Power* as a thoroughly decent chap *and* as a wholly committed comrade in the class war triggered by the Depression and the collapse of the second Labour Government. As noted in Chapter Two, there is some evidence that Strachey knew Mountbatten, but the latter was too wary to associate himself with the fellow-travelling left, notwithstanding a shared contempt for Chamberlain's continued appeasement of the Axis dictators. As for Zuckerman, despite his familiarity with grand country houses the length and breadth of England, on no occasion pre-war was he introduced to Dickie and Edwina. He would surely have remembered, and they would doubtless have found his easy manner congenial and appealing – when necessary, the master of assimilation wore his learning lightly on his sleeve.[45]

In early 1939, as in so many other matters, the Government began to take notice, and Bernal came in from the cold. That spring the Home Office appointed him to Sub-Committee A, constituted 'to study the physics of explosion, blast and penetration'. Needless to say, by the time Zuckerman revived 'The Tots and Quots' the following November the question of whether one was for or against war was irrelevant, for all but the most one-eyed supporter of the Soviet Union. Now the key issue was what role the nation's scientists could play within the overall war effort. Blackett, no longer semi-detached, would eventually brief his fellow diners on 'the analysis and planning of actual operations', in other words, operational research. For the moment, however, members built on initiatives taken by Bernal and Zuckerman in the winter of 1938–9, notably a memo to the War Office on 'Science and Defence' drafted jointly with the eminent military commentator Basil Liddell-Hart. While the minister, Lesley Hore-Belisha, warmly welcomed the document, he pointed out that he was in no position to promote its contents across Whitehall.[46] By the time 'The Tots and Quots' commissioned its two leading lights to produce at breakneck speed a Penguin Special on *Scientists At War*, the generals had long since got rid of Hore-Belisha and the Panzers had finally rolled into Dunkirk. Events bore out Bernal and Zuckerman's central argument that a national emergency as dire as 'Our Finest Hour' demanded the full mobilisation of the nation's most precious assets, one of which was its scientific community. Whether meeting in London or Oxford, 'The Tots and Quots' gained in importance as its members assumed ever greater responsibility within the Churchill coalition's war machine. In its original incarnation Lindemann would have viewed the club as a hotbed of unpatriotic quasi-Bolsheviks, with the honourable exception of its founder – 'The Prof' was also a fellow of Christ Church, and always enjoyed Zuckerman's company at High Table. Yet as early as March 1940 Lindemann was prepared to forget old quarrels and accept an invitation to dine.[47] Within a year, however, fresh differences would emerge, and the old divisions harden. Thus, Zuckerman's club never acquired establishment approval, and this is probably what made it such a dynamic body: 'The Tots and Quots' was a convenient forum for establishing common agreement on what precisely 'operational research' was. In time the club also became a counterweight to Combined Operations, Mountbatten's scientific advisers using dinner table discussion as an avenue for airing ideas re the wider implication of those projects enjoying priority status inside Richmond Terrace.

In the spring of 1940 Desmond Bernal and his fellow investigators were focused full-time on accurately predicting the consequences of bomb blast and shock waves.

At the same time Zuckerman was establishing his reputation as an expert on the physiological consequences of explosions, including wound ballistics. With cruel irony Bernal's team chose Coventry as their focus for study, and, following the catastrophic raid of 14–15 November, found themselves in the unique position of being able to compare their casualty and bomb damage projections with the harsh reality of a city in ruins. The experience of London, Coventry, and south coast ports like Southampton convinced Bernal and his fellow researchers that a systematic process of recording bomb damage was required. Zuckerman was thus instrumental in setting up the Casualty Survey, based at Guy's Hospital, and in due course he assumed control of the Oxford Extra-Mural Unit (OEMU) – rather than a quaint wartime centre for lifelong learning, this was in fact an intellectual powerhouse for quantifying the human and material consequences of sustained aerial bombardment. Although surveys undertaken under the auspices of the Ministry of Home Security were primarily intended to improve civil defence, they proved equally useful in designing ordnance, namely the development of high explosive bombs that matched or even exceeded the destructive capacity of those currently reining down on British cities.[48]

Over the next 18 months Bernal and Zuckerman became increasingly concerned with the offensive potential of their respective projects, not least the detailed surveys of Birmingham and Hull. In arriving at its final conclusions the OEMU utilised data from the Home Office's Bomb Census and detailed daily analysis of how the two cities functioned under conditions of acute duress. Results and a final report, *Field Study of Air Raid Casualties*, appeared in the spring of 1942. The survey findings fuelled a ferocious quarrel between Lord Cherwell on one side, and on the other Henry Tizard and Patrick Blackett, the latter discreetly supported by Dudley Pound. Both sides already loathed each other anyway, but they differed fundamentally over Cherwell's argument that the *Luftwaffe*'s only modest success in disrupting munitions production constituted a powerful argument for intensifying Bomber Command's assault upon German cities. The resource implications were immense, hence the First Sea Lord questioning Portal's insistence on demoting Coastal Command's needs and prioritising the production of heavy bombers. Bernal and Zuckerman were appalled that Cherwell, who had been instrumental in facilitating such a thorough investigation of conditions in Birmingham and Hull, was seemingly intent on subverting the inductive process – that, with a cavalier disregard for scientific method, Churchill's most influential acolyte was reinterpreting the findings simply to support the Air Staff in their insistence that the RAF could bring Germany to its knees. They greatly admired the sceptical Tizard for being so independent minded – at the time he was still Portal's chief scientific adviser. The finer details regarding one of *the* key debates within Whitehall across the whole of the war need not concern us here. Suffice it to say, that both Bernal and Zuckerman felt powerless, and increasingly disillusioned. Although there was unfinished business, particularly for Zuckerman in his capacity as director of the OEMU, it was time to move on. Henry Tizard appreciated the extent to which both men's hands were tied so long as his old adversary remained so close to the Prime Minister: in 1942 Cherwell was appointed Paymaster-General, and a year later he joined the War Cabinet. At the height of the quarrel Tizard took the initiative, astutely identifying where the complementary talents of Bernal and Zuckerman might best be employed. He sowed the seed in Mountbatten's mind that experts on the effects of bombing were uniquely qualified to advise those in the vanguard of taking the war to the Germans. They had the expertise acquired in the course of the Blitz, but they also had the intellectual capital and transferable skills which enabled them to undertake whatever tasks the CCO deemed appropriate.[49]

At the Ministry of Defence in the early 1960s civil servants regularly complained that the 'Zuckbatten Axis' was well-nigh impossible to break down. The CDS and his Chief Scientific Adviser consolidated a friendship and a working partnership that survived intact until the day the IRA struck – following which Zuckerman was inconsolable. From the mid-1950s onwards Sir Solly filled the advisory role vacated by Peter Murphy (surprisingly, between 1943 and 1954 the two men only met twice, hence Edwina never really getting to know her husband's smartest ally).[50] In public Mountbatten declared Zuckerman the cleverest man in the world. In private he valued greatly his friend's shrewdness and sagacity. Self-assured, coldly analytical, and deeply sceptical, Zuckerman had the ability to go straight to the heart of the problem – Polaris or Profumo, he would take any crisis in his stride, and advise accordingly.[51] Even before leaving South Africa the Jewish-born intellectual was already an outsider. On the surface he assimilated brilliantly, but the arrogance, ambition, and capacity to intrigue – as his biographer has pointed out, all traits shared with Mountbatten – camouflaged a self-awareness that Lord Zuckerman would never be entirely at home among the great and the good of his adopted land.[52] He was too intelligent to try and be more English than the English, but he had the perspicacity and mental equipment to sense when another outsider was trying just that little bit too hard. In this respect he had the measure of his master. Zuckerman wrote revealingly about Mountbatten even before he died, but his later thoughts on the man displayed a laudable aversion to hagiography.[53] It's clear that on a number of occasions before – but more especially after – Mountbatten retired, Zuckerman's precious words of wisdom compensated for an obvious absence of sound judgement. Never did a deluded elderly gentleman have greater cause to thank his old friend for intervening than the notorious occasion in May 1968 when press tycoon Cecil King sought Mountbatten's support for a coup to depose the Wilson Government. It was King's foil at IPC, *Daily Mirror* editor-in-chief Hugh Cudlipp, who first revealed Zuckerman's denunciation of 'such treasonable nonsense', and his insistence that Dickie 'Throw them out'. An indignant Zuckerman soon left, and Mountbatten quickly came to his senses.[54]

Given the enormous debt Mountbatten owed to Zuckerman by the time he died, it's ironic that initially the anatomist was very much number two in the package proposed by Tizard. When Bernal was asked to come and work as a scientific liaison officer in the Experimental and Developmental Section he agreed to join only if his professorial partner came too. Technically their boss was Tom Hussey, but from the outset they enjoyed a direct line to Mountbatten: inside an acronym-obsessed organisation Bernal and Zuckerman were respectively XSA1 and XSA2, reporting to CXD, but ultimately accountable within COHQ to CCO! Ironically, once ensconced in Richmond Terrace the two friends found themselves working on separate projects, and it soon became obvious that Bernal was seen as the senior researcher – he was quickly moved into his own office. This was perfectly acceptable to Zuckerman, who was still technically responsible for the statistical unit in Oxford. On his first encounter with Mountbatten he was surprised to find a refreshing lack of top-brass self-importance. He already knew Robert Henriques, and Tony Head was another friendly face, but there was clearly resistance within Combined Operations Headquarters to decidedly independent scientific advisers with no obvious military background.[55]

Prejudice was no doubt reinforced by the unorthodox appearance and occasionally eccentric behaviour of 'Sage' Bernal and of Geoffrey Pyke. The latter, of whom more anon, had been the first scientist recruited by Mountbatten, on the recommendation of Leo Amery. The long-haired, rumple-suited Bernal may have come across to the unenlightened as something of a rum cove, but with Pyke they truly broke the mould. The CCO must have sensed rumblings of discontent as in May 1942 he issued a minute emphasising the centrality to the planning process of independent and properly informed technical advice: 'This is an experiment to which I attach great importance as I am anxious to link up the scientists from the very beginning of operational planning so that when their scientific knowledge is required they may be completely in the picture.'[56] The atmosphere began to change, and soon scientists were seen in a positive light, as reinforcing COHQ's carefully cultivated image of unconventionality. More importantly, it was clear that the likes of Bernal and Zuckerman were blessed with brilliant minds, and that they learnt fast – *very* fast. A key moment was when Bernal refused to advise on measurement of beach gradients unless he was properly informed as to the purpose of the exercise. Once fully briefed he came up with a wholly original answer, based on regular aerial reconnaissance of tidal activity. Word quickly spread that if you put these chaps fully in the picture then they would solve your problems in ways beyond the compass of most military minds.[57]

Bernal's influence within Combined Operations stretched far beyond specific research projects. As we shall see, in later life Zuckerman chose to play down his old friend's importance. Nevertheless, he acknowledged that Bernal had energised the whole organisation: 'He imparted a point of view, a way of seeing things – the same quality which characterised his whole life as a scientist. He had an amazing capacity for knowing what questions to ask, and a brilliant ability to know where to seek an answer. He had a clear eye, encyclopaedic knowledge, and an incredible memory.' From the outset Mountbatten made time for Bernal, 'one of the most engaging personalities I have ever known'. Here was a man of intellect and integrity, and an unsung hero: 'his most pleasant quality was his generosity. He never minded slaving away on other people's ideas, helping to decide what could or could not be done, without himself being the originator of any of the major ideas on which he actually worked. This may be why his great contribution to the war effort has not been properly appreciated.'[58] Another obvious reason is Bernal's break with the British defence establishment after 1945: his Cold War commitment to nuclear disarmament entailed energetic propagandising on behalf of the Soviet-backed World Peace Council. No wonder Zuckerman, Ultra-secure and operating at the highest levels inside Whitehall, kept his one-time collaborator at a distance. Bernal's postwar friends may have been questionable, but his intentions were laudable – ironically, the 'big science' he and Blackett saw as fundamental to winning the war *and* to winning the peace created the unique circumstances in which nuclear Armageddon became a reality.[59]

Zuckerman soon found, 'Combined Ops a happy place, and friends one made there remained friends for life'. He was in awe of Mountbatten's energy, enthusiasm, attention to detail, and ability to motivate even the humblest operative within his command.[60] A somewhat inauspicious start to his career at Combined Operations entailed a detailed statistical analysis, using number crunchers at OEMU, to determine how many nights in each month offered optimum conditions for cross-Channel commando raids. In later years Mountbatten found it hilarious that Zuckerman handed him his report with the words, 'Well, it turns out that there never will be a night suitable for a small raid'. Whether he saw the joke at the time is open to question. Zuckerman most certainly did not, as much of his early work, whether advising the commandos on night vision and ration packs, or calculating the ordnance necessary to silence Alderney's defensive batteries, was not intellectually challenging in the way that his previous research clearly had been. Alan Brooke thankfully vetoed the idea of sending a Guards brigade to the Channel Islands, but Zuckerman now had a clearer insight into the direct application of operational research.[61]

Zuckerman's probability model for calculating the appropriate level of preliminary bombardment formed the basis for far more ambitious planning once the decision was made early in 1943 to attack Italy's southernmost island, Pantelleria. His 283 page report advised on the most cost-effective form of bombing, factoring in the need to ensure that sufficient superstructure survived in order to support the occupying forces. The complete success of the operation, carried out in June 1943 ahead of Husky, secured Zuckerman's reputation as an operational planner and established his credibility as a military scientist – from now on every door in the defence sphere was open to him. Arthur Tedder, Supreme Air Commander in the Mediterranean, was especially impressed by Zuckerman's intellect. The air marshal had already been struck by the adviser's independence of mind when he submitted a devastating critique of the Desert Air Force's failure to disrupt the Axis forces' retreat from El Alamein. Throughout the first half of 1943 Zuckerman spent long periods in north Africa, initially with Bernal and later alone. Thus began a gradual withdrawal from Combined Operations, and attachment to the RAF – in May 1943, against Mountbatten's advice, Zuckerman accepted the honorary rank of group captain. Both Tedder and Leigh-Mallory made increasing demands on his time, and he was rarely in London. A final meeting with Mountbatten took place in the Mediterranean when the CCO flew out to witness the invasion of Sicily – after dinner the two men talked for several hours in Dickie's bedroom, neither of them aware that it would be three years before they next met. Zuckerman's formal break with COHQ only arrived in August 1943 when he joined the Allied Air Forces' planning staff for Overlord. Newly arrived in Kandy, Mountbatten wrote urging him to join SEAC, but Zuckerman saw the real action as taking place closer to home: on 6 June 1944 he would find himself in the invasion War Room targeting suitable aiming points within the battle area.[62]

Brains and integrity stopped Zuckerman from arguing that D-Day planners drew heavily upon the lessons learnt at Dieppe. He acknowledged how deeply Mountbatten felt about the disaster, while at the same time making clear that the great man bore much of the responsibility for what went wrong.[63] Zuckerman seemingly had no idea that Bernal was involved in planning for the raid. Crude analysis of the density and constituency of the Dieppe beaches formed the basis for Bernal's far more sophisticated fieldwork when charged with locating the most suitable landing places for a full-scale invasion. Operation Jubilee exposed the multiple problems generated by landing a large body of men and machines on a steeply sloping sand or shingle beach. Bitterly acknowledging the inadequacies of aerial reconnaissance, between Dieppe and D-Day Bernal acquired an encyclopaedic knowledge of sea and sand, studiously analysing deposits surreptitiously scooped from Normandy *plages*. Beach reconnaissance would ultimately generate a sizeable operation within COHQ – and, as land speed record-breaker Sir Malcolm Campbell was deemed to have an unrivalled knowledge of beach surfaces, Dickie duly invited him to join the show.[64]

Despite their presence at the chaotic initial exercise, both advisers were eager to sail with the Jubilee task force. Their request was turned down, and Mountbatten was singularly unmoved when 'Sage' complained that he was placing the needs of the press above those of his scientists. Zuckerman's lasting anger over Dieppe was shared by Bernal. As soon as the full extent of the disaster became clear the two scientists were ordered down to Newhaven. All night and into the next day they documented the shocking scenes on the quay as crippled naval and assault craft came alongside, unloading commandos and Canadians, and transferring a ceaseless stream of wounded and shell-shocked into the waiting ambulances. Appalled by Mountbatten's insistence that the raid be seen in a positive light, only his promise of a no-holds-barred inquest tempered their protests. Ever the Renaissance man, 'Sage' focused upon the damage sustained by all shipping involved in the operation, whether big or small. Zuckerman and his statisticians in Oxford conducted a quantitative survey of half the nearly 1,000 casualties who managed to make it home. The final report confirmed the vulnerability of landing craft crews, and the havoc created once they were disabled; it also highlighted the disproportionate impact of German mortar fire.[65] Zuckerman found the survey a grim and unsatisfactory exercise which, once submitted, was largely ignored: 'But years after, I remembered our sombre study when I stood under the Dieppe cliffs where so many had died.'[66]

While Zuckerman viewed Bernal and a later recruit, Max Perutz, as cutting-edge scientists whose intellectual DNA matched his own, he placed Geoffrey Pyke in a category all of his own – 'a man of a vivid and uncontrollable imagination, and a totally uninhibited tongue'. Yet he was never dismissive of someone with whom he worked quite closely, and he understood why at a particular point in time Pyke and Mountbatten forged the unlikeliest of partnerships – an alliance of eccentricity and ego lost in the mists of time until resurrected in *Turbulence*, Giles Foden's fictional representation of wartime weathermen reconciling the mysteries of quantum mechanics with the hellish responsibility of forecasting the most opportune moment at which to launch Overlord.[67]

Geoffrey Pyke looked every inch the disorganised eccentric with his large glasses, manic stare, straggly beard, and complete lack of even the most basic dress sense. Writing in the late 1950s, with the full cooperation of former colleagues at Combined Ops, Pyke's biographer was too polite to speculate upon his subject's mental condition. However, Pyke's mode of behaviour, and his acute nervous breakdown at the onset of the Depression, strongly suggests bipolar disorder. Bernal had first encountered his future colleague at a Bloomsbury gathering in 1926. At the time fevered share dealings funded the experimental Malting House School in Cambridge. However, Pyke's mathematical agility allowed him to make and to lose a small fortune on the metal exchanges. Although somewhat adrift in the 1930s, he nevertheless managed to mobilise a campaign against German-backed anti-semitism, and to found the Voluntary Industrial Aid scheme as a means of supporting Republican Spain – his ideas for sustaining the loyalist war effort offered an insight into his thinking once he arrived at Richmond Terrace. The onset of a wider European war saw Pyke bombarding ministries with a myriad of ideas, and a campaign in *Reynold's News* for a radically fresh approach to mass shelter building. Among his wildest proposals was one that caught the eye of Leo Amery: the suggestion that specially equipped commandos in northern Norway could tie up substantial enemy forces.[68] Keyes had previously rubbished the notion of COHQ masterminding an operation deep inside the Arctic Circle, but Mountbatten was to prove more open-minded – he acted on Amery's suggestion that Pyke was a man worth inviting to lunch. Tieless and sockless, down at heel, and with frayed trousers flapping about his ankles, an unfazed Pyke announced himself to his immaculately suited host with the words, 'Lord Mountbatten you need me on your staff because I am a man who thinks'.[69]

Mountbatten wanted Pyke to talk about Norway, but he began speculating on whether the appointment of such a provocative figure to Combined Operations might prove a useful shock tactic. It's questionable whether the gamble paid off, as almost everyone working inside COHQ viewed Pyke as a crank; and this prejudiced their perception of Bernal and Zuckerman until they established their credentials as serious scientists. Mountbatten's aides found it infuriating that their boss spent so much time with Pyke, and appeared oblivious to the man's lack of even the most basic social skills. They felt the CCO indulged someone whose value to the organisation was questionable, and were astonished that Mountbatten should visit Pyke's chaotic, rubbish-strewn flat whenever recurrent pleurisy obliged the guru to remain in bed. Bombarded with what he labelled 'Pykeries', Mountbatten scrutinised every crazy idea, fearful of overlooking the one really clever suggestion. Acutely aware of Downing Street's ceaseless demand for fresh and imaginative schemes, Mountbatten saw Pyke as one means of keeping Churchill off his back. Just occasionally the flight of fantasy became real, and at that point the professional scientists were called in.[70]

Such was the case with 'Project Plough', Pyke's proposal for a marauding force behind enemy lines in Norway. What caught the Prime Minister's imagination was, firstly, that here was an operation ideally suited to keeping the Canadians occupied, and secondly, that troops already hardened to Arctic conditions could evade the enemy by travelling at great speed on snowmobiles propelled by Archimedean screws. Churchill was convinced by Bernal's single-sheet distillation of what was an epic project proposal. Pyke was incapable of writing concisely, witness a 3,500 word memo to Mountbatten in advance of meeting with Marshall on 11 April 1942 to discuss Norway. Harry Hopkins was at the same Chequers conference. He found the PM in sparkling form, observing of 'Project Plough' that, 'Never in the history of human conflict will so few immobilise so many'. Not having met Pyke, Churchill insisted that this newly-discovered genius be sent to the United States immediately in order to start work on his revolutionary vehicle. Officials inside COHQ moved heaven and earth to get Pyke across the Atlantic before the end of the month. Predictably, the trip proved a disaster, and only direct intervention by Mountbatten prevented the project from collapsing. Over the longer term SOE became the US Army's British partner; and in August 1943 a Canadian-American joint force trialled the 'Weasel' tracked cargo carrier on the Aleutian Islands prior to special operations in Europe. Screw-driven snow transport in Norway never became a reality, but to be fair to Pyke there was an outcome – and 15 years later, similar vehicles would enable the Fuchs-Hillary expedition to bisect Antarctica.[71]

Mountbatten worked hard to appease those Americans appalled by his adviser's tactlessness and obvious organisational incompetence: he apologised profusely to Washington for the absence of social interaction, while at the same time refusing to accept Pyke's resignation. When visiting the capital in June Mountbatten recommended his maverick man of ideas to Roosevelt, and even risked introducing him to Eisenhower. Before the CCO left for London Pyke made him promise to read a memo that he was still working upon: it transpired that his mind was no longer on Norway, but was preoccupied with the Allied air forces' inability to provide comprehensive convoy protection. The memo landed on the top man's desk on 24 September 1942. Later that autumn, to the dismay of Mountbatten's staff, its author would reappear in Richmond Terrace, bloody but unbowed.[72]

Boundary-breaking boffins on the Combined Ops front line (2): 'Habbakuk' and 'Mulberry'

Pyke's correspondence with Mountbatten is unique, the former informing the latter what needs to be done in a prolix yet matter-of-fact fashion. There is a refreshing absence of deference, and no obvious acknowledgement of the CCO's status and authority ('Dear Mountbatten …'). Mountbatten once promised to devote a maximum of 30 minutes to any document Pyke sent him, after which he would delegate.[73] Totalling over 55,000 words, Pyke's memo from America soon found itself in the hands of Zuckerman and Bernal. In both appearance – 232 pages of typed foolscap interleaved with blue or red-inked scribblings to Mountbatten – and content, the 'Habbakuk' memorandum was truly fantastical. Remarkably, Bernal condensed this long, rambling exposition into a single sheet evaluation, no doubt taking on board Pyke's favourite quotation from G.K. Chesterton: 'Father Brown laid down his cigar and said carefully: "It isn't that they can't see the solution. It is that they can't see the problem".[74]

With the Battle of the Atlantic still raging, Pyke addressed the absence of adequate air cover by proposing a giant, unsinkable aircraft carrier made of reinforced ice. He complemented his basic proposal with ever more incredible scenarios, involving frozen super-freighters, ice fortresses, and super-hard lock-breakers. A further nod to science fiction was the use of 'supercooled water' as a deadly weapon. The notion of literally petrifying opponents by spraying the enemy with liquid water cooled below its normal freezing point was, and is, truly fantastic – attempts to emulate cloud formation only ever generate minuscule amounts. All Pyke's flights of fantasy fell by the wayside as attention focused upon the central idea, of a 'bergship' with a hull 30 feet thick and half a mile long. Slow but impregnable, this frozen leviathan would contain hangars, workshops, freezing plants, and living quarters. Research by Howard Mark, an old colleague of Bernal in New York, had suggested that a small amount of sawdust or wood pulp could significantly enhance the tensile strength of a sheet of ice, which, if struck, would no longer shatter upon impact. Furthermore, the insulating shell of soggy wood pulp made the mixture, later christened 'Pykrete', far more resistant to melting than pure ice. The down side, as Max Perutz soon discovered, was that even reinforced ice sags as a consequence of gravitational pull; hence the carrier's need for an insulating skin, and a refrigeration plant to feed its labyrinthine system of cold air ducts.[75]

Artificial icebergs seemed a crazy idea, but could it work? Zuckerman was sceptical but Bernal was by no means dismissive. That was enough for Mountbatten, who took the idea to the Prime Minister. Churchill was equally enthusiastic, speculating on the potential for circumventing Pyke's proposal by simply cutting giant landing strips out of the Arctic ice sheet. Clearly viewing 'Habbakuk' as just not worth the fight, the Chiefs endorsed the Prime Minister's directive of 7 December 1942. In no time at all a high-powered committee was established, and an ambitious pilot programme agreed. Cherwell and Zuckerman were the most unenthusiastic members of the 'Habbakuk' committee, and their indifference to the project allowed Pyke and Bernal to oversee a huge programme of research and development. Now almost wholly forgotten, 'Habbakuk' was in the vanguard of wartime trans-Atlantic scientific collaboration. As with Britain's involvement in the Manhattan Project, Canada was deemed a vital junior partner. After all, the Canadians had the capacity to construct a sizeable plant in sub-zero temperatures. In fact Churchill made clear to Mountbatten that Ottawa should always take precedence over Washington. For nigh on 12 months the CCO defended his pet project's accelerating costs, constantly courting a receptive Churchill in order to counter objections from Cherwell and the Chiefs of Staff.[76]

Meanwhile, still working on peacetime research in Cambridge was someone uniquely qualified to work with Bernal and Pyke on this bizarre project. In 1936 Max Perutz had left his native Vienna to work on x-ray crystallography at the Cavendish Laboratory. Bernal considered the Jewish refugee his most brilliant student, and over the succeeding 60 years Perutz's achievements and accolades would eclipse those of his mentor. He shared Zuckerman's ability to communicate complex ideas clearly, concisely, and coherently: from his early days briefing Mountbatten on the mysteries of Pykrete, he would become one of the late twentieth century's key science communicators. Perutz's 1962 Nobel Prize for Chemistry applauded his research into the three-dimensional structure of molecules, but it also acknowledged his pioneering work as a glaciologist: as early as 1938 he had wintered in the Swiss Alps to study how snowflakes falling on a glacier become large grains of ice. In 1940 Perutz's research had been rudely interrupted when he was first of all interned on the Isle of Man and then incarcerated in a Canadian POW camp. He could easily have been embittered by the whole experience, but from January 1941 he was back at the Cavendish eagerly awaiting a call to arms.[77]

That call came 12 months later, when Perutz found himself summoned to Piccadilly, and an appointment inside the Albany. Waiting to receive him was Geoffrey Pyke, whose response to the loan of such a fashionable apartment was, in his own inimitable fashion, simply to trash the place. This otherworldly and at the same time mysterious character issued a vague invitation on behalf of Lord Louis Mountbatten to advise Combined Operations about glaciers. Max Perutz heard no more for nearly a year, during which time Pyke went on his calamitous mission to the United States and drafted the 'Habbakuk' memo. Perutz was now sworn to secrecy and invited to join a project known only to Pyke, Bernal, and Mountbatten. This was of course a great exaggeration, as must have become clear when Perutz's proposal for a laboratory to manufacture reinforced ice generated an immediate response: requisition of a huge meat store five floors beneath Smithfield Market, and technical support from a team of young commandos headed by an equally youthful Cambridge physicist. Only when Perutz had established his credentials as a team leader did Douglas Grant, once a naval architect but by this time serving as secretary to the project's burgeoning committees, persuade Harold Wernher that their star researcher really ought to be put in the picture.[78]

To the CCO's delight, once Perutz had access to Howard Mark's research findings he provided plentiful supplies of shatter-proof Pykrete. Legend has it that Mountbatten took a piece to Chequers, and demonstrated its strength while Churchill lay luxuriating in the bath. Sir Stafford Cripps – never a man eager to share his ablutions, but nevertheless a member of the War Cabinet until late 1942 – enthused over the offensive potential for reinforced ice. Nor for once was the Admiralty wholly scornful of Dickie's latest wheeze: A.V. Alexander was hostile, but Their Lordships reserved judgement. With Churchill cracking the whip, naval architects worked to ever more ambitious specifications: an ability to ride once in a century tidal waves; a torpedo-proof hull up to 40 feet; a flight deck at least 50 feet above the water, 200 feet wide, and 2,000 feet long in order to accommodate heavy bombers; a cruising range of up to 7,000 miles; and a minimum speed of seven knots in order to avoid drift, with power provided via turboelectric steam generators capable of supplying 33,000 horsepower to no fewer than 26 electric motors, each independently powering a nacelle-housed ship's screw. The slide rules calculated that this monstrous man-made iceberg would boast a displacement of 2,200,000 tons, which was 26 times that of the *Queen Elizabeth*, then the largest ship afloat! Incredibly, by the summer of

1943 detailed plans had been drawn up for the 'bergship', but one insoluble problem remained – although steerage via variable speed from the motors made sense for a vessel 15 storeys high, the Royal Navy continued to insist upon a rudder.[79]

By the time Pyke left for Canada in late February 1943, he was a man with a mission. Earlier in the winter a serious bout of jaundice had left him stranded in the Albany apartment. Astonishingly, a bedside conference call brought Bernal, Zuckerman, Tom Hussey, Sir Harold Wernher, and the Chief of Combined Operations. The latter assured an impatient Pyke that work on 'Habbakuk' was progressing as fast as humanly possible. Like 'some jaundiced Christ', the fevered prophet protested that, '"Without faith nothing will come of this project"':

> 'But I have faith', replied Mountbatten. 'Yes', said Pyke, 'but have the others got faith?, and turning to Harold Wernher he asked solemnly, 'Have you got faith, Brigadier?' Poor Wernher did not know what to say, but before he could utter a word, C.C.O. chipped in with the remark 'Wernher's on my staff to see that I am not over-lavish with my own faith'.[80]

Briefed by Desmond Bernal before he left for the Middle East, Mountbatten's first concern was to ensure that Mackenzie King, Canada's veteran premier, should also keep the faith.[81] Any doubts held by the High Commissioner had already been shattered – even if the Pykrete hadn't. The Hon. Vincent Massey had been conveyed in cognito to Smithfield, and bundled into an insulated flying suit. He was then invited to hammer the reinforced ice as hard as he could. Mountbatten and Wernher enthusiastically joined in, the faith-challenged brigadier bringing the show to a dramatic conclusion by firing a bullet into the block, creating merely a dent.[82]

The Canadians were by now crucial to the success of the project, and Mountbatten was clearly fearful of the damage Pyke could wreak if left in North America on his own. He signalled Bernal to leave Zuckerman in Cairo, and to meet up with Pyke in New York. Zuckerman urged 'Des' not to go, insisting that 'Habbakuk' was a nonsense, and that to leave now would see the end of a uniquely productive partnership – on both counts he was right. Nevertheless, sending 'Sage' halfway round the world was a shrewd move on Mountbatten's part as, by the time he returned to brief Churchill in late May, a 1,100 ton prototype was under construction in Alberta. With the Canadians confident that 'Habbakuk' could be a reality inside a year, materials were being stockpiled and detailed plans drawn up for an inaugural vessel to be built in Newfoundland. Yet at the same time there was no real sense of urgency in Ottawa, and Bernal remained sceptical about 1944 as a launch date. His doubts were reinforced by Perutz's growing concern over creep – in other words, the sagging problem. While Bernal kept his colleague in check on the banks of Lake Patricia, Mountbatten found himself placating the Chief of Naval Construction: it was widely known that Pyke had cabled the CCO labelling one of his keenest adversaries 'an old woman'. The irate admiral stormed across to Richmond Terrace demanding Pyke's head on a platter, but the ever-loyal Mountbatten resolutely refused to sack him.[83]

Figure 10.1: Canadian premier Mackenzie King hosts Churchill, Roosevelt, and their staffs at the first Quebec conference, August 1943 – no Mountbatten, so did he take the photograph?

To his credit Mountbatten was no fair-weather friend. He never dismissed Pyke's ideas out of hand, witness the 50-page memo on 'power-driven rivers' which the CCO passed on to Bernal for careful scrutiny: 'Sage' applauded the theory of long pipelines from supply ships using compressed air to pump ashore fuel or cylindrical containers, but advised that in practice such an unorthodox system of transportation would encounter insurmountable problems.[84] Nor was Mountbatten offended by Pyke's readiness to mock him, not least Dickie's claim that he and Edwina were no different from anybody else: recommended bedside reading in mid-1943 was a brilliant parody of Soviet propaganda, paying tribute to the late 'Comrade Louis Mountbatten, aged 101 ... one of the most enthusiastic converts to proletarian revolution during the great struggle of 1949–50'.[85] When Pyke's contract with the Admiralty ended abruptly in June 1944, from halfway around the world Mountbatten intervened to ensure that he was treated fairly and properly recompensed.[86]

Mountbatten was loyal, but not stupid. In July 1943 he acted on Max Perutz's advice to take Bernal not Pyke to any high-level encounters with the Americans. The US Navy, relegated to the trans-Atlantic triad's non-executive partner, was unconvinced of the need let alone the viability of 'Habbakuk'. The Admiralty, having designed the vessel, now baulked at the cost. Perutz, who in any case was still wrestling with the creep problem, had calculated that to build the first 'bergship' would take 12,000 men 50 weeks, at a cost of £2 million; the Treasury later tripled that figure. Perutz was the obvious person to deal directly with the Americans, but so far had been denied a visa given his formal status as an enemy alien. Bernal appeared ready to go along with Pyke's crazier schemes, notably a merger of 'Habbakuk' and 'Project Plough': while 'Trojan Horses' raced around inside the Arctic Circle, a fleet of reinforced ice ships would facilitate the rapid seizure of the whole Norwegian coastline. A scarcely sage-like suggestion was that Pyke attend Churchill's final meeting with the Joint Planners before the PM's departure for Canada on 5 August 1943. Mountbatten wisely vetoed Pyke's presence at any meeting, but by now he was torn between his continued faith in the wondrous powers of Pykrete and a growing belief that its inventor was living in a fantasy world – for the Admiralty that belief had long since become a firm conviction. Pyke was henceforth kept at ocean's distance from both the Americans and the Canadians, but steps were taken to secure British citizenship for COHQ's rising star – a quiet word with the Home Office set wheels in motion. Perutz would be part of the 'Habbakuk' team despatched to New York in September 1943. Bernal preceded his colleagues by a month: Mountbatten ordered him to get a haircut, buy a decent suit, and stow his kit on the *Queen Mary*. He was surely the oddest member of the 150-strong British delegation attending the 'Quadrant' conference, scheduled for the second half of August. The venue for the next Anglo-American summit was the Château Frontenac, Quebec city's majestic cliff-top hotel high above the St Lawrence – and, thanks to the dogged persistence of Mountbatten and Bernal, 'Habbakuk' was on the agenda.[87]

One intriguing 'what if' is whether, while crossing the Atlantic, Bernal bumped into another great eccentric added to the passenger list at the last moment. Presumably he did because Mountbatten invited the Chindits' founder, Orde Wingate, to meet Tom Hussey and the rest of the Combined Ops team. For Churchill the one general capable of giving the Japanese a bloody nose was a Lawrentian free spirit, and a natural ally of young Dickie Mountbatten. The CCO thus found himself dealing with someone as brimming with self-belief as himself. It's perhaps not so surprising therefore that he never really warmed to Wingate, even if they did share a similarly unorthodox approach to waging war. The same, incidentally, was true of the Dambusters' commanding officer, Guy Gibson, another last-minute addition to Churchill's party. [88] On the other hand, given Wingate's pro-Zionist activities when policing in Palestine, perhaps Edwina preferred to give 'Gideon' the benefit of the doubt; in fact they only met on one occasion, when the pioneer of deep penetration behind enemy lines lunched at Chester Street following Dickie's appointment to SEAC. At sea a month earlier, a charismatic Wingate had left his COHQ audience in awe of the Chindits' forbearance when isolated inside the dense Burmese jungle.[89]

Bernal had been ordered to keep a low profile, and two days out from Southampton the CCO announced his presence in a typically theatrical fashion. Following a briefing by Tom Hussey on artificial harbours, Mountbatten informed his fellow chiefs that 'the greatest expert in the world' just happened to be on board. 'Sage' was duly summoned from below decks, and we shall return to his role in the development of the 'Mulberry' harbour. Nor was this his only appearance before the COSC as the *Queen Mary* cautiously steamed westwards. Two days later, wisely avoiding mention of Pyke's wackier schemes, Bernal made a spirited defence of 'Habbakuk'. No doubt to the irritation of the CIGS the project was added to the conference agenda, with Mountbatten deputed to write a briefing paper. Throughout the Quadrant conference Bernal's priority was Overlord, but on 19 August an especially strained meeting of the Combined Chiefs of Staff concluded with proof of the power of Pykrete. The chairman was furious that Mountbatten was so insistent on delivering his paper. Brooke was then left speechless when Dickie's all-action delivery ended with his firing a pistol at a block of ice. Shards shot out in all directions, but the real danger came when he aimed at a block of reinforced ice – the bullet ricocheted around the room, just missing Portal. Another airman, Hap Arnold, had already hurt himself trying to smash the same block with an axe supplied by Bernal. Arnold's scream of pain, followed quickly by revolver shots, led one of the assorted aides gathered outside the room to scream, 'My God! They've now started shooting!' Nor did this mark the end of the affair – on the final day of the conference Bernal was taken by Churchill to demonstrate the thermal properties of Pykrete to Roosevelt. As the block stood impregnable in an antique silver punch bowl filled from an equally ancient pitcher of boiling water, a beaming Prime Minister revelled in the ingenuity of British invention. This was indeed the high water mark of 'Habbakuk'.[90]

The Combined Chiefs of Staff authorised a board to oversee production, and 'Mahomet' (Mountbatten loved codenames as much as he loved acronyms) ordered the whole team to New York – regrettably, 'John the Baptist' was to remain in England. Pyke, unable to comprehend why the Americans had vetoed his continued involvement, blamed Bernal. Ironically, the 'Sage' was desperate to get home, and genuinely concerned for his friend's future welfare. Bernal recognised that Mountbatten's imminent departure from Combined Operations left Pyke unprotected, and more crucially, left 'Habbakuk' at the hands of the Admiralty and the Naval Department. By Christmas Bob Laycock, Mountbatten's successor at COHQ, would have sealed Pyke's fate by transferring him to the Admiralty; on the first stage of a downward spiral that would end with the poor man's suicide in 1948. With Zuckerman already gone, Bernal would remain as the CCO's sole scientific adviser, working almost exclusively on Overlord. In September 1943 he rejected Mountbatten's request to join SEAC on a temporary basis, and on two further occasions he turned down invitations to fly out and advise on establishment of an operational research unit. Freddie Morgan had initially indicated a willingness to let Bernal go, but as planning of the invasion gathered momentum his technical advice became so crucial that absence abroad was out of the question. Instead, Bernal bridged the distance with a regular flow of detailed advice for the SEAC Supreme Commander. He finally flew out to the Far East in October 1944. 'Sage' remained there until late December, advising on the imminent Arakan offensive:

experience gained on D-Day was directly applied to the planned landings at Akyab. Both Mountbatten and Bill Slim judged his contribution invaluable.[91]

Late 1943 would also see Pyke's great vision melt away, with Bernal unintentionally starting the process. 'Sage' was despatched south to bring the Americans back on board (a vacant hotel bedroom conveniently becoming available for surely Dickie's oddest ad hoc adviser, the newly-arrived Bunny Phillips).[92] At a key meeting in Washington the impartial, gloriously otherworldly academic was convinced that sceptics from the Naval Department had not made their case strongly enough. As Mountbatten recalled: 'Bernal, who had become so expert in proclaiming the points in favour of Habbakuk, now, with his Jesuitical mind, volunteered to produce all the points against it as well. The criticisms of the project were so powerful that they turned the scales against it and I had a telegram from the Prime Minister, Mr Churchill, saying that "The next time you come to a Combined Chiefs of Staff Conference, you must not bring your Scientific Advisers with you".' Perutz noted Mountbatten's pride in his adviser's 'prodigious knowledge and his original approach to any kind of problem'; yet there was also an inability to recognise, 'that Bernal's one great failing was a lack of critical judgement'. Similarly, the CCO was at fault for indulging the Cartesian Pyke's 'arrogant conviction that an intelligent human being could reason his way through any problem …'.[93] Perutz might also have noted that, in terms of basic common-sense and *real politik*, Solly Zuckerman was a very different political animal from his erstwhile colleagues. Bernal's most recent biographer has argued that during the Cold War an ambitious and worldly-wise Zuckerman distanced himself from his old ally, belittling the major contribution 'Sage' had made to establishing precisely when and where the D-Day landings should occur. Thus Zuckerman's memorial service 'tribute' somehow managed to be both measured and mean. An elderly Mountbatten, although inclined to adopt a more generous – and thus a more accurate – assessment of Bernal's achievements at COHQ, merely tempered his friend's begrudging remarks. Tom Hussey proffered a more spirited defence, but only in private.[94]

As soon as the US Navy denounced 'Habbakuk' as a false prophet, Perutz quit Washington, and then quit Combined Operations. The Americans and the Admiralty torpedoed the project because it required such an enormous volume of steel, and building smaller, albeit more vulnerable aircraft carriers was a far cheaper option. Crucially, Allied access to airfields on the Azores, and the development of long-range aircraft, ensured adequate protection for exposed convoys in mid-Atlantic. Pyke moved on to the next pipedream. Max Perutz moved back to Cambridge: 'sad at first that my eagerness to help in the war against Hitler had not found a more effective outlet, but later relieved to have worked on a project that at least never killed anyone.' Having witnessed at first hand the centralised planning model advocated by Blackett and Bernal, after the war Perutz would foster a more flexible, laissez-faire system of research and development. Ironically, the ethos he cultivated at the Laboratory of Molecular Biology, of hiring very bright people, giving them a supportive infrastructure, and then seeing what they came up with, is strongly reminiscent of Mountbatten's bottom-up approach on his arrival at COHQ.[95]

Years later Solly Zuckerman discussed with Perutz whether 'Habbakuk' would have survived had Dickie remained in London. He was convinced that the answer was yes, in that, 'It was too grand an idea for him to abandon'. Covering his tracks, Mountbatten himself maintained that the 'Mulberry' artificial harbour was a far greater gamble – the idea only seemed less outrageous because it was put into practice, and it worked.[96] It remains a persuasive argument. After all, Pyke's 'power-driven rivers' seem a crazy notion, even when one has seen the technical spec; but the concept was only one stage on from PLUTO, the 'Pipe Line Under the Ocean' that daily pumped a million gallons of fuel across the Channel in the summer of 1944. Mountbatten always insisted that he had come up with that particular idea, and those supposedly party to his original grand wheeze were more than happy to humour him.[97] One inspired staff officer mocked his master's tendency to claim responsibility for every idea and invention. Because the poem's gentle humour was in a roundabout way complimentary, Mountbatten loved reciting it, especially on television:

Mountbatten was a likely lad,
A nimble brain Mountbatten had,
And this most amiable trait:
Of each new plan which came his way
He'd always claim in accents pat
'Why, I myself remembered that!'
Adding when he remembered it,
For any scoffer's benefit,
Roughly the point in his career
When he'd conceived the bright idea,
As 'August 1934'
Or 'Some time during the Boer War'.[98]

The CCO never laid claim to the 'Swiss Roll', the huge drum of flexible roadway powered by giant catherine-wheels that wreaked havoc whenever it was tested – failure to synchronise firing of the two engines meant the Behometh rolled everywhere but up the beach. Yet Mountbatten could with justice maintain that expensive design failures were necessary if Combined Operations was to uncover the rare gem, most notably the two 'Mulberry' harbours taken to Normandy in June 1944.[99]

To be fair, Mountbatten never laid claim to the original notion of floating harbours, instead attributing the idea to Jock Hughes-Hallett. The latter recalled an engineer by the name of Guy Maunsell sowing the seeds in 1940, but identified a service in Westminster Abbey three years later as the eureka moment when he resolved the post-Dieppe dilemma of how to sustain an invasion without access to a port. However, this was nearly 12 months after Churchill issued his 'Piers for Use on Beaches' minute; heralded by his most blinkered admirers as the inspiration for 'Mulberry'. No it wasn't, and neither was it a direct response to Mountbatten informing the PM that his notion of a floating pier had been blocked at the highest level. Even Michael Harrison, who in writing a history of 'Mulberry' invariably interpreted Mountbatten's every word as gospel, demurred over this particular version of events. Although, to be fair, Eisenhower recalled how in the spring of 1942 there remained deep scepticism as to the feasibility of a taskforce boasting its own port. Also, Tom Hussey did identify one vital and cost-effective suggestion made by the CCO, namely the sinking of blockships to create protective breakwaters.[100]

Where Churchill did make a difference was in pointing out to Mountbatten that ten months after his original minute precious little progress had been made in agreeing on a single design for artificial harbours. Two months later the PM rebuked all four chiefs of staff for a collective failure to coalesce the diverse development projects taking place under the auspices of the War Office and the Admiralty. In identifying 'Mulberry' as the preferred design, with its huge concrete caissons that formed a floating inner harbour wall (the 'Phoenixes'), and two flexible steel roadways that surmounted four giant floating piers (the 'Whales'), Churchill played a key role in kick-starting the project. For all his grand ideas Hughes-Hallett had to defer to the nuts-and-bolts man, one Major Steer-Webster, later the War Office's Director of Experimental Engineering. The unsung hero, Steer-Webster relied heavily on Bernal's current research into wave formation. Mountbatten brought engineer and applied scientist together, and performed the role of minder whenever the 'Mulberry' mastermind wheeled his scale models down the corridors of power. Crucially, at the Rattle conference in June 1943 Mountbatten acted as an advocate for the new technology, enthusiastically endorsing Hussey and Hughes-Hallett's technical depositions. He fulfilled a similar function at Quadrant, this time relying on Bernal for technical advice. 'Sage' had already convinced Churchill and the COSC of the case for an artificial harbour courtesy of a bathroom experiment aboard the *Queen Mary*.[101]

Although the man-made harbour at St Laurent was wrecked by the great gale that lashed the post-invasion beaches on 19 June 1944, its British partner at Arromanches remained intact and invaluable. Needless to say, Mountbatten always insisted that the Americans hadn't properly bolted together what was an impressively solid logistical asset. While the likes of Harold Wernher would assume a far greater role in what was after all a vast undertaking – remarkably, all components were ready in just eight months – Mountbatten could justifiably claim some of the credit for 'Mulberry' proving such a stunning success. Unfortunately, he too often claimed *all* the credit, most notably in an *Observer* interview to mark his retirement as CDS in 1965.[102] Yes, in advance of Overlord, as in every other aspect of Combined Operations R and D, the CCO was a mover and shaker, laudably receptive to new ideas and intellectually equipped to absorb technical detail – given his career path within the Royal Navy Mountbatten was well-qualified to interpret hard data, and to comprehend the practical application of often abstruse theoretical physics. Crucially, he understood the fundamental concept of operational research. At the same time he was gamely hands-on, intervening directly where necessary. For example, Churchill was appalled to learn that his newest chief of staff had arrived at a COSC meeting fresh from test-driving a one-man submarine.[103] Yet surely Mountbatten's greatest achievement was to recruit a team of exceptionally talented scientists and engineers, each one of whom made a significant contribution to the success of interim operations and eventually of Overlord itself.[104] To be fair to their boss, he was never averse to acknowledging the unique qualities of those serving under his command in a technical and advisory capacity. Any expression of appreciation, admiration, or even awe was always genuine – after all a huge ego negates any need for false modesty.

Every ego, large or small, needs massaging when appropriate. 'Pug' Ismay returned from France in July 1944 stunned by the scale of the logistical exercise taking place both sides of the Channel. It was breathtaking, and, as he pointed out to Mountbatten, an operation scarcely conceivable only two years before: 'So that's a great feather in your cap, Dickie.'[105] Such flattery was welcome, but Mountbatten especially prized a telegram despatched from the Prime Minister's train on the evening of 12 June 1944. He ensured that it appeared in both the internal history of Combined Operations, and in the published version; and it enjoyed pride of place in the televised story of his life.[106] Churchill, Smuts, and Brooke had made their first visit to the Normandy beachhead, the latter's diary offering an evocative, moving, and at the same time highly amusing, account of their adventures ashore at Monty's HQ and off-shore in Philip Vian's barge ('Close by was a monitor with a 14″ gun firing away into France. Winston said he had never been on one of His Majesty's ships engaging the enemy and insisted on going aboard. Luckily we could not climb up …'). After 'a wonderfully interesting day', the party dined in Portsmouth with George Marshall, Hap Arnold, and Ernie King, the Americans having returned from a parallel expedition further along the coastline.[107] Before departing for Victoria five of the most powerful men in the western world drafted a joint cable to SEAC's Supreme Allied Commander. It's hard to imagine the idea originating with Alan Brooke, and both tone and sentiments suggest only one author. Since the summer of 1941 the romantic sentimentalist in Downing Street had seen young Dickie as a blue-blooded Mercury of the 'special relationship', and this was very much a trans-Atlantic *hommage*. Yet in his memoirs Churchill attributed authorship to Marshall, the dominant figure in the American military machine. A glowing Mountbatten noted in his diary that he had just received, 'the nicest telegram of my life'. As Bernard Fergusson later remarked, no doubt with his patron's approval: 'It was a handsome, a gracious signal: and it was perhaps especially pleasant to have Admiral King's name among the signatories.'[108] For all Mountbatten's faults and false moves, George Marshall's message constitutes a suitable coda to the story of Combined Ops under its most flamboyant commander:

> Today we visited the British and American armies on the soil of France. We sailed through vast fleets of ships with landing-craft of many types pouring more and more men, vehicles and stores ashore. We saw clearly the manoeuvre in process or rapid development. We have shared our secrets in common and helped each other all we could. We wish to tell you at this moment in your arduous campaign that we realise that much of this remarkable technique and therefore the success of the venture has its origins in developments effected by you and your staff of Combined Operations.[109]

11

CONCLUSION

Pastures new

The title of this book draws heavily upon hindsight: 'apprentice war lord' clearly suggests that the first half of Mountbatten's life can be seen as preparation for a position of over-arching command. Critics of his record as Supreme Allied Commander, South East Asia, have of course argued that he never was a 'war lord' per se. In other words, that Mountbatten may have fulfilled valuable roles boosting troop morale and oiling the wheels of inter-Allied collaboration, but beyond that his wartime impact was limited – real power lay either at operational level, witness Slim's impressive control of events in Burma 1944–5, or in Washington and London via the Combined Chiefs and their political masters.[1] Yes, Mountbatten's own contentious version of events, reheated by later admirers such as Richard Hough, exaggerated his power and influence; but to reduce his command to little more than stirring speeches and conference glad-handing is to diminish certain very real achievements, not least his enlightened view of regional nationalism following the Japanese surrender. Mountbatten had no obvious 'end of empire' agenda, even if Edwina was clearly convinced that things could never be the same again.[2] Nevertheless, an open-minded view of anti-colonialist dissent, as forged in resistance to Japanese hegemony, contrasted starkly with those unreconstructed imperialists eager to restore the pre-1942 ante, whatever the cost. Thus, in the aftermath of war the future viceroy stated his credentials. Clausewitz was neither the first nor the last to note how the enlightened war lord must impose authority and exercise acuity both before and after the moment of victory.[3]

Mountbatten did in fact serve as a peacetime war lord, albeit using the term in a far looser sense than is applicable to overseeing a theatre of conflict at the climax of a devastating global conflagration. From 1959 to 1965 he served as the second Chief of the Defence Staff. His original three-year appointment was renewed so as to provide a degree of continuity at a time of significant change within the defence establishment: soon after the Ministry of Defence was created in 1964, Mountbatten belatedly retired. Harold Macmillan's redefinition of the role had meant that Mountbatten was the first defence chief to be visibly more than just *primus inter pares*, establishing a template for the authority and standing of the CDS as we understand it today.[4] This enhancement of power was evident throughout the final quarter of the last century, with the momentum maintained into the current. It's scarcely conceivable that a young Dickie Mountbatten could have imagined a defence staff, let alone a defence supremo. Equally, for most if not all of his time at Combined Operations his ambitions could scarcely have embraced ultimate responsibility for the Allied war effort across southern Asia. There was no inevitability about Mountbatten's appointment to SEAC, just as there was no obvious intention to secure command of a defence hierarchy which didn't even exist until 1956. Notwithstanding the book's title, the preceding chapters contain no teleological sub-text; and yet of course throughout the first half of his career there was one prize that Mountbatten never lost sight of.

In the summer of 1943 he refocused upon his principal ambition: if he was ever to become First Sea Lord he had to get his naval career back on track. Hence an ever more frustrated CCO stalked Dudley Pound as the *Queen Mary* steamed towards what Mountbatten perceived as a watershed conference: post-Quadrant, Combined Operations could anticipate seeing its wings clipped as the three services geared up for the great offensive. An unusually deferential Mountbatten sought command of a big ship; and yet polite lobbying generated no more than the vaguest acknowledgement from a visibly ailing Pound.[5]

Although no-one suspected it at the time, these were the First Sea Lord's final months. For a sick man in late middle age Mountbatten represented youth, health, and the future.[6] He was also an unwelcome reminder of how much Pound's own position depended upon the continued goodwill of the Prime Minister. No wonder Dickie's appearance on deck prompted muttered apologies and a hasty retreat. A further cause for withdrawal was that Pound was privy to conversations at the very highest level regarding Mountbatten's suitability as a supreme commander. At a time when, following the failure of the first Arakan offensive, the morale of British forces in the Far East was at its lowest ebb, did the man who had turned Combined Operations around have the qualities necessary to rebuild confidence and to convince the two commanders-in-chief, Wavell and Auchinleck, that attack was the best means of defence? For the Prime Minister, appointing an effective counterweight to the senior generals in the field was a priority: there was an immediate need for fresh thinking and a vital infusion of 'vigour and authority'.[7]

The idea of a supreme commander had originated in the India Office, the secretary of state urging Churchill in late May to take urgent action. Leo Amery's suggestion of Mountbatten was, 'brushed aside ... on the ground that his health is bad and that he was not big enough'.[8] Downing Street's answer indicates the severity of the CCO's pneumonia, and just how long it took him to regain full fitness. But more telling is the belief as late as the spring of 1943 that Mountbatten lacked weight and gravitas when dealing at the very highest level with Allied politicians and commanders. Working in his favour was that Washington felt frustrated by the taciturn Wavell, and saw that the only way to facilitate effective Anglo-American military collaboration was to parachute in someone with the necessary authority to resolve the current impasse. Trans-Atlantic discussions focussed as much upon policy as personalities, and the command structure of SEAC was only resolved after both sides met in Quebec.[9] Clearly Mountbatten was a figure well-regarded within the White House, but he was by no means the obvious choice. Preferred candidates on both sides of the Atlantic pushed Mountbatten well down the pecking order. Both Alan Brooke and Churchill agreed on Sholto Douglas as their first choice; the Americans said no, but the CIGS never wavered in his belief that the airman would have done a better job than Mountbatten.[10]

With Douglas out of the running, the job was Andrew Cunningham's if he wanted it. The trouble was that he didn't. ABC was very much the Combined Chiefs' choice once Eisenhower made clear that Tedder was going nowhere. Brooke battled to persuade Cunningham that he should change his mind, and to dissuade Churchill from vetoing a naval appointee. The CIGS failed on both counts, hence the decision not to push James Somerville's candidacy when the Americans questioned his suitability. Given the Prime Minister's insistence that sailors were singularly unqualified for the task in hand, it's ironic that, once a long list of generals and air marshals had been exhausted, his thoughts should turn again to Mountbatten.[11] Presumably, Churchill rationalised his change of heart by claiming that the Chief of Combined Operations enjoyed a unique insight into the workings of the military mind. Ironically, one person convinced that Mountbatten lacked the right qualifications was Cunningham. On learning of the appointment ('a political job, of course') he anticipated failure, surmising that this meant the end of Mountbatten's service career. Four years later, he would feel the same way when Attlee announced the name of the new viceroy.[12]

A month earlier, Brooke had been equally astonished when, only a day out from Southampton, Churchill had solemnly declared that Mountbatten was the man to sort out SEAC. A telegram to the Deputy Prime Minister confidently stated that Mountbatten's appointment would delight the President and excite the general public. Attlee, backed by Eden, urged caution, and revived the case for Cunningham. Yet once it was clear that Winston had made his mind up, both men signalled agreement. Back home the War Cabinet may have acquiesced but aboard the *Queen Mary* the Chief of the Imperial General Staff was yet to back down. An eager ally was the incandescent P.J. Grigg. The War Office's senior civil servant turned secretary of state was an old adversary of Combined Operations, whose grievances dated back to the jerrican fiasco. Brooke spent the rest of the voyage endeavouring to change the Prime Minister's mind, and continued to do so even after Churchill secured FDR's agreement. Neither of the other two chiefs showed any great enthusiasm; unlike their American counterparts, whose previously favourable impression of Mountbatten was confirmed by his graciousness towards them throughout the Quebec conference. Pound would have preferred Cunningham, but was content (and probably relieved) to see Mountbatten's name go forward. Similarly, Portal had no objection given that neither Douglas nor Tedder was in the running. Brooke on the other hand felt sure Mountbatten 'lacked balance for such a job', hence the selection of a no-nonsense chief of staff was crucial to the success of his mission – a view the appointee would soon come to endorse.[13] With Churchill's approval Brooke and Ismay orchestrated the recruitment of an experienced and battle-hardened staff officer, the reluctant

Henry Pownall, to act as Dickie's right-hand man. Although at the outset a prickly relationship, in the end the combination worked. Thus Pownall tempered a decidedly jaundiced first impression, and, while never a believer, quietly admired the way his new boss hit the ground running. By the time ill health necessitated his return home in late 1944 the administrator extraordinaire had acquired a healthy respect for the high-profile front man, in what was from the outset an unlikely partnership. Brooke, on the other hand, was still unconvinced, noting in May 1944 that, 'Mountbatten will be a constant source of trouble to us and will never really fit the bill as Supreme Commander'.[14]

Brooke's feelings were no doubt affected by the fact that presidential endorsement of Mountbatten's appointment came in the same meeting that Roosevelt insisted supreme command of Overlord must be given to Marshall.[15] In the end it was Eisenhower who took up the post, but Brooke was devastated that the promised prize had been snatched away. Churchill broke the news in an uncharacteristically unsentimental and unsympathetic fashion, and then called in Mountbatten. The latter was genuinely taken aback by the Prime Minister's proposal, requesting 24 hours to think it over: "'Why?" he asked. "Don't you think you can do it?" I replied that I had a congenital weakness for thinking I could do anything.' No change there then, but Mountbatten needed to know whether he was being hung out to dry – did he have support from the British, and crucially, the American chiefs of staff? Despite mixed messages from within the COSC, it was clear that from the White House down he had both administration and military on board. Crucially, on the British side 'Pug' Ismay reassured him that he was 'big enough to handle the job'. Shocked yet exultant ('It is the first time in history that a naval officer has been given supreme command over land and air forces. It will mean another stripe …'), he finally said yes.[16]

Encouraged by Edwina, even before leaving Quebec Mountbatten was clarifying the terms of his appointment. At the same time he started work on a memorandum to the Chiefs of Staff, recommending alternative models for the organisation of Combined Operations following his departure. The new supremo did indeed secure another stripe, but only after Pound insisted that promotion to full admiral remain acting and unconfirmed. Predictably, Mountbatten sought promotion in the other two services, and equally predictably the Army and the RAF refused to upgrade the honorary ranks he had been given as Chief of Combined Operations. Advice flowed in from an assortment of generals, even if Mountbatten's fellow admirals were more circumspect in their response to his good news. Fond farewells were made to Richmond Terrace, his staff at COHQ seeing him off in style. Several old hands, like Wildman-Lushington, were due to follow their master out as soon as authorisation came through and transport became available. To Dickie's delight he learnt that Al Wedemeyer would be Pownall's deputy, acting as Washington's man on the spot.[17]

Meanwhile Edwina played the perfect hostess as old Asia hands arrived at Chester Street for audience with the Supreme Commander. At the same time, however, the woman in black gently rebuffed her husband's pleas that she travel out with him. As the St John's most senior nurse the Superintendent-in-Chief remained a pivotal figure in the maintenance and improvement of civil defence, let alone basic living conditions. Not even news of Bunny Phillips' timely posting to India prompted a change of heart. When the day came for Dickie to leave, Edwina chose not to see him off. He flew out on 2 October 1943, after a farewell luncheon in Downing Street. Mountbatten arrived in Delhi four days later, following a brief stop in Baghdad. An audacious challenge lay ahead, but, unlike his arrival in the Indian capital five years later, this time he faced it alone.[18]

High politics and pivotal relationships

With the staff car already outside No. 10 waiting to whisk Dickie to Northolt, the Chief of the Imperial General Staff toasted his good health and wished him well. In a general atmosphere of bonhomie, relations between the two men were by no means rancorous. Just over a fortnight earlier Mountbatten had written to Brooke, expressing his, 'heartfelt thanks for your guidance, patience, and helpful criticism during the eighteen months which I have had the honour of to sit under your Chairmanship on the Chiefs of Staff's Committee'. Furthermore, by proving 'such a good friend', the CIGS had given Mountbatten the confidence to undertake, 'the very difficult task which I am now taking on'. Gratitude extended to, 'having allowed me to retain my honorary commission in the Army which I value so highly'. No more needed to be said, but Mountbatten could never resist the grand gesture: the King had authorised his wearing the buttons of all three services on his tropical kit, so could Brooke furnish him with one of his, plus a signed photograph to commemorate their 18 months partnership? Needless to say, if the general ever felt like a spot of fly-fishing then he should simply call Edwina on Sloane 7871 or Romsey 8. Another power-wielding ornithologist, Sir Edward Grey, had contrived to catch trout on the Test and at the same time scour the skies for rare sightings – but always from the vantage point of his own fishing lodge. Quite simply, there was no way the future Lord Alanbrooke would ever let himself become indebted to Broadlands benevolence. He simply responded with a brief yet generous letter, thanking Mountbatten for, 'the wonderful advance the Combined Operations made under your able guidance'. As we have seen, nine months later Brooke added his name to the post-invasion message drafted by his American counterpart and enthusiastically endorsed by Churchill. It was near enough the last kind word that the CIGS expressed regarding his junior sparring partner, and in any case it would have been churlish and impolitic not to sign – whatever his private thoughts, Brooke had no option but to endorse Marshall's warm appreciation of the former CCO's contribution to Overlord.[19]

Distance did little to relieve tension, and if anything Mountbatten's capacity to irritate and infuriate Brooke intensified. Contrary to the impression given in a recent account of the Burma campaign, from the outset the two men were rarely in agreement.[20] Brooke became less inhibited in his diary entries following Pound's death and the arrival of Andrew Cunningham at the Admiralty. The new First Sea Lord and the Chief of the Imperial General Staff constituted a formidable partnership, Brooke carrying away 'nothing but the very happiest recollections of all my dealings' with ABC. The latter was lauded as loyal, trustworthy, and a man of impeccable integrity: 'the staunchest of campaigners when it came to supporting a policy agreed to amongst ourselves, no matter what inclement winds might be brought to bear on it'.[21] Stern, and tested repeatedly in the heat of battle, Pound's successor was not the sort of chap to break ranks and brief presidential aides on how he fundamentally disagreed with his fellow chiefs of staff – as previously suggested, Brooke *must* have learnt of Mountbatten's unprofessional behaviour at the Casablanca conference. Time and again Cunningham clashed with Churchill over the PM's readiness to extend Mountbatten's powers, including de facto command of the Pacific Fleet, which Britain had insisted should have a visible role in the final defeat of Imperial Japan. Brooke invariably supported his colleague's efforts to rein Dickie in, not least because he tired of ceaseless turf wars inside SEAC Headquarters; as he noted in June 1944, 'It is astonishing how petty and small men can be in connection with questions of command'.[22]

The end of the war in Europe brought SEAC into sharper focus, and Brooke was damning of Mountbatten when he flew back to attend the Potsdam summit and later COSC meetings in London. The two men clashed throughout a stormy conference at the War Office on 8 August 1945 when Brooke adamantly refused to take Mountbatten's side against Cunningham. The following day Bill Slim had an appointment with the CIGS, during which the latter, 'rubbed into him my dislike for "prima donna generals" and "film star generals". I hope he will take it to heart'. No doubt Brooke had Monty in mind, but it's not hard to identify the main focus of his ire given the following day's dismissal of Dickie: 'I find it very hard to be pleasant when he turns up! He is the most crashing bore I have met on a committee, is always fiddling about with unimportant matters [like buttons?], and wasting other people's time.'[23] Mountbatten had a thick hide but he knew how Brooke felt towards him; and he was by no means impervious to criticism. Thus, he was genuinely hurt when, following the surrender of Japan, Brooke and Portal requested that he resign his honorary ranks – an idea torpedoed by an indignant George VI.[24]

The CIGS of course wrote far worse things about Churchill, but either at the time or in his notes after the war he invariably tempered or withdrew his criticism – 'Brookie' never allowed the Prime Minister's multiple failings to detract from history's judgement that indisputably he was a great man. Commenting upon Marshall, Eisenhower, and Alexander, Brooke invariably identified positive character traits to compensate for their perceived failings as grand strategists. In the most obvious parallel with Mountbatten, the ennobled Alanbrooke always acknowledged that Montgomery's attributes as a fighting general far outweighed his failings as a monstrous egotist. Yet the CIGS's diaries and his postwar 'Notes on my life' display scarcely a hint of goodwill towards Mountbatten, with scant recognition of those redeeming qualities that endeared him to so many rank-and-file service personnel – in other words, those sailors and squaddies beyond his immediate acquaintance. Arthur Bryant's post-Suez expurgated and sanitised editions of Alanbrooke's diaries suppressed his client's sniping of the then First Sea Lord.[25] Yet Mountbatten was never so vainglorious that he became blind to his enemies. Decorum was duly maintained, but in 1963 Alanbrooke died. The gloves were off, and Mountbatten hit back, albeit in a relatively low-key fashion. After all the one-time CIGS's antipathy was not at that time in the public domain, and in any case the Chief of the Defence Staff dare not offend the Army, who to a man (and woman) revered the architect of victory.

Michael Harrison, author of *Mulberry The Return in Triumph*, was a freelance writer who, judging by his dust-jacket profile, had a remarkably high opinion of himself. For Harrison the Mulberry harbours symbolised the triumph of forward-thinking visionaries over a military establishment whose instinctive caution had brought Britain to its knees. From Ray Murphy to Bernard Fergusson, any writer promising to portray Mountbatten of Burma's military career in a positive light could anticipate full cooperation. Not surprisingly, therefore, the CDS provided Harrison with access to every key figure inside COHQ.[26] Whole sections of the book were based upon lengthy interviews with Hughes-Hallett and Harold Wernher; but the most remarkable chapter was the first – an on-the-record interview in which from the opening paragraph Mountbatten placed himself at the heart of the Overlord preparations, claiming full credit for Mulberry:

> It was necessary, said Mountbatten, that before one wrote a word about the Invasion, something should be most clearly understood. The Normandy landings, the Chief of Defence Staff said, were, in their conception, in their location, in their techniques and the equipment needed for them and the training of their forces, basically a Combined Operations job. This might sound, he added, like boasting – and perhaps it was. But it was also the truth.[27]

An uncritical – and clearly very grateful – Harrison portrayed the former Chief of Combined Ops as one of the nation's truly outstanding leaders, even at one point comparing him with Napoleon.[28] Such shameless inflation of his hero's reputation would have been of little consequence, had he not caricatured the Chiefs of Staff as Blimpish objectors to any proposal for crossing the Channel. Thus the CIGS's refusal to mount a diversionary attack on the Cherbourg peninsula prompted Harrison to observe: 'His reasons were sound – but so were those of Pétain and Laval when they chose friendship with Hitler. Brooke, in short, had that "defensive mentality" which, in Churchill's opinion, had caused the demoralisation of the French government and the French armed forces.' This was an astonishing claim, matched by similarly derogatory comments elsewhere in the book.[29] Surely fear of libel would have forced Harrison to tone down his remarks had the recently deceased field marshal still been alive. Elsewhere in the book Bernard Paget and Sholto Douglas received similarly rough treatment, both men depicted as the real villains in the Dieppe disaster, which, needless to say, was seen as a necessary lesson in the build-up to D-Day. Nor did Charles Portal escape retribution: by 1945 his malevolent envy was on a par with that of the CIGS.[30] Mountbatten was scarcely the hidden hand – his accusing finger was visible on almost every page. In a crowded field *Mulberry The Return in Triumph* stood out. It set a new standard of hagiography, rarely equalled since. Today the only reason this book should be remembered is that, behind the authorial bluster, we find an unforgiving Dickie Mountbatten quietly wreaking revenge on his old adversary, the late Lord Alanbrooke.

Sensitive to the wishes of his gold-braided *consigliere*, Harrison was uncharacteristically silent regarding Pound and Cunningham. Both men of course knew Mountbatten far better than Alan Brooke ever did. Admittedly after May 1941 most of ABC's wartime dealings with the tyro chief of staff were at a distance; but Cunningham had observed the fast-rising, fast-tracked Commander Mountbatten at close quarters in the Mediterranean long before he returned to Malta as a flotilla captain with a great deal to prove. The *Kelly*'s mixed fortunes in the spring of 1941 simply reinforced a hard-headed scepticism regarding her master's seamanship and sound judgement. Unfairly perhaps, the destruction of the 5th Flotilla off Crete was seen by Cunningham as confirmation that Mountbatten somehow lacked the initiative, vision, and tactical nous so evident in a naturally gifted commander like Philip Vian. The latter, no doubt to Cunningham's intense satisfaction, declined Churchill's invitation to succeed Mountbatten as CCO because he desired to remain at sea. Vian, who at the commencement of hostilities was a flotilla captain and at the end commanded the Pacific Fleet's carrier squadron, enjoyed an eventful and impressive fighting war. Mountbatten, for all the glittering prizes, must surely have envied Vian's achievements in every theatre of operations, and the high regard in which he was held throughout the Service, not least in the eyes of the First Sea Lord.[31] As we've seen, Mountbatten always sought Cunningham's approval, and cultivated the impression of a close working and personal relationship. The reality was far from the truth, with ABC for a long time reluctant to support the notion of Mountbatten's appointment as First Sea Lord.[32] Worthy but unglamorous, neither Chatfield nor Pound were adequate role models, and, despite a change of heart, Mountbatten could never forget that Jellicoe settled for a draw at Jutland. Cunningham was thus the obvious figure to look up to once the young Lord Louis realised that his first great hero was deeply flawed. Perhaps Cunningham and his errant captain had more in common than they realised, but before considering this possibility we should recall certain striking similarities between Mountbatten and the man he once saw as invincible.

Chapter Three identified the more obvious parallels between Mountbatten and David Beatty, but they ranged far beyond a shared penchant for rich wives, fast ships, and imaginative tailors. Both men secured key promotions in unorthodox circumstances. Each gained and then lost Churchill's goodwill, while at the same time enjoying and exploiting royal patronage. Beatty especially disguised a sharp intellect under a patina of philistinism, and to a degree the same might be said of Mountbatten. In action they mixed courage and folly, each compensating for disappointment in command at sea with tangible achievement in senior appointments on land. Crucially, both men more than held their own when dealing with even the most senior ministers and their advisers. Interestingly, they shared a common vision of inter-service collaboration and a unified defence establishment. It should also be noted that both men behaved in a manner that, day by day, if not hour by hour, ranged from the admirable to the abhorrent. Where Beatty and Mountbatten differed profoundly was in the latter's credentials as a man of science. Indifferent to scientific ideas, and ignorant of key precepts of ordnance and naval engineering, Beatty partially redeemed himself when First Sea Lord; but in action during the Great War his failure to engage wholly with the new technology contrasted sharply with Jellicoe's professionalism and natural caution.[33]

In this respect Beatty had more in common with Cunningham who, while in every respect a superior sailor, also questioned a younger generation's enthusiastic embrace of the new and unorthodox. As the admiral who despatched the Fleet Air Arm to Taranto, ABC could scarcely be considered hostile to fresh ideas (even though planning of that particular pre-emptive strike dated back to the mid-1930s). From 1941 he deliberately stationed himself ashore in North Africa, recognising the need to be an integral part of the Mediterranean command structure and communications/intelligence networks. Nevertheless, he saw the technological imperative as always secondary to certain fundamental and unchanging values of seamanship and command. Unlike Mountbatten, he was never a gadgets man.[34]

Having said that, the differences between the two men were by no means profound.[35] Cunningham would have been reluctant to concede that he had much in common with Mountbatten, other than their absence when Jellicoe's mighty dreadnoughts finally locked horns with the High Seas Fleet. Yet the two men shared a passion for destroyers, and a rare concern inside the Navy for the mechanics of amphibious operations: for the older man service in the Dardanelles was a formative influence, while for his eager young acolyte Gallipoli signalled a watershed in inter-service rivalry – the Senior Service had a duty to collaborate closely with the 'pongoes' in safely setting military units ashore, and if necessary lifting them off again. Cunningham demonstrated the strength of that commitment in Greece and again in Crete. Mountbatten meanwhile saw his best intentions shredded on the blood-soaked beaches of Dieppe. As Chapter Three made clear, the Great War was a hugely formative influence, but Mountbatten had no experience of command under fire in the same way that Cunningham did. Nevertheless Lord Louis' North Sea adventures led him to share ABC's conviction that fleet communications required radical improvement, as did the Royal Navy's capacity to engage with the enemy at night. Similarly, both men ended the First World War even more convinced of the need to keep the lower decks well-informed and content, albeit via very different approaches to man management – Cunningham's starched-collar paternalism reflected his Victorian upbringing, contrasting starkly with the more relaxed Mountbatten's dependence on humour and a staged intimacy. Both men displayed a professional zeal and a single-minded dedication to the task, but in very different ways. Age and personality explained Mountbatten's flamboyant displays of modernity and of an often staged unorthodoxy, and yet he shared Cunningham's qualities of focus and wholehearted application to the task in hand. Where he differed from Cunningham was in rarely recognising when that wholehearted application was likely to cause offence or resentment, witness the well-meaning yet wholly insensitive ambition to ensure his first command won every competition it contested. ABC would have known when to stop, and graciously concede to one's rivals in the interest of on-shore harmony and flotilla morale. Cunningham, however, was no trimmer, witness a scarcely disguised distaste for Churchill, invariably dismissed as a mere amateur strategist. The First Sea Lord stood his ground when dealing with bullies like Ernie King, so that, albeit by different methods, he proved as adept as Mountbatten in handling the Americans.[36]

Where they differed profoundly was in Cunningham's enviable capacity for consistently choosing tried and tested aides, and his consequent refusal to micro-manage. Mountbatten's record in this respect was far from perfect, especially at Combined Operations. At COHQ, and in every posting thereafter, his staff far exceeded the number appropriate to the mission. Even when he was aided by highly talented individuals all too often he usurped command, and he rarely resisted the temptation to intervene. As a commander-in-chief Mountbatten needed the detachment and the distance that came naturally to Cunningham, by instinct a more reflective – as well as a more modest – man. Yet even the greatest general looks to his or her legacy. Hence, Cunningham proved as keen as Mountbatten in ensuring that the correct version of events entered the historical record. He collaborated closely with Stephen Roskill on the official history of the Royal Navy during the Second World War, and recruited the ex-destroyer captain turned freelance writer Taprell Dorling to ghost-write a best-selling autobiography.

Someone else set on getting his story straight was Anthony Eden, A.J.P. Taylor famously renaming his appeasement memoirs, 'Making Faces at the Dictators'. To say that Dickie and Anthony had a tortured relationship is an understatement, yet until 1945 it was on the whole amicable. As seen in Chapter Four, Mountbatten stiffened Eden's back before and after his resignation as Foreign Secretary in February 1938. The young naval commander was by instinct an anti-appeaser, not least because family ties had exposed the potency of an ultra-nationalist ideology in seducing a defeated and dispirited nation – from bottom to top. As a serving officer Mountbatten had to exercise caution. Not so Eden, and yet for much of 1938–9 he displayed a similar degree of discretion. As we have seen, Edwina never really had much time for him, but Dickie genuinely rejoiced in Eden's restoration to office, not least his return to the Foreign Office. The problems really began after the war, over India. Whatever his private views, Eden could not be seen as dissenting from Churchill's unremitting hostility to the speed with which His Majesty's Government handed back the jewel in the crown. In 1972 Mountbatten was busy preparing to film a definitive overview of his career. He pestered an irascible Lord Avon to confirm that, upon the retiring governor-general's final arrival home from New Delhi, the Tory heir apparent had telephoned the VIP lounge at Heathrow to offer discreet congratulations on a job well done. Eden repeatedly insisted that he was incapable of recalling a phone call he might or might not have made 24 years earlier, but Mountbatten refused to take no for an answer.[37] Although age is a mitigating factor, this persistence was astonishingly insensitive given the two men's strained relations.

When Eden finally became Prime Minister in 1955 an early engagement was a family weekend at Broadlands with the Nehrus. The strained social gathering set the tone as, although Eden considered his friendship with Dickie was now back on an even keel, 'Edwina is so very left and so full of prejudice e.g. against Pakistan that conversation is difficult'.[38] Eden's second official biographer suggested that early in his premiership senior officials inside Buckingham Palace perceived 'the wicked uncle' as exercising a malign influence over the young Elizabeth II. In retirement, Eden came to believe that, over a long weekend at Broadlands in late July 1956, Mountbatten briefed the Queen on the folly of invading Egypt in retaliation for Nasser's nationalisation of the Suez Canal; yet only 24 hours earlier a disingenuous First Sea Lord had advised senior cabinet ministers on how speed and surprise could secure rapid control of the waterway. Ironically, while accepting the Army's advice that the proposed 'Commando action' was far too risky, an increasingly harassed Prime Minister had considered Mountbatten's impulsive nature and questionable judgement a price worth paying given the sure-footedness of his staff work. Ultimately, however, Eden came to believe the First Sea Lord, 'presumed too much on their pre-war acquaintanceship, was prone to expecting special treatment and sidestepped military conventions, notably in respect of the military's duty to submit to political control'.[39] Eden's worst fears were confirmed by Mountbatten's emotionally-charged insistence on 2 November that, in line with the wishes of 'the overwhelming majority of the United Nations', military operations should cease forthwith. Special pleading that as a serving officer he had suppressed serious doubts about the Cabinet's firm line left a no doubt incandescent Eden unconvinced, even when a postscript added in green ink:

> You can imagine how hard it is for me to break with all service custom and write direct to you in this way, but I feel so desperate about what is happening that my conscience would not allow me to do otherwise.[40]

With the invasion force already en route from Malta, Eden telephoned Broadlands the next morning to say that it was too late.[41] Back in Whitehall on the Monday morning Mountbatten submitted his resignation, and was told in no uncertain terms by Lord Hailsham that he must stay in post and get on with the job in hand. The First Lord of the Admiralty confided to Eden that, 'I think it would be disastrous to relieve him now, which is the only other possible course'.[42] In 1968 Eden drafted a lengthy memorandum on the Suez crisis in which he squashed the rumour that, 'the Queen, as a result of the promptings of Mountbatten, had telephoned her concerns to me during the Suez crisis'. Four years later, Mountbatten privately noted that in 1956 Eden was 'physically and mentally ill' and 'going dotty': it was in fact, 'Staggering what one mad PM can do'. Wary of revealing his true feelings in front of a film crew, and with Lord Avon still seemingly fighting fit, Mountbatten wisely altered the cue cards – and then placed the unexpurgated text in his archive.[43]

Ironically, Eden was more and more convinced that, if Mountbatten wasn't 'ga-ga' at the time of Suez, then he had become so since: the man was 'a congenital liar', actively encouraging journalist and royal biographer Robert Lacey to portray the Queen as opposed to military intervention over Suez and yet constrained by her constitutional status from opposing the Prime Minister's preferred course of action.[44] Although seriously ill with cancer, Eden confronted Mountbatten on 13 June 1976 in the Provost's Lodge at Eton. It was the last occasion upon which the two old men were to meet. Mountbatten was emollient but unrepentant, even when Eden threatened legal action should Lacey's forthcoming book imply royal dissatisfaction with his handling of the crisis.[45] Despite a fusillade of letters from a dying Eden to Sir Martin Charteris, the Queen's Secretary, and to Robert Lacey, the latter clearly followed the Mountbatten line in *Majesty*, his bulky contribution to the Silver Jubilee celebrations. Sarah Bradford's landmark biography, *Elizabeth*, provided circumstantial evidence that her subject deemed the Suez invasion 'idiotic'; while Ben Pimlott's authoritative *The Queen* named Charteris as his source for Mountbatten telling Her Majesty that ministers 'are being absolutely lunatic', and for her officials' belief that she thought Eden was mad.[46] The unstated question of course is whether the Prime Minister, during his weekly audiences at Buckingham Palace in the autumn of 1956, lied over the level of collusion with France and Israel, or was merely economical with the truth. As befits a biographer commissioned by Lady Avon to revisit these tempestuous events, D.R. Thorpe noted that a highly contestable 'accepted truth' rests almost solely on the evidence of two of Eden's harshest critics: 'When Suez came under the historical spotlight, both Mountbatten and Charteris – now old men – were keen to put down markers, establishing their position on the "right" side of the barricades.'[47]

Of course such a statement could apply to just about every facet of Dickie Mountbatten's career, not least his rollercoaster relationship with Churchill. While still in Quebec Mountbatten had found time to note his good fortune in enjoying the trust of the Prime Minister, and crucially, the best wishes of the Chiefs of Staff. The approval of his peers, 'has now begun to make me feel that your decision in this case may turn out to be as right as it has certainly been in all other cases'. Clearly, any lingering doubts over SEAC had been well and truly dispelled – such a revealing statement displays either laudable self-confidence or breathtaking arrogance. Mountbatten added that he would have felt ill-equipped to accept Churchill's offer had he not experienced, 'the rare privilege of being allowed to sit for 18 months at the feet of the greatest master of strategy and war this century has produced. Nor have I overlooked your method of applying the spur to the sluggish war horse'.[48] Given his natural appreciation of all Churchill had done for him Mountbatten's hyperbole is understandable, and yet somehow one can not imagine a Philip Vian or a Charles Lambe getting quite so carried away.

The thought must have crossed Stephen Roskill's mind when an elderly Mountbatten reflected upon a relationship that dated back to his years at Osborne. Because he had known Churchill since he was a child he never felt intimidated by him, unlike 'most people, even Chiefs of Staff'. This no doubt would have been news to Alanbrooke and Cunningham, had they still been alive. Lack of fear left Mountbatten confident to say 'some pretty drastic things' when alone with the PM. This frankness was further rooted in the fact that Churchill, 'knew I backed him through thick and thin when his voice was crying in the wilderness against Hitler and Mussolini, and so our relationship was really rather extraordinary'. Yes, Chatfield encouraged a desk-bound Mountbatten to use Churchill's formidable lobbying skills in the late 1930s, but there is nothing to suggest any broader agenda. In old age being recognised as a discreet critic of Chamberlain's policy was no longer enough. Thus Mountbatten reinvented himself as a member of that tiny circle which had remained loyal to the post-1940 icon of anti-appeasement. He admitted to Roskill that at Buckingham Palace in July 1948 the then Leader of the Opposition had angrily informed him that, "'What you did in India is as though you had struck me across the face with a riding whip.'" Churchill then turned his back, walked away, and refused even to communicate with Edwina for the next seven years. Yet predictably, after Mountbatten was appointed First Sea Lord, 'we became real friends again'.[49]

Most prominent personalities, as they get older, display a refreshing candour about past dealings with friends and colleagues. Mountbatten never threw caution to the wind. Just as he refused to acknowledge a mistake, so he fought hard to maintain an increasingly fragile myth of consensuality, conviviality, and camaraderie – he got on well with everyone, and in turn they got on well with him. From his first posting patronage was a critical factor in Mountbatten's successful career, and Churchill would prove the patron *extraordinaire*.[50] To suggest that 1947 marked a watershed in Winston's well-being towards him was unthinkable to a grateful beneficiary in the autumn of his years, forever excavating and reshaping a crowded and eventful past.

As we have seen, the likes of Andrew Roberts and David Reynolds have savaged Mountbatten, insisting that Churchill's sentimental attachment to the younger Battenberg clouded his judgement, revealing a residual guilt over Prince Louis' harsh treatment in 1914. Shielding Mountbatten from Admiralty criticism of his record as a flotilla captain was bad enough; but far worse was facilitating his promotion to senior posts for which he was singularly unqualified. Serving at sea he had unnecessarily placed men's lives at risk, and elevation to Chief of Combined Operations ensured appallingly fatal consequences. Appointment as Supreme Commander failed to generate a Far Eastern Dieppe, but Japan's surrender prior to planned landings on the Malayan peninsula left the charge sheet still open. The argument of critics like Reynolds is simple: at Churchill's behest Mountbatten was promoted well beyond his natural ability, and Downing Street (in tandem with Buckingham Palace) bore ultimate responsibility for his failures at Combined Operations or South East Asia Command. Thus the rise and rise of Dickie Mountbatten reflected a serious misjudgement on the part of the Prime Minister, confirming Churchill's remarkable capacity to over-ride the doubts of his most senior military advisers.[51] Admirers of Mountbatten such as Richard Hough and Ian McGeoch would of course point to very real achievements in the years 1941–6, viewing any obvious success as testimony to the shrewdness and sagacity of a great wartime leader; someone bold enough to dismiss the old guard, and confident enough to cultivate the young and talented.

Movies and modernity

Mountbatten was talented, although never so gifted as he clearly thought he was. He was unashamedly aspirational, which is a polite way of saying extremely ambitious.

Even his harshest critics would concede that he was always hard-working. Was he young? No he wasn't – not by today's standards (prime ministers in their early forties), or even those of a wartime emergency – but he conveyed a youthful image. Mountbatten's good looks can never be ignored; and if manners maketh the man then here was someone whose success depended disproportionately upon a natural charm, and careful cultivation of a popular persona. The latter entailed an early acknowledgement of the need to control one's emotions, albeit at the cost of a fierce backlash when away from the public gaze. Those close to Mountbatten were familiar with a very different and a far more complex individual than the smiling, courteous, feel-good patrician who could work a room, lift a ship's company, or even silence a mob. An inner circle of acolytes, like Sir John Hughes-Hallett or Alan Campbell-Johnson, were fiercely loyal, and lifelong keepers of the flame.[52] Others who worked closely with Mountbatten, such as Robert Henriques and *Jupiter*'s Anthony Pugsley, looked back on an especially bruising and unhappy experience. As we have seen, Mountbatten later acknowledged that his behaviour at Richmond Terrace was often appalling, a short fuse attributable to long hours and remorseless stress. A sharp tongue might be excused, but not the vanity and conceit. Admirers either ignored or laughed away the worst excesses.[53]

Others were less generous, the shrewder sceptic espying the inferiority complex of a half-German aristocrat intent on working his way from the periphery to the heart of the Royal Family; while at the same time rapidly ascending towards the very highest levels of power within a British state bloodied but by no means unbowed. Writing several years after Mountbatten's death, Solly Zuckerman perceptively noted that, 'Despite the way he bore himself, and the apparent certainty in his manner, Dickie sometimes did not seem to understand how he fitted into the company around him. He wanted to be liked, but could not understand why his peers so often failed to comply'.[54] In a generous if characteristically rambling profile, written for the *Evening Standard* in 1943 but later withdrawn, Geoffrey Pyke saw in Mountbatten's personality a troubling juxtaposition of supreme self-confidence and disarming modesty: 'it is his arrogance which binds him to his fellow men, and his humility which on occasion separates him from them.'[55] Humility is not a word frequently associated with Mountbatten of Burma, but Pyke was acknowledging an unqualified respect for expertise, witness the CCO's readiness to defend Bernal, and of course the writer himself.

There is a further paradox: the first five decades of Mountbatten's life were played out against a backdrop of imperial twilight, and yet at the same this was a scion of the old order imbued with an aura of mid-Atlantic modernity. Here was the young buck turned trusted envoy traversing a global estate still obeisant to his second cousin, the King-Emperor, courtesy of a Pan-Am Clipper. Casablanca was the last great conference of the war where the British were in the driving seat, and even the most junior chief of staff felt confident of gaining the President's ear. For someone whose preferred career options were the sea or the studio, the summit location was a fitting setting for Hollywood's finest film of 1943: at SEAC Mountbatten screened *Casablanca* to secure the Viceroy's goodwill, unintentionally confirming Archie Wavell's worst fears regarding low-brow mass entertainment.[56] Here was the incomprehension of a reserved, unusually well-read general when confronted with popular culture in the raw, whether it be home-grown or, as in this case, imported from the far side of 'the Pond'. Wavell of course hailed from the cautious and conservative propertied classes of late Victorian England – a generation so cautious and conservative that he himself was deemed mildly eccentric when he compiled a best-selling volume of improving verse.[57] Mountbatten on the other hand effortlessly embraced the hedonism of the Jazz Age. He never fell victim to the *zeitgeist*, being far too sensible and disciplined; but even as an old man he still knew how to have a bloody good time.

Figure 11.1: The dying days of the Jazz Age – Dickie, Edwina, and the Prince of Wales on the Isle of Wight, 7 September 1929

Hornblower notwithstanding, Mountbatten was a reluctant reader. Averse to calm reflection, his hinterland was pictorial and mechanical, rarely literary and artistic.[58] History was cinematic not academic. Had he pursued an active and rigorous engagement with the past then one result might well have been a more balanced perspective on his own place in history. Geoffrey Pyke, on the eve of his benefactor's departure for India, lamented Mountbatten's intellectually debilitating 'inability, almost a refusal, to contemplate'. This was a 'strange and exotic creature' whose rapid mental reflexes made it, 'difficult for him not to form immediate opinions: to maintain that temporary agnosticism so essential a part of the scientific method'. Here, not for the last time, was a veiled charge of impetuosity, in tandem with an assertion that Mountbatten was all too often a poor judge of character. Although Pyke's profile revealed as much about the writer as it did his unlikely companion, sometimes even the barmiest boffin can conjure up the apposite *aperçu*. Thus, 'In his dreams he is a Promethean. In reality he has not yet learnt to stand alone'.[59]

Even a proto-Prometheus could recognise at least one failing. The young Dickie had no illusions that his much-vaunted matinee-idol looks were a guarantee of thespian talents – and if he did, then Charlie Chaplin quickly disabused him. However, as we have seen, he was captivated by the production process, and this extended beyond the cinema into popular music and even on occasion theatre.[60] This fascination chimed with a lifelong interest in all means of communication, hence in retirement his pioneering of cable television, promotion of BAFTA, and creation of the National Electronics Research Council.[61] All three enterprises embodied a wholehearted engagement with the technology appropriate to facilitating the transmission of information, whether for education, instruction, or pure entertainment.

Mountbatten lived at a time when much of that technology derived from indigenous research and development, witness the formidable contribution of applied science to the success of Combined Operations. Operational research, of which Mountbatten was in many ways the godfather, confirmed hard-pressed British scientists' remarkable ability to adapt to wartime conditions and demands. British science and engineering emerged from the Second World War enjoying an unprecedented degree of international esteem, witness the volume of knowledge transfer across the Atlantic. Nevertheless, much that was new and appealing, whether for civilian or military application, emanated from America. Like Mountbatten's passion for the movies, interest lay as much in the production process as in the original creative idea. One obvious example was the CCO's eagerness in 1941–2 to harness US shipbuilding techniques as speedily as possible in order to boost Combined Operations' complement of landing craft.

The United States had a material and cultural lure, but there was a psychological and emotional attraction as well. Americans exercised power and authority in a discernibly different way from their counterparts in Britain. Like Churchill, Mountbatten was an everyman aristocrat who instinctively empathised with the less formal, more intimate manner adopted by the likes of Al Wedemeyer. The notion of a senior officer in His Majesty's armed forces 'going colonial' was bound to generate suspicion, even distaste. Yet, conveying an impression of concern was vital to effective man (and woman) management in an era when the foot soldiers of empire – in the 'mother country' as well as in the Dominions – were far less deferential than their fathers' cannon-fodder generation. Even better was to convert that concern for the welfare of the individual into direct intervention, thereby consolidating the impression that here was a commanding officer who cared. For all his many failings, Mountbatten enjoyed just such a reputation throughout the lower decks. Later, that same mixture of affection, respect, and deference, tempered by an instinctive wariness and occasional scorn, could be found in the Nissen huts and the tents of

Argyllshire and the Arakan. From subaltern to field marshal, every competent, self-respecting officer would insist on prioritising the interests of the men and women under his/her command, and yet Mountbatten's mid-Atlantic manner and style was strikingly different.

If Mountbatten was popularly regarded as a charming man, then the skilful and professional deployment of that charm owed as much to New World manipulation as it did to *noblesse oblige*. If the British Empire and Commonwealth was to survive wholly or in part, along the way transmogrifying into a fresh geopolitical, even post-imperial, entity, then it required a radical shift in the nature of administration and control. David Winner has argued persuasively that Noel Coward, driven to despair by Suez, conspired in a further erosion of imperialism, turning it into 'a kind of jokey, postmodernist version of the same thing'. Romsey's most privileged film fan would have seen *The Italian Job*, and got the joke; but Mountbatten's patriotism was always far more sophisticated than that of the Windsor-obsessed 'Mr Bridger'.[62] Even prior to the war he suspected a healthy injection of American egalitarianism was vital to maintaining the familiar, if not necessarily the status quo. Here was a conscientious courtier, and eager servant of his sovereign (some would say over-eager, especially in December 1936), who effortlessly reconciled a lifelong weakness for the trappings of invented tradition with the warm embrace of modernity. His politics can best be viewed through an American prism, suggesting as they do the confused identity of a blue-blooded New Dealer and a Republican Boston brahmin. It's scarcely surprising that Mountbatten got on equally well with White House wheeler-dealers like Harry Hopkins, and uniformed chief executives like Wedemeyer and 'Ike'. Eisenhower has been described as exemplifying, 'The modern commander as manager (mediating between generals and politicians, and balancing the conflicting demands on grand strategy) …'.[63] Mountbatten strove hard to secure similar status, its reward the exercise of raw power on the grand stage. As seen in Chapter Nine, Nigel Hamilton's expanded indictment of Mountbatten included his imposition of a defiantly 'modern', Washington-inspired model of command. A hybrid COHQ was at odds with, and ostensibly inferior to, Monty's more hands-on command structure, his battle headquarters subtly tailored to a tried, tested, and distinctively British mechanism for waging war.

The present chapter has already noted that the jury remains out on the degree of authority exercised by Mountbatten at SEAC. Certainly, before his arrival in the Far East there were only brief moments when his views really counted, most obviously when serving as Churchill's envoy in Washington. Even on these occasions he was the emissary not the imperial legate. For the first half of the war Mountbatten was still very much the apprentice war lord – and when in mid-1941 he became a junior power broker it was only by the skin of his teeth. Yet, despite all the misadventures, Captain 'D' had never faced disciplinary action, or even a formal court of inquiry. Avoidance of serious sanction, let alone a court martial, suggests something more than just a charmed life; patronage, privilege, and publicity all combined to provide a blanket of protection that stretched from The Mall to Fleet Street. In a conspiracy of Admiralty resignation and Fleet Street flag-waving, Mountbatten successively turned

a grimly inauspicious turn of events into heart-warming triumphs of derring do.
Pound's eventual offer of a state-of-the-art aircraft carrier confirmed what everyone
across the Service had known for years: that this was no ordinary career-minded naval
officer, his ambitions focused on some far-distant landmark. Rarely was Cromwell's
adage that, 'A man never rises so high as when he does not know where he is going',
less appropriate. What Cunningham could never understand is why, given these
obvious advantages, Mountbatten refused to remain focused upon the job in hand,
namely working his way up the ladder.

Churchill provided the patronage, but he never kidded himself that Mountbatten
was a superior sailor – clearly, of his generation there were men much better
equipped to command HMS *Illustrious*. Far fewer officers, however, could enjoy a
natural empathy with Americans, generating a reciprocal goodwill. Here was a rare
commodity, to be put to good use, albeit within clearly defined parameters. Thus,
in 1942–3 when, thanks to the British Empire's final heroic fling in the Western
Desert, Churchill and his chiefs retained a disproportionate influence over the
future direction of the war, the CCO always remained an agent, never a real player.
Brooke's mastery of martial diplomacy, and his wholly unique working and personal
relationship with the Prime Minister, rendered him well-nigh unchallengeable. Any
influence Mountbatten might have exercised over grand strategy was negated by the
Chairman of the COSC's prejudice against an 'adviser' enjoying access to such an
august body. Furthermore, the Chief of the Imperial General Staff remained firmly
convinced that Dickie's credentials as a commander-in-chief were deeply flawed. Yet
the impetuosity which so appalled Brooke was viewed by Churchill as a real strength:
in 1941 and again in 1943 he needed a Beatty not a Jellicoe – not a sure-footed grand
fleet commander, but someone who could bang heads and make a loud noise. Brooke
was unconvinced, and by no means alone in believing that Mountbatten had been
promoted too fast too soon. Here, however, was an informed viewpoint. At the
time, and for many years after the war, those critics most dismissive of Mountbatten's
attributes and achievements invariably did so from a platform of partial knowledge,
plus also of course, pure envy. Few enjoyed the insight and intuition of Andrew
Cunningham, and as we've seen even ABC eventually came around to endorsing
Mountbatten's appointment as First Sea Lord.

In establishing the assets required of a great admiral, and thus a great leader,
Nelson's most distinguished biographer quoted with approval Jackie Fisher's
insistence that seamanship was never a primary requirement: 'He needs good sailors
under him.' Andrew Lambert identified mental toughness as a necessary prerequisite,
especially when dealing with more senior officers, and with their political masters.
Nelson was an exception to the rule in that there is no obligation upon a great leader
to be an attractive personality. There is, however, a requirement, 'to translate insight
and decision into action and success'; and here we get to the heart of what constitutes
genuine leadership: 'the ability to engage with the moral and mental resources of the
people who alone can make a fighting force great, inspiring them with the conviction
that their cause is just, their equipment effective and their commander successful.'[64]

Here was an admiral who clearly had the necessary mental toughness, and a capacity to ride roughshod over those who stood in his way. He used every means at his disposal to get what he wanted, all too often turning to Buckingham Palace in order to outflank his superiors. Guileful and quick-witted, Mountbatten's single-minded determination fostered the impression of a singularly untrustworthy character. Rightly or wrongly, this was a view commonly expressed throughout the decade that Mountbatten served as First Sea Lord and later as Chief of the Defence Staff.[65] Macmillan was happy to enjoy a weekend away from No. 10 casting his fly over the Test, yet he found his host, 'a strange character ... who tries to combine being a professional sailor, a politician and a royalty. The result is that nobody trusts him'.[66]

The seeds had of course been sown much earlier. Combined Operations confirmed a taste for chicanery acquired during the abdication crisis, and more especially, the Admiralty's aggressive campaign to regain control of the Fleet Air Arm. In the corridors of power Mountbatten tread a fine line between legitimate lobbying and manipulative political manoeuvring. Even prior to retirement he demonstrated how ruthless he could be in challenging or silencing anyone prepared to question his skilfully tailored version of events. Late in life, when 'fancy about the past had a strong tendency to replace the reality', Mountbatten left himself open to fierce criticism, even ridicule. Thus, 'he was wont to confuse what he would have liked to have happened with what actually did happen'.[67] Ironically, the unprincipled advocacy, let alone the inflated claims, undermined what was often a convincing case for the defence. An exception must be made for the debacle at Dieppe, where Combined Operations' justification for remounting the raid was always open to question. The suggestion that Operation Jubilee really did offer lessons for Overlord seemed increasingly implausible once Mountbatten began exaggerating D-Day's indebtedness to the biggest blot in his copybook.

For the first 18 months of the war Mountbatten's undoubted courage was tainted by foolhardiness, his remarkable capacity for crippling destroyers clearly corrosive in terms of each crew's self-confidence. Yet, even if the *Kelly*'s wardroom grew more wary of its captain, morale remained remarkably high throughout the rest of the ship. Reading seamen's and petty officers' correspondence reveals the immense respect shown towards Mountbatten. Talking to surviving veterans confirms an untarnished affection. Similarly, even the most jaundiced observer of Combined Operations conceded that morale remained unusually high, even in the aftermath of Dieppe – having said that, few residents of Richmond Terrace had crossed the Channel, and those who did were mainly off-shore. By the summer of 1943 the Chief of Combined Operations may have generated an aura of success among his immediate staff, but the same was scarcely true of either the Commandos or the Canadians. While members of the Special Service Brigade retained a healthy scepticism in the company of the CCO, most audiences were readily convinced that their cause was just, *and* that they now had the kit necessary to hit back. Commandos aside, Mountbatten was preaching to the converted. Had Dieppe not cast its long shadow, he might justifiably have claimed to match Andrew Lambert's criteria. Hence the added significance of the challenge waiting in the Far East: could he convey that same energy, drive, and above all, conviction when faced with a far larger and far more demoralised fighting force than he had inherited from Roger Keyes two years earlier? Although the Supreme Commander had some grasp of the task facing him in south-east Asia, the sheer scale of the mission only really hit him in the first few weeks after his arrival. For all his mishaps at sea, Mountbatten remained the eternally lucky man. Needless to say, privilege and position enabled him to ride his luck. Providentially, SEAC offered him a rare opportunity to display great leadership: in even the fiercest conflagration theatre commanders are few and far between. Yet at the moment of his appointment in late summer 1943 no-one could really know whether Mountbatten's career to date constituted an adequate preparation for what was clearly a post of immense responsibility. Many of course had their doubts. Mountbatten had served a 30-year apprenticeship, but the crucial question was whether he had the humility to look back upon a succession of formative experiences, and learn from his mistakes. Surely *that* was the true test of greatness ...

NOTES

Chapter One

1 Arguably the writing was on the wall as early as the end of the Boer War, and certainly the end of the Great War, as demonstrated in Ronald Hyam, *Britain's Declining Empire: The Road to Decolonisation, 1918–68* (CUP, Cambridge, 2007), part 1. How stubbornly such a conclusion was resisted at the very highest level is revealed in Anthony Eden's mid-1952 cabinet memorandum on 'British Overseas Obligations', as dissected in Peter Hennessy, *Having It So Good Britain in the Fifties* (Penguin/Allen Lane, London, 2006), pp. 38–42.

2 David Cannadine, 'Lord Mountbatten' in *The Pleasures of the Past* (Fontana, London, 1990), p. 67

3 In 1946 and 1951 Mountbatten privately stated how well qualified he was to be prime minister. Lord Zuckerman, 'Admiral of the Fleet Earl Mountbatten of Burma', *Six Men Out of the Ordinary* (Peter Owen, London, 1992), pp. 142–3.

4 Mountbatten claimed that Attlee offered him a cabinet post on 26 February 1949, and that Macmillan made the same suggestion on 3 November 1962 while weekending at Broadlands. Wilson cleared the Rhodesia post with the Queen in October 1965, and an unenthusiastic provisional governor-general then drafted a list of staff to take with him to Salisbury. Lord Mountbatten, briefing card on jobs offered, 1972, Mountbatten papers, MB1/L149.

5 Report of the Irish ambassador in London, Donal O'Sullivan, on his conversation with Lord Mountbatten, [?] 1972, National Archives in Dublin, quoted in Henry McDonald, 'Royal blown up by IRA "backed united Ireland"', *Guardian*, 29 December 2007.

6 Andrew Roberts, 'Lord Mountbatten and the Perils of Adrenalin' in *Eminent Churchillians* (Phoenix, London, 1995), pp. 78–132 is a fierce denunciation of Mountbatten's performance as the last viceroy by a vocal champion of Britain's record in India as a civilising influence and benign colonial power. Almost as offensive is the patronising of an intellectually challenged SEAC C-in-C in Max Hastings, *Nemesis: The Battle for Japan, 1944–45* (Harper Press/HarperPerennial, London, 2007/8), pbk edn, pp. 68–9.

7 Since first drafting this chapter I have discovered a deeply hostile reference to 'the Mountbattens (the Orléanists of Britain)' in Harold Macmillan, *The Macmillan Diaries The Cabinet Years 1950–57*, ed. Peter Catterall (Pan, London, 2003), 9 August 1951, p. 93.

8 Mountbatten is cruelly depicted as an absurdity left over from a singularly ungilded age in A.N. Wilson, *Our Times The Age of Elizabeth II* (Hutchinson, London, 2008), pp. 253–9.

9 For example, a heavily promoted drama-documentary offered a surprisingly flattering portrayal of the last viceroy given that few commentators today would offer unqualified endorsement of Mountbatten's viceregal performance: *The Last Days of the Raj* (Carl Hindmarch, Channel 4, UK, 2007). At the same time sales in Pakistan remain buoyant for *Lord Mountbatten's Deceit*, a pirated version of Andrew Roberts' hatchet-job; resentment

towards the perfidious Viceroy and his 'promiscuous' wife reinforced by sixtieth anniversary soul-searching: Tariq Ali, 'Pakistan at Sixty', *London Review of Books*, 4 October 2007. On a residual loathing of the Mountbattens among old India hands, see Patrick French, *Liberty Or Death India's Journey to Independence and Division* (HarperCollins, London, 1997), pp. 285–6.

10   For example, the conference proceedings of Alan Campbell-Johnson, 'Mountbatten: the Triple Assignment, 1942–1948. A Recorder's Reflections' in C.M. Woolgar (ed.), *Mountbatten On The Record* (University of Southampton, Southampton, 1997), pp. 1–20.

11   Interview with Alan Campbell-Johnson quoted in French, *Liberty Or Death*, p. 286.

12   Hugh Massingberd, *Daydream Believer Confessions of a Hero-Worshipper* (Macmillan, London, 2001), pp. 146–51.

13   *In Which We Serve* (Noel Coward/David Lean, Two Cities, UK, 1942).

14   Ray Murphy, *The Last Viceroy The Life and Times of Rear-Admiral The Earl Mountbatten of Burma* (Jarrolds, London, 1948), p. 15; Neil Huxter, 'Smith, Cecil Lewis Troughton [*pseudo.* Cecil Scott Forester], *Oxford Dictionary of National Biography* (OUP, Oxford, 2004), www. oxforddnb.com. Other novelists educated at Dulwich were Raymond Chandler, and the fictional recorder of the College's cricketing accomplishments, P.G. Wodehouse.

15   William Pattinson, *Mountbatten and the Men of the 'Kelly'* (Patrick Stephens, Wellingborough, 1986), p. 108; C.S. Forester, *The Ship* (Martyn Joseph, 1943/Penguin, London, 1949), pp. 25, 38–9, 49–51, 55, 103–5 and 128; Rear-Admiral Lord Mountbatten to C.S. Forester, 5 June 1944, Mountbatten papers, MB1/C101. In actual fact Nicholas Montserrat's *The Cruel Sea* (Cassell, London, 1951) gives a far better insight in to life aboard a destroyer, even though HMS *Compass Rose* is actually a corvette.

16   Murphy, *The Last Viceroy*, pp. 7 and 9–20; Philip Ziegler (ed.), *Personal Diary of Admiral the Lord Louis Mountbatten Supreme Allied Commander South-East Asia 1943–1946* (Collins, London, 1988), 6–11 February 1946, p. 294.

17   Murphy, *The Last Viceroy*, pp. 15–20; Rear-Admiral Lord Mountbatten to Admiral of the Fleet the Lord Chatfield, 31 August 1946, Mountbatten papers, MB1/E110.

18   Ray Murphy to Rear-Admiral Lord Mountbatten, 19 September 1947, and Rear-Admiral Lord Mountbatten to Ray Murphy, 31 August and 20 December 1946, and 20 October 1947, ibid.; Brian Connell, *Manifest Destiny A Study in Five Profiles of the Rise and Influence of the Mountbatten Family* (Cassell, London, 1953); Rear-Admiral Lord Mountbatten to Everett C. Somers, 17 September 1953, Mountbatten papers, MB1/H199.

19   Rear-Admiral Lord Mountbatten to Ray Murphy, 9 July and 20 October 1947, and to Peter Murphy, 20 October 1947, ibid., MB1/E110; A.N. Wilson, *After the Victorians: 1901–1953* (Hutchinson, London, 2005), pp. 493–4; James Lees-Milne, *James Lees-Milne Diaries, 1942–1954*, ed. Michael Bloch (John Murray, London, 2006/7), pbk edn, 25 November 1942, p. 58: footnote speculation that 'M.B.' in an S-M anecdote told by John Gielgud was Mountbatten, who 'was known to have these tastes'.

20   On Noel Coward's affair with Prince George, Duke of Kent, see Philip Hoare, *Noel Coward A Biography* (Sinclair-Stevenson, London, 1995), pp. 122–3.

21   Rear-Admiral Lord Mountbatten to Ray Murphy, 20 October 1947, Mountbatten papers, MB1/E110.

22   Tom Driberg, *Ruling Passions* (Jonathan Cape, London, 1977), pp. 213–27; and re Driberg's role as a republican apologist for the Royal Family, see Francis Wheen, *Tom Driberg His Life and Indiscretions* (Chatto and Windus, London, 1990), pp. 211–15. After Driberg left Saigon in 1945, Mountbatten noted that, 'I shall never cease to bless the day when Mike Wardell persuaded me to break my rule about MPs-cum-war-correspondents!': quoted in ibid., p. 215.

23   Janet Morgan, *Edwina Mountbatten A Life of Her Own* (HarperCollins, London, 1991), pp. 192–5; Anne Chisholm and Michael Davie, *Lord Beaverbrook A Life* (Alfred A. Knopf, New York, 1993), pp. 254–5, 265 and 282–4; Lord Beaverbrook to Michael Wardell,

30 June 1955, quoted in A.J.P. Taylor, *Beaverbrook* (Hamish Hamilton, London, 1972/ Penguin, London, 1974), pbk edn, p. 814, and to Tom Driberg MP, 1 August 1952, quoted in Philip Ziegler, *Mountbatten The Official Biography* (Collins, London, 1985), p. 489; Tom Driberg, *Beaverbrook A Study in Power and Frustration* (Weidenfeld and Nicolson, London, 1956), pp. 268. Wartime editor Michael Foot insisted in 2003 that, despite Beaverbrook's denial to the 1947 royal commission on the press, the *Evening Standard*'s blacklist included Mountbatten, Coward, and Paul Robeson: quoted in Matthew Sweet, *Shepperton Babylon The Lost Worlds of British Cinema* (Faber, London, 2005), pbk edn, p. 173.

24 Lord Mountbatten, briefing card on Lord Beaverbrook, 1972, Mountbatten papers, MB1/ L149. Re the Duke of Kent, see: Hoare, *Noel Coward*, p. 382, and Jonathan Petropoulos, *Royals and the Reich The Princes Von Hessen in Nazi Germany* (OUP, Oxford, 2006), p. 73.
25 Lord Beaverbrook to Max Aitken, 20 April 1958, quoted in Taylor, *Beaverbrook*, p. 815.
26 Chisholm and Davie, *Lord Beaverbrook*, p. 441; Beaverbrook quoted in Taylor, *Beaverbrook*, pp. 689–90; Lord Mountbatten, briefing card on Lord Beaverbrook, 1972, Mountbatten papers, MB1/L149; Macmillan, *The Macmillan Diaries*, 9 August 1951, p. 93.
27 Wheen, *Tom Driberg*, pp. 275–92; Tom Driberg, *Beaverbrook A Study in Power and Frustration*, pp. 292–4, and *Ruling Passions*, p. 224; correspondence between Tom Driberg and the First Sea Lord, 1955–9, Mountbatten papers, MB1/I24; and re *Reynolds News* rebuttals of *Daily Express* and *Sunday Express* attacks on the CDS, 1958–9, see ibid., MB1/B73. On Mountbatten's extensive role in drafting the section in *Beaverbrook* on the Dieppe raid and his feud with Beaverbrook, see Chapter Nine.
28 Taylor, *Beaverbrook*, p. 815; Chisholm and Davie, *Lord Beaverbrook*, pp. 493–4; Driberg, *Ruling Passions*, pp. 224–5; Morgan, *Edwina Mountbatten*, pp. 206 and 218.
29 See miscellaneous correspondence, and transcripts of Mountbatten reminiscences, in series MS350, Alan Campbell-Johnson papers.
30 *The Life and Times of Lord Mountbatten 4: The Stormy Winds* (Peter Morley, Rediffusion, UK, 1969). On the filming of the series see Ziegler, *Mountbatten*, pp. 667–70.
31 Brian Bond, 'John Terraine', *Guardian*, 1 January 2004; John Terraine, *The Life and Times of Lord Mountbatten* (Hutchinson/Arrow, London, 1968/70).
32 Admiral of the Fleet the Earl Mountbatten of Burma, Foreword, *Mountbatten Eighty Years in Pictures* (Macmillan, London, 1979), p. 7.
33 Bibliographical note, ibid., p. 218; Larry Collins and Dominique Lapierre, *Freedom at Midnight* (Collins, London, 1975). Friends and relations, including a reluctant Her Majesty, were pressed to read a book, which, 'is remarkable chiefly for the faithfulness with which it portrays the history of the period as Lord Mountbatten would have wished it to be seen'; a truly Jeevesian description, to be found in Ziegler, *Mountbatten*, pp. 666–7. Correspondence with co-authors and press clippings re *Freedom at Midnight*, Mountbatten papers, MB1/K15 and K15A-E.
34 French, *Liberty Or Death*, p. 286.
35 Richard Hough, *Louis and Victoria* (Hutchinson, London, 1974). The other recommended title was Kenneth Poolman, *Kelly* (William Kimber, London, 1954), for which Mountbatten wrote a foreword.
36 For example, Richard Hough to Admiral Lord Mountbatten, 14 October 1975 and 25 April 1976, Mountbatten papers, MB1/K9A.
37 Richard Hough to Admiral Lord Mountbatten, 22 September 1975, and miscellaneous correspondence with Mollie Travis, 1975, ibid.; Richard Hough (ed.), *Queen Victoria Advice to a Granddaughter* (Heinemann, London, 1975).
38 Lord Brabourne, letter to *The Bookseller* quoted in 'William Hickey', *Daily Express*, 7 July 1980; Weidenfeld and Nicolson/Richard Hough promotional material quoted in 'Lord Brabourne and Others v. Hough' in Michael Fish (ed.), *Fleet Street Reports of Industrial Property Cases from the Commonwealth and Europe [1981] F.S.R. Vol. 7* (European Law Centre, London, 1981), pp. 81–6.

39 Richard Hough, Foreword, *Mountbatten Hero of Our Time* (Weidenfeld and Nicolson, London, 1981), p. xiii.

40 Ray Monk (biographer of Bertrand Russell and Ludwig Wittgenstein), 'Getting inside Heisenberg's head' in A.L. Macfie (ed.), *The Philosophy of History* (Palgrave Macmillan, Basingstoke, 2006), pp. 237–52.

41 Richard Hough, Foreword, *Edwina Countess Mountbatten of Burma* (Weidenfeld and Nicolson, 1983), pp. xiii–xiv. On Mary Ashley as a 'pretty, self-centred fantasizer', see Morgan, *Edwina Mountbatten*, p. 24; and on inaccuracies in *Edwina*, see Marjorie, Countess of Brecknock, to Lord Brabourne, 19 February 1985, Mountbatten papers, MB1/K41A. The cousin and closest friend had herself overseen an early tribute: Marjorie, Countess of Brecknock, *Edwina Mountbatten: Her Life in Pictures* (Macdonald, 1961).

42 Richard Hough, *Mountbatten Hero of Our Time* (Pan, London, 1981); private information. Arguably three times given a later, albeit less contentious volume: ibid., *Bless Our Ship Mountbatten and the Kelly* (Hodder and Stoughton, London, 1991).

43 Brian Hoey, *Mountbatten The Private Story* (Sidgwick and Jackson, London, 1994), pp. vii, ix, and 1–10. In anticipation of the thirtieth anniversary of Mountbatten's assassination, a paperback edition appeared in 2008, boasting extravagant claims of the author's closeness to his subject and bearing predictable cover puffs from Andrew Roberts and Hugo Vickers: Brian Hoey, *Mountbatten The Private Story* (History Press, London, 2008), pbk edn.

44 Anthony Lambton, *The Mountbattens The Battenbergs and Young Mountbatten* (Constable, London, 1989), pp. 9–25 and 226–44.

45 See Chapter Five. Obituary of Vice-Admiral Sir Ian McGeoch, *Daily Telegraph*, 17 August 2007; Vice-Admiral Sir Ian McGeoch, *The Princely Sailor Mountbatten of Burma* (Brassey's, London, 1996), pp. 52–4. To mark the thirtieth anniversary of its subject's death the book was republished under a new name and with a foreword by the Countess Mountbatten: Ian McGeoch, *Mountbatten of Burma Captain of War Guardian of Peace* (J.H. Haynes and Co., London, 2009), pbk edn.

46 'Some comments by Admiral of the Fleet the Earl Mountbatten of Burma on his relationship with the late Admiral of the Fleet Viscount Cunningham of Hyndhope', August 1966, Alan Campbell-Johnson papers, MS350/A3002/2/1/9.

47 On Alan Brooke's frequent exasperation when dealing with Mountbatten see Part Four, but for a sample of his diary descriptions try 'quite irresponsible, suffers from the most desperate illogical brain, always producing red herrings …' Field Marshal Lord Alanbrooke, *War Diaries 1939–1945*, eds. Alex Danchev and Daniel Todman (Weidenfeld and Nicolson, London, 2001), 8 January 1943, p. 357.

48 Morgan, *Edwina Mountbatten*, p. 17

49 Promotional material for Shashi Joshi, *The Last Durbar A Dramatic Presentation of the Division of British India* (OUP, Karachi, 2006).

50 *Gandhi* (Richard Attenborough, Columbia Pictures, USA, 1982); *The Last Days of the Raj*; *Lord Mountbatten, The Last Viceroy* (Tom Clegg, George Walker TV Productions/Mobil, UK/USA, 1985) and David Butler, *Lord Mountbatten, The Last Viceroy* (Methuen, London, 1985). Nicol Williamson starred as Mountbatten in 1985 and James Wilby in 2007.

51 Stanley Wolpert, *Shameful Flight The Last Years of the British Empire in India* (OUP, Oxford, 2006), pp. 10–11, 129–31, 134–41, 151–6, 176 and 188.

52 Alex von Tunzelmann, *Indian Summer The Secret History of the End of an Empire* (Simon and Schuster/Pocket Books, 2007/8), pbk edn.

53 Patrick French, *Younghusband The Last Great Imperial Adventurer* (HarperCollins, London, 1995) and *Liberty or Death*.

54 Attlee quoted in von Tunzelmann, *Indian Summer*, p. 150.

55 Ibid., pp. 148 and 202.

56 Ibid., pp. 7 and 226.

57 Alex von Tunzelmann quoted in Ed Caesar, 'Indian Summer: story of the Mountbattens', *Sunday Times*, 29 June 2008.

58 von Tunzelmann, *Indian Summer*, pp. 276–7.

59 Tina Brown, *The Diana Chronicles* (Century, London, 2007), pp. 81–2, 86, and 201; Sarah Bradford, *Diana* (Penguin, London, 2007), pp. 48, 53–4, 57 and 174.

60 Penny Junor, *The Firm The Troubled Life of the House of Windsor* (HarperCollins, London, 2005), pp. 63,66, 68–9, 72, 74 and 109.

61 *The Queen's Wedding* (Julia Harrington, Menton Productions, UK, 2007). The programme purported 1947 to be a crisis year for the Royal Family; and on the strength of this claim a repeat was scheduled for Boxing Day as part of Channel 4's Windsor-themed evening entertainment.

62 Timothy Knatchbull, *From A Clear Blue Sky: Surviving the Mountbatten Bomb* (Hutchinson, London, 2009). As well as losing a brother, two grandparents, and his friend Paul Maxwell, Knatchbull was blinded in one eye. While the author's *Tatler* feature and radio appearances may have been courtesy of his publisher's marketing department, the same was not the case for all newspaper coverage. A *Daily Telegraph* story on 27 August was clearly lifted from a BBC interview, but more substantial was an earlier report revealing the whereabouts of convicted assassin Thomas McMahon, freed as a consequence of the Good Friday peace agreement: Andrew Alderson and Kathryn Johnston, 'Killer of Lord Mountbatten enjoys freedom, 30 years on from IRA murder', *Sunday Telegraph*, 9 August 2009.

63 Conversation with the Countess Mountbatten, 17 July 2007.

64 Morgan, *Edwina Mountbatten*, pp. 227, 438, and 446–9.

65 Ibid., p. 230.

66 Ziegler, *Mountbatten*, pp. 15–17 and 751–6.

67 Ziegler could legitimately claim to have passed fierce examination by his establishment peers: Robert Blake (*The Times*), Michael Howard (*TLS*), John Keegan (*Sunday Times*), Elizabeth Longford (*Literary Review*) and Max Beloff (*Books and Bookmen*); plus across the Atlantic the acclaim of a Nobel Prize laureate in the shape of Kenneth Galbraith's *Washington Post* review.

68 Ziegler, *Mountbatten*, p. 315; Wheen, *Tom Driberg*, p. 211.

69 Mountbatten quoted in von Tunzelmann, *Indian Summer*, p. 363; Noel Coward to Commander Lord Louis Mountbatten, 21 June 1934, Mountbatten papers, MB1/A48.

70 Cannadine, *The Pleasures of the Past*, pp. 60 and 64–7; David Cannadine in *The Last Viceroy*, part 2 (Susan Marling, Just Radio, UK, 2004), BBC Radio 4, 21 August 2004.

71 Philip Ziegler, *Mountbatten Revisited* (Harry Ransom Humanities Research Center, Austin Texas, 1995), pp. 5–6; Nigel Hamilton, *Monty The Making of a General 1887–1942* (Hamish Hamilton, London, 1981), p. 547.

72 Brian Loring Villa, *Mountbatten and the Dieppe Raid 1942* (OUP, Oxford, 1989); private information.

73 Roberts, 'Lord Mountbatten and the Perils of Adrenalin', p. 65; Ziegler, *Mountbatten Revisited*, p. 9; ibid., 'Foreword to 2001 edition', *Mountbatten The Official Biography* (Phoenix Press, London, 2001), pbk edn, pp. xi-xii.

74 Roberts, 'Lord Mountbatten and the Perils of Adrenalin', pp. 55 and 135–6.

75 Ibid., pp. 91–111; Ziegler, *Mountbatten Revisited*, pp. 16–23; ibid., 'Foreword to 2001 edition', *Mountbatten*, pbk edn, pp. xii–xiv; ibid., *Mountbatten*, pp. 700–1. On Radcliffe's retrospective view of the Raj, and the extent to which late in life he was haunted by his 1947 arbitration, see Hennessy, *Having It So Good*, pp. 272–4.

76 Ralph Waldo Emerson, 'Heroism', *Emerson's Essays* (Dent, London, 1971), p. 141; Philip Ziegler (ed.), *From Shore to Shore The Final Years The Diaries of Earl Mountbatten of Burma, 1953–1979* (Collins, London, 1989).

77 Isaiah Berlin, 'The Hedgehog and the Fox', *Russian Thinkers* (Penguin, London, 1979), pbk edn, pp. 41–2. On *Queen* magazine's August 1959 naming of Mountbatten as a prominent member of 'the Establishment' see Dominic Sandbrook, *Never Had It So Good A History of Britain from Suez to the Beatles* (Little, Brown, London, 2005), p. 532.

78 Berlin, 'Hedgehog and the Fox', p. 22.

79 Ziegler, *Mountbatten*, p. 700.

80 For the most thorough public investigation of the circumstances surrounding the assassination, see *The Day Mountbatten Died*, a BBC2 documentary broadcast on 18 June 2004.

81 Re the First Sea Lord's views and actions during the Suez crisis see Ziegler, *Mountbatten*, pp. 537–547. On divisions within the Chiefs of Staff Committee, and Mountbatten's characteristic lack of discretion when addressing the Imperial Defence College, see Hennessy, *Having It So Good*, pp. 431–52. Admiral Lord Mountbatten to Anthony Eden, 2 November 1956, in briefing card on Suez 1972, Mountbatten papers, MB1/L149.

Chapter Two

1 Ashley Hicks quoted in Hoey, *Mountbatten The Private Story*, p. 46.

2 Misc. papers re 'Arrangements for Lord Mountbatten's funeral', Mountbatten papers, MB1/K381; interviews with Ronald Allison, John Barrett, and Sir John Titman in Hoey, *Mountbatten The Private Story*, pp. 37–41.

3 'I can't help thinking how much he would have enjoyed today': Countess Mountbatten quoted in Pattinson, *Mountbatten and the Men of the 'Kelly'* ; Barbara Cartland quoted in Hoey, *Mountbatten The Private Story*, p. 46.

4 Mountbatten's tribute in the *Daily Telegraph*, 5 June 1972, quoted in a balanced and informative summary of research into, and the debate surrounding, the extent of the Windsors' prewar and wartime dealings with Nazi Germany's leadership, intelligence services, and [pro-NSDAP] aristocrats: Petropoulos, *Royals and the Reich*, pp. 206–18.

5 Ziegler, *Mountbatten*, p. 679; Greg King, *The Duchess of Windsor The Uncommon Life of Wallis Simpson* (Aurum, London, 1999), pbk edn, pp. 458 and 466.

6 Ibid., p. 475; Hoey, *Mountbatten The Private Story*, p. 138; Ziegler (ed.), *From Shore to Shore The Diaries of Earl Mountbatten of Burma, 1853–1979*, 29 May 1972, pp. 250–1. HM's private secretary was Sir Martin Charteris, who noted the point made by the BBC's Harry Middleton that foreign – republican – heads of state such as Nixon and Pompidou had already paid tribute to the late Duke.

7 Hugo Vickers, *Elizabeth, The Queen Mother* (Hutchinson, London, 2005), p. 364. Vickers also quotes the Queen Mother's verdict: 'So like Edwina, she always did everything with a splash!'

8 Ziegler, *Mountbatten*, p. 681; King, *The Duchess of Windsor*, pp. 488–9; Hoey, *Mountbatten The Private Story*, pp. 137–8; Charles Higham, *Mrs Simpson Secret Lives of the Duchess of Windsor* (Sidgwick and Jackson, London, 2004), revised 1988 edn, pp. 483–7. For a judicious assessment of the August 1945 document-hunting mission carried out by Buckingham Palace's Sir Owen Morshead and Anthony Blunt, see Petropoulos, *Royals and the Reich*, pp. 337–44.

9 The heads and/or heirs of the royal families of Great Britain and Ireland, Norway, Sweden, Greece, Bulgaria, Italy, Romania, Spain, The Netherlands, Denmark, Monaco, Belgium, Luxembourg, and Liechtenstein: names listed in Hoey, *Mountbatten The Private Story*, p. 42.

10 Petropoulos, *Royals and the Reich*, pp. 248 and 283–7.

11 Ziegler, *Mountbatten*, pp. 22–4; Robert K. Massie, *Castles of Steel Britain, Germany and the Winning of the Great War at Sea* (Pimlico, London, 2005), pbk edn, pp. 165–9; John B. Hattendorf, 'Admiral Prince Louis of Battenberg (1912–1914)' in Malcolm H. Murfett (ed.), *The First Sea Lords From Fisher to Mountbatten* (Praegar, New York, 1995), pp. 75–6;

Admiral of the Fleet Lord Fisher to J.A. Spender, 25 October 1911, quoted in ibid., p. 76. The most recent Unionist First Lord insisted that 'a better Englishman does not exist': Lord Selborne to Winston Churchill, 29 November 1911, quoted in Randolph S. Churchill, *Winston S. Churchill Vol. II Young Statesman 1901–1914* (Heinemann, London, 1967), p. 552.

12   Admiral Lord Mountbatten to Stephen Roskill, 4 October 1976, quoted in Stephen Roskill, *Churchill and the Admirals* (Collins, London, 1977), p. 24.

13   Ibid., pp. 21–4 and 27; Massie, *Castles of Steel*, pp. 169–70.

14   Hattendorf, 'Admiral Prince Louis of Battenberg (1912–1914)', pp. 77–83.

15   Ziegler, *Mountbatten*, pp. 23–4; Mountbatten quoted in Terraine, *The Life and Times of Lord Mountbatten*, p. 21.

16   Petropoulos, *Royals and the Reich*, pp. 3–4, 18–19, 21–2, 93–5, 119, 287–97, 189–94, 200–2, and 341–2.

17   'Lu' was instructed by Ambassador Ribbentrop to exploit his extensive social contacts in London, not least his familiarity with the Royal Family. During 1937–8 he successfully cultivated the Duke of Kent. Ibid., pp. 160–1, 423–4 n. 141, and 201.

18   Sarah Bradford, *King George VI* (Weidenfeld and Nicolson, London, 1989), p. 166; Petropoulos, *Royals and the Reich*, pp. 205–18 and 225–6.

19   Roskill, *Churchill and the Admirals*, pp. 34–6; Massie, *Castles of Steel*, pp. 170–5.

20   Ibid., pp. 175–8; Hattendorf, 'Admiral Prince Louis of Battenberg (1912–1914)', pp. 85–8; Martin Gilbert, *Winston S. Churchill Vol. III 1914–16* (Heinemann, London, 1971), pp. 144–5 and 147–53.

21   Vice Admiral Sir David Beatty to Lady Ethel Beatty, [?] November 1914, quoted in McGeoch, *The Princely Sailor,* p. 11.

22   Roberts, 'Lord Mountbatten and the Perils of Adrenalin', p. 56; Cannadine, 'Lord Mountbatten', p. 60; David Reynolds, *In Command of History Churchill Fighting and Writing the Second World War* (Penguin/Allen Lane, London, 2004), p. 348.

23   Admiral Prince Louis of Battenberg to Admiral Sir John Jellicoe, quoted in Massie, *Castles of Steel*, p. 176.

24   Mountbatten quoted in Terraine, *The Life and Times of Lord Mountbatten*, p. 34; Churchill, *Winston S. Churchill Vol. II*, p. 553.

25   Connell, *Manifest Destiny*, pp. 20, 44–52 and 128–31; Murphy, *Last Viceroy*, pp. 33–4; Mountbatten quoted in Terraine, *The Life and Times of Lord Mountbatten*, p. 34; transcript of interview with Kenneth Harris for first issue of the *Observer*'s magazine, [?] July 1964, Alan Campbell-Johnson papers, MS350/A2096/20; Hough, *Mountbatten: Hero of our Time*, p. 31.

26   A fellow cadet of Prince Albert and future Noble Prize laureate recalled that high quality teaching took place in 'the confident expectation that the naval arms race with Germany then in full swing would inevitably lead to war': Patrick Blackett quoted in Mary Jo Nye, *Blackett, War, and Politics in the Twentieth Century* (Harvard University Press, Cambridge Mass., 2004), p. 17. Blackett came second in his class at Osborne, and top at Dartmouth.

27   A.P. Boissier was Mountbatten's 'Tutor', appointed after the 1902 Selborne Scheme for a 2+2 naval education on the Isle of Wight and at Dartmouth was implemented in September 1903. Re Osborne pre-war, see ibid., pp. 17–20; Evan Davies, 'The Selborne Scheme: The Education of the Boy' and Geoff Sloan, 'One of Fisher's Revolutions: The Education of the Navy' in Peter Hore (ed.), *Patrick Blackett Sailor, Scientist and Socialist* (Frank Cass, London, 2003), pp. 16–37 and 44–7, and Michael Partridge, *The Royal Naval College Osborne A History 1903–1921* (Sutton, Stroud, 1999).

28   Re Mountbatten's unpopularity at Osborne: private information.

29   G.S. Hugh-Jones to Admiral Lord Mountbatten, 7 September 1954, and Bernard Braine to Philip Ziegler, 2 September 1983, quoted in Ziegler, *Mountbatten*, p. 36; Mountbatten

quoted in Hough, *Mountbatten: Hero of our Time*, p. 31; Roberts, 'Lord Mountbatten and the Perils of Adrenalin', p. 56; Cannadine, 'Lord Mountbatten', p. 60.

30 See Chapter Three re Mountbatten's first destroyer command.

31 Ziegler, *Mountbatten*, p. 54.

32 Bradford, *King George VI*, pp. 85–6 and 148.

33 Philip Ziegler (ed.), *The Diaries of Lord Louis Mountbatten 1920–1922 Tours with the Prince of Wales* (Collins, London, 1987), 'Preface', pp. 9–10, and *King Edward VIII The Official Biography* (Collins, London, 1999), pp. 124–5.

34 Lord Louis Mountbatten to the Marchioness of Milford Haven, [?] 1920, quoted in ibid., p. 164.

35 Ibid., 15 July 1920, quoted in Ziegler, *Mountbatten*, pp. 54–5.

36 Ziegler (ed.), *The Diaries of Lord Louis Mountbatten 1920–1922*, 'Preface', pp. 11–12; Prince of Wales to Mrs Freda Dudley Ward, 17 March and 18 April 1920 in Rupert Godfrey (ed.), *Letters from a Prince: Edward, Prince of Wales to Mrs Freda Dudley Ward, March 1918–January 1921* (Little, Brown and Company, London, 1998), pp. 256 and 280; Bradford, *King George VI*, pp. 86–7.

37 'I feel perfectly miserable about the whole of that awful business ... I burned my boats long ago in trying to make my master see sense; but I do very much care about his future, which I am completely fogged about, and I can see *no* daylight': Admiral Sir Lionel Halsey to Commander Lord Louis Mountbatten, 28 December 1936, Mountbatten papers, MB1/A110.

38 Prince of Wales to Mrs Freda Dudley Ward, 28 August 1920 in Godfrey (ed.), *Letters from a Prince*, p. 376.

39 Ziegler (ed.), *The Diaries of Lord Louis Mountbatten 1920–1922*, 'Preface' and 'Editor's note', pp. 10 and 13.

40 Ibid., commentary, p. 165; Prince of Wales to Mrs Freda Dudley Ward, 29 June 1920, in Godfrey (ed.), *Letters from a Prince*, p. 340.

41 Ziegler, *King Edward VIII*, p. 136.

42 Ziegler (ed.), *The Diaries of Lord Louis Mountbatten 1920–1922*, commentary, p. 166.

43 Morgan, *Edwina Mountbatten*, pp. 116, 187, 19–20, 17–18, 25–6, and 90–8.

44 George V's permission was a technicality under the Royal Marriages Act, and it was granted on 14 March. Ibid., pp. 103–16; Ziegler (ed.), *The Diaries of Lord Louis Mountbatten 1920–1922*, 13, 15, 17 and 18 February, and 13 and 15 March 1922, pp. 255–7 and 266; Mountbatten quoted in Terraine, *The Life and Times of Lord Mountbatten*, pp. 60–2; Cannadine, 'Lord Mountbatten', p. 61.

45 Ziegler, *King Edward VIII*, pp. 142, 160, and 137–40. 'Of all the Staff I must say that I like Fruity best so I was highly delighted when David fixed up yesterday to take him on to Japan as extra A.D.C. and then home in the *Renown* ...': Ziegler (ed.), *The Diaries of Lord Louis Mountbatten 1920–1922*, 24 January 1922, p. 247.

46 For the impact upon both HRH and his ADC of experiencing the boycott in Allahabad, consequently reinforcing their shared support for a hard-line response to Indian nationalism; and for Mountbatten's still uneasy relations with colleagues, see ibid., 12 and 17 December 1921, pp. 213 and 220–1.

47 The hapless Montagu was tainted by scandal given that his future wife, Venetia Stanley, had been the focus of Asquith's affection for much of his premiership; while Isaacs had attracted extensive criticism – often deeply anti-semitic – for his involvement with Lloyd George in the Liberal Government's most serious pre-war scandal, namely the accusation of insider trading in Marconi shares.

48 Ziegler (ed.), *The Diaries of Lord Louis Mountbatten 1920–1922*, 6 March, 8 and 10 January, and 22 March 1922, pp. 263, 234–5, and 269.

49 For the Japanese naval attaché at Taranto on 11 November 1940, the Fleet Air Arm was still an invaluable role model. Ibid., 12 April 1922, pp. 278–9.

50   'The crowd gave David a wonderful reception, and thanks to the efforts of the penny press they even gave me a cheer in places with suitable remarks like "She's waiting for you"': ibid., 21 June 1922, p. 307.

51   Ziegler, *Mountbatten*, pp. 92–3 and 95, and *King Edward VIII*, p. 199.

52   Memo by Lord Mountbatten, 1 December 1969, quoted in ibid., pp. 226–7, and Lord Louis Mountbatten to the Dowager Marchioness of Milford Haven, 1 September 1935, quoted in Ziegler, *Mountbatten*, p. 93; ibid., p. 95; Morgan, *Edwina Mountbatten*, pp. 254–5.

53   See Chapter Four. Mountbatten quoted in Terraine, *The Life and Times of Lord Mountbatten*, p. 90.

54   Ziegler, *King Edward VIII*, p. 281; Bradford, *King George VI*, pp. 166–7; Oliver Warner, *Admiral of the Fleet The Life of Sir Charles Lambe* (Sidgwick and Jackson , London, 1969), p. 69.

55   Noel Coward to Lord Louis Mountbatten, 19 November 1936, quoted in Ziegler, *Mountbatten*, p. 94; Bradford, *King George VI*, pp. 170–1.

56   Lord Louis Mountbatten to King Edward VIII, 7 December 1936, and Lady Edwina Mountbatten diary, 10 December 1936, quoted in Ziegler, *Mountbatten*, p. 94; Duff Hart-Davis (ed.), *King's Counsellor Abdication and War: The Diaries of Sir Alan Lascelles* (Weidenfeld and Nicolson/Phoenix, London, 2006/2007), pbk edn, 5 March 1943, p. 109; 'List of reminiscences dictated by Lord Mountbatten: The Abdication of King Edward VIII', August 1966, Alan Campbell-Johnson papers, MS350/A3002/2/1/9.

57   Bradford, *King George VI*, p. 491; Petropoulos, *Royals and the Reich*, pp. 22–3

58   Ziegler, *Mountbatten*, p. 93; Higham, *Mrs Simpson*, pp. 195–6.

59   See Chapter Four re Mountbatten passing *The Week* on to Anthony Eden. Patricia Cockburn, *The Year of the Week* (Penguin, London, 1971), pbk edn, pp. 220–3; Claud Cockburn, *I, Claud ... The Autobiography of Claud Cockburn* (Penguin, London, 1967), pbk edn [including 1956 memoir *A Discord of Trumpets*], pp. 158–9.

60   Ibid.; Hugh Thomas, *John Strachey* (Eyre Methuen, London, 1973), p. 161; Adrian Smith, 'Harold Macmillan and Munich', *Dalhousie Review*, summer 1989, vol. 68, no. 3, pp. 235–47.

61   Cockburn, *I Claud*, pp. 158–9; Thomas, *John Strachey*, p. 161.

62   Cockburn, *I Claud*, pp. 159–61; Cockburn, *The Year of The Week*, pp. 222–3; Ziegler, *Mountbatten*, p. 93; Higham, *Mrs Simpson*, pp. 195–6.

63   Ibid.

64   *The Life and Times of Lord Mountbatten 4: The Stormy Winds*; Mountbatten quoted in Terraine, *The Life and Times of Lord Mountbatten*, p. 92; King Edward VIII announcement of abdication, BBC Home Service broadcast, 10 December 1936; Hoey, *Mountbatten The Private Story*, p. 149.

65   The Windsors gleefully applied Richard Nixon's derogatory nick-name to Mountbatten. Vickers, *Elizabeth, The Queen Mother*, p. 166.

66   Mountbatten quoted in John Wheeler-Bennett, *King George VI* (Macmillan, London, 1958), pp. 293–4, and in Terraine, *The Life and Times of Lord Mountbatten*, p. 92; 'List of reminiscences dictated by Lord Mountbatten: The Abdication of King Edward VIII', ibid.. Mountbatten briefed both Wheeler-Bennett and Frances Donaldson, the Duke of Windsor's first biographer.

67   Lord Louis Mountbatten to King George VI, 11 December 1936, quoted in Ziegler, *Mountbatten*, p. 94.

68   'The speed with which he transferred his allegiance from Fort Belvedere to the new residents of Buckingham Palace almost left burn marks on the carpet ... he could not afford to be in the losing camp.' Roberts, 'Lord Mountbatten and the Perils of Adrenalin', p. 58; Morgan, *Edwina Mountbatten*, p. 256.

69   'List of reminiscences dictated by Lord Mountbatten: The Abdication of King Edward VIII', ibid.; Lord Louis Mountbatten to Duke of Windsor, 5 May 1937, quoted in Ziegler,

Mountbatten, p. 96, and to Harold Nicolson, [?] 1937, quoted in Bradford, *King George VI*, p. 244; Morgan, *Edwina Mountbatten*, p. 256.

70 Vickers, *Elizabeth, The Queen Mother*, p. 167; Bradford, *King George VI*, p. 245.

71 Puzzlingly, given the expressed preference for Metcalfe, after the Windsors' private viewing of *The Life and Times* the Duke asked Mountbatten why he had refused to be best man. Vickers, *Elizabeth, The Queen Mother*, p. 166.

72 Hoey, *Mountbatten The Private Story*, pp. 148–9; Bradford, *King George VI*, pp. 365–6; Mountbatten quoted in ibid., p. 382.

73 Ibid., pp. 422–3; Hoey, *Mountbatten The Private Story*, pp. 149–50; Vickers, *Elizabeth, The Queen Mother*, pp. 268–9 and 393–4.

74 Queen Elizabeth's alleged remark re Edwina quoted in ibid., p. 394; Evelyn Waugh, *Vile Bodies* (Chapman and Hall, London, 1930); on Noel Coward representing the Mountbattens on stage and screen see Chapter Six; Vickers, *Elizabeth, The Queen Mother*, pp. 268–9.

75 For example, speeches collected in Stanley Baldwin, *On England* (Hodder and Stoughton, London, 1926/Penguin, London, 1937), and Baldwin's paean to the National Government in the newsreel, 'The Prime Minister takes stock' (Movietone, UK, November 1937) – the latter a complacent 'fireside chat' which clearly assumes Madrid is about to fall to the Nationalists, and gives not the slightest hint that a major constitutional crisis is about to explode.

Chapter Three

1 Mountbatten quoted in Terraine, *The Life and Times of Lord Mountbatten*, p. 28; Ziegler, *Mountbatten*, pp. 36–9.

2 In 1908–9 Beatty had been Prince Louis Battenberg's not especially admiring captain on the pre-dreadnought HMS *Queen Elizabeth*. One of his second son's names was Louis, and the compliment extended to Beatty asking his C-in-C to sponsor the infant. Stephen Roskill, *Admiral of the Fleet Earl Beatty The Last Naval Hero An Intimate Biography* (Collins, London, 1980), pp. 42–3. For a judicious assessment of Beatty, man and sailor, see Andrew Lambert, 'Ruthless Bounder: David Beatty (1871–1936)' in *Admirals The Naval Commanders Who Made Britain Great* (Faber, London, 2008), pp. 335–78.

3 Ziegler, *Mountbatten*, pp. 36–41.

4 Winston S. Churchill, *The World Crisis Volume 1 1911–1914* (Thornton Butterworth, London, 1923), p. 93; Hew Strachan, *The First World War Volume 1: To Arms* (OUP, Oxford, 2001), pp. 381 and 391; Captain S.W. Roskill, RN, *The Strategy of Sea Power Its Development and Application* (Collins, London, 1962), pp. 104–5 and 132.

5 While resident in Paris Mountbatten communicated only in French, adopting a policy of total immersion in the city's language and culture. 'Preliminary Examination of Navy Candidates in Modern Languages', RN Malta, 31 July 1933, and results of Civil Service Commission interpreter examination, 16 January 1934, Mountbatten papers, MB1/A110; Princess Victoria Battenberg to Prince Louis Battenberg, 26 June 1916: full letter quoted in Ziegler, *Mountbatten*, p. 41.

6 Roskill, *The Strategy of Sea Power*, pp. 108–9; Strachan, *The First World War Vol. 1*, pp. 381–2. A more senior colleague of Roskill viewed both organisation and performance more sympathetically: [Vice-Admiral] B.B. Schofield, *British Sea Power Naval Policy in the Twentieth Century* (Batsford, London, 1967), pp. 69–71.

7 Paul Kennedy, *The Rise and Fall of British Naval Mastery* (Macmillan/Fontana, London, 1983/1992), pbk edn, pp. 288–9 and 300–2. For a contrary view, that British industry and agriculture was sufficiently strong as to more than offset the impact of unrestricted submarine warfare, see Niall Ferguson, *The Pity of War* (Penguin, London, 1998), pbk edn, pp. 282–3.

8 Strachan, *The First World War Vol. 1*, pp. 387 and 487; Kennedy, *The Rise and Fall*, pp. 288 and 296–7.

9 Ferguson, *The Pity of War*, pp. 283–4; Kennedy, *The Rise and Fall*, pp. 297–8; Schofield, *British Sea Power*, pp. 69 and 51.

10 Roskill, *The Strategy of Sea Power*, pp. 117–21; Ian F.W. Beckett, *The Great War 1914–1918* (Pearson, London, 2001), pbk edn, pp. 182–5; Andrew Gordon, *The Rules of the Game Jutland and British Naval Command* (John Murray, London, 1996), pp. 46–7, 80–97, 505–6, 567 and 563. Monographs abound but the fullest account of the battle can still be found in A.J. Marder, *From the Dreadnought to Scapa Flow Volume 3 Jutland and After*, revised edn. (OUP, Oxford, 1978), and the most exciting in Massie, *Castles of Steel*, pp. 553–684. Gordon, op. cit., provides a forensic, and sardonic analysis of the battle.

11 Kennedy, *The Rise and Fall*, pp. 292–3. Ironically, despite a short sortie on 18 October 1916 meeting no opposition, Scheer became less adventurous once redeployment of U-boats to the Atlantic denied his capital ships a suitably dense submarine screen.

12 Admiral Sir John Jellicoe to A.J. Balfour, 4 June 1916, quoted in Bryan Ranft, 'The Royal Navy and the War at Sea' in John Turner (ed.), *Britain and the First World War* (Unwin Hyman, London, 1988), pbk edn, p. 64. Balfour concluded that neither surface fleet controlled the North Sea, leaving 'joint occupation' to their respective submarines. Beckett, *The Great War*, p. 183. On the contrast with Nelson's navy see Admiral Lord Chatfield, *The Navy and Defence: The Autobiography of Admiral of the Fleet Lord Chatfield* (William Heinemann, London, 1942), pp. 148–9.

13 On HMS *New Zealand*'s impressive performance at Jutland, see Massie, *Castles of Steel*, pp. 579–605, with a more qualified view in Gordon, *The Rules of the Game*, pp. 429–30. Mountbatten quoted in Terraine, *The Life and Times of Lord Mountbatten*, p. 38.

14 Strachan, *The First World War Vol. 1*, pp. 385–8.

15 Chatfield, *The Navy and Defence*, pp. 106, 108 and 123–4.

16 'Obviously I thought this was a "cover up" for their failure to get properly into action.' Lord Mountbatten, 'The Battle of Jutland 31st May 1916 Some remarks written by the Admiral of the Fleet the Earl Mountbatten of Burma 51 years after the battle in 1967', Milford Haven papers, Misc. 3 (40), Imperial War Museum.

17 Mountbatten quoted in Terraine, *The Life and Times of Lord Mountbatten*, pp. 38–40; Ziegler, *Mountbatten*, pp. 42–3.

18 Admiral of the Fleet Lord Mountbatten to Alfred Temple Patterson, 9 July 1970, Mountbatten papers, MB1/K12.

19 No fewer than eight future First Sea Lords and two 'near misses' saw action at Jutland. Gordon, *The Rules of the Game*, p. 575.

20 Ernle Chatfield , 27 November 1916, and [?] 1922, quoted in Ziegler, *Mountbatten*, pp. 47, and Alfred Temple Patterson to Lord Mountbatten, 15 October 1970, Mountbatten papers, MB1/K12; Chatfield, *The Navy and Defence*, p. 84; Winston S. Churchill, *The Second World War Volume I The Gathering Storm* (Cassell, London, 1948), pp. 124–8 and 463. On Chatfield's claim to be the most effective First Sea Lord since Fisher, see G.A.H. Gordon, *British Seapower and Procurement Between the Wars* (Macmillan, Basingstoke, 1988), particularly pp. 109–13, and Eric J. Grove, 'Admiral Sir (later Baron) Ernle Chatfield (1933–1938)' in Murfett (ed.), *The First Sea Lords From Fisher to Mountbatten*, pp. 157–72.

21 At Jutland this failure to protect magazines was deemed by Mountbatten *the* major factor regarding 'the disaster to our Battle Cruisers': Lord Mountbatten, 'The Battle of Jutland 31st May 1916'. On Beatty's irresponsibility in this matter see Lambert, 'Ruthless Bounder: David Beatty', pp. 354–60.

22 Supported by a laudably principled warrant officer gunner, Chatfield was unusually stringent in the safety procedures adopted for HMS *Lion*: ibid., p. 354, and Gordon, *British Seapower and Procurement*, p. 123. Lord Mountbatten, 'Some remarks'; Mountbatten quoted in Terraine, *The Life and Times of Lord Mountbatten*, pp. 38 and 40; tour diary, 19

August 1976, quoted in Ziegler, *Mountbatten*, p. 43; Prince Louis Battenberg to Mr [?] Pocock, 27 May 1917, Mountbatten papers, MB1/A9. On post-battle tension between the two admirals, and the postwar historiography of Jutland, see Gordon, *The Rules of the Game*, pp. 508–13 and 539–61.

23 Gordon, *The Rules of the Game*, p. 108. The ambitious nature of these screenings is shown by the fact that not only did Prince George secure D.W. Griffith's *Intolerance* to show for seven nights in April 1918, but he even had HMS *Lion*'s name superimposed on the film's elaborate programme. Original programme, 8–14 April 1918, in Mountbatten papers, MB1/A9. On a lifelong obsession with the film industry, both in the UK and Hollywood, see Adrian Smith, 'Mountbatten goes to the movies: the cinema as a vehicle for promoting the heroic myth', *Historical Journal of Film, Radio and Television*, August 2006, vol. 26, no. 3, pp. 395–416.

24 The original idea was to commission the Topical Film Company, on the grounds that the RN had a good working relationship with the makers of the popular weekly newsreel *Topical Budget*. Sub. Lt Lord Louis Mountbatten, 'Signal Training by Cinematograph Idea', 1 February 1920, and reply re paper from Alec Hunt, Secretary to the Admiralty, 23 December 1920, Mountbatten papers, MB1/A10. Mountbatten shot his own version, which, along with a 'weekly newsreel' from HMS *Renown*, was included in *The Life and Times of Lord Mountbatten: 3 The Azure Main* (Peter Morley, Rediffusion TV, UK, 1969) .

25 One reason Beatty transferred his flag from the *Iron Duke* to a newer, faster ship was that the ship's company could barely disguise its disappointment at Jellicoe's departure. On his captain's deep and lasting admiration, see Chatfield, *The Navy and Defence*, pp. 105, 108, 115–16 and 172.

26 The Beattys were guests at the Mountbattens' wedding, as confirmed by an unflattering photograph in their nephew's tribute: Charles Beatty, *Our Admiral A Biography of Admiral of the Fleet Earl Beatty* (W.H. Allen, London, 1980). For short profiles of Jellicoe and Beatty, see Massie, *Castles of Steel*, pp. 56–71 and 83–96. Roskill saw Mountbatten as the only modern admiral to match Beatty's high profile, but argued that there the comparison ended as the former's 'purely *naval* commands never rose higher than a Destroyer Flotilla.' Roskill, *Admiral of the Fleet Earl Beatty*, p. 370.

27 On Mountbatten, Keyes, and the latter's belief that 'I had never met a keen, dashing polo-player who was not also a good officer', see Ziegler, *Mountbatten*, pp. 77–9; 1928–9 correspondence re RNPA, Mountbatten papers, MB1/A108.

28 Massie, *Castles of Steel*, pp. 63 and 95–6; Chatfield, *The Navy and Defence*, pp. 153–4.

29 *Chronicles of the Queen Elizabeth*, December 1917, original proposal for 'a gun room paper', and programme for *Three Peeps*, Mountbatten papers, MB1/A9; Ziegler, *Mountbatten*, pp. 44–5; Ranft, 'The Royal Navy and the War at Sea', pp. 66 and 68.

30 Ibid., p. 46; Mountbatten quoted in Terraine, *The Life and Times of Lord Mountbatten*, pp. 46–7; Ranft, 'The Royal Navy and the War at Sea', p. 61.

31 Lord Louis Mountbatten to Marquess of Milford Haven, 4 December 1917, quoted in Ziegler, *Mountbatten*, p. 45; Hough, *Mountbatten*, pp. 38–9; Mountbatten quoted in Terraine, *The Life and Times of Lord Mountbatten*, p. 38.

32 Ibid., p. 51; Ziegler, *Mountbatten*, pp. 46–7; 'Statement of Sub-Lieutenant LFAVN Mountbatten RN to Treasury Solicitor: H.M.S. "P31" and "Steam Hopper Yves"', in reply to request of 10 July 1919, Mountbatten papers, MB1/A10. Personnel report of Lt. Commander T.G. Carter, 5 December 1919, quoted in Ziegler, *Mountbatten*, p. 47.

33 Christ's was chosen as its Master, Sir Arthur Shipley, was not only the university vice-chancellor, and thus the instigator of the RN scheme, but also a family friend. Mountbatten became an honorary fellow of the college in 1946.

34 Brian Cathcart, *The Fly in the Cathedral How a small group of Cambridge Scientists won the race to split the atom* (Penguin, London, 2005), pbk edn, pp. 13–16 and 138; Patrick Blackett,

'Boy Blackett' and Andrew Brown, 'Blackett at Cambridge' in Hore (ed.), *Patrick Blackett*, pp. 11–12 and 97–101.

35 Mountbatten in Terraine, *The Life and Times of Lord Mountbatten*, p. 52. As well as RN officer Prince Albert, future Duke of York, his younger brother, the future Duke of Gloucester, was also in residence at Southacre just outside Cambridge, and undertaking undergraduate courses. Both were in regular contact with the less inhibited Mountbatten. Bradford, *King George VI*, p. 85.

36 Nye, *Blackett Physics, War and Politics in the Twentieth Century*, pp. 25–6. An equivalent of the 'Heretics' for Mountbatten was the exclusive club for privileged iconoclasts, the Pitt Club.

37 A politically immature Mountbatten's first foray in to public speaking was to defend the Ulster Unionists at a Milton Society debate on 14 November 1919. McGeoch, *The Princely Sailor*, pp. 13–14.

38 John Gross, *The Rise and Fall of the Man of Letters English Literary Life Since 1800* (Pelican, London, 1973), pbk edn, pp. 205–9; Ziegler, *Mountbatten*, pp. 48–9.

39 On the obsolescence and unreliability of RN signals technology six months into the war, see Strachan, *The First World War Vol. 1*, pp. 391–3 and 434–5; and on Beatty's involvement in an almost ceaseless signalling controversy, see Gordon, *The Rules of the Game*, pp. 80–97, 133–46, 487–9, 506–7 and 566; Lord Mountbatten, 'The Battle of Jutland 31st May 1916'.

40 Ibid.; Mountbatten quoted in Terraine, *The Life and Times of Lord Mountbatten*, p. 68.

41 Ziegler, *Mountbatten*, pp. 98–9; Kennedy, *The Rise and Fall*, p. 333; Churchill, *The Second World War Volume I*, pp. 124 and 534–6; 'Lord Mountbatten's comments on Commander Bousfield's "The Story of H.M.S. Kelly and Captain (D) 5th Destroyer Flotilla"', 10 September 1966, Mountbatten papers, MB1/B11E.

42 Mountbatten quoted in Terraine, *The Life and Times of Lord Mountbatten*, pp. 35–7; Kennedy, *The Rise and Fall*, p. 303–4; Roskill, *The Strategy of Sea Power*, pp. 122–6 and 133–4; Massie, *Castles of Steel*, pp. 426–91; Oliver Warner, *Cunningham of Hyndhope A Memoir* (John Murray, London, 1967), p. 227.

43 Kennedy, *The Rise and Fall*, pp. 309–11; Ziegler (ed.), *The Diaries of Lord Louis Mountbatten 1920–1922*, 12 April 1922, p. 278.

44 Ibid., 12 and 22 April and 10 May 1922, pp. 278, 287–8 and 300. In 1969 Mountbatten claimed to have written a 'most-secret report' on the *Mutsu*, but it does not survive in Admiralty files at the National Archives. Kennedy, *The Rise and Fall*, pp. 316 and 321; Mountbatten quoted in Terraine, *The Life and Times of Lord Mountbatten*, p. 67.

45 Always 'Dear Dickie' – Cunningham was the only admiral to address him by his surname. Sir Dudley Pound to Lord Louis Mountbatten, 19 September 1936 and 1 December 1939, Mountbatten papers, MB1/A111.

46 Mountbatten in Terraine, *The Life and Times of Lord Mountbatten*, pp. 57–8; Ziegler, *Mountbatten*, p. 60.

47 Terraine, *The Life and Times of Lord Mountbatten*, p. 67; Hough, *Mountbatten*, pp. 67–8; Captain Gilbert Stephenson quoted in Ziegler, *Mountbatten.*, pp. 76–7.

48 Correspondence with Douglas Fairbanks, 1923–4, Mountbatten papers, M1/A107; Mountbatten quoted in Terraine, *The Life and Times of Lord Mountbatten*, p. 69; Ziegler, *Mountbatten*, pp. 76–7.

49 Morgan, *Edwina Mountbatten*, pp. 151–78.

50 Ibid., pp. 180–1; Material re HM Signals School, Portsmouth, 1924–5, Mountbatten papers, M1/A88/1.

51 Ibid., pp. 184–5; Ziegler, *Mountbatten*, pp. 77–8 and 109; Hough, *Mountbatten*, pp. 68–9; Mountbatten, *Mountbatten Eighty Years in Pictures*, p. 109; Jonathan Glancey, *Spitfire The Biography* (Atlantic Books, London, 2006), pp. 24–5. Appropriately Lawrence's home base was RAF Mount Batten in Plymouth.

52 Terraine, *The Life and Times*, p. 69; Chatfield, *The Navy and Defence*, p. 159.

53 Morgan, *Edwina*, pp. 188–9, 62, 77–8; Ziegler (ed.), *The Diaries of Lord Louis Mountbatten 1920–1922*, 3 February 1922, p. 250; Hough, *Mountbatten*, pp. 77–8; Mountbatten quoted in Terraine, *The Life and Times of Lord Mountbatten*, pp. 74–5; Herbert Spencer and 'Marco', *An Introduction to Polo* (J.A. Allen, London, 2000).

54 Lord Brabourne quoted in Hoey, *Mountbatten The Private Story*, p. 210.

55 A composite portrait drawn from ibid., pp. 92–4; Morgan, p. 140 and passim; Ziegler, *Mountbatten*, particularly pp. 50–2, 111 and passim.

56 Mountbatten quoted in Terraine, *The Life and Times of Lord Mountbatten*, p. 63; Ziegler, *Mountbatten.*, p. 79.

57 Lord Louis Mountbatten to Andrew Yates, 13 October 1926, quoted in ibid., p. 80; Lt Commander Peter Kemp in Hough, *Mountbatten*, pp. 77–8.

58 Ibid., pp. 95–9; Morgan, *Edwina*, pp. 200–6; Mountbatten in Terraine, *The Life and Times of Lord Mountbatten*, p. 75; Ziegler, *Mountbatten*, p. 80.

59 Mountbatten telephoned his cousin, Queen Ena, for help, but was put through to a confused Alfonso. The Royal Guard despatched by the King to the Ritz promptly arrested the doctor; and the military governor, arriving in full dress uniform, insisted on overseeing the birth. Morgan, *Edwina*, pp. 209–10; Mountbatten quoted in Terraine, *The Life and Times of Lord Mountbatten*, p. 75–6.

60 Ibid., p. 77.; Morgan, *Edwina*, pp. 209–10; Ziegler, *Mountbatten*, pp. 110–15; Hoey, *Mountbatten The Private Story*, pp. 83–6 and 122–3.

61 Mountbatten quoted in Terraine, *The Life and Times of Lord Mountbatten*, p. 77; Ziegler, *Mountbatten*, pp. 81–2; Material re HM Signal School, Portsmouth, 1929–31, Mountbatten papers, M1/A88/1.

62 McGeogh, *The Princely Sailor*, p. 22. Report of Captain, HM Signal School, Portsmouth, 1 January 1930, quoted in Ziegler, *Mountbatten*, p. 81, and 1931 Admiralty personnel report quoted in Terraine, *The Life and Times of Lord Mountbatten*, p. 77.

Chapter Four

1 Mountbatten quoted in Terraine, *The Life and Times of Lord Mountbatten*, pp. 78–9.

2 Mountbatten, diary, 29 September 1931, quoted in Ziegler, *Mountbatten*, p. 84; Chatfield, *The Navy and Defence,* pp. 242–3; Mountbatten quoted or via invented dialogue in Hough, *Mountbatten*, pp. 91–2; Vice-Admiral Sir Ernle Chatfield recommendation for promotion, 10 October 1932, and Michael Hodges to Lord Mountbatten, 10 September 1970, quoted in Ziegler, op. cit., pp. 85 and 84; Lord Mountbatten to Alfred Temple Patterson, 9 July and 5 October 1970, Mountbatten papers, MB1/K12.

3 Morgan, *Edwina*, pp. 221–3.

4 Ziegler, *Mountbatten*, pp. 83–4; Mountbatten quoted in Terraine, *The Life and Times of Lord Mountbatten*, p. 79. A Lt. J Mansfield Robinson actually came up with the idea of a giant receiver on the *Royal Oak*, connected to a network of local transmitters, but his boss attracted most of the plaudits. The same technical wizard devised a scheme whereby the fleet's film projectors could be adapted for sound at a fraction of the commercial cost. Material re Fleet Wireless Officer, Mediterranean, HMS *Elizabeth*, 1931–2, Mountbatten papers, M1/A88/1.

5 Chatfield, *The Navy and Defence,* pp. 248–9.

6 Morgan, *Edwina*, pp. 250–1, 222–3, and 233–6.

7 Arthur J. Marder, 'The Influence of History on Sea Power: The Royal Navy and the lessons of 1914–1918' in *From the Dardanelles to Oran Studies of the Royal Navy in War and Peace 1915–1940* (OUP, Oxford, 1974), pp. 35–6 and 48; '… the inescapable lesson, of course, was that our failure to make essential signals had been well-nigh disastrous'. Mountbatten quoted in Terraine, *The Life and Times of Lord Mountbatten*, pp. 80–1; Lord Mountbatten, 'Some remarks'; ibid., 'The Battle of Jutland 31st May 1916; Lambert, 'Ruthless Bounder: David Beatty', pp. 373–5.

8   Lord Louis Mountbatten to Dowager Marquess of Milford Haven, 9 July 1934, quoted in Ziegler, *Mountbatten*, p. 87.

9   Reminiscences of H.T. Baillie-Grohman, Thomas Iremonger, E.G. Roper, and Admiral Sir Richard Onslow, quoted in Ziegler, *Mountbatten*, pp. 87–8.

10 For example Admiral Sir William Fisher, Mediterranean Fleet C-in-C, aboard *Daring*, and Somerville aboard *Wishart*: Mountbatten, diary, 9 July 1934, quoted in ibid., p. 88, and Rear-Admiral James F. Somerville to Lord Louis Mountbatten, 6 April 1936, Mountbatten papers, MB1/A111. McGeoch, *The Princely Sailor*, pp. 18–19.

11 Ziegler, *Mountbatten*,, pp. 88–9; Hough, *Mountbatten*, p. 98.

12 E.P. Thompson, *The Making of the English Working Class* (Pelican, London, 1980), second pbk edn, p. 12; Hoey, *Mountbatten The Private Story*, p. 170.

13 Beyond gunnery the only obvious points of comparison between Dickie Mountbatten and Patrick O'Brian's fictional hero, 'Lucky Jack' Aubrey, are a shared passion for new technology, a mutual talent for effective man management, and an ability to fall asleep in minutes. At Combined Operations could O'Brian, in one of his many guises, have ever met the C-in-C?

14 Hough, *Mountbatten*, p. 99; Mountbatten quoted in Terraine, *The Life and Times of Lord Mountbatten*, p. 83. See Chapters Eight and Nine re Baillie-Grohman's criticism of Mountbatten's decision to resurrect the raid on Dieppe.

15 Ibid., p. 83.

16 Ziegler, *Mountbatten*, p. 89.

17 Ibid., pp. 89–90; Hough, *Mountbatten*, p. 101. Hough saw neither Mountbatten nor his father as fitting neatly in to the Royal Navy in the early decades of the last century, seeing their professionalism as a then alien continental characteristic, and speculating that a public school education might have provided 'the peculiar British masculine ethic and style of behaviour' they so clearly lacked. Even more contestable is the author's claim that in the 1930s Mountbatten might have felt more at home in an ultra-efficient, ostensibly apolitical German Navy! Ibid., pp. 101–2.

18 'He took all the fun out of Fleet Regattas because he never left anything for the other chap. He had to have every trophy and then crowed about it.' A 'former colleague' quoted in Hoey, *Mountbatten*, p. 171. Another unnamed source claimed that, to avoid informing the Admiralty, Mountbatten paid the full cost of repairs when the *Wishart* collided with another destroyer in an unauthorised race: Roberts, 'Lord Mountbatten and the Perils of Adrenalin', pp. 57–8.

19 Admiral Viscount Cunningham, *A Sailor's Odyssey The Autobiography of Admiral of the Fleet Viscount Cunningham of Hynhope K.T., G.C.B., O.M., D.S.O.* (Hutchison, London, 1951); Lord Mountbatten quoted in Warner, *Cunningham of Hyndhope*,, pp. 74–5.

20 Michael Simpson, 'Viscount Cunningham of Hyndhope', *Oxford Dictionary of National Biography* (OUP, Oxford, 2004), www.oxforddnb.com ; Warner, *Cunningham of Hyndhope*, pp. 75 and 79; John Winton, *Cunningham The Greatest Admiral Since Nelson* (John Murray, London, 1998), pp. 58–7 and 140–75; Rear-Admiral Andrew Cunningham to Helen Browne [?] October 1938 in Warner, op. cit., pp. 87–8. As C-in-Cs Chatfield and Fisher were equally insistent that the Mediterranean Fleet be highly trained in night fighting: Marder, 'The Influence of History', pp. 36–7.

21 Rear-Admiral Andrew Cunningham to Lord Louis Mountbatten, 2 July 1937, Mountbatten papers, MB1/A109.

22 Rear-Admiral Andrew Cunningham to Lord Louis Mountbatten, 13 April 1936, ibid.; Warner, *Cunningham*, p. 273.

23 The Controller, Admiral Sir Reginald Henderson, was empowered to over-rule a Naval Staff hostile to radical changes in design as a consequence of his close working relationship with the First Sea Lord. Grove, 'Admiral Sir (later Baron) Ernle Chatfield', p. 158. Hough, *Mountbatten*, pp. 102–5. This is a rare occasion when the author's own naval experience

ensures a fuller and more informed account than is available in the official biography. Admiral of the Fleet Lord Mountbatten, memo to author, 1978, in D.K. Brown, *A Century of Naval Construction: the History of the Royal Corps of Naval Constructors 1883–1983* (Conway Maritime Press, London, 1983), pp. 149–50 and 192–3.

24 Ibid.; Pattinson, *Mountbatten and the Men of the Kelly*, pp. 75–6.

25 A.P. Cole to Lord Louis Mountbatten, 17 November 1939, Mountbatten papers, MB1/B5. Cole suggested future contact via his home address and telephone, and enclosed private notes with official communiqués which he urged Mountbatten to destroy. Ibid., 13 November 1939.

26 Rear-Admiral Andrew Cunningham to Lord Louis Mountbatten, 16 September 1935, Mountbatten papers, MB1/A109

27 Kennedy, *The Rise and Fall*, pp. 339–43; Gordon, *British Seapower and Procurement*, pp. 76–95; Roskill, *The Strategy of Sea Power*, pp. 146–8; Schofield, *British Sea Power*, pp. 133–6; Arthur J. Marder, 'The Royal Navy and the Ethiopian Crisis of 1935–1936' in *From the Dardanelles to Oran*, pp. 69–70, 82–7. 'Arguably' under-gunned in that David Edgerton refutes such a suggestion, articulating a now common view that capital expenditure on construction and modernisation of capital ships between the wars remained remarkably high, and ensured the potency and power of the Royal Navy as a global force. David Edgerton, *Warfare State Britain, 1920–1970* (Cambridge University Press, Cambridge, 2006), pbk edn, pp. 33–41.

28 'HMS Wishart Report of Proceedings 21st–24th December 1935 (Visit to Bizerta)', 24 December 1935, ADM116/3398, National Archives; Marder, 'The Royal Navy and the Ethiopian Crisis', pp. 78 and 88–94; Mountbatten quoted in Terraine, *The Life and Times of Lord Mountbatten*, p. 84.

29 Rear-Admiral Andrew Cunningham to Lord Louis Mountbatten, 13 April 1936, Mountbatten papers, MB1/A109. For a detailed account of mid-1930s naval operations in the Mediterranean, see Arthur Marder, 'The Royal Navy and the Ethiopian Crisis of 1935–1936' in *From the Dardanelles to Oran*, pp. 64–104.

30 Edwina left Malta on 31 November 1936 because she was bored not scared, and she needed to recover her children from a supposedly safe hotel in Hungary. Morgan, *Edwina*, p. 247.

31 Ziegler, *Mountbatten*, p. 91; Hough, *Mountbatten*, pp. 106–7; Mountbatten quoted in Terraine, *The Life and Times of Lord Mountbatten*, p. 84; Kennedy, *The Rise and Fall*, p. 342; Reynolds, *Churchill Fighting and Writing the Second World War*, p. 116; Michael Simpson, *A Life of Admiral of the Fleet Andrew Cunningham A Twentieth-Century Naval Leader* (Frank Cass, London, 2004), pp. 32–3.

32 Admiral Dudley Pound, and Rear-Admiral James F. Somerville, to Lord Louis Mountbatten, 19 and 14 September 1936, Mountbatten papers, MB1/A111.

33 Lord Louis to Edwina Mountbatten, 5 February 1936, and Rear-Admiral J.F. Somerville's recommendation for promotion, 27 June 1936, quoted in Ziegler, *Mountbatten*, p. 92; Rear-Admiral James F. Somerville to Lord Louis Mountbatten, 2 July 1937, Mountbatten papers, MB1/A109.

34 Rear-Admiral Andrew Cunningham, and Admiral Sir Roger Keyes, to Lord Louis Mountbatten, 2 and 3 July 1937, ibid.

35 In retirement Mountbatten identified in pencil congratulatory messages from his contemporaries at Dartmouth and those officers previously senior in service that henceforth he outranked! Miscellaneous letters and telegrams, Mountbatten papers, MB1/A44. 30 June 1937 diary entry quoted in Ziegler, *Mountbatten*, p. 98.

36 Mountbatten quoted in Terraine, *The Life and Times of Lord Mountbatten*, p. 85.

37 Commander Connolly Abell-Smith to Lord Louis Mountbatten, 18 January 1936, Mountbatten papers, MB1/A109; Admiral Lord Chatfield, *The Navy and Defence Vol. II: It Might Happen Again* (William Heinemann, London, 1947), p. 102.

38   Air Division paper quoted by Mountbatten in Terraine, *The Life and Times of Lord Mountbatten*, p. 88.

39   Grove, 'Admiral Sir (later Baron) Ernle Chatfield', pp. 164–5; Ziegler, *Mountbatten*, p. 97; Churchill, *The Second World War Volume I*, p. 124. Hoare resigned as Foreign Secretary over the pact agreed with Pierre Laval, but on the understanding that Baldwin would soon restore him to the cabinet. As a former air minister he was sympathetic to the RAF retaining partial control of the FAA, but proved open to persuasion.

40   Marder, 'The Influence of History', pp. 56–7; Bryan M. Raft, 'Admiral David Early Beatty (1919–1927) in Murfett (ed.), *The First Sea Lords*, pp. 134–5; Roskill, *Admiral of the Fleet Earl Beatty*, pp. 317–18.

41   Again this view would be challenged by David Edgerton, arguing that the distinction between adapted and purpose-built carriers was largely immaterial in terms of combat effectiveness, and that the RN remained the premier exponent of naval air power throughout the interwar period. Edgerton, *Warfare State*, pp. 31–2.

42   In theory the western Mediterranean was the responsibility of the French Navy, but after 1935 the Admiralty suspected their ally's operational capability. The 1937 Nyon Conference encouraged Eden to hope the French Navy might boost its presence in the Mediterranean should RN ships be despatched east of Suez. Roskill, *The Strategy of Sea Power*, pp. 148–9 and 150–1; Kennedy, *The Rise and Fall*, pp. 333–4, 338, 340, and 345; Earl of Avon, *The Eden Memoirs: Facing the Dictators* (Cassell, London, 1962), pp. 496–7.

43   Aircraft were designed to fit the carrier, rather than the other way round, and thus compared poorly with RAF monoplane designs. Admiralty-Air Ministry tension re R and D and production was matched by persistent problems over personnel and training. Schofield, *British Sea Power*, pp. 152–4 and 157–8; Grove, *The Royal Navy Since 1815*, pp. 155–7 and 173–6; Ziegler, *Mountbatten*, pp. 97–8; Sean Greenwood, 'Sir Thomas Inskip as Minister for the Co-ordination of Defence, 1936–39' in Paul Smith (ed.), *Government and the Armed Forces in Britain 1856–1990* (Hambledon Press, London, 1996), pp. 164–6.

44   Martin Gilbert, *Winston S. Churchill Vol. V 1931–1939* (Heinemann, London, 1976), pp. 852–3; Churchill, 'Appendix B My Note on the Fleet Air Arm' in *The Second World War Volume I*, pp. 534–6. The memorandum is mistakenly dated 1936. Reynolds, *In Command of History*, pp. 115–16.

45   Sir Samuel Hoare to Lord Louis Mountbatten, 28 May 1937, Mountbatten papers, MB1/A110; A. Duff Cooper, *Old Men Forget The Autobiography of Duff Cooper (Viscount Norwich)* (Rupert Hart-Davis, London, 1954), pp. 209–10 and 218.

46   Greenwood, 'Sir Thomas Inskip', p. 166; Sir Samuel Hoare to Lord Louis Mountbatten, 28 May 1937, quoted in Ziegler, *Mountbatten*, p. 98; Schofield, *British Sea Power*, pp. 158–9.

47   Grove, 'Admiral Sir (later Baron) Ernle Chatfield', pp. 164–5. For an exaggerated assessment, see Hough, *Mountbatten*, pp. 108–9. Ziegler, *Mountbatten*, p. 98.

48   Dinner at Adsdean on 6 November 1936 saw Dickie speak twice with 'David' on the telephone while Edwina entertained the Second Sea Lord. Mountbatten, diary, 13 and 16 October and 6 November 1936, quoted in ibid., p. 99.

49   Marder, 'The Influence of History', pp. 58–60.

50   Number 10 was furious that journalists visiting *Ark Royal* were told that the absence of off-duty sailors was a consequence of fears that Germany was about to launch a pre-emptive strike. Ziegler, *Mountbatten*, p. 100; miscellaneous RNFC early correspondence, Mountbatten papers, MB1/L160.

51   Mountbatten quoted in Terraine, *The Life and Times of Lord Mountbatten*, pp. 94 and 97.

52   Ibid., p. 97. On the history of Typex, see John Terraine, *The Right of the Line The Royal Air Force in the European War 1939–1945* (Wordsworth, London, 1997), pbk edn, pp. 39–43.

53   Schofield, *British Sea Power*, p. 156; Gordon, *British Seapower and Procurement*, pp. 224–5.

54   Ibid.; Ziegler, *Mountbatten*, p. 99; McGeoch, *The Princely Sailor*, pp. 31–2; Mountbatten quoted in Terraine, *The Life and Times of Lord Mountbatten*, pp. 95–6. Mountbatten even

helped Gazda apply to become a British national. He introduced his new friend to leading figures in the National Government, witness a visit to the Air Ministry on 8 July 1938 to lobby Sir Kingsley Wood. A high-level delegation visiting Oerlikon, and photographed extensively by Mountbatten in the mountains above Zurich, included General Lord Gort, the CIGS. Mountbatten papers, MB1/A53. On gunners' and captain's view of the Oerlikons, see Pattinson, *Mountbatten and the Men of the Kelly*, p. 93.

55 Personnel reports of Naval Air Division Deputy Director, 11 April 1938, and of Admiral Kennedy-Purvis, 16 February 1939, quoted in Ziegler, *Mountbatten*, p. 104; 'List of Officers attending 1939 Higher Commanders Course', Mountbatten papers, MB1/A111.

56 'Lord Mountbatten's comments'; Mountbatten quoted in Terraine, *The Life and Times of Lord Mountbatten*, pp. 84–5.

57 Morgan, *Edwina*, pp. 211 and 248; Lady Edwina Mountbatten, 1 January 1936, quoted in Ziegler, *Mountbatten*, p. 117.

58 Arthur Marwick, 'Middle Opinion in the Thirties: Planning, Progress and Political "Agreement"', *English Historical Review*, vol. 71 no. 2, April 1964, pp. 285–98; Smith, 'Harold Macmillan and Munich: the open conspirator' , pp. 235–47.

59 Kenneth Young (ed.) *The Diaries of Sir Robert Bruce Lockhart Vol. 1 1915–1938* (Macmillan, London, 1973), 7 October 1936 and 24 September 1936, pp. 356 and 355–6; Mountbatten quoted in Terraine, *The Life and Times of Lord Mountbatten*, p. 90.

60 Lord Louis Mountbatten to Prince Louis of Hesse [cousin, and cultural attaché, German Embassy], 10 May 1937, quoted in Ziegler, *Mountbatten*, p. 102.

61 Also present were Princess Marina, Duchess of Kent, and a young Prince Philip, the future Duke of Edinburgh travelling to the funeral from his German-Scottish public school, Gordonstoun. Petropolous, *Royals and the Reich*, pp. 94–5 and 281.

62 Kazuo Ishiguro, *The Remains of the Day* (Faber, London, 1989). Richard Griffiths, *Fellow Travellers of the Right British Enthusiasts for Nazi Germany 1933–39* (OUP, Oxford, 1983), pbk edn, pp. 184–6, 224–5 and 339–40; documentation re JEC protest meeting at Whitechapel Art Gallery, 1 April 1933, and Aubrey Stanhope to Lord Mount Temple, 4 April 1933, Broadlands archives, BR81/15. 'His wrong-headed approach of appeasement to the Nazis caused his daughter, Edwina, and the family, great distress.' From a note by Lord Mountbatten, 27 June 1966, on the back of a signed photograph of Hitler given to Lord Mount Temple 30 years earlier. Mountbatten papers, MB1/A110.

63 Re Mount Temple and the AGF, see Martin Pugh, *Hurrah for the Blackshirts! Fascists and Fascism in Britain Between the Wars* (Jonathan Cape, London, 2005), pp. 269–71 and 277–78.

64 According to Hough Mountbatten claimed two assets: 'I was of German descent and, like my father, understood the German mind. I was well-informed, and thanks to my position and my relationship to the Court, I had the ear of powerful men – others as well as Winston.' Hough, *Mountbatten*, p. 111.

65 Anthony Adamthwaite, 'The British Government and the media 1937–1938', *Journal of Contemporary History*, vol. 18 no. 2 , 1983, pp. 281–97; Lynne Olson, *Troublesome Young Men The Churchill Conspiracy of 1940* (Bloomsbury, London, 2007/2008), pbk edn, pp. 118–25.

66 Lord Louis Mountbatten, 'Synopsis for "March of Time" film on the Royal Navy', 22 March 1939, and Raimund von Hofmannsthal to Lord Louis Mountbatten, 18 and 25 March 1939, Mountbatten Papers, MB1/A67. S.P. MacKenzie, *British War Films 1939–1946* (London, 2001), p. 63. After the newsreel was finally released Mountbatten insisted on the Royal Navy's need to generate yet more film publicity: Nigel Nicolson (ed.), *Harold Nicolson Diaries and Letters 1939–45* (Collins, London, 1967), 7 December 1939, pp. 47–48.

67 *The Life and Times of Lord Louis Mountbatten 2: The Azure Main* (Peter Morley, Thames TV, UK, 1969).

68 On the historiography of Appeasement see individual national and thematic essays in Robert Boyce and Joseph A. Maiolo (eds), *The Origins of World War Two The Debate Continues* (Palgrave, Basingstoke, 2003). 'Cato', *Guilty Men* (Victor Gollancz/Penguin,

London, 1940/1998), pp. 7–14. Frank Owen, the *Evening Standard* editor who, along with fellow Beaverbrook journalists Michael Foot and Peter Howard, comprised 'Cato', was later recruited by Mountbatten to edit *SEAC*, the forces newspaper distributed across the south-east Asia theatre of operation. *In Which We Serve* (Noel Coward/David Lean, Two Cities, UK, 1942).

69 Mountbatten in *The Life and Times of Lord Mountbatten 3: The Stormy Winds* (Peter Morley, Rediffusion, UK, 1969).

70 Mountbatten quoted in Terraine, *The Life and Times of Lord Mountbatten*, p. 93; A. Duff Cooper to Lord Louis Mountbatten, 9 September 1938 and 17 March 1939, Mountbatten papers, MB1/A88/1 and MB1/A109.

71 Duff Cooper, *Old Men Forget*, p. 243; Lord Louis Mountbatten to A. Duff Cooper, 1 October 1939, quoted in ibid., p. 245. The same letter was quoted at length by Mountbatten himself in Terraine, *The Life and Times of Lord Mountbatten*, p. 95, and in Ziegler, *Mountbatten*, p. 104, clearly with a view to confirming its author's anti-appeasement credentials. On the Navy's respect for Duff Cooper as a service minister prepared to fight his corner, see Greenwood, 'Sir Thomas Inskip', pp. 178–80, and John Charmley, *Duff Cooper The Authorized Biography* (Weidenfeld and Nicolson, London, 1986), pp. 105–12.

72 Duff Cooper papers, Churchill Archives Centre, Cambridge. Charmley, *Duff Cooper*, pp. 108 and 132–4. For an argument that in the *Evening Standard* Duff Cooper did a disservice to the Royal Navy by portraying the Treasury in an unfairly harsh light, see Gordon, *British Seapower and Procurement*, pp. 259–60.

73 Avon papers, University of Birmingham; Lord Avon in *The Life and Times of Lord Mountbatten 3: The Stormy Winds*; Avon, *Facing the Dictators*, passim.

74 Anthony Eden in a 1922 letter to Lady Eden, and in a diary entry for 6 February 1955, quoted in D.R. Thorpe, *Eden The Life and Times of Anthony Eden First Lord of Avon, 1897–1977* (Chatto and Windus, London, 2003), pp. 52 and 458; Lady Mountbatten quoted in Morgan, *Edwina*, p. 461. On the King's and Queen's view of Eden, see Roberts, *Eminent Churchillians*, p. 16.

75 Lord Mountbatten, 1972 correspondence with Lord Avon, and briefing card on Suez, Mountbatten papers, MB1/L149. Derogatory typed references to 'Eden going dotty' were amended in pencil to neutral observations on the PM's state of mind. On the two men's final clashes, see Chapter Eleven.

76 Admiral of the Fleet Lord Mountbatten, 'Meeting with Mr. Eden and Lord Cranborne at Broadlands – September 1938', 10 September 1964, Allan Campbell-Johnson papers, MS350/A2096/20; Ziegler, *Mountbatten*, p. 103.

77 Anthony Eden to Lord Mountbatten, 22 August 1938, Mountbatten papers, MB1/A109.

78 For a sustained argument that Eden desired an early return to office, hence his determination 'to give no new overt offence to Chamberlain and in no way to rival Churchill as a critic', see David Carlton, *Anthony Eden A Biography* (Allen Lane, London, 1981), pp. 142–50; and Olson, *Troublesome Young Men*, pp. 109, 132, and 180–3. A.J.P. Taylor, no admirer of Eden, suggested *Facing the Dictators* should be retitled 'Making faces at the dictators'.

79 'He [Churchill] knew I backed him through thick and thin when his voice was crying in the wilderness against Hitler and Mussolini, and so our relationship was really rather extraordinary ...': Lord Mountbatten to Captain Stephen Roskill, 4 October 1976, Mountbatten papers, MB1/K20B.

80 Mountbatten, 'Meeting with Mr. Eden and Lord Cranborne at Broadlands – September 1938'.

81 Robert Rhodes James, *Anthony Eden* (Weidenfeld and Nicolson, London, 1986), pp. 213–17; Duff Cooper, *Old Men Forget*, p. 250.

82 Morgan, *Edwina*, pp. 273–6.

83   Board of Admiralty signal to the Fleet, 3 September 1939, in Churchill, *The Second World War Volume I*, pp. 320–1. The new First Lord was in the War Cabinet, unlike Eden, a reluctant Dominions Secretary.

Chapter Five

1   Lord Louis Mountbatten to Lady Edwina Mountbatten, 2 September 1939, quoted in Ziegler, *Mountbatten*, p. 124.
2   Roskill, *Churchill and the Admirals*, pp. 93–4.
3   Hough, p. 118; Nicolson (ed.), *Harold Nicolson*, 7 December 1939, p. 47; Churchill, *The Second World War Volume I*, pp. 364–5 and 406–7.
4   Increased contact was partly the consequence of Edwina's early wartime work with the Depot for Knitted Garments for the RN, chaired by Lady Betty Pound. Morgan, *Edwina Mountbatten*, p. 278.
5   Reynolds, *In Command of History*, pp. 113–19; Nicolson (ed.), *Harold Nicolson*, 7 December 1939, p. 47.
6   Lord Louis Mountbatten to Anthony Eden, 15 February 1940, and Anthony Eden to Lord Louis Mountbatten, 8 January 1940, quoted in Ziegler, *Mountbatten*, p. 134; Mountbatten's 1975 reminiscences in Hough, *Mountbatten*, pp. 118–20.
7   In an attempt to induce cabinet action Eden was urged to back Churchill's combative approach over violation of Norwegian neutrality. Lord Louis Mountbatten to Anthony Eden, 15 February 1940, Mountbatten papers, MB1/A110.
8   '... no construction of HA [i.e. high-angle anti-aircraft] fire can be countenanced which might prejudice LA [i.e. low-angle ship-to-ship] performance until such time as aircraft threaten the successful accomplishment of destroyers' main object – the delivery of torpedo attack ...', i.e. 1914 thinking: Admiralty specification quoted in Hough, *Bless Our Ship*, p. 46; Rear-Admiral A.F. Pugsley, *Destroyer Man* (Weidenfeld and Nicolson, London, 1957), pp. 33–4.
9   Ibid., pp. 27–9.
10 Poolman, *The Kelly*, pp. 91–2. Mountbatten did insist on a drying-room for the ratings. For a former signalman's amusing, even iconoclastic account of day to day life on the *Kelly* mess decks see John Knight, *The Kelly: Mountbatten's Ship* (John Knight, London, 1997). Knight painted a picture of culinary chaos in the galley, and a general air of foreboding every time 'Louis' promised his hapless crew they would soon see action.
11 For a full list of yards spread around Britain building 'K' class ships, see McGeoch, *The Princely Sailor*, p. 34.
12 Mountbatten quoted in Terraine, *The Life and Times of Lord Mountbatten*, p. 99; Pattinson, *Mountbatten and the Men of the 'Kelly'*, pp. 76–7
13 Rear Admiral Philip Burnett quoted in ibid., pp. 75–7; Hough, *Bless Our Ship*, pp. 48–9; correspondence between Lord Louis Mountbatten and Lt-Commander Philip Burnett, 1938–40, Mountbatten papers, MB1/B1 and MB1/B2.
14 Correspondence between Lord Louis Mountbatten and Lt-Commander Mike Evans, 1938–40, ibid.
15 Ziegler, *Mountbatten*, p. 122.
16 Captain Edward Dunsterville quoted in Pattinson, *Mountbatten and the Men of the 'Kelly'*, pp. 78–81. Although loyal to Mountbatten, Dunsterville saw all too clearly the feet of clay; see his healthy scepticism in Roberts, 'Lord Mountbatten and the Perils of Adrenalin', pp. 59–60.
17 Captain Alastair Robin quoted in op. cit., p. 81.
18 Arrangements for the visit of A.P. Cole and Sir Edward Bridges: Lord Louis Mountbatten to Lt. Alastair Robin, 9 June 1939, Mountbatten papers, MB1/B1.
19 Poolman, *The Kelly*, pp. 37–9.

20 Rocky Wilkins and Ron Hall quoted in Pattinson, *Mountbatten and the Men of the 'Kelly'*, pp. 43–4.

21 The RNFC's Arthur Jarratt arrived in Hebburn 'very anxious to see how a film programme can be worked on a small ship': Lord Louis Mountbatten to Lt Alastair Robin, 15 May and 9 June 1939, Mountbatten papers, MB1/B8 and MB1/B1. A petty officer edited the daily *KDF* [K Destroyer Flotilla] *News*.

22 Kinross/Mountbatten begins, 'In my experience, I have always found that you cannot have an efficient ship unless you have a happy ship, and you cannot have a happy ship unless you have an efficient ship. That is the way I intend to start this commission, and that is the way I intend to go on …': *In Which We Serve* (Noel Coward/David Lean, Two Cities, UK, 1942).

23 Mountbatten quoted in Terraine, *The Life and Times of Lord Mountbatten*, p. 99.

24 Ibid.; diary of CPO[1939–41, Able later Leading Seaman] Sid Mosses, sent to Mountbatten in 1977 and replicated in Pattinson, *Mountbatten and the Men of the 'Kelly'*, pp. 21–31. A later example of Mountbatten leading by example was cleaning his torpedoed ship of body parts in Hebburn dry dock, May 1940: reminiscence of CPO H.V. Rogers in Hough, *Mountbatten*, p. 124.

25 Mountbatten quoted in Terraine, *The Life and Times of Lord Mountbatten*, p. 99; Poolman, *The Kelly*, pp. 60–1 – and assumed by both Philip Ziegler and Richard Hough to be the correct version of events.

26 Ibid, pp. xi–xii; Admiral Lord Louis Mountbatten, 'Preface', ibid., p. vi.

27 Rear Admiral Philip Burnett quoted in Pattinson, *Mountbatten and the Men of the 'Kelly'*, pp. 199–200; Ziegler, *Mountbatten*, pp. 124–5; Hough, *Bless Our Ship*, pp. 58–9.

28 Martin Gilbert, *Finest Hour Winston S. Churchill 1939–1941 Volume VI* (William Heinemann, London, 1983), pp. 12–13; reminiscence of Captain Edward Dunsterville in Ziegler, *Mountbatten*, p. 125

29 Roskill, *Churchill and the Admirals*, p. 94; Churchill, *The Second World War Volume I*, pp. 362–3.

30 Captain S.W. Roskill, *The Navy at War 1939–1945* (Collins, London, 1960), pp. 41–2.

31 Hough, *Bless Our Ship*, pp. 64–6.

32 Ibid., pp. 66–7; Hough, *Mountbatten*, p. 116; Morgan, *Edwina Mountbatten*, pp. 274–5.

33 Ziegler, *Mountbatten*, p. 126.

34 Reminiscences of Captain Edward Dunsterville in ibid., and in Hough, *Bless Our Ship*, p. 68.

35 Ziegler, *Mountbatten*, pp. 126–7.

36 A.P. Cole to Lord Louis Mountbatten, 13 November 1939, Mountbatten papers, MB1/B5.

37 Some of the ship's company heard Joyce on Berlin Radio correctly place the *Kelly* back on the Tyne. Poolman, *The Kelly*, p. 102.

38 Pugsley, *Destroyer Man*, pp. 30–1.

39 Rear Admiral Philip Burnett quoted in Pattinson, *Mountbatten and the Men of the 'Kelly'*, p. 199. Mountbatten, exaggerating the roll and reducing the speed, recalled that, 'I left it rather late and I thought the Luftwaffe would be on our trail …': commentary on Mosses diary, 1977, replicated in Pattinson, *Mountbatten and the Men of the 'Kelly'*, p. 32.

40 Morgan, *Edwina Mountbatten*, p. 276.

41 Admiral Lord Louis Mountbatten to W.E. Stoneham, 3 February 1965, Mountbatten papers, MB1/B11A; Hough, *Bless Our Ship*, pp. 69–70.

42 Mountbatten quoted in Terraine, *The Life and Times of Lord Mountbatten*, p. 99.

43 Hough, *Bless Our Ship*, p. 70; Ziegler, *Mountbatten*, p. 127.

44 Mountbatten quoted in Terraine, *The Life and Times of Lord Mountbatten*, p. 101; Poolman, *The Kelly*, pp. 106–7.

45 Ibid.; reminiscence of Captain Maurice Butler-Bowdon in Ziegler, *Mountbatten*, p. 127.

46 Ibid., p. 128: Mountbatten at 1978 Kelly Reunion Association annual dinner quoted in Pattinson, *Mountbatten and the Men of the 'Kelly'*, p. 161.

47 Mountbatten quoted in Terraine, *The Life and Times of Lord Mountbatten*, p. 101.

48 Poolman, *The Kelly*, pp. 106–7; speech replicated in Hough, *Bless Our Ship*, p. 71, and Ziegler, *Mountbatten*, pp. 127–8.

49 Mountbatten complained loudly on learning that *Kingston*'s captain had been admonished for his magnanimous treatment of U-35's rescued crew. McGeoch, *The Princely Sailor*, p. 38.

50 Morgan, *Edwina Mountbatten*, p. 276.

51 Ibid., pp. 279–81.

52 Hough, *Bless Our Ship*, p. 73.

53 Diary of Vice-Admiral Sir Alastair Ewing quoted in Ziegler, *Mountbatten*, pp. 128–9; McGeoch, *The Princely Sailor*, pp. 38–9.

54 Ibid., pp. 36 and 38; Pattinson, *Mountbatten and the Men of the 'Kelly'*, p. 56.

55 Roskill, *The Navy at War 1939–1945*, p. 66. Warburton-Lee was an old friend and rival from the Mediterranean Fleet whose death greatly distressed Mountbatten, to whom Hough attributed the spurious comment, 'What a way to go!' Hough, *Bless Our Ship*, p. 80.

56 Roskill, *Churchill and the Admirals*, pp. 100–2 and 295–9; Lord Louis Mountbatten to Anthony Eden, 15 February 1940, ibid.

57 Diaries of Captain R.A.B. [later Admiral Sir Ralph] Edwards, 7 April 1940, quoted in Roskill, *Churchill and the Admirals*, p. 101.

58 Ibid., p. 143.

59 Sir John Colville, *The Fringes of Power Downing Street Diaries 1939–1955* (Hodder and Stoughton, London, 1985), 10 May 1940, pp. 121–3; Robert Rhodes James (ed.), *Chips The Diaries of Sir Henry Channon* (Penguin, London, 1970), pbk edn, 10 May 1940, pp. 121–3.

60 Churchill, *The Second World War Volume I*, pp. 465–519. For a sharply critical assessment of Churchill's performance see Roskill, *Churchill and the Admirals*, pp. 97–108. Reynolds, *In Command of History*, pp. 121–6.

61 Roskill, *The Navy at War 1939–1945*, p. 68; Lieutenant-General Sir Adrian Carton de Wiart, *Happy Odyssey* (Jonathan Cape, London, 1950), p. 174; Churchill, *The Second World War Volume I*, p. 500.

62 Roskill also blamed the crude aircraft attack prediction system, the High Angle Control System, but equally crucial was the absence of radar proximity fuses in AA shells until later in the war. Grove, *The Royal Navy since 1915*, p. 186.

63 Diary of Lord Louis Mountbatten, 2 and 4 May 1940, quoted in Ziegler, *Mountbatten*, p. 129; Hough, *Bless Our Ship*, pp. 80–1.

64 McGeoch, *The Princely Sailor*, p. 41; Mountbatten quoted in Terraine, *The Life and Times of Lord Mountbatten*, p. 101.

65 Reminiscence of Captain Edward Dunsterville in Hough, *Bless Our Ship*, p. 82. Carton de Wiart's first but thankfully not last choice of transport was the *Afridi* and not the *Kelly*, presumably to remain with his men as long as possible. Interestingly, the official history praised the courage of the three French transports, and made no mention of the *Kelly*'s role: Captain S.W. Roskill, *The War at Sea 1939–1945 Vol. I The Defensive* (HMSO, London, 1954), pp. 189–90.

66 Morgan, *Edwina Mountbatten*, p. 281.

67 Mountbatten made exaggerated claims for his ability to evade Stuka attacks, as well as insisting that the *Kelly* shot down a Ju87 once free of the fiord – a claim disputed by his officers. Lord Louis Mountbatten quoted in Hough, *Bless Our Ship*, p. 83; Rear Admiral Philip Burnett quoted in Pattinson, *Mountbatten and the Men of the 'Kelly'*, p. 200.

68 In addition eight large merchantmen were lost, including two troopships and two tankers. Roskill, *The Navy at War 1939–1945*, p. 71.

69 While the Royal Navy had 58 cruisers and 100 destroyers in September 1939 (with a nearly 50 per cent increase in total complement intended by the end of 1941), it had only 38 submarines. Roskill, *The Strategy of Sea Power*, pp. 162–3; Kennedy, *The Rise and Fall of British Naval Mastery*, pp. 346–7, 358–9 and 367; Grove, *The Royal Navy since 1915*, pp. 184–7.

70 Lord Louis Mountbatten to Commanding General, *Kandahar*, 17 May 1939, MB1/B11B, Mountbatten papers. The 5th was awash with aristocrats as the Marquess of Graham served on *Kandahar* and the Earl of Antrim on *Kashmir*; and Lord Hugh Beresford succeeded Burnett as the recommissioned *Kelly*'s first lieutenant.

71 Reminiscence of Vice-Admiral Sir Geoffrey Robson in Ziegler, *Mountbatten*, pp. 129–30; Captain (D), Fifth Destroyer Flotilla, 'H.M.S. Kelly Report of Proceedings 8th May–13th May 1940, 20 May 1940, Mountbatten papers, MB1/B11B.

72 Reminiscence of Captain Edward Dunsterville in Hough, *Bless Our Ship*, p. 92; McGeoch, *The Princely Sailor*, p. 42.

73 Ibid.; reminiscences of Vice-Admiral Sir Geoffrey Robson and Captain Edward Dunsterville in Ziegler, *Mountbatten*, pp. 129–30.

74 Ibid.; Captain (D), Fifth Destroyer Flotilla, 'H.M.S. Kelly Report of Proceedings 8th May-13th May 1940, ibid.; Admiral of the Fleet Lord Mountbatten, memo to author, 1978, in Brown, *A Century of Naval Construction*, p. 193; Lord Mountbatten to Countess of Brecknock, 5 June 1973, Mountbatten papers, MB1/B11B.

75 Mountbatten at first believed all on the *Kandahar* presumed there to be no survivors: Captain Lord Louis Mountbatten, 'The Epic of the Kelly', dictated to Lady Patricia Mountbatten, [?] May 1940, ibid.

76 Closing the circle, Mountbatten ordered *Jupiter* to tow HMS *Express* back to harbour. Reminiscences of Vice-Admiral Sir Geoffrey Robson in Ziegler, *Mountbatten*, p. 130, and of Lieutenant C.J. Jones in Hough, *Mountbatten*, p. 125.

77 'Try to imagine for a moment what the plight of the Kelly would have been had the Bulldog not turned up in the fog and darkness.' Mountbatten, 'The Epic of the Kelly', Mountbatten papers, MB1/B11B.

78 Captain (D), Fifth Destroyer Flotilla, 'H.M.S. Kelly Report of Proceedings 8th May–13th May 1940, ibid.

79 Mountbatten quoted in Terraine, *The Life and Times of Lord Mountbatten*, p. 104; Hough, *Bless Our Ship*, pp. 91–2.

80 Morgan, *Edwina Mountbatten*, p. 281.

81 George VI was so impressed by the vindication of longitudinal over transverse strength that he tried but failed to secure Cole a knighthood. Mountbatten, memo to author, 1978, in Brown, *A Century of Naval Construction*, p. 194; Lord Mountbatten to Countess of Brecknock, 5 June 1973, ibid.; Mountbatten quoted in Terraine, *The Life and Times of Lord Mountbatten*, p. 104.

82 Ibid., pp. 104–5; Mountbatten, diary, 13 and 15 May 1940, quoted in Ziegler, *Mountbatten*, pp. 131–2; HMS *Kelly* [and *Javelin* – two letters] ratings' correspondence, Mountbatten papers, MB1/B9.

83 Diary of Lady Edwina Mountbatten, May–June 1940, quoted in Morgan, *Edwina Mountbatten*, pp. 281–2; ibid., pp. 283–5 and 289–90; Ziegler, *Mountbatten*, pp. 134–6.

84 The total attendance of officers and of men respectively, and their response to individual films, embraced the whole flotilla and was recorded in detail. 'Features – ships' reports up to 31st July 1941', Mountbatten papers, MB1/B8.

85 Reminiscence of Captain Maurice Butler-Bowdon in Ziegler, *Mountbatten*, p. 127; Pattinson, *Mountbatten and the Men of the 'Kelly'*, p. 45; Lord Louis to Lady Edwina Mountbatten [no date], quoted in Morgan, *Edwina Mountbatten*, p. 288.

332 MOUNTBATTEN

332 MOUNTBATTEN

86 Hitler postponed 'Operation Sealion' indefinitely on 17 September 1940. Pugsley, *Destroyer Man*, pp. 49–50. Captain (D) would be accompanied on the bridge by his flotilla staff, notably his signals officer.

87 Ibid., p. 50; anonymous admiral quoted by Mountbatten in Terraine, *The Life and Times of Lord Mountbatten*, p. 104.

88 Captain (D), Fifth Destroyer Flotilla, 'H.M.S. Kelly Report of Proceedings 8th May–13th May 1940, ibid.; reminiscence of Vice-Admiral Sir Charles Hughes Hallett in Ziegler, *Mountbatten*, p. 132.

89 Reminiscence of Commander B.P. Skinner [salvage officer, 1940] in ibid., p. 131.

90 'British grit in a British ship BEAT ALL', *Daily Mirror*, 7 December 1940.

91 Lawson Carr, 'Sailor on Horseback is Destroyer Hero', *Everybody's Weekly*, 19 July 1941.

92 Captain Philip Vian, and Admiral Sir Charles Forbes, to Captain Lord Louis Mountbatten, 4 June 1940, and 31 May 1940, Mountbatten papers, MB1/B9.

93 Reminiscence of Vice-Admiral Sir Charles Hughes Hallett, and Admiral Sir Charles Forbes quoted, in Ziegler, *Mountbatten*, p. 132.

94 Lord Louis to Lady Edwina Mountbatten, 13 August 1940, and to King George VI, 19 October 1940, quoted in ibid., pp. 132–3 and 137.

95 1941 New Year's Honours List *Gazette* citation quoted in Bob Whinney, *The U-Boat Peril An Anti-Submarine Commander's War* (Blandford Press, Poole, 1986), p. 63; Lord Louis to Lady Edwina Mountbatten, 2 January 1941, quoted in Ziegler, *Mountbatten*, p. 140. Roskill, *Churchill and the Admirals*, pp. 118–22.

96 Encouraged by George VI in his letter to Churchill of 29 October 1940 quoted in Roberts, 'Lord Mountbatten and the Perils of Adrenalin', p. 62.

97 Mountbatten, diary, 9 December 1940, and Lord Louis to Lady Edwina Mountbatten, 11 December 1940, quoted in Ziegler, *Mountbatten*, p. 139. The PM's official biographer erroneously placed Mountbatten at Chequers a week later: Gilbert, *Finest Hour*, p. 938; Colville, *The Fringes of Power*, 14–15 December 1940, pp. 314–15.

98 Ziegler, *Mountbatten*, p. 140.

99 Commander Henry King [HMS *Kashmir*], quoted in Captain Maurice Butler-Bowdon (ed.), 'The action between British and German Destroyers off the Lizard: November 29th 1940', August 1966, Mountbatten papers, MB1/B11D.

100 Ziegler, *Mountbatten*, pp. 137–8; Pugsley, *Destroyer Man*, pp. 52–4; McGeoch, *The Princely Sailor*, p. 43.

101 Account of the engagement based upon: ibid., pp. 46–8; Butler-Bowdon (ed.), 'The action between British and German Destroyers off the Lizard: November 29th 1940', and Captain Lord Louis Mountbatten, 'Report [No. 0320.U.] of proceedings of destroyer action on the morning of 29th November 1940', Mountbatten papers, MB1/B11D; and Pugsley, *Destroyer Man*, pp. 55–63.

102 Ziegler suggested that the noise of the 5th's destroyers approaching at speed prompted the Germans to act swiftly, but efficient radar was the key to their alertness. Ziegler, *Mountbatten*, p. 139.

103 Hough, *Bless Our Ship*, p. 103; Pugsley, *Destroyer Man*, pp. 55–63; Commander Henry King, quoted in Butler-Bowdon (ed.), 'The action between British and German Destroyers off the Lizard: November 29th 1940'.

104 Mountbatten, 'Report [No. 0320.U.].

105 Whinney [in attendance with Vian], *The U-Boat Peril*, p. 63; Admiral Dunbar Naismith and 1940 Admiralty Docket, quoted in Butler-Bowdon (ed.), 'The action between British and German Destroyers off the Lizard: November 29th 1940'.

106 'Lord Mountbatten's comments on Commander Bousfield's "The Story of H.M.S. Kelly and Captain (D) 5th Destroyer Flotilla"', and Admiral Lord Louis Mountbatten to Lieutenant A.G.G. Vanrenen [*Javelin* sub-lieutenant, and NI interrogator of Bartel],

6 November 1947, and to Captain Maurice Butler-Bowdon, 13 September 1971, Mountbatten papers, MB1/B11.

107 Admiral Lord Louis Mountbatten to Captain Maurice Butler-Bowdon, 23 July 1971, and to Lieutenant A.G.G. Vanrenen, 23 June 1976; 'Night action in the Channel on 29th November 1940. Recollections of Captain (then Lieutenant) Butler-Bowdon', 23 September 1971; ibid.

108 Hough, *Bless Our Ship*, p. 103; Ziegler, *Mountbatten*, p. 139; McGeogh, *The Princely Sailor*, pp. 47–8. Phillips had clashed with Mountbatten in December 1939 when the latter refused to take responsibility for the *Kelly* being disabled by a mine. Commander Robin Bousfield, 'The Story of H.M.S. Kelly and Captain (D) 5th Destroyer Flotilla', Mountbatten papers, MB1/B11E.

Chapter Six

1 Morgan, *Edwina Mountbatten*, pp. 290–5.

2 Ziegler, *Mountbatten*, p. 140. Leading Signalman John Knight, 'wasn't the only one who wasn't keen on going back to the Kelly. One reaction was "What! And get blown up again?"'. Knight, *The Kelly: Mountbatten's Ship*, p. 15.

3 Poolman, *The Kelly*, pp. 148–9.

4 Gilbert, *Winston S. Churchill Volume III*, p. 148. The First Lord already despised Beresford for his antipathy towards Jackie Fisher.

5 Pattinson, *Mountbatten and the Men of the 'Kelly'*, p. 47; 'L.M.', 'Obituary: Personal Tributes – Lt. Lord Hugh Beresford RN', *The Times*, 16 July 1941; Poolman, *The Kelly*, pp. 150–3 and 160–1.

6 Ibid.; Hough, *Bless Our Ship*, pp. 107–8.

7 The twin Oerlikon AA cannon fired 500 HE tracer shells a minute, at twice the muzzle velocity of its rivals. Between 1950 and 1979 Mountbatten wrote over 800 letters to Wilkins re the KRA. Poolman, *The Kelly*, p. 170; Pattinson, *Mountbatten and the Men of the 'Kelly'*, pp. 43–4, 58–61, 66–73 and 135–46. For West's memoir and his captain's response, see ibid., pp. 89–93 and 119–20. Years later Mountbatten arranged for West's widow to scatter his ashes from an admiral's barge. Ibid., p. 121.

8 Grove, *The Royal Navy since 1815*, p. 191; Roskill, *The Navy at War 1939–45*, pp. 123–4, and *The War at Sea 1939–1945*, pp. 373–9.

9 Lord Louis Mountbatten's account of events in Bousfield, 'The Story of HMS Kelly'; Ziegler, *Mountbatten*, p. 141; Hough, *Bless Our Ship*, pp. 110–12; Roskill, *The War at Sea 1939–1945*, pp. 376–9. On Roskill's failure to mention the *Kelly*'s role at Namsos, see Chapter Five footnote 66 – the ship has only two entries in the index of *The War at Sea 1939–1945 Vol. I*.

10 The *Abdiel* laid over 300 mines. Ibid., p. 393; Lord Louis Mountbatten's account of events in Bousfield, 'The Story of HMS Kelly'; Hough, *Bless Our Ship*, pp. 111–12.

11 Ibid., pp. 113–14.

12 Roskill, *The War at Sea 1939–1945*, pp. 241–5 and 419–24, and *Churchill and the Admirals*, pp. 150–84. Matapan was another battle just missed by Mountbatten, who later claimed the 5th received such a warm welcome on arriving from Gibraltar as 'we were the first to do so for a long time', thereby ignoring the convoy that slipped in to Valletta on 23 March 1941. Mountbatten quoted in Terraine, *The Life and Times of Lord Mountbatten*, p. 104. Re civil-military tensions arising out of Mers el-Kebir, see Arthur J. Marder, 'Oran, 3 July 1940: Mistaken Judgement, Tragic Misunderstanding, or Cruel Necessity' in *From Dardanelles to Oran Studies of the Royal Navy in War and Peace 1915–1940* (Oxford University Press, Oxford, 1974), pp. 179–288.

13 Captain Lord Louis Mountbatten to Robert Neville, 8 May 1941, quoted in Ziegler, *Mountbatten*, p. 142.

14   Ibid.; Rear Admiral G.W.G. Simpson, *Periscope View* (Macmillan, London, 1972), p. 139; Mountbatten quoted in Terraine, *The Life and Times of Lord Mountbatten*, pp. 104–5. In a test of nerve the then Commander George Simpson had to brief a freshly arrived Lord Louis as the bombs fell around them. Finally commonsense prevailed. Mountbatten's official biographer noted that in old age he simply could not resist writing on the fly-leaf of *Periscope View* that, 'As soon as Simpson had left the shelter I returned to the *Kelly*'. Ziegler, *Mountbatten*, p. 141.

15   McGeogh, *The Princely Sailor*, pp. 49–50.

16   Roskill, *The Navy at War 1939–45*, pp. 149–51; Hough, *Bless Our Ship*, pp. 110–12; James Holland, *Fortress Malta An Island Under Siege 1940–1943* (Phoenix, London, 2004), pp. 34–5, 64–5, 158, and 298–301; Captain Lord Louis Mountbatten to Robert Neville, 8 May 1941, quoted in Ziegler, *Mountbatten*, p. 142; Monckton in 1947 on his friendship with Mountbatten, see Lord Birkenhead, *Walter Monckton: the life of Viscount Monckton of Brenchley* (Weidenfeld and Nicolson, London, 1969), p. 226. While Mountbatten's postwar correspondence with Mabel Strickland is deposited in the papers at the University of Southampton, it's noticeable that there are no letters from the first half of the 1940s.

17   Robin Broadhurst, 'Admiral Sir Dudley Pound 1939–1943' in Murfett (ed.), *The First Sea Lords From Fisher to Mountbatten*, p. 198; Admiral A.B. Cunningham to Admiral Sir Dudley Pound, 26 April 1941, in Michael Simpson (ed.), *The Cunningham Papers Selections from the private and official correspondence of Admiral of the Fleet Viscount Cunningham of Hyndhope, O.M., K.T., G.C.B., D.S.O. and two bars Vol. 1 The Mediterranean Fleet, 1939–42* (Ashgate/Navy Records Society, Aldershot, 1999), p. 359.

18   Captain Lord Louis Mountbatten to Vice-Admiral Phillips [including Cunningham's warning and promise], 16 May 1941, quoted in Ziegler, *Mountbatten*, p. 142; Admiral A.B. Cunningham to Admiral Sir Dudley Pound, 11 March and 18 May 1941, in Simpson (ed.), *The Cunningham Papers*, pp. 301 and 406: in the first letter Mountbatten was rejected as a potential Chief of Staff, MF, through being 'very junior still' and not as sound as his successful rival; Hough, *Bless Our Ship*, pp. 136–7.

19   Roskill, *The War at Sea 1939–1945*, pp. 440–2.

20   Hough, *Bless Our Ship*, pp. 152–3; Ziegler, *Mountbatten*, pp. 143 and 145. 'Account of the sinking of H.M.S. "Kelly" on 23rd May 1941 in the Battle of Crete given by the captain, Lord Louis Mountbatten, to his sister, the Queen of Sweden', 1941 – amended 1966, Mountbatten papers, MB1/B11E. With the *Kelly* sunk, her captain still contrived to claim compensation for lost kit worth £420 – an unusually large sum but, he insisted, a conservative estimate: Captain Lord Louis Mountbatten to the Secretary of the Admiralty, [?] July 1941, ibid., MB1/B8.

21   Mountbatten quoted in Terraine, *The Life and Times of Lord Mountbatten*, p. 105; Hough, *Bless Our Ship*, pp. 149–56; Admiral Sir Andrew Cunningham, 'The effects of German intervention, 1941', in Simpson (ed.), *The Cunningham Papers*, pp. 423–4 and 432–3. Cunningham judged the break up of a concentrated force in order to rescue survivors a key tactical error, and the decision to do so effectively ended the career of the admiral commanding the squadron: ibid., p. 423.

22   Ibid., p. 434; Roskill, *The War at Sea 1939–1945*, p. 443.

23   Admiral Sir Andrew Cunningham quoted in Warner, *Admiral of the Fleet The Life of Sir Charles Lambe*, p. 101; Roskill, *Churchill and the Admirals*, p. 185; Mountbatten quoted in Trefor Evans (ed.)/Lord Killearn [Sir Miles Lampson], *The Killearn Diaries 1934–1946* (Sidgwick and Jackson, London, 1972), 31 May 1941, p. 180: Air Marshal Sir Arthur Longmore made way as Air Officer C-in-C, ME, for Arthur Tedder.

24   Mountbatten quoted in Terraine, *The Life and Times of Lord Mountbatten*, p. 105.

25   Ibid., pp. 106–7; 'Account of the sinking of H.M.S. "Kelly" on 23rd May 1941'. The 4,500 word letter to Queen Louise of Sweden is one of at least six published or unpublished,

formal or personal, accounts Mountbatten either wrote or dictated between 1941 and 1969: see manuscripts in folder MB1/B11E of the Mountbatten papers.

26 Ibid.

27 Ibid.; Pattinson, *Mountbatten and the Men of the 'Kelly'*, p. 67: Garner always insisted his remark wasn't aimed at Mountbatten. Captain Edward Dunsterville and Captain Aubrey St Clair-Ford quoted in Hough, *Bless Our Ship*, pp. 160–1, 163 and 164. For Mountbatten's initial claims to have been machine-gunned, see Evans (ed.), *The Killearn Diaries 1934– 1946*, 31 May 1941, p. 180 and Colville, *The Fringes of Power*, 21 July 1941, p. 403; see also the *Kipling* officers' very different versions of events as quoted in Roberts, 'Lord Mountbatten and the Perils of Adrenalin', p. 63. Mountbatten quoted in Murphy, *Last Viceroy*, p. 16; Knight, *The Kelly: Mountbatten's Ship*, p. 25.

28 Hough, *Bless Our Ship*, pp. 164–5; 'Account of the sinking of H.M.S. "Kelly" on 23rd May 1941'.

29 Mountbatten quoted in Terraine, *The Life and Times of Lord Mountbatten*, p. 105; 'Account of the sinking of H.M.S. "Kelly" on 23rd May 1941'; 'Obituary: Personal Tributes – Lt. Lord Hugh Beresford RN', *The Times*, 16 July 1941: on the same day Mountbatten paid tribute to the three other officers lost, including his secretary and the ship's surgeon.

30 'Account of the sinking of H.M.S. "Kelly" on 23rd May 1941'; 1943 wireless testimony of Coxswain William Lawlor quoted in Ziegler, *Mountbatten*, p. 145.

31 Admiral Lord Louis Mountbatten quoted in Warner, *Cunningham of Hyndhope A Memoir*, p. 157.

32 'Account of the sinking of H.M.S. "Kelly" on 23rd May 1941'; Captain Lord Louis Mountbatten to Patricia Mountbatten, 5 June 1941, quoted in Ziegler, *Mountbatten*, p. 147; farewell speech at Dhekelia replicated in Poolman, *The Kelly*, p. 210. 'If I did not have communistic tendencies before, that was when they began to sprout ...': Knight, *The Kelly: Mountbatten's Ship*, p. 26.

33 Evans (ed.), *The Killearn Diaries 1934–1946*, 31 May 1941, p. 180; Vice-Admiral Sir James Somerville to Admiral Sir Andrew Cunningham, 12 June 1941, in Simpson (ed.), *The Cunningham Papers*, p. 479.

34 Travel arrangements for Egypt to UK via Lagos, 1 June 1941, Mountbatten papers, MB1/ B11E.

35 Colville, *The Fringes of Power*, 21 June 1941, p. 403; Gilbert, *Finest Hour*, p. 1118; Mountbatten quoted in Terraine, *The Life and Times of Lord Mountbatten*, pp. 110–11; Morgan, *Edwina Mountbatten*, p. 296.

36 Ibid., pp. 294–5; F. Wooley [Chief Medical Officer], *The One-Hundred and Sixth Annual Report of the Royal South Hants and Southampton Hospital, 1942* (Southern Newspapers Ltd, Southampton, 1942), p. 19.

37 Admiral Lord Louis Mountbatten quoted in Warner, *Cunningham of Hyndhope A Memoir*, p. 157; Cunningham, *A Sailor's Odyssey*, pp. 373–4; Cunningham quoted in Ziegler, *Mountbatten*, p. 146.

38 Ibid., pp. 146–7; Hough, *Bless Our Ship*, pp. 173–5; McGeoch, *The Princely Sailor*, pp. 52–4.

39 For example, Dunsterville's assessment in Roberts, 'Lord Mountbatten and the Perils of Adrenalin', p. 60 and Pattinson, *Mountbatten and the Men of the 'Kelly'*, p. 200. A healthy sceptic re Mountbatten, Philip Burnett nevertheless questioned whether Dunsterville had correctly heard Cunningham's comment to him at dinner, as did another flotilla staff officer James Turnbull: ibid., p. 199.

40 A German broadcast claiming the *Kelly* had been sunk with all hands led Edwina briefly to fear the worst, and for 24 hours the children in New York believed their father to be dead. Signal to 'Lady Louis', 25 May 1941, Mountbatten papers, MB1/B11E; Graham Payn and Sheridan Morley (eds.), *The Noel Coward Diaries* (Weidenfeld and Nicolson/Phoenix, London, 1985/1998), pdk edn, 3 July 1941, p. 7.

41 Ibid.

42 On the filming of *In Which We Serve* see Kevin Brownlow, *David Lean A Biography* (Richard Cohen Books, London, 1996), pp. 151–68, Hoare, *Noel Coward*, pp. 322–31, and best of all, MacKenzie, *British War Films*, pp. 72–81; also Coward's enlightening and yet less than frank version of events in *Future Indefinite* (William Heinemann, London, 1954), reprinted in Noel Coward, *The Autobiography of Noel Coward* (Mandarin, London, 1992), pp. 420–32.

43 Mountbatten's influence is reflected in the speed with which Coward found himself in Plymouth - less than three days after leaving Broadlands with a rough outline of 'White Ensign': Payn and Morley (eds.), *The Noel Coward Diaries*, 28–29 July and 1 August 1941, pp. 9–10; Coward, *The Autobiography*, pp. 480–1 and 426–7.

44 Lean also relied on Mountbatten when reworking the last of Coward's several drafts into a shooting script: 'Even after all these years a sort of tingle of electricity goes through me when I think of that man coming into a room and starting to talk. And he gave us a lot of help behind the scenes.' David Lean quoted in Brownlow, *David Lean*, p. 156.

45 Payn and Morley (eds), *The Noel Coward Diaries*, 28 October and 12 December 1941, pp. 12–13. On Coward's account of his court cases, and Mountbatten and his fellow officers' indifference to 'palpable celebrity-baiting', see Coward, *The Autobiography*, pp. 427–31.

46 Payn and Morley (eds.), *The Noel Coward Diaries*, 17 December 1941, p. 14. 'As usual he was wise and clear, and said that he would handle the whole affair … Dickie's militant loyalty, moral courage and infinite capacity for taking pains, however busy he is, is one of the marvels of this most unpleasant age': ibid., 22 December 1941, pp. 14–15.

47 Vice-Admiral Lord Louis Mountbatten to Noel Coward, 2 October 1942, Mountbatten papers, MB1/C58.

48 Payn and Morley (eds.), *The Noel Coward Diaries*, 8 April 1942, p. 16; Coward, *The Autobiography*, pp. 422–3. Following the King's visit Mountbatten reported that he and Churchill were full of admiration for what Coward was doing, and that the PM was 'most distressed' over his humiliation in court. Vice-Admiral Lord Louis Mountbatten to Noel Coward, 16 April 1942, ibid. Bernard Miles interview in *Filming For Victory: British Cinema, 1939–45* (Christopher Frayling, BBC2 TV, UK, 1986).

49 Ziegler, *Mountbatten*, p. 171; Bernard Miles interview; Coward, *The Autobiography*, pp. 425–426; miscellaneous correspondence with the Admiralty, Board of Trade, and Ministry of Labour, Mountbatten papers, MB1/C58; Graham Payn with Barry Day, *My Life With Noel Coward* (Applause, London, 1994), p. 154. Lean and Neame were appalled when Coward readily accepted Mountbatten's suggestion that the film's title be taken from the Royal Navy's morning prayer. Brownlow, *David Lean*, pp. 166 and 159.

50 On the positive response of both the Admiralty and the film critics, see MacKenzie, *British War Films*, pp. 80–81. Brownlow, *David Lean*, pp. 167–168; Jeffrey Richards and Dorothy Sheridan (eds.), *Mass Observation at the Movies* (Routledge and Kegan Paul, London, 1987), p. 220.

51 Brian Loring Villa floated the unconvincing idea that Mountbatten saw Coward's film as a vehicle for securing his elevation above the other service chiefs. Villa, *Unauthorized Action*, pp. 200–1.

52 On a shift in public perception of the Royal Navy, 1941–42, see MacKenzie, *British War Films*, pp. 81–82.

53 Payn and Morley (eds), *The Noel Coward Diaries*, 25 September 1942, p. 18; Coward, *The Autobiography*, p. 421.

54 Ibid., p. 422; Ziegler, *Mountbatten*, p. 172.

55 Ibid. Like Mountbatten, Kinross announces that 'out of 240 men on board this ship, 239 behaved as they ought', but gives the unnamed yet ashamed Richard Attenborough a second chance on the grounds that the captain must be at fault for not ensuring every crew member knew what was expected of him once in action.

56 Michael Powell, *Million-Dollar Movie The Second Volume of his Life in Movies* (William Heinemann, London, 1992), p. 260. Despite his disappointment over Lean's defection Powell liked the film, but felt Coward casting himself 'had spoilt the ship with a ha'pence of tar'. When the *Daily Express* campaigned against 'me writing and acting Lord Louis Mountbatten' [note the absence of disguise] Coward secured powerful support within the Admiralty and the MoI on his own initiative: Payn and Morley (eds.), *The Noel Coward Diaries*, 2 and 17–18 September 1941, pp. 10–11. Criticism of *In Which We Serve* largely focused upon Coward's performance, for example, see Richards and Sheridan (eds), *Mass Observation at the Movies*, pp. 257 and 267.

57 Hoare, *Noel Coward*, p. 326.

58 Celia Johnson as Alix Kinross is preparing her stiff upper lip for *Brief Encounter*, memorably switching to discussion of the chintz when her husband concedes that a war is likely; her two perfect children are implausibly named Bobbie and Lavinia. Ironically, the lower middle-class and working-class domestic scenes are far more convincing. *Hands Across The Sea A Light Comedy in One Scene* from *To-night at 8.30* (1935) in Noel Coward, *Plays: Three* (Eyre Methuen, London, 1979), pp. 306–33. Payn with Day, *My Life With Noel Coward*, p. 151. Mountbatten was again recreated on stage as a 'bright young thing', along with Coward, in Jeremy Kingston's *Making Dickie Happy*, performed at London's Rosemary Branch pub theatre in September–October 2004 – 'The Master' would have been horrified at the venue.

59 Coward, *The Autobiography*, pp. 421–2. An indication of frosty relations is that Edwina's extremely thorough biographer, Janet Morgan, makes no reference to Coward after late 1944.

60 Payn and Morley (eds.), *The Noel Coward Diaries*, 30 May 1966, p. 632.

61 Admiral Lord Louis Mountbatten to Noel Coward, 11 September 1953, Mountbatten papers, MB1/H66; Payn and Morley (eds.), *The Noel Coward Diaries*, 1 October 1953, p. 221.

62 Correspondence with relatives of personnel killed on HMS *Kelly*, 1941–42, Mountbatten papers MB1/B4 and MB1/B6.

63 Pattinson, *Mountbatten and the Men of the 'Kelly'*, pp. 181–9 and 147.

64 Miscellaneous correspondence and press clippings re Tom Kelly and Alan Price, *Kelly-A Musical Documentary* (15 July 1977, South Shields) and *Kelly*, (Peter West, BBC2–The Lively Arts, 12 February 1978), Mountbatten papers, MB1/B80.

65 For details of Kelly theme pubs and hotels, see Pattinson, *Mountbatten and the Men of Kelly*, p. 147. The principal website is www.battleships-cruisers.co.uk/hms_kelly, providing a short history of the *Kelly*, a message noticeboard independent of the Reunion Association, and a facility to order online four specially commissioned prints.

66 Pattinson, *Mountbatten and the Men of the 'Kelly'*, pp. 66–73, 135–46, 159–61, 170–2, and 11–15.

67 HRH Prince of Wales quoted in ibid., p. 10. *Mountbatten and the Men of the 'Kelly'* was a coffee table book published in 1986 with a foreword by Prince Charles, the Association's second president, and a preface by Philip Ziegler. Its author, Bill Pattinson, was a destroyer veteran who had been enthused by Mountbatten to join Combined Operations, and who collaborated closely with Rocky Wilkins in producing the Association's fullest and most lasting tribute to Captain (D).

68 Admiral of the Fleet Lord Louis Mountbatten, inscription accompanying '*Kelly* at Namsos' (Mark Myers, 1979).

Chapter Seven

1 Morgan, *Edwina Mountbatten*, pp. 290–3; Hough, *Edwina*, pp. 150–3, 157, and 154.

2 von Tunzelmann, *Indian Summer*, p. 114.

3 '... politically, she talked tripe, and pretended to be against all monarchy ... How easy it seems for a semi-royal millionaires, who has exhausted all the pleasures of money and position to turn almost Communist!': Rhodes James (ed.), *Chips*, 19 September 1944, p. 480.

4 Steven Fielding, 'The Second World War and popular radicalism: the significance of the "Movement away from Party"', *History*, vol. 80 no. 258, 1995, pp. 38–58; Peter Clarke, *The Cripps Version The Life of Sir Stafford Cripps 1889–1952* (Allen Lane/Penguin, London, 2002/2003), pbk edn, pp. 257–370.

5 Rhodes James (ed.), *Chips*, 20 and 25 February 1942, pp. 394–5.

6 Alanbrooke, *War Diaries*, 25 February 1942, p. 233; C.E. Lucas Phillips, *The Greatest Raid of All* (William Heinemann/Pan, 1958/2000), pbk edn, p. 35; Admiral of the Fleet the Earl Mountbatten of Burma, 'Foreword' in ibid., p. xv.

7 Ibid., p. 21; Edwina was being instructed to lobby Syfret, and to lunch the First Lord of the Admiralty, A.V. Alexander, over a month before the *Kelly* was sunk: Ziegler, *Mountbatten*, pp. 148–9.

8 Ibid., p. 149.

9 Ibid.; 'Remarks by Captain Mountbatten', [?] 1941, Mountbatten papers, MB1/B14.

10 Morgan, *Edwina Mountbatten*, pp. 299–300 and 304.

11 'Remarks by Captain Mountbatten'; Ziegler, *Mountbatten*, pp. 149–50; Commander [?] Robert Neville [Intelligence Division, Naval Staff] to Captain Lord Louis Mountbatten, 27 September 1941, Mountbatten papers, MB1/B8.

12 Morgan, *Edwina Mountbatten*, pp. 303–5; Captain Lord Louis Mountbatten to Rear Admiral H. Pott [Washington Embassy naval attaché], 9 October 1941, and 'Remarks by Captain Mountbatten', Mountbatten papers, MB1/B14; Commander C.R.L. Parry [ADC to naval attaché?] to Captain Lord Louis Mountbatten, 17 January 1942, ibid.: 'you have no idea how much they [Annapolis midshipmen] enjoyed your lecture there, they'd never heard anything like it in their lives before.'

13 Hough, *Mountbatten*, pp. 144–5; unsigned note from the Washington Embassy [Lord Halifax?] to Rt. Hon. Brendan Bracken, 27 October 1941, quoted in Ziegler, *Mountbatten*, pp. 150–1.

14 Ibid., p. 150; Mountbatten quoted in Terraine, *The Life and Times of Lord Mountbatten*, p. 112.

15 Admiral H.R. Stark USN to Admiral of the Fleet Dudley Pound, 15 October 1941, Mountbatten papers, MB1/B14.

16 'No period in the 5th Destroyer Flotilla in this war left me so utterly exhausted as eight days in the U.S. Pacific Fleet': Captain Lord Louis Mountbatten to Rear Admiral H. Pott, 9 October 1941, ibid.; Morgan, *Edwina Mountbatten*, p. 305.

17 Mountbatten quoted in Terraine, *The Life and Times of Lord Mountbatten*, p. 112; Captain Lord Louis Mountbatten to Rear Admiral H. Pott, 9 October 1941, op. cit.

18 Morgan, *Edwina Mountbatten*, pp. 305–6; Prime Minister to Harry Hopkins, 10 October 1941, quoted in Ziegler, *Mountbatten*, p. 151.

19 Prime Minister to Captain Lord Louis Mountbatten, 10 October 1941, quoted in Terraine, *The Life and Times of Lord Mountbatten*, p. 112; Ziegler, *Mountbatten*, p. 151.

20 F.D. Roosevelt to Winston S. Churchill, 15 October 1941, in Warren F. Kimball (ed.), *Churchill and Roosevelt The Complete Correspondence I. Alliance Emerging* (Collins, London, 1984), p. 250.

21 Morgan, *Edwina Mountbatten*, pp. 307–8 and 309–10; 'This is an extraordinary man with the *instinct* and the *industry* necessary for modern warfare': David Eccles to Sybil Eccles, 24 October 1941, quoted in Ziegler, *Mountbatten*, p. 152.

22 Churchill quoted in Terraine, *The Life and Times of Lord Mountbatten*, pp. 112–13. This version of events tallies with Mountbatten's diary entry at the time, and the account he gave to Combined Operation's semi-official historian some time in 1959 or 1960. Ziegler,

Mountbatten, p. 156; Bernard Fergusson, *The Watery Maze The Story of Combined Operations* (Collins, London, 1961), p. 87.

23 Ibid., pp. 87–8.

24 COSC, directive on the role of Adviser of Combined Operations, 16 October 1941, COS (41) 629, replicated in ibid., pp. 89–90 and Ziegler, *Mountbatten*, pp. 156–7.

25 On the history, role, and status, of the CIGS and the COSC respectively, and Brooke's interpretation of his constitutional and military position as head of the Army and chair of the COSC, see David Fraser, *Alanbrooke* (HarperCollins, London 1982/1997), pbk edn, pp. 176–88.

26 Fergusson, *The Watery Maze*, pp. 32–5 and 51.

27 Roskill, *Churchill and the Admirals*, p. 178; Prime Minister to General H. Ismay, 6 June 1940, quoted in Winston S. Churchill, *The Second World War Vol. II Their Finest Hour* (Cassell, London, 1949), p. 217.

28 Prime Minister to General Hastings Ismay, 4 June 1940, quoted in ibid., p. 214.

29 Prime Minister to General Hastings Ismay, 6 June 1940, quoted in ibid., p. 217; Fergusson, *The Watery Maze*, p. 47.

30 Ministry of Information (MoI), *Combined Operations, 1940–1942* (HMSO, London, 1943), pp. 8–9; Fergusson, *The Watery Maze*, pp. 37–45.

31 Only briefly number two as in November 1940 Bourne resumed his post as RM Adjutant-General.

32 Fergusson, *The Watery Maze*, pp. 48–9 and 57–8; MoI, *Combined Operations*, pp. 10–12.

33 Fergusson, *The Watery Maze*, pp. 57–8, 54–5 and 76–7.

34 Ibid., p. 56; Roskill, *Churchill and the Admirals*, p. 178.

35 See the complaint of Admiral Sir William James in Ziegler, *Mountbatten*, p. 154.

36 Lord Lovat, *March Past A Memoir* (Weidenfeld and Nicolson, London, 1978), p. 189.

37 Fergusson, *The Watery Maze*, pp. 60, 74–5, 77, and 80; Roskill, *Churchill and the Admirals*, p. 176.

38 First Sea Lord and C-in-C Mediterranean Fleet correspondence quoted in Fergusson, *The Watery Maze*, p. 95, and Roskill, *Churchill and the Admirals*, p. 176.

39 Unimpressed when the Director took him to Inverary, Brooke always believed that each Commando should constitute a 'divisional battle patrol'; but he begrudgingly accepted a papering over of the cracks once Keyes was gone: Alanbrooke, *War Diaries*, 28 August, 23–25 September and 5 November 1941, pp. 179, 185 and 196.

40 Fergusson, *The Watery Maze*, pp. 77–8; MoI, *Combined Operations*, pp. 33–6.

41 Fergusson, *The Watery Maze*, pp. 78–82.

42 Exchange of correspondence, September-October 1941 between Prime Minister and Director of Combined Operations quoted in ibid., pp. 83–5; Mountbatten quoted in Terraine, *The Life and Times of Lord Mountbatten*, p. 115; Roskill, *Churchill and the Admirals*, pp. 176–7.

43 Lovat, *March Past*, p. 215.

44 Churchill invited Brooke to become CIGS at Chequers in mid-November (with Mountbatten also a guest): Alanbrooke, *War Diaries*, 16 November 1941, p. 199; ibid., 5 March 1942, p. 236; Winston S. Churchill, *The Second World War Vol. III The Grand Alliance* (Cassell, London, 1950), pp. 480–1.

45 Mountbatten interview quoted in Ziegler, *Mountbatten*, pp. 157–8.

46 At Westminster the PPS to the First Lord of the Admiralty and a former RN officer, Rex Fletcher MP [later Lord Winster], spread malicious gossip about Mountbatten's promotion: Ben Pimlott (ed.), *The Second World War Diary of Hugh Dalton 1940–45* (Jonathan Cape, London, 1986), 19 November 1941, p. 317.

47 Ziegler, *Mountbatten*, p. 158; Admiral-of-the-Fleet Sir Dudley Pound to the Prime Minister, 7 March 1942, quoted in Roskill, *Churchill and the Admirals*, p. 204; Hough, *Mountbatten*, p. 149.

48 'Some Reflections on Combined Operations', addendum to Lt. Gerald C. Butler to Commodore G.L. Warren, 25 October 1941, Mountbatten papers, MB1/B24.

49 Hough, *Mountbatten*, p. 146; Ziegler, *Mountbatten*, p. 156.

50 Mountbatten on being briefed by Keyes at COHQ, quoted in Hough, *Mountbatten*, p. 146 and in Terraine, *The Life and Times of Lord Mountbatten*, pp. 114–15.

51 Correspondence of Admiral-of-the-Fleet Sir Roger Keyes with the Prime Minister and General Hastings Ismay, October 1941, quoted in Ziegler, *Mountbatten*, p. 155.

52 Ibid., pp. 157–8; Alanbrooke, *War Diaries*, 17 and 18 February and 5 and 7 March 1941, pp. 230–1 and 236–7.

53 An SOE liaison officer was lost on the Dieppe raid. Pimlott (ed.), *The Second World War Diary of Hugh Dalton*, 19 November 1941, p. 317; M.R.D. Foot, *The Special Operations Executive 1940–46* (Greenwood Press/Pimlico, London, 1984/1999), pbk edn, pp. 44–5; Lucas Phillips, *The Greatest Raid Of All*, pp. 59–60; Commander D.S. Wyatt to [?], 11 November 1964, Mountbatten papers, MB1/B54; Kenneth Young (ed.), *The Diaries of Sir Robert Bruce Lockhart 2: 1939–1965* (Macmillan, London, 1980), 2 January 1942, p. 133.

54 Pimlott (ed.), *The Second World War Diary of Hugh Dalton*, 9 January 1942, pp. 345–8.

55 Adrian Smith, 'Command and Control in Postwar Britain: Defence Decision-Making in the United Kingdom, 1945–1984', *Twentieth Century British History*, vol. 2 no. 3, 1991, pp. 303–12.

56 Interview with Major Arthur Marshall [COHQ Security] quoted in Ziegler, *Mountbatten*, p. 161.

57 Vice-Admiral John Hughes-Hallett, 'Before I Forget – Combined Operations' manuscript, 1971, Mountbatten papers, MB1/B47, p. 112

58 Commodore (C), Adviser on Combined Operations, policy document, paras 1–9, and COSC, directive on Combined Operations, 9 December 1941, COS (41) 732, MB1/B13, Mountbatten papers.

59 Lucas Phillips, *The Greatest Raid Of All*, pp. 18–19; Hughes-Hallett, 'Before I Forget', pp. 106 and 111.

60 Fergusson, *The Watery Maze*, p. 123; Commodore (C), Adviser on Combined Operations, policy document, op. cit.; 1943 shipping data (courtesy of Rear Admiral R.E. Horan, *The Naval Review*, January 1961) quoted in McGeoch, *The Princely Sailor*, p. 90.

61 On the R and D, commissioning, and construction of Combined Operations' fleet of landing ships and landing craft during Mountbatten's tenure, see Fergusson, *The Watery Maze*, pp. 93, 109–18, 149, and 235–6, and 'Transcript of Lord Mountbatten's speech at the Mediterranean LCI(L) Reunion Dinner, London, 15th October, 1977', Mountbatten papers, MB1/B53B.

62 Ibid.; Fergusson, *The Watery Maze*, p. 93.

63 Ibid., pp. 90–1; McGeoch, *The Princely Sailor*, p. 64. 'I had a lover's quarrel and reconciliation with Col. Lushington and was feeling very deeply devoted to him': Evelyn to Laura Waugh, 13 September 1940 in Mark Amory (ed.), *The Letters of Evelyn Waugh* (Weidenfeld and Nicolson/Penguin, London, 1980/1982), pbk edn, p. 139.

64 Hughes-Hallett, 'Before I Forget', p. 112.

65 Robert Henriques, *From A Biography of Myself* (Secker and Warburg, London, 1969).

66 Fergusson, *The Watery Maze*, p. 91.

67 Ibid., pp. 91–3 and 189–91.

68 Hughes-Hallett, 'Before I Forget', p. 120. Casa Maury also contributed a large body of photo-reconnaissance information on St Nazaire gathered when 19 Group's Air Intelligence Officer: Lucas Phillips, *The Greatest Raid Of All*, pp. 26, 28 and 23–4.

69 Miscellaneous private papers (1) re Marquis de Casa Maury, Mountbatten papers, MB1/B25.

70 Marquis de Casa Maury to Commodore Lord Louis Mountbatten, 19 November 1941, ibid.

71   Morgan, *Edwina Mountbatten*, p. 297; miscellaneous private papers (2) re Marquis de Casa Maury, Mountbatten papers, MB1/B26.

72   Commander Ian Fleming RNVR established his credibility with career officers by serving as a highly competent assistant to the Director of the Naval Intelligence Division, Rear Admiral John Godfrey. Foot, later an intelligence officer for the SAS, was recruited by de Casa Maury largely because he was 'socially acceptable'. On Combined Operations' day-to-day contact with parallel organisations such as SOE, see M.R.D. Foot, *Memories of an S.O.E. Historian* (Pen and Sword Military, Barnsley, 2008), pp. 69–76.

73   Active from 1914 to 1919, the PID was revived by the Foreign Office; Murphy was in regular contact with Casa Maury: miscellaneous private papers (2) re Marquis de Casa Maury, op cit.

74   Ziegler, *Mountbatten*, pp. 162–3.

75   Fergusson, *The Watery Maze*, p. 189.

76   Even at a distance Brockman would fulfil this function for the rest of Mountbatten's life, providing information and advice, and when necessary acting as his lordship's intermediary.

77   Henriques, *From A Biography of Myself*, p. 54.

78   Admiral Lord Mountbatten to Captain Robin Todhunter, 14 February 1978, Mountbatten papers, MB1/B49.

79   Lovat, *March Past*, p. 238.

80   Goronwy Rees, *A Bundle of Sensations Sketches in Autobiography* (Chatto and Windus, London, 1960), p. 143.

81   Evelyn Waugh, *Officers and Gentlemen* (Chapman and Hall, 1955): volume 2 of *The Sword of Honour Trilogy* (Everyman's Library, New York, 1994), p. 272. 'Marchmain House' signals the principal location for *Brideshead Revisited*, written in 1944 after Waugh had left Combined Operations.

82   Fergusson, *The Watery Maze*, pp. 1 and 124; Lovat, *March Past*, pp. 233–6 and 187. For differing accounts of Mountbatten's role in Waugh's enforced departure, see Humphrey Carpenter, *The Brideshead Generation Evelyn Waugh and his Friends* (Weidenfeld and Nicolson, London, 1989), pp. 350–1 and Selina Hastings, *Evelyn Waugh A Biography* (Sinclair-Stevenson, London, 1994), pp. 450–1, both versions drawing upon Lovat, *March Past*, pp. 233–6; ibid., p. 187. For an example of Waugh's appalling behaviour inside Richmond Terrace, see Foot, *Memories of an S.O.E. Historian*, p. 72.

83   Ziegler, *Mountbatten*, p. 165; Fergusson, *The Watery Maze*, pp. 120–3; Young (ed.), *The Diaries of Sir Robert Bruce Lockhart 2*, 15 June 1942, p. 174.

84   At Mountbatten's behest the Admiralty ordered 20 million jerricans for 'Overlord': 'C.M. & S.F. Activities 1942–1944 at COHQ and SHAEF', [N.D.], p. 6, Mountbatten papers, MB1/B50. Commodore Lord Louis Mountbatten to Sir Harold Wernher, 24 March 1942; note by Mountbatten re 'Sir Harold Wernher's Papers', [?] 1970, ibid.; Hughes-Hallett, 'Before I Forget', p. 142. Fergusson, *The Watery Maze*, pp. 127–8. Wernher insisted that his battle with the War Office's Sir John Grigg left the latter a powerful 'antagonist and opponent' of both himself and Mountbatten: interview with Sir Harold Wernher in Michael Harrison, *Mulberry The Return in Triumph* (W.H. Allen, London, 1965), pp. 89–97.

85   See Chapter Nine.

86   Hughes-Hallett, 'Before I Forget', pp. 132–4; Fergusson, *The Watery Maze*, p. 131.

87   Ibid., pp. 107–8; MoI, *Combined Operations*, pp. 52–65.

88   Fergusson, *The Watery Maze*, p. 131; Hughes-Hallett, 'Before I Forget', pp. 118–19 and 132–3; Alanbrooke, *War Diaries*, 28 March, 8 April and 6 May 1942, and pp. 242, 245 and 255.

89   Hughes-Hallett, 'Before I Forget', p. 133. On Mountbatten's mission to Washington in July 1942, see Chapter Eight.

90 Ibid., pp. 131–2; MoI, *Combined Operations*, pp. 65–70. The major from the Airborne Division who commanded the assault force was John Frost, of the Cameronians, later famous for holding the bridge at Arnhem.

91 Author's note in Lucas Phillips, *The Greatest Raid of All*, pp. x–xi; Jeremy Clarkson's commentary in *Jeremy Clarkson: The Greatest Raid Of All Time* (Richard Pearson, BBC, UK, 2007).

92 Hughes-Hallett, 'Before I Forget', pp. 119 and 122–3; Lucas Phillips, *The Greatest Raid Of All*, pp. 20–22; Fergusson, *The Watery Maze*, p. 134. Both authors were much-decorated brigadiers who in retirement became prolific writers of military history.

93 Lucas Phillips, *The Greatest Raid Of All*, p. 265.

94 MoI, *Combined Operations*, pp. 71–97: by far the fullest section in the 1943 booklet; Fergusson, *The Watery Maze*, p. 136.

95 C.E. Lucas Phillips, *Cockleshell Heroes* (William Heinemann/Pan, 1956/2000), pbk edn, p. 10; Ziegler, *Mountbatten*, p. 167.

96 Correspondence with Captain Thomas Hussey, Mountbatten papers MB1/B49; Fergusson, *The Watery Maze*, pp. 192–3; David Edgerton, *Warfare State: Britain, 1920–1970* (CUP, Cambridge, 2005). A qualified engineer, Nevil Norway/Shute's career in aeronautics informed the majority of his novels: see Nevil Shute, *Slide Rule: The Art of an Engineer* (William Heinemann, London, 1954).

97 Lucas Phillips, *Cockleshell Heroes*, pp. 14–15. The CODC had previously operated as the Inter-Services Training and Development Centre.

98 Lucas Phillips, *Cockleshell Heroes*, pacem.; Fergusson, *The Watery Maze*, p. 137; Ziegler, *Mountbatten*, p. 168.

99 Lucas Phillips, *Cockleshell Heroes*, pp. 13–15 and 74.

100 The anonymous MoI author makes only one extended reference to Mountbatten: MoI, *Combined Operations*, p. 52; *The Cockleshell Heroes* (José Ferrer, Warwick Films/Columbia, UK, 1955); Robert Murphy, *British Cinema and the Second World War* (Continuum, London, 2000), pbk edn, pp. 225–6; Admiral of the Fleet the Earl Mountbatten of Burma, 'Foreword' in Lucas Phillips, *Cockleshell Heroes* [no page number].

101 Winston S. Churchill to F.D. Roosevelt, 1 April 1942, quoted in Winston S. Churchill, *The Second World War Vol. IV The Hinge of Fate* (Cassell, London/Curtis Brown, New York, 1951), US edn, p. 166.

102 First Sea Lord to the Prime Minister, 7 March 1942, PREM 3/119/6, quoted in Reynolds, *In Command of History*, p. 343.

103 Alanbrooke, *War Diaries*, 5, 11 and 12 March 1942, and Alanbrooke's subsequent note re diary entry for 5 March 1942, pp. 236, 238–9, and 236.

104 Anonymous colleague of Mountbatten ('who ordinarily stood in awe of no man but the King, approached Brooke with considerable caution') quoted in Ziegler, *Mountbatten*, pp. 169–70; Fraser, *Alanbrooke*, pp. 180, 185 and 189.

105 Prime Minister to the First Sea Lord, 8 March 1942, PREM 3 119/6, quoted in Reynolds, *In Command of History*, p. 343; and to the Chiefs of Staff, [?] March 1942, PREM 3 330/2, quoted in Fergusson, *The Watery Maze*, p. 124, and Ziegler, *Mountbatten*, p. 169.

106 Ibid., p. 170.

107 Mountbatten quoted in Hough, *Mountbatten*, pp. 150–1 and Terraine, *The Life and Times of Lord Mountbatten*, pp. 120–1.

108 Roskill, *Churchill and the Admirals*, pp. 142–3; Reynolds, *In Command of History*, pp. 342–4; Rear-Admiral John Godfrey's 1956 and 1964 correspondence re Pound's possible replacement, quoted in Ziegler, *Mountbatten*, pp. 175–6.

109 Olson, *Troublesome Young Men*, pp. 335–40. For an excellent profile of Amery, as seen through the prism of a fraught lifelong friendship with Churchill, see ibid., pp. 111–18.

110 John Barnes and David Nicholson (eds), *The Empire at Bay The Leo Amery Diaries 1929–1945* (Hutchinson, London, 1988), 8 February, 8 and 15 April, and 27 May 1942, pp. 770,

804, 809, and 814; Rt Hon Leo Amery to Vice-Admiral Lord Louis Mountbatten, 30 April 1942, MB1/B15, Mountbatten papers; 'The Higher Military Direction of the War' – paper attached to Captain J. Hughes Hallett to Chief of Combined Operations, 25 April 1942, ibid.

111 Hughes-Hallett, 'Before I Forget', p. 134, and interviewed in *The Life and Times of Lord Mountbatten 5: United We Conquer* (Peter Morley, Rediffusion, UK, 1969).

112 Mountbatten quoted in Terraine, *The Life and Times of Lord Mountbatten*, pp. 118–19; Vice-Admiral Lord Louis Mountbatten to Patricia Mountbatten, 20 March and 3 April 1942, quoted in Ziegler, *Mountbatten*, p. 170.

113 Edwina to Patricia Mountbatten, [?] March 1942, quoted in Morgan, *Edwina Mountbatten*, p. 317.

114 Ibid., pp. 317–18.

115 Ibid., pp. 318–19; Hough, *Edwina*, p. 161.

Chapter Eight

1 Sergeant George Cook, quoted in Max Arthur (ed.), *Forgotten Voices of the Second World War* (Ebury Press, London, 2004), p. 188.

2 Fraser, *Alanbrooke*, pp. 201–6. For an overview of Anglo-American relations re the defeat of Hitler, see Andrew Roberts, *Masters and Commanders: How Roosevelt, Churchill, Marshall and Alanbrooke Won the War in the West* (Allen Lane, London, 2008).

3 Alanbrooke, *War Diaries*, 9, 10, 14, and 16 April, and 17 and 20–24 July 1942, pp. 246–50 and 281–5.

4 For FDR the Torch landings would ideally have occurred just before and not just after the mid-term congressional elections. Max Hastings, 'How They Won', *New York Review of Books*, 22 November 2007.

5 For an argument that a 200-year tradition of waging war was foolishly abandoned in the early twentieth century, see John Charmley, *Splendid Isolation? Britain and the Balance of Power 1874–1914* (Hodder and Stoughton, London, 1999). For a more balanced assessment, see Michael Howard, *The Continental Commitment: The Dilemma of British Defence Policy in the Era of the Two World Wars* (M.T. Smith/Pelican, London, 1972/1974), pbk edn.

6 David Reynolds, 'Churchill, Roosevelt and the Alliance', in *From World War to Cold War Churchill, Roosevelt, and the International History of the 1940s* (OUP, Oxford, 2006/2007), pbk edn, p. 56.

7 Fraser, *Alanbrooke* , p. 508; David French, *Raising Churchill's Army The British Army and the War Against Germany 1919–1945* (OUP, Oxford, 2000/2001), pbk edn, pp. 203–11; Hastings, 'How They Won'.

8 John Keegan, *Six Armies in Normandy From D-Day to the Liberation of Paris* (Jonathan Cape/Pimlico, London 1982/1992), pbk edn, pp. 31–4 and 36–7.

9 Reynolds, 'Churchill, Roosevelt and the Alliance', pp. 56–7; Rupert Smith, *The Utility of Force The Art of War in the Modern World* (Allen Lane/Penguin, London, 2005/2006), pbk edn, pp. 88–9.

10 On FDR's sensitive handling of the crisis, see Churchill, *The Second World War Vol. IV*, p. 312. Marshall's immediate offer to Brooke of an armoured division for the Middle East demonstrates how quickly he amended his 'concentration' approach: Alanbrooke, *War Diaries*, 21 June 1942, p. 269.

11 On the new CIGS's reading of the strategic significance of the ships' sinking, see ibid., 10 and 20 December 1941, pp. 210 and 213. 'One thing Mountbatten said struck me very much ... in his view ships from the Mediterranean fleet would have disposed of the Japanese attack without difficulty' – and this coming from someone who only just managed to survive Crete! Barnes and Nicholson (eds), *The Empire at Bay*, 15 April 1942, p. 809.

12 Alanbrooke, *War Diaries*, 8 May 1942, pp. 255–6.

13   Ziegler, *Mountbatten*, p. 177.

14   Alanbrooke, *War Diaries*, 28 March 1942, p. 242.

15   Admiral of the Fleet Lord Mountbatten to Captain Stephen Roskill, 23 August 1977, Mountbatten papers, MB1/K20; Hughes-Hallett, 'Before I Forget', p. 147.

16   Ziegler, *Mountbatten*, p. 181; Alanbrooke, *War Diaries*, 8 April 1942, pp. 245–6.

17   F.D. Roosevelt to Winston S. Churchill, 18 March 1942, in Kimball (ed.), *Churchill and Roosevelt The Complete Correspondence I*, p. 421.

18   One argument is that Stalin knew an early Second Front was impossible but used the demand as a means of embarrassing the British, 'and then simply cashing in on the compensations that were certain to be delivered as a result of Britain's being unable to deliver'. Villa, *Unauthorized Action*, p. 69.

19   On the importance the PM placed on Hopkins as 'the main prop and animator of Roosevelt himself', see Churchill, *The Second World War Vol. III*, pp. 20–2.

20   Marshall shared Hopkins' fears, within the Joint Chiefs of Staff fighting off King and Macarthur's call for Bolero to be scaled down. Keegan, *Six Armies in Normandy*, pp. 41–2.

21   Ibid., pp. 37–8; Alanbrooke, *War Diaries*, 14 April 1942, p. 248; Mountbatten quoted in Terraine, *The Life and Times of Lord Mountbatten*, p. 124.

22   Prime Minister's aide-mémoire to the Soviet Government, 11 June 1942, CAB120/64, National Archives, quoted in Churchill, *The Second World War Vol. IV*, p. 279.

23   Keegan, *Six Armies in Normandy*, pp. 38–41; Villa, *Unauthorized Action*, p. 70.

24   Alanbrooke, *War Diaries*, 20, 22 and 24 July 1942, pp. 282, 283–4 and 285.

25   Prime Minister's aide-mémoire to the Soviet Government, 11 June 1942.

26   Ibid.

27   Chiefs of Staff Committee, 1 June and 1 July 1942, COS (42), paras 48 and 62, quoted in Ziegler, *Mountbatten*, p. 183; Alanbrooke, *War Diaries*, 1 July 1942, p. 275; Winston S. Churchill to F.D. Roosevelt to Winston S. Churchill, 28 May 1942, in Kimball (ed.), *Churchill and Roosevelt The Complete Correspondence I.*, p. 494.

28   Mountbatten quoted in Hough, *Mountbatten*, p. 153; Keegan, *Six Armies in Normandy*, p. 42.

29   David Reynolds, 'The President and the King: The Diplomacy of the British Royal Visit of 1939', in *From World War to Cold War*, pp. 137–47.

30   General Albert Wedemeyer quoted in Ziegler, *Mountbatten*, pp. 179 and 180.

31   Ibid., pp. 180 and 184. Wedemeyer didn't trust *any* British officer, always insisting that a witness be present at inter-Allied meetings: Michael [Lord] Adeane, COHQ staff officer in Washington, 1942, quoted in Ziegler, *Mountbatten*, p. 184.

32   Hallett, 'Before I Forget', pp. 148–50; Robin Neillands, *The Dieppe Raid The Story of the Disastrous 1942 Expedition* (Aurum, 2005), p. 36

33   Mountbatten quoted in Terraine, *The Life and Times of Lord Mountbatten*, p. 125. The same story was recounted to the author, almost word for word, in Hough, *Mountbatten*, p. 152.

34   At the same time, volunteers from the US Army's newly-formed elite force, the Rangers, arrived to begin commando training in Scotland. After Mountbatten's visit to Washington in June 1942, the US Navy's highest ranking authority on amphibious operations was seconded to COHQ, Admiral H. Kent Hewitt.

35   Ziegler, *Mountbatten*, p. 180.

36   Dwight D. Eisenhower, *Crusade in Europe* (Heinemann, London, 1948), p. 75. The CIGS recorded Eisenhower's visit, but made no mention of his *faux pas*: Brooke, *War Diaries*, 28 May 1942, p. 261.

37   Eisenhower lobbying on behalf of Mountbatten, quoted in Ziegler, *Mountbatten*, p. 182.

38   Hughes-Hallett, 'Before I Forget', p. 158.

39   Wedemeyer quoted in Ziegler, *Mountbatten*, p. 184; Keegan, *Six Armies in Normandy*, pp. 43–4; Admiral Lord Louis Mountbatten to President F.D. Roosevelt, [?] June 1942,

Mountbatten papers, MB1/B13; Mountbatten quoted in Terraine, *The Life and Times of Lord Mountbatten*, pp. 126–7.

40 Ibid., p. 126.

41 Wedemeyer quoted in Ziegler, *Mountbatten*, p. 184.

42 Ibid., p. 184; Alanbrooke, *War Diaries*, 13 June 1942, p. 265.

43 Mountbatten summarised the outcome of his White House meeting, as described to the PM: Admiral Lord Louis Mountbatten to President F.D. Roosevelt, [?] June 1942.

44 Henry Stimson's account of the 21 June 1942 meeting, quoted in Ziegler, *Mountbatten*, pp. 184–5; Alanbrooke, *War Diaries*, 21 June 1942, p. 268.

45 Churchill, *The Second World War Vol. IV*, p. 220–3; Villa, *Unauthorized Action*, pp. 122–3.

46 Neillands, *The Dieppe Raid*, pp. 75–6; Lord Beaverbrook to Winston S. Churchill, 14 September 1941, quoted in Taylor, *Beaverbrook*, pp. 621–2; Keegan, *Six Armies in Normandy*, pp. 45–6. In early March 1942 the Army had rubbished COHQ's parallel suggestion of seizing Cherbourg: Hughes-Hallett, 'Before I Forget', pp. 132–3.

47 Neillands, *The Dieppe Raid*, pp. 71–2; Alanbrooke, *War Diaries*, 12 and 15 August 1942, pp. 299–300 and 303.

48 Hughes-Hallett, 'Before I Forget', p. 118.

49 Mountbatten quoted in Hough, *Mountbatten*, p. 157.

50 Neillands, *The Dieppe Raid*, pp. 91–2.

51 C.P. Stacey, *The Canadian Army, 1939–45* (Department of National Defence, Ottawa, 1948), p. 57. COHQ's semi-official history claimed another reason for choosing Dieppe was that it would not be considered a suitable port to seize when invasion did take place. If so, this calls into questions the value of the lessons learnt. Fergusson, *The Watery Maze*, p. 169.

52 Brooke, *War Diaries*, 23 and 13 May 1942, pp. 260 and 257; Hughes-Hallett, 'Before I Forget', p. 152.

53 B.L. Montgomery, *The Memoirs of Field Marshal The Viscount Montgomery of Alamein, K.G.* (Collins, London, 1958), pp. 75–7; 'Note by Field-Marshal Montgomery on the Dieppe Raid: August 1962', quoted in Nigel Hamilton, *The Full Monty Volume I: Montgomery of Alamein, 1887–1942* (Allen Lane/Penguin Press, London, 2001), p. 433.

54 Hamilton, *The Full Monty*, p. 444; Rees, *A Bundle of Sensations*, pp. 138–51.

55 Villa, *Unauthorized Action*, p. 295, ft. 16. In March 1942 Hughes-Hallett had wisely turned down the new CCO's promise to secure him fast-track promotion, negating the need for any external Admiralty appointments: Hughes-Hallett, 'Before I Forget', p. 133.

56 'Note by Field-Marshal Montgomery on the Dieppe Raid: August 1962'; Rees, *A Bundle of Sensations*, pp. 141–4 and 156–7. Rees observed the raid from the bridge of the destroyer HMS *Garth*.

57 Montgomery, *The Memoirs of Field Marshal The Viscount Montgomery of Alamein, K.G.*, p. 77.

58 Correspondence of Major Walter Skrine, August 1958, quoted in Hamilton, *The Full Monty*, pp. 433 and 441–3; Hughes-Hallett, 'Before I Forget', pp. 152–3.

59 Ibid., p. 154; Villa, *Unauthorized Action*, p. 13.

60 Ibid., pp. 11–12.

61 Fergusson, *The Watery Maze*, p. 170; Rees, *A Bundle of Sensations*, pp. 141–2 and 148–51.

62 On Leigh-Mallory and the legacy for Dieppe of the 'Big Wing' controversy within Fighter Command, see ft. 94. When arguing with generals Leigh-Mallory drew on his infantry experience on the Western Front. Fergusson, *The Watery Maze*, p. 171; Hughes-Hallett, 'Before I Forget', p. 155.

63 Ibid.; Montgomery, *The Memoirs of Field Marshal The Viscount Montgomery of Alamein, K.G.*, p. 76; Hamilton, *The Full Monty*, pp. 444–5.

64 Hughes-Hallett, 'Before I Forget', p. 155; Rees, *A Bundle of Sensations*, pp. 145–6.

65 Hamilton, *The Full Monty*, pp. 445–6.

66 Admiral Sir Dudley Pound, quoted in Earl Mountbatten of Burma, 'Dieppe: The Inside Story', *Legion Magazine*, November 1973, pp. 10–15 and 45–8; Villa, *Unauthorized Action*, pp. 95–96 and 125.

67 Ibid., pp. 125–6. Correspondence re Vice Admiral H.T. Baillie-Grohman in Mountbatten papers, MB1/B15; Vice Admiral H.T. Baillie-Grohman to editor, *RUSI Journal*, February 1953.

68 For example, Neillands, *The Dieppe Raid*, p. 97, and Ziegler, *Mountbatten*, pp. 189–90.

69 Neillands, *The Dieppe Raid*, pp. 57–64 and 94–5.

70 Mountbatten interviewed in *Dieppe 42 Aux yeux du present* (Pierre Gavreau, Radio-Québec, 1976) and *Dieppe 1942* (Terence Macartney-Filgate, CBC, 1979); 'Note by Field-Marshal Montgomery on the Dieppe Raid: August 1962'; Ronald Atkin, *Dieppe 1942 The Jubilee Disaster* (Macmillan, London, 1980), pp. 12–13.

71 Hughes-Hallett, 'Before I Forget', pp. 55–6.

72 Ibid., pp. 164–5. Contrary to Hughes-Hallett's recollection, a now apprehensive Roberts needed reassurance from Crerar: Villa, *Unauthorised Action*, pp. 190–1.

73 Hughes-Hallett, 'Before I Forget', 164–5; Rees, *A Bundle of Sensations*, pp. 151–7; Fergusson, *The Watery Maze*, p. 172; Hamilton, *The Full Monty*, pp. 446–9.

74 Fergusson, *The Watery Maze*, p. 173; Atkin, *Dieppe 1942*, pp. 33–5.

75 Villa, *Unauthorised Action*, pp. 191–2.

76 Ibid., pp. 193–4.

77 'Note by Field-Marshal Montgomery on the Dieppe Raid: August 1962'; Fraser, *Alanbrooke*, pp. 257–9; Rees, *A Bundle of Sensations*, pp. 153–4 and 149.

78 Hughes-Hallett, 'Before I Forget', pp. 167–8; Mountbatten in 1972 interview, quoted in Ziegler, *Mountbatten*, p. 190 and in Atkin, *Dieppe 1942*, p. 37.

79 Neillands, *The Dieppe Raid*, pp. 111–12; Villa, *Unauthorized Action*, pp. 192–8.

80 Correspondence between Ramsay and Mountbatten, 25 and 27 July 1942 quoted in ibid., p. 198; Ferguson, *The Watery Maze*, p. 174; Hughes-Hallett, 'Before I Forget', pp. 146, 165, 168 and 171; Atkin, *Dieppe 1942*, pp. 37–8.

81 Hughes-Hallett, 'Before I Forget', p. 168.

82 Neillands, *The Dieppe Raid*, pp. 112–20; Peter J. Henshaw, 'The British Chiefs of Staff and the Preparation of the Dieppe Raid, March-August 1942: Did Mountbatten Really Evade the Committee's Authority', *War and History*, 1994, vol. 1, no. 2, pp. 204–5. Unlike Henshaw, Villa questioned Mountbatten's claim that by 27 July the COSC had granted him final authority to remount Rutter as Jubilee: Villa, *Unauthorised Action*, pp. 44 and 45.

83 Minutes of COSC meeting, 20 July 1942, quoted in ibid., p. 184.

84 Henshaw, 'The British Chiefs of Staff and the Preparation of the Dieppe Raid', pp. 205–7.

85 Villa, *Unauthorised Action*, p. 185; Hughes-Hallett, 'Before I Forget', p. 177.

86 The basic outline of Jubilee's final plan draws upon Fergusson, *The Watery Maze*, pp. 174–5; Christopher Buckley, *Norway The Commandos Dieppe* (HMSO, London, 1952/1977), pbk edn, pp. 231, 234–8; and Neillands, *The Dieppe Raid*, p. 102–5.

87 'Instructions to cutting out force', Mountbatten papers, MB1/B34. The 150–ton Chasseurs, carrying a 75mm gun and machine guns, formed the core of the Free French Navy in June 1940.

88 Informed on 2 July 1942 of the arrival of 10th Panzer Division in Amiens, only four hours from Dieppe, Montgomery had argued that Rutter be a one-tide affair. Hamilton, *The Full Monty*, p. 450.

89 Lovat, *March Past*, pp. 239–43.

90 Neillands, *The Dieppe Raid*, pp. 166–72.

91 At 900 tons Hunt constituted a small destroyer class. An accompanying gunboat carried just two 4-inch guns (plus a howitzer), and a solitary sloop only one. The four newly-commissioned steam gunboats despatched to Dieppe were lightly armed and, as it

transpired, highly vulnerable. Lieutenant-Commander Peter Scott, *The Battle of the Narrow Seas A History of the Light Coastal Forces in the Channel and the North Sea, 1939–1945* (Country Life Ltd, London, 1945), pp. 92–108.

92 The Beatty curse re ordnance remained: the LCTs carried [unpacked] Bren guns but the Canadian AA gunners arrived on board trained to fire Bofors: Atkin, *Dieppe 1942*, p. 67.

93 Ibid., pp. 66–7. Fliers from the Dominions were joined by Free French, Poles, and Norwegians. Astonishingly, ground troops included Sudeten Germans, as intelligence-gatherers for Lovat's Commandos – a role repeated on D-Day.

94 With the Battle of Britain at its height Leigh-Mallory's 12 Group failed to secure a major tactical switch by Fighter Command to Douglas Bader's 'Big Wing' principle of deploying the maximum number of fighter squadrons in advance of the enemy's arrival over England. Leigh-Mallory nevertheless replaced Keith Park at 11 Group in December 1940, assuming command of Fighter Command exactly two years later. Terraine, *The Right of the Line*, pp. 194–205; John Ray, *The Battle of Britain Dowding and the First Victory, 1940* (Cassell, 1994), pbk edn, pp. 145–69. John P. Campbell, *Dieppe Revisited A Documentary Investigation* (Frank Cass, London, 1993), pp. 205–7; Fergusson, *The Watery Maze*, pp. 174–5.

95 Ibid., p. 175.

96 Atkin, *Dieppe 1942*, pp. 65–6 and 69; Campbell, *Dieppe Revisited*, pp. 170–1; Atkin, op. cit., pp. 135–6, 140 and 146. Sir Henry Tizard at an early stage squashed the crazy idea of two of his most valuable scientists, including R.V. Jones, being parachuted into Berneval. Campbell, op. cit., p. 125. Fleming wrote a lengthy account of the Dieppe raid for internal circulation within NID, and made clear to friends his future preference for waging war from behind a desk. Andrew Lycett, *Ian Fleming* (Weidenfeld and Nicolson/Phoenix, London, 1995/1996), pbk edn, pp. 139–41.

97 The revived spa town is located in approximately the same part of the French coastline as Dieppe, and it's clearly not coincidental that the Ultra insider gave SMERSH's sadistic card shark the code name 'Le Chiffre' ('The Cipher'): Ian Fleming, *Casino Royale* (Jonathan Cape, London, 1953). A more hapless villain, Major Dexter Smythe, is an interrogator on cross-Channel commando raids and joins a thinly disguised 30AU: Ian Fleming, *Octopussy* (Jonathan Cape, London, 1966). One 'Red Indian' memoirist was possibly Bond's model: Patrick Dalzel-Job, *Arctic Snow to Dust of Normandy* (Pen and Sword, London, 1997).

98 Neillands, *The Dieppe Raid*, pp. 104–5; Lovat, *March Past*, p. 239; Villa, *Unauthorised Action*, pp. 11–12.

99 Fergusson, *The Watery Maze*, p. 176.

100 Campbell, *Dieppe Revisited*, pp. 30, 167, and 185–8.

101 Account of 3 Commando assault on the eastern battery drawn from Neillands, *The Dieppe Raid*, pp. 129–47 and Atkin, *Dieppe 1942*, pp. 74–92; Captain J. Hughes-Hallett to C-in-C, RN Portsmouth, 'Dieppe Raid: despatch by Naval Force Commander', 30 August 1942, [Supplement to *London Gazette*, 38045, 12 August 1947], Mountbatten papers, MB1/B47.

102 Scott, *The Battle of the Narrow Seas*, p. 101; Neillands, *The Dieppe Raid*, p. 171.

103 Ibid., pp. 151–2; Lovat, *March Past*, pp. 238–40.

104 Ibid., pp. 240–1; Major Derek Mills-Roberts quoted in ibid., p. 256.

105 Scott, *The Battle of the Narrow Seas*, p. 101; Lovat, *March Past*, p. 245; Neillands, *The Dieppe Raid*, pp. 156–62. For a lively account of 4 Commando's assault on the eastern battery, and how Captain Pat Porteous won the VC, see Atkin, *Dieppe 1942*, pp. 93–112.

106 Lovat, *March Past*, p. 273; Lord Lovat [filmed on Orange Beach] quoted in *Dieppe 1942* (Terence Macartney-Filgate/CBC/Canada/1977); Lovat, op. cit., p. 274.

107 Ibid., pp. 272–7. For praise of General Von Runstedt's Special Order, and of coastal commander Colonel-General Haase's 'Special Alert', in anticipating an Allied incursion, see ibid., pp. 276 and 278.

108 Neillands, *The Dieppe Raid*, pp. 173–6; Atkin, *Dieppe 1942*, p. 115.

109 Hughes-Hallett, 'Before I Forget', p. 195.

110 Ibid., p. 185; 'Report on Informal Enquiry held on board HMS "Queen Emma" on 21st August 1942', 22 August 1942, Mountbatten papers, MB1/B33.

111 Neillands, *The Dieppe Raid*, pp. 181 and 184; Atkin, *Dieppe 1942*, pp. 116–33.

112 Neillands, *The Dieppe Raid*, pp. 179–80 and 182–3; Buckley, *Norway The Commandos Dieppe*, p. 248.

113 The account of events on Green Beach draws upon ibid., pp. 249–52, Atkin, *Dieppe 1942*, pp. 134–9, and Neillands, *The Dieppe Raid*, pp. 188–206 and 245.

114 The most evocative account of the withdrawal is in Atkin, *Dieppe 1942*, pp. 214–23.

115 Neillands, *The Dieppe Raid*, pp. 205–6; Atkin, *Dieppe 1942*, pp. 147–9.

116 Admittedly, there were also some very poor soldiers at Pourville, but largely because they were from support units working with the Todt Organisation. See South Saskatchewan recollections of fighting in and around the village, quoted in ibid., pp. 139–40.

117 COHQ had suggested destroying the first line of defence by obsolescent heavy tanks packed with explosives crashing in to the sea wall. However impractical the idea its main advocate always insisted that, 'If only this proposal had been adopted the outcome might have been very different'. Hughes-Hallett, 'Before I Forget', p. 154.

118 The following account of events on Red and White Beaches draws upon: Atkin, *Dieppe 1942*, pp. 150–213, Buckley, *Norway The Commandos Dieppe*, pp. 253–61, and Neillands, *The Dieppe Raid*, pp. 208–45.

119 Ibid., pp. 224–34.

120 For the most vivid account of the Calgary Tanks' and the sappers' nightmare at Dieppe, see Atkin, *Dieppe 1942*, pp. 159–76.

121 Atkin, *Dieppe 1942*, pp. 185–9

122 Jacques Mordal, writing on the raid in 1962, and quoted in ibid., p. 190.

123 Hughes-Hallett, 'Before I Forget', pp. 186–7.

124 Neillands, *The Dieppe Raid*, pp. 243–4.

125 Hughes-Hallett, 'Before I Forget', pp. 186–8.

126 Neillands, *The Dieppe Raid*, pp. 246–50, and Atkin, *Dieppe 1942*, pp. 211–12.

127 Neillands, *The Dieppe Raid*, pp. 255–60, and Atkin, *Dieppe 1942*, pp. 224–34, 236–7 and 241–50.

128 Ibid., pp. 235–6, 250–2, and 254. An alternative global figure, presumably including Allied air casualties, is 4,131, quoted in Neillands, *The Dieppe Raid*, p. 2. Captured equipment included 20 tanks, seven scout cars, a truck, 170 machine-guns, 130 mortars, 42 anti-tank rifles, and 170 rifles: op. cit., p. 253.

129 COHQ, 'Combined Report on the Dieppe Raid', C.B. 04244, 15 October 1942, paras 312, 318 and 321–2, Mountbatten papers, MB1/B65.

130 Atkin, *Dieppe 1942*, pp. 199–209; Terraine, *The Right of the Line*, pp. 560–5. For air ace 'Johnnie' Johnson's graphic account of flying four testing patrols over Dieppe, during a raid he deemed 'a complete failure', see J.E. Johnson, *Wing Leader* (Chatto and Windus, London, 1956/Goodall, London, 2000), pbk edn, pp. 140–5. The problem of fighters operating for very short periods at the extreme of their range was finally solved by fitting a Griffon engine and fuel drop-tanks to later variants of the Mustang.

Chapter Nine

1 Young (ed.), *The Diaries of Sir Robert Bruce Lockhart Vol. 2*, 2 January 1942, p. 133.

2 Lovat, *March Past*, pp. 228–9.

3 Most spectacularly in the cover photo-story for *Illustrated London News*, 25 April 1942.

4 'Commando Chief Lord Louis Mountbatten', *News Review*, 23 April 1942, cover and pp. 5–6; 'Deux espoirs anglais: Lord Mountbatten and Wavell', *La Semaine*, [?] 1942 – article sent to CCO in November 1942 and circulated for comment.

5 See 'Mountbatten and his Commandos' cover stories in *Reader's Digest* [June?] 1942, and *Time*, 8 June 1942.

6 Tribute to the accredited war correspondent in *The Bulldozer The Magazine of Combined Operations*, No. 10, March 1943.

7 Villa, *Unauthorised Action*, p. 23. Fairbanks served four months in the Atlantic before his secondment to COHQ, working on camouflage. He ended the war a much-decorated commander in the USNVR – idolising Mountbatten (and Edwina), his lengthy wartime letters attracted only perfunctory acknowledgement, and yet he was happy to receive any sort of reply. Douglas Fairbanks Jnr, speeches on American intervention 1940–1, and correspondence with CCO and SEAC C-in-C, Mountbatten papers, MB1/C105/1–10 and 11–48.

8 Richard Cockett, *David Astor and The Observer* (André Deutsch, London, 1991), pp. 90–2 and 100.

9 On Orwell's close personal relationship with Astor, 1941–50, see ibid., pp. 94–5, 113–14 and 125–30.

10 Hughes-Hallett, 'Before I Forget', p. 194; George Orwell, diary, 22 August 1942, in Richard J. Aldrich (ed.), *Witness To War Diaries of the Second World War in Europe and the Middle East* (Doubleday, London, 2004), p. 343.

11 M. Bondarenko, London correspondent of Tass, the Soviet news agency, refused an invitation when COHQ denied him advance knowledge of his final destination. Atkin, *Dieppe 1942*, p. 66.

12 *Britain/London Can Take It!* (Humphrey Jennings and Harry Watt, GPO/Crown Film Unit, UK, 1940); Angus Calder, *The Myth of the Blitz* (Jonathan Cape /Pimlico, London, 1991/1992), pbk edn, pp. 209–33.

13 Quentin Reynolds, report on Dieppe, *Reader's Digest*, May 1943, pp. 81–96, and *Dress Rehearsal The Story of Dieppe* (Random House, New York, 1943), p. 12.

14 A.B. Austin, *We Landed At Dawn* (Angus and Robertson, London, 1943).

15 Ross Munro, *Gauntlet to Overlord The Story of the Canadian Army* (MacMillan, Toronto, 1945); Atkin, *Dieppe 1942*, pp. 257 and 66; Wallace Reyburn, *Glorious Chapter: the Canadians at Dieppe* (Harrap, Toronto, 1943) – also published by Harrap in Britain as the best-selling *Rehearsal for Invasion: An Eyewitness Story of the Dieppe Raid*.

16 Wallace Reyburn to the editor, *Sunday Telegraph*, 27 August 1967.

17 Hughes-Hallett, 'Before I Forget', pp. 194–5.

18 J.R.M. Butler, *Grand Strategy Vol. 3 Pt. 2* (HMSO, London, 1964) p. 641; CCO to Prime Minister, 20 August 1942, quoted in Gilbert, *Road To Victory*, p. 211. 'Great air battle. Many casualties and some successes.' Mountbatten, diary, 20 August 1942, quoted in Ziegler, *Mountbatten*, p. 191.

19 Prime Minister to Deputy Prime Minister, 21 August 1942, quoted in Churchill, *The Second World War Vol. IV*, p. 420; Hart-Davis (ed.), *King's Counsellor*, 20 August 1942, pp. 47–8; Alanbrooke, *War Diaries*, 19 August 1942, p. 309; Barnes and Nicholson (eds), *The Empire at Bay*, 20 August 1942, p. 829.

20 Atkin, *Dieppe 1942*, pp. 254–60.

21 Ibid., p. 259.

22 Hughes-Hallett, 'Before I Forget', p. 195; Alanbrooke, *War Diaries*, 17 September 1942, p. 322; COHQ, 'Combined Report', paras 1–375.

23 A future Librarian of the House of Commons, Hilary St George Saunders was no superannuated Westminster apparatchik. He held the MC, had written pre-war thrillers under the *nom de plume* 'Francis Breeding', was author of the Air Ministry's best-selling *The Battle of Britain*, and would later produce a popular history of the Commandos: *The Green Beret* (Michael Joseph, 1949).

24 COHQ, 'Military Lessons to be Drawn from the Assault on Dieppe', November 1942 [incorporating forces commanders' priorities in joint memorandum to CCO, 'Combined operations against Dieppe'], Mountbatten papers, MB1/B33; Admiral Lord Mountbatten to Major General Sir Hastings Ismay, 24 December 1942, ibid., MB1/B18.

25 Prime Minister to Major General Sir Hastings Ismay, 22 [?] December 1942, PREM 3/256, National Archives, quoted in Atkin, *Dieppe 1942*, p. 26.
26 Ministry of Information, 'Home Intelligence Division Weekly Report', Nos 99–106, 27 August-15 October 1942 [microfilm], Hartley Library special collections, University of Southampton. A special thanks to former tutee Rob Smith for drawing my attention to Dieppe's prominence in these reports.
27 Admiral Lord Mountbatten to General Sir Alan Brooke, 31 August 1942, Mountbatten papers, MB1/B17.
28 Alanbrooke, *War Diaries*, 23 October, 9 October, 25 November, 22 and 23 October, and 22 December 1942, pp. 332, 328, 343–4, 332 and 350.
29 Ibid., 23 December 1942, p. 350; Neillands, , *The Dieppe Raid*, pp. 265–6.
30 Major General Sir Hastings Ismay to Admiral Lord Louis Mountbatten, 22 December 1942, Mountbatten papers, MB1/B18.
31 Admiral Lord Louis Mountbatten to Major General Sir Hastings Ismay, 24 December 1942 [inc. copy of CCO's letter to General Sir Alan Brooke, 31 August 1942], ibid.
32 As argued, for example, in Neillands, , *The Dieppe Raid*, p. 97.
33 Hughes-Hallett, 'Before I Forget', pp. 165–6; Alanbrooke, *War Diaries*, 30 June 1942, p. 275: the meeting was rendered insignificant when the PM announced an imminent trip to the Middle East.
34 Admiral Lord Louis Mountbatten to Major General Sir Hastings Ismay, 'Enclosure to letter of 24th December 1942', Mountbatten papers, MB1/B18; COHQ, 'Combined Report', paras 11–24, 27 and 46.
35 'Operation "Jubilee" – The Combined Plan, 31st July 1942', Mountbatten papers, MB1/B32; Neillands, *The Dieppe Raid*, pp. 8–11 and 265–7.
36 Brigadier General Dollard Menton quoted in William Whitehead and Terence Macartney-Filgate (eds), *Dieppe 1942 Echoes of Disaster* (Personal Library, Toronto, 1979/Drew Publishing, London, 1982), p. 42.
37 'The Germans punished mistakes – always.' 21st Army field commander quoted in Max Hastings, 'Up Against 'the Finest Soldiers in the World'', *The New York Review of Books*, 3 April 2008 [review title quoting General Alexander to Brooke, Monte Cassino, March 1944].
38 Miscellaneous files and correspondence re Wing Commander Marquis de Casa Maury, Mountbatten papers, MB1/C46 and B26/27. Murphy was almost certainly engaged in propaganda work for the Political Warfare Executive under the cover of the PID: Foot, *Memories of an SOE Historian*, p. 180.
39 COHQ, 'Combined Report', para. 43; for a judicious assessment of the Intelligence Section's performance, see F.H. Hinsley et al., *British Intelligence in the Second World War Its Influence on Strategy and Operations Volume Two* (HMSO, London, 1981), pp. 696–700.
40 Major Ernest Magnus quoted in Whitehead and Filgate (eds), *Dieppe 1942*, p. 43; Rees, *A Bundle of Sensations*, pp. 152–3; Hamilton, *The Full Monty*, pp. 441 and 447; Campbell, *Dieppe Revisited*, pp. 130–1.
41 Rear-Admiral H.T. Baillie-Grohman quoted in ibid., pp. 26–7
42 Hinsley et al, *British Intelligence in the Second World War*, pp. 696–7.
43 Campbell, *Dieppe Revisited*, pp. 52–3; Villa, *Unauthorized Action*, pp. 205–6.
44 Miscellaneous files and correspondence re Wing Commander Marquis de Casa Maury, Mountbatten papers, B26/27.Evelyn Waugh, dedication to Major-General Sir Robert Laycock, *Officers and Gentlemen*.
45 Ziegler, *Mountbatten*, p. 194.
46 COHQ, 'Combined Report', para. 43; Neillands, *The Dieppe Raid*, pp. 96–7, 273, and 12–13.
47 'I talked to Leigh-Mallory, my air adviser, and he said the chances of even hitting Dieppe are small, let alone of hitting the targets you want … all it would do would be to block the

streets and my tanks would never get through.' General J.H. Roberts quoted in Whitehead and Filgate (eds), *Dieppe 1942*, p. 40.

48 For example, Hughes-Hallett, 'Before I Forget', pp. 155, 156 and 164; Beryl M. Goldsmith to the editor, *Daily Telegraph*, 12 December 1980.

49 COHQ, 'Combined Report', paras 324–75; Hughes-Hallett, 'Before I Forget', pp. 195–200.

50 Hamilton, *The Full Monty*, pp. 438–44.

51 In his last year as the Tory member for Croydon East, Hughes-Hallett gave scant indication of his role at Dieppe, omitting mention of Combined Operations from his *Who's Who* entry.

52 CBC film transcript: Mountbatten of Burma, 'The Dieppe Raid', *The Naval Review*, January 1963, pp. 35–40. Canadian documentaries on Dieppe made by CBC (1963), ABC (1967), Radio-Québec (1976), and CBC (1977); plus in Britain, *Dieppe 1942* (Tony Broughton, BBC, 1972).

53 Admiral of the Fleet Lord Mountbatten to Tony Broughton, 6 September 1976, Mountbatten papers, MB1/B63. *The Life and Times of Lord Mountbatten 5: United We Conquer* (Peter Morley, Rediffusion, UK, 1969).

54 See the extravagant claims of an old man in *Dieppe 1942* (Terence Macartney-Filgate, CBC, 1979), broadcast as two 90 minute programmes in the winter of 1979, having previously been screened at that year's Edinburgh Film Festival; with the commentary and interviews replicated in Whitehead and Filgate (eds), *Dieppe 1942*, p. 174.

55 Admiral of the Fleet Lord Mountbatten to Major General Gilbert W. Embury USAR, 15 July 1973, Mountbatten papers, MB1/B36.

56 Campbell, *Dieppe Revisited*, p. 201.

57 Publication of *The War at Sea* prompted Tom Hussey and Bob Laycock to send the series editor a point-by-point critique of what they saw as a belittling treatment of Combined Operations. Roskill wrote an equally lengthy and almost wholly unrepentant rebuttal of Laycock's criticisms. As CDS Mountbatten wisely chose to remain above the fray; although when all relevant correspondence entered the Broadlands archives in July 1977 he sent Roskill a belated corrective. Major General Sir Robert E. Laycock to Sir James Butler, 6 April 1962, and Captain Stephen Roskill to Major General Sir Robert E. Laycock, 17 April 1962, Mountbatten papers, MB1/56; Admiral of the Fleet Lord Mountbatten to Captain Stephen Roskill, 8 September 1977, ibid., MB1/B49.

58 *History of the Combined Operations Organisation 1940–1945* (Amphibious Warfare Headquarters, London, 1956 – restricted circulation), Mountbatten papers, MB1/B47: originally drafted by retired Rear Admiral H.E. [Pat] Horan in conjunction with the Secretary to the Chief of Amphibious Warfare. 1950–1 correspondence between Mountbatten and Alan Campbell-Johnson re a book on Combined Operations, ibid., MB1/57.

59 1956–61 correspondence re recruiting an author in the absence of an official history, and assistance to Bernard Fergusson in the research, writing, and redrafting of his commissioned book, Mountbatten papers, MB1/57; miscellaneous correspondence between the CDS and Brigadier B.E. Fergusson re research and writing of *The Watery Maze*, 1958–61, ibid., MB1/55 and MB1/56. All involved in the enterprise were greatly disappointed when Fergusson's book failed to sell in large numbers – arguably the tide had turned, and 'true accounts' of wartime derring-do were no longer as popular as in the mid-1950s.

60 Fergusson, *The Watery Maze*, pp. 182–4.

61 Ibid., pp. 185 and 184.

62 McGeoch, *The Princely Sailor*, pp. 79–81.

63 As argued in Douglas Porch, *Hitler's Mediterranean Gamble: The North African and the Mediterranean Campaigns in World War II* (Weidenfeld and Nicolson, London, 2004).

64 For a detailed and convincing refutation of Mountbatten's claim that Operation Jubilee moulded Overlord, see Campbell, *Dieppe Revisited*, pp. 200–27.

65 Ibid., p. 221.

66 Terence Robertson, *Dieppe: the Shame and the Glory* (Hutchinson, London, 1963). In Canada the book had been serialised in the *Weekend Magazine*, to mark the raid's twentieth anniversary. Robertson was highly critical of Mountbatten, airing his views on Canadian TV in the 'Close Up' series' investigation of Dieppe (CBC, Canada, 9 September 1962). This film was screened at the British Film Council Theatre on 27 May 1963, but generated little interest.

67 Mountbatten of Burma, 'Dieppe: The Inside Story', pp. 10–15 and 45–8. Publication of a slightly amended version in the March 1974 issue of the *RUSI Journal* generated correspondence between Mountbatten and the University of Toronto's Colonel C.P. Stacey, Mountbatten papers, MB1/B62.

68 Admiral of the Fleet Lord Mountbatten unedited interview with Terence Macartney-Filgate, 1978, quoted in Villa, *Unauthorized Action*, p. 240.

69 Wallace Reyburn to the editor, *Sunday Telegraph*, 27 August 1967.

70 Vice-Admiral J. Hughes-Hallett and Wallace Reyburn to the editor, *Sunday Telegraph*, 10 and 17 September 1967; Admiral of the Fleet Lord Mountbatten to Vice-Admiral J. Hughes-Hallett, 5 September 1967, Mountbatten papers, MB1/B64.

71 Vice-Admiral J. Hughes-Hallett and Commander David Joel to the editor, *Sunday Telegraph*, 1 and 8 October 1967; Vice-Admiral J. Hughes-Hallett to Michael Berry, 26 September 1967, and Admiral of the Fleet Lord Mountbatten to Vice-Admiral J. Hughes-Hallett, 10 October 1967, Mountbatten papers, MB1/B64.

72 Villa, *Unauthorized Action*, p. 18; Hamilton, *The Full Monty*, p. 467.

73 Ibid., p. 467.

74 Mountbatten interviewed in *Dieppe 42 Aux yeux du present* (Pierre Gavreau, Radio-Québec, 1976).

75 'I could have gone to Prime Minister Winston Churchill and complain but I did not do that, because I had enough confidence in the different people involved to think that they knew what they were doing.' Ibid.; Admiral of the Fleet Lord Mountbatten to John Swettenham [Canadian War Museum], 15 April 1976, Mountbatten papers, MB1/B62.

76 Field Marshal Lord Montgomery interviewed on CBC TV's *Close Up*, 9 September 1962, quoted in Atkin, *Dieppe 1942*, p. 267.

77 'Note by Field-Marshal Montgomery on the Dieppe Raid: August 1962', quoted in Hamilton, *The Full Monty*, pp. 433–6.

78 Montgomery, *The Memoirs of Field Marshal The Viscount Montgomery of Alamein, K.G.*, pp. 75–7.

79 Ronald Lewin, *Montgomery as Military Commander* (B.T. Batsford, London, 1971), pp. 39–4; Percy Howard, 'Will 1959 be Mountbatten's year?', *Daily Express*, 28 December 1958; Admiral of the Fleet Lord Mountbatten to Field Marshal Viscount Montgomery, 25 February and 4 March 1959, and Field Marshal Viscount Montgomery to Admiral of the Fleet Lord Mountbatten, 27 February 1959, Mountbatten papers, MB1/B73.

80 Fergusson, *The Watery Maze*, p. 171; Hamilton, *Monty*, pp. 554, 547 and 555.

81 Hamilton, *The Full Monty*, p. 453; Villa, *Unauthorized Action*, p. 303 f. 4; Leo Amery to PM, 8 April 1942, quoted in Barnes and David Nicholson (eds), *The Empire at Bay*, p.84. Unlike Hamilton, Villa ultimately rejects the supremo argument.

82 Hamilton and Richard Hough both claimed that Mountbatten put pressure on the historical division within the Admiralty responsible for staff histories, in a fruitless attempt to secure a more sympathetic judgement on the raid. Hamilton, *The Full Monty*, pp. 441–2; Hough, *Mountbatten: Hero of Our Time*, p. 157.

83 Hamilton, *The Full Monty*, pp. 427–73.

84 A.N. Wilson has proved an unusually brutal critic, as in Wilson, *Our Times*, pp. 253–9.

85 To take but one example, the uncomplimentary portrayal of the outgoing First Sea Lord in Percy Howard, 'Will 1959 be Mountbatten's year?', *Daily Express*, 28 December 1958 [plus unflattering Cummings caricature] – prompting a rapid rebuttal in Tom Driberg's column, *Reynolds News*, 5 January 1959. It is extremely rare, even today, for a service chief to receive hostile treatment in the British press, let alone the level of criticism Beaverbrook deemed acceptable – his reporters were given a clear signal that the newly-appointed CDS remained a legitimate target.

86 Hamilton, *Monty*, p. 547, quoted in Roberts, 'Lord Mountbatten and the Perils of Adrenalin', p. 68.

87 Peter Murphy to Admiral of the Fleet Lord Mountbatten, [?] January 1955, Mountbatten papers, MB1/I24, quoted in Roberts, ibid., p. 70.

88 Tom Driberg to Admiral of the Fleet Lord Mountbatten, 13 January and 9 February 1954, and 4 January 1955, Mountbatten papers, MB1/I24; Tom Driberg, *Beaverbrook*, pp. 288–91, and *Ruling Passions*, pp. 213–27; Wheen, *Tom Driberg*, pp. 211–21 and 275–91.

89 Campbell, *Dieppe Revisited*, p. 68.

90 Neillands, *The Dieppe Raid*, p. 97.

91 COHQ's inability to provide full and up-to-the-minute intelligence was the one criticism Ziegler shared with Brian Loring Villa, although he refused to accept that Combined Operations' failure to liaise closely with 'the highest authorities in the intelligence and counter-intelligence fields' demonstrated the degree to which its CCO was acting unilaterally: Philip Ziegler, *Mountbatten Revisited* (The Harry Ransom Humanities Research Center, University of Texas at Austin, USA, 1995), pp. 10–11; Villa, *Unauthorised Action*, p. 265.

92 Roberts, 'Lord Mountbatten and the Perils of Adrenalin', pp. 65–9; Lovat, *March Past*, p. 282; Hughes-Hallett, 'Before I Forget', p. 166.

93 For a trenchant critique of Roberts' recent work, arguing that his real strength as a historian lies in biography – as signalled at the outset of his career by his life of Halifax – see Richard Evans, 'Tank Traps', *Times Literary Supplement*, 21/28 August 2009.

94 Andrew Roberts, *'The Holy Fox' A Life of Lord Halifax* (Weidenfeld and Nicolson, 1991). As well as Roberts' television and radio broadcasts re India, his most controversial 'film essay' was the fortieth-anniversary short documentary, *Suez: A Personal View* (BBC2, UK, 1996).

95 Campbell, *Dieppe Revisited A Documentary Investigation*, pacem.

96 Ibid., p. 33.

97 Villa, *Unauthorised Action*, p. 302 f. 4.

98 Ibid., pp. 204–6; Anthony Cave Brown, *Bodyguard of Lies* (Harper Collins, London, 1975); Campbell, *Dieppe Revisited*, pp. 13–17, 19–20, 22, 47, 58–9, 161–6 and 179; Stephen Roskill, 'The Dieppe raid and the question of German foreknowledge', *RUSI Journal*, 1964, vol. CIX no. 633, pp. 27–31. Perhaps as Lord Beaverbrook's final parry, David Irving was commissioned to write three articles, which appeared in the *Evening Standard* on 1, 2 and 14 October 1963. This was long before Ultra became public knowledge, after which he repeated his contentious claim re Dieppe in *Hitler's War* (Viking Press, London, 1977), and in a letter to the *Daily Telegraph* on 2 September 1989.

99 For example, Villa, *Unauthorised Action*, pp. 176–86.

100 Speculation within Chapter Three ranges from Churchill orchestrating absences abroad to coincide with military defeats, through his appointment of Cripps as Leader of the House so that frequent Commons statements would maximise his rival's propensity to make malapropisms, to his privately encouraging Mountbatten to revive plans for the attack on Dieppe. The chapter's fundamental misreading of Attlee's character and intentions (and arguably of Eden's) was compounded by factual errors, for example, a premature ennobling of the FO's PUS, Sir Alexander Cadogan.

101 Ibid., pp. 201, 200, 71–3, and 123–4.

102 Ibid., pp. 31–3, 43–5 and 265.

103 Henshaw, 'The British Chiefs of Staff and the Preparation of the Dieppe Raid', pp. 209–10.

104 Roskill, *The War at Sea 1939–45*, p. 243; *History of the Combined Operations Organisation*, p. 40; Butler, *Grand Strategy*, p. 639; Hinsley et al, *British Intelligence in the Second World War*, p. 697; Henshaw, 'The British Chiefs of Staff', pp. 208–9 and 210–11.

105 Ibid., pp. 211–12 and 198–9.

106 Ibid., pp. 198–9 and 206–8.

107 Ibid., pp. 212–14.

108 Philip Ziegler, review of *Unauthorised Action Mountbatten and the Dieppe Raid 1942* in *Spectator*, 10 March 1990, Foreword to 2001 Edition, *Mountbatten The Official Biography*, pp. xi–xiv, and *Mountbatten Revisited*, pp. 10–11; Villa, *Unauthorised Action*, pp. 43 and 46.

109 Private information.

110 Villa, *Unauthorised Action*, pp. 19–22 and 28–40; Ziegler, *Mountbatten Revisited*, pp. 10–11; Churchill, *The Second World War Vol. IV*, pp. 411–13.

111 Villa, *Unauthorised Action*, p. 39; Churchill, *The Hinge of Fate*, pp. 412–13.

112 'Cato', *Guilty Men*: Beaverbrook always denied any involvement in Michael Foot and his fellow pamphleteers' blistering denunciation of appeasement; a connection with Mountbatten is that co-author Frank Owen later edited *SEAC*. On Churchill's unforgiving portrait of Stanley Baldwin, but surprisingly gentle treatment of Neville Chamberlain, see Philip Williamson, 'Baldwin's reputation: politics and history, 1937–1967', *The Historical Journal*, 2004, vol. 47 no. 1, pp. 127–68.

113 Reynolds, *In Command of History*, pp. 345–8.

114 Ibid., p. 348.

Chapter Ten

1 Fergusson, *The Watery Maze*, pp. 223, 159–60, 261 and 384; CCO to General Sir Alan Brooke, 10 and 15 March, and 4 May 1943, and to VCIGS [General Sir Archibald Nye], 26 May 1943, Mountbatten papers, MB1/B17; Brigadier R.E. Laycock to CCO, 31 March 1943, inc. paper on reorganisation of the Special Service Brigade, ibid. Some RM units not absorbed into the Commandos were assigned to landing craft duties in order to alleviate the acute shortage of crews. On a detailed description of the SSB's evolving structure, within an impressively succinct history of wartime special forces, see Tim Moreman, *British Commandos 1940–1946* (Osprey, London, 2006).

2 Prime Minister to Chief of Combined Operations, 1 May 1943, quoted in ibid., p. 224.

3 For example, see Haydon-Mountbatten exchange of 7–8 October 1942, Mountbatten papers, MB1/B28.

4 Ibid., p. 207; Fergusson, *The Watery Maze*, pp. 225–6 and 221.

5 Alanbrooke, *War Diaries*, 22 December 1942, p. 350; McGeoch, *The Princely Sailor*, pp. 83–4.

6 Morgan, *Edwina*, p. 320; Ziegler, *Mountbatten*, pp. 211–12. See entries between 5 and 27 April 1943 in Alanbrooke, *War Diaries*, pp. 392–6.

7 Ibid., 9 July 1942 and 21 June 1943, pp. 278 and 422; Henriques, *From a Biography of Myself*, pp. 155–7 and 132.

8 Alanbrooke, *War Diaries*, 3 September 1942, p. 317; Mountbatten's Washington message: Winston S. Churchill to Harry Hopkins [?] September 1942, quoted in McGeoch, *The Princely Sailor*, pp. 85–6.

9 Fergusson, *The Watery Maze*, pp. 199 and 208

10 Ibid., pp. 215 and 229–36. The LCT(R) was an important invention, even if reloading proved a lengthy process: firing in 26 seconds 840 (later 1080) rockets at over 3,000 metres, its firepower was the equivalent of a bombardment by 80 cruisers or 240 destroyers; each

rocket had an effect 25 per cent greater than that of a six-inch shell: ibid., p. 236. Stephen Roskill, *The War at Sea 1939–45 Vol. 3 Part 1 The Offensive* (HMSO, London, 1960), p. 119.

11 Alanbrooke, *War Diaries*, 23 December 1942 and note to 13 January 1943, pp. 350 and 358; Fraser, *Alanbrooke*, pp. 283–4 and 294.

12 Alanbrooke, *War Diaries*, notes to 12 and to 13 January 1943, and 21 January 1943, pp. 357–8 and 365; Harry Hopkins quoted in Ziegler, *Mountbatten*, p. 203.

13 Fraser, *Alanbrooke*, pp. 294–5; Alanbrooke, *War Diaries*, 21 January 1943 and note, pp. 365–6.

14 Ibid., 22 January 1943, pp. 366–7; Harry Hopkins quoted in Ziegler, *Mountbatten*, p. 203.

15 For example, Alanbrooke, *War Diaries*, 19 February and 10 March 1943, pp. 383 and 388.

16 Brigadier Antony Head and Major Robert Henriques quoted in Fergusson, *The Watery Maze*, p. 241.

17 Mountbatten anecdote in ibid., pp. 241–2.

18 Morgan, *Edwina*, p. 321.

19 Close observation of the invasion's initial stages: 'afforded me invaluable experience and a much increased understanding of the problems and difficulties of major Combined Operations': CCO, 'Operation 'Husky' Memorandum by Chief of Combined Operations', para. 36, Mountbatten papers, MB1/B31.

20 Mountbatten anecdote for possible use by HRH Prince of Wales at El Alamein reunion, ibid., MB1/N73.

21 Fergusson, *The Watery Maze*, p. 250.

22 Ibid., p. 219.

23 Lt-Gen. Sir Frederick Morgan, *Overture to Overlord* (Hodder and Stoughton, London, 1950) p. 31, 76 and 143; Admiral Lord Mountbatten quoted in Harrison, *Mulberry*, pp 126–8; Morgan, op. cit., p. 49.

24 Ibid., p. 92; Fergusson, *The Watery Maze*, pp. 222 and 264; Chiefs of Staff directive, 24 May 1943, quoted in Ziegler, *Mountbatten*, p. 212; Alanbrooke, *War Diaries*, footnote to 23 April 1943, p. 383; 'American made some difficulty about Morgan running the show as it might detract from his energies in preparing plans for 1944!!': ibid.

25 CCO-COSSAC correspondence, 1943, Mountbatten papers, MB1/B19; Morgan, *Overture to Overlord*, p. 181; Fergusson, *The Watery Maze*, pp. 201–3 and 268–9.

26 Ibid., pp. 39, 43 94 , 218 and 265 ; Fraser, *Alanbrooke*, pp. 314–18; Alanbrooke, *War Diaries*, 21 May 1943, p. 408.

27 Fergusson, *The Watery Maze*, pp. 265–70; Morgan, *Overture to Overlord*, p. 142–3.

28 Fergusson, *The Watery Maze*, pp. 270–2; Morgan, *Overture to Overlord*, p. 142–3.

29 Admiral Lord Louis Mountbatten to General Sir Bernard Montgomery, 4 February 1944, Mountbatten papers, MB1/N77, and quoted in Harrison, *Mulberry*, p. 128.

30 Morgan, *Overture to Overlord*, pp. 143–9; Ziegler, *Mountbatten*, p. 694.

31 COSSAC report to Chiefs of Staff, Parts I–III, 3 August 1943, quoted in Fergusson, *The Watery Maze*, pp. 281–2. The CIGS displayed his usual healthy scepticism upon receiving Morgan's report and briefing: Alanbrooke, *War Diaries*, 4 August 1943, p. 435.

32 Sir Harold Wernher quoted in Harrison, *Mulberry*, p. 130.

33 Lord Zuckerman quoted in Nye, *Blackett Physics, War, and Politics in the Twentieth Century*, p. 84. On Blackett and the origins of OR, see Richard Ormerod, 'The father of operational research' in Hore (ed.), *Patrick Blackett*, pp. 187–200.

34 Edgerton, *Warfare State*; and chapters 5–6 in David Edgerton, *The Shock of the Old Technology and Global History Since 1900* (Profile, London, 2006/2008), pbk edn. For Blackett's wartime thinking re the organisation and methodology of operational research, see P.M.S. Blackett, *Studies of War* (Hill and Wang, New York, 1962).

35 Adrian Fort, *PROF The Life of Frederick Lindemann* (Jonathan Cape/Pimlico, London 2003/2004), pbk edn, pp. 136–47; Paul Crook, 'The case against area bombing' in Hore (ed.), *Patrick Blackett*, pp. 167–86 For an insider's account of the notorious Tizard-

Lindemann quarrel, so debilitating to science policy-making in mid-century Britain, see: C.P. Snow, *Science in Britain* (Oxford University Press, Oxford, 1961).

36 On the deep antipathy between the two men, see Fort, *PROF* , pp. 146, 251 and 274.

37 Zuckerman, 'Admiral of the Fleet Earl Mountbatten', pp. 162–3.

38 Robert Anderson, 'Blackett in India: thinking strategically about new conflicts' in Hore (ed.), *Patrick Blackett*, pp. 226–37, and Nye, *Blackett Physics, War, and Politics in the Twentieth Century*, pp. 160–7.

39 Mary Jo Nye, 'Blackett, Patrick Maynard Stuart', *Oxford Dictionary of National Biography* (OUP, Oxford, 2004), www.oxforddnb.com.

40 Chief of the Defence Staff, speech to annual dinner of the Royal Society, 30 November 1962; Professor Sir Solly Zuckerman, 'Statement in support of candidature', Royal Society, 9 March 1966; Professor Patrick Blackett to Admiral Lord Mountbatten, 31 March 1966, and reply, 10 April 1966. Mountbatten papers, MB1/M36.

41 Andrew Brown, *J.D. Bernal The Sage of Science* (Oxford University Press, Oxford, 2005/2007), pbk edn, pp. 188–9.

42 Fort, *PROF* , pp. 1–65, 113–33 and 159–82.

43 On Lindemann's role in the damning Butt Report on Bomber Command, see ibid., pp. 237–40, and Brown, *J.D. Bernal*, pp. 194–6.

44 Ibid., pp. 92–4, 104, 111, 121–4, 126, and 129–35; Solly Zuckerman, *From Apes To Warlords An Autobiography 1904–46* (Heinemann/Collins, London, 1978/1988), pbk edn, p. 60.

45 Ibid., pp. 52 and 54; Brown, *J.D. Bernal*, pp. 112 and 133. In 1938, when Blackett left London University to take up the Langworthy Chair at Manchester, Bernal moved down from Cambridge to succeed his friend as Professor of Physics at Birkbeck College: ibid., pp. 156–7.

46 Zuckerman, pp. 109 and 101–2.

47 Ibid., pp. 111–12; Brown, *J.D. Bernal*, pp. 175–6 and 196.

48 Ibid., pp. 129–36 and 190–3; Zuckerman, *From Apes To Warlords*, pp. 113–30 and 134–9.

49 Ibid., pp. 139–48; Brown, *J.D. Bernal*, pp. 196–204; Fort, *PROF*, pp. 239–57; CDS speech to the Royal Society, 30 November 1962; John Peyton, *Solly Zuckerman A Scientist Out of the Ordinary* (John Murray, London, 2001), p. 36.

50 Zuckerman, 'Admiral of the Fleet Earl Mountbatten', pp. 148. The two meetings did involve lengthy conversations, at Christ Church in the summer of 1946 and in mid-1951 at Admiralty House. Edwina first met Zuckerman when he was invited to lunch in May 1943, and rarely saw him again: ibid., pp. 142–3.

51 Re Polaris, see Richard Maguire, 'An enlightenment scientist in an irrational world: Lord Zuckerman and the British Government's nuclear weapons programme', unpublished paper, Mountbatten Centre for International Studies, University of Southampton. Re the Profumo scandal, Mountbatten passed on to Douglas Fairbanks Jnr. Zuckerman's advice not to take legal action over newspaper allegations of his involvement: '… he thinks you would be mad to risk further publicity unless you had 100% case [sic], and from what you told me, you haven't.' Admiral Lord Mountbatten to Douglas Fairbanks Jnr, 31 July 1963, Mountbatten papers, MB1/J161.

52 Peyton, *Solly Zuckerman*, pp. 140–1.

53 For example, 'Mountbatten masked determination with charm, finesse, and when needed, guile', and the frank conclusion explaining why his friend *was* a great man but nevertheless flawed: Zuckerman, 'Admiral of the Fleet Earl Mountbatten', pp. 131 and 166–7.

54 Ibid., pp. 160–2, and Solly Zuckerman, *Monkeys, Men and Missiles An Autobiography 1946–88* (W.W. Norton, New York, 1999), pp. 463–4. Cudlipp's account forms the basis for Philip Ziegler's assessment of an episode that clouded Mountbatten's later years: Ziegler, *Mountbatten*, pp. 659–62. See also Stephen Dorrill and Robin Ramsay, *Smear! Wilson and the Secret State* (Grafton, London, 1992), and an authoritative account of events in Ruth

Dudley Edwards, *Newspapermen Hugh Cudlipp, Cecil Harmsworth King and the Glory Days of Fleet Street* (Secker and Warburg, London, 2003).

55 Brown, *J.D. Bernal*, pp. 208–11; Zuckerman, 'Admiral of the Fleet Earl Mountbatten', p. 136, and *From Apes To Warlords*, pp. 150–3.

56 CCO minute, [?] May 1942, quoted in ibid., p. 152.

57 Ibid., p. 153; Brown, *J.D. Bernal*, pp. 210–11.

58 'John Desmond Bernal Tribute by Lord Zuckerman O.M., K.C.B., F.R.S.', 24 January 1972, p. 7, and 'Memories of Desmond Bernal by Admiral of the Fleet The Earl Mountbatten of Burma, K.G., O.M., D.S.O., F.R.S.', 1972, p. 4, Mountbatten papers, MB1/B52.

59 See Eric Hobsbawm, 'Red Science', *London Review of Books*, 9 March 2006.

60 Zuckerman, 'Admiral of the Fleet Earl Mountbatten', pp. 136–7.

61 CDS speech to the Royal Society, 30 November 1962; Zuckerman, *From Apes To Warlords*, pp. 155–6; Alanbrooke, *War Diaries*, 6 May 1942, p. 255.

62 Fergusson, *The Watery Maze*, pp. 237–40; Zuckerman, *From Apes To Warlords*, pp. 156 and 176–207. An unforgiving Air Staff ordered Zuckerman not to discuss D-Day planning with Blackett: Nye, *Blackett Physics, War, and Politics in the Twentieth Century*, p. 84.

63 Zuckerman, 'Admiral of the Fleet Earl Mountbatten', p. 140.

64 Brown, *J.D. Bernal*, pp. 214–15 and 239–46.

65 Ibid., pp. 213–15; Zuckerman, 'Admiral of the Fleet Earl Mountbatten', p. 140, and *From Apes To Warlords*, pp. 156–8.

66 Ibid., p. 158.

67 Ibid., pp. 150–1; Giles Foden, *Turbulence* (Faber and Faber, London, 2009). Foden's major departure from actual events is to extend the 'Habbakuk' project into 1944 in order for his central character, Henry Meadows, to move almost directly from working with Pyke to forecasting a brief break in the bad weather that is delaying D-Day.

68 Brown, *J.D. Bernal*, pp. 26 and 208–9; David Lampe, *Pyke The Unknown Genius* (Evans Brothers, London, 1959), pp. 15–88.

69 Ibid., p. 88.

70 Lampe, *Pyke*, pp. 96–105; Ziegler, *Mountbatten*, p. 198.

71 Ibid., pp. 110–26, 153 and 156–8; Brown, *J.D. Bernal*, pp. 211–12. Pyke's voluminous memos and proposals may be found in Mountbatten papers, MB1/C209.

72 Lampe, *Pyke*, pp. 141–4; Brown, *J.D. Bernal*, p. 215.

73 Geoffrey Pyke to C-in-C SEAC, 8 June 1944, Mountbatten papers, MB1/C209.

74 Attachment to Geoffrey Pyke, 'Mammoth Unsinkable Vessel with Functions of a Floating Airfield', August 1942, ibid.; scrawled across the first page in blue and red ink was a message for Mountbatten: 'This Memorandum – however dogmatic its focus, is intended as everything I have written for you, as a catalyst of the ideas of other people. No idea is a good one which does not breed its successors', ibid. Confusion remains as to whether 'Habbakuk' is a reference to a character in Voltaire's *Candide*, or a misspelt nod to the Old Testament prophet Habakuk: Fergusson, *The Watery Maze*, pp. 145–6.

75 Pyke, 'Mammoth Unsinkable Vessel with Functions of a Floating Airfield'; Brown, *J.D. Bernal*, pp. 215–16; Max F. Perutz, 'Enemy Alien' in *I Wish I'd Made You Angry Earlier Essays on Science, Scientists, and Humanity* (Cold Spring Harbor Laboratory Press, New York, 1998), pp. 90 and 89.

76 Zuckerman, *From Apes To Warlords*, pp. 158–9; PM to General Sir Hastings Ismay, 7 December 1942, quoted in Perutz, 'Enemy Alien', p. 88: CCO to Lord Cherwell, [?] 1942, in Fort, *PRO*, p. 236. For the CIGS's view of, 'One of Dickie Mountbatten's bright ideas!', see Alanbrooke, *War Diaries*, 9 August 1943, p. 438.

77 Tim Lewens, 'Launch the Icebergs!', *London Review of Books*, 15 November 2007; Perutz, 'Enemy Alien', pp. 80–2.

78   Ibid., pp. 82–4; meeting with Wernher re Perutz's security clearance described in Lt Cmd.
      Douglas Grant to Geoffrey Pyke, 22 February 1943, quoted in Georgina Ferry, *Max
      Perutz and the Secret of Life* (Chatto and Windus, London, 2007), p. 102.
79   Brown, *J.D. Bernal*, p. 218; Ziegler, *Mountbatten*, p. 210; 'bergship' specification given in
      Perutz, 'Enemy Alien', pp. 89–90; for the Admiralty's July 1943 'Habbakuk' blueprints,
      see file ADM1/15236, National Archives.
80   Zuckerman, *From Apes to Warlords*, p. 159.
81   For Pyke's bizarre encounters with Canada's wartime PM, see ibid., p. 158, and Perutz,
      'Enemy Alien', p. 84.
82   Ferry, *Max Perutz*, p. 103. Douglas Grant requested mufti so as not to attract the attention
      of Smithfield porters. Massey was familiar to film fans as the Canadian speaking at the
      start of Humphrey Jennings' widely-screened documentary, *Listen To Britain* (Crown Film
      Unit, UK, 1941).
83   Zuckerman, *From Apes to Warlords*, pp. 164–5; Lampe, *Pyke*, pp. 144–50; Brown, *J.D. Bernal*,
      pp. 225–7; Ferry, *Max Perutz*, p. 104; Perutz, 'Enemy Alien', p. 85.
84   Lampe, *Pyke*, pp. 144–50, pp. 162–3 and 167–9; Geoffrey Pyke, 'Power-driven Rivers', [?]
      1943, Mountbatten papers, MB1/C209. Pyke later sent Mountbatten detailed plans for a
      gigantic pneumatic tube to despatch men and material from Burma to China, which was
      duly subjected to serious technical review: Memo to Supreme Allied Commander, South
      East Asia, 'The Military Significance of Power-Driven-Rivers. With Particular Reference
      to The War in the Far East', 8 June 1944, and acknowledgement, 28 July 1944, ibid.
85   Geoffrey Pyke to CCO, 16 June 1943, and attached 'Extract from:- Obituary Notice of
      The Late Commissar for National Defence, THE TIMES (Official organ of the British
      Soviet Republic of the U.S.S.R.)', Mountbatten papers, MB1/B15.
86   Geoffrey Pyke to Supreme Allied Commander, South East Asia, 14 June 1944, and reply,
      28 July 1944, Mountbatten papers, MB1/C209.
87   Ferry, *Max Perutz*, pp. 105–7; Perutz, 'Enemy Alien', pp. 91 and 92; Geoffrey Pyke to
      CCO, 3 August 1943, and attached draft paper: 'Has the relation of Norway to the
      strategy of the rest of the war been so fully worked out that it contributes the maximum
      to that strategy?', Mountbatten papers, MB1/C209s; Brown, *J.D. Bernal*, pp. 231–2.
88   Trevor Royle, *Orde Wingate Irregular Soldier* (Weidenfeld and Nicolson, 1995), pp. 262–4.
      A more benevolent CIGS nevertheless saw the Chindit leader's last-minute invitation to
      Canada as a waste of everyone's time, and with Mountbatten and the other chiefs had
      already vetoed Churchill's proposal that Wingate be made overall army commander in SE
      Asia: Alanbrook, *War Diaries*, 4 August and 25 July 1943, pp. 436 and 433; Royle, op. cit.,
      pp. 283, 296–7, 303–4, and 307.
89   Churchill arranged for Lorna Wingate, an even more committed Zionist than her
      husband, to join the *Queen Mary*; her dinner-table evangelising for Israel infuriated 617
      Squadron's CO. John Bierman and Colin Smith, *Fire in the Night Wingate of Burma, Ethiopia,
      and Zion* (Radom/Pan, London, 1999/2000), pbk edn, pp. 313–18, 325; Morgan, *Edwina
      Mountbatten*, p. 323; Ziegler, *Mountbatten*, p. 217.
90   Brown, *J.D. Bernal*, pp. 232–4; Alanbrook, *War Diaries*, added commentary to entry for 19
      August 1942, pp. 445–6; Lampe, *Pyke*, pp. 144–7. Churchill claimed that the bullet nearly
      hit Portal, and another source identified Admiral King; whereas Douglas Grant claimed it
      struck him and the CCO himself: Ferry, *Max Perutz*, p. 106.
91   Ibid., pp. 106–10; Brown, *J.D. Bernal*, pp. 235–9, 243, 245, and 255–63 ; CCO to Lt.
      General F.E. Morgan, 24 August 1943, and reply 4 September 1943, Mountbatten papers,
      MB1/B19; C-in-C SEAC to J.D. Bernal, 23 December 1944, quoted in Brown, op. cit.,
      p. 263.
92   'I think he is enjoying being in the midst of this weird party, and it is lovely having him
      as I can discuss my terrific problems with him …': Dickie to Edwina re Bunny Phillips,
      quoted in Morgan, *Edwina Mountbatten*, p. 322.

93 'Memories of Desmond Bernal', ibid.; Perutz, 'Enemy Alien', pp. 91 and 95;

94 Brown, *J.D. Bernal*, pp. 477–84 ; 'John Desmond Bernal Tribute', ibid. Zuckerman even privately questioned Blackett's achievements: Brown, op. cit., pp. 483–4.

95 'Memories of Desmond Bernal', ibid.; Perutz, 'Enemy Alien', p. 95; Lewens, 'Launch the Icebergs!'

96 Zuckerman, 'Admiral of the Fleet Earl Mountbatten', p. 139; Harrison, *Mulberry*, p. 16; Fergusson, *The Watery Maze*, pp. 286–7.

97 Captain Thomas Hussey to Admiral Lord Mountbatten, 21 December 1967, Mountbatten papers, MB1/B49; interview with Geoffrey Lloyd, quoted in Ziegler, *Mountbatten*, pp. 208–9. Lloyd was the minister responsible for the Petroleum Warfare Department who, at a demonstration on Salisbury Plain in April 1942, was supposedly asked by Mountbatten if his engineers could lay a pipeline across the Channel – an idea submitted to the COSC two months later.

98 Quoted in Terraine, *The Life and Times of Lord Mountbatten*, p. 130.

99 Mountbatten quoted in Harrison, *Mulberry*, p. 18.

100 Hughes-Hallett quoted in ibid., pp. 16 and 79; Churchill, *The Second World War Vol. V*, p. 59; Harrison, op. cit., pp. 118–20; Eisenhower, *Crusade in Europe*, p. 258; Captain Thomas Hussey to Admiral Lord Mountbatten, 27 October 1967, Mountbatten papers, MB1/B49.

101 Churchill, *The Second World War Vol. V*, pp. 59–61, 465, and 467 – previous minutes from PM to CCO re progress were despatched on 26 September and 1 December 1942; Brown, *J.D. Bernal*, pp. 228–9; Harrison, *Mulberry*, pp. 135 and 138–9; Fergusson, *The Watery Maze*, pp. 278–80 and 284–6; Brown, op. cit., pp. 232–3; 'Memories of Desmond Bernal', ibid.

102 Harrison, *Mulberry*, pp. 18 and 130–2: a fawning author insisted that an *Observer* sub-editor had omitted the CDS's qualifying remarks.

103 Hough, *Mountbatten: Hero of Our Time*, pp. 159–60.

104 On Overlord as a 'planning triumph' for Combined Operations' scientific advisers, see COHQ, 'Overloard Bulletins' Y/36 and Y/39, autumn 1944, quoted in Brown, *J.D. Bernal*, p. 254.

105 General Hastings Ismay to Admiral Lord Louis Mountbatten, 6 July 1944, Mountbatten papers, MB1/C295.

106 Quoted in: anon., *History of Combined Operations*, p. 74; Fergusson, *The Watery Maze*, p. 350; and Terraine, *The Life and Times of Lord Mountbatten*, pp. 130–1.

107 Winston S. Churchill, *The Second World War Vol. VI Triumph and Tragedy* (Curtis Brown, New York, 1954), pp. 11–13: Churchill erroneously recorded the date of the visit as 10 June. Alanbrooke, *War Diaries*, 12 June 1944, pp. 556–8. For the CIGS's grim humour that day regarding Churchill, see the anecdote in Fraser, *Alanbrooke*, p. 395.

108 Churchill, *The Second World War Vol. VI* , p. 13; Philip Ziegler (ed.), *Personal Diary of Admiral the Lord Louis Mountbatten Supreme Allied Commander, South-East Asia, 1943–1946* (Collins, London, 1988), 10–15 June 1944, p. 111; Fergusson, *The Watery Maze*, p. 350.

109 Quoted in ibid., and Ziegler, *Mountbatten*, p. 215.

Chapter Eleven

1 For a recent downgrading of Mountbatten's significance in the grand scheme of things, see Hastings, *Nemesis*, pacem.

2 Christopher Bayly and Tim Harper, *Forgotten Armies Britain's Asian Empire and the war with Japan* (Allen Lane/Penguin, London, 2004/2005), pbk edn, pp. 431–2; Morgan, *Edwina Mountbatten*, pp. 366, 369 and 372–3.

3 On the prescience of Clausewitz's observations re problems facing the victorious commander, see Hew Strachan, *Carl Von Clausewitz's On War A Biography* (Atlantic Books, London, 2007), pbk edn, pp. 172–5 and 189.

4 Thus since 1963 the CDS has been the only five-star officer on active service. Smith, 'Command and Control in Postwar Britain', p. 307.

5 Mountbatten quoted in Terraine, *The Life and Times of Lord Mountbatten*, p. 132, and Hough, *Mountbatten: Hero of Our Time*, p. 162.

6 On a fishing tribute in Canada a jaunty Mountbatten would save an exhausted Pound from falling down a ravine. Alanbrooke, *War Diaries*, note added to 12 August 1943, p. 440.

7 Ibid., 21 May 1943, p. 408; PM to General Sir Hastings Ismay, 26 July 1943, quoted in Ziegler, *Mountbatten*, pp. 217–18. Wavell's military command ended when he was appointed Viceroy in June 1943.

8 Leo Amery diary, 31 May 1943, quoted in Christopher Thorne, *Allies of a Kind The United States, Britain and the war against Japan, 1941–1945* (Hamish Hamilton, London, 1978), p. 298.

9 Alanbrooke, *War Diaries*, 14 May 1943, p. 403; Thorne, *Allies of a Kind*, pp. 298–9; Bayly and Harper, *Forgotten Armies*, pp. 291–2.

10 Ibid., p. 299; Alanbrooke, *War Diaries*, note added to 17 June, and 5, 13 and 15 July 1943, pp. 421, 426, 429 and 430.

11 Warner, *Cunningham of Hyndhope*, p. 222; Alanbrooke, *War Diaries*, 14 July 1943, p. 429; Ziegler, *Mountbatten*, p. 220.

12 'It is a poor business but I think most people in the service have just laughed': Admiral Sir Andrew Cunningham to Admiral Whitworth [?] September 1943, quoted in McGeoch, *The Princely Sailor*, p. 97, as evidence that even the greatest warriors have chinks in their armour; 'Some comments by Admiral of the Fleet the Earl Mountbatten of Burma'.

13 Alanbrooke, *War Diaries*, 6 August 1943, p. 437; Martin Gilbert, *Road to Victory: Winston S. Churchill 1941–1945* (London, Heinemann, 1986), p. 467; Ziegler, *Mountbatten*, pp. 220–2; Alanbrooke, op. cit., 15 August 1943, p. 441; Ismay quoted in Young (ed.), *The Diaries of Sir Robert Bruce Lockhart 2*, 21 February 1946, p. 527.

14 Brian Bond (ed.), *Chief of Staff The Diaries of Lieutenant-General Sir Henry Pownall Vol. Two* (Leo Cooper, London, 1974), introduction, and 14 September 1943, pp. xiii–xviii and 108–9; Alanbrooke, *War Diaries*, 31 May 1944, p. 552. On the strategic dimension to Brooke's opposition, see Bayly and Harper, *Forgotten Armies*, pp. 292–3.

15 Before he died Alanbrooke gave the impression that the PM's agreement to American supreme command of Overlord was a quid pro quo for Mountbatten's appointment: Arthur Bryant, *The Turn of the Tide, 1939–1943* (Collins, London, 1957), p. 707.

16 Alanbrooke, *War Diaries*, note added to 15 August 1943, pp. 441–2; Mountbatten quoted in Terraine, *The Life and Times of Lord Mountbatten*, pp. 132–3, and in Ziegler, *Mountbatten*, p. 217; Ismay quoted in, Young (ed.), *The Diaries of Sir Robert Bruce Lockhart 2*, 21 February 1946, p. 527; Dickie to Edwina, 18 August 1943, quoted in Morgan, *Edwina Mountbatten*, p. 322.

17 Fergusson, *The Watery Maze*, pp. 291–3; Thorne, *Allies of a Kind*, p. 300; Ziegler, *Mountbatten*, pp. 224–6

18 Ibid.; Morgan, *Edwina Mountbatten*, pp. 322–3. On Mountbatten's reception in Delhi, see Bayly and Harper, *Forgotten Armies*, pp. 293.

19 CCO to CIGS, 16 September 1943, Mountbatten papers, MB1/B17 and CIGS to CCO, 18 September 1943, ibid., MB1/C50.

20 Robert Lyman, *The Generals: From Victory to Defeat, Leadership in the Burma Campaign, 1941–45* (Constable, London, 2008), p. 191.

21 Alanbrooke, *War Diaries*, note added to 21 October 1943, pp. 462.

22 Ibid., 21 June 1944, p. 561.

23 Ibid., 24 and 27 July, and 7,8, 9 and 10 August 1945, pp. 711, 712, and 715–16.

24 Recollection of General Sir Leslie Hollis, quoted in Harrison, *Mulberry*, pp. 146–7.

25 Arthur Bryant, *The Turn of the Tide*, and *Triumph in the West* (Collins, London, 1959).

26 Harrison, *Mulberry*, acknowledgements, pp. 11–12.

27 Ibid., p. 13.

28 Ibid., pp. 140–1.

29 Ibid., pp. 31–6, 145, and 146–7.

30 Ibid., pp. 116–21.

31 Lambert, 'Transcendent Talent: Andrew Cunningham (1883–1963)', p. 407; Peter Gretton, 'Vian, Sir Philip Louis', *Oxford Dictionary of National Biography* (OUP, Oxford, 2004), www.oxforddnb.com.

32 Ziegler, *Mountbatten*, pp. 521–4; 'Some comments by Admiral of the Fleet the Earl Mountbatten of Burma'.

33 This comparison draws heavily upon the judicious assessment of Beatty in Lambert, 'Ruthless Bounder: David Beatty', pp. 335–78.

34 Lambert, 'Transcendent Talent: Andrew Cunningham (1883–1963)', pp. 383 and 417.

35 This comparison of Mountbatten with Cunningham draws heavily upon a second judicious assessment by Andrew Lambert, in ibid., pp. 379–420.

36 Ibid., pp. 410–11.

37 Correspondence between Lord Avon and Admiral Lord Mountbatten, spring 1972, Mountbatten papers, MB1/L149.

38 Diary of Sir Anthony Eden, 6 February 1955, quoted in Thorpe, *Eden*, p. 458.

39 Ibid., pp. 458, 479–80, and 493–4.

40 First Sea Lord to the Prime Minister, 2 November 1956, Mountbatten papers, MB1/L149.

41 Mountbatten notes on Suez, spring 1972, ibid.

42 Admiral Lord Mountbatten to Lord Hailsham, 4 November 1956, and reply 5 November 1956, ibid.; First Lord of the Admiralty to the Prime Minister, 5 November 1956, PREM11/1090, National Archives, and quoted in Thorpe, *Eden*, p. 532.

43 Lord Avon, memo on Suez, 9 September 1968, quoted in ibid.; Mountbatten notes on Suez, spring 1972, Mountbatten papers, MB1/L149.

44 Lord Avon to Robert Lacey [?] January 1976, quoted in Thorpe, *Eden*, p. 585.

45 Carlton, *Anthony Eden*, pp. 364–5; Ziegler (ed.) *From Shore to Shore*, 13 June 1976, pp. 340–1.

46 Robert Lacey, *Majesty Elizabeth II and the House of Windsor* (Hutchinson , London, 1977), p. 238; Sarah Bradford, *Elizabeth A Biography of Her Majesty* (Heinemann, London, 1996), p. 234; Ben Pimlott, *The Queen A Biography of Elizabeth II* (Harper Collins , London, 1996), pp. 254 and 255; Thorpe, *Eden*, pp. 585–8.

47 Ibid., p. 588.

48 CCO to PM, 28 August 1941, Mountbatten papers, MB1/N41.

49 Admiral of the Fleet Lord Mountbatten to Captain Stephen Roskill, 4 October 1946, ibid., MB1/K208.

50 M.R.D. Foot observed his old boss at Churchill's funeral, Mountbatten's 'ravaged face clearly indicating, "Gentlemen don't cry in public, but if they did then I should be floods"'. Foot, *Memories of an S.O.E. Historian*, p. 140.

51 Reynolds, *In Command of History*, pp. 345–8.

52 For example, the bland endorsement from Mountbatten's principal naval aide while his old boss was still alive: Vice-Admiral Sir Ronald Brockman, 'Mountbatten' in Field Marshal Sir Michael Carver (ed.), *The War Lords Military Commanders of the Twentieth Century* (Weidenfeld and Nicolson, London, 1976), pp. 357–74.

53 Mountbatten's last confidant, Solly Zuckerman, confirmed that his friend was often short-tempered in his dealings with domestic staff, but insisted that he, 'was fully aware of his major warts ... his vanities'. Zuckerman, 'Admiral of the Fleet Earl Mountbatten of Burma', p. 163.

54 Ibid., p. 166.

55   Geoffrey Pyke, unpublished profile of Mountbatten, autumn 1943, replicated in Lampe, *Pyke*, p. 166.

56   Smith, 'Mountbatten goes to the movies', p. 401.

57   A.P. Wavell (ed.), *Other Men's Flowers* (Jonathan Cape, London, 1944).

58   Zuckerman, 'Admiral of the Fleet Earl Mountbatten of Burma', p. 167.

59   Pyke, unpublished profile of Mountbatten, replicated in Lampe, *Pyke*, pp. 166–7.

60   Mountbatten contrasts with the genuinely creative 'Max', a US Army captain who post-Iraq resigned his commission to attend film school, informing his West Point mentor that, 'It amazes me how much a film set runs and operates like a military unit. Commands, phonetic alphabet, chain of command, etc.'. The tutor later extended the parallels, noting how many Hollywood titans like Walsh and De Mille, 'behaved as if they were generals in the field'. Elizabeth D. Samet, *Soldier's Heart Reading Literature Through Peace and War at West Point* (Farrar, Straus and Giroux, New York, 2007), p. 251.

61   On Mountbatten's misguided intention to seek a stipend as chair of the NERC, and his aggressive lobbying on the Council's behalf, see Zuckerman, 'Admiral of the Fleet Earl Mountbatten of Burma', pp. 158–9.

62   Quoting with approval John Lahr's claim that Coward was synonymous with English cultural history between the wars, Winner suggests that in the 1969 film, he passed 'this baton of Englishness' on to Michael Caine. David Winner, *Those Feet An Intimate History of English Football* (Bloomsbury, London, 2005/2006), pbk edn, pp. 197–8. The Turin police's chaotic response to the bullion raid has echoes of *In Which We Serve*'s lower deck scorn for 'the Eyties': ibid., p. 199. With *The Italian Job* and reports of an anti-Wilson conspiracy each providing inspiration, an elderly Mountbatten makes an unflattering appearance in a recent addition to British cinema's comedy-thriller sub-genre, the failed heist: *The Bank Job* (Roger Donaldson, Lion's Gate, UK, 2008).

63   Paul Hirst, *War and Power in the 21st Century* (Polity, 2001), pbk edn, p. 24.

64   Andrew Lambert, 'Epilogue', *The Admirals*, p. 423.

65   Zuckerman, 'Admiral of the Fleet Earl Mountbatten of Burma', pp. 131 and 146–7.

66   Harold Macmillan quoted in ibid., p. 166.

67   Ibid., pp. 151 and 164.

BIBLIOGRAPHY AND FILMOGRAPHY

Mountbatten [Battenberg] family autobiographical and biographical material

Papers of Admiral of the Fleet the Earl Mountbatten of Burma, University of Southampton

Papers of Admiral of the Fleet the Earl Mountbatten of Burma, Liddell Hart Archives, King's College London

Papers of Lady Edwina Mountbatten, University of Southampton

Broadlands archives [Lord Mount Temple], University of Southampton

Milford Haven papers, Imperial War Museum

Admiral of the Fleet the Earl Mountbatten of Burma, Foreword, *Mountbatten Eighty Years in Pictures* (Macmillan, London, 1979)

Admiral of the Fleet the Earl Mountbatten of Burma, *The Diaries of Lord Louis Mountbatten 1920-1922 Tours with the Prince of Wales*, ed. Philip Ziegler (Collins, London, 1987)

Admiral of the Fleet the Earl Mountbatten of Burma, *Personal Diary of Admiral the Lord Louis Mountbatten Supreme Allied Commander South-East Asia 1943-1946*, ed. Philip Ziegler (Collins, London, 1988)

Admiral of the Fleet the Earl Mountbatten of Burma, *From Shore to Shore The Final Years The Diaries of Earl Mountbatten of Burma, 1953-1979*, ed. Philip Ziegler (Collins, London, 1989)

CBC film transcript: Mountbatten of Burma, 'The Dieppe Raid', *The Naval Review*, January 1963

Earl Mountbatten of Burma, 'Dieppe: The Inside Story', *Legion Magazine*, November 1973

'L.M.', 'Obituary: Personal Tributes – Lt. Lord Hugh Beresford RN', *The Times*, 16 July 1941

Herbert Spencer and 'Marco', *An Introduction to Polo* (J.A. Allen, London, 2000)

Marjorie, Countess of Brecknock, *Edwina Mountbatten: Her Life in Pictures* (Macdonald, 1961)

Lord Brabourne, letter to *The Bookseller* quoted in 'William Hickey', *Daily Express*, 7 July 1980

Lord Brabourne and Others v. Hough' in Michael Fish (ed.), *Fleet Street Reports of Industrial Property Cases from the Commonwealth and Europe [1981] F.S.R. Vol. 7* (European Law Centre, London, 1981)

David Butler, *Lord Mountbatten, The Last Viceroy* (Methuen, London, 1985)

Brian Connell, *Manifest Destiny A Study in Five Profiles of the Rise and Influence of the Mountbatten Family* (Cassell, London, 1953)

Brian Hoey, *Mountbatten The Private Story* (Sidgwick and Jackson, London, 1994)

Richard Hough, *Bless Our Ship Mountbatten and the Kelly* (Hodder and Stoughton, London, 1991)

Richard Hough, *Edwina Countess Mountbatten of Burma* (Weidenfeld and Nicolson, London, 1983)

Richard Hough, *Louis and Victoria* (Hutchinson, London, 1974)

Richard Hough, *Mountbatten Hero of Our Time* (Weidenfeld and Nicolson/Pan, London, 1981)

Richard Hough (ed.), *Queen Victoria Advice to a Granddaughter* (Heinemann, London, 1975)

Timothy Knatchbull, *From A Clear Blue Sky: Surviving the Mountbatten Bomb* (Hutchinson, 2009)

Anthony Lambton, *The Mountbattens The Battenbergs and Young Mountbatten* (Constable, London, 1989)

Brian Loring Villa, *Mountbatten and the Dieppe Raid 1942* (OUP, Oxford, 1989)

Vice-Admiral Sir Ian McGeoch, *The Princely Sailor Mountbatten of Burma* (Brassey's, London, 1996)

Janet Morgan, *Edwina Mountbatten A Life of Her Own* (HarperCollins, London, 1991)

Pamela Mountbatten, *India Remembered A Personal Account of the Mountbattens During the Transfer of Power* (Pavilion, London, 2007)

Ray Murphy, *The Last Viceroy The Life and Times of Rear-Admiral The Earl Mountbatten of Burma* (Jarrolds, London, 1948)

William Pattinson, *Mountbatten and the Men of the 'Kelly'* (Patrick Stephens, Wellingborough, 1986)

John Terraine, *The Life and Times of Lord Mountbatten* (Hutchinson/Arrow, London, 1968/1970)

Philip Ziegler, *Mountbatten The Official Biography* (Collins, London, 1985)

Philip Ziegler, *Mountbatten The Official Biography*, second edition (Phoenix Press, London, 2001)

Philip Ziegler, *Mountbatten Revisited* (Harry Ransom Humanities Research Center, Austin Texas, 1995)

Primary source material
Admiralty papers, National Archives
Prime Ministerial papers, National Archives

Ministry of Information papers, National Archives

Avon papers, University of Birmingham

Alan Campbell-Johnson papers, University of Southampton

+ miscellaneous private and copies of official documents held within the Mountbatten papers, University of Southampton

Anon., *History of the Combined Operations Organisation 1940–1945* (Amphibious Warfare Headquarters, London, 1956 – restricted circulation)

Field Marshal Lord Alanbrooke, *War Diaries 1939–1945*, eds Alex Danchev and Daniel Todman (Weidenfeld and Nicolson, London, 2001)

Richard J. Aldrich (ed.), *Witness To War Diaries of the Second World War in Europe and the Middle East* (Doubleday, London, 2004)

Leo Amery, *The Empire at Bay The Leo Amery Diaries 1929–1945*, eds John Barnes and David Nicholson (Hutchinson, London, 1988)

Max Arthur (ed.), *Forgotten Voices of the Second World War* (Ebury Press, London, 2004)

A.B. Austin, *We Landed At Dawn* (Angus and Robertson, London, 1943)

Earl of Avon, *The Eden Memoirs: Facing the Dictators* (Cassell, London, 1962)

Stanley Baldwin, *On England* (Hodder and Stoughton, London, 1926/Penguin, London, 1937)

Isaiah Berlin, 'The Hedgehog and the Fox', *Russian Thinkers* (Penguin, London, 1979)

P.M.S. Blackett, *Studies of War* (Hill and Wang, New York, 1962)

Sir Robert Bruce Lockhart, *The Diaries of Sir Robert Bruce Lockhart Vol. 1 1915–1938*, ed. Kenneth Young (Macmillan, London, 1973)

Sir Robert Bruce Lockhart, *The Diaries of Sir Robert Bruce Lockhart Vol. 2: 1939–1965*, ed. Kenneth Young (Macmillan, London, 1980)

Arthur Bryant, *The Turn of the Tide, 1939–1943* (Collins, London, 1957)

Arthur Bryant, *Triumph in the West* (Collins, London, 1959)

Christopher Buckley, *Norway The Commandos Dieppe* (HMSO, London, 1952/1977)

Alan Campbell-Johnson, 'Mountbatten: the Triple Assignment, 1942–1948. A Recorder's Reflections' in C.M. Woolgar (ed.), *Mountbatten On The Record* (University of Southampton, Southampton, 1997)

Lieutenant-General Sir Adrian Carton de Wiart, *Happy Odyssey* (Jonathan Cape, London, 1950)

'Cato', *Guilty Men* (Victor Gollancz/Penguin, London, 1940/1998)

Sir Henry Channon, *Chips The Diaries of Sir Henry Channon*, ed. Robert Rhodes James (Penguin, London, 1970)

Admiral Lord Chatfield, *The Navy and Defence: The Autobiography of Admiral of the Fleet Lord Chatfield* (William Heinemann, London, 1942)

Admiral Lord Chatfield, *The Navy and Defence Vol. II: It Might Happen Again* (William Heinemann, London, 1947)

Winston S. Churchill, *The Second World War Volume I The Gathering Storm* (Cassell, London, 1948)

Winston S. Churchill, *The Second World War Vol. II Their Finest Hour* (Cassell, London, 1949)

Winston S. Churchill, *The Second World War Vol. III The Grand Alliance* (Cassell, London, 1950)

Winston S. Churchill, *The Second World War Vol. IV The Hinge of Fate* (Cassell, 1951)

Winston S. Churchill, *The Second World War Vol. V Closing the Ring* (Cassell, London, 1952)

Winston S. Churchill, *The Second World War Vol. VI Triumph and Tragedy* (Cassell, London, 1954)

Winston S. Churchill, *The World Crisis Volume 1 1911–1914* (Thornton Butterworth, London, 1923)

Winston S. Churchill and F.D. Roosevelt, *Churchill and Roosevelt The Complete Correspondence I. Alliance Emerging*, ed. Warren F. Kimball (Collins, London, 1984)

Claud Cockburn, *I, Claud … The Autobiography of Claud Cockburn* (Penguin, London, 1967)

Patricia Cockburn, *The Year of the Week* (Penguin, London, 1971)

Sir John Colville, *The Fringes of Power Downing Street Diaries 1939–1955* (Hodder and Stoughton, London, 1985)

Noel Coward, *The Autobiography of Noel Coward* (Mandarin, London, 1992)

Noel Coward, *The Noel Coward Diaries*, eds Graham Payn and Sheridan Morley (Weidenfeld and Nicolson/Phoenix, London, 1985/1998)

Admiral Viscount Cunningham, *The Cunningham Papers Selections form the private and official correspondence of Admiral of the Fleet Viscount Cunningham of Hynhope, O.M., K.T., G.C.B., D.S.O. and two bars Vol. 1 The Mediterranean Fleet, 1939–42*, ed. Michael Simpson (Ashgate/Navy Records Society, Aldershot, 1999)

Admiral Viscount Cunningham, *A Sailor's Odyssey The Autobiography of Admiral of the Fleet Viscount Cunningham of Hynhope K.T., G.C.B., O.M., D.S.O.* (Hutchison, London, 1951)

Hugh Dalton, *The Second World War Diary of Hugh Dalton 1940–45*, ed. Ben Pimlott (Jonathan Cape, London, 1986)

Patrick Dalzel-Job, *Arctic Snow to Dust of Normandy* (Pen and Sword, London, 1997)

Tom Driberg, *Beaverbrook A Study in Power and Frustration* (Weidenfeld and Nicolson, London, 1956)

Tom Driberg, *Ruling Passions* (Jonathan Cape, London, 1977)

Alfred Duff Cooper, *Old Men Forget The Autobiography of Duff Cooper (Viscount Norwich)* (Rupert Hart-Davis, London, 1954)

Dwight D. Eisenhower, *Crusade in Europe* (Heinemann, London, 1948)

Ralph Waldo Emerson, 'Heroism', *Emerson's Essays* (Dent, London, 1971)

Robert Henriques, *From A Biography of Myself* (Secker and Warburg, London, 1969)

Captain J. Hughes-Hallett to C-in-C, RN Portsmouth, 'Dieppe Raid: despatch by Naval Force Commander', 30 August 1942, supplement to *London Gazette*, 38045, 12 August 1947

M.R.D. Foot, *Memories of an S.O.E. Historian* (Pen and Sword Military, Barnsley, 2008)

J.E. Johnson, *Wing Leader* (Chatto and Windus, London, 1956/Goodall, London, 2000)

Lord Killearn, *The Killearn Diaries 1934–1946*, ed. Trefor Evans (Sidgwick and Jackson, London, 1972)

John Knight, *The Kelly: Mountbatten's Ship* (John Knight, London, 1997)

Sir Alan Lascelles, *King's Counsellor Abdication and War: The Diaries of Sir Alan Lascelles*, ed. Duff Hart-Davis (Weidenfeld and Nicolson/Phoenix, London, 2006/2007)

James Lees-Milne, *James Lees-Milne Diaries, 1942–1954*, ed. Michael Bloch (John Murray, London, 2006/7)

Lord Lovat, *March Past A Memoir* (Weidenfeld and Nicolson, London, 1978)

Harold Macmillan, *The Macmillan Diaries The Cabinet Years 1950–57*, ed. Peter Catterall (Pan, London, 2003)

Hugh Massingberd, *Daydream Believer Confessions of a Hero-Worshipper* (Macmillan, London, 2001)

Ministry of Information, *Combined Operations, 1940–1942* (HMSO, London, 1943)

B.L. Montgomery, *The Memoirs of Field Marshal The Viscount Montgomery of Alamein, K.G.* (Collins, London, 1958)

Lt-Gen. Sir Frederick Morgan, *Overture to Overlord* (Hodder and Stoughton, London, 1950)

Ross Munro, *Gauntlet to Overlord The Story of the Canadian Army* (MacMillan, Toronto, 1945)

Harold Nicolson, *Harold Nicolson Diaries and Letters 1939–45*, ed. Nigel Nicolson (Collins, London, 1967)

Graham Payn with Barry Day, *My Life With Noel Coward* (Applause, London, 1994)

Michael Powell, *Million-Dollar Movie The Second Volume of his Life in Movies* (William Heinemann, London, 1992)

Max F. Perutz, *I Wish I'd Made You Angry Earlier Essays on Science, Scientists, and Humanity* (Cold Spring Harbor Laboratory Press, New York, 1998)

Lieutenant-General Sir Henry Pownall, *Chief of Staff The Diaries of Lieutenant-General Sir Henry Pownall Vol. Two*, ed. Brian Bond (Leo Cooper, London, 1974)

Prince of Wales, *Letters from a Prince: Edward, Prince of Wales to Mrs Freda Dudley Ward, March 1918–January 1921*, ed. Rupert Godfrey (Little, Brown and Company, London, 1998)

Rear-Admiral A.F. Pugsley, *Destroyer Man* (Weidenfeld and Nicolson, London, 1957)

Goronwy Rees, *A Bundle of Sensations Sketches in Autobiography* (Chatto and Windus, London, 1960)

Wallace Reyburn, *Glorious Chapter: the Canadians at Dieppe* (Harrap, Toronto, 1943)

Quentin Reynolds, *Dress Rehearsal The Story of Dieppe* (Random House, New York, 1943)

Jeffrey Richards and Dorothy Sheridan (eds), *Mass Observation at the Movies* (Routledge and Kegan Paul, London, 1987)

Lieutenant-Commander Peter Scott, *The Battle of the Narrow Seas A History of the Light Coastal Forces in the Channel and the North Sea, 1939–1945* (Country Life Ltd, London, 1945)

Nevil Shute, *Slide Rule: The Art of an Engineer* (William Heinemann, London, 1954)

Rear Admiral G.W.G. Simpson, *Periscope View* (Macmillan, London, 1972)

C.P. Snow, *Science in Britain* (Oxford University Press, Oxford, 1961)

Hilary St George Saunders, *The Green Beret* (Michael Joseph, 1949)

C.P. Stacey, *The Canadian Army, 1939–45* (Department of National Defence, Ottawa, 1948)

Evelyn Waugh, *The Letters of Evelyn Waugh*, ed. Mark Amory (Weidenfeld and Nicolson/Penguin, London, 1980/1982)

Bob Whinney, *The U-Boat Peril An Anti-Submarine Commander's War* (Blandford Press, Poole, 1986)

F. Wooley, *The One-Hundred and Sixth Annual Report of the Royal South Hants and Southampton Hospital, 1942* (Southern Newspapers Ltd, Southampton, 1942)

Lord Zuckerman, *Six Men Out of the Ordinary* (Peter Owen, London, 1992)

Solly Zuckerman, *From Apes To Warlords An Autobiography 1904–46* (Heinemann/Collins, London, 1978/1988)

Solly Zuckerman, *Monkeys, Men and Missiles An Autobiography 1946–88* (W.W. Norton, New York, 1999)

Secondary source material

Books

Ronald Atkin, *Dieppe 1942 The Jubilee Disaster* (Macmillan, London, 1980)

Christopher Bayly and Tim Harper, *Forgotten Armies Britain's Asian Empire and the war with Japan* (Allen Lane/Penguin, London, 2004/2005)

Charles Beatty, *Our Admiral A Biography of Admiral of the Fleet Earl Beatty* (W.H. Allen, London, 1980)

Ian F.W. Beckett, *The Great War 1914–1918* (Pearson, London, 2001)

John Bierman and Colin Smith, *Fire in the Night Wingate of Burma, Ethiopia, and Zion* (Radom/Pan, London, 1999/2000)

Lord Birkenhead, *Walter Monckton: the life of Viscount Monckton of Brenchley* (Weidenfeld and Nicolson, London, 1969)

Robert Boyce and Joseph A. Maiolo (eds), *The Origins of World War Two The Debate Continues* (Palgrave, Basingstoke, 2003)

Sarah Bradford, *Diana* (Penguin, London, 2007)

Sarah Bradford, *Elizabeth A Biography of Her Majesty* (Heinemann, London, 1996)

Sarah Bradford, *King George VI* (Weidenfeld and Nicolson, London, 1989)

Andrew Brown, *J.D. Bernal The Sage of Science* (Oxford University Press, Oxford, 2005/2007)

D.K. Brown, *A Century of Naval Construction: the History of the Royal Corps of Naval Constructors 1883–1983* (Conway Maritime Press, London, 1983)

Tina Brown, *The Diana Chronicles* (Century, London, 2007)

Kevin Brownlow, *David Lean A Biography* (Richard Cohen Books, London, 1996)

J.R.M. Butler, *Grand Strategy Vol. 3 Pt. 2* (HMSO, London, 1964)

Angus Calder, *The Myth of the Blitz* (Jonathan Cape /Pimlico, London, 1991/1992)

John P. Campbell, *Dieppe Revisited A Documentary Investigation* (Frank Cass, London, 1993)

David Cannadine, *The Pleasures of the Past* (Fontana, London, 1990)

David Carlton, *Anthony Eden A Biography* (Allen Lane, London, 1981)

Humphrey Carpenter, *The Brideshead Generation Evelyn Waugh and his Friends* (Weidenfeld and Nicolson, London, 1989)

Field Marshal Sir Michael Carver (ed.), *The War Lords Military Commanders of the Twentieth Century* (Weidenfeld and Nicolson, London, 1976)

Brian Cathcart, *The Fly in the Cathedral How a small group of Cambridge Scientists won the race to split the atom* (Penguin, London, 2005)

Anthony Cave Brown, *Bodyguard of Lies* (HarperCollins, London, 1975)

John Charmley, *Duff Cooper The Authorized Biography* (Weidenfeld and Nicolson, London, 1986)

John Charmley, *Splendid Isolation? Britain and the Balance of Power 1874–1914* (Hodder and Stoughton, London, 1999)

Anne Chisholm and Michael Davie, *Lord Beaverbrook A Life* (Alfred A. Knopf, New York, 1993)

Randolph S. Churchill, *Winston S. Churchill Vol. II Young Statesman 1901–1914* (Heinemann, London, 1967)

Peter Clarke, *The Cripps Version The Life of Sir Stafford Cripps 1889–1952* (Allen Lane/ Penguin, London, 2002/2003)

Richard Cockett, *David Astor and The Observer* (André Deutsch, London, 1991)

Larry Collins and Dominique Lapierre, *Freedom at Midnight* (Collins, London, 1975)

Stephen Dorril and Robin Ramsay, *Smear! Wilson and the Secret State* (Grafton, London, 1992)

Ruth Dudley Edwards, *Newspapermen Hugh Cudlipp, Cecil Harmsworth King and the Glory Days of Fleet Street* (Secker and Warburg, London, 2003)

David Edgerton, *The Shock of the Old Technology and Global History Since 1900* (Profile, London, 2006/2008)

David Edgerton, *Warfare State Britain, 1920–1970* (Cambridge University Press, Cambridge, 2006)

Niall Ferguson, *The Pity of War* (Penguin, London, 1998)

Bernard Fergusson, *The Watery Maze The Story of Combined Operations* (Collins, London, 1961)

Georgina Ferry, *Max Perutz and the Secret of Life* (Chatto and Windus, London, 2007)

M.R.D. Foot, *The Special Operations Executive 1940–46* (Greenwood Press/Pimlico, London, 1984/1999)

Adrian Fort, *PROF The Life of Frederick Lindemann* (Jonathan Cape/Pimlico, London 2003/2004)

David Fraser, *Alanbrooke* (HarperCollins, London 1982/1997)

David French, *Raising Churchill's Army The British Army and the War Against Germany 1919–1945* (OUP, Oxford, 2000/2001)

Patrick French, *Liberty Or Death India's Journey to Independence and Division* (HarperCollins, London, 1997)

Patrick French, *Younghusband The Last Great Imperial Adventurer* (HarperCollins, London, 1995)

Martin Gilbert, *Winston S. Churchill Vol. III 1914–16* (Heinemann, London, 1971)

Martin Gilbert, *Winston S. Churchill Vol. V 1931–1939* (Heinemann, London 1976)

Martin Gilbert, *Finest Hour Winston S. Churchill 1939–1941 Volume VI* (William Heinemann, London, 1983)

Martin Gilbert, *Road to Victory Winston S. Churchill 1941–1945 Volume VI* (London, Heinemann, 1986)

Jonathan Glancey, *Spitfire The Biography* (Atlantic Books, London, 2006)

Andrew Gordon, *The Rules of the Game Jutland and British Naval Command* (John Murray, London, 1996)

G.A.H. Gordon, *British Seapower and Procurement Between the Wars* (Macmillan, Basingstoke, 1988)

Peter Gretton, 'Vian, Sir Philip Louis', *Oxford Dictionary of National Biography* (OUP, Oxford, 2004)

Richard Griffiths, *Fellow Travellers of the Right British Enthusiasts for Nazi Germany 1933–39* (OUP, Oxford, 1983)

John Gross, *The Rise and Fall of the Man of Letters English Literary Life Since 1800* (Pelican, London, 1973)

Nigel Hamilton, *The Full Monty Volume I: Montgomery of Alamein, 1887–1942* (Allen Lane/Penguin Press, London, 2001)

Nigel Hamilton, *Monty The Making of a General 1887–1942* (Hamish Hamilton, London, 1981)

Michael Harrison, *Mulberry The Return in Triumph* (W.H. Allen, London, 1965)

Max Hastings, *Nemesis: The Battle for Japan, 1944–45* (Harper Press/HarperPerennial, London, 2007/8)

Selina Hastings, *Evelyn Waugh A Biography* (Sinclair-Stevenson, London, 1994)

Peter Hennessy, *Having It So Good Britain in the Fifties* (Penguin/Allen Lane, London, 2006)

Charles Higham, *Mrs Simpson Secret Lives of the Duchess of Windsor* (Sidgwick and Jackson, London, 2004)

F.H. Hinsley et al, *British Intelligence in the Second World War Its Influence on Strategy and Operations Volume Two* (HMSO, London, 1981)

Paul Hirst, *War and Power in the 21st Century* (Polity, 2001)

Philip Hoare, *Noel Coward A Biography* (Sinclair-Stevenson, London, 1995)

James Holland, *Fortress Malta An Island Under Siege 1940–1943* (Phoenix, London, 2004)

Peter Hore (ed.), *Patrick Blackett Sailor, Scientist and Socialist* (Frank Cass, London, 2003)

Michael Howard, *The Continental Commitment: The Dilemma of British Defence Policy in the Era of the Two World Wars* (M.T. Smith/Pelican, London, 1972/1974)

Neil Huxter, 'Smith, Cecil Lewis Troughton [*pseudo.* Cecil Scott Forester], *Oxford Dictionary of National Biography* (OUP, Oxford, 2004)

Ronald Hyam, *Britain's Declining Empire: The Road to Decolonisation, 1918–68* (CUP, Cambridge, 2007)

David Irving, *Hitler's War* (Viking Press, London, 1977)

Shashi Joshi, *The Last Durbar A Dramatic Presentation of the Division of British India* (OUP, Karachi, 2006)

Penny Junor, *The Firm The Troubled Life of the House of Windsor* (HarperCollins, London, 2005)

John Keegan, *Six Armies in Normandy From D-Day to the Liberation of Paris* (Jonathan Cape/Pimlico, London 1982/1992)

Paul Kennedy, *The Rise and Fall of British Naval Mastery* (Macmillan/Fontana, London, 1983/1992)

Greg King, *The Duchess of Windsor The Uncommon Life of Wallis Simpson* (Aurum, London, 1999)

Robert Lacey, *Majesty Elizabeth II and the House of Windsor* (Hutchinson, London, 1977)

Andrew Lambert, *Admirals The Naval Commanders Who Made Britain Great* (Faber, London, 2008)

David Lampe, *Pyke The Unknown Genius* (Evans Brothers, London, 1959)

Ronald Lewin, *Montgomery as Military Commander* (B.T. Batsford, London, 1971)

C.E. Lucas Phillips, *Cockleshell Heroes* (William Heinemann/Pan, 1956/2000)

C.E. Lucas Phillips, *The Greatest Raid of All* (William Heinemann/Pan, 1958/2000)

Andrew Lycett, *Ian Fleming* (Weidenfeld and Nicolson/Phoenix, London, 1995/1996)

Robert Lyman, *The Generals: From Victory to Defeat, Leadership in the Burma Campaign, 1941–45* (Constable, London, 2008)

Terence Macartney-Filgate (eds), *Dieppe 1942 Echoes of Disaster* (Personal Library, Toronto, 1979/Drew Publishing, London, 1982)

S.P. MacKenzie, *British War Films 1939–1946* (Continuum, London, 2001)

Arthur J. Marder, *From the Dardanelles to Oran Studies of the Royal Navy in War and Peace 1915–1940* (OUP, Oxford, 1974)

Arthur J. Marder, *From the Dreadnought to Scapa Flow Volume 3 Jutland and After*, revised edn. (OUP, Oxford, 1978)

Robert K. Massie, *Castles of Steel Britain, Germany and the Winning of the Great War at Sea* (Pimlico, London, 2005)

Ray Monk, 'Getting inside Heisenberg's head' in A.L. Macfie (ed.), *The Philosophy of History* (Palgrave Macmillan, Basingstoke, 2006)

Tim Moreman, *British Commandos 1940–1946* (Osprey, London, 2006)

Malcolm H. Murfett (ed.), *The First Sea Lords From Fisher to Mountbatten* (Praegar, New York, 1995)

Robert Murphy, *British Cinema and the Second World War* (Continuum, London, 2000)

Robin Neillands, *The Dieppe Raid The Story of the Disastrous 1942 Expedition* (Aurum, 2005)

Mary Jo Nye, 'Blackett, Patrick Maynard Stuart', *Oxford Dictionary of National Biography* (OUP, Oxford, 2004)

Mary Jo Nye, *Blackett, War, and Politics in the Twentieth Century* (Harvard University Press, Cambridge Mass., 2004)

Lynne Olson, *Troublesome Young Men The Churchill Conspiracy of 1940* (Bloomsbury, London, 2007/2008)

Michael Partridge, *The Royal Naval College Osborne A History 1903–1921* (Sutton, Stroud, 1999)

Jonathan Petropoulos, *Royals and the Reich The Princes Von Hessen in Nazi Germany* (OUP, Oxford, 2006)

John Peyton, *Solly Zuckerman A Scientist Out of the Ordinary* (John Murray, London, 2001)

Ben Pimlott, *The Queen A Biography of Elizabeth II* (HarperCollins , London, 1996)

Kenneth Poolman, *Kelly* (William Kimber, London, 1954)

Douglas Porch, *Hitler's Mediterranean Gamble: The North African and the Mediterranean Campaigns in World War II* (Weidenfeld and Nicolson, London, 2004)

Martin Pugh, *Hurrah for the Blackshirts! Fascists and Fascism in Britain Between the Wars* (Jonathan Cape, London, 2005)

John Ray, *The Battle of Britain Dowding and the First Victory, 1940* (Cassell, 1994)

David Reynolds, *From World War to Cold War Churchill, Roosevelt, and the International History of the 1940s* (Oxford, OUP, 2006/2007)

David Reynolds, *In Command of History Churchill Fighting and Writing the Second World War* (Penguin/Allen Lane, London, 2004)

Robert Rhodes James, *Anthony Eden* (Weidenfeld and Nicolson, London, 1986)

Andrew Roberts, *Eminent Churchillians* (Phoenix, London, 1995)

Andrew Roberts, *'The Holy Fox' A Life of Lord Halifax* (Weidenfeld and Nicolson, 1991)

Andrew Roberts, *Masters and Commanders: How Roosevelt, Churchill, Marshall and Alanbrooke Won the War in the West* (Allen Lane, London, 2008)

Terence Robertson, *Dieppe: the Shame and the Glory* (Hutchinson, London, 1963)

Stephen Roskill, *Admiral of the Fleet Earl Beatty The Last Naval Hero An Intimate Biography* (Collins, London, 1980)

Stephen Roskill, *Churchill and the Admirals* (Collins, London, 1977)

Stephen Roskill, *The War at Sea 1939–45 Vol. 3 Part 1 The Offensive* (HMSO, London, 1960)

Captain S.W. Roskill, RN, *The Strategy of Sea Power Its Development and Application* (Collins, London, 1962)

Captain S.W. Roskill, *The War at Sea 1939–1945 Vol. I The Defensive* (HMSO, London, 1954)

Trevor Royle, *Orde Wingate Irregular Soldier* (Weidenfeld and Nicolson, 1995)

Elizabeth D. Samet, *Soldier's Heart Reading Literature Through Peace and War at West Point* (Farrar, Straus and Giroux, New York, 2007)

Dominic Sandbrook, *Never Had It So Good A History of Britain from Suez to the Beatles* (Little, Brown, London, 2005)

B.B. Schofield, *British Sea Power Naval Policy in the Twentieth Century* (Batsford, London, 1967)

Michael Simpson, *A Life of Admiral of the Fleet Andrew Cunningham A Twentieth-Century Naval Leader* (Frank Cass, London, 2004)

Michael Simpson, 'Viscount Cunningham of Hyndhope', *Oxford Dictionary of National Biography* (OUP, Oxford, 2004)

Paul Smith (ed.), *Government and the Armed Forces in Britain 1856–1990* (Hambledon Press, London, 1996)

Rupert Smith, *The Utility of Force The Art of War in the Modern World* (Allen Lane/ Penguin, London, 29005/2006)

Hew Strachan, *Carl Von Clausewitz's On War A Biography* (Atlantic Books, London, 2007)

Hew Strachan, *The First World War Volume 1: To Arms* (OUP, Oxford, 2001)

Matthew Sweet, *Shepperton Babylon The Lost Worlds of British Cinema* (Faber, London, 2005)

A.J.P. Taylor, *Beaverbrook* (Hamish Hamilton, London, 1972/Penguin, London, 1974)

John Terraine, *The Right of the Line The Royal Air Force in the European War 1939–1945* (Wordsworth, London, 1997)

Hugh Thomas, *John Strachey* (Eyre Methuen, London, 1973)

E.P. Thompson, *The Making of the English Working Class* (Pelican, London, 1980)

Christopher Thorne, *Allies of a Kind The United States, Britain and the war against Japan, 1941–1945* (Hamish Hamilton, London, 1978)

D.R. Thorpe, *Eden The Life and Times of Anthony Eden First Lord of Avon, 1897–1977* (Chatto and Windus, London, 2003)

John Turner (ed.), *Britain and the First World War* (Unwin Hyman, London, 1988)

Hugo Vickers, *Elizabeth, The Queen Mother* (Hutchinson, London, 2005)

Alex von Tunzelmann, *Indian Summer The Secret History of the End of an Empire* (Simon and Schuster/Pocket Books, London, 2007/8)

Oliver Warner, *Admiral of the Fleet The Life of Sir Charles Lambe* (Sidgwick and Jackson, London, 1969)

Oliver Warner, *Cunningham of Hyndhope A Memoir* (John Murray, London, 1967)

John Wheeler-Bennett, *King George VI* (Macmillan, London, 1958)

Francis Wheen, *Tom Driberg His Life and Indiscretions* (Chatto and Windus, London, 1990)

A.N. Wilson, *After the Victorians: 1901–1953* (Hutchinson, London, 2005)

A.N. Wilson, *Our Times The Age of Elizabeth II* (Hutchinson, London, 2008)

David Winner, *Those Feet An Intimate History of English Football* (Bloomsbury, London, 2005/2006)

John Winton, *Cunningham The Greatest Admiral Since Nelson* (John Murray, London, 1998)

Stanley Wolpert, *Shameful Flight The Last Years of the British Empire in India* (OUP, Oxford, 2006)

Philip Ziegler, *King Edward VIII The Official Biography* (Collins, London, 1999)

Newspaper, magazine, and journal articles

Anon., 'British grit in a British ship BEAT ALL', *Daily Mirror*, 7 December 1940

Anon., 'Commando Chief Lord Louis Mountbatten', *News Review*, 23 April 1942

Anon., 'Deux espoirs anglais: Lord Mountbatten and Wavell', *La Semaine*, [?] 1942

Anon., 'Mountbatten and his Commandos', *Reader's Digest* [June?]1942

Anon., 'Mountbatten and his Commandos', *Time*, 8 June 1942

Anon., Mountbatten cover photo-story *Illustrated London News*, 25 April 1942

Anon., obituary of Vice-Admiral Sir Ian McGeoch, *Daily Telegraph*, 17 August 2007

Anon., tribute to the accredited war correspondent, *The Bulldozer The Magazine of Combined Operations*, No. 10, March 1943

Andrew Alderson and Kathryn Johnston, 'Killer of Lord Mountbatten enjoys freedom, 30 years on from IRA murder', *Sunday Telegraph*, 9 August 2009

Anthony Adamthwaite, 'The British Government and the media 1937–1938', *Journal of Contemporary History*, vol. 18 no. 2 , 1983

Tariq Ali, 'Pakistan at Sixty', *London Review of Books*, 4 October 2007

Brian Bond, 'John Terraine', *Guardian*, 1 January 2004

Ed Caesar, 'Indian Summer: story of the Mountbattens', *Sunday Times*, 29 June 2008

Lawson Carr, 'Sailor on Horseback is Destroyer Hero', *Everybody's Weekly*, 19 July 1941

Tom Driberg, column, *Reynolds News*, 5 January 1959

Richard Evans, 'Tank Traps', *Times Literary Supplement*, 21/28 August 2009

Max Hastings, 'How They Won', *New York Review of Books*, 22 November 2007

Max Hastings, 'Up Against "the Finest Soldiers in the World"', *New York Review of Books*, 3 April 2008

Eric Hobsbawm, 'Red Science', *London Review of Books*, 9 March 2006.

Percy Howard, 'Will 1959 be Mountbatten's year?', *Daily Express*, 28 December 1958

Henry McDonald, 'Royal blown up by IRA "backed united Ireland"', *Guardian*, 29 December 2007

Peter J. Henshaw, 'The British Chiefs of Staff and the Preparation of the Dieppe Raid, March-August 1942: Did Mountbatten Really Evade the Committee's Authority?', *War and History*, vol. 1, no. 2, 1994

Tim Lewens, 'Launch the Icebergs!', *London Review of Books*, 15 November 2007

Arthur Marwick, 'Middle Opinion in the Thirties: Planning, Progress and Political "Agreement"', *English Historical Review*, vol. 71 no. 2, April 1964

Quentin Reynolds, report on Dieppe, *Reader's Digest*, May 1943

Stephen Roskill, 'The Dieppe raid and the question of German foreknowledge', *RUSI Journal*, vol. CIX no. 633, 1964

Adrian Smith, 'Command and Control in Postwar Britain: Defence Decision-Making in the United Kingdom, 1945–1984', *Twentieth Century British History*, vol. 2 no. 3, 1991

Adrian Smith, 'Harold Macmillan and Munich', *Dalhousie Review*, vol. 68 no. 3, summer 1989

Adrian Smith, 'Mountbatten goes to the movies: the cinema as a vehicle for promoting the heroic myth', *Historical Journal of Film, Radio and Television*, vol. 26 no. 3, August 2006

Philip Williamson, 'Baldwin's reputation: politics and history, 1937–1967', *The Historical Journal*, vol. 47 no. 1, 2004

Philip Ziegler, review of *Unauthorised Action Mountbatten and the Dieppe Raid 1942*, *Spectator*, 10 March 1990

Unpublished papers

Richard Maguire, 'An enlightenment scientist in an irrational world: Lord Zuckerman and the British Government's nuclear weapons programme', Mountbatten Centre for International Studies, University of Southampton

Fiction and verse

Ian Fleming, *Casino Royale* (Jonathan Cape, London, 1953)
Ian Fleming, *Octopussy* (Jonathan Cape, London, 1966)
Giles Foden, *Turbulence* (Faber and Faber, London, 2009)
C.S. Forester, *The Ship* (Martyn Joseph, 1943/Penguin, London, 1949)
Kazuo Ishiguro, *The Remains of the Day* (Faber, London, 1989)
Nicholas Montserrat, *The Cruel Sea* (Cassell, London, 1951)
Evelyn Waugh, *Vile Bodies* (Chapman and Hall, London, 1930)
Evelyn Waugh, *Put Out More Flags* (Chapman and Hall, London, 1942)
Evelyn Waugh, *Men At Arms* (Chapman and Hall, London, 1952)
Evelyn Waugh, *Officers and Gentlemen* (Chapman and Hall, 1955)
A.P. Wavell (ed.), *Other Men's Flowers* (Jonathan Cape, London, 1944)

Theatre

Noel Coward, *Hands Across The Sea A Light Comedy* in *One Scene* in *To-night at 8.30*, Phoenix Theatre, London, 1936, in *Plays: Three* (Eyre Methuen, London, 1979)
Tom Kelly and Alan Price, *Kelly-A Musical Documentary*, South Shields, 15 July 1977
Jeremy Kingston, *Making Dickie Happy*, Rosemary Branch Pub/Theatre, London, September-October 2004

Film, radio, and television

The Bank Job (Roger Donaldson, Lion's Gate, UK, 2008)
Britain/London Can Take It! (Humphrey Jennings and Harry Watt, GPO/Crown Film Unit, UK, 1940)
The Cockleshell Heroes (José Ferrer, Warwick Films/Columbia, UK, 1955)
The Day Mountbatten Died (Timewatch team, BBC2, UK, 2004)
Dieppe 42 Aux yeux du present (Pierre Gavreau, Radio-Québec, Canada, 1976)
Dieppe 1942 (Tony Broughton, BBC, UK, 1972)
Dieppe 1942 (Terence Macartney-Filgate, CBC, Canada, 1979)
Filming For Victory: British Cinema, 1939–45 (Christopher Frayling, BBC2, UK, 1986)
Gandhi (Richard Attenborough, Columbia Pictures, USA, 1982)
In Which We Serve (Noel Coward/David Lean, Two Cities, UK, 1942)
Jeremy Clarkson: The Greatest Raid Of All Time (Richard Pearson, BBC2, UK, 2007)
Kelly (Peter West, BBC2, UK, 1978)
The Last Days of the Raj (Carl Hindmarch, Channel 4, UK, 2007)
The Last Viceroy, parts 1–2 (Susan Marling, Just Radio/BBC Radio 4, UK, 2004)
The Life and Times of Lord Mountbatten, episodes 1–12 (Peter Morley, Rediffusion, UK, 1969)

Listen To Britain (Humphrey Jennings, Crown Film Unit, UK, 1941)

Lord Mountbatten, The Last Viceroy (Tom Clegg, George Walker TV Productions/ Mobil, UK/USA, 1985)

'The Prime Minister takes stock', *Movietone News* (Movietone, UK, November 1937)

The Queen's Wedding (Julia Harrington, Menton Productions, UK, 2007)

Suez: A Personal View (Andrew Roberts, BBC2, UK, 1996)

INDEX